2013 Children's Writer's & Illustrator's MARKET®

P9-CSV-481

includes a 1-year online subscription to **Children's Writer's & Illustrator's Market** on

WritersMarket.com

Where & How to Sell What You Write

THE ULTIMATE MARKET RESEARCH TOOL FOR WRITERS

To register your *2013 Children's Writer's & Illustrator's Market* book and **start your 1-year online genre only subscription**, scratch off the block below to reveal your activation code, then go to www.WritersMarket.com. Find the box that says "Have an Activation Code?" then click on "Sign Up Now" and enter your contact information and activation code. It's that easy!

CM-T52RR431

UPDATED MARKET LISTINGS FOR YOUR INTEREST AREA
EASY-TO-USE SEARCHABLE DATABASE • RECORD-KEEPING TOOLS
PROFESSIONAL TIPS & ADVICE • INDUSTRY NEWS

Your purchase of *Children's Writer's & Illustrator's Market* gives you access to updated listings related to this genre of writing (valid through 12/31/13). For just $9.99, you can upgrade your subscription and get access to listings from all of our best-selling Market books. Visit **www.WritersMarket.com** for more information.

WritersMarket.com

Where & How to Sell What You Write

Activate your WritersMarket.com subscription to get instant access to:

- **UPDATED LISTINGS IN YOUR WRITING GENRE:** Find additional listings that didn't make it into the book, updated contact information and more. WritersMarket.com provides the most comprehensive database of verified markets available anywhere.

- **EASY-TO-USE SEARCHABLE DATABASE:** Looking for a specific magazine or book publisher? Just type in its name. Or widen your prospects with the Advanced Search. You can also search for listings that have been recently updated!

- **PERSONALIZED TOOLS:** Store your best-bet markets, and use our popular recording-keeping tools to track your submissions. Plus, get new and updated market listings, query reminders, and more—every time you log in!

- **PROFESSIONAL TIPS & ADVICE:** From pay rate charts to sample query letters, and from how-to articles to Q&A's with literary agents, we have the resources freelance writers need.

YOU'LL GET ALL OF THIS WITH YOUR INCLUDED SUBSCRIPTION TO

WritersMarket.com

Where & How to Sell What You Write

13CMI0M

25TH ANNUAL EDITION

2013 Children's Writer's & Illustrator's MARKET

Chuck Sambuchino, Editor

WRITER'S DIGEST
BOOKS

WritersDigest.com
Cincinnati, Ohio

2013 CHILDREN'S WRITER'S & ILLUSTRATOR'S MARKET. Copyright © 2012 by F+W Media Inc. Published by Writer's Digest Books, an imprint of F+W Media Inc., 10151 Carver Road, Suite 200, Cincinnati, Ohio 45242. Printed and bound in the United States of America. All rights reserved. No part of this book may be reproduced in any form or by any electronic or mechanical means including information storage and retrieval systems without permission in writing from the publisher, except by a reviewer, who may quote brief passages in a review.

Publisher & Editorial Director, Writing Community: Phil Sexton

Writer's Market website: www.writersmarket.com
Writer's Digest website: www.writersdigest.com
Writer's Digest Bookstore: www.writersdigestshop.com
Guide to Literary Agents Blog: www.guidetoliteraryagents.com/blog

Distributed in Canada by Fraser Direct
100 Armstrong Avenue
Georgetown, Ontario, Canada L7G 5S4
Tel: (905) 877-4411

Distributed in the U.K. and Europe by F&W Media International
Brunel House, Newton Abbot, Devon, TQ12 4PU, England
Tel: (+44) 1626-323200, Fax: (+44) 1626-323319
E-mail: postmaster@davidandcharles.co.uk

Distributed in Australia by Capricorn Link
P.O. Box 704, Windsor, NSW 2756 Australia
Tel: (02) 4577-3555

ISSN: 0897-9790
ISBN-13: 978-1-59963-599-6

Attention Booksellers: This is an annual directory of F+W Media, Inc. Return deadline for this edition is December 31, 2013.

Edited by: Chuck Sambuchino
Cover designed by: Jessica Boonstra
Interior designed by: Claudean Wheeler
Production coordinated by: Greg Nock
Cover illustration by: Joshua Roflow

CONTENTS

INTERVIEWS

RESOURCES

MARKETS AND MORE

FROM THE EDITOR

While the publishing industry is in a state of transition, the children's book market continues to blossom and grow. Kids are reading more, and a greater number of children's books are getting published now than ever before. That's inspiring news if you're crafting or illustrating a story! Lots of debut authors find success each year.

Along with the hundreds of markets you've come to expect in *CWIM*, I also made an effort to gather great writing advice so you can craft the best book possible. To give you this advice, I enlisted the help of SCBWI regional advisors worldwide. In a gigantic interview roundup, you'll find wisdom and advice from 22 different SCBWI advisors around the globe. It's an article you don't want to miss. After you examine the roundup, don't forget our other articles on illustration and craft—along with all the author interviews and roundups.

Also in this edition of *CWIM*, I've tried to focus on two things that I believe will help you on your journey: 1) Throughout the "Agents & Art Reps" market section, I've spotlighted new/newer literary agents who are actively looking to build their roster of clients. These new reps are smart targets for unpublished writers seeking agents. 2) I've focused a good deal of attention on how to build your writer platform and use social media, as doing so will make you a more attractive author to publishers.

Please stay in touch with me at guidetoliteraryagents.com/blog and on Twitter (@chucksambuchino). I love hearing feedback and success stories. Until we next meet, good luck on your writing journey!

Chuck Sambuchino
literaryagent@fwmedia.com
Editor, *Guide to Literary Agents / Children's Writer's & Illustrator's Market*
Author, *How to Survive a Garden Gnome Attack* (2010); *Red Dog / Blue Dog* (2012); *Create Your Writer Platform* (2012)

PHOTO: Al Parrish

HOW TO USE
CWIM

//

As a writer, illustrator or photographer first picking up *Children's Writer's & Illustrator's Market*, you may not know quite how to start using the book. Your impulse may be to flip through the book and quickly make a mailing list, then submit to everyone in hopes that someone will take interest in your work. Well, there's more to it. Finding the right market takes time and research. The more you know about a market that interests you, the better chance you have of getting work accepted. We've made your job a little easier by putting a wealth of information at your fingertips. Besides providing listings, this directory includes a number of tools to help you determine which markets are the best ones for your work. By using these tools, as well as researching on your own, you raise your odds of being published.

USING THE INDEXES

This book lists hundreds of potential buyers of freelance material. To learn which companies want the type of material you're interested in submitting, start with the indexes.

Editor and Agent Names Index

This index lists book and magazine editors and art directors as well as agents and art reps, indicating the companies they work for. Use this index to find company and contact information for individual publishing professionals.

Age-Level Index

Age groups are broken down into these categories in the Age-Level Index:

- **PICTURE BOOKS OR PICTURE-ORIENTED MATERIAL** are written and illustrated for preschoolers to 8-year-olds.

- **YOUNG READERS** are for 5- to 8-year-olds.
- **MIDDLE READERS** are for 9- to 11-year-olds.
- **YOUNG ADULT** is for ages 12 and up.

Age breakdowns may vary slightly from publisher to publisher, but using them as general guidelines will help you target appropriate markets. For example, if you've written an article about trends in teen fashion, check the Magazines Age-Level Index under the Young Adult subheading. Using this list, you'll quickly find the listings for young adult magazines.

Subject Index

But let's narrow the search further. Take your list of young adult magazines, turn to the Subject Index, and find the Fashion subheading. Then highlight the names that appear on both lists (Young Adult and Fashion). Now you have a smaller list of all the magazines that would be interested in your teen fashion article. Read through those listings and decide which ones sound best for your work.

Illustrators and photographers can use the Subject Index as well. If you specialize in painting animals, for instance, consider sending samples to book and magazine publishers listed under Animals and, perhaps, Nature/Environment. Because illustrators can simply send general examples of their style to art directors to keep on file, the indexes may be more helpful to artists sending manuscript/illustration packages who need to search for a specific subject. Always read the listings for the potential markets to see the type of work art directors prefer and what type of samples they'll keep on file, and obtain art or photo guidelines if they're available through the mail or online.

Photography Index

In this index, you'll find lists of book and magazine publishers that buy photos from free-lancers. Refer to the list and read the listings for companies' specific photography needs. Obtain photo guidelines if they're offered through the mail or online.

USING THE LISTINGS

Many listings begin with symbols. Refer to the handy pull-out bookmark (shown later in this article).

Many listings indicate whether submission guidelines are available. If a publisher you're interested in offers guidelines, get them and read them. The same is true with catalogs. Sending for and reading catalogs or browsing them online gives you a better idea of whether your work would fit in with the books a publisher produces. (You should also look at a few of the books in the catalog at a library or bookstore to get a feel for the publisher's material.)

⊕ market new to this edition

Ⓐ market accepts agented submissions only

🏆 award-winning market

🍁 Canadian market

🌐 market located outside of the U.S. and Canada

◗ online opportunity

💬 comment from the editor of *Children's Writer's & Illustrator's Market*

◐ publisher producing educational material

◑ book packager/producer

ms, mss manuscript(s)

SCBWI Society of Children's Book Writers and Illustrators

SASE self-addressed, stamped envelope

IRC International Reply Coupon, for use in countries other than your own

b&w black & white (photo)

(For definitions of unfamiliar words and expressions relating to writing, illustration and publishing, see the Glossary.)

Especially for artists & photographers

Along with information for writers, listings provide information for illustrators and photographers. Illustrators will find numerous markets that maintain files of samples for possible future assignments. If you're both a writer and an illustrator, look for markets that accept manuscript/illustration packages and read the information offered under the **Illustration** subhead within the listings.

If you're a photographer, after consulting the Photography Index, read the information under the **Photography** subhead within listings to see what format buyers prefer. For example, some want 35mm color transparencies, others want black-and-white prints. Note the type of photos a buyer wants to purchase and the procedures for submitting. It's not uncommon for a market to want a résumé and promotional literature, as well as tearsheets from previous work. Listings also note whether model releases and/or captions are required.

DUTTON CHILDREN'S BOOKS

Penguin Group (USA), Inc., 375 Hudson St., New York NY 10014. **Website:** www.penguin.com/youngreaders. **Contact:** Lauri Hornik, president and publisher. Estab. 1852. Dutton Children's Books publishes fiction and nonfiction for readers ranging from preschoolers to young adults on a variety of subjects. Publishes hardcover originals as well as novelty formats. Dutton Children's Books has a diverse, general-interest list that includes picture books, and fiction for all ages and occasional retail-appropriate nonfiction. 15% of books from first-time authors.

   ◯ "Cultivating the creative talents of authors and illustrators and publishing books with purpose and heart continue to be the mission and joy at Dutton."

FICTION Dutton Children's Books has a diverse, general interest list that includes picture books; easy-to-read books; and fiction for all ages, from first chapter books to young adult readers. Recently published *Skippyjon Jones, Lost in Space*, by Judy Schachner (picture book); *Thirteen*, by Lauren Myracle (middle grade novel); *Paper Towns*, by John Green (young adult novel); and *If I Stay*, by Gayle Forman (young adult novel).

NONFICTION Query with SASE.

HOW TO CONTACT Query letter only; include SASE.

TERMS Pays royalty on retail price. Offers advance.

ADDRESSES AND WEBSITES

SPECIFIC CONTACT NAMES

INFO ON WHAT A PUBLISHER HANDLES

TERMS AND FINANCES

QUICK TIPS FOR WRITERS & ILLUSTRATORS

If you're new to the world of children's publishing, buying *Children's Writer's & Illustrator's Market* may have been one of the first steps in your journey to publication. What follows is a list of suggestions and resources that can help make that journey a smooth and swift one:

1. MAKE THE MOST OF *CHILDREN'S WRITER'S & ILLUSTRATOR'S MARKET.* Be sure to read "How to Use This Book" for tips on reading the listings and using the indexes. Also be sure to take advantage of the articles and interviews in the book. The insights of the authors, illustrators, editors and agents we've interviewed will inform and inspire you.

2. JOIN THE SOCIETY OF CHILDREN'S BOOK WRITERS AND ILLUSTRATORS. SCBWI, more than 19,000 members strong, is an organization for both beginners and professionals interested in writing and illustrating for children. It offers members a slew of information and support through publications, a website, and a host of Regional Advisors overseeing chapters in almost every state in the U.S. and a growing number of locations around the globe (including France, Canada, Japan and Australia). SCBWI puts on a number of conferences, workshops, and events on the regional and national levels (many listed in the Conferences & Workshops section of this book). For more information, contact SCBWI, 8271 Beverly Blvd., Los Angeles CA 90048, (323)782-1010, or visit their website: scbwi.org.

3. READ NEWSLETTERS. Newsletters, such as *Children's Book Insider*, *Children's Writer* and the *SCBWI Bulletin*, offer updates and new information about publishers on a timely basis and are relatively inexpensive. Many local chapters of SCBWI offer regional newsletters as well. (See Helpful Books & Publications later in this book for contact information on the newsletters listed above and others.) For information on regional SCBWI newsletters, visit scbwi.org and click on "Publications."

4. READ TRADE AND REVIEW PUBLICATIONS. Magazines like *Publishers Weekly* (which offers two special issues each year devoted to children's publishing and is available on newsstands), *The Horn Book* and *Booklinks* offer news, articles, reviews of newly published titles and ads featuring upcoming and current releases. Referring to them will help you get a feel for what's happening in children's publishing.

5. READ GUIDELINES. Most publishers and magazines offer writer's and artist's guidelines that provide detailed information on needs and submission requirements, and some magazines offer theme lists for upcoming issues. Many publishers and magazines state the availability of guidelines within their listings. Send a self-addressed, stamped envelope (SASE) to publishers who offer guidelines. You'll often find submission information on publishers' and magazines' websites.

6. LOOK AT PUBLISHERS' CATALOGS. Perusing publishers' catalogs can give you a feel for their line of books and help you decide where your work might fit in. If catalogs are available (often stated within listings), send for them with a SASE. Visit publishers' websites, which often contain their full catalogs. You can also ask librarians to look at catalogs they have on hand. You can even search Amazon.com by publisher and year. (Click on "book search" then "publisher, date" and plug in, for example, "Lee & Low" under "publisher" and "2012" under year. You'll get a list of Lee & Low titles published in 2012, which you can peruse.)

7. VISIT BOOKSTORES. It's not only informative to spend time in bookstores—it's fun, too! Frequently visit the children's section of your local bookstore (whether a chain or an independent) to see the latest from a variety of publishers and the most current issues of children's magazines. Look for books in the genre you're writing or with illustrations similar in style to yours, and spend some time studying them. It's also wise to get to know your local booksellers; they can tell you what's new in the store and provide insight into what kids and adults are buying.

8. READ, READ, READ! While you're at that bookstore, pick up a few things, or keep a list of the books that interest you and check them out of your library. Read and study the latest releases, the award winners and the classics. You'll learn from other writers, get ideas and get a feel for what's being published. Think about what works and doesn't work in a story. Pay attention to how plots are constructed and how characters are developed or the rhythm and pacing of picture book text. It's certainly enjoyable research!

9. TAKE ADVANTAGE OF INTERNET RESOURCES. There are innumerable sources of information available on the Internet about writing for children (and anything else you could possibly think of). It's also a great resource for getting (and staying) in touch with other writers and illustrators through listservs, blogs, social networking sites and e-mail, and it can serve as a vehicle for self-promotion. (Visit some authors' and illustrators' sites for ideas. See "Useful Online Resources" in this book for a list of websites.)

10. CONSIDER ATTENDING A CONFERENCE. If time and finances allow, attending a conference is a great way to meet peers and network with professionals in the field of children's publishing. As mentioned above, SCBWI offers conferences in various locations year round. (See scbwi.org and click on "Events" for a full conference calendar.) General writers' conferences often offer specialized sessions just for those interested in children's writing. Many conferences offer optional manuscript and portfolio critiques as well, giving you a chance for feedback from seasoned professionals. See the Conferences & Awards section for information on SCBWI and other conferences. The section features a Conferences & Workshops Calendar to help you plan your travel.

11. NETWORK, NETWORK, NETWORK! Don't work in a vacuum. You can meet other writers and illustrators through a number of the things listed above—SCBWI, conferences, online. Attend local meetings for writers and illustrators whenever you can. Befriend other writers in your area (SCBWI offers members a roster broken down by state)—share guidelines, share subscriptions, be conference buddies and roommates, join a critique group or writing group, exchange information and offer support. Get online—sign on to listservs, post on message boards and blogs, visit social networking sites and chatrooms. Exchange addresses, phone numbers and e-mail addresses with writers or illustrators you meet at events. And at conferences, don't be afraid to talk to people, ask strangers to join you for lunch, approach speakers and introduce yourself, or chat in elevators and hallways.

12. PERFECT YOUR CRAFT AND DON'T SUBMIT UNTIL YOUR WORK IS ITS BEST. It's often been said that a writer should try to write every day. Great manuscripts don't happen overnight; there's time, research and revision involved. As you visit bookstores and study what others have written and illustrated, really step back and look at your own work and ask yourself—honestly—*How does my work measure up? Is it ready for editors or art directors to see?* If it's not, keep working. Join a critique group or get a professional manuscript or portfolio critique.

13. BE PATIENT, LEARN FROM REJECTION, AND DON'T GIVE UP! Thousands of manuscripts land on editors' desks; thousands of illustration samples line art directors' file drawers. There are so many factors that come into play when evaluating submissions. Keep in mind that you might not hear back from publishers promptly. Persistence and patience are important qualities in writers and illustrators working toward publication. Keep at it—it will come. It can take a while, but when you get that first book contract or first assignment, you'll know it was worth the wait. (For proof, read the "First Books" article later in this book!)

BEFORE YOUR FIRST SALE

If you're just beginning to pursue your career as a children's book writer or illustrator, it's important to learn the proper procedures, formats and protocol for the publishing industry. This article outlines the basics you need to know before you submit your work to a market.

FINDING THE BEST MARKETS FOR YOUR WORK

Researching publishers thoroughly is a basic element of submitting your work successfully. Editors and art directors hate to receive inappropriate submissions; handling them wastes a lot of their time, not to mention your time and money, and they are the main reason some publishers have chosen not to accept material over the transom. By randomly sending out material without knowing a company's needs, you're sure to meet with rejection.

If you're interested in submitting to a particular magazine, write to request a sample copy or see if it's available in your local library or bookstore. For a book publisher, obtain a book catalog and check a library or bookstore for titles produced by that publisher. Most publishers and magazines have websites that include catalogs or sample articles (websites are given within the listings). Studying such materials carefully will better acquaint you with a publisher's or magazine's writing, illustration and photography styles and formats.

Most of the book publishers and magazines listed in this book offer some sort of writer's, artist's or photographer's guidelines for a self-addressed, stamped envelope (SASE). Guidelines are also often found on publishers' websites. It's important to read and study guidelines before submitting work. You'll get a better understanding of what a particular publisher wants. You may even decide, after reading the submission guidelines, that your work isn't right for a company you considered.

SUBMITTING YOUR WORK

Throughout the listings, you'll read requests for particular elements to include when contacting markets. Here are explanations of some of these important submission components.

Queries, cover letters & proposals

A query is a no-more-than-one-page, well-written letter meant to arouse an editor's interest in your work. Query letters briefly outline the work you're proposing and include facts, anecdotes, interviews or other pertinent information that give the editor a feel for the manuscript's premise—enticing her to want to know more. End your letter with a straightforward request to submit the work, and include information on its approximate length, date it could be completed, and whether accompanying photos or artwork are available.

In a query letter, think about presenting your book as a publisher's catalog would present it. Read through a good catalog and examine how the publishers give enticing summaries of their books in a spare amount of words. It's also important that query letters give editors a taste of your writing style. For good advice and samples of queries, cover letters and other correspondence, consult the article "Crafting a Query" in this book, as well as *Formatting & Submitting Your Manuscript, 3rd Ed.* and *How to Write Attention-Grabbing Query & Cover Letters* (both Writer's Digest Books).

- **QUERY LETTERS FOR NONFICTION.** Queries are usually required when submitting nonfiction material to a publisher. The goal of a nonfiction query is to convince the editor your idea is perfect for her readership and that you're qualified to do the job. Note any previous writing experience and include published samples to prove your credentials, especially samples related to the subject matter you're querying about.
- **QUERY LETTERS FOR FICTION.** For a fiction query, explain the story's plot, main characters, conflict, and resolution. Just as in nonfiction queries, make the editor eager to see more.
- **COVER LETTERS FOR WRITERS.** Some editors prefer to review complete manuscripts, especially for picture books or fiction. In such cases, the cover letter (which should be no longer than one page) serves as your introduction, establishes your credentials as a writer, and gives the editor an overview of the manuscript. If the editor asked for the manuscript because of a query, note this in your cover letter.
- **COVER LETTERS FOR ILLUSTRATORS AND PHOTOGRAPHERS.** For an illustrator or photographer, the cover letter serves as an introduction to the art director and establishes professional credentials when submitting samples. Explain what services you can provide as well as what type of follow-up contact you plan to make, if any. Be sure to include the URL of your online portfolio if you have one.

- **RÉSUMÉS.** Often writers, illustrators and photographers are asked to submit résumés with cover letters and samples. They can be created in a variety of formats, from a single page listing information to color brochures featuring your work. Keep your résumé brief, and focus on your achievements, including your clients and the work you've done for them, as well as your educational background and any awards you've received. Do not use the same résumé you'd use for a typical job application.
- **BOOK PROPOSALS.** Throughout the listings in the Book Publishers section, publishers refer to submitting a synopsis, outline and sample chapters. Depending on an editor's preference, some or all of these components, along with a cover letter, make up a book proposal.

A *synopsis* summarizes the book, covering the basic plot (including the ending). It should be easy to read and flow well.

An *outline* covers your book chapter by chapter and provides highlights of each. If you're developing an outline for fiction, include major characters, plots and subplots, and book length. Requesting an outline is uncommon, and the word is somewhat interchangeable with "synopsis."

Sample chapters give a more comprehensive idea of your writing skill. Some editors may request the first two or three chapters to determine if they're interested in seeing the whole book. Some may request a set number of pages.

Manuscript formats

When submitting a complete manuscript, follow some basic guidelines. In the upper-left corner of your title page, type your legal name (not pseudonym), address and phone number. In the upper-right corner, type the approximate word count. All material in the upper corners should be single-spaced. Then type the title (centered) almost halfway down that page, the word "by" two spaces under that, and your name or pseudonym two spaces under "by."

The first page should also include the title (centered) one-third of the way down. Two spaces under that, type "by" and your name or pseudonym. To begin the body of your manuscript, drop down two double spaces and indent five spaces for each new paragraph. There should be one-inch margins around all sides of a full typewritten page. (Manuscripts with wide margins are more readable and easier to edit.)

Set your computer to double-space the manuscript body. From page two to the end of the manuscript, include your last name followed by a comma and the title (or key words of the title) in the upper-left corner. The page number should go in the top right corner. Drop down two double spaces to begin the body of each page. If you're submitting a novel, type each chapter title one-third of the way down the page. For more information on manuscript formats, read *Formatting & Submitting Your Manuscript, 3rd Ed.* (Writer's Digest Books).

Picture book formats

The majority of editors prefer to see complete manuscripts for picture books. When typing the text of a picture book, don't indicate page breaks and don't type each page of text on a new sheet of paper. And unless you are an illustrator, don't worry about supplying art. Editors will find their own illustrators for picture books. Most of the time, a writer and an illustrator who work on the same book never meet or interact. The editor acts as a go-between and works with the writer and illustrator throughout the publishing process. *How to Write and Sell Children's Picture Books*, by Jean E. Karl (Writer's Digest Books), offers advice on preparing text and marketing your work.

If you're an illustrator who has written your own book, consider creating a dummy or storyboard containing both art and text, and then submit it along with your complete manuscript and sample pieces of final art (color photocopies or computer printouts—never originals). Publishers interested in picture books specify in their listings what should be submitted. For tips on creating a dummy, refer to *How to Write and Illustrate Children's Books and Get Them Published*, edited by Treld Pelkey Bicknell and Felicity Trotman (North Light Books), or Frieda Gates' book, *How to Write, Illustrate, and Design Children's Books* (Lloyd-Simone Publishing Company).

Writers may also want to learn the art of dummy-making to help them through their writing process with things like pacing, rhythm and length. For a great explanation and helpful hints, see *You Can Write Children's Books*, by Tracey E. Dils (Writer's Digest Books).

Mailing submissions

Your main concern when packaging material is to be sure it arrives undamaged. If your manuscript is fewer than six pages, simply fold it in thirds and send it in a #10 (business-size) envelope. For a SASE, either fold another #10 envelope in thirds or insert a #9 (reply) envelope, which fits in a #10 neatly without folding.

Another option is folding your manuscript in half in a 6x9 envelope, with a #9 or #10 SASE enclosed. For larger manuscripts, use a 9x12 envelope both for mailing the submission and as a SASE (which can be folded in half). Book manuscripts require sturdy packaging for mailing. Include a self-addressed mailing label and return postage. If asked to send artwork and photographs, remember they require a bit more care in packaging to guarantee they arrive in good condition. Sandwich illustrations and photos between heavy cardboard that is slightly larger than the work. The cardboard can be secured by rubber bands or with tape. If you tape the cardboard together, check that the artwork doesn't stick to the tape. Be sure your name and address appear on the back of each piece of art or each photo in case the material becomes separated. For the packaging, use either a manila envelope, a foam-padded envelope, brown paper or a mailer lined with plastic air bubbles. Bind nonjoined edges with reinforced mailing tape and affix a typed mailing label or clearly write your address.

Mailing material first class ensures quick delivery. Also, first-class mail is forwarded for one year if the addressee has moved, and it can be returned if undeliverable. If you're concerned about your original material safely reaching its destination, consider other mailing options such as UPS. No matter which way you send material, never send it where it requires a signature. Agents and editors are too busy to sign for packages.

Remember, companies outside your own country can't use your country's postage when returning a manuscript to you. When mailing a submission to another country, include a self-addressed envelope and International Reply Coupons, or IRCs. (You'll see this term in many listings in the Canadian & International Book Publishers section.) Your postmaster can tell you, based on a package's weight, the correct number of IRCs to include to ensure its return. If it's not necessary for an editor to return your work (such as with photocopies), don't include return postage.

Unless requested, it's never a good idea to use a company's fax number to send manuscript submissions. This can disrupt a company's internal business. Study the listings for specifics and visit publishers' and market websites for more information.

Keeping submission records

It's important to keep track of the material you submit. When recording each submission, include the date it was sent, the business and contact name, and any enclosures (such as samples of writing, artwork or photography). You can create a record-keeping system of your own or look for record-keeping software in your area computer store.

Keep copies of articles or manuscripts you send together with related correspondence to make follow-up easier. When you sell rights to a manuscript, artwork or photos, you can "close" your file on a particular submission by noting the date the material was accepted, what rights were purchased, the publication date and payment.

Often writers, illustrators and photographers fail to follow up on overdue responses. If you don't hear from a publisher within their stated response time, wait another month or so and follow up with a note asking about the status of your submission. Include the title or description, date sent and a SASE for response. Ask the contact person when she anticipates making a decision. You may refresh the memory of a buyer who temporarily forgot about your submission. At the very least, you'll receive a definite "no" and free yourself to send the material to another publisher.

Simultaneous submissions

If you opt for simultaneous submissions—sending the same material to several publishers at the same time—only submit to publishers who state in their submission guidelines that they accept simultaneous submissions. In such cases, always specify in your cover letter that you've submitted to more than one editor/agent.

It's especially important to keep track of simultaneous submissions, so if you get an offer on a manuscript sent to more than one publisher, you can instruct other publishers to withdraw your work from consideration.

AGENTS & ART REPS

Most children's writers, illustrators and photographers, especially those just beginning, are confused about whether to enlist the services of an agent or representative. The decision is strictly one that each writer, illustrator or photographer must make for herself. Some are confident with their own negotiation skills and believe acquiring an agent or rep is not in their best interest. Others feel uncomfortable in the business arena or are not willing to sacrifice valuable creative time for marketing.

About half of children's publishers accept unagented work, so it's possible to break into children's publishing without an agent. Writers targeting magazine markets don't need the services of an agent. In fact, it's practically impossible to find an agent interested in marketing articles and short stories—there simply isn't enough financial incentive.

One benefit of having an agent, though, is it may speed up the process of getting your work reviewed, especially by publishers who don't accept unagented submissions. If an agent has a good reputation and submits your manuscript to an editor, that manuscript will likely bypass the first-read stage (which is generally done by editorial assistants and junior editors) and end up on the editor's desk sooner.

When agreeing to have a reputable agent represent you, remember that she should be familiar with the needs of the current market and evaluate your manuscript/artwork/photos accordingly. She should also determine the quality of your piece and whether it is saleable. When your manuscript sells, your agent should negotiate a favorable contract and clear up any questions you have about payments.

Keep in mind that however reputable the agent or rep is, she has limitations.

Representation does not guarantee sale of your work. It just means an agent or rep sees potential in your writing, art or photos. Though an agent or rep may offer criticism or advice on how to improve your work, she cannot make you a better writer, artist or photographer.

Literary agents typically charge a 15 percent commission from the sale of writing; art and photo representatives usually charge a 25–30 percent commission. Such fees are taken from advances and royalty earnings. If your agent sells foreign rights or film rights to your work, she will deduct a higher percentage because she will most likely be dealing with an overseas agent with whom she must split the fee.

Be advised that not every agent is open to representing a writer, artist or photographer who lacks an established track record. Just as when approaching a publisher, the manuscript, artwork or photos, and query or cover letter you submit to a potential agent must be attractive and professional looking. Your first impression must be as an organized, articulate person. For listings of agents and reps, turn to the Agents & Art Reps section.

For additional listings of art reps, consult *Artist's & Graphic Designer's Market*; for photo reps, see *Photographer's Market*; for more information and additional listings of literary agents, see *Guide to Literary Agents* (all Writer's Digest Books).

RUNNING YOUR BUSINESS

The basics for writers & illustrators.

A career in children's publishing involves more than just writing skills or artistic talent. Successful authors and illustrators must be able to hold their own in negotiations, keep records, understand contract language, grasp copyright law, pay taxes and take care of a number of other business concerns. Although agents and reps, accountants and lawyers, and writers' organizations offer help in sorting out such business issues, it's wise to have a basic understanding of them going in. This article offers just that—basic information. For a more in-depth look at the subjects covered here, check your library or bookstore for books and magazines to help you. We also tell you how to get information on issues like taxes and copyright from the federal government.

CONTRACTS & NEGOTIATION

Before you see your work in print or begin working with an editor or art director on a project, there is negotiation. And whether negotiating a book contract, a magazine article assignment, or an illustration or photo assignment, there are a few things to keep in mind. First, if you find any clauses vague or confusing in a contract, get legal advice. The time and money invested in counseling up front could protect you from problems later. If you have an agent or rep, she will review any contract.

A contract is an agreement between two or more parties that specifies the fees to be paid, services rendered, deadlines, rights purchased and, for artists and photographers, whether original work is returned. Most companies have standard contracts for writers, illustrators and photographers. The specifics (such as royalty rates, advances, delivery dates, etc.) are typed in after negotiations.

Though it's OK to conduct negotiations over the phone, get a written contract once both parties have agreed on terms. Never depend on oral stipulations; written contracts protect both parties from misunderstandings. Watch for clauses that may not be in your best interest, such as "work-for-hire." When you do work-for-hire, you give up all rights to your creations.

When negotiating a book deal, find out whether your contract contains an option clause. This clause requires the author to give the publisher a first look at her next work before offering it to other publishers. Though it's editorial etiquette to give the publisher the first chance at publishing your next work, be wary of statements in the contract that could trap you. Don't allow the publisher to consider the next project for more than 30 days and be specific about what type of work should actually be considered "next work." (For example, if the book under contract is a young adult novel, specify that the publisher will receive an exclusive look at *only* your next young adult novel.)

Book publishers' payment methods

Book publishers pay authors and artists in royalties, a percentage of either the wholesale or retail price of each book sold. From large publishing houses, the author usually receives an advance issued against future royalties before the book is published.

After your book has sold enough copies to earn back your advance, you'll start to get royalty checks. Some publishers hold a reserve against returns, which means a percentage of royalties is held back in case books are returned from bookstores. If you have a reserve clause in your contract, find out the exact percentage of total sales that will be withheld and the time period the publisher will hold this money. You should be reimbursed this amount after a reasonable time period, such as a year. Royalty percentages vary with each publisher, but there are standard ranges.

Book publishers' rates

First-time picture book authors can expect advances of $500–20,000; first-time picture book illustrators' advances range from $2,000–15,000. Rates go up for subsequent books. Experienced authors can expect higher advances. Royalties for picture books are generally about five percent (split between the author and illustrator) but can go as high as 10 percent. Those who both write and illustrate a book, of course, receive the full royalty. Advances for novels can fetch advances of $1,000–100,000 and 10 percent royalties.

As you might expect, advance and royalty figures vary from house to house and are affected by the time of year, the state of the economy and other factors. Some smaller houses may not even pay royalties, just flat fees. Educational houses may not offer advances or may offer smaller amounts. Religious publishers tend to offer smaller advances than trade publishers. First-time writers and illustrators generally start on the low end of the scale, while established and high-profile writers are paid more. For more information, SCBWI members can request or download SCBWI publication "Answer to Some Questions About Contracts." (Visit scbwi.org.)

Pay rates for magazines

For writers, fee structures for magazines are based on a per-word rate or range for a specific article length. Artists and photographers have a few more variables to contend with before contracting their services.

Payment for illustrations and photos can be set by such factors as whether the piece(s) will be black and white or four-color, how many are to be purchased, where the work appears (cover or inside), circulation, and the artist's or photographer's prior experience.

Remaindering

When a book goes out of print, a publisher will sell any existing copies to a wholesaler who, in turn, sells the copies to stores at a discount. When the books are "remaindered" to a wholesaler, they are usually sold at a price just above the cost of printing. When negotiating a contract with a publisher, you may want to discuss the possibility of purchasing the remaindered copies before they are sold to a wholesaler, then you can market the copies you purchased and still make a profit.

KNOW YOUR RIGHTS

A copyright is a form of protection provided to creators of original works, published or unpublished. In general, copyright protection ensures the writer, illustrator or photographer the power to decide how her work is used and allows her to receive payment for each use.

Essentially, copyright also encourages the creation of new works by guaranteeing the creator power to sell rights to the work in the marketplace. The copyright holder can print, reprint or copy her work; sell or distribute copies of her work; or prepare derivative works such as plays, collages or recordings. The Copyright Law is designed to protect work (created on or after January 1, 1978) for her lifetime plus 70 years. If you collaborate with someone else on a written or artistic project, the copyright will last for the lifetime of the last survivor plus 70 years. The creators' heirs may hold a copyright for an additional 70 years. After that, the work becomes public domain. Works created anonymously or under a pseudonym are protected for 120 years, or 95 years after publication. Under work-for-hire agreements, you relinquish your copyright to your employer.

Copyright notice & registration

Although it's not necessary to include a copyright notice on unregistered work, if you don't feel your work is safe without the notice (especially if posting work online), it is your right to include one. Including a copyright notice—(©) (year of work, your name)—should help safeguard against plagiarism.

Registration is a legal formality intended to make copyright public record, and it can help you win more money in a court case. By registering work within three months of publication or before an infringement occurs, you are eligible to collect statutory damages and attorney's fees. If you register later than three months after publication, you will qualify only for actual damages and profits.

Ideas and concepts are not copyrightable, only expressions of those ideas and concepts can be protected. A character type or basic plot outline, for example, is not subject to a copyright infringement lawsuit. Also, titles, names, short phrases or slogans, and lists of contents are not subject to copyright protection, though titles and names may be protected through the Trademark Office.

You can register a group of articles, illustrations or photos if it meets these criteria:
- the group is assembled in order, such as in a notebook
- the works bear a single title, such as "Works by (your name)"
- it is the work of one writer, artist or photographer
- the material is the subject of a single claim to copyright

It's a publisher's responsibility to register your book for copyright. If you've previously registered the same material, you must inform your editor and supply the previous copyright information; otherwise, the publisher can't register the book in its published form.

For more information about the proper way to register works and to order the correct forms, contact the U.S. Copyright Office, (202)707-3000. For information about how to use the copyright forms, request a copy of Circular I on Copyright Basics. All of the forms and circulars are free. Send the completed registration form along with the stated fee and a copy of the work to the Copyright Office.

For specific answers to questions about copyright (but not legal advice), call the Copyright Public Information Office at (202)707-3000 weekdays between 8:30 a.m. and 5 p.m. EST. Forms can also be downloaded from the Library of Congress website: copyright. gov. The site also includes a list of frequently asked questions, tips on filling out forms, general copyright information, and links to other sites related to copyright issues.

The rights publishers buy

The copyright law specifies that a writer, illustrator or photographer generally sells one-time rights to her work unless she and the buyer agree otherwise in writing. Many publications will want more exclusive rights to your work than just one-time usage; some will even require you to sell all rights. Be sure you are monetarily compensated for the additional rights you relinquish. If you must give up all rights to a work, carefully consider the price you're being offered to determine whether you'll be compensated for the loss of other potential sales.

Writers who only give up limited rights to their work can then sell reprint rights to other publications, foreign rights to international publications, or even movie rights, should the opportunity arise. Artists and photographers can sell their work to other markets such as paper product companies who may use an image on a calendar, greeting card or mug. Illustrators and photographers may even sell original work after it has been published. There are a number of galleries throughout the U.S. that display and sell the original work of children's illustrators.

Rights acquired through the sale of a book manuscript are explained in each publisher's contract. Take time to read relevant clauses to be sure you understand what rights each contract is specifying before signing. Be sure your contract contains a clause allowing all rights to revert back to you in the event the publisher goes out of business. (You may even want to have the contract reviewed by an agent or an attorney specializing in publishing law.)

The following are the rights you'll most often sell to publishers, periodicals and producers in the marketplace:

FIRST RIGHTS. The buyer purchases the rights to use the work for the first time in any medium. All other rights remain with the creator. When material is excerpted in this way (from a soon-to-be-published book in this manner) for use in a newspaper or periodical, first serial rights are also purchased.

ONE-TIME RIGHTS. The buyer has no guarantee that she is the first to use a piece. One-time permission to run written work, illustrations or photos is acquired, and then the rights revert back to the creator.

FIRST NORTH AMERICAN SERIAL RIGHTS. This is similar to first rights, except that companies who distribute both in the U.S. and Canada will stipulate these rights to ensure that another North American company won't come out with simultaneous usage of the same work.

SECOND SERIAL (REPRINT) RIGHTS. In this case, newspapers and magazines are granted the right to reproduce a work that has already appeared in another publication. These rights are also purchased by a newspaper or magazine editor who wants to publish part of a book after the book has been published. The proceeds from reprint rights for a book are often split evenly between the author and his publishing company.

SIMULTANEOUS RIGHTS. More than one publication buys one-time rights to the same work at the same time. Use of such rights occurs among magazines with circulations that don't overlap, such as many religious publications.

ALL RIGHTS. Just as it sounds, the writer, illustrator or photographer relinquishes all rights to a piece—she no longer has any say in who acquires rights to use it. All rights are purchased by publishers who pay premium usage fees, have an exclusive format, or have other book or magazine interests from which the purchased work can generate more mileage. If a company insists on acquiring all rights to your work, see if you can negotiate for the rights to revert back to you after a reasonable period of time. If they agree to such a proposal, get it in writing. Note: Writers, illustrators and photographers should be wary of "work-for-hire" arrangements. If you sign an agreement stipulating that your work will be done as work-for-hire, you will not control the copyrights of the completed work—the company that hired you will be the copyright owner.

FOREIGN SERIAL RIGHTS. Be sure before you market to foreign publications that you have sold only North American—not worldwide—serial rights to previous markets. If so, you are free to market to publications that may be interested in material that's appeared in a North American-based periodical.

SYNDICATION RIGHTS. This is a division of serial rights. For example, if a syndicate prints portions of a book in installments in its newspapers, it would be syndicating second serial rights. The syndicate would receive a commission and leave the remainder to be split between the author and publisher.

SUBSIDIARY RIGHTS. These include serial rights, dramatic rights, book club rights or translation rights. The contract should specify what percentage of profits from sales of these rights go to the author and publisher.

DRAMATIC, TELEVISION AND MOTION PICTURE RIGHTS. During a specified time, the interested party tries to sell a story to a producer or director. Many times options are renewed because the selling process can be lengthy.

DISPLAY RIGHTS OR ELECTRONIC PUBLISHING RIGHTS. They're also known as "Data, Storage and Retrieval." Usually listed under subsidiary rights, the marketing of electronic rights in this era of rapidly expanding capabilities and markets for electronic material can be tricky. Display rights can cover text or images to be used in a CD or online, or they may cover use of material in formats not even fully developed yet. If a display rights clause is listed in your contract, try to negotiate its elimination. Otherwise, be sure to pin down which electronic rights are being purchased. Demand the clause be restricted to things designed to be read only. By doing this, you maintain your rights to use your work for things such as games and interactive software.

SOURCES FOR CONTRACT HELP

Writers organizations offer a wealth of information to members, including contract advice:

SOCIETY OF CHILDREN'S BOOK WRITERS AND ILLUSTRATORS members can find information in the SCBWI publication "Answers to Some Questions About Contracts." Contact SCBWI at 8271 Beverly Blvd., Los Angeles CA 90048, (323)782-1010, or visit their website: scbwi.org.

THE AUTHORS GUILD also offers contract tips. Visit their website: authorsguild.org. (Members of the guild can receive a 75-point contract review from the guild's legal staff.) See the website for membership information and application form, or contact The Authors Guild at 31 E. 28th St., 10th Floor, New York NY 10016, (212)563-5904. Fax: (212)564-5363. E-mail: staff@authorsguild.org.

STRICTLY BUSINESS

An essential part of being a freelance writer, illustrator or photographer is running your freelance business. It's imperative to maintain accurate business records to determine if you're making a profit as a freelancer. Keeping correct, organized records will also make your life easier as you approach tax time.

When setting up your system, begin by keeping a bank account and ledger for your business finances apart from your personal finances. Also, if writing, illustration or photography is secondary to another freelance career, keep separate business records for each.

You will likely accumulate some business expenses before showing any profit when you start out as a freelancer. To substantiate your income and expenses to the IRS, keep all invoices, cash receipts, sales slips, bank statements, canceled checks and receipts related to travel expenses and entertaining clients. For entertainment expenditures, record the date, place and purpose of the business meeting, as well as gas mileage. Keep records for all purchases, big and small. Don't take the small purchases for granted; they can add up to a substantial amount. File all receipts in chronological order. Maintaining a separate file for each month simplifies retrieving records at the end of the year.

Record keeping

When setting up a single-entry bookkeeping system, record income and expenses separately. Use some of the subheads that appear on Schedule C (the form used for recording income from a business) of the 1040 tax form so you can easily transfer information onto the tax form when filing your return. In your ledger, include a description of each transaction—the date, source of income (or debts from business purchases), description of what was purchased or sold, the amount of the transaction, and whether payment was by cash, check or credit card.

Don't wait until January 1 to start keeping records. The moment you first make a business-related purchase or sell an article, book manuscript, illustration or photo, begin tracking your profits and losses. If you keep records from January 1 to December 31, you're using a calendar-year accounting period. Any other accounting period is called a fiscal year.

There are two types of accounting methods you can choose from—the cash method and the accrual method. The cash method is used more often: You record income when it is received and expenses when they're disbursed.

Using the accrual method, you report income at the time you earn it rather than when it's actually received. Similarly, expenses are recorded at the time they're incurred rather than when you actually pay them. If you choose this method, keep separate records for "accounts receivable" and "accounts payable."

Satisfying the IRS

To successfully—and legally—work as a freelancer, you must know what income you should report and what deductions you can claim. But before you can do that, you must prove to the IRS you're in business to make a profit, that your writing, illustration or photography is not merely a hobby. The Tax Reform Act of 1986 says you should show a profit for three years out of a five-year period to attain professional status. The IRS considers these factors as proof of your professionalism:

- accurate financial records
- a business bank account separate from your personal account
- proven time devoted to your profession
- whether it's your main or secondary source of income
- your history of profits and losses
- the amount of training you have invested in your field
- your expertise

If your business is unincorporated, you'll fill out tax information on Schedule C of Form 1040. If you're unsure of what deductions you can take, request the IRS publication containing this information. Under the Tax Reform Act, only 30 percent of business meals, entertainment and related tips, and parking charges are deductible. Other deductible expenses allowed on Schedule C include: car expenses for business-related trips; professional courses and seminars; depreciation of office equipment, such as a computer; dues and publication subscriptions; and miscellaneous expenses, such as postage used for business needs.

If you're working out of a home office, a portion of your mortgage interest (or rent), related utilities, property taxes, repair costs and depreciation may be deducted as business expenses—under special circumstances. To learn more about the possibility of home office deductions, consult IRS Publication 587, Business Use of Your Home.

The method of paying taxes on income not subject to withholding is called "estimated tax" for individuals. If you expect to owe more than $500 at year's end and if the total amount of income tax that will be withheld during the year will be less than 90 percent of the tax shown on the current year's return, you'll generally make estimated tax payments. Estimated tax payments are made in four equal installments due on April 15, June 15, September 15, and January 15 (assuming you're a calendar-year taxpayer). For more information, request Publication 533, Self-Employment Tax.

The Internal Revenue Service's website (irs.gov) offers tips and instant access to IRS forms and publications.

Social Security tax

Depending on your net income as a freelancer, you may be liable for a Social Security tax. This is a tax designed for those who don't have Social Security withheld from their paychecks. You're liable if your net income is $400 or more per year. Net income is the difference between your income and allowable business deductions. Request Schedule SE, Computation of Social Security Self-Employment Tax, if you qualify.

If completing your income tax return proves to be too complex, consider hiring an accountant (the fee is a deductible business expense) or contact the IRS for assistance. (Look in the White Pages under U.S. Government—Internal Revenue Service or check their website, irs.gov.) In addition to offering numerous publications to instruct you in various facets of preparing a tax return, the IRS also has walk-in centers in some cities.

Insurance

As a self-employed professional, be aware of what health and business insurance coverage is available to you. Unless you're a Canadian who is covered by national health insurance or a full-time freelancer covered by your spouse's policy, health insurance will no doubt be one of your biggest expenses. Under the terms of a 1985 government act (COBRA), if you leave a job with health benefits, you're entitled to continue that coverage for up to 18 months; you pay 100 percent of the premium and sometimes a small administration fee. Eventually, you must search for your own health plan. You may also choose to purchase disability and life insurance. Disability insurance is offered through many private insurance companies and state governments. This insurance pays a monthly fee that covers living and business expenses during periods of long-term recuperation from a health problem. The amount of money paid is based on the recipient's annual earnings.

Before contacting any insurance representative, talk to other writers, illustrators or photographers to learn which insurance companies they recommend. If you belong to a writers' or artists' organization, ask the organization if it offers insurance coverage for professionals. (SCBWI has a plan available to members in certain states. Look through the Clubs & Organizations section for other groups that may offer coverage.) Group coverage may be more affordable and provide more comprehensive coverage than an individual policy.

AGENTS TELL ALL

Literary agents answer some common (and not-so-common) questions.

by *Chuck Sambuchino, Ricki Schultz and Donna Gambale*

Whether during their travels to conferences or on their personal blogs, literary agents get a lot of questions from writers—some over and over. Below is a roundup of such questions answered by some of the top children's agents in the business.

ON STARTING STRONG

When you're reviewing a partial fiction manuscript, what do you hate to see in Chapter 1?

I hate to see a whiny character who's in the middle of a fight with one of their parents, slamming doors, rolling eyes and displaying all sorts of other stereotypical behavior. I hate seeing character "stats" ("Hi, I'm Brian. I'm 10 years and 35 days old with brown hair and green eyes."). I also tend to have a hard time bonding with characters who talk to the reader ("Let me tell you about the summer when I …").

—**KELLY SONNACK** *is a literary agent with the Andrea Brown Literary Agency*

In YA and teen, what are some page 1 clichés you come across?

The most common problem I see is a story that's been told a million times before, without any new twists to make it unique enough to stand out. Same plot, same situations, same set up = the same ol' story. For example: abusive parents/kid's a rebel; family member(s) killed tragically/kid's a loner; divorced parents/kid acts out. Another problem I often see is when the protagonist/main characters don't have an age-appropriate voice. For example: If your main character is 14, let him talk like a 14-year-old. And lastly, being unable to "connect" with the main character(s). For example: Characters are too whiny or bratty, or a character shows no emotion/angst.

—**CHRISTINE WITTHOHN** *is the founder of Book Cents Literary*

What are some Chapter 1 clichés you often come across when reading a partial manuscript?

One of my biggest pet peeves is when writers try to stuff too much exposition into dialogue rather than trusting their abilities as storytellers to get information across. I'm talking stuff like the mom saying, "Listen, Jimmy, I know you've missed your father ever since he died in that mysterious boating accident last year, but I'm telling you, you'll love this summer camp!" So often writers feel like they have to hook the reader right away. In some ways that's true, but in others you can hook a reader with things other than explosions and big secrets being revealed. Good, strong writing and voice can do it, too.

—**CHRIS RICHMAN** *is a literary agent with Upstart Crow Literary*

Tell me about some Chapter 1 clichés that you come across from time to time that immediately make you stop reading.

The "information dump" is one—paragraphs of information about the protagonist, the protagonist's parents, background information about the protagonist's situation. Often, this information is unnecessary, and if it is necessary, a blend of telling and showing, along with a measured unfolding of information, is a stronger approach. Another is starting the first chapter with the wrong action. Writers are often instructed to start a story in the middle of the action, but it's important that it be the right action. For example, I recently read a manuscript in which the protagonists embark on a dangerous outing in the first chapter. But since I didn't have a clear sense yet for the significance of this outing, the action was undermined and I wasn't invested in the outcome. It was a crucial scene, but the author needed to back up and start with completely different action that placed me more firmly in the world of the story. Finally, I stop reading when the first chapter starts with the protagonist saying something like, "Hi, my name is (fill in the blank)."

—**JEN ROFE** *is an agent with Andrea Brown Literary Agency*

What are some reasons you stop reading a YA manuscript?

Once I've determined that the writing is strong enough, it's usually a question of plot (we receive many works that are derivative or otherwise unoriginal) or voice. As we know from the young adults in our lives, anything that sounds even vaguely parental will not be well received. And there's nothing worse than narration that reads like a text message from a grandmother. In the past month, I've received 29 YA partials. Looking back on my notes, I see that I rejected eight for writing, seven for voice, six for derivative or unoriginal plots, four because they were inappropriate for the age group, and two that simply weren't a good fit for the agency but may find a home elsewhere. Then there were two I liked and passed them on to others in my office. Also, I think a lot of writers, seeing the success of *Twilight*, have tried to force their manuscripts into this genre. I know you've heard it before, but it's so true: Write what you are meant to write—don't write what you think will sell.

—JESSICA SINSHEIMER *is a literary agent with the
Sarah Jane Freymann Literary Agency*

ON VOICE, CONCEPT AND SUBJECT MATTER

I've heard that nothing is taboo anymore in young adult books and you can write about topics such as sex and drugs. Is this true?

I would say this: Nothing is taboo if it's done well. Each scene needs to matter in a novel. I've read a number of "edgy" young adult books where writers seem to add in scenes just for shock value and it doesn't work with the flow of the rest of the novel. "Taboo" subjects need to have a purpose in the progression of the novel—and of course, need to be well written! If it does, then yes, I would say nothing is taboo. Taboo topics do, however, affect whether the school and library market will pick up the book—and this can have an effect on whether a publisher feels they can sell enough copies.

—JESSICA REGEL *is a literary agent with the Jean V. Naggar Literary Agency*

What are three of the biggest mistakes you see writers make when writing for kids/teens?

I find being very preachy is a big turnoff for me. Nine and a half times out of ten, when a query letter for a YA or MG starts talking about all the lessons the novel will teach kids, I reject it. Literature can be very powerful and it can teach lessons, but I think it is most important to focus on writing something that kids will want to read first. I've also seen a lot of things lately set in the '80s or '90s that don't need to be; I think it is because this is when the writers remember being teenagers. However, it is important to remember that a 15-year-old now was born in 1997. The '90s are historical fiction to them, and if the story can work at all set in 2011, it probably should be. Finally—and this isn't a mistake, per se—but writing an authentic teenage voice is very difficult, and I see a lot of writers struggling with it. If there is one thing YA and MG writers should practice and work to perfect, it is writing a teenage voice.

—LAUREN MACLEOD *is an agent with The Strothman Agency*

What are some subjects or styles of writing that you rarely receive in a submission and wonder why more writers don't tackle such a subject/style?

In terms of style and execution, I'd love to see more MG and YA submissions use innovative narrative strategies deliberately and well. For example: alternating voices/points of view, or a structure that plays with narrative time. Kids are sophisticated readers.

Books that engage them on the level of storytelling, as well as story, could break out. In terms of subject matter, I don't see as many stories as you'd think about multicultural families and friendships. I'd also love to see more YA submissions depict awkward, funny and real—rather than flat and glossy—teen romance.

—**MICHELLE ANDELMAN** *is a literary agent with Regal Literary*

Regarding submissions, what do you see too much of? What do you see too little of?

I'm definitely looking for projects with something timeless at their core, whether it's the emotional connection a reader feels to the characters, or the universal humor, or issues that are relevant now and will still be relevant years from now. Can readers truly understand what it's like to be the prince of Denmark? Probably not, but they can identify with feeling disconnected from a dead loved one and the anger at watching him be replaced by a conniving uncle. I want stories that, no matter what the setting, feel true in some way to the reader. I definitely see too many people trying to be something else. I used to make the mistake of listing Roald Dahl as one of my favorite writers from my childhood, but I've found that just inspires a bunch of Dahl knockoffs. And trust me, it's tough to imitate the greats. I get far too much emulation of Dahl, Snicket, Rowling, and whatever else has worked in the past. It's one thing to aspire to greatness; it's another to imitate it. I want people who can appeal to me in the same way as successful writers of yore, with a style that's their own. I see too few writers willing to take chances. I just finished Markus Zusak's wonderful novel, *The Book Thief*. It breaks so many so-called rules for kids' books—there are tons of adult characters and points of view, it's a historical at heart, and it's narrated by Death for crying out loud. It's one of the best young adult novels I've read recently.

—**CHRIS RICHMAN** *is a literary agent at Upstart Crow Literary*

Are there any subjects you feel are untapped and would, therefore, be a refreshing change from the typical multicultural story?

When I was a [bookstore buyer], I was tired of certain subject matters only because those subjects have been explored so well, so often, that you really needed to bring something special to the page to make anyone take notice. Send me a story about some modern immigrant stories, some multi-generational stuff, like the YA novels of Carlos Ruiz Zafon. There are deeply rich stories about being an outsider, and yet how assimilation means a compromise and loss. I'd also love to see more issues of race discussed in modern terms, where there is the melting pot happening across the U.S., yet the tensions are still there, like the fear of the other. I think these stories, when done well, are universal stories, as we all feel that way at some point. Look at Junot Diaz's *The Brief Wondrous Life of Oscar Wao* as exhibit A.

—**JOE MONTI** *is a literary agent with Barry Goldblatt Literary*

ON PICTURE BOOKS & ILLUSTRATIONS

Do you often get queries from authors who have also illustrated their children's book? Are the illustrations usually of enough quality to include them with the submission to publishers?

I do receive many queries from author/illustrators, or from authors who aren't necessarily illustrators but fail to understand that they don't have to worry about submitting illustrations. But most often I find that most illustrators are not the best at coming up with compelling storylines or can't execute the words like a well-seasoned writer (or vice versa: The better writers usually are not the best illustrators).

—**REGINA BROOKS** *is the founder of Serendipity Literary*

With picture books, I suspect you get a lot of submissions and most of them get rejected. Where are writers going wrong?

Rhyming! So many writers think picture books need to rhyme. There are some editors who won't even look at books in rhyme, and a lot more who are extremely wary of them, so it limits an agent on where it can go and the likelihood of it selling. It's also particularly hard to execute perfectly. Aside from rhyming, I see way too many picture books about a family pet or bedtime.

—**KELLY SONNACK** *is a literary agent with the Andrea Brown Literary Agency*

Many people tend to try their hand at children's writing and picture books, but it's often said that writing such books is much more difficult than writers first consider. Why is this so?

I suspect the common thinking goes that if a writer "knows" children, she can write for them. But a successful children's author doesn't simply "know" children—what makes them tick, what their internal and emotional lives are like—she also knows children's literature. She's an avid reader, so she's familiar with what's age-appropriate and authentic to her category of the market. If she's writing a picture book, she's a skilled visual storyteller and can offer up a plot, character, relationship or emotional arc in miniature—but still, and this is the difficult part, in full.

—**MICHELLE ANDELMAN** *is a literary agent with Regal Literary*

What can writers do to increase their chances of getting a picture book published?

I know it sounds simplistic, but write the very best picture books you can. I think the market contraction has been a good thing, for the most part. I'm only selling the very best picture books my clients write—but I'm definitely selling them. Picture books are generally skewing young, and have been for some time, so focus on strong read-alouds and truly kid-friendly styles. I'm having a lot of luck with projects that have the feel of being created by an author-illustrator even if the author is not an artist, in that they're fairly simple, have all kinds of room for fun and interpretation in the illustrations, and have a lot of personality. I see a lot of picture book manuscripts that depend too heavily on dialogue, which tends to give them the feel of a chapter book or middle grade novel. The style isn't a picture book style.

—**ERIN MURPHY** *is the founder of the Erin Murphy Literary Agency*

ON CHILDREN'S NONFICTION

Can you give us some 101 tips on writing nonfiction for kids?

You can write about almost anything when it comes to children's nonfiction, even if it's been done before. But you need to come at the subject from a different angle. If there is already a book on tomatoes and how they grow, then try writing about tomatoes from a cultural angle. There are a ton of books on slavery, but not many on slaves in Haiti during the Haitian Revolution. (Is there even one? There's an idea—someone take it and query me!) Another thing to always consider is your audience. Kids already have textbooks at school, so you shouldn't write your book like one. Come at the subject in a way that kids can relate to and find interesting. Humor is always a useful tool in non-fiction for kids. Adding to a series is a great way to get started as a writer of nonfiction. But it can't hurt to research the market and try to come up with an idea of your own.

—**JOANNA STAMPFEL-VOLPE** *is an agent with New Leaf Literary*

You're looking for nonfiction for young adults, such as picture book biographies. Can you give a few good examples of this for people to read and learn from?

The most important thing to me is that the nonfiction reads like fiction—that there is a "story behind the story." For example, Pamela S. Turner's *George Schaller: Life in the Wild*, from FSG/Kroupa (2008), is a biography of the great field biologist George Schaller. The book explores Dr. Schaller's career both as a scientist and as an advocate for vanishing wildlife. Appealing to children who are interested in animals, science, adventure and the outdoors, each chapter of the book will also be a "mini-biography" of the species being studied. Several of Pamela's other books study certain environments or animals and make science fun and interesting for kids.

—**CARYN WISEMAN** *is a literary agent with the Andrea Brown Literary Agency*

ON CHILDREN'S WRITING CATEGORIES

You seek books with dystopian themes. That seems to be a healthy area of market—particularly in YA. Why do you think this is so? As well, what do you see for the future? Will it always be so hot?

YA topics and trends are cyclical, but I think dystopian is always relevant and in-demand. It's funny that the term "science fiction" is still not "cool" or commercial, still relegated to genre fiction—but *dystopian*—suddenly that word is very cool. Do people not realize that most of it is science fiction? Or magical realism? In that sense, the theme has been hot forever.

It's fascinating to ponder the question "what if?" These books make us think about the world and humanity—how people act toward each other when pushed to the brink, when fighting for survival. It's so interesting to think how quickly these societies we've built could break down and we'd be left with the most basic human instincts.

—**MELISSA SARVER** *is an agent with Elizabeth Kaplan Literary*

If someone asked about the line between middle grade and young adult, how would you explain the difference?

Is there a line? It seems to me there is scale more than a line. An editor said to me recently that if the main character is 14, it automatically gets shelved in YA in the chain stores. There's a line. But I work with authors whose light and wholesome novels, with teen main characters, are read mostly by tweens; and others whose novels are populated by middle graders going through such intense experiences that the readership skews to the high end of MG/low end of YA. I try to focus on helping my clients make their stories the best stories they can be rather than fitting them into boxes. The line sometimes feels like a moving target, and the writer has little control over it; better to focus on what you can control, which is how good it is. That said, characters should feel as though they are truly the age they are supposed to be—and that age *today*. Kids are savvier than they used to be even five or 10 years ago. They are exposed to more and more at a younger age. Writers should respect their readership accordingly.

—**ERIN MURPHY** *is the founder of the Erin Murphy Literary Agency*

Can you explain exactly how chapter books differ from middle grade?

There is a lot of overlap between categories, so the difference between older chapter books and younger middle grade is often just a matter of marketing. Younger chapter books are for kids who have graduated from easy readers and are starting to read more fluently. They usually have 8–10 short chapters, each with a cliffhanger ending. They are often a series, like Captain Underpants or Magic Tree House, and can be lightly or heavily illustrated. Middle grade is for readers in the 8–12 age group. They can have a complex plot and subplot, and while often humorous, they can certainly be more serious. The vocabulary is more sophisticated than chapter books, and the emphasis is on character. *The Qwikpick Adventure Society* by Sam Riddleburger (Dial) is an example of a middle grade book in which the targeted reader is at the younger end of the spectrum. At the older end of the middle grade spectrum is "tween." It's realistic, often contemporary, often edgier than traditional middle-grade, and deals with identity issues, school-based situations, family vs. friends, and just how hard it is to be 12.

—**CARYN WISEMAN** *is a literary agent with the Andrea Brown Literary Agency*

Does "tween" exist as a category?

Tween *does* exist, and various publishers even have specific tween imprints in place. As for queries, the same standard holds true for me in terms of tween as it does with YA or MG: If the voice is authentic, then I'm probably interested. However, I do look more at plot with tween novels. Right now, it's not enough just to have a great tween voice—the storyline also needs to be unique enough to stand out in the marketplace.

—**MEREDITH KAFFEL** *is a literary agent at DeFiore and Company*

ON EVERYTHING ELSE

What's your best piece of advice for new writers who wish to submit their work to agents?

My best one word of advice: professionalize. A new writer who has done her homework on the children's market ahead of time, and submits to agents in a way that suggests a professional approach to a writing career, is going to stand out. Professionalizing may mean doing a few different things that make all the difference: joining a critique group that can help you polish your manuscript before you query, researching and approaching agents according to submission guidelines, crafting a query that aims to pique interest in—rather than fully explain—your project, and joining the Society of Children's Book Writers & Illustrators (SCBWI).

—**MICHELLE ANDELMAN** *is a literary agent with Regal Literary*

One of the areas you seek is young adult. That is a healthy market—and has been for quite some time. However, what do you see for the future? Will it always be so hot?

It's hot; it's just that the competition is huge. Especially in the paranormal romance genre. I think that the YA market will continue to grow in the future, and we will see more variety and dimension in the work that is offered to this market. Authors who are targeting this market really need to bring the groundbreaking stories in order to be competitive due to the saturation factor in the paranormal genre. The window is still open; it's just not open as wide.

—**JENNIFER SCHOBER** *is a literary agent with Spencerhill Associates*

What do you see for the future of young adult literature?

A shift to enhanced e-book domination. My older kids are 9 and 13, and while they love stories and enjoy reading, they also like the computer and the iPad and the television more—in spite of having parents and stepparents that are all voracious readers. Young adult authors are going to have to abandon the urge to be old-school about their writing, in most cases, if they want to find a healthy audience among tomorrow's kids. I've personally got little use for links to music and video and other material I consider extraneous, but the minds of kids today work completely differently than they did even just 10 years ago, for better or for worse. It's just a different, more fragmented requirement for all entertainment.

—**DAVID DUNTON** *is a literary agent at Harvey Klinger, Inc.*

Best piece of advice we haven't talked about yet?

Don't hold back from your passion. Too many folks get caught up in what the marketplace is supposedly looking for, and they lose sight of what they're trying to write. That, and read your drafts (Note the plural usage!) aloud for imperfections of language and cadence. It's an old horse, but not done enough because it may take you days to finish—but the results are astounding.

—**JOE MONTI** *is a literary agent with Barry Goldblatt Literary*

CHUCK SAMBUCHINO (chucksambuchino.com, @chucksambuchino on Twitter) edits the *Guide to Literary Agents* (guidetoliteraryagents.com/blog) as well as the *Children's Writer's & Illustrator's Market*. His pop-humor books include *How to Survive a Garden Gnome Attack* (film rights optioned by Sony) and *Red Dog / Blue Dog: When Pooches Get Political* (reddog-bluedog.com). Chuck's other writing books include *Formatting & Submitting Your Manuscript, 3rd. Ed.*, as well as *Create Your Writer Platform* (fall 2012). Besides that, he is a husband, guitarist, dog owner, and cookie addict.

RICKI SCHULTZ (rickischultz.com) is an Ohio-based freelance writer and recovering high school English teacher. She writes young adult fiction and, as coordinator of The Write-Brained Network (writebrainednetwork.com), she enjoys connecting with other writers.

DONNA GAMBALE works an office job by day, writes young adult novels by night, and travels when possible. She is a contributing editor for the Guide to Literary Agents Blog and freelances as a copyeditor and proofreader of both fiction and nonfiction. She is the author of a mini kit, *Magnetic Kama Sutra* (Running Press, 2009). You can find her online at firstnovelsclub.com, where she and her critique group blog about writing, reading, networking and the rest of life.

PICTURE BOOK PACING

The 20 ultimate editing tools for your work.

....

by Jodell Sadler

When writers consider the best of the best picture books, there are certain features they all have in common: great pacing and great writing. When writers and illustrators focus on pacing (how a story moves, slows, speeds or halts) and the award-winning tools writers have been using for years, it moves the art and words of a story to a whole new level of *Wow!* Studied individually, these 20 ultimate editing tools allow writers to connect with readers, decrease word counts, and bring out the rhythm and heart of their stories in a well-paced picture book.

VERBAL PACING TOOLS

EVERY WORD MATTERS. Each word of a picture book impacts readers, so each word must be chosen purposefully. But when writers move into the nuances of words and explore them fully, we see that one word elates us, breaks our hearts, or adds the essential rhythm needed, as seen in *The LOUD Book!* by Deborah Underwood. Two words pause and point to an irony in *My Cat, the Silliest Cat in the World* by Gilles Bachelet. As readers read, "My cat is very fat, very sweet, and very, very silly," they see that cat is actually an elephant. Three words speed and add aural energy in *Get Busy, Beaver!* by Carolyn Crimi: " 'Go, go, go,' said Pa Beaver." Three words may also slow over three spreads, as "Roar!" repeats in *Oliver Finds His Way* by Phyllis Root to increase tension as Oliver finds himself absolutely lost.

REPETITION RACES. Repetition adds rhythmic beats and creates patterns. Repetition alerts readers to what is important, or pivotal, to a story, while also inviting readers to join in by repeating these lines for themselves. It also builds structure and invites readers to interact with words—and may even act as a pacing marker to highlight changes in a character's emotional journey.

In *Kitten's First Full Moon*, Kevin Henkes uses a repetitive line as a pacing marker. "Still, there was the little bowl of milk, just waiting" breaks up the challenges Kitten faces and marks important emotional changes within his story. Kitten tries and tries and ultimately gives up her search for her big bowl of milk. Once she reaches home and readers reach the climax of the story, the line shifts to "… and there was a great big bowl of milk on the porch …" and the pacing of this line slows. A page turn shows the milk: "… just waiting for her." Another page turn says, "Lucky Kitten!"

RHYTHM ROCKS. Rhythm in a children's book is not a bonus item. It's essential. Rhythm adds beats and energy that make a book fantastic. Rhythmic sounds and emotions are key elements as picture books are listened to as well as read aloud. As readers hear the words of story, they notice pauses and beats, and the words merge with meaning—creating rhythmic strings that are, perhaps, as beautiful as a song.

There are many ways to create rhythm: a repetitive line, parallel structuring, or a three-series are a few. Alliteration, beats, and word choice create rhythm in *Up North at the Cabin* by Marsha Wilson Chall: "From the dock I dive headfirst, / skimming over sand that swirls behind me. / Anchored at the bottom, upside down, / I am an acrobat in a perfect handstand. / Then rising in a sea of air-bubble balloons, / I float on a carpet of waves."

RHYME? Rhyme must be used with care and caution. Near rhyme is a miss, while true rhyme calls for careful word choice and 100 percent commitment to beats, meter, and story. When the rhyme sings, the author serves up a speedy and satisfying read. *Doggone Dogs!* by Karen Beaumont is a great example. "As the morning sun / peeks through the dark … / Doggone dogs begin to bark. / NO, DOGS! / DOWN, DOGS! / SIT, DOGS! / Hey! / Doggone dogs do not obey."

QUESTIONS CREATE THE QUEST. Questions may be used to pull readers through a story. Questions alert readers toward something specific, offer surprise, or even pose the contrary. They create performances readers will love and may become an entire premise for a story like in *It's A Book* by Lane Smith: "Do I need a password?"

A story that uses questions to serve up surprise is *Where's My Mummy?* by Carolyn Crimi. A young mummy plays a game of hide and shriek before bed. Big mummy hides, while little mummy counts bandages. When little mummy creeps out, a rhythmic onomatopoeia previews a repetitive question: "Clank clink clank / Woo boo woo / Clank Clink CLOO / Mama Mummy, is that you?" Before the page turn, these words also beg the question: If not Mummy, who?

SETTING DEVELOPS TIME AND PLACE. Setting creates a sense of place while it also serves as an innovative pacing tool. When fully explored, setting adds variety and excitement, and it can break up story in interesting, non-linear ways, and this benefits readers. Setting can move readers in time and place, to and fro and back again, or create two different settings that run simultaneously but come together at the climax.

Two different settings merge in *One Dark Night* by Lisa Wheeler, which begins with rhythm and a thrill. "In a wee little house, / In a wee little hole, / Lived a wee little mouse / and a wee little mole …" Readers turn the page and discover a second setting introduced: "Meanwhile … / In a BIG GIANT lair, / Near a BIG GIANT glen, / Lived a BIG GIANT bear. / In this BIG GIANT den …" These alternating settings build tension as readers learn these natural-born enemies will soon meet up, and they begin to wonder: What will happen then?

DETAILS DO DOUBLE DUTY. Details provide an opportunity to share a lot of information in few words. They weave in fabulous wordplay, add rhythm, reveal character, or act as a pacing marker. Details slow the reader as needed to enhance the emotional trajectory of a story. A detail that serves double-duty is found in *Banjo Granny*. Sarah Martin Busse and Jacqueline Briggs Martin write, "She [Granny] put on her thousand-mile shoes." This immediately announces Granny's long journey and her determined spirit.

DESCRIPTIONS DANCE. Descriptions normally slow the pace and allow time for the reader to process information that's important to the story, but what's key is that descriptions may also speed story and create a whole, believable world built out of words, depending on how writers use literary devices to craft fabulous word strings.

In *Looking for a Moose,* Phyllis Root invites readers to "TROMP STOMP! TROMP STOMP!" through the woods—but not just any woods: "treesy-breezy, tilty-stilty, wobbly-knobbly woods, " which are Root's very original, built-out-of-words woods filled with rich rhythm, onomatopoeia, alliteration, assonance and consonance. Root's words exude tone and energy and become so infectious they frolic.

DIALOGUE REVEALS CHARACTER. Dialogue draws the reader in. It reveals character and speeds the pace of a story. Most often writers forget to consider the use of contrary dialogue. In *By Cunning and Craft: Sound Advice and Practical Wisdom for Fiction Writers,* Peter Selgin says, "Be adversarial. The essence of most strong dialogue can be distilled down to the following two-word exchange: 'Please—' / 'Maybe.' "

Readers experience this in *Duck! Rabbit!* by Amy Krouse Rosenthal. "Hey, look! A duck! / That's not a duck. / That's a rabbit! / Are you kidding me? / It's totally a duck. / It's for sure a rabbit. / See, there's his bill. / What are you talking about? / Those are ears, silly." The art joins with the words to discuss the many ways of seeing.

OBJECTS DO MORE. Objects reveal character. They can be endowed objects or pacing markers; they can also represent the obstacles a character has to overcome. Objects within a story help readers make connections. In *I Want My Hat Back* by Jon Klassen, Bear looks for an object he desires: a red pointy hat. While Bear's hat remains the focus, the mission becomes clear when readers reach a red page that reads, "I have seen my hat." Bear knows where his hat is and if he gets it back, he realizes there will be a very amusing price to pay.

POWER OF THREES. Writers need to power up the power of threes and please readers. A three series is satisfying, and there are so many ways to use a three: words, verbs, lists—even obstacles. A three series adds rhythm and flair to a manuscript.

In *Wemberly Worried,* Kevin Henkes begins his story with a three: "Wemberly worried about everything. Big things, little things, and things in between." In *Birdie's Big Girl Shoes*, Sujean Rim says, "She [Birdie] loved her crocodile pumps and her summer peep-toes and all her strappy sandals" and alerts readers that Birdie loves designer shoes. In *Banjo Granny*, Granny overcomes three obstacles: "And she started out to cross one river, one mountain, and a desert." Threes simply satisfy and should be used often.

VISUAL PACING TOOLS

LISTS LURE READERS IN. A list is a list. But a list is also more than a list. A list is an undervalued and under-utilized pacing tool. It may slow the reader and build tension, reveal character, or become an interactive game. A list of words can join with the art on one page or extend over a few spreads to slowly share a change in the emotional trajectory.

In *A Sick Day for Amos McGee,* Philip C. Stead excavates story down to a list that reveals the heart of friendship. "He [Amos] would play chess with the elephant / (who thought and thought before making a move), / run with the tortoise (who never ever lost), / sit quietly with the penguin / (who was very shy), / lend a handkerchief to the rhinoceros / (who always had a runny nose), / and, at sunset, read stories to the owl / (who was afraid of the dark)." Readers learn Amos plays nice with others, supports his friends, cares, and entertains.

Writers may also use a contrary list, as seen in *Leonardo the Terrible Monster* by Mo Willems. "He [Leonardo] didn't have 1,642 teeth, like Tony. / He wasn't big, like Eleanor. / And he wasn't just plain weird, like Hector." So much can be done with a list.

WHITE SPACE EVOKES EMOTION. White space paces with immediacy. It forces readers to entertain expressions, feelings, and emotional journeys. When nothing appears on a page besides a character, the focus shifts to facial expressions, positioning, and body language. That's all there is for readers to consider. The pacing halts, and the character's plight reveals itself like a freeze frame.

In *Leonardo the Terrible Monster*, readers learn that Leonardo is terrible. He looks for the "perfect candidate" to terrify. After a page turn, readers meet Sam. Sam is shown alone. He's singled out. Found. Mo Willems takes control and lets the emotional intensity of this moment resonate with his readers. Horn Book and *Kirkus* reviewer Robin Smith writes, "These animators (I am talking to you, Mo Willems and John Rocco) who write picture books have a special gift of pacing. They know when to stop putting words on the page."

PAGE TURNS = SURPRISE. The page turn is integral to the picture book. It's a built-in pause that provides a hide-and-reveal relationship with readers. Writers have the opportunity to surprise, spook, build suspense, compare and contrast, or create an interactive game. When writers see all that is possible in this one tool, they are able to make great strides in their writing. In Jan Brett's *The Mitten,* readers are surprised as more and more ever-larger critters push their way into a white knitted mitten: first a mole, then a rabbit, a hedgehog, an owl, and so on, which begs the question: What's next? In *I Ain't Gonna Paint No More!* Karen Beaumont uses the page turn to create a guessing game. As we begin to play with these twenty tools, we start to see many more ways to interact with readers.

UNSPOKEN CHARACTERS. Unspoken characters may carry story, slow the pacing, and add an additional layer to a story. Unspoken characters move the story beyond the words and create a bonus feature that also allows readers to engage in the story at a higher level.

In *A Sick Day for Amos McGee* by Philip C. Stead, Caldecott Award-winning illustrator Erin Stead introduces two characters not mentioned in the text: Mouse and Bird. Mouse checks a pocket watch, waits at a mini bus stop, holds pompoms as Tortoise crosses the finish line, wipes Rhino's eye, rides Tortoise's shell, sits below the bed when Amos wakes, and looks on as the animals surprise him. Meanwhile, Bird appears as well, inviting readers in on a game of hide and seek.

ART AMPLIFIES. Art must marry the words of a story, but not replicate. Art is best when it follows the intensity of a scene, or dares to differ or even carry the story alone. In the Caldecott Award-winning book, *Where The Wild Things Are,* Maurice Sendak reinforces the story's intensity through the bold presentation of the art.

In *Ways of Telling*, Leonard Marcus asks Sendak, "Over the course of the book, the pictures change in size, and eventually the pictures displace the words altogether. Is that meant to reflect Max's development in the story?"

Sendak explains, "As Max's rage engorges him, those pictures fill the page. When his anger turns to a kind of wild jungle pleasure, the words are pushed off the page altogether. And then, he deflates (as does the art) like any normal child; he's getting hungry, he's getting tired, and he wants to go back home."

GRAPHICS GET ATTENTION. The picture book is a physical form: horizontal, vertical, and may be rotated or flipped. When writers explore graphics, they realize words may become art, a graphic element on the page, divide up a scene, or go large. Both art and words may enhance story. A page may be graphically broken up into small segments to slow the pace, as seen in *SWIM! SWIM!* by James Proimos. A goldfish named Lerch searches for a friend in the pebbles, a diver, and the page breaks up, frame by frame, until the cat gets hold of him ... for lunch? Dinner? Or a heart-felt ending?

While *SWIM! SWIM!* shares a comic book feel, the graphics in Mo Willem's *Leonardo the Terrible Monster* transform words into a graphic that slows story. As Leonardo thinks he has scared the "tuna salad" out of Sam, Sam's rant appears huge, in bold-lettered pastels behind him and this screams for readers to take notice.

INTERACTIVE GAMES. When we begin to see the picture book as a performance, we can really find ingenious ways to inspire more interactive fun. As books launch as e-books and apps, new ways to interact, engaging readers through art and words, will become even more important. In *Looking for a Moose*, Phyllis Root asks, "Have you ever seen a moose—a long-leggy moose—a branchy-antler, dinner-diving, bulgy-nose moose?" She breaks down these descriptive phrases to use them as building blocks. She writes, "We don't see any long-leggy moose." Then writes, "We don't see any long-leggy, dinner-diving moose," and so on. Meanwhile, illustrator Randy Cecil hides long-leggy legs among trees. He dips dinner-divers in the swamp. He hides branchy-antlers in the bushes. And soon readers know they will find bulgy noses alongside the hilltop ... for once the reader catches on, this picture book offers page after page of surprise.

CONTRARY FLIPS. Contrary flips are fun art or word reversals. Words may run opposite to the art of a story. The art may alert the reader of a sneaky trick played on a character within a story. The best contrary flip is Peter Brown's *Children Make Terrible Pets,* where he explores the most unexplored pet experience yet: children. The pet says, "He was impossible to potty train," and the boy, shown standing in a litter box, says, "Squeak." This provides the reader with oodles of fun. Another quick example is found in *Emma Kate* by Patricia Polacco, when the imaginary friend isn't revealed until the end.

HUMOR. When it comes to pacing and influencing story, humor can be used in the art and words. Some of the best humor is created when readers notice something the writer or illustrator lets them in on, or when something is held back. Humor is all about honing the pauses and page turns to evoke a giggle or two verbally or visually. In David LaRochelle's *The Best Pet of All*, the main character wants a dog. He asks every day, and finally "On Thursday, I asked my mom if I could have a dragon." Once found, the dragon comes with many ill-suited behaviors and Mom wants him to leave. When the dragon finally does, a dog enters the scene, and readers see the dragon giving the thumbs up over the fence. This way, they are aware dragon was in on this all along.

PICTURE BOOK DUMMIES. The picture book dummy allows writers and illustrators the opportunity to play, testing their work for word placement, pacing, and page turns. Writers can divide story up, play around with the story arc, and really decide what text will fall on each page. They may also consider if the text may be broken up differently to create surprise or interaction, or to enhance story.

When we explore the best of the best picture books, these 20 tools stand out. When writers are looking to craft a great story, with great writing and great pacing—as well as heart. When writers focus on each of these tools in turn, they not only move the art and words of their story to a whole new level of *Wow!* They see more: Connections start to click, word counts decrease, and the rhythm and heart of story starts to shine through.

JODELL SADLER earned her MFA in Writing for Children & Young Adults from Hamline University, 2009, works as a adjunct professor at the University of Phoenix and Rasmussen college, hosts Picture Book Pacing Tutorials with Writer's Digest, and teaches Picture Book Pacing and Editing Courses Online: pacingpicturebooks.com. She's the author of *Picture Book Lunch: 20 Delicious Pacing Tools For Writing Picture Books to Wow*, available as an e-book on Amazon. (This article is excerpted from her e-book.)

SOCIAL MEDIA ROUNDUP

The value of blogging, Twitter, and more.

....

by Kristen Grace

Writer and illustrators are now expected to be the masters of their own publicity. But with round-the-clock Twitter updates, Google+ hangouts, Facebook fan pages, and what seems like an endless supply of reading material dished out on author's blogs, it's hard to know where yet another aspiring author fits into the vast online landscape. How much time do you need to spend cultivating your online prescience? Do you need an account on every site? How much exposure is too much? We've invited four online writer/illustrator personalities to share their thoughts and personal guidelines for making the online community work for you.

SARAH OCKLER is the bestselling author of young adult novels *Twenty Boy Summer, Fixing Delilah*, and *Bittersweet*. Her books have been translated into several languages and have received numerous accolades, including ALA's Best Fiction for Young Adults, Girls' Life Top 100 Must Reads, ABA's Indie Next and more. When she's not writing or reading, Sarah enjoys taking pictures, hugging trees and road-tripping through the country with her husband, Alex. Visit her website at sarahockler.com or find her on Twitter or Facebook.

LINDSAY WARD has a BFA in Illustration from Syracuse University. She has illustrated a handful of children's picture books including *The Yellow Butterfly* (Bright Sky Press) by Mehrnaz S. Gill, *A Garden for Pig* (Kane/Miller) by Kathryn Thurman, and the covers of both STAR Academy books by Edward Kay (Random House Canada). Lindsay's most recent books *Pelly and Mr. Harrison Visit the Moon* (Kane/Miller) and *When Blue Met Egg* (Dial Books for Young Readers) were both written and illustrated by her. Her upcoming book with Dial Books for Young Readers will be released in 2013. You can visit her on the web at lindsaymward.com or see her blog at respectthecupcake.blogspot.com.

RAYMOND BEAN is a father, teacher and the Amazon best-selling author of the Sweet Farts Series. His books have ranked #1 in children's humor, humorous series, and fantasy and adventure. The Sweet Farts series is consistently in Amazon's top 100 books for children. Foreign editions of his books have been released in Germany and Korea. Editions for Italy, Brazil and Turkey will be released soon. His School Is a Nightmare digital series launched in November of 2011. He writes for kids who claim they don't like reading. You can e-mail him at raymondbeanbooks@gmail.com.

KATE MESSNER is the award-winning author of more than a dozen current and forthcoming books for children and teens. Her titles include E.B. White Read Aloud award-winner *The Brilliant Fall of Gianna Z., Sugar and Ice*, and *Eye of the Storm* with Walker-Bloomsbury; the popular Marty McGuire chapter book series and *Capture the Flag* with Scholastic; and picture books like *Sea Monster's First Day* and *Over and Under the Snow*, an ALSC and *NY Times* Notable Children's Book and 2012 SCBWI Golden Kite Award winner with Chronicle Books. A TED 2012 speaker and former middle school English teacher, Kate is a frequent presenter at writing and education conferences. She also loves visiting classrooms and libraries in person and via Skype to talk about reading and writing with kids. You can follow her on Twitter (@katemessner) and learn more at her website: katemessner.com.

What social media outlets are you currently using? Which is your favorite? Which do you think is the most effective outlet to reach readers and buyers? Why?

OCKLER: I use Twitter, a Wordpress blog, Goodreads, YouTube and a limited Facebook fan page with no connected profile. My favorites—and consequently the most successful for me—are Twitter and the blog.

Now, here's a secret every aspiring and published author should know: The reason for their effectiveness has little to do with Twitter or Wordpress as media platforms and everything to do with authenticity and effort. Readers (especially teens) can spot insincerity a mile away, and if an author is using social media merely out of an obligation to pedal books, she's going to fail. Similarly, if authors don't actively cultivate their social sites, readers will stop showing up. There are lots of ways to reach readers and buyers, but the bottomline best strategy is pretty simple, online and off: Show up. Be yourself.

WARD: Currently I use Facebook, Twitter and my blog as my social media outlets. I have two Facebook profiles, one as an author/illustrator and one for my personal life. Although I am on Facebook from time to time I prefer Twitter as a way to reach the public in terms of upcoming events, new books and other book-related news. My blog enables me to expand on the promotion of my books, events, and everyday thoughts on writing and illustrating that Twitter would not allow because of the character limit.

BEAN: I have accounts with Facebook, Twitter and Skype. I also have a website and in my view, Amazon.com is also a form of social media. It's a hub where my readers can write reviews, read about my books and find links to my other social media sites.

Since my audience is generally reluctant readers between the ages of eight and 12, the goal of my social media efforts is to reach parents, teachers and librarians trying to find books that will motivate those reluctant readers.

MESSNER: I have a blog that's connected to my website, as well as Facebook, Twitter, Goodreads and Pinterest accounts. I'd have a tough time choosing a favorite of those because they all connect me with different kinds of readers and gatekeepers, and in different ways. I love my blog because it's a place to share the stories behind books— the research tidbits and photographs that may not make it into a book, even though I love them. And I think it's also a place where readers can see "Author= Kate" as a real person, too.

Tell us a little about how you came to this point. How did you get into social media in the first place? How did your use of it evolve to promote your books and make connections?

OCKLER: My use of the sites evolved along with my publication journey—once I had a book deal, I started meeting other authors online, and once that book hit the shelves, I was connecting more with actual teen readers, book bloggers, librarians and booksellers. Connecting is the key word—I try not to look at social media strictly as a promotional tool. Sure, promotion happens and it's important, and I definitely share links about new books and reviews and other related news, but I also chat about other authors' books, writing advice, food, television and the random stuff of life.

WARD: Up until recently I was a bit of a hermit when it came to promotion and social media. There are times when I am on Twitter and I see people who spend all day on there and I wonder how they get any work done. It takes a lot of self-discipline to write and/or illustrate from home because you have to step away from the TV or Internet and actually get work done. For this reason I stayed away from social media in the beginning of my career, until I realized how incredibly powerful and helpful it could be. I generally use my social media outlets as ways to discuss what is going on with me as an author/illustrator.

BEAN: When I first self-published in 2008 I used very little social media. I had a basic website with a contact link and that was about it. I didn't even have a Facebook account until fairly recently.

My experience was unique in that I wrote my first book, *Sweet Farts,* under a pen name. I didn't tell friends, family or colleagues about the book for over a year. My hunch was that if I wrote a book that young readers really enjoyed, they would promote it through word of mouth. I was very fortunate that my hunch paid off. My approach was unconventional, and I was fortunate that the book found an audience.

MESSNER: I was never involved in social media sites before I had books to promote, and really, that's why I started exploring territory like Facebook and Twitter. But once I started my blog and later on, joined Facebook, Twitter, GoodReads and Pinterest, I found that I really loved being part of those communities of teachers, librarians, parents and book lovers.

How much time each day (or week) do you dedicate to tweeting, blogging, updating, etc? How do you make sure you limit your time so you can actually write?

OCKLER: I don't have a set number of hours dedicated to social media—I just pop on when I feel like saying hello or when I have something interesting to share. For me, catching up with the Twitter stream often feels like grabbing a cup of coffee with friends—and then suddenly you look out the coffee shop window and it's dark, and they're about to close, and you realize you didn't get any work done, and now your latte's cold.

WARD: I generally don't really dedicate a specific amount of time to social media. I tweet when I have something to announce or share, which I usually do in the morning when I am spending time on e-mails and such. As for my blog, I try to post an entry every Wednesday if possible. The key to having a blog is maintaining it, which can be very difficult when work is busy. However, no one will read your blog if you only post twice a year. I think the best way to approach social media without it taking over your life is to give yourself a certain amount of time each day to do it and try to stick to that schedule.

BEAN: I try to limit how much and how often I post to Facebook, Twitter, etc. I have lesson plans to write and papers to grade! If I have a new cover to share or a new book coming out, I'll share it. If I hit a bestseller list somewhere, I'll post it and thank my readers.

MESSNER: I try to blog at least once a week, but it's often more than that if I'm doing a lot of book events or research trips and I'm excited to share photos. Aside from those blog entries, which may take anywhere from 10 minutes to an hour to write, I probably spend about an hour a day on social media, answering Tweets and Facebook messages, and posting updates and links. Writing always comes first, though.

What kinds of content are you offering readers that's making your efforts a success? How has your content and social media outreach changed or become better over time?

OCKLER: Before I was published, my blog was just a place to chat about my day or share the challenges of writing a YA novel while working a corporate gig. But now, I have a much wider audience that includes not only people I know in real life, but teen readers, librarians, book bloggers, booksellers, publishers, other published authors and aspiring writers seeking advice or anecdotes about the journey.

I try to blog about things that will appeal to these different audiences—maybe an article on finding an agent for the aspiring writers, followed by a review or giveaway of a YA book I loved for my teen readers, or a personal anecdote about something funny that happened that day just because. Twitter is more of a constant stream of chatter, like an ongoing conversation that can shift gears at any moment, and it's fun to jump in on other people's threads or retweet an interesting article, or comment on the latest episode of "The Walking Dead."

WARD: I try to offer my followers my perspective on things. Write what you know, which I know sounds like a cliché but it's true. I would never post a blog entry on tips for writing a YA novel because I don't know the first thing about it. Generally I try to offer my input on writing picture books and illustration, because that is what I feel comfortable with. My blog also tends to be more about what is going on in my life as an author/illustrator, which I think makes me seem more real and accessible to my readers.

BEAN: I try to always write my books with the reluctant reader in mind. I try to write content they'll talk about, and their parents and teachers will recommend.

MESSNER: I assume the people who are following me are interested in the kinds of books I write, so I try to ask myself, "What would be of interest to readers who like my books?" As someone who taught middle school for 15 years, I work especially hard to make teachers' and librarians' lives easier, sharing book recommendations, links and resources that they can use with students in the classroom.

What opportunities or connections have befallen you that you can directly attribute to your work through social media and blogging?

OCKLER: One experience that really stands out is the Speak Loudly campaign. In September 2010, Laurie Halse Anderson's incredible novel, *Speak*, was challenged in the Republic, Missouri school district along with Kurt Vonnegut's *Slaughterhouse-Five* and my novel, *Twenty Boy Summer*. Teacher Paul Hankins started the #SpeakLoudly hashtag on Twitter to spread the word about the challenges and encourage people to speak out against them. Through the Twitter conversation and all the ensuing blog posts, I "met" tons of readers, teachers, librarians and parents in the district. A year later, after the challenge was fully investigated by the school board, *Speak* was finally reinstated, but *Twenty Boy Summer* and *Slaughterhouse-Five* were both banned. The Springfield-Greene County Library that serves Republic invited me to visit during Banned Books Week in 2011, as did the Kurt Vonnegut Memorial Library in Indianapolis.

WARD: I have had conversations with editors and art directors that I don't think I would have had, had we not started chatting via social media. It's amazing what you can connect with another person about. And who knows what will come of those conversations.

BEAN: I've made connections with other writers in my genre. It's amazing how easily you can connect with others using social media. I've heard from teachers and readers all over the world thanks to Facebook, Twitter and my website. The first Sweet Farts book was released in Germany under the title *Stinker*. The illustrator of the German version found me on Facebook. I don't think he and I would have ever connected before social media.

MESSNER: I actually got a book deal thanks to my blog. I like to share my writing process, especially when it comes to revision, because I know how helpful it can be for a teacher to have examples of real authors revising to show students who are reluctant writers. So whenever I can, I post revision stories and photos of my marked-up manuscripts, with tips for student writers. One day, I got an e-mail from the acquisitions editor at Stenhouse, asking if I'd be interested in writing a book to demystify the revision process.

My Twitter feed and blog have also led to school visits and other speaking invitations. I've also presented on using social media to connect readers and authors at a number of national conferences for teachers, librarians and writers.

Let's say you're addressing a group of new writers. How should budding authors and illustrators be using social media to further their career? What would you tell them? (In other words, what did you wish you knew at the beginning of your journey?)

OCKLER: Social media is a great way to connect with readers and colleagues, but if you're not writing anything for us to read, all the "follows" and "likes" in the world aren't going to further your career. Only your books can do that.

WARD: Go on the Internet and see what is out there, spend time reading some blogs, tweeting, and see what people are discussing in the industry. And then close your computer and do what you do. Write. Illustrate. Focus. Because you are never going to write your book if you are tweeting all day. Pull what you can from social media but don't let it run your life.

MESSNER: Be interesting, friendly and helpful—and social media will work for you. Share a variety of ideas, news, links and photos. When you have good news about your books, share that, too. Celebrate other writers' good news at least as often as you celebrate your own, and share book recommendations for lots of titles that you didn't write.

Do you set any rules for yourself when interacting online? If so, what are they?

OCKLER: I try to follow the rule of common sense, which means I don't share overly personal information or air my dirty laundry (and that's not a pun on my work pajamas). It's one thing to be authentic and honest, but it's another thing entirely to report every single opinion, thought, location, desire, fear, mother's maiden name, meal, doctor visit, relationship details, scars … you get the idea! Social networking is a great way to connect with other book lovers, but no matter how chummy and informal it feels, it's not a venue for opening up every aspect of our lives to outside observation, commentary and icky corporate data mining.

WARD: The only rule I really have for myself when it comes to social media is how much I share, especially when it comes to my personal life. I would never tweet or post something on Facebook that I wouldn't want anyone in the world to be able to read. I am a firm believer in keeping your private life separate from your professional life. Also, when it comes to tweeting, I don't force conversations with editors just because I really admire them and I want to talk to them. There is a fine line between polite conversation and being intrusive or pushy.

MESSNER: In everything I do online, I remember that I write books for kids. You'll read about a huge variety of things on my social media feeds—how I write, what I'm reading, trips I'm taking and what I'm learning about—everything from tornadoes to airport security to venomous snakes. But you'll never read anything on my blog or any of my social media feeds that a teacher couldn't share with a class full of fifth graders.

How do you approach other writers and illustrators to develop online connections? How do others approach you?

OCKLER: For the most part, young adult authors and illustrators are really friendly and open online, so it's pretty easy to connect. I might read and comment on another author's blog, post a review of his work on mine, or just start following him on Twitter. Authors find me in much the same way. From there, it's easy to build a rapport because we're all chatting about similar writerly interests: books, authors, movies, chocolate, coffee—stuff like that.

WARD: Generally, if I want to tell someone how great I think their work is or something along those lines I will say it, even if I don't know them. At the end of the day, we as writers and illustrators want to know that people are appreciating and enjoying our work and what better way to do that than connecting with each other about it. Most of my online connections have developed through other people. Either we share the same agent, participate in a book club together, have met in passing at a conference or something along those lines. And from there I meet their connections. The circle keeps on growing.

MESSNER: Authors and illustrators who maintain blogs and Twitter feeds are pretty much universally delighted to be followed, so there's no reason you can't follow and interact with anyone you admire online. Facebook can be a little trickier because people set up accounts there with different expectations. Some authors share photos of their kids with family members via Facebook and may feel strange about having many "friends" they've never met in real life. But many—most, I'd guess—are happy to have readers, teachers, librarians, booksellers and fellow writers as friends. When you add someone you don't know personally on Facebook, it's not a bad idea to send a message along with the request. Just a quick note saying "I love your books" or "I heard you speak at such-and-such a conference …" to let the person know that you're already a friend in the literary world.

When you're viewing other people's blogs and Twitter accounts and Facebook profiles, where are other writers going wrong in their outreach, in your opinion?

OCKLER: The first mistake is when writers commandeer social media strictly for the hard sell. It's great to share news about a new book, retweet a glowing review, chat about a work in progress or answer reader questions—after all, readers and fans connect online because they *want* to hear about an author and her books. But if a Twitter stream is full of "buy my book, buy my book, buy my book" with no genuine personality or real reciprocity in the conversation, that's a huge turnoff and the quickest way to alienate readers and lose fans.

The second mistake is when writers set up dozens of different social media accounts just because they feel they have to, and then struggle with updating or participating in any meaningful way. When authors abandon their social media accounts, or they just post the same few links to every single media outlet, it becomes a waste of everyone's time and after awhile, readers will venture elsewhere.

WARD: I definitely think that when people are inappropriate about other writers' work or have a bad experience with someone in the industry and talk about it on a public forum, such as Facebook or Twitter, that reflects badly. Obviously there are going to be reviews and blog posts that tear apart your work. If you publish something, that means everyone is allowed to have an opinion on it unfortunately. But keep in mind that you never know who is reading your posts or tweets about said agent/writer/illustrator/editor. You don't want to be known for bad-mouthing peers in the industry.

MESSNER: I know people approach social media with different expectations, but I have to be honest—I cringe when I see someone who writes books for children or teens tweeting a string of expletives or blogging about how they were drunk the night before. It makes it difficult for teachers and librarians to share your online links with students.

The other mistake I see enthusiastic new writers making is tweeting only about their books. I've heard people compare social media outlets to cocktail parties, and I think that's a good metaphor. When you're at a social gathering, you want to hang out with people who are interesting—who talk about lots of different things and share neat ideas. If some of them wrote books, you'd be interested in hearing about those, for sure. But you probably wouldn't spend very long talking with someone who blabbed on about his or her book and nothing else all night long. Social gatherings online are no different.

KRISTEN GRACE is a contributor to *Writer's Digest* and is currently earning her Master's Degree in English at Miami University of Ohio. You can check out her blog at kegrace.wordpress.com or follow her on Twitter (@kayeeegee).

WHY ILLUSTRATORS SHOULD BLOG

by Teresa Kietlinski

Attention aspiring picture book illustrators: next time you are in the studio staring at a blank paper or screen, let some visitors in. Your artist blog can turn your solitary studio into a happening virtual studio tour. And before you know it, your blog will inspire others while they inspire you.

A blog is the best free tool you have to break into children's book publishing today. With proper blogging, you can demonstrate that you have the skills, knowledge, and desire to illustrate picture books. Blogs are unique in that they allow art directors, editors, agents, and representatives the opportunity to see if there is an "instant connection" with you as a person and an artist. The art that you post lets visitors see what and how you illustrate—but it is the writing that gives insight on your thought process, your personality, and ultimately a peek into the kinds of projects you would like to work on in the future.

SETTING GOALS

Let's be honest, most artists are "artists"—not writers by nature. Blogging with a consistent frequency each week can seem overwhelming to visual communicators at first. But like all things, the more you practice writing the easier it becomes. The benefit to writing regularly is simple: blogging flexes your writing muscles and makes you a well rounded communicator. Being an excellent communicator—both visually and verbally—will help you succeed in the children's book industry.

It is no secret that blog maintenance can be a time-consuming part of an illustrator's day, but only if you allow it to be. Setting schedules that are feasible will make the blogging experience fun and stress free.

Start by setting reasonable goals and be consistent with your postings. Consistency will help build a steady audience of readers and keep you on "task" when it is time to blog. Try to post on a same day(s) of the week so your blog fans will know when to expect new posts. Can you update your site once a week? Twice a week? Can you post a new sample every Monday? Can you review a new book every Friday? Set calendar reminders on your phone or computer to remind you what to post and when until your blogging becomes a fun habit. How much time are you willing to dedicate to maintaining a blog presence?

GROUP BLOGGING

Be honest with yourself. If you are not the most consistent blogger or have commitment issues, find another artist or two or three who share your sensibilities and passion and become blog buddies. With the right blog buddy (or buddies) the task of maintaining may actually turn out to be a treat—blogs offer a way of connecting with real people who share your passion and goals. You can inspire one another.

Writers everywhere are joining writer's groups and sharing the responsibility of posting and updating blogs—and artists should get on board with this useful trend. Not only does blog sharing help take some writing pressure off of one individual, but it also helps to create a safe community of likeminded souls where ideas can be shared. Group blogs act like a virtual "circle time" creating a supportive community for your work and ideas.

SHARING THE PROCESS

The key is to keep your blog posts simple. There is no need to delve into 20-20 investigative reporting style posts—what all visitors (especially art directors, agents and fellow artists) will respond to is hearing your unique voice. What makes you special? What makes you *you*?

Blogs—unlike websites that can get outdated quickly—allow readers to get a sense of who you are as a person and an artist at that moment.

So when you post a new art sample, share the process with your readers. Where did the idea come from? What inspired you to draw this particular piece? What did the sketch look like? What does the finish look like? Are you currently working on a book project? If you aren't working a project, are you still adding samples to your blog? How consistent are the samples? Are they sequential or stand-alone? What story are you trying to convey? Is this sample the start of a story? Or is this piece a character who hasn't found his/her "story" yet? You never know who will stumble upon your website and which sample might spark a potential book deal.

Always continue to post doodles, drawings, sketches—by sharing these important moments, the moment an idea starts, you are drawing people into your creative space. There is nothing more personal or inspiring than seeing an artist's idea take shape.

CONTENT FLEXIBILITY

If you find something that inspires you unrelated to books, share that with your readers, too. Sometimes inspiration can come from non-children's book sources as well. But be sure to keep the off-topic blogs professional to some degree.

Writing about children's book industry events will let readers know you are learning the trade. Are you attending conferences? If so, who spoke at this conference? What did he or she have to say? What tidbit can you share with others? Do you belong to an illustrators group? Are you reading other picture books? What library books have you checked out recently? What is your favorite bookshop? Why? What book visits have you attended? What blogs do you follow? What book made you laugh today?

Postings like these help readers get to know you while helping you establish credibility in the eyes of publishing professionals.

Ultimately, your blog goal should be letting visitors get to know you as an artist and person. If you are serious about getting published, the best tool that you have is keeping your posts relevant and updating your blog samples frequently.

The life of an artist can be very solitary—but only if you let it. Blog regularly and open yourself up to new possibilities.

TERESA KIETLINSKI (on Twitter as @keresakie) is a literary agent at Prospect Agency (prospectagency.com), where she represents writers and illustrators.

ILLUSTRATORS & AUTHORS

Dividing details in picture books.

....

by Sue Bradford Edwards

It seems simple. A picture book is the sum of two parts, the text and the illustrations. The author and illustrator each depend on the other to carry part of the story.

It seems simple.

But, it's not.

"This is one of the most difficult and intangible parts of picture book making, and what makes the picture book form so unique: The factual and emotional information in the book does not come solely from the words. All we writers, illustrators, and editors of picture books are on a quest we cannot accomplish alone: to marry the words and pictures perfectly, inextricably," says Arthur A. Levine Books editor, Cheryl Klein, in her presentation *Words, Wisdom, Art and Heart: Making a Picture-Book Cookie.*

Successfully completing a picture book means bringing together the work of a diverse group of professionals, each of whom will shape the story until it sings. For this to happen, the author must first understand which details come from the text and which details fall under the control of the illustrator.

YOURS OR MINE?

Dividing the detail is pretty straightforward. If it's visual, it probably belongs to the illustrator. This means that you can describe your character's appearance, their school, or their yard in visual detail if and only if it is vital to the story.

Is the visual detail in your manuscript truly vital to the plot? Or is it just the way you laid the story down after imagining it one scene at a time? Many writers, myself included, imagine their story scene by scene, like a movie. "When you are writing picture books, it's helpful to have a picture in your head, but there's a point where you need to let that go," says Charlesbridge Associate Editor Randi Rivers.

Illustrations are visual, so illustrators get most of the visual detail. So what? Writers get everything else. "All sensory details except visual are my territory. I get to use sound effects, onomatopoeia, strong smells, textural details such as smooth or rough, and tastes when appropriate. I especially love the kinesthetic details, how it feels to move in space, I can and by using the right verbs," says author Darcy Pattison. Used effectively, sound, smell, taste, texture and movement impact everything from character to setting.

PICTURE BOOKS TO CHECK OUT

One of the best ways to learn what details the writer brings to a story as compared to the illustrator is to study picture books. Study them. Don't just read them casually. "Read a picture book without looking at the illustrations," says Charlesbridge associate editor Randi Rivers, "and then go back and look at the illustrations but don't read the story. What did you get each time? Can you see what the illustrator added and the author didn't say?"

Be careful which books you study, however. "Be aware that author/illustrators write different sorts of stories than just authors. The author/illustrator can leave out much more text than you'll be able to, says author Darcy Pattison. "When I write the same type of abbreviated story, I get rejections that say, *This is too slight. This needs to be fleshed out more.* Explanations in the cover letter aren't the same as a sample illustration. So, when you study picture books as models for how to write, look for those written and illustrated by someone else. Of course if you're an author-illustrator, then study those picture books by author-illustrators."

Here is a list to start you on your way:

BOOKS BY AN AUTHOR/ILLUSTRATOR

Barbara Berger's *Grandfather Twilight*
Lauren Child's Clarice Bean books
Anna Dewdney's *Llama, Llama Red Pajama*
Laura McGee Kvasnosky's Zelda and Ivy books
Nina Laden's *The Night I Followed the Dog*
Peggy Rathman's *Officer Buckle and Gloria*
Maurice Sendak's *Where the Wild Things Are*

BOOKS BY AN AUTHOR AND A SEPARATE ILLUSTRATOR

Jessica Clerk's *The Wriggly, Wriggly Baby,* illustrated by Laura Rankin
Doreen Cronin's *Click Clack Moo: Cows that Type,* illustrated by Betsy Lewin

> Lois Grambling's *Can I Bring My Pterodactyl to School, Ms. Johnson?*, illustrated by Judy Love
>
> Mary Ann Hoberman's *The Seven Silly Eaters*, illustrated by Marla Frazee
>
> David LaRochelle's *The End*, illustrated by Richard Egielski
>
> Reeve Lindbergh's *The Day the Goose Got Loose*, illustrated by Steven Kellogg
>
> Darcy Pattison's *The Journey of Oliver K. Woodman* and *Searching for Oliver K. Woodman*, illustrated by Joe Cepeda
>
> Rick Walton's *Bertie Was a Watchdog*, illustrated by Arthur Robins; *So Many Bunnies*, illustrated by Paige Miglio; *A Very Hairy Scary Story*, illustrated by David Clark; and *Just Me and 6,000 Rats*, illustrated by Mike Gordon and Carl Gordon.

MORE THAN SKIN DEEP

Characterization can easily sound like an APB: "Be on the lookout for a 5-year-old male. He is slender with brown hair and green eyes. He was last seen wearing a denim jacket." While picture book readers need these details, they normally get them not from the text but from the illustration.

"Visual characterization—what the characters look like, what their expressions are—will be shown in illustrations," says Klein. "The text supplies verbal and behavioral characterization. Who a character is, as seen in her words or actions."

This encourages the author to show the character in more meaningful ways. "How are you envisioning the character when you write the story? Do you know that she has brown hair and wears a yellow coat or do you know she's funny and afraid of spiders?" asks Rivers. "In other words, don't rely solely on a physical description to get across who she is unless the description has something to do with a plot point."

This is why author Lisa Wheeler includes a brief visual description for her animal characters. "I let the reader know up front what type of animal I am writing about when I am using anthropomorphism," she says. "But I steer clear of specifics on clothing, colors, etc. For instance, I might say the character has a hat, if a hat is important to the plot, but it is best to leave it up to the illustrator as to what kind of hat." Thus she lays down what the character *is* but leaves as much visual control as possible to the illustrator.

It is up to the author to seize the opportunity to lay out habits, likes and dislikes that create depth of character. This allows the illustrator to add another layer by bringing in the visual detail. Characters thus deeply drawn stride through the world of their stories.

YOU ARE HERE

As with the characters themselves, even without visual detail, the writer maintains surprising control of the manuscript's setting. Although the writer may not determine if the character's house is blue or white, he or she does establish where the story takes place. City or country. Gym or playground. Past or present. The author not only selects the setting, but is the first to describe it. "What does it smell like? What do you hear?" asks Rivers. "Use the senses that can't be captured by illustration."

Not only do these specifics anchor the story in a specific place, but carefully chosen, they establish the mood of the story. "By careful selection of specific details, I can create the story's mood," says Pattison. "For example, think about how you would describe a playground and create a happy versus a scary mood. It's the same playground; the difference is in the selection of details. Illustrators only get the leftover visual stuff and, actually, I dictate a lot for them by the careful selection of action words and by creating moods."

The skilled author does this without inflating the word count. "I would never say in my text, 'The dark clouds hung overhead and the flowers began bending in the breeze.' That kind of description is told through the illustration and it would be a waste of space to say it in the text," says author/illustrator Todd Aaron Smith. If the main character must face a bully on the playground, perhaps the slide is hulking or looming. A playground where a birthday party is held may have a glimmering slide and singing swings. "The text helps in achieving the emotional content of the story," says Smith, "and the illustrations are for visually conveying these emotions."

Once established by the author, the illustrator heightens the mood by selecting which details to illustrate. "A good illustration shows the highest point of emotional interest and active tension in a scene," says Klein. "Suppose a text reads 'Cheryl ran through the park, leaped across the ravine, somersaulted through the daffodils, stood up, and started running again. But the man was still behind her.' But in a picture book, the illustrator has to choose—and so he'd probably go with the point where Cheryl was leaping across the ravine, because that's the moment with the most tension and excitement."

For the illustrator to do this well, the writer must include a variety of action and emotion. "It is important to give the illustrator enough action and emotion to illustrate. Don't squeeze it all in the beginning. You need to do it spread after spread after spread," says author/illustrator Joan Holub. "Move from place to place, even if it's two places and you go back and forth. For instance, in *Skippyjon Jones*—you see a lot of different aspects of his room as setting."

TESTING FOR BALANCE

Details of smell, taste, touch and sound. Details selected to show mood and emotion. Varied action. How can the author be sure she's selected the right details and distributed them evenly through the text?

"Look at every line of your story, every word, and make sure it wouldn't be better represented in the illustrations," says author Rick Walton. "Make sure that it needs to be in the text for the story to work."

One tool can help the author judge pacing and analyze a manuscript line by line. "Make a test dummy," says Holub. "That will show you so quickly if there is too much text on one spread and not enough on the other." Study the manuscript one spread at a time to evaluate your details and how they work to establish tone and mood.

If a spread is wordy, this may be a place to trim. "Make cuts in places where you have lots of description and see if the story still flows," says Wheeler. "It probably flows better! Any word or line that does not move the story forward is probably expendable. Beware of 'stage directions' in your story. This is one of those things that we tend to miss when revising our picture books. You text doesn't have to tell readers that 'Billy opened the door, stepped onto the porch, walked down the sidewalk and headed to town.' In a picture book, just say 'Billy headed to town.' The artist will take care of the rest.

Study your text spread by spread. Do you have sensory detail? Action? Emotion? Details carefully chosen give subtle cues that influence the illustrator in creating his or her work.

CHANGING FOR THE BETTER

Now that we've examined how authors influence illustration, it's time to look at the reverse, when the illustration influences the text. Although it isn't the case with every picture book, an illustrator's work can mean making changes to the text.

At times, this happens because details that originally appeared in the text have been duplicated in the illustrations. "With a mystery I recently edited, there were certain things that had to appear in the illustrations," says Rivers. Once the details appeared in the illustrations, the author could remove them from the text, and Rivers asked for cuts. "I've done that with most of the books I've edited because the tendency is for tighter texts," she says. "It's important to keep things in the text until you see what the illustrator is going to pick to illustrate."

Making cuts this late in the picture book process is an art. "Look for things that don't influence the voice or the humor. Taking out words can help with pacing and the emotion," says Rivers. "If you want to build drama, sometimes you want the text to be shorter and punchier."

Sometimes the editor asks the author to alter the text to match the illustrator's specialty. "My editor once came to me and asked if we could change the characters in one of my books from kids into bunnies, because they'd found an illustrator who did cute bunnies," says Walton. "I made the changes, adapted the text appropriately, and it became my best selling book, *So Many Bunnies*."

Changes may also be requested because the illustrator has contradicted certain textual details. The decision to go against the text usually comes about when details as established in the text would yield a sub-standard illustration. "In one book, I described a truck as being gray and a toad as being brown. The finished art was vibrant, with a blue truck and green toad. I went back and rewrote my rhyme accordingly," says Wheeler. "I wouldn't have added those color details except that, for meter and rhyme, they were words that served a purpose. When the colors got changed, I realized that it was a good choice by the illustrator to keep with the vibrancy of the book. Changing rhyming text is never easy, but in this case, it was worthwhile."

This give and take between writer and illustrator marries the text and the illustration to form a seamless picture book. For this give-and-take to take place, the author must have faith. "You have to trust that the illustrator will put as much into the book as you have," says Rivers. "They are just as smart, funny and witty, but they will show this visually in a way that complements your text.

This faith allows the author to hand over the control the illustrator needs to truly create. "You want the illustrator to feel like it is a true collaboration, that it is as much their book as yours," says Walton. "If they do, they will put more effort into the work, make the work their own, add dimensions that will make the book richer, better, more successful."

Pattison agrees and hopes that each illustrator she works with will bring her characters to life for generations of kids. This level of collaboration can happen only where both creative parties have the space to shine. In a picture book, this means handing visual details to the illustrator and using all else to the greatest possible effect.

ILLUSTRATION NOTES

Tempted to include detailed illustration notes with your text?

"There is a long debate about whether authors can include visual notes—things the illustrations should include that do not belong in the text," says Arthur A. Levine Books editor Cheryl Klein. "Editors dislike it because, I must tell you, it often feels like if you give an author a visual inch, he will take a mile. He will describe shot angles. He will write character descriptions. And obviously the only thing keeping him from illustrating this book is the fact that he can't draw. So if you can avoid having visual notes, do."

If you still want to include illustration notes, Charlesbridge associate editor Randi Rivers has a request. "Type the manuscript with the notes and give it to a friend to read aloud. You'll see how they lose the thread of the story," she says. "When I lose interest in the story, I don't read it all the way through." If an editor can't follow your story from beginning to end, you've just botched a potential sale.

There are times when illustration notes *are* needed. "If the visual action is essential to the story, describe that action in your cover letter or at the appropriate point in the story, briefly," says Klein. "Then let the rest of the manuscript stand on its own."

Respect the expertise the illustrator brings to the job and an editor may ask for illustration notes. "*Noah's Square Dance* is a danceable square dance," says Rick Walton, "and my editor requested that I, with the help of my wife, who is more logical than I am, prepare notes that showed where each of the characters would be in the dance sequence. This helped the illustrator place the characters in the scenes."

Even with illustration notes, the picture book remains a collaboration.

SUE BRADFORD EDWARDS works to leave room for the illustrations from her office in St. Louis, Miss. Visit her at suebradfordedwards.com. Her blog about writing, One Writer's Journey, can be found at suebe.wordpress.com.

WRITING BUDDIES

Team up with another writer for encouragement and success.

....

by Carmela Martino

When my friend Sue confessed a few months ago that she had trouble motivating herself to write, I could definitely relate. I'd faced a similar challenge while working on a young adult historical novel. After eking out a rough draft, I spent a year trying to motivate myself to do the much-needed rewrite, with minimal success. Then, in January 2011, April Halprin Wayland (one of my co-bloggers) posted about a six-step plan for working with a "Writing Buddy" (See tinyurl.com/7rgyjtv.) Soon after reading her blog post, I found my own Writing Buddy, and within six months I completed the rewrite.

I adapted April's six-step plan to the following to best suit my own needs and schedule:

1. Find a Writing Buddy.

I wanted a Writing Buddy who would hold me accountable—someone who would be both encouraging and demanding. (See sidebar, "Tips for Choosing a Writing Buddy.") For the relationship to be mutually beneficial, my Buddy had to also be serious about accomplishing her own writing goals. I turned to Leanne Pankuch, a member of my critique group. Leanne is a wonderful writer, but she struggled with trying to write while working full-time. She loved the idea of our being Buddies.

2. Write three *specific, measurable* goals for each week.

It took some trial and error to learn how to set **specific, measurable** goals that **truly motivated me**. For example, one of my first week's goals was:

- Spend at least six hours revising my young adult novel—this includes thinking and planning time, but not research time.

I accomplished my goal that week, but I didn't have much to show for those six hours of work. After discussing the results with my Buddy during our check-in (see Step 6), I modified this goal for the following week to:

- Add at least 500 words/day on at least three days for a minimum of 1,500 additional words. (Current word count: 61,022.)

For me, a word-count goal was much more motivating than a time-oriented goal. When Friday afternoon rolled around and I hadn't reached my word count, I resolved to get up early on Saturday to accomplish it before my check-in with Leanne. And I succeeded!

3. Set a deadline.

Leanne and I set our work week to run from Sunday through Saturday, and our deadline is always some time Saturday afternoon.

4. Select a "salary" to pay yourself.

In her blog post April advised, "... pay yourself every week whether you've completed all three commitments or not. Don't business execs get paid even when they've had an unproductive week? It happens. This is not about whipping yourself. This is about encouraging yourself."

I thought this was a fun idea. My typical "salary" is $5 toward my writing retreat fund. My fund has already paid for three retreats!

5. Share your goals with each other.

Leanne and I do this via e-mail, usually on Sunday or Monday.

6. Check in with each other at the end of the week.

Every Friday, Leanne and I schedule our weekend phone appointment. Knowing we'll be checking in often motivates me to make an extra push, something I never did when I didn't have someone to hold me accountable. I asked Leanne if this was true for her, too. She wrote back, "If the week is winding down and I still haven't made my goal, then I'll sometimes even—gasp!—leave the shirts at the cleaners, tell my husband to make us some cream of wheat for dinner, leave the dishes for tomorrow, and knock out those last few hundred words—just so I can tell you I made it!"

To my surprise, our weekly phone conversations evolved into more than simple check-ins. Leanne and I also talk about our process. We share not only the day-to-day challenges that threaten our goals, but also the difficulties we face with the writing itself. Talking through our plot and character problems often helps us find solutions.

Our Buddy relationship has done much more than merely increase our productivity. The additional benefits we've reaped include: learning how to set realistic goals that suit our circumstances, personalities, and writing styles; putting an end to procrastination; relieving some of the loneliness of being a writer; and being able to enjoy our free time without the nagging guilt of unmet goals.

My relationship with Leanne has been so successful that when my friend Sue mentioned her motivation problem, I suggested she get a Writing Buddy, too. She now checks in regularly via Skype with her Buddy, who lives in another state. They've both boosted their productivity, and you can, too, by following the above steps.

SIDEBAR: THE BUDDY SYSTEM

Here are some things to consider when choosing your Writing Buddy:

- Would the person you have in mind be willing and able to make a serious commitment to the Buddy relationship?
- Would you be comfortable sharing your writing goals and struggles with this person?
- Would being accountable to this person help motivate you, either because you wouldn't want to disappoint her or him, or because you'd be embarrassed to fail in front of this person?
- On the flip side, would this person be understanding and encouraging if you didn't achieve your goals, for whatever reason?
- Would the person work with you to apply the steps listed in "Boost Your Productivity with a Writing Buddy" in a way that suits both your needs?

If, like me, you're lucky enough to be in a critique group, I suggest you look for your Writing Buddy within your group. If you're not in a critique group, are you a member of any writing organizations, such as the Society of Children's Book Writers and Illustrators (SCBWI), where you might find a compatible buddy? Still no prospects? Consider friends who may need motivation sticking with creative goals in areas other than writing, such as illustrating, knitting, quilting, etc.

It may take some work to find your Buddy, but the rewards will be worth your effort!

CARMELA MARTINO (carmelamartino.com) is a writer and writing teacher. She writes short stories, poetry, picture books, nonfiction, and novels for children and young adults. She completed her MFA in Writing from Vermont College in 2000. Carmela's first children's novel, *Rosa, Sola*, was published by Candlewick Press in 2005.

BUILDING YOUR AUTHOR PLATFORM

Gain visibility and network with others.

....

by Mary Kole

"Platform" is one of those buzzwords that you hear all over the place. It's on blogs and at conferences, confounding fiction writers everywhere. First and foremost, it's much more important for nonfiction scribes. That is a fact. When you put together a nonfiction book proposal, the publisher really wants to know how many people you can reach and *sell books to.* That's a crucial concern at acquisitions. Professionals with big networks, popular bloggers, experts with connections, people who have caught the media spotlight—those are the writers who can impress editors with the promise of big nonfiction sales.

Most aspiring fiction writers are different. They're not selling themselves, they're selling a story. In most cases, the fiction market really is all about the book and not about the personality behind it. The John Green kind of "cult of personality" only happens to authors once they've built up momentum in the marketplace.

The average fiction writer's big platform is, "I like to write fiction," and that's OK. Unless you happen to be an expert in a subject matter that plays into your novel's setting or theme, or you've got writing credits in a different market (adult fiction, nonfiction, journalism), or you're famous, you're not going to have any more platform than that.

Just like a query letter does not have the power to make or break you as a fiction writer, a platform isn't the end all and be all. A small platform won't get in the way of an acquisition if the book is brilliant, and a large platform does not have the power to land you a book deal if your book is horrible. (Unless, of course, you're a celebrity or on the Jersey Shore. A sad truth but it's part of today's commercially driven reality.)

Let me repeat: Fiction lives and dies by the manuscript itself.

THE DANGERS OF PLATFORM BEFORE YOU'RE READY

Let's say you're an unpublished writer chasing publication. You don't have a book or a deal to blog about yet, but you've heard that writers need platform and Internet presence, and you've heard that blogs get you friends and Web traffic, and you've also heard about this Twitter thing. Yet it sounds overwhelming. You wonder if you have enough to blog about and worry if you have the time to keep up with all this social networking.

Still, the blogosphere sounds like so much fun and you think maybe you'll attract an agent by being all over Facebook all the time. So you sink your precious writing hours into social media. And you comment on other people's blogs—like you've heard you're supposed to—in the hopes that they'll flock to yours. You get a few friends here and there and make a few connections.

But where is *your book* in all of this digital gallivanting?

Oh, that's right. You're trying to be a professional writer. Not a blogger.

The cautionary tone in my voice is no accident. If platform is stressing you out, go back to focusing on the writing. This might sound strange coming from me, because I have the modern trifecta of blog/Facebook/Twitter at my fingertips pretty much daily, but stay with me. (Not all of us feel this way, so please take my opinion with a generous grain of salt.)

I hardly ever look at the blogs of people who query me unless they can give me some kind of impressive fact, like "30,000 people visit this blog per month," or "I draw a daily Web cartoon and have a following," or "I've created an interactive game that gets 5,000 plays a day," or whatever. I'll check for Web presence if I'm considering offering representation, but I don't have all day to sit around and cruise writer blogs.

If you're iffy on blogging, I say don't do it. There are too many bad blogs, blogs about people's cats, blogs about the day's word count, blogs with amateur book reviews, blogs by people who think they need a blog, etc., out there already. Don't add one more to the pile. Blogs without useful information or blogs by a clearly reluctant author are the worst.

The Internet is a living thing. For example, blogs take your most recent entry and post it first. For the savvy, content-rich blog, that's great. For the half-hearted blog, that's bad. Readers can log on and see the exact date when you lost your zest for it. And I'd say that a site last updated years ago is worse than no blog at all. It makes you seem out-of-date, irrelevant … maybe even dead.

Plus, a lot of blogs are self-centered, and that's *fine*, but a truly personal blog limits your reach. If there's one thing I've learned about the Internet from actually working at dot coms for six years, it's that users come to the Internet to see, "What's in it for me?" They want valuable content that speaks to their needs.

Most writing blogs—and most blogs in general—are about the writer of the blog, not about the user. I write my blog to give readers valuable content because I know that's what people want from me. At the end of the day, they don't care about my personal life. I know my readers visit me for writing and publishing advice, so that's what I dish up.

ONLINE PLATFORM DOS AND DON'TS

Here's a quick rundown of considerations for when you do decide to kick your platform up a notch.

DO:

- **Leverage everything you do**—blog about school visits, author events, books you're reading, movies you see that have a good writing take-away, your agent search, milestones of your book's journey to publication (check with your editor, though, to make sure you're allowed to post cover images and other production-related stuff).
- **Use pictures or cover images to liven up your posts.** If you're an illustrator, share sketches and finishes, talk about your process, talk about the tools you use, show works in progress.
- **Tweet or Facebook or post interesting links you find**, don't just talk about yourself.
- **Ask other people to create content for you**—host blog tours, have guest blogs, do interviews, and bring added value by using your blog to spotlight fun and different people who fit in with the theme of your blog.
- **Write about things that might hook a wider audience**—I give conference tips and lessons from outside kidlit sometimes, just to mix things up.
- **Do contests and giveaways**—remember, people are always asking "What's in it for me?" when they read blogs.
- **Use your blog as a place to talk about interesting things** you're learning about your book's subject matter, or research you're doing, or topical articles. For example, if butterflies are a huge part of your novel, post about migrations that are going on that month, etc.

DON'T:

- **Rant or talk endlessly about yourself**—make your blog a place that other people will want to visit. Besides, if you rant about how hard it is to get published or what scum publishing professionals are, it'll come back to bite you. The agent who clicks on the link in your query will think you're a negative and difficult person … not a positive business partner who will be a joy to work with.
- **Force it.** Again, there are too many blogs online to try and add yours to the heap if you're not committed. You're better off not having one instead of doing a bad or unenthusiastic job.

- **Leave your blog hanging**. Blogs are hungry little monsters. If you can't update at least once a week, you should think about a static website.
- **Get on a promotion soapbox.** Use Facebook and Twitter to get in touch with friends, fans and writing buddies. Don't use your Facebook as a platform that constantly blasts sales pitches for your work. If your profile looks like a marketing channel, readers and friends will tune you out.
- **Exist in isolation.** When you're starting to blog, reach out. Respond to comments on Twitter. Post comments on the blogs of people who comment on your blog. Read other blogs. You can't expect the "social" part of social media to be a one-way street.

This should at least get you thinking about how much social media you really need and how much to get involved in. It's a slippery slope. Some people start and can't stop, others start and can't wait to stop.

Find your own style but never, ever lose sight of the writing.

YOUR PLATFORM AUDIENCE

There's also the question of audience. Teens hang out online but they're more interested in social networking with friends, so there's little conclusive data on how they interact with writer blogs. If you write middle grade fiction, the audience for your online presence won't be kids at all. You'll hit other writers, book bloggers, parents, librarians, booksellers and teachers.

Unpublished writing blogs do foster community among other unpublished writers. You can gripe about rejections, brag about word count, share your successes and frustrations and make friends. While that's nice for you, it has little value to an agent or editor who comes to visit.

If you have a blog where you can give people really valuable content, tips and things to make their lives better (or at least to give them good cocktail party conversation), do it. If you are just thinking of blogging because everyone else does it or you heard that agents won't consider you unless you have a blog, don't.

BE CAREFUL WITH YOUR TIME

Social networking can be a timesuck. You can go pretty far down the rabbit hole with tweets and Facebook updates and adding photos everywhere. Then you lose sight of the thing that's really going to get you published: writing.

Focus on your writing. And if you feel the need to be online, which you should, at least in some small way, put up a static three-page site: a main landing page with info about your work, an "About Me" page and a contact page. That's it, and it should be cheap to make a website that actually looks good and professional.

Once you're under contract with a publisher, of course, every-thing changes. You'll need to shift into two modes, a) marketing Debut Novel, and b) writing Follow-up Novel. You'll have stuff to say. You'll have a book to sell. You'll have events to publicize. You'll have readers who want to know more about you. But that's after. Building a plat-form now, before you have a book, is superfluous. I'm all about writers getting themselves out there and starting to participate in the world and build buzz, but that's not what I'm selling when I sell your fiction.

For the time being, don't bow to platform pressure if you really don't feel comfortable blogging or tweeting or Facebooking. Unless, of course, you want to. If that's the case, just make sure your content is geared toward your audience. And make sure it's good content. That's at the heart of building an online presence.

8 WAYS TO BUILD YOUR PLATFORM

Here are resources you can use or join in order to start building your platform:

1. Start your own static three-page website.
2. Start a blog. (I use the self-hosted WordPress.org because I love the control and in-terface, but you can also use free WordPress.com, Blogspot or Tumblr.)
3. Start a Twitter account.
4. Make sure you're on Facebook.
5. Get involved with an online writing group or message board.
6. Write articles and get them published in children's magazines, on other people's blogs, or in your local SCBWI bulletin (for magazine markets, see page XX).
7. Collect e-mail addresses via your website and put together a simple (yet content-rich) newsletter to send out once a month.
8. Do public speaking, school visits or volunteer at the library—anything that connects you to kids or books or both.

MARY KOLE is a literary agent for Movable Type Management (mtmgmt.net). Formerly, she was an agent at the Andrea Brown Literary Agency. Mary runs Kidlit.com, a website for writers of children's books, and is the author of *Writing Irresistible Kidlit: The Ultimate Guide to Crafting Fiction for Young Adult and Middle Grade* (Writer's Digest Books, fall 2012). As an agent, Mary represents outstanding young adult works, middle grade novels, and picture books.

CRAFTING A QUERY

How to write a great letter.

....

by Kara Gebhart Uhl

So you've written a book. And now you want an agent. If you're new to publishing, you probably assume that the next step is to send your finished, fabulous book out to agents, right? Wrong. Agents don't want your finished, fabulous book. In fact, they probably don't even want *part* of your finished, fabulous book—at least, not yet. First, they want your query.

A query is a short, professional way of introducing yourself to an agent. If you're frustrated by the idea of this step, imagine yourself at a cocktail party. Upon meeting someone new, you don't greet them with a boisterous hug and kiss and, in three minutes, reveal your entire life story including the fact that you were late to the party because of some gastrointestinal problems. Rather, you extend your hand. You state your name. You comment on the hors d'oeuvres, the weather, the lovely shade of someone's dress. Perhaps, after this introduction, the person you're talking to politely excuses himself. Or, perhaps, you become best of friends. It's basic etiquette, formality, professionalism—it's simply how it's done.

Agents receive hundreds of submissions every month. Often they read these submissions on their own time—evenings, weekends, on their lunch break. Given the number of writers submitting, and the number of agents reading, it would simply be impossible for agents to ask for and read entire book manuscripts off the bat. Instead, a query is a quick way for you to, first and foremost, pitch your book. But it's also a way to pitch yourself. If an agent is intrigued by your query, she may ask for a partial (say, the first three chapters of your book). Or she may ask for your entire manuscript. And only then may you be signed.

As troublesome as it may first seem, try not to be frustrated by this process. Because, honestly, a query is a really great way to help speed up what is already a monumentally slow-paced industry. Have you ever seen pictures of slush piles—those piles of unread queries on many well-known agents' desk? Imagine the size of those slush piles if they held full manuscripts instead of one-page query letters. Thinking of it this way, query letters begin to make more sense.

Here we share with you the basics of a query, including its three parts and a detailed list of dos and don'ts.

PART I: THE INTRODUCTION

Whether you're submitting a 100-word picture book or a 90,000-word novel, you must be able to sum up the most basic aspects of it in one sentence. Agents are busy. And they constantly receive submissions for types of work they don't represent. So upfront they need to know that, after reading your first paragraph, the rest of your query is going to be worth their time.

An opening sentence designed to "hook" an agent is fine—if it's good and if it works. But this is the time to tune your right brain down and your left brain up—agents desire professionalism and queries that are short and to the point. Remember the cocktail party. Always err on the side of formality. Tell the agent, in as few words as possible, what you've written, including the title, genre and length.

Within the intro you also must try to connect with the agent. Simply sending 100 identical query letters out to "Dear Agent" won't get you published. Instead, your letter should be addressed not only to a specific agency but a specific agent within that agency. (And double, triple, quadruple check that the agent's name is spelled correctly.) In addition, you need to let the agent know why you chose her specifically. A good author-agent relationship is like a good marriage. It's important that both sides invest the time to find a good fit that meets their needs. So how do you connect with an agent you don't know personally? Research.

1. Make a connection based on an author or book the agent already represents.
Most agencies have websites that list who and what they represent. Research those sites. Find a book similar to yours and explain that, because such-and-such book has a similar theme or tone or whatever, you think your book would be a great fit. In addition, many agents will list specific topics they're looking for, either on their websites or in interviews. If your book is a match, state that.

2. Make a connection based on an interview you read.
Search by agents' names online and read any and all interviews they've participated in. Perhaps they mentioned a love for X and your book is all about X. Or, perhaps they mentioned that they're looking for Y and your book is all about Y. Mention the specific

interview. Prove that you've invested as much time researching them as they're about to spend researching you.

3. Make a connection based on a conference you both attended.

Was the agent you're querying the keynote speaker at a writing conference you were recently at? Mention it, specifically commenting on an aspect of his speech you liked. Even better, did you meet the agent in person? Mention it, and if there's something you can say to jog her memory about the meeting, say it. And better yet, did the agent specifically ask you to send your manuscript? Mention it.

Finally, if you're being referred to a particular agent by an author who that agent already represents—that's your opening sentence. That referral is guaranteed to get your query placed on the top of the stack.

PART II: THE PITCH

Here's where you really get to sell your book—but in only three to 10 sentences. Consider the jacket flap and its role in convincing readers to plunk down $24.95 to buy what's in between those flaps. Like a jacket flap, you need to hook an agent in the confines of very limited space. What makes your story interesting and unique? Is your story about a woman going through a midlife crisis? Fine, but there are hundreds of stories about women going through midlife crises. Is your story about a woman who, because of a midlife crisis, leaves her life and family behind to spend three months in India? Again, fine, but this story, too, already exists—in many forms. Is your story about a woman who, because of a midlife crisis, leaves her life and family behind to spend three months in India, falls in love with someone new while there and starts a new life—and family?—and then has to deal with everything she left behind upon her return? *Now* you have a hook.

Practice your pitch. Read it out loud, not only to family and friends, but to people willing to give you honest, intelligent criticism. If you belong to a writing group, workshop your pitch. Share it with members of an online writing forum. Know anyone in the publishing industry? Share it with them. Many writers spend years writing their books. We're not talking about querying magazines here, we're talking about querying an agent who could become a lifelong partner. Spend time on your pitch. Perfect it. Turn it into jacket-flap material so detailed, exciting and clear that it would be near impossible to read your pitch and not want to read more. Use active verbs. Write your pitch, put it aside for a week, then look at it again. Don't send a query simply because you finished a book. Send a query because you finished your pitch and are ready to take the next steps.

DOS AND DON'TS FOR QUERYING AGENTS

DO:

- Keep the tone professional.
- Query a specific agent at a specific agency.
- Proofread. Double-check the spelling of the agency and the agent's name.
- Keep the query concise, limiting the overall length to one page (single space, 12-point type in a commonly used font).
- Focus on the plot, not your bio, when pitching fiction.
- Pitch agents who represent the type of material you write.
- Check an agency's submission guidelines to see how it would like to be queried—for example, via e-mail or mail—and whether or not to include a SASE.
- Keep pitching, despite rejections.

DON'T:

- Include personal info not directly related to the book. For example, stating that you're a parent to three children doesn't make you more qualified than someone else to write a children's book.
- Say how long it took you to write your manuscript. Some best-selling books took 10 years to write—others, six weeks. An agent doesn't care how long it took—an agent only cares if it's good. Same thing goes with drafts—an agent doesn't care how many drafts it took you to reach the final product.
- Mention that this is your first novel or, worse, the first thing you've ever written aside from grocery lists. If you have no other publishing credits, don't advertise that fact. Don't mention it at all.
- State that your book has been edited by peers or professionals. Agents expect manuscripts to be edited, no matter how the editing was done.
- Bring up screenplays or film adaptations; you're querying an agent about publishing a book, not making a movie.
- Mention any previous rejections.
- State that the story is copyrighted with the U.S. Copyright Office or that you own all rights. Of course you own all rights. You wrote it.
- Rave about how much your family and friends loved it. What matters is that the agent loves it.
- Send flowers, baked goods or anything else except a self-addressed stamped envelope (and only if the SASE is required).
- Follow up with a phone call. After the appropriate time has passed (many agencies say how long it will take to receive a response) follow up in the manner you queried—via e-mail or mail.

PART III: THE BIO

If you write fiction, unless you're a household name or you've recently been a guest on "Oprah," an agent is much more interested in your pitch than in who you are. If you write nonfiction, who you are—more specifically, your platform and publicity—is much more important. Regardless, these are key elements that must be present in every bio:

1. Publishing credits

If you're submitting fiction, focus on your fiction credits—previously published works and short stories. That said, if you're submitting fiction and all your previously published work is nonfiction—magazine articles, essays, etc.—that's still fine and good to mention. Don't be overly long about it. Mention your publications in bigger magazines or well-known literary journals. If you've never had anything published, don't say you lack official credits. Simply skip this altogether and thank the agent for his time.

2. Contests and awards

If you've won many, focus on the most impressive ones and the ones that most directly relate to your work. Don't mention contests you entered and weren't named in. Also, feel free to leave titles and years out of it. If you took first place at the Delaware Writers Conference for your fiction manuscript, that's good enough. Mentioning details isn't necessary.

3. MFAs

If you've earned or are working toward a Master of Fine Arts in writing, say so and state the program. Don't mention English degrees or online writing courses.

4. Large, recognized writing organizations

Agents don't want to hear about your book club and the fact that there's always great food, or the small critique group you meet with once a week. And they really don't want to hear about the online writing forum you belong to. But if you're a member of something like the Romance Writers of America (RWA), the Mystery Writers of America (MWA), the Society of Children's Book Writers and Illustrators (SCBWI), the Society of Professional Journalists (SPJ), etc., say so. This shows you're serious about what you do and you're involved in groups that can aid with publicity and networking.

5. Platform and publicity

If you write nonfiction, who you are and how you're going to help sell the book once it's published becomes very important. Why are you the best person to write it and what do you have now—public speaking engagements, an active website or blog, substantial cred in your industry—that will help you sell this book?

Finally, be cordial. Thank the agent for taking the time to read your query and consider your manuscript. Ask if you may send more, in the format she desires (partial, full, etc.).

Think of the time you spent writing your book. Unfortunately, you can't send your book to an agent for a first impression. Your query *is* that first impression. Give it the time it deserves. Keep it professional. Keep it formal. Let it be a firm handshake—not a sloppy kiss. Let it be a first meeting that evolves into a lifetime relationship—not a rejection slip. But expect those slips. Just like you don't become lifelong friends with everyone you meet at a cocktail party, you can't expect every agent you pitch to sign you. Be patient. Keep pitching. And in the meantime, start writing that next book.

KARA GEBHART UHL (karagebhartuhl.com) was formerly a managing editor at *Popular Woodworking Magazine* and, later, *Writer's Digest* magazine. Kara now freelance writes and edits for trade and consumer publications from her 100-year-old foursquare in Fort Thomas, KY. She also actively writes about the joys and challenges of raising a 3-year-old daughter and twin 1-year-old boys at pleiadesbee.com, which is part of Cincinnati.com's Locals on Living blog network. An essay she wrote, which she originally read for WVXU's "This I Believe" program, will be published in the forthcoming *This I Believe: Life Lessons* (Wiley; fall 2011). You can read more of her work at karagebhartuhl.com.

Dear Ms. MacLeod,

I am seeking literary representation and hope you will consider my tween novel, REAL MERMAIDS DON'T WEAR TOE RINGS.

First zit. First crush. First … mermaid's tail?

1 Jade feels like enough of a freak-of-nature when she gets her first period at almost fifteen. She doesn't need to have it happen at the mall while trying on that XL tankini she never wanted to buy in the first place. And she really doesn't need to run into Luke Martin in the Feminine Hygiene Products **2** aisle while her dad Googles "menstruation" on his Blackberry **4** .

3 But "freak-of-nature" takes on a whole new meaning when raging hormones and bath salts bring on another metamorphosis—complete with scales and a tail. And when Jade learns she's inherited her mermaid tendencies from her late mother's side of the family, it raises the question: if Mom was once a mermaid, did she really drown that day last summer?

Jade is determined to find out. Though, how does a plus-sized, aqua-phobic mer-girl go about doing that, exactly … especially when Luke from aisle six seems to be the only person who might be able to help?

5 REAL MERMAIDS DON'T WEAR TOE RINGS is a light-hearted fantasy novel for tweens (10-14). It is complete at 44,500 words and available at your request. The first ten pages and a synopsis are included below my signature. I also have a completed chapter book for boys (MASON AND THE MEGANAUTS), should that be of interest to you.

My middle grade novel, ACADIAN STAR, was released last fall by Nimbus Publishing and has been nominated for the 2009/2010 Hackmatack Children's Choice Book Award. I have three nonfiction children's books with Crabtree Publishing to my credit (one forthcoming) as well as an upcoming early chapter book series. Thank you for taking the time to consider this project.

Kind regards,
Hélène Boudreau
www.heleneboudreau.com

1 One of the things that can really make a query letter stand out is a strong voice, and it seems that is one of the things writers struggle with the most. Hélène, however, knocked it out of the park with her query letter. I find young readers are very sensitive to inauthentic voices, but you can tell by just the first few paragraphs that she is going to absolutely nail the tween voice in the manuscript—you can see this even by the way she capitalized Feminine Hygiene Products **2** .

3 The first time I read this query, I actually did laugh out loud. Instead of merely promising me RMDWTR was funny (which it absolutely is), Hélène showed me how funny she can be, which made me want to request the manuscript even before I got to her sample pages.

I also loved how clearly and with just a few words she could invoke an entire scene. Hélène doesn't tell us Jade gets embarrassed in front of a local hunk, she plops us right down in the middle of the pink aisle with the well-intentioned but hopelessly nerdy Dad **4** . I felt this really spoke to her talents—if she could bring bits of a query to life, I couldn't wait to see what she could do with a whole manuscript. **5** And on top of all of this, she had a phenomenal title, a bio that made it very clear she was ready to break out, and a hook so strong it even made it onto the cover!

SAMPLE QUERY NO. 2: YOUNG ADULT
AGENT'S COMMENTS: MICHELLE HUMPHREY (MARTHA KAPLAN LITERARY)

Dear Ms. Humphrey,

I'm contacting you because I've read on various writing websites that you are expanding your young adult client list.

In LOSING FAITH, fifteen-year-old Brie Jenkins discovers her sister's death may not have been an accident ❶. At the funeral, an uncorroborated story surfaces about Faith's whereabouts the night of her tragic fall from a cliff. When Brie encounters a strange, evasive boy ❸ at Faith's gravesite, she tries to confront him, but he disappears into a nearby forest.

Brie searches out and questions the mysterious boy, finding more information than she bargained for: Faith belonged to a secret ritualistic group, which regularly held meetings at the cliff where she died. Brie suspects foul play, but the only way to find out for sure is to risk her own life and join the secret cult. ❷

LOSING FAITH (76k/YA) will appeal to readers of ❹ John Green's LOOKING FOR ALASKA and Laurie Halse Anderson's CATALYST. My published stories have won an editor's choice award in *The Greensilk Journal* and appeared in *Mississippi Crow* magazine. I'm a member of Romance Writers of America, where my manuscript is a finalist in the Florida chapter's Launching a Star Contest. For your convenience, I've pasted the first chapter at the bottom of this e-mail. Thank you for your time and consideration.

Sincerely,
Denise Jaden
www.denisejaden.com ❺

Everything about Denise's query appealed to me. She gave me a quick sentence about why she chose to query me, and then went right into the gist of her novel. ❶ Her "gist" is very much a teaser, or like the back blurb of a book. She gives plot clues without revealing too much of the plot. She keeps the plot points brief and keeps the teaser moving; most important is where she ends—on a note that makes the agent curious to know more. ❷ Denise also gives us vivid characters ❸ in this teaser: the smart, investigative protagonist, Brie; the mysterious boy at the gravesite; the sister, Faith, who's not what she seems. By creating hints of vivid characters and quick engaging plot points in a paragraph, Denise demonstrates her storytelling ability in the query—and I suspected it would carry through to her novel. ❹ Denise includes some other elements that I like to see in queries: comparisons to other well-known books (two or three is enough) and credentials that show her ability to write fiction. ❺ I like, too, that she included her website—I often visit websites when considering queries.

Dear Ms. Roth,

A boy with a hidden power and the girl who was sent to stop him have 24 hours to win a pickle contest.

1 12-year-old Pierre La Bouche is a *cornichon*. That's French for "pickle," but it also means "good-for-nothing." A middle child who gets straight C's, he's never been No. 1 at anything. When the family farm goes broke, grandfather Henri gives Pierre a mission: to save the farm by winning an international pickle contest.

2 En route to the contest, Pierre meets Aurore, the charming but less-than-truthful granddaughter of a rival farmer. She's been sent to ensnare Pierre, but after a wake up call from her conscience, she rescues him. Together, they navigate the ghostly Paris catacombs, figure out how to crash-land a plane, and duel with a black-hearted villain who will stop at nothing to capture their pickles. In their most desperate hour, it is Pierre's incredible simplicity that saves the day. Always bickering but becoming friends, Pierre and Aurore discover that anything is possible, no matter how hard it may seem.

3 *Pickle Impossible* is complete at 32,500 words. I'm a technical writer by day, optimistic novelist by night. Recently, I've interviewed a host of pickle makers and French natives. My own pickles are fermenting in the kitchen. I grew up in Toronto and live with my wife and children in Israel.

Thank you for your consideration. I hope to hear from you.

Kind Regards,

Eli Stutz

1 The first paragraph introduces the main character and the set-up. He uses concrete things to describe Pierre. He throws in the French flair of the book right away. And he doesn't beat around the bush to tell me what Pierre has to accomplish. **2** The second delves a little deeper into the plot. It gives me the complication that will drive the story forward—someone is out to stop Pierre. And then Eli accomplishes the most important trick here: He gives me some fun examples of what will happen in the book without summarizing the entire plot. That is key because I don't want to read the whole book in the query letter. But he gives me flavor. **3** The bio paragraph is straight to the point, not overcrowded with his whole life history, and also ties light-heartedly right back to the subject of the book. I loved that he tried fermenting his own pickles. (He later told me they weren't very good.) Here's the kicker. The total word count on this letter is 242 words. 242! Look how much he fits into 242 words. There's plot, character, personality and quirk. From this tightly written letter I know I'm going to get a fun, zany story. Those of you who wanted 250 words just to pitch your book, take heed! Shorter is better.

SYNOPSIS WORKSHOP

Compose an effective novel summary.

....

by Chuck Sambuchino

Before you submit your novel to an agent or publisher, there are things you need to do. First and foremost, you must finish the work. If you contact an agent and she likes your idea, she will ask to see some or all of the manuscript. You don't want to have to tell her it won't be finished for another six months. If your novel is complete and polished, it's time to write your query and synopsis. After that, you're ready to test the agent and editor waters.

How you submit your novel package will depend on each agent or publisher's specified submission guidelines. You'll find that some want only a query letter; others request a query letter and the complete manuscript; some prefer a query letter plus three sample chapters and a synopsis; and still others request a query letter, a few sample chapters, an outline *and* a synopsis. All want a SASE (self-addressed, stamped envelope) with adequate postage, unless they request an electronic submission. To determine what you need to submit, visit the agent or publisher's website for guidelines, or consult a current edition of a market resource such as *Novel & Short Story Writer's Market*, *Writer's Market* or *Guide to Literary Agents*. These sources have submission specifications that come straight from the editors and agents telling you just what to send, how to send it and when to anticipate a response.

Be prepared to send at least a query letter, a synopsis and three consecutive sample chapters. These are the most important—and most requested—parts of your novel package. You may not need to send them all in the same submission package, but you probably will need to use each of them at one time or another, so prepare everything before you start submitting. Here we'll focus on what writers often find the most difficult component of their novel submission package: the synopsis.

DEFINING SYNOPSIS

The synopsis supplies key information about your novel (plot, theme, characterization, setting), while also showing how these coalesce to form the big picture. You want to quickly tell what your novel is about without making an editor or agent read the novel in its entirety.

There are no hard and fast rules about the synopsis. In fact, there's conflicting advice about the typical length of a synopsis. Most editors and agents agree, though: The shorter, the better.

When writing your synopsis, focus on the essential parts of your story, and try not to include sections of dialogue unless you think they're absolutely necessary. (It's OK to inject a few strong quotes from your characters, but keep them brief.) Finally, even though the synopsis is only a condensed version of your novel, it must seem complete.

Keep events in the same order as they happen in the novel (but don't break them down into individual chapters). Remember that your synopsis should have a beginning, a middle and an ending (yes, you must tell how the novel ends to round out your story).

That's what's required of a synopsis: You need to be concise, compelling and complete, all at the same time.

CRAFTING TWO SYNOPSES

Because there is no definitive length to a synopsis, it's recommended you have two versions: a long synopsis and a short synopsis.

In past years, there used to be a fairly universal system regarding synopses. For every 35 or so pages of your manuscript, you would have one page of synopsis explanation, up to a maximum of eight pages.

So, if your book was 245 pages, double-spaced, your synopsis would be approximately seven pages. This was fairly standard, and allowed writers a decent amount of space to explain their story. You should write a synopsis following these guidelines first. This will be your long synopsis.

The problem is that during the past few years, agents started to get busier and busier, and now they want to hear your story now-now-now. Many agents today request synopses of no more than two pages. Some even say one page, but two pages is generally acceptable. To be ready to submit to these agents, you'll also need to draft a new, more concise summary—the short synopsis.

So, once you've written both, which do you submit? If you think your short synopsis is tight and effective, always use that. However, if you think the long synopsis is actually more effective, then you will sometimes submit one and sometimes submit the other. If an agent requests two pages max, send only the short one.

If she says simply, "Send a synopsis," and you feel your longer synopsis is superior, submit the long one. If you're writing plot-heavy fiction, such as thrillers and mysteries, you might really benefit from submitting a longer, more thorough synopsis.

Your best bet on knowing what to submit is to follow the guidelines of the agency or publisher in question.

FORMATTING ELECTRONIC SUBMISSIONS

Some editors or agents might ask you to submit your synopsis via e-mail or on a CD. The editor or agent can provide you with specific formatting guidelines indicating how she wants it sent and the type of files she prefers.

If an agent or editor does request an electronic submission, keep the following four points in mind:

1. Follow the same formatting specs as for a paper (hard copy) synopsis submission.
2. When sending your synopsis via e-mail, put the name of your novel in the subject line (but don't use all capital letters—it's just obnoxious).
3. Send the synopsis as an attachment to your e-mail unless the agent requests you cut and paste it in the e-mail body.
4. Include a cover letter in the body of your e-mail, and your cover page and table of contents in the file along with the synopsis.

PUTTING IT ALL TOGETHER

Now you know the basics of synopsis writing. Read on for explanations of mistakes to avoid in your synopsis, as well as an example of what a well-crafted, properly formatted synopsis should look like.

Article excerpted from *Formatting & Submitting Your Manuscript, 3rd edition* © 2009 by **CHUCK SAMBUCHINO AND THE EDITORS OF WRITER'S DIGEST BOOKS**, with permission from Writer's Digest Books.

MISTAKES TO AVOID IN YOUR SYNOPSIS

John Q. Writer ①
123 Author Lane
Writerville, USA 95355 ②

Officer on the Run ③

Investigative officer ④ David Black doesn't know where to begin when he gets word Police Chief John Murphy is found dead on his bed—with a silver bullet between his eyes and half-inch nail marks running down his back. Black has to answer two questions: Who would kill the Chief, and why?

It turns out quite a few people aren't too pleased with the Chief. He's been on the force for 23 years and no doubt made some enemies. On the home front, the Chief was completely out of control. He'd lost all affection for his wife, Mary, who was once the apple of his eye.

Black interviews all of the women that the Chief had affairs with, whom he called his "Seven Deadly Sins," and finds no leads until Marlene Preston, the Chief's seventh "sin." ⑤ She reveals how the Chief repeatedly would handcuff her arms and legs to four metal poles under the bleachers at the school football stadium. Black drinks himself into a stupor and pours out his problems to a young barmaid, who tells him that the Chief deserved to die.

Black continues investigating the Chief and uncovers all kinds of sordid details. ⑥ The killer is revealed at the end, and it is a total shock and surprise ⑦ to all, especially Black. ⑧

① The genre of the novel is not mentioned, nor is the word length. ② Phone number and e-mail address are missing; make sure the agent or editor will be able to contact you. ③ The title of the book should be in all caps, or at the very least bold and italicized. ④ The first time a character is introduced, the name should be in all caps. ⑤ Pivotal plot points are glossed over—they should be highlighted. ⑥ Be sure to reveal your novel's ending. ⑦ A short synopsis is preferable, but this is actually too short; it doesn't give enough information about the characters or the plot to make it compelling. ⑧ The characters' motivations and emotions aren't conveyed at all in this synopsis, leaving the editor or agent to think, "Why should I care about these characters?"

THE MAKING OF A SUCCESSFUL SYNOPSIS

John Q. Writer   **2** Mystery
123 Author Lane   70,000 words
Writerville, CA 95355
(323) 555-0000
johnqwriter@e-mail.com **1**

> **1** List contact information on the top left corner of first page. **2** Include novel's genre and word length here. **3** Avoid numbering the first page. **4** Center title in all caps. **5** Use all caps the first time a character is introduced. **6** Double-space all text. **7** Establish a good hook, introduce important characters and set up a key conflict.

4 OFFICER ON THE RUN
Synopsis

Investigative officer **5** DAVID BLACK doesn't know where to begin when he gets word Police Chief JOHN MURPHY is found dead on his bed—with a silver bullet between his eyes and half-inch nail marks running down his back. Black has to answer two questions: **6** Who would kill the Chief, and why? **7**

It turns out quite a few people aren't too pleased with the Chief. He'd been on the force for 23 years and no doubt made some enemies. All the townspeople called him Bulldog because he looked like a pit bull, and certainly acted like one.

Countless stories passed through City Hall about how the Chief wouldn't hesitate to roll up his cuffs and beat suspects into submission until they would confess to a crime. That was his method and it worked. He could take control of any person and any situation.

Except his wife and his marriage. On that front, the Chief was completely out of control. He'd lost all affection for his wife, MARY, who was once the apple of his eye but now weighs in at 260 lbs. That was fine with the Chief—the less he had to see Mary, the more time for his own pursuits. But he really had only one pursuit: younger women. That fact he didn't hide. He'd often brag to guys on the force about being the only Chief in the history of law enforcement to "burn through seven dispatchers in just as many years." He even called them his "Seven Deadly Sins." Little did he know that one day they'd all be suspects for his murder.

❷ Black interviews all seven women and finds no leads until MAR-
LENE PRESTON, the Chief's "Seventh Deadly Sin," reveals how the
Chief repeatedly would handcuff her arms and legs to four metal poles
under the bleachers at the school football stadium. Marlene says she's
never told anyone about any of it. Black then interrogates ❸ the six other "sins" to see if they had also been physically mistreated. They all say
the Chief never tried anything like that with them.

> ❶ Format headers with your name, the title, the word "Synopsis" and the page number. ❷ Begin text three lines below the header. ❸ Write your synopsis in third person, present tense. ❹ In a long synopsis, begin a new scene or twist with the start of a new paragraph (there is not enough room to do this in a short synopsis).

Black drinks himself into a stupor and pours out his problems to a
young barmaid, SARAH, who just happens to be the best friend of the
Police Lieutenant's daughter, KELLY LIEBERMAN. Sarah tells Black
the Chief deserved to die and that he was a jerk, especially to Kelly when
she'd baby-sit for the Chief and his wife. According to Sarah, the Chief
used to talk dirty to Kelly and then warn her not to tell her father because LIEUTENANT
LIEBERMAN was in line for a promotion.

Black interviews Kelly. She denies the Chief did anything but make a few lewd comments
on occasion. When Black approaches Kelly's father, Lieutenant Lieberman says Kelly never
mentioned a word about the Chief. Black returns to talk with Kelly and asks why she's never
mentioned anything to her father. She says she's afraid he'd get upset at her for bringing it up.
Black presses further, asking Kelly if the Chief ever did anything other than verbally harass her.
Kelly says no.

❹ Black decides to walk back under the bleachers to the spot where Marlene says the Chief repeatedly handcuffed her. There, he notices two sneaker shoestrings on the ground by the four poles
Marlene pointed out. The strings had been tied in knots and then cut. Black shows the strings to
Marlene and asks if the Chief ever tied her to the poles with them. "Not once," she says. "Handcuffs
every time."

CONFERENCES

Get the most out of a writing event.

....

by Mary Kole

You've finally taken the plunge and decided to invest in a writers' conference. Or perhaps you're planning this year's conference schedule and hitting all your favorite events. Great! There's no better way to network with publishing professionals, meet fellow writers, learn about the current marketplace, and get a jolt of inspiration for your craft.

When you're choosing your next conference, keep in mind that there are two major types: big group and small group. The big group conferences feature breakout speaker sessions, panels and other information-packed classes for large audiences of writers. Small group conferences, like workshops or retreats, often break attendees into smaller classes and focus directly on participants' writing samples.

I go to dozens of events every year as a faculty member and can share a few tips to help you get the most from your experience at both types of events. Read below for hints on big conferences, small workshops, pitching and aligning your expectations.

BIG CONFERENCES

At a big group conference, you'll be going to sessions with dozens or hundreds of your writing peers. This was the case at the DFW Writers' Conference (dfwwritersconference.org), the Society of Children's Book Writers and Illustrators (scbwi.org) New York and Los Angeles national conferences, the Florida Writers Association Conference (floridawriters.net), the San Diego Writers' Conference (writersconferences.com), the Writer's Digest Writers Conference (writersdigest.com/conferences-events), and many more. Independent regional conferences and big writing groups like the Romance Writers of America (rwa.org) often host these types of events, too.

Sessions at big conferences range from the general—perhaps "Trends in the Children's Marketplace"—to the specific—"Humor for Picture Book Illustrators." You'll also get informational sessions from agents and editors about their agencies, tastes and houses. Big conferences can be overwhelming, and the issue is often too many great sessions to choose from!

Here's how you make the most of a big conference:

- **MIX UP YOUR SCHEDULE:** Check the schedule with an eye toward variety. Mix craft seminars with talks by publishing bigwigs. If a session isn't satisfying you, it's perfectly OK to get up and visit a concurrent one. Make sure you go to all of the panels, too.

- **MINGLE:** Even if you're naturally shy, you'll get more out of a big event by meeting other writers, talking to the professionals, asking questions during sessions (we love getting smart questions!) and otherwise putting yourself out there. Writing is a solitary pursuit, but this isn't the time to hold back on the socializing!

- **PRINT BUSINESS CARDS.** Whether you get a set designed or use free services like VistaPrint (vistaprint.com) you'll want something with your name and e-mail to give out. Staying in touch with people is Networking 101, and if you don't have them, you'll end up regretting it.

- **MEET YOUR NEW CRITIQUE GROUP.** Connect with other writers at the event so you can exchange pages after you go home and the conference buzz wears off.

I urge every writer to go to a big conference at least once. You'll get relevant information, meet other writers and rub elbows with agents and editors. Such a massive event is also a jolt of creative inspiration, which is worth the price of admission every time.

SMALL CONFERENCES, WORKSHOPS AND RETREATS

Smaller conferences and workshops focus on an attendee's work in a hands-on environment. Here, you'll be in small groups with a writing teacher or publishing professional and you'll work on your writing sample in a critique setting.

Workshops and retreats are great because you're getting personalized advice on your writing. You're also working in small groups. These events are intense—lots of information to soak up, lots of critique to give, lots of interactions with writers and faculty—but totally worth it. The Andrea Brown Literary Agency hosts the Big Sur Writing Workshop twice a year (December and March, henrymiller.org) on the beautiful Northern California Coast, and I am always amazed by how much writers evolve from Friday to Sunday. There's nothing quite like a focused workshop to really take craft to the next level.

I've seen the same happen at other workshops I've attended, like the SCBWI LA Retreat, the SCBWI New York Writers Intensive, and the workshops put on by the Highlights Foundation (highlightsfoundation.org) on their secluded property in Pennsylvania. That's the other benefit of small conferences: They're often held in scenic locations that are perfect for courting your muse.

Here are my tips for taking advantage of a small group workshop or retreat:

- **COME READY TO WORK.** A retreat should be relaxing, right? Wrong! While you'll benefit from a gorgeous setting or a lot of personal attention, you should also come with a notepad, a laptop and your regular writing tools. Attendees are often inspired to make changes to their writing sample mid-workshop, so make sure you're equipped to do so.

- **ADJUST YOUR CRITIQUE ATTITUDE.** Writers learn to revise—the biggest skill in a working author's toolbox—by first looking constructively at the work of others. Don't just sit in workshop waiting for them to talk about your work. Actively critique, participate, examine and analyze the work of your fellow writers. They'll return the favor, and your editorial eye will be that much sharper as a result, which you'll need to finesse your own work.

- **USE THE FACULTY.** We show up to a retreat weekend knowing that our time belongs to the attendees. You'll have unprecedented access to authors, agents and editors. Ask questions, really drill into craft topics and take full advantage of the faculty's knowledge base.

Whether it's your first retreat or your tenth, you'll leave the weekend with new connections and a deeper understanding of your work and the bigger writing craft.

PITCHING

You'll most likely have the opportunity to pitch the faculty at both kinds of conferences. My biggest piece of advice on this fraught writing topic is: relax. Seriously. I've had people burst out crying during a pitch. I've had people mumble their memorized monologue into their laps. People read off of cue cards. People shake. People forget their words.

Don't do any of the above. Just talk to me. Tell me about your book. Pique my curiosity. Have a conversation and make a personal connection … *that's* what I'll remember as I head off to the airport. I have experienced thousands of pitches. Don't put undue pressure on yourself to knock my socks off or get an offer of representation right off the bat. Just being casual and interesting is enough. And for goodness sake, don't worry about memorizing your lines or fret if you misremember them. Only you know how it's supposed to go, so don't put so much emphasis on getting every word right.

Once you loosen up and talk to me, you'll be ahead of the pack.

KNOW BEFORE YOU GO

As an agent, I wish more writers went into conferences with the right attitude. You should be prepared to have fun, make new friends, network with the pros, pitch casually, leave with new ideas to take your work to the next level. You shouldn't go in expecting a contract or a big break. You shouldn't pack your suitcase with 20 copies of your full manuscript and spend all weekend trying to slip them to faculty. That's unrealistic. If you ever leave a conference feeling *crushed* and unable to go on, you need to revise your expectations. You don't have to be a "conference success story" in order to have a successful conference.

The benefits of a conference are inspiration and knowledge. You may see the positive effects immediately, or you may wake up with a brainstorm months after the event. Either way, a conference is something every writer should invest in at least once in their career.

See you on the conference circuit!

MARY KOLE is a literary agent for Movable Type Management (mtmgmt.net). Formerly, she was an agent at the Andrea Brown Literary Agency. Mary runs Kidlit.com, a website for writers of children's books, and is the author of *Writing Irresistible Kidlit: The Ultimate Guide to Crafting Fiction for Young Adult and Middle Grade* (Writer's Digest Books, fall 2012). As an agent, Mary represents outstanding young adult works, middle grade novels, and picture books.

FIRST BOOKS

Hear from debut authors of picture books, middle grade and young adult.

by Chuck Sambuchino

There's something fresh and amazing about debut novels that's inspiring to other writers. It's with that in mind that we collected eight successful debuts from the past year and sat down to ask the authors questions about how they broke in, what they did right and what advice they have for scribes who are trying to follow in their footsteps. These are writers of picture books, middle grade stories and young adult novels—same as you—who saw their work come to life through hard work and determination. Read on to learn more about their individual journeys.

PICTURE BOOKS

① GINA BELLISARIO (GINABELLISARIO.COM)

The Twelve Days of Christmas in Illinois (STERLING CHILDREN'S)

QUICK TAKE: "For the holidays, Mia sets off with her cousin on an authentically Illinois road trip, collecting gifts to the tune of a classic carol with a Land of Lincoln twist."

WRITES FROM: Outside of Chicago.

PRE-BOOK: I have a background in journalism and teaching, so my pre-*Illinois* writings include articles in newspapers and educator magazines. But before college (and even kindergarten), I wrote children's stories. Learning picture book structure came later, thanks to my literary agent's teachings.

TIME FRAME: Completing the first draft took about a month. I already knew how the draft should look, well before I wrote it. *The Twelve Days of Christmas in Illinois* is one of many titles in an established series, so I was able to reference other titles.

ENTER THE AGENT: I did an Internet search for "children's literary agents." Kelly Sonnack [of the Andrea Brown Literary Agency] popped up. Because our writing tastes seemed similar, I submitted a picture book manuscript. A rejection letter returned, with revision advice and an invitation to resubmit. I followed Kelly's advice, resubmitted, and … YESSS! She asked if I'd consider revising the manuscript with her. Several rewrites later, she offered representation.

WHAT YOU LEARNED: The clichéd phrase, "never give up," is underrated. If a writer wants his/her work published, that phrase is a *must* to live by. For me, it meant reading picture books with starred reviews, figuring out my story arc and taking rejection letters into consideration (without letting them squash my author dreams).

WHAT YOU DID RIGHT: Kelly gave revision advice; I accepted it with open ears.

PLATFORM: Because *Illinois* celebrates state history and town landmarks, I'm reaching out to representatives of the book's destinations. Elementary teachers, too!

NEXT UP: I have four books coming out in 2013. They are part of an eight-book series from Millbrook Press. Each title is about a community helper, and the series is a fantastic teaching tool for grades K-2.

② ERIC PINDER (ERICPINDER.COM)

If All the Animals Came Inside (LITTLE, BROWN)

QUICK TAKE: "Kangaroos, lemurs, lions, elephants and every other creature you can think of rush inside a family's house to play, startling the parents and delighting the kids as fun mayhem ensues."

WRITES FROM: Northern New Hampshire.

PRE-BOOK: My career focus was on creative nonfiction, with plans for a novel. But then a funny thing happened. All my friends started having kids. Suddenly their houses were full of books by Seuss and Boynton and Carle. Listening to friends read to their children, I could hear and admire the music in the words. Picture books are a lot like poetry. When you write a picture book, you're basically using words as a musical instrument. I picked up some old classics and some new titles and thought, "Wow! These are really good." And that got me started on some picture books of my own.

TIME FRAME: From first draft to published book took about three years. I lost count of the number of revisions. That first draft started as homework during my first semester in the Writing for Children & Young Adults MFA program at Vermont College of Fine Arts.

ENTER THE AGENT: My agent is Ammi-Joan Paquette of the Erin Murphy Literary Agency.

WHAT YOU LEARNED: The biggest difference between publishing a book for grownups and a picture book is the illustrator's role, which is just as important as the author's. I didn't know who the illustrator would be until months after signing the contract. When I found out I'd be sharing a book with Marc Brown, that was a very big (and very pleasant) surprise.

PLATFORM: I had some practice doing talks and presentations at schools and libraries, and a network of librarians ready to invite me back. That's one good way to get publicity for a new book. I've had a Web page for about eight years, and I try to update it and add things semi-regularly, to keep people checking in to see what's new. Twitter and an author page on Facebook are newer endeavors, but they're also good ways to build and interact with an audience.

NEXT UP: Finishing up a middle grade mystery novel and a funny memoir about teaching writing. And, of course, I'm going to keep writing picture books. I was wrestling a dragon onto the page earlier this morning.

MIDDLE GRADE

3 CAROLINE STARR ROSE
(CAROLINESTARRROSE.COM)

May B. (**SCHWARTZ & WADE**)

QUICK TAKE: "When a terrible turn of events leaves May Betterly all alone, she must try to find food—and courage—to make it through the approaching winter."

WRITES FROM: Albuquerque, N.M.

PRE-NOVEL: I'd written three middle grade novels and seven picture books before selling *May B.* With no agent or leads, I (believe it or not) stopped teaching to try writing full time.

TIME FRAME: I started writing in 2007. I wrapped up the first draft in fall 2008. Most of my writing I did in a 3'x4' closet "office"—my tiny private corner of the house.

ENTER THE AGENT: I found Michelle Humphrey [of ICM] through the Guide to Literary Agents Blog. (Thanks, Chuck!)

BIGGEST SURPRISE: *May B.* was scheduled to publish September 2011 with Random House imprint, Tricycle Press. When Tricycle closed in November 2010, the book was orphaned. Fortunately mine was one of several titles kept on by Random House (and is now with imprint Schwartz and Wade). While waiting for a month to learn the fate of my book, a friend reminded me of the themes of *May B.*: surviving, overcoming, trying when you're not sure of the outcome but pushing forward still. In a lot of ways, May Betterly— an unsure, unreal, old-fashioned child—taught me what it means to be brave.

WHAT YOU DID RIGHT: I was manically optimistic that the next editor or agent would want to work with me, kept submitting and kept writing.

PLATFORM: I'm a part of two debut novelists groups, the Class of 2k12 and the Apocalypsies. I'm also a member of SCBWI. I blog about writing, reading and the publication process at carolinebyline.blogspot.com.

NEXT UP: I'm about to go on submission with a middle grade about a girls' club and a picture book about the Louisiana wetlands.

4 MIKE JUNG (CAPTAINSTUPENDOUS.WORDPRESS.COM)

Geeks, Girls, and Secret Identities (**SCHOLASTIC**)

QUICK TAKE: "Three 12-year-old guys discover that the alter ego of their hometown superhero, Captain Stupendous, is actually a 12-year-old girl."

WRITES FROM: Oakland, Calif.

PRE-BOOK: I've dabbled in creative writing my entire life—short stories, songs, playwriting classes in college, snarky and inappropriate e-mail at work—but I'd never attempted to publish anything before, and *Geeks* was my first attempt at writing a novel.

TIME FRAME: I first had the idea of writing a children's book *way* back in 1996, then spent 10 years daydreaming about it. When my daughter was born in 2006, I realized that it was never going to happen unless I fully, unequivocally committed to making it happen. Over the next few years I wrote 26 versions of the first page, four rewrites of the first 50 pages, and finally a complete manuscript, which I intensely revised three times before signing with my agent.

ENTER THE AGENT: EMLA agent Ammi-Joan Paquette contacted me after reading whatever lunacy I was spouting on my blog back in 2009.

WHAT YOU DID RIGHT: The single biggest thing I've tried to do is be honest. I've given honest feedback to others' work, and I've tried to honestly express all my positive feelings for all the great children's books out there and the people who create them. I believe the presence of that kind of positive energy is one of the best things about the kidlit community.

NEXT UP: I have a piece in the *Dear Teen Me* anthology (Zest Books, November 2012) and I'm also a contributor for *Break These Rules*, an anthology edited by fellow EMLA client Luke Reynolds that's forthcoming in fall of 2013.

YOUNG ADULT

5 MARIE LU (MARIELU.ORG)

Legend (**PUTNAM**)

QUICK TAKE: "In a dark, futuristic United States, a 15-year-old girl prodigy is chosen to hunt down a famous 15-year-old boy criminal."

WRITES FROM: Pasadena, Calif.

TIME FRAME: *Legend* came to me after I watched *Les Miserables* on TV one afternoon in 2009. After I finished the first draft (which took about five months) and before I got back revisions, I distracted myself by making a Facebook game set in the *Legend* world.

ENTER THE AGENT: I first met the amazing Kristin Nelson [of Nelson Literary] in college at a writers' conference. She rejected my first novel but took me on for my second!

SURPRISES: How unbelievably good copyeditors are at spotting kinks in a story.

WHAT YOU DID RIGHT: Kristin and I were trying in vain to sell one of my older stories. While rejections slowly trickled in for that one, I forced myself to start on a new story instead of waiting around. That new story was *Legend*. Best decision I ever made!

DO DIFFERENT NEXT TIME: I wouldn't have spent so long dwelling on my first unpublished manuscript. I learned that the most important thing to do when you know a story isn't working is to put it away, and write a new, better one!

PLATFORM: I'm a big fan of deviantART, a large online community of great folks where I've gained about 15,000 watchers for my blog and art/writing uploads. I'm also a Flash artist, so I like to make games and trailers for *Legend* that viewers can share online.

NEXT UP: I have several ideas swirling in my head, so I'm not sure which I'll tackle first. This time the story might be set in the past, but with magic. Mafias might be involved.

⑥ MICHELLE HODKIN (MICHELLEHODKIN.COM)
The Unbecoming of Mara Dyer (SIMON & SCHUSTER)

QUICK TAKE: "16-year-old Mara Dyer doesn't believe life can get any stranger than waking up in a hospital with no memory of how she got there. It can."

WRITES FROM: South Florida

PRE-BOOK: This was the first book I ever attempted to write. Previously, I was practicing as an attorney—specifically, working on civil anti-terrorism litigation.

ENTER THE AGENT: In February 2010, I entered a Backspace Conference Scholarship contest by submitting my first pages of *The Unbecoming of Mara Dyer*, and Diana Fox of Fox Literary was one of the judges. She requested the manuscript before I was told that I was selected as one of the contest finalists. I sent the manuscript to her and she offered me representation two weeks later.

WHAT YOU LEARNED: To be honest, the biggest surprise is that I'm a published author. Three years ago, I couldn't have fathomed that my life would look like this. It's been a wonderful and surreal journey.

WHAT YOU DID RIGHT: I worked obsessively on my manuscript every day for 10 months. I wanted to make the thrilling aspects genuinely thrilling and the romantic aspects deeply romantic. But at the end of the day, I wrote the story I felt I *had* to write and wrote the book that only I *could* write, and I hope my passion is felt by the reader.

DO DIFFERENT NEXT TIME: I spent a lot of time making tiny, superficial tweaks to the manuscript and worrying about whether it was actually, completely finished. I think I would have saved myself a lot of anxiety had I had more confidence back then.

PLATFORM: I have a blog and I'm on Twitter, but I can't say I engage in either platform specifically to gain readership. I do it because I enjoy it; getting to interact with readers, industry professionals and other writers is a bonus.

NEXT UP: The sequel is due out in Fall 2012!

⑦ ROBIN MELLOM (ROBINMELLOM.COM)

Ditched (HYPERION)

QUICK TAKE: "A girl finds herself lying in a ditch the morning after prom with no memory of the last 12 hours, which she soon learns included a Tinkerbell tattoo, a dog-swapping escapade and a disappearing prom date."

WRITES FROM: Central Coast, Calif.

PRE-BOOK: I wrote lighthearted middle grade fiction for several years, which was how I landed my agent. While submitting, my agent suggested I try writing a funny teen novel.

TIME FRAME: I wrote *Ditched* in about five months. I knew exactly how I wanted it to end but wasn't sure of the specific events that would get me there. I went ahead and wrote an opening chapter, listing five of the most random things I could think of (a three-legged Chihuahua, In-N-Out Burger, etc.) figuring I would change them later, but they all ended up being big plot points, so *thumbs up* for randomness!

ENTER THE AGENT: I met Jill Corcoran of The Herman Agency several years ago at the SCBWI national conference. She was looking specifically for humorous middle grade, so we were a perfect match.

WHAT YOU LEARNED: The community of writers is such a supportive environment. There's not a sense of competition but rather a feeling that the more books there are available to teen readers the better. Authors are fans of one another and very often become good friends.

WHAT YOU DID RIGHT: I listened to my agent's advice. It had never occurred to me to try my humorous writing for teens instead of middle grade. She saw something in my writing I didn't realize I had in me. Finding the *right* project and being willing to put the others aside made all the difference.

DO DIFFERENT NEXT TIME: I wouldn't have stressed quite so much over the rejections. Finding an editor who truly *gets* what you're doing is the ultimate goal. And my editor was worth the wait.

NEXT UP: A middle grade series, The Classroom (2012), as well as the companion novel to *Ditched*, titled *Busted*.

⑧ KIMBERLY PURCELL (KIMPURCELL.COM)

Trafficked **(VIKING JUVENILE)**

QUICK TAKE: "Stranded in a foreign land with no money and nobody who can help her, Hannah must find a way to save herself from her new status as a modern-day slave."

WRITES FROM: Westchester, N.Y.

PRE-BOOK: I worked briefly as a journalist. Later, while I was teaching ESL [English as a second language], my students talked to me about how they'd been mistreated, and I became interested in the issue of modern-day slavery.

TIME FRAME: From the very beginning stages of researching this book to the final copyedit, it took eight years. In the middle of all that, I gave birth to two children and wrote during their naps.

ENTER THE AGENT: My husband met my agent, Kate Lee at ICM, and asked if I could send her my novel. Fortunately, she called me and said she loved it. I was shocked. I had sent an earlier novel out to a bunch of agents, and even had some personal referrals, but no one took it.

WHAT YOU LEARNED: I always thought if you got a great agent—and Kate Lee is indeed great—I'd be set. It didn't happen this way. Kate sent it out to six editors and all of them passed on it. I agreed with the editors' comments and didn't want it to keep being rejected, so I re-imagined the main character and rewrote the book from scratch. Later, I was with friends on the subway talking about my novel and how my agent was about to send it back out. There was a young woman sitting a few seats away glancing our way. I could tell she was listening. When we got off the train at the same spot, she came up to me and said, "I'm an editor and I heard you talking about your novel. Do you have an editor?" I said I didn't and she gave me her card. You can imagine my surprise when I read "Penguin" on her card. I never thought I would meet an editor of a huge publishing house in this way.

WHAT YOU DID RIGHT: I never stopped writing or putting myself out there. I think that's the difference between a published writer and an unpublished writer—the published writer hears the word, "No," but interprets it as, "Not yet."

PLATFORM: I have a website and a blog. Also, I'm using Twitter a lot and building relationships in the literary community.

NEXT UP: I'm writing a paranormal thriller.

CHUCK SAMBUCHINO (chucksambuchino.com, @chucksambuchino on Twitter) edits the *Guide to Literary Agents* (guidetoliteraryagents.com/blog) as well as the *Children's Writer's & Illustrator's Market*. His pop-humor books include *How to Survive a Garden Gnome Attack* (film rights optioned by Sony) and *Red Dog / Blue Dog: When Pooches Get Political* (reddog-bluedog.com). Chuck's other writing books include *Formatting & Submitting Your Manuscript, 3rd. Ed.*, as well as *Create Your Writer Platform* (fall 2012). Besides that, he is a husband, guitarist, dog owner, and cookie addict.

GARTH NIX

On co-writing and choosing the right books for the right ages.

....

by Kristen Grace

Before becoming a full-time writer, Garth Nix worked at nearly every level of the book publishing industry including stints as a literary agent, marketing consultant, book editor and book publicist. His first novel, *Sabriel*, was released in 1995 and won the Aurealis Award for best young adult novel and best fantasy novel. Since then, he has published the next two books in the Old Kingdom Chronicles, *Lirael* in 2001 and the *New York Times* best-selling *Abhorsen* in 2003.

His other books include The Keys to the Kingdom and The Seventh Tower series, the sci-fi thriller *Shade's Children*, and more. His most recent works include *Troubletwisters*, released in 2011 with co-author Sean Williams, and *A Confusion of Princes*, a young adult space opera that Nix is currently working to promote.

Here he gives his thoughts about the young adult genre, his process for creating realistic worlds, and the joys of working with a co-author. For more information on Nix, you can visit his website at garthnix.com and follow him on Twitter @garthnix.

On your website, you outline your process for writing a book in great detail. How has this process changed over the years? Do you approach writing full series differently than writing a single book?

"The Nine Stages of a Garth Nix Novel" and "How I Write," which are up on garthnix. com, are still basically how I write a book, though of course there have been variations with different novels. I tend to do less hand writing than I once did, so I no longer have complete handwritten manuscript books, but I do still write with a pen on paper when I find a chapter or section particularly challenging, or for some reason I can't type on a computer.

The main difference with writing series (or sequels) is that I spend a lot of time re-reading the previous books! With The Keys to the Kingdom for example, I found I needed to re-read all the previous books every time I was working on a new book, so I ended up re-reading the first book at least six times. But I did this rather than keeping spreadsheets of the characters, places and so on, which is how other authors have done it, so as always, there are many different ways to work on a series or sequence of books.

Your stories feature a variety of protagonists, from the teenage girls of the Abhorsen series to a young boy in the Keys to the Kingdom series. How do you choose your protagonist's age and gender? How do you approach writing stories from such different perspectives?

I'm very story-focused, so I tend to discover my characters as I go along, rather than knowing a lot about the characters beforehand. So I typically work out who I need for the story, rather than working out what story a character might have, and this sets the age and gender of the protagonist. To some degree this is all instinctive, I start thinking of a story, a character emerges from that, and they are what they are, though I might tweak the age to make it fit the story better.

In terms of writing stories from different perspectives, it's probably more accurate to say I use different viewpoint characters rather than different perspectives. Here, I am again led by the story. I simply try to imagine my protagonist's actions and emotions given the situation I have put them in and what I already know about them, and where I want the story to go. I only use as much character introspection or third-person observation as is necessary to carry that story forward, and no more. This imagining is based upon observation and knowledge of how real people behave, talk and reveal themselves; but also from experiencing many other people's fictional characters, in film and television as well as books. In general, I would say that humans are more similar than they are different, regardless of age and gender, and small but accurate details of behavior, appearance, speech and thought will take you a long way towards a believable character.

The beginning of a novel is crucial for finding an agent and a publisher, and for hooking readers. What do you suggest for writers struggling with how to open their novel? How do you decide where your story will begin?

My advice would be just to write from where you think the story starts, but be prepared to throw away, condense or change what you have written if it turns out the story doesn't feel interesting until later on. Even if you do have to throw out three chapters,

or 10,000 words or whatever, the chances are that you needed to write those words in order to get to the real beginning.

Many of your books have strong magical foundations. How did you go about developing the magical rules and mythologies that are so central in stories like the Abhorsen series?

Many fantasy writers spend a lot of time developing their magic systems and invented world and so forth before they write anything of the story, and this is a tried and trusted method. However, in my case I typically work a lot of this stuff out as I write the story, rather than before. That said, I think I equip myself to do this by reading a lot of history, myth and legend, so that I have a lot of 'real world' potential mythological and magical beliefs to draw upon, and reinvent or transform for my own purposes.

If you use magical ideas or myths that have some resonance with existing myth, legend or history, it will work better for the reader. The trick is to build upon these foundations, or transform elements of them, so they have the resonance but also feel new and not just something lifted holus bolus from familiar material.

You've suggested that your younger readers start with the Seventh Tower series or the Keys to the Kingdom series, and that your older readers start with the Abhorsen series or Shade's Children. What is your reasoning for this distinction? When writing, do you keep specific age groups in mind?

I don't think books have age ranges, despite the publishing industry's tendency to label books in this way. For example, a book might be labeled for 9-12 year olds. But this suggests that it is not suitable for a 13-year-old or an adult, which in most cases is not true. Rather than an age range, I think books have an entry level, a reading age (which may not be chronological age) when a book becomes accessible. But there should be no upper age limit, because many good children's books have a lot to offer older readers, and re-readers who are coming back to a book.

This is because good books have multiple layers of story and meaning. At the entry age level the reader might only really get the adventure or the top layer of a story, but a more experienced reader (or someone re-reading when they are older) will find multiple layers that will expand upon that surface reading.

I think my Seventh Tower books have an entry level of about 8+, and the Keys to the Kingdom about 9+, but the Abhorsen books and *Shade's Children* are more complex and have more sophisticated and mature content, so the entry level is 13 or 14+.

The latter books are young adult, and as I have said elsewhere, I think YA is a subset of adult fiction, not of children's fiction. They are books for adults that are particularly attractive to younger adults but not limited to them, and they are not for younger children.

What's your favorite murdered darling from your books—a character, scene, plot, or even a single line that you really wanted to keep but ultimately had to cut?

If something has to go, it has to go! I am cold-blooded in this regard. In one of my Keys to the Kingdom books the editor, David Levithan, pointed out that one character could be entirely removed without losing any part of the story. All that character's dialogue, all their actions, were inconsequential window-dressing. So out they went. Possibly being an ex-editor myself helps in this regard.

What made you decide to team up with Sean Williams to write the Troubletwisters series? What has your experience been working with a co-author? How has it differed from writing on your own?

Sean and are I are old friends. We met at a writers' festival in 1997 or 1998 and ever since have discussed various story ideas for books, screenplays and television that we could write together. None of them ever really felt like the right project until we started talking about *Troubletwisters*. Writing is such a solitary occupation that co-writing is very tempting, just for the fun of it, if you can find the right person (or persons) to work with. In the case of Sean and myself, we have similar tastes, we have professional work habits, and we respect each other's work. It's probably also important that we both have our own books, so everything—particularly ego—is not invested in the co-written books. The only thing that you absolutely must have in any co-writing partnership is a written agreement!

Can you describe that moment when you knew you wanted to be a writer?

I don't think there was any one moment. I wrote stories from a very young age; it seemed a natural offshoot of reading. I wrote the kind of stories that I liked to read, and just kept on doing it. So I became a writer because I wrote a lot, and kept on doing more and more of it. But in terms of actually wanting it to be the major pursuit of my life, I decided when I was about 19 that I would attempt to write novels, and try to get them published. But I also realized that this might not work out in terms of earning a living, so I also pursued a career in publishing (with a diversion for a while into IT, PR and marketing), so for a long time I had a dual career track. It is a good thing that you don't need to be full-time to get books written, because often the day job is an economic necessity. I wrote at least a dozen novels while I had very busy day jobs, by dedicating a few hours two nights a week, and most Sunday afternoons. Eventually, I was able to become a full-time writer, but you can't plan for that to happen. All you can do is do the work, target your key business partners (agents and publishers) carefully, hope for some luck, and persevere.

What is the most useful advice you've ever received as an author?

A great deal of the advice I've benefited from came early on in my career from reading about authors, or reading their autobiographies, or reading about publishing. Though it is old now, and very out of date in some ways, Stanley Unwin's *The Truth About Publishing* still has considerable good advice about the reality of writing and publishing. Robert Heinlein's rules of writing (easily found on the Internet) were also useful, though I would disagree about not rewriting except to editorial order.

The most useful advice I can pass on is that there are many, many different ways to write, many different roads to publication, and many different kinds of success. No one set of advice, or any particular author's experience, may work for any other author.

What's next for you?

I've just started on the publicity or pre-publicity trail for my YA science fiction novel *A Confusion of Princes*, out in April/May 2012, so I've been attending festivals and so on and will be doing a lot more of that. I've also just finished working on the third Troubletwisters novel with Sean Williams, the second one that came out in June 2012.

At the moment I'm mostly working on *Clariel*, another book set in the Old Kingdom, which takes place several hundred years before *Sabriel*. But I'm also concurrently writing a few short stories, making notes for some other possible books and a couple of television ideas, slowly adding a few scenes to a feature screenplay, and jotting down fragments of prose for who knows what.

....

KRISTEN GRACE is a contributor to *Writer's Digest* and is currently earning her Master's Degree in English at Miami University of Ohio. You can check out her blog at kegrace.wordpress.com or follow her on Twitter (@kayeeegee).

....

TAMORA PIERCE

How creating memorable characters draws your readers in.

....

by Kristen Grace

Tamora Pierce has penned and published 27 young adult novels, introducing readers to the worlds of Tortall and Emelan in series such as The Song of the Lioness and the Circle of Magic quartet. Her work frequently features strong female characters because, as Pierce explains, there just aren't enough of them out there.

Her characters continue to be memorable for readers, with female knights Alanna and Kel, the young spy Beka Cooper, and the Circle of Magic wizards (Sandry, Tris, Daja and Briar)—many of whom, Pierce says, are based on real people in her life, or actors from the big screen.

Her first novel, *Alanna: The First Adventure*, was published in 1983. Since then, she has been featured on and topped *The New York Times* Children's Chapter Books bestseller list, as well as being on the *Publishers Weekly* Children's Fiction Bestsellers and *The Wall Street Journal*'s fiction bestseller list.

She has been generous enough to share her thoughts on interacting with her fans, developing strong characters and her own personal struggles with plot.

For more information about Pierce, you can visit tamora-pierce.com.

You maintain a strong presence online on sites like Goodreads and LiveJournal. How important do you think it is for authors to interact with their readers? Do you find that your fans have an impact on the stories you choose to write?

There are plenty of authors out there who don't interact with fans—who don't tour, who don't do appearances—yet still manage careers. I began to interact with fans not for my career, but because I knew how much it would have meant to me to have a moment with or a letter from an author I admired. I continue to do so now because I have a lot of fun with my fans. They are a very cool bunch—passionate, idealistic, imaginative, intelligent. I would be a dullard if I didn't like them.

They do have a certain amount of impact on what I write, in that I often include something I know will please them in particular, or I include aspects of characters I know will speak to them (hair color, weight, height, personality traits), or I bring back a beloved character from other books when they add to the current story. I told my second story of a girl knight because when I asked a group of fans if they would be interested if I tackled such a story, their response was so enthusiastic that I knew I was on the right track. I also consult fans when I'm trying to remember where and when I said something, or if I said it, and I'm not willing to read 14 books to look it up. They know the books better than I do, and they're always happy to tell me what I need.

Walk us through your writing process. Do your story ideas come first? Your characters? Where do you go from there? And has it changed since you first wrote *The Song of the Lioness*?

When I wrote *Song*, I wrote the first scene, and the next, and so on, until I fetched up at the ending of the book (732 pages later—it started as a single adult novel before I turned it into four YA books). I basically followed the story. The main character, a sword-slinging girl, was one I'd been trying to write a book about since 7th grade; this was the first time it really worked. I never thought ahead more than a few scenes at a time, so I was writing to see how it came out.

I haven't written a book that way since. By the time I began to think about The Immortals quartet, I had a year or so to plan before I began to write. I chose my main character—it always begins with the main character—and in developing her, or his, traits, abilities, flaws, family background, I start seeing the main secondary characters and the main conflict. By the time I begin to write now, I've been thinking about the book for at least four to six years (I like multi-book contracts, which gives me plenty of time to plan future work). I know the main character, the main secondary characters, the overarching plot for the series if there is one, and the plot for each book in the series (my first editor, Jean Karl, schooled me to have a plot that's resolved in each book of a series, and I do not stray from her path). I study on future works during idle moments (dish-

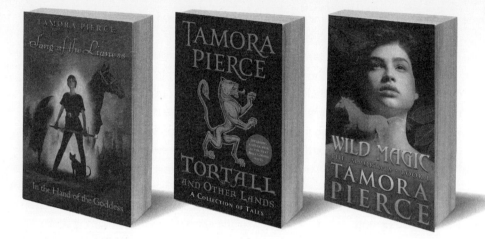

washing, showering, driving, flying, when I should be doing something else), then talk to others about it when I think it's ready to be talked about, until everything's in place.

My first drafts always begin with a scene that shows the main character doing something that tells us something about her, or him. The first scene in *Wild Magic* shows Daine from Onua's point of view, a shy young country girl who is looking for a job and who handles Onua's frisky mountain ponies very easily. In the scenes that begin my first Circle of Magic book, we see each of the four protagonists at the point where their support systems abandon them, followed by scenes where each discover their first touches of magical power.

Every book I write is a character's struggle for mastery of skills and self, a struggle for respect from peers and teachers, and a search for her or his place in the greater world. Often this requires traumatic events, the grounding for which has come from something that has fascinated me for years—medieval warfare, slavery, colonialism, epidemic disease, forest fires, serial murder, trade wars, earthquakes. While I turn my ideas over in my head, I will also work out the traumatic series of greater events that will be the greater tests for my characters. I will require other research as I write—talking to people, searching online, collecting images, reading—but the heavy ground-work gets done in those years when I'm writing something else.

With so many books under your belt, how do you go about making each cast of characters fresh and unique? How do you keep them all straight?

I have to work to make them unique. I review my former characters in my head and consider what I haven't covered to bring to my new character. I also base most of my characters on actors or the characters they play, performers, people I have known, fans and photos I've taken from magazines. I get photos of all of these unless they are people

I know so well I can remember their faces vividly, and I keep their photos in files online or in a cabinet behind my desk.

When it comes time to "cast" a character, I get the right file for the age, sex and ethnic group, and go through the photos until the right one grabs me. Or sometimes I will see someone as a particular character: when I saw actor Noah Wyle on "E.R.," during years I was feeding crows in Riverside Park, I asked my husband if he didn't think Wyle looked like a prince of crows. I have since figured out that crows don't believe in royalty, but Nawat from my Trickster duet has turned out to be a very popular character, even with his penchant for offering girls juicy bugs as courtship presents.

Using this method of creating characters also gives me something interesting to talk about with fans. They're always curious to find out who I based particular characters on. I usually wind up a parade of the more expected ones—the young Jodie Foster as Beka Cooper, Vincent D'Onofrio's Bobby Goren as the captain of the royal guard in *Trickster's Queen*, Susan Sarandon as the Empress in *The Will of the Empress*, my younger sister as Alanna—with the ones that are good for a laugh, Mitch Pileggi's Assistant Director Skinner from "The X-Files" as Kel's first training master (known to the pages as "the Stump"), and Ozzy Osbourne as the evil Emperor in The Immortals. For some reason kids find these two in particular to be hilarious. Of course, characters always evolve away from who I base them on, so I can use this moment as an entry into the writing process, which is a double bonus.

When it comes to important characters, I have a form biography sheet on my computer system. I fill one in for those characters, including things like family background, skills, height, build, the description when they first appear, friends, enemies, magic if any, verbal tics, weapons, etc. If they appear in different series (I didn't know this would happen when I started, but I do now), I add the new material. It saves me a lot of humiliating trips to my LiveJournal to ask the fans where I introduced so-and-so and if I mention such-and-such about them. (My fans like to gloat over these senile moments of mine.)

There is one thing about my characters that seems to hold true no matter what other elements differ. They are all mule-headed. They have to be, to survive what happens to them. I can't see a weak-willed character doing it, otherwise.

What has been your most challenging book (or series) to write? What made it challenging? On the flipside, what was your easiest? Why do you think that is?

Most challenging was the most recent, the Beka Cooper trilogy. The journal form near about drove me nuts. At first it was simply first person, which was bad enough. Up until I began to think about the books, I reserved first person for short stories, for the most part, because I perceive first person as being a more emotional form. My Random House editor, Mallory Loehr, suggested that I try the Beka books as first person. Even though

I complain like a mule over her suggestions, I like to follow them because she gets me to stretch as a writer. I don't ever want to be doing the same thing over and over.

I don't remember any series being easy. With the Circle books there was always the research of each of the four kids' crafts, as well as writing the first quartet to give equal time to each of them. In the second quartet, the trick was to find new crafts for their students and new ways to teach them, with new problems arising, which differed from the students in the other books. In *Protector of the Small* I struggled to keep Kel's journey very different from Alanna's, while maintaining a careful hand with hazing. Also, I was being kept to 200-page manuscripts, and I reached page 180 without having finished Kel's first year as a page (she had three more to go in what had taken Alanna one book). I either had to cut a lot or find a good reason why Kel's first year was broken off from her four years as a page. Until I got to Beka, Aly of the *Trickster* books made me crazy because she is the character most unlike me: charming, witty, flirty, manipulative, sly, mysterious, graceful, a spy. I was simply too much like her mother, Alanna. Writing espionage plots was hard, too, because a good spy does not ride up to problems and hit them on the head with a stick. She can never be seen to be doing anything.

On the other hand, if it was easy, I'd probably worry I was doing something wrong.

Your books often follow the growth and development of strong young women. Do you know from the start what kind of people your characters will become, or do they surprise you by the end?

My experience with people has been that by the time they are teenagers, you can see the seeds of what they will become if they are given an opportunity and even a modicum of encouragement. They will pursue their dreams and build their own spaces in the world. That's what I write about—how they go about it, the pitfalls, how things never turn out as they expect them to. Alanna planned to be a warrior maiden riding around the world fighting evil, not a mother with achy bones making it so punitive for people to demand trial by combat from the king that they would welcome the rule of courts and magistrates. Kel thought to become Alanna, not to become a commander of troops and in charge of a refugee camp. Sandry wanted to be a mage, not a teacher, not a vice-seneschal and associate criminalist at her uncle's court. Daja wanted to be a trader and a good daughter to her culture, yet she is blissfully happy at work beating out hot metal in a forge. And so on. And Numair is about to have his entire life's dream taken away.

What would you say is a writing weakness of yours? How do you go about overcoming it?

Plot. I hate plot. This is why I can only write books by starting at the beginning, going through the middle, and fetching up at the end, because I'm excavating the plot along with the reader. It's why I also borrow plot elements from elsewhere: history, battles, biographies, the tracks of natural events, and so on. I used the unfolding of an epidemic, gleaned from my obsession with epidemic disease, to provide the rough plot structure for *Briar's Book*. I took elements from the lives of Elizabeth I and Catherine the Great for *The Will of the Empress* and the Trickster books. The Chinese conquest of Tibet is providing the grounding for my current book, *Battle Magic*. My fascination with true crime has provided the plot underpinnings for The Circle Opens quartet and the Beka Cooper books.

What's something you wish you had known when you first started writing?

That for a long time I wouldn't finish most of what I started, and that this was both normal and OK. I wouldn't have thought I was such a failure for leaving so many things unfinished. I also wish I had known that we can only write what makes us happy, and we have to ignore what others think we should be writing. We are the only ones we get to please for a really long time, so it's important that we entertain ourselves, listen to our guts, and write what we like.

What do you think is the reason your novels appeal to readers of all ages, not just young adults?

I pretty much write straight across, and whoever gets it, gets it. Because I write teen heroes I'm classed as a YA writer, but they live in medieval-esque worlds, where you were an adult when you were 14. Thus my characters are making their way in the adult world, so adults get the struggles they're undergoing.

What was the best piece of writing advice you've ever received?

My boss when I worked for a literary agency, Phyllis Westberg, gave it to me: "Read aloud." You catch so much more than you do when you simply correct on the page or the screen, so I do that as well as hand corrections.

What's next for you?

Right now, *Battle Magic*, a stand-alone Circle of Magic novel featuring my 16-year-old male plant mage, Briar, his teacher, Rosethorn, and his student, a stone mage, Evvy. Once that's done, I'm back in the Tortall universe with a book about Numair, the male hero of The Immortals quartet, in the years preceding that quartet.

KRISTEN GRACE is a contributor to *Writer's Digest* and is currently earning her Master's Degree in English at Miami University of Ohio. You can check out her blog at kegrace.wordpress.com or follow her on Twitter (@kayeeegee).

KIERSTEN WHITE

On why your writing process can change from book to book.

....

by Frankie Mallis

When Kiersten White was waiting to hear back from editors about her novel on submission, a new idea and voice came to her. That voice was Evie, and three weeks later that idea would become the *New York Times* bestseller *Paranormalcy*. *Paranormalcy* debuted in August 2010, and since then Kiersten has completed six more books, two more telling Evie's story and four novels departing from the *Paranormalcy* world.

Kiersten's easygoing online presence and sense of humor has endeared her to her large fan base. But in all seriousness, she is an incredibly hard worker, one who doesn't quit until the job is done, and one who can finish projects incredibly fast—she wrote one whole novel in seven days.

Here Kiersten talks about her sometimes insane work habits, her advice for writers, and what it's like to be such a fast writer whose life changed just as fast from an unknown hopeful to one of the most sought after young adult writers today. For more information on White, check out kierstenwhite.com.

Paranormalcy was such a fun and unique breakout novel. Can you tell us how you got the idea and how you began writing?

Typically I buy my ideas in a back alley of Chinatown. Everything is done in cash, and the remains of serial numbers have been filed off. A bit shady, perhaps, but I've always liked finding a good deal.

Alternately, I had another book on submission and needed something to keep from going crazy, so I decided to go wild and write a book with paranormal elements that was also funny, because I hadn't read many of them in the young adult market and wanted to see if I could do it. Three weeks later I had a finished draft.

When you began telling Evie's story in *Paranormalcy*, did you always know there'd be more books? And now that *Endlessly* completes the trilogy ... will we ever hear more from Evie?

I wrote *Paranormalcy* to stand on its own, hoping that would make it an easier sell, but I hoped for a trilogy. Fortunately HarperTeen offered for all three books without so much as a series outline. I had always planned on a three-part story arc for Evie, and was so pleased to have the opportunity to write her story just that way.

That being said, it was only a three-book arc, and I have no plans to write sequels or prequels of any kind. I have four books coming out in 2013 and 2014; two are stand-alones and two are part of a new dark thriller series. I adore Evie like mad, but her story, for me, is done with *Endlessly*.

Paranormalcy was not your first completed novel. How has your writing process changed? Can you describe what your writing process looks like? Do you outline?

I've found my writing process differs with every book. Some I have to force myself to sit and write every day. Some I have to force myself to do things other than write (like eating and showering). Some I've written mostly by hand. Most I've tapped out curled up on the couch or outside with my laptop.

The only thing that remains consistent is this: I write, first and foremost, to entertain myself. Because of this I do not outline; if there are no surprises, how can I stay entertained?

Typically I start with an idea. Most of the time this is less plot-based and more feeling-based, such as, I want to write a book about an impossible relationship, or, I want to write a book about that stage in teenagerhood when you realize your parents aren't perfect and have a hard time forgiving them for being human. After that I wait for a voice. If I don't have a voice that speaks to me it doesn't matter how much I like the plot—I cannot write.

What did your journey from deciding to write to actual publication look like?

Two kids, four books, five years, seven wrist braces, 20 pounds and a whole lot of Dr Pepper.

Did you have any idea when you started *Paranormalcy* it would become so successful?

I actually wrote *Paranormalcy* while another book of mine was on submission with editors. I assumed that one would sell and that it would be years before I could go back to *Paranormalcy*. So, no. I wrote it just for fun, and I think that's what made it special!

Writing with a preconceived notion or anticipation of "success" is the surest way to kill any joy you have in creation. I try my hardest when drafting to disconnect from anything other than the story. Not all of my books will (or should) be published. I'm OK with that, because I learned something from each one and loved each one while I was writing. The career success is just a (massive, overwhelmingly delightful) bonus.

What part about becoming not only a published author, but a bestselling author most surprised you?

I think the realization that there is a part of you now open for public access is a very strange one that takes a lot of coming to terms with. Never before in my life had I been in a position where I didn't know the people who knew me. Now there are thousands of people who at least know who I am, many of whom feel like they know me to some degree from my writing and social media presence. Honestly, sometimes I feel guilty about it. Sometimes it makes me tired, worrying that I'm going to disappoint them. But mostly I'm just so grateful that people enjoy my writing and support my career.

You're pretty well known for finishing novels in short periods of time—like nine days. Can you talk a little about your speed-write novels?

Mind Games, out early 2013, was written in nine days last summer. But that's not taking into account the fact that I cannibalized the concepts of two trunk novels of mine, or that it was based on an idea I'd been playing with for the last decade. A whole lot of time and writing went into those nine days! That book was just over 50,000 words, and has actually stayed almost entirely intact with no significant structural or narrative changes. I write very complete first drafts.

The fastest I've ever written a novel was one I wrote this past February in seven days, clocking in at about 64,000 words. That one genuinely came out of nowhere. I don't write all my novels that quickly (my longest took me a year-and-a-half), but the ones that come out in a mad giddy rush do always feel a bit special to me.

Of course, after I finish I crash, completely drained, and have a hard time doing much of anything for weeks. My brain has two working modes: very very fast, or not at all. I'd like a happy medium.

Which part of the writing process do you find the most challenging? And how do you go about conquering it?

Starting! I conquer it by … starting. Really, any book is impossible until it is finished. Any edit is overwhelming until it is finished. If I can get myself to just start, I know I can find my way through it.

But … napping is way easier, isn't it?

Growing up which books were your favorite to read? Which writers did you admire? Which writers do you most admire now?

I loved reading books that took me to a world I didn't live in, and I think the same thing applies as much now as it did when I was young. My favorite books are the ones that not only let me escape reality, but increasingly that fill me with a sort of writerly awe. If I shut a book and think, "I could never in a million years have written this," odds are I'll be crazy about it. Recent favorites include Gayle Forman, Laini Taylor, Holly Black, E. Lockhart, Markus Zusak, Patrick Ness, Neil Gaiman and John Green.

Can you describe in your gut the moment you knew you wanted to be a writer?

A bit like indigestion, but with a more productive outcome.

In all seriousness, no. I've never wanted to be a writer, because I always felt I already was one, for as long as I can remember. I don't think a writer is something you decide to become. It's something you do, something that's a part of you, something that you couldn't figure out how not to do.

What was the best piece of writing advice you ever got, and what advice would you give to writers?

Write the next thing. Seriously. While you are waiting for an agent, or a book deal, or whatever it is you are waiting for, write the next thing.

My advice is this: Stories are made in first drafts. Books are made in editing. Learn your craft and always try to improve.

All of your stories so far have been young adult. Would you ever consider writing for a different audience or genre?

Up to now I've done everything I said I wouldn't: write YA, write in first person, write in present tense, go back to third person. I'm not going to go on the record ruling anything out! But right now I have no desire or plans to write outside of YA. It's what I love reading and what I love writing, and I'm deeply passionate about creating for that particular audience. That being said, I'm always looking for new ways to stretch myself creatively, and love finding a challenge within what I write. I do hop genre a lot, from paranormal romance to dark thrillers to mythology-based stories to historical fantasy. It's one reason I love YA: anything goes, and readers are far more accepting of things outside of their typical "type" of book.

Do you ever see yourself pursuing another form of art outside of writing?

Though I draw a mean stick-figure unicorn, no. Writing is hardwired into my brain and I have no desire to create elsewhere.

If you could redo one moment in your writing career, what would it be?

I spent all of 2010 spinning my wheels and freaking out about the *Paranormalcy* release. I edited two books but didn't create anything new. I think I needed to go through that to realize that all of these things we obsess over as writers don't matter much in the end. What matters is the writing. A year from now I won't remember how many e-mails I answered, or which blogs featured my books, or even what my Amazon rankings were on a given day. But I will have everything that I created, and that is a wonderful thing indeed.

FRANKIE MALLIS is a young adult writer based in Philadelphia. When not writing, she can be found belly dancing, baking vegan food or teaching creative writing at Arcadia University. She also runs a small children's library on the weekends. Frankie is represented by Laura Rennert at the Andrea Brown Literary Agency. For more information visit frankiediane.blogspot.com.

PATRICIA C. WREDE

On research and the art of the opening.

....

by Kristen Grace

///

Patricia C. Wrede has explored all kinds of literary landscapes in her books, from Regency England in her Cecelia and Kate and Magic and Malice books, to the wild frontier in her Frontier Magic series. She's also given us new worlds to explore in her Lyra books, and most notably, The Enchanted Forest Chronicles.

Her first book, *Shadow Magic*, was published in 1982, the same year she became a founding member of the Interstate Writers' Workshop, aka the Scribblies. Wrede belonged to the group for what she says were "five extremely productive years."

Wrede also spent a number of years working as a financial analyst and writing in her spare time until she made the switch to become a full-time writer in 1985. Her most recent series, Frontier Magic, explores the life of Eff who moves with her family to learn magic at the edge of the expanding U.S. frontier, dangerously close to the magical divide that separates them from the wild. Here she shares her research methods and how she approaches beginnings, as well as some unique opportunities she's had as a writer.

For more information on Wrede, visit pcwrede.com.

How did you go about getting published for the first time? What was the process like? Do you have any advice for first time writers trying to break in to the market?

I wrote a novel; I polished it up; I typed up a clean copy (this was before computers); I sent it out to my first-choice editor and publishing house. It came back a year and a half later with a very nice rejection letter. I sent it out again, and it bounced within three weeks. I sent it out again, and again, and … eventually it sold.

The process of getting published in the traditional publishing industry hasn't changed much. It's very discouraging, especially if you don't move on to the next thing right away. If you have all your hopes and ambitions centered in the one book you just finished, you want to haunt the mailbox, and you worry, and it's absolutely crushing when the rejections arrive. If you start something new as soon as you've dumped the first one in the mail, then by the time the rejection arrives, you're excited about the new thing and you can think, "Well, yeah, they didn't like this, but what I'm writing *now* is so much better!" It's not quite as discouraging.

So the main advice I'd have is twofold: first, start something new the minute the most recently finished thing is in the mail, and second, be persistent and keep the finished stuff in the mail. The one way to be absolutely sure that something won't sell is to keep it at home on your computer. Editors don't do house-to-house searches for manuscripts.

Can you describe your writing process? How has it changed since you published your first novel, *Shadow Magic*?

My writing process has been mostly the same (with a couple of exceptions): I think and dither and try out different characters and ideas in my head until something starts to come together; then I sit down and write an outline, usually about five pages of "… and then he does this and then she goes there …" plot summary stuff. Once I'm fairly satisfied with that, I sit down and write the first chapter. Then I look at the outline, see that the chapter has nothing to do with the outline, and throw the outline away. I write another outline, write the second chapter, and again have to throw the outline away. I repeat this several more times until I finally get tired of rewriting the outline, and then I just finish the book.

I still have to do plot summaries or outlines, even though by this time I know perfectly well that I'm not going to follow them. I don't seem to need quite as many as I used to, so maybe by the time I've done another 10 or 15 books, I'll be able to just do one, but I think I'll always need something. I've decided that my backbrain needs something to rebel against.

You say that ideas are the easy part of writing. For you, what's the hardest part? How do you work past it?

Generally speaking, the hardest part is sitting down and starting, and what I do is just do it, the same as I would at any other job. Inspiration is lovely when it happens, but you can't count on it, any more than you can count on being in the mood to flip hamburgers or do a bunch of filing or photocopying at a day job. If you're working in an office, you go in whether you feel like it or not, and you do the work whether you feel like it or not. I have to treat my writing the same way; if I don't, then putting it off for a day becomes putting it off for a week and then a month and the next thing I know, I have a deadline in two weeks and I'm only a quarter of the way through the manuscript.

Nine times out of ten, if I'm "blocked" the problem isn't that I don't know what happens next, it's that I know and don't want to write it. I hate writing transitions and council scenes, but nobody is going to do them for me. Putting them off just makes them harder. It's a whole lot easier to keep the momentum going if I write something every day, even if it's just a paragraph (though I generally shoot for three or four pages).

What has been your most challenging book (or series) to write? What made it challenging? On the flipside, what was your easiest? Why do you think that is?

The easiest one so far was *Sorcery and Cecelia*, largely because a) I only had to write half of it, and b) we [myself and co-author Caroline Stevermer] didn't know we were writing a book; as far as we knew, we were playing a game and having a blast doing it. We didn't figure out that we'd written a novel until it was all over. Also, the writing went *much* faster than it normally does, because there was no down time. Usually, if I were tearing through something that fast, I'd have to stop every two or three days and think for a while. With the letter game, I'd get to the point where I needed to stop and think, and I'd hand it off to Caroline. So while I was thinking, she was working, and vice versa.

The hardest is tougher to pin down. I like doing books that feel stretchy, even though I complain a lot while I'm writing them. The Frontier Magic books were stretchy in a couple of ways; first, my viewpoint character started off rather more shy and uncertain than my main characters usually are, and second, I was playing with more recent history, which is a lot more familiar to most of my readers than the backgrounds I've used before.

What is your process for doing research for novels set in semi-historical settings like *Mairelon the Magician* and the Kate and Cecy books? What kind of research did you have to do for *Thirteenth Child*

The Regency period of British history has fascinated me for a long time. I've read Jane Austen's books multiple times, as well as a lot of other fiction and nonfiction in and about the period. When I first decided to write a novel set in London in the early 1800s, I reread several of my general sources on what life was like in the period, mostly books on the social history of England. Then I read biographies and autobiographies, starting with several about Jane Austen and then branching out into books on Lord Wellington and the Prince Regent (later George IV). I asked my friends for recommendations.

Then I hit the library, looking for specific things, like a street map of London in 1817 and books on period slang. *The 1811 Dictionary of the Vulgar Tongue* turned out to be invaluable for writing Kim's dialogue. Along the way, I kept running across other fas-

cinating things that I hadn't known to look for. Mairelon's wagon, for instance, came out of a thin little book on the period equivalent of RVs, which I found in the gift shop of a museum I'd gone to in order to look at some of the paintings and period pieces they had on display.

Once I start actually writing the book, I keep having to stop every so often and look something up. I tend to do this sort of thing in chunks; I'll write for a couple of weeks, marking every place I need to check a description, and then I'll spend a week going through my sources looking stuff up and fixing the manuscript. It gives me something useful to do when I get tired or stuck.

The process for *Thirteenth Child* was very much the same, except I started with books and videos on the flora and fauna of the most recent Ice Age, and then went on to autobiographies of local pioneers. In some ways it was a lot easier, because I live in the Twin Cities and there are a lot of local resources about the real-life settling of the Northern Plains.

What's something you wish you had known when you first started writing?

That you don't *have* to learn your craft writing short fiction before you can write a novel. That was the conventional wisdom at the time I started, and I tried, I really did. But I'm a natural novelist, and short stories are really hard for me. The best ones I managed at that time were essentially plot outlines for novels. I learned my craft writing novels, and I didn't figure out how to write short stories until after I had written and sold five novels.

Nowadays, the short story market has shrunk and I see people being told the opposite—that you *have* to start off writing novels because there's no short fiction market. This is just as bad for the natural short story writers as being told I *had* to write short was for me. Almost everyone finds that one length comes more easily than the others, and it's a lot easier to learn your craft if you play to your strength.

What's your favorite murdered darling from your books—a character, scene, plot or even a single line that you really wanted to keep but ultimately had to cut?

I don't know. I've cut things, and hated cutting them, but once they're cut I let go, because the book is always better for having them out. I keep a "scraps" file while I'm writing for the things I can't bear to lose, but I don't think I've ever actually gone back to it during the writing, and certainly I never look at it once the story is done.

The closest I can come is a character who was supposed to be in *Across the Great Barrier*—a Cathayan magician who was supposed to come to my heroine's home town to teach at the college for a while. Unfortunately, I couldn't figure out a reason strong enough to justify her coming all the way from Cathay (China) to the edge of the Columbian frontier; she was an important person and a powerful magician, and she had much better things to do. So I had to invent a different person to take the teaching job. My Cathayan magician and her aides do finally show up in *The Far West*, but I couldn't persuade her to stick around for more than a couple of chapters. I still regret that a little; she has a lot of background and personality that there just wasn't time to get onto the page.

How did you get into writing Star Wars novelizations? What was that experience like in comparison to creating a story from scratch?

The editor in charge of the department at Scholastic that had bought the license for the middle-school novelizations called me and asked if I'd like to do one. I have no idea how they settled on me; it was totally out of the blue as far as I was concerned. After I picked my jaw up off the floor, I said "Sounds interesting; talk to my agent," and she did. After I did the first one, they asked if I'd like to do the second.

Writing the books was a lot more difficult than I expected. I had copies of the most recent screenplay, and the LucasBooks people were extraordinarily helpful about answering my questions, but sometimes the answer was "We're sorry; George hasn't made that up yet." And of course they were really just starting to work on a lot of the special effects, so there were quite a few places where "What does X look like?" didn't have an answer yet.

The biggest problem, though, turned out to be viewpoint. I wanted to keep the books in close third-person, but the camera is omniscient, and there were quite a few scenes where the focus shifted from one character to another in the middle, which made it difficult to decide who to use as the viewpoint. On the other hand, I never had to worry about where the plot was going or what the dialog was going to be, which made it all go a lot faster.

The other big difficulty was that because George Lucas wrote the script and directed it himself, he didn't have to put in a lot of description for certain scenes. There's a huge battle at the end of the first movie that goes on for about five minutes, and all the script said was "The Jedi fight." I had to make it up and hope I was close.

Watching the movies afterward was one of the most surreal experiences of my life. I'd been through the shooting script so many times that I knew every line of dialogue that had been cut or changed in the editing room—and there were quite a few of them. It kept jerking me out of the movie.

The beginning of a novel is crucial for finding an agents and a publisher, and for hooking readers. What do you suggest for writers struggling with how to open their novel? How do you decide where your story will begin?

Stories begin when something changes. Characters who are living happily or miserably in the same unchanging situation may make for a nice character sketch, but they usually don't provide much in the way of a plot or story. It's only when something happens, or they have to make a decision, or their circumstances change in some way, that the story begins.

The opening scene usually takes place just before, just after or just at that moment of change, unless the author is deliberately opening in the middle for some reason. Which one to pick depends on the story, the voice and the author's personal preference. There isn't a rule for this; that's part of what makes writing an art as well as a craft.

I've written books all four ways: The Enchanted Forest books all start a little before the moment when things start to change for my main characters, sometimes as much as a chapter before; *Caught in Crystal* starts at the moment of change, with the arrival of a magician at my viewpoint character's inn; *Mairelon the Magician* starts shortly after the moment of change, which was when the main character was hired to perform the burglary that gets her involved with the other characters; and *The Seven Towers* starts *en medias res*, with one of the viewpoint characters galloping through the woods trying to evade pursuit. I didn't spend a lot of time thinking about where to open each one; it was always pretty obvious what I needed to do.

The first scene is important for hooking readers, editors and publishers, but I think there's too much emphasis on this aspect, to the point where some writers forget that the point is to set the tone of the story you're telling. I *could* have opened any of those books in a different place, but if I had, either the books would have come out very differently, or else there would have been a mismatch between the style and tone that the opening leads the reader to expect and the actual story I was telling, to the detriment of the book as a whole. The important thing, to my mind, is getting the story in my head down on paper as truly as I can, not manipulating the story in my head to turn it into something I think will sell.

There's also an overemphasis on opening with action, especially in genre fiction. You can hook readers in a lot of ways: with a character, with a mystery, with an appealing voice, with an unexpected or startling situation, with an interesting background, etc. It doesn't have to be action. Also, you aren't stuck with what you put down when you first start writing. A number of my friends write a book, then routinely go back and cut the entire first chapter, because once the book is written, it's obvious that the "first chapter" was really just scaffolding, and the story actually opens wherever Chapter Two started.

You mentioned in an interview that *Dealing With Dragons* was a prequel and the plot was already set when you wrote it, but *Talking to Dragons* was a much more "make-it-up-as-you-go" experience. When you first started the Enchanted Forest Chronicles, did you know it would be a series? If so, how did that affect the way you wrote the story?

Talking to Dragons was very much written on the fly. I had a title, a voice and a character, and I had no idea what was going on until I was three-quarters of the way through the book. It was very scary; I don't normally work that way.

I didn't intend it to be a series. I hardly ever do. I write a book, and then I have all this leftover information about the characters and where they're going and what could happen next, and my editors and readers want more, so I do another one. It's practically part of my process. By the time I finished *Talking to Dragons*, I'd had the usual series of thoughts about what might come next, but I didn't have anything really planned, and I doubt that I'd have written more if Jane Yolen hadn't come around wanting a story for an anthology. She told me to write "something like that dragon book," and there was a character I really liked who hadn't had much on-stage time, so I did a short story about her (Cimorene). Then Jane was asked to edit a line of books for Harcourt Brace, and came back wanting me to expand the short story into a novel, and the rest is history.

The only time I ever actually set out to write a series right from the start was with the Frontier Magic books. I had to think about the plot and the ramifications of various incidents in *Thirteenth Child* a lot more carefully than I usually do, because I had this three-book plot arc to steer. Normally, I plot one book at a time, and if I get to Chapter 20 and decide that I need a new character, I can go back and mention him/her in Chapters 2, 5, 9, 14 and 18 so that he/she doesn't come out of nowhere. With three books under contract, the first book was finished and out well before I was done writing *Across the Great Barrier,* and long before I'd even begun writing *The Far West*. I couldn't go back and add things, or change what I'd said about various characters or the way magic worked, if it turned out I needed things to be different in the middle of the last book. So I had to make sure that things didn't need to be different, which meant sticking more closely to my plans than I usually do.

What's next for you?

More books! I have a list of about 20 or 30 books I really want to write, and it keeps getting longer all the time. Now that I've finished the Frontier Magic trilogy, I'm thinking about setting my next book somewhere totally imaginary, instead of doing the sort of alternate-pseudo-historical backgrounds I've been using. This cuts my options down from 20 to 10 or 12, I think. And that assumes I won't have a better idea between now and when I start the next story.

KRISTEN GRACE is a contributor to *Writer's Digest* and is currently earning her Master's Degree in English at Miami University of Ohio. You can check out her blog at kegrace.wordpress.com or follow her on Twitter (@kayeeegee).

RAE CARSON

On worldbuilding, tense, voice, and more.

....

by Ricki Schultz

Since Rae Carson's first novel, *The Girl of Fire and Thorns* (Greenwillow Books), was released in September 2011, it has set bookshelves ablaze. But being a successful young adult author is more than just writing, she says.

And she would know: Within six months of its debut, *The Girl of Fire and Thorns* was not only a finalist for the Morris, Cybils and Andre Norton Awards, but it also appeared on ALA's Top Ten Best Fiction for Young Adults list. As well, Carson herself was named a *Publishers Weekly* Flying Start author in Fall 2011.

So, how does she do it?

Currently anticipating the release of the second installment in the Fire and Thorns trilogy (*The Crown of Embers*) and hard at work on the conclusion, the Ohio-based author took some time to discuss her work and give pointers to aspiring writers of teen literature.

With conferences, speaking engagements, interviews and multiple projects on the horizon, what does your typical writing week look like? How do you get it all done?

It's different every day, which is as frustrating as it is fun. I have no routine to fall back on when I feel exhausted or overwhelmed. I admit that I struggled for a while. Now, though, I make a list each night of what I hope to accomplish the next day. It's a short list—only two or three items. (Too many items, and I get overwhelmed and end up playing games on my iPod.) For instance, today's list is: 1) finish *CWIM* interview, 2) deposit Polish [foreign rights] advance, and 3) write 1,200 words on contracted novella.

Walk us through your writing process. Do your story ideas come first? Your characters? And where do you go from there?

Characters always come first for me. I must feel that a character is a real human being, with wants and needs that often conflict, before the plot elements form in my mind. Then I structure the plot around my vision for the character's arc. My husband, who is also a novelist, has an opposite process. Plot or premise comes first for him, and he structures the character arcs around his ideas. I think it's important for writers to figure out whichever element of storytelling sings to them most and indulge it shamelessly, allowing it to be their inspiration.

Your character names are all very unique and feel very much like they belong within the world you've constructed. How do you come up with them? It feels like there was more involved in the creation of names like Jacián, Cosmé, Ximena, etc., than simply going to Babynames.com!

Thanks! Yes, I did some research for this. I wanted them to have Spanish-sounding names, but I threw in some Aztec and Basque influences to distinguish between the novel's fictional regions and to give some names a more exotic flair.

Elisa not only has an authentically teen voice, but she also has one that feels very accessible to the contemporary teen. Although she's living in this fantastic world, the voice you've created appeals to *all* readers, not just science fiction/fantasy fans. How did you find her voice? And what advice would you have for someone trying to develop a voice appropriate for a young adult book?

As they hit puberty, teens' perception broadens to include not just self but the whole world. They become hyper-aware that they're not the center of the universe, which creates enormous conflict—especially for teens who have grown up in a sheltered, economically privileged environment. There's this creeping suspicion that they don't *matter* nearly as much as they thought they did, and the search for significance becomes central to the coming-of-age experience. I think the voice of a fictional teen should reflect this conflict. There should be hints of self-doubt, of hope for the future, of pride-but-also-trepidation for the burgeoning self, of suspicion of authority, etc. At the same time, teens are as diverse as any group of humans, and it's important to infuse a voice with some individuality as well as universal teen struggles.

You also don't write "down" to the young readers. How do you balance using sophisticated words/concepts without losing your authentically YA voice?

I don't balance it at all! I made exactly two tiny word-choice edits to make the book more audience-friendly. Other than that, I allowed the book to be as complex as the story demanded. Teens are very bright, and they absorb new concepts like sponges. In fact, after seeing general responses to the book, I have to conclude that grown-ups struggled with the more sophisticated political and religious social science than my teen readers did.

The Girl of Fire and Thorns is written in first-person present tense. Why did you choose this tense? What benefits do you think it has, and how would you say it enhances your story?

Funny you should ask. I had a false start in traditional past tense; it just didn't feel right. Elisa's struggles are so personal—physically and emotionally—that I needed to move inside her head even more. Once I hit on present tense, the immediacy gave me the jolt I needed, and her story unfolded a lot more naturally.

Talk to us a little bit about how you approach worldbuilding. You do a fantastic job of illustrating Orovalle and Joya d'Arena without overwhelming the reader. What methods do you use to construct your world? Any tips on how to go about sprinkling in details without becoming description heavy?

It helped me to base these countries on real places, i.e., Spanish Morocco, the Yucatan peninsula, the American southwestern desert. So the geography, clothing, even food all fell into place.

One thing I tell aspiring authors is to allow your characters to think like people who live in a different world than you do. For instance, when I am physically exhausted, my long association with sports makes me feel like I've been pummeled in a football game. But Elisa, who grew up in a desert, feels like she's been flayed in a sandstorm. Our world colors our perceptions—and even our personal metaphors.

Throughout the course of the novel, Elisa deals with bigger issues, such as religion, sibling rivalry, growing up without a mother, as well as body issues—just like many modern teens. *The Girl of Fire and Thorns* is not, however, an issue book. How do you go about weaving in these details without becoming preachy? Is this a conscious decision, or are you just good at it?

I cannot abide a preachy book! And yet, as authors, our worldviews inevitably creep into our writing. I'll just be honest and say that, yes, there were a few minor deletions I made to the original manuscript because they felt like author-intrusion. One thing that helps me keep my preachiness in check is to remember that my book is not my platform. My book is a vehicle, which provides me with a platform. So, even though I don't come out and say, "I don't believe a girl needs to have a boyfriend to have a happy ending" in the book itself, I've been able to say this in interviews (like this one) and during speaking engagements. Some authors believe they should never address hot-button

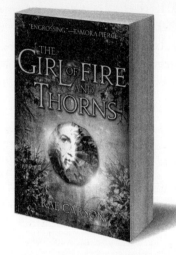

issues openly, and I think this is a valid artistic choice. But it s not my choice. I intend to continue addressing things like body image, female power, religion, etc., but I will do so with the hope that my books are merely a jumping off place for these discussions rather than hammers of morality.

How do you go about your research?

I don't know how anyone wrote anything research-intensive before the Internet! With just a few clicks, I can get a map or a picture or a statistical table. I love living in the future. A couple of tips, though:

1) Take special interest classes—online, at a community college, at your local crafts store or stables, whatever. You will be amazed at how organically your specialty knowledge will permeate your writing. In fact, I strongly recommend that future authors major in coursework other than English or Creative Writing. Anyone can learn to write with practice and determination. But attaining a broad knowledge base upon which to build worlds is more challenging.

2) Indulge your inner nerd. Do not be ashamed to follow the Wikipedia spiral until you suddenly realize you've lost three hours just clicking links. Watch obscure documentaries on Netflix. Tour museums. I firmly believe that pampered intellectual curiosity is the very best foundation from which to launch a writing career.

The Girl of Fire and Thorns is the first installment of the Fire and Thorns trilogy. When writing a series, there has to be a fair amount of planning involved. How do you know what to reveal about the overarching plot and when?

I'm still writing the third book, so maybe I should revisit this question when I'm done! But for now, I'll say that I've been über-aware that my pace of reveals needs to stretch throughout the trilogy. Big twists or important plot points have to be spaced far enough apart that they don't muddy each other and lose power, but close enough together that a plot-oriented reader will not lose interest. This is an area where a good editor becomes your best friend and richest treasure. Mine is very good about pointing out passages that need tightening or emphasizing or even rearranging.

As well, even though most people picking up *The Crown of Emberss*, which will be released in September 2012, will likely have read *The Girl of Fire and Thorns*, there is always the pressure to make each book in a series work as a stand-alone, for any new readers. That said, how do you approach working in backstory? Any suggestions on how to make sure you're incorporating everything you need in order to make each book a stand-alone success?

There are a few schools of thought on this. Mine is that too much backstory kills a book by slowing the pacing to a crawl. This is especially deadly in a young adult novel, where pacing is generally faster than in adult books. My first draft of *The Crown of Embers* had a lot of backstory, which I tried to weave in at appropriate intervals. Because these books are in first person, the backstory must come at a time when the protagonist might naturally be thinking about it. Otherwise, it's stiff and jolting. I was very happy with the result. That said, I still ended up cutting a lot of it to speed things up. I feel like the *conflicts* of book two stand alone well enough—if not the tiny details—and although reading the first book would enhance the experience of reading the second, it is not required.

What would you say is a writing weakness of yours—and how do you overcome it?

My biggest weakness is second-guessing everything I write and allowing myself to be crippled by doubt. I am learning, gradually, to let myself write poorly. I am learning to rest in the understanding that I now have a whole team at my back (beta readers, editor, my own stubborn determination) that will help me polish my work into something I'm proud of.

What's one thing you wish you'd known when you were starting out writing?

I wish I'd know how much of my job as an author would be not-writing! There are interviews, social media, website updates, reading/blurbing other books, contract proposals, foreign rights, self-employment records and taxes, edits, copyedits, page proofs ... It requires much better time management and triaging skills than I had when I started out. But I wouldn't trade it for anything; it's the best job in the world.

RICKI SCHULTZ (rickischultz.com) is an Ohio-based freelance writer and recovering high school English teacher. She writes young adult fiction and, as coordinator of The Write-Brained Network (writebrainednetwork.com), she enjoys connecting with other writers.

JESSICA DAY GEORGE

How nine years of writing led to success.

....

by Kristen Grace

Jessica Day George spent nine years trying to break into the adult fantasy market before she wrote her first young adult novel, *Dragon Slippers*, published in 2007 (Bloomsbury) and received the Whitney Award for Best Book by a New Author. Since then, she has embraced her love for children's literature and gone on to publish the rest of the Dragon Slipper series as well as the Princess series and her two standalone books, *Sun and Moon, Ice and Snow*, and *Tuesdays at the Castle*.

She has extensively studied German and Norwegian, and maintains a great love of fairy tales, which inspired her modern retellings of the "East of the Sun, West of the Moon" in *Sun and Moon, Ice and Snow*, and the "Twelve Dancing Princesses" in her Princess series.

Before being published, George worked at a wedding invitation factory, a video store, libraries and bookstores, and in a school office, all while pursuing her love of writing. She is an avid knitter and works hard to balance her writing life with her life as a mother of three. "But mostly," she says, "it's all about the books."

Here she shares her writing process, her long path to publication and how her love of knitting found its way into her stories.

For more information about George, visit her website at jessicadaygeorge.com or follow her on Twitter at @JessDayGeorge.

What is your writing process like? How has it changed since you published your first novel, *Dragon Slippers*?

My writing process is to jump screaming into a book as soon as the idea comes. I've never been an outliner, I like to go from Chapter 1 to The End, but when it's all done I'll do some revising, add in a new chapter or take one out. I'm much better at rough drafts, though, so I must admit I rely heavily on my editor now. Since *Dragon Slippers*, I've added two more children (for a total of three), so instead of having a set writing time, I just have to be prepared any minute of the day to dive right into the current work-in-progress and charge ahead for as long as the kids let me!

What has been your most challenging book (or series) to write? What made it challenging? On the flipside, what was your easiest? Why do you think that is?

Writing *Dragon Flight* was terrifying. I had never written a sequel before, and trying to get it just right, to make it "match" *Dragon Slippers* made me a little nuts. Every line of dialogue, I thought: does this sound like so-and-so? Is this funny enough? Too funny? Is there enough action? Too much action? Also, the easiest thing I've ever written was *Dragon Slippers*. That book just downloaded into my brain one night, and I felt like I was taking dictation from a higher power, it was so easy to write!

In your books you often create entire worlds that include multiple countries and intricate politics, such as Sleyne and Vhervhine in *Tuesdays at the Castle*, and the entire continent of Ionia in *Princess of the Midnight Ball*. How do you go about building these worlds and establishing their magical rules?

Ionia is a cheat! It's based on early 19th century Europe. I used my years of German classes to construct the kingdom of Westfalin, and my love of Regency romances for Breton. There's not a great deal of magic in practice in Ionia, but I always try to incorporate something physical (knitting, charms, herbs). Most of the time, I just base a country on an existing country and then start adding bits.

What's your favorite murdered darling from your books—a character, scene, plot or even a single line that you really wanted to keep but ultimately had to cut?

Oh, I saved both victims! I don't really remember most parts that end up being cut, but the subplot with Lily and Heinrich from *Princess of the Midnight Ball* almost got the axe. At first there was only one mention of Heinrich in the beginning of the book, and then he appeared at the end, and my editor thought it was confusing and asked me to cut it. Instead I added more hints throughout, determined to give Lily her own romance (and an explanation for her skill with a pistol), and my editor said that she was not going to stand in the way of young love after all, so Lily and Heinrich got their story.

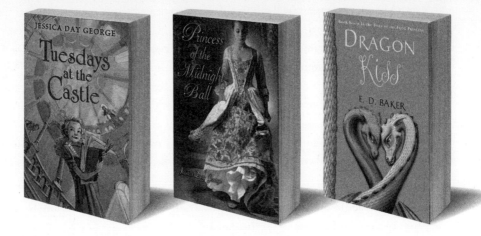

What do you suggest for writers struggling with how to open their novel? How do you decide where your story will begin?

You want to begin with a bang, to grab readers' attention. But sometimes a great opening line has to wait a bit. If you're trying too hard for that opening punch, it will be obvious. You may want to write the rest of the story, or the bits that you already have in your head, and then come back and see where and how the story should begin, in light of what you've already written.

You say that you wrote six novels before *Dragon Slippers* was published. How did you go about getting published for the first time? What was the process like? Do you have any advice for first time writers trying to break in to the market?

In my case, it was finding the right genre. My first six novels were all adult fantasy, and my rejection letters often said, "You're a good writer, but this just didn't quite work." I was suddenly inspired to write *Dragon Slippers* and as soon as I did, I knew I had hit on something good. I took the manuscript to a writing conference (Writing and Illustrating for Young Readers) before it was even finished, and had a great deal of interest from the editors there. But I also met someone who was setting up a smaller workshop where attendees could have one-on-one pitch sessions with an editor from Bloomsbury Children's. I went, and she bought it, and it was wonderful! But the key here was that I had found my niche, writing-wise, and then I found the right editor for it. Both my editor and the person organizing the workshop said, "This is a very Bloomsbury book." You have to find the editor or agent who is interested in the kind of book you've written, and then go after them!

What's something you wish you had known when you first started writing?

I wish I had known that my persistence would pay off. It would have made the years of struggle easier to handle. But I really do wish that someone had said to me, before I spent nine years trying to break into the adult market, Honey, you love kids books, write something for younger readers.

You include a knitting pattern with your book *Princess of the Midnight Ball* and actually reference where it corresponds with the story. How did you decide to include such an interesting supplement? What was the process for putting that together like?

As soon as I came up with the idea for retelling "The Twelve Dancing Princesses" from the soldier's point of view, I knew that I wanted him to be a knitter. (As recently as WWI, they taught soldiers to knit as part of their training.) I had just seen a pattern similar to the black wool chain that is vital to my book and wanted to incorporate something like it in the story, and thought that including the pattern would be both fun and give readers a chance to see what it looked like in person. In the end I decided to include all the patterns so that readers could "knit along" with the main character. At first we put them in the book, after each chapter where Galen is depicted knitting, but that distracted from the story, so we put most of them on my website instead. I tried to find basic items that a beginning knitter could try, and wrote very simple instructions for them, like a hat, a scarf and a pair of socks. I did a test knit of each of the items, and had a friend who was just learning to knit read over them to see if she understood.

Tuesdays at the Castle seems to be aimed at a much younger age group than your other novels. How much do you keep your reader in mind as you write?

Generally I'm writing for me. I try to write a story that appeals to me, as a reader, and don't worry about the genre or the age group in the early stages. Some of the books end up on the older end of the spectrum, and some the younger. When I'm revising, I get a feel for the age group and try then to make sure that the jokes seem age appropriate, the language, and voice, etc.

What's next for you?

The third (and final) book about the Ionian princesses, *Princess of the Silver Woods,* will be out in fall of 2012, and right now I'm working on the sequel to *Tuesdays at the Castle.*

....

KRISTEN GRACE is a contributor to *Writer's Digest* and is currently earning her Master's Degree in English at Miami University of Ohio. You can check out her blog at kegrace.wordpress.com or follow her on Twitter (@kayeeegee).

....

MARISSA MEYER

On why a strong focus can be a writer's greatest weapon.

....

by Frankie Mallis

 Marissa Meyer's debut novel *Cinder*, the first title in her Lunar Chronicles series, debuted in January 2012 with Feiwel and Friends. The books, starring Cinder, a futuristic cyborg Cinderella retell famous fairy tales, giving them each a science fiction twist. *Cinder* was met with great reviews and even landed Meyer on the *New York Times* bestseller list soon after its release.

Now with *Cinder* under her belt and plans for the remaining Lunar Chronicles, Meyer is living her dream life as a full-time writer with her husband and cats in Tacoma, Washington. Here she talks about her early, life-long love of fairy tales, the writing assignment that accidentally led to the story of *Cinder*, her years of craft study, followed by her whirlwind journey from unpublished writer to *New York Times* bestselling author. To learn more about Meyer and her writing, check out her website: marissameyer.livejournal.com.

Cinder was such a fun and unique break out novel. Can you tell us how you got the idea for the novel and how you began writing?

I got the idea for *Cinder* when I entered a writing contest a few years back. The administrator had made a list of ten items, and entries had to include at least two of them. For my short story, I chose to set it in the future and include a fairy-tale character—the story I wrote for that contest became a sci-fi retelling of Puss in Boots, which is one of my favorite fairy tales. Interestingly, I would later come to find that only two stories had been entered for that contest ... and mine didn't win! But it was a lot of fun to write and it gave me the idea to write an entire series of futuristic fairy tales.

When you began writing *Cinder*, did you know there'd be more than one book in the series?

Yes. My original plan had been to write each book as a stand-alone story, set in the same futuristic world but with separate characters and plots. However, the more I brainstormed and plotted the books, the more they started to overlap. Snow White's wicked stepmother began terrorizing Little Red Riding Hood, Rapunzel's prince befriended Cinderella, etc., until pretty soon I was seeing the series as one ongoing plotline, with Cinderella acting as the main protagonist throughout.

You must love fairy tales. Can you talk about your history with them and which fairy tales are your favorite?

I think my obsession with fairy tales began when I saw Disney's *The Little Mermaid* in theaters as a child. I loved the movie, and not long after that someone gave me a little book of fairy tales, including Hans Christian Andersen's "Little Mermaid." Well, anyone who's read the tale knows that it does *not* share Disney's happy ending, and that both shocked and fascinated me. I've been intrigued with the darker and more gruesome versions of the tales ever since, and even took a Fairy Tale and Fantasy Literature course in college that focused a lot on the symbolism and subconscious meanings behind the stories. Some favorites include "Cinderella" (of course), "Bluebeard," and "Brier Rose," a.k.a. Sleeping Beauty.

Was *Cinder* your first novel? If not, from that first novel to the writing of *Cinder*, did your writing process change? Can you describe what your writing process looks like now? Do you outline?

Cinder was my first completed novel—though I have many unfinished novels along without about 45 works of "Sailor Moon" fanfiction, which is really how I "got my start" as a writer. I started writing fanfic when I was 14 years old, and back then I was a pantser, but after awhile I realized that my stories turned out a lot better when I gave them some forethought. I've been a serious outliner ever since. Probably the biggest difference between *Cinder* and anything that came before it is the amount of revisions that went into it. I completely rewrote the manuscript twice, along with a few heavy revision rounds, and countless editing and polishing rounds. As I work on the rest of the series, I find my outlines becoming even more detailed and structured, as the later books have lots of characters and subplots to keep track of. Having a plan keeps me focused, while still allowing me room to be creative if the story takes an unexpected turn.

What did your journey from deciding to write to actual publication look like?

I always wanted to be a writer, from the time that I was a little kid and first learned that such a job existed. I decided to attempt my first novel when I was a teenager, and I thought it was going to be easy—that I'd no doubt be published before I graduated from high school. Ha! It obviously didn't work that way. It would be ten years of learning the craft and abandoning novels that weren't working before I had the idea for *Cinder*. Once I had the idea, it took about two years to write it (during which time I also wrote the first drafts of books 2 and 3).

On the other hand, once the book was ready to go to agents, my writing journey started to happen very fast. It took two months to sign with an agent, and I ended up signing with the first agent I'd queried. We worked together on the submission materials for two weeks and she went out with it on a Friday—we had our first offer the following Monday. The series went to auction soon after that. From the first query letter sent to the book deal was just under three months.

Did you have any idea when you started *Cinder*, you were writing a *New York Times* bestseller?

Ha! Yes and no. I think every writer goes into a book with hope that it could hit a nerve and be met with enthusiasm. I remember a time when money was tight, I turned to my husband (boyfriend at the time) and joked, "Don't worry, someday I'll be a bestselling author." But at the same time, no matter how much you dream it, you never *really* believe it will happen to you. And then it happens, and it's completely surreal.

Since being published, how has your life changed?

In every way! I was able to quit my day job and become a full-time writer. I've gone on book tour, been on the radio and TV, presented at schools and conferences, met hundreds of wonderful readers and writers in the world of children's literature, and on and on. It's all been a dream come true.

What part about becoming not only a published author, but a bestselling author most surprised you?

Although I know it shouldn't have been a surprise, I was caught off-guard by the blurb requests that started rolling in from authors and editors. Obviously, I know that writers receive blurb requests and I always like reading the blurbs on a book that I'm interested in, but it was one element of the writing life that I'd never imagined for myself. The idea that my opinion matters enough to go on someone else's front cover is still baffling to me, but also flattering, of course. And it's a lot of fun getting sneak peeks at upcoming titles.

What has been your craziest moment as a published author?

On the day that *Cinder* released, I drove to Seattle to visit the local bookstores, sign copies, and meet booksellers. At the very first store I went into—not fifteen minutes after the store had opened—the clerk was able to find all but one of the books that they were supposed to have in stock. I signed what they had and was just getting ready to leave

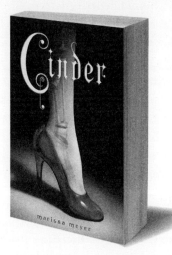

when I noticed a guy sitting by the escalator … and he was reading my book! It was very bizarre, and I think that was the moment I first realized that this whole publishing thing was real, and that my book was out in the world for anyone and everyone to read and enjoy. (And yes, I did introduce myself to him and sign the book.)

What do you feel is your greatest strength as a writer and how have you cultivated that strength?

I'm a very determined, goal-oriented person, and am able to stay focused until I accomplish what I've set my mind to. This comes in handy for every aspect of the writing life, whether it's writing a first draft, meeting a deadline, or promoting the novel. I'm always breaking my goals into small tasks and monitoring my progress. I sometimes think that lack of focus can be a writer's greatest enemy, and I'm lucky that it's not something I normally struggle with.

Which part of the writing process do you find the most challenging? And how do you go about conquering it?

I generally find the starting to be the most difficult part of the process. I enjoy revising and editing, because I'm always looking for that moment when I feel like I've really created something worthwhile. But the beginning is scary—when you don't know if what seems like a good idea now is still going to seem like a good idea two years from now. Nothing is more daunting than a blank page! That's one of the reasons I outline. If I have an idea of what needs to happen on that blank page, it takes away a lot of the worry. And of course, there's the ever-constant chant in the back of my head, reminding me that *everything* can be fixed in revisions.

Growing up which books were your favorite to read? Which writers did you admire? Which writers do you most admire now?

A few childhood favorites were *Charlie and the Chocolate Factory*, *The Little House on the Prairie*, *The Hobbit* and The Lord of the Rings, The Chronicles of Narnia, and later Goosebumps. I don't know that I "admired" writers as a child—I doubt I gave the writer any thought at all! But I adored any book that could make me lose myself in the story and forget where I was. I still admire writers who manage to accomplish that, along with those who are able to bring effortless (or what seems effortless!) humor into their books, as I think humor is one of the most difficult things to get right. Some favorites are John Green, J.K. Rowling, Louis Sachar and Gail Carson Levine.

Can you describe in your gut the moment you knew you wanted to be a writer?

Honestly, I don't remember a time when I *didn't* want to be a writer. I often feel like every decision I've made in my life has been with the intent of bringing me to this moment.

What was the best piece of writing advice you ever got, and what advice would you give to writers?

I'm not sure where I first heard it, but the idea that every character is the hero of their own story has always stuck with me. If your protagonist is the only person leading an interesting life, then you've probably assembled a rather dull and cliché cast of characters. Rather, imagine that every secondary character, every "extra," even every villain sees themselves as the hero of their own life. To think of them that way instantly adds a whole dimension to their character and forces you to question their history, motivations and desires.

As for what advice I can offer, it's the oldest advice in the book, but I also think it's the most relevant: Write as much as you can. Read as much as you can. It's the only way to learn what works for you and what doesn't.

Would you ever consider writing books for children or adults? Would you ever write outside of your genre?

I would consider writing anything that called out to me as a story that needed to be told, regardless of age group, although for the foreseeable future I plan on sticking with young adult. As for genre, I hope to have the opportunity to explore many genres throughout my career. *Cinder* combines science fiction and fairy tales, two genres I've had a lot of fun with, but I also have ideas for historicals, fantasies, contemporaries and everything in between. We'll see what calls to me next.

Do you ever see yourself pursuing another form of art outside of writing?

Not as a career, although I do enjoy different types of crafting and decorating.

If you could redo one moment in your writing career, what would it be?

I would have designed my home office with more storage in mind. Between ARCs, swag, author copies, stationery and shipping supplies, we writers sure accumulate a lot of stuff. What a mess!

FRANKIE MALLIS is a young adult writer based in Philadelphia. When not writing, she can be found belly dancing, baking vegan food or teaching creative writing at Arcadia University. She also runs a small children's library on the weekends. Frankie is represented by Laura Rennert at the Andrea Brown Literary Agency. For more information, visit frankiediane.blogspot.com.

KRISTIN O'DONNELL TUBB

Research is the key to getting it done right.

....

by Ricki Schultz

Self-proclaimed research "geek" Kristin O'Donnell Tubb does it all: she writes, she mothers, she speaks at workshops ... and she still has time to pay the bills and do the occasional load of laundry. Well, after the writing has been done.

Although her first two novels are middle-grade historicals, Tubb's upcoming book, *The 13th Sign* (Feiwel & Friends/Macmillan), is a fantasy.

For Tubb, it's all about research—from unlocking character to cultivating setting to shaping plot—and she was nice enough to discuss her process as well as impart what works for her when writing for kids.

What does your typical writing week look like? How do you get it all done?

You know those pictures of highways that shoot across the desert straight as an arrow? My writing week looks like the dotted, fading, roadkill-laced, pothole-strewn line down the middle of that road. I have young children, so I write when they are in school/preschool. No grocery shopping, no bill-paying, no personal errands of any kind when they are in school. (At least, I try to stick to that.) Writing is a priority to me, so I treat it as one. On the days when I can, I write every moment I have to myself. It often requires overlooking a messy home or a pile of mail. But those things will still be there later. Those things will be there *always*. Ideas must be chased past Mt. Laundry.

Walk us through your writing process. Do your characters tend to come first, or your story ideas? And where do you go from there? Do you outline? Conduct

character interviews? Do writing exercises to unlock certain plot elements or character traits, etc.?

I wish I could say I have a tried-and-true writing process, but that's not exactly the case. For me, each book comes to life a little differently. But I do tend to get a story idea first: with *Autumn Winifred Oliver Does Things Different*, it was: how does someone's home become a national park? With *Selling Hope*, the term "comet pills" and the idea of a hoax centered around Halley's Comet sparked the story. And for my fantasy debut, *The 13th Sign*, it was why and to what extent people believe in horoscopes. From there, I usually start researching: the Great Smoky Mountains National Park, vaudeville, the zodiac calendar.

Research usually gives me a good idea of who my main character will be; while doing research, I ask myself, "Who would be the worst possible person to put in this scenario?" The worst person, of course, provides the most story conflict. Research tends to unlock much of the plot for me as well, and I research stories anywhere from six months (*The 13th Sign*) to two years (*Autumn*).

After that, yes, I absolutely outline. I use the term "outline" loosely—it's more of a scene-by-scene story map that helps keep me focused. I write slowly, too. Once I finish writing a scene, I look at the scene that comes next on the outline. I think about that scene, a lot, between writing times—at the grocery store, doing dishes, driving, etc. I record ideas using a voice recorder app on my phone, so when it's time to sit and write, I usually have a fairly good idea of how the scene will look and feel.

Cross-eyed Jane of *Selling Hope* as well as Beef, Uncle John, and Uncle John Too of *Autumn Winifred Oliver Does Things Different* are all unique character names that work very well within your worlds. How do you come up with character names?

Naming characters is one of my favorite parts of writing! A character's name or nickname should reflect that person and his/her circumstances, if possible. Autumn's name came from the Smoky Mountains in the fall, my favorite time of year there. The trees are tiny explosions of red and yellow and orange—fiery, like Autumn. Hope's name is a bit more obvious—she's peddling hope to strangers in the form of anti-comet pills. And in The 13th Sign, the main character is named Jalen, which means "healer." Healing plays a major role in the story. I usually know who my character is and the role he or she plays before I know his/her name. Once you know the details, the name can usually appear.

As you mentioned, you are a plotter—not a pantser. What methods do you use to plot when an idea strikes you?

I am a plotter, through and through. I use my voice recorder quite a bit when I'm driving or cleaning to record plot points. But I'm primarily old school: I research

and outline using 3x5 notecards. I know you can do this with certain computer programs, but I haven't figured out how to make them work for me in the same way that I use traditional cards. While researching, I record both facts and ideas for scenes. (Research unlocks many scene ideas for me.) Once the research phase is finished, I have a stack of scenes and a stack of facts. (I should say a "shoebox" of each. I keep them in shoeboxes. It's all very high-tech.) I lay the notecards out on the floor, starting with the scenes, and then figure out the best places to use my facts. This becomes my rough outline. The story will change as it's being written, but those notecards are the skeleton of the story.

You mentioned that your upcoming novel is a fantasy. How was the planning of this one different from your historicals?

The 13th Sign is still based in fact; it is the story of the little-known thirteenth sign of the zodiac, Ophiuchus, and how its addition to the zodiac calendar shifts almost everyone's horoscope sign. But the research for this book was different from researching an historical in that I studied personality theory and modern-day belief systems (hefty stuff!). So the research didn't spark as many plot ideas as reading about a concrete time and place tends to. It became a challenge, then, when I turned from research to plotting. For both *Autumn* and *Selling Hope*, I had an abundance of scene ideas by the time I'd finished researching. But after I felt I had enough knowledge to write about each personality of the zodiac, I still didn't have a plot.

So I started writing. And rewriting. And rewriting. Luckily my editor, Liz Szabla, is a very patient and talented woman. She guided me through four (five?) major rewrites of this book, until it finally started to take shape. *The 13th Sign* came to life much differently than Autumn and Selling Hope. With historicals, chronology is usually king, and if you search hard enough, you can usually find a factual answer to fill in a plot hole. But with fantasy, anything is possible. Anything! I found it a challenge to reign in that kind of power. But it's also freeing, the idea that in fantasy, there are far fewer facts to contradict. Writing different genres taps into different realms of creativity, and I hope to have the opportunity to explore both for a long time.

In both your books out now, you have recurring elements that seem to push along the plot and reveal character (Autumn's "rules" or tags at the beginning of each chapter about why she does things "different," and Hope's internal one-liners, which are usually mean—and hilarious). Talk to us about these. For what purpose did you use them?

Autumn and Hope both deal with some pretty serious stuff—Autumn's family home is being seized by the government to form a national park, and Hope is running a con on strangers, swearing to protect them from the dangers of Halley's Comet with her "anti-comet pills." It's not always easy to write comic relief into stories like these, and personally, I need comic relief in tough times. Those tags and one-liners help achieve that, I hope. Plus, yes, it's part of their characterization. Most of us have sayings or mantras that we refer back to when we need a mental boost, something that propels us forward on bad days. The fact that Autumn always "does things different" and that Hope thinks in terms of one-line zingers gives hints at setting and voice.

Speaking of voice, how do you write with an authentically middle grade voice? What advice would you have for someone trying to recreate a voice appropriate for those works?

Voice, to me, is the key that unlocks a story. It's difficult to fully understand a character and his/her motivations if the voice isn't clear. And voice comes from the main character—where they live, what experiences they've had, how they act and react to the obstacles placed in their way. When I do writing workshops, I remind the participants that they aren't the ones telling the story—their characters do that, even in third person point-of-view. Instead, as writers, our job is to write down the story as our character tells it to us.

Middle grade voices aren't much different from the voices in YA or adult, actually. By that I mean, as humans, we all have the same basic needs and wants. But those needs and wants change and morph as we grow. (Notice I didn't say "evolve." Our wants don't necessarily become more important!) The key to capturing an authentic middle-grade voice, I think, is to remember what's important to a middle-grader: family, friends, spirituality, the importance of being noticed, the importance of being special or good at something. Vocabulary and word count aren't so much an issue as authentic word usage (for your character) and a sufficient number of words to tell the story.

Along those same lines, you use some dialect—specifically within *Autumn Winifred Oliver Does Things Different*—which enhances Autumn's voice. Can you speak to that a bit? What kinds of decisions went in to what to use and when to use colorful words/phrases that would give Autumn such a unique sound and really tie into the time period with which you're dealing?

> A large part of research, for me, is compiling a vocabulary list. The list usually ends up being several pages long, and has everything in it from brand names and phrases to adjectives and adverbs—anything that sounds uniquely like the place and time of my story. (This helps for all kinds of stories, I've noticed—not just historicals. For *The 13th Sign*, I collected words like "drench" and "thrummed"—words that evoke the same feelings I hope to achieve in the story.)
>
> It can be difficult, though, adding the right amount of spice to your story. Too much, and the flavor is overkill. I decided that for Autumn, spelling the words they way they would've been pronounced (like "cain't") or using words like "ain't" outside of dialogue just saturated the story too much. A sprinkle of salt goes a long way!

I noticed, particularly in *Autumn Winifred Oliver Does Things Different*, you gave characters certain characteristics or tics that helped identify them. For instance, Katie, Autumn's sister, tugs on her earlobe. Was this on purpose? Talk to us about why you used little details like these. Also, what are some other characteristics in you've used that function in the same way?

> I love character tics! They are a quick—and relatively easy—way to add an extra splash of characterization to stories. Katie is brash girl, but her earlobe tugs show her sensitive side. Gramps sucks his teeth audibly and frequently, showing that he lives out loud and doesn't really care to fit in with what's customary. I got to have a *ton* of fun with this in *The 13th Sign*, because it deals largely with the personalities as defined by each horoscope sign. When the main character Jalen is a Sagittarius, she twirls her fingers in her hair—to me, more of a withdrawn, reserved habit. But when she becomes an Ophiuchus (yes, the characters switch horoscope signs!), she is a loud knuckle-cracker. These shifts were so much fun to write for each character. Habits and tics like these are the heart of "show, don't tell."

What methods do you use to approach weaving in backstory? Any rules you follow or tips to impart?

> Ah, backstory. Our nemesis, our best friend. The only rule I try to follow is not to introduce it before it is absolutely necessary. If we need a slice of backstory in order to understand a scene, yes, weave it in. But if you understand the scene without any backpedaling at all, save it until you need it. And you only need it once. Trust that your reader will remember what they read.

Backstory, to me, is related to motivation. What happened in the past is driving what our characters want now. Make certain that the backstory of a character aligns with his or her wants. Otherwise, it serves no purpose.

Can you speak about setting a bit? How do you feel your settings enhance your characters and plots?

Setting is a character and can be developed just as vividly. It is one of the strongest tools a writer has—use it! For both *Autumn* and *Selling Hope*, the setting is the plot. Autumn's home in Cades Cove is wanted by farmers, loggers, and the government, and Autumn and her family cope with that. In *Selling Hope*, Hope runs her con in order to escape her setting, the vaudeville circuit. And in *The 13th Sign*, the setting is New Orleans—a mystical, voodoo atmosphere whose geography and historical landmarks play a huge role in the plot. If your story can be set anywhere, ask yourself if there's any way you can make your setting work harder for you. It is a major driver for everything from plot to voice.

As you've mentioned, you cover some unique topics in both *Selling Hope* and *Autumn Winifred Oliver Does Things Different*: from logging to vaudeville acts! You obviously need to know a great deal about these subjects in order to write about them in such an authentic way. That said, how do you go about all the research you do?

Those who know me know I am a research geek—I absolutely love the idea of putting on white gloves to hold a photograph taken in 1934, the dizzy feeling you get as microfiche spins by, finding the answer to a question after weeks of searching. I say on my website that I'm basically a dork who would still be going to school if they'd let me!

As for databases and other sources, every book has its own research path. But there are a few tried-and-true places I visit to begin. The Library of Congress has a wonderful database and website: loc.gov. They even have an Ask the Librarian feature that is amazing. I asked for their help when I needed to know how one would start a late 1920s-era car. They e-mailed me a PDF of an entire operating manual for a 1928 Plymouth! I not only knew how to start the car, I knew how to fix it!

Many larger cities now have great historical websites thanks to historical societies and museums. Chicago's is exemplary: chicagohs.org. Even if your story isn't set in Chicago, you can get an idea of an era by studying the cars, the clothing and other details in the photos they've made available online.

I also love studying old advertisements for hairstyles, jewelry, hats, clothing, kitchens, cars, brand names, and more. Advertisements capture the ideals of an era in a way that news stories don't.

And some of my "super-secret" research outlets are classified ads, eBay, and YouTube. These are great resources for brand names, prices, setting details, and learning how to perform skills that one has never performed (as in *The 13th Sign*, when I needed to know how one "turns on" a hot air balloon).

While your books aren't "issue books," you do deal with a few heavier issues as well as some elements that could be used in the classroom—particularly since your books are historical (you even have a spot for educators on your website!). How do you approach these issues in your writing without becoming too teachy or preachy (which you do not become)?

Thank you. I think that one of the biggest dangers we have—we adults who write for children—is to write in a "trust me, I know" tone. No one likes to be addressed with that tone. For me, the way to avoid being too teachy is to present multiple sides of an issue, to have the protagonist ask lots of questions, and to have many of the answers be undesirable or unclear. That is how most of our challenges present themselves in our own lives: as uncertain change. I think readers are more likely to identify with characters who face uncertainty with questions and doubt than those who face it with an inflexible drive for "right."

One hot topic in writing for kids seems to be swearing. While your books aren't littered with swear words, they do appear. What are your thoughts on this? How do you determine whether or not to use swear words, and how do you know when you've used enough?

Swear words, like any other type of word choice, are a tool in the writer's toolbox. Just like any tool, if you use it too frequently, it wears down and becomes ineffective. But used sparingly, they can really characterize someone. As a parent, I'm sensitive to the use of curse words in stories. But as a writer, I feel I must be true to how my characters act and react. Hope's boss on the vaudeville circuit, Mr. Whitting, is a tough nut. It's not realistic for him to say, "Drat!" when Hope and Buster Keaton steal his car. But if he were to curse on every other page (he doesn't), it would steal from the more dramatic moments when he does.

What would you say is a writing weakness of yours? How do you go about overcoming it?

Plotting is one of my weaknesses. Amping up the tension, realistically and in a nonpredictable manner, is something I struggle with. Research helps me overcome a lot of plot problems; reading about the subject will usually spark a scene a two. I also like to experiment by playing with scenes, writing them two or three different ways. Writing is fun, and sometimes you can come up with something great (as opposed to something there), if you just play around with the scene for a bit. And if none of it works, I walk away for a while. I'm not the kind of person who can bully my way through the mud. If a scene is murky, if my plot is getting too thick, I might need a break for a few days to see it more clearly when I return.

What's one thing you wish you'd known when you were starting out writing?

I wish I'd known how wonderful the people in this industry are, because I would've started writing much sooner in my life! The children's literature community is one of the most supportive, creative, caring, and open communities I've ever had the honor to be a part of. From my wonderful agent Josh Adams; to my amazing editors and publicists; to my fellow SCBWI members; to online forums; to my fabulous critique group; to the booksellers, out there pairing kids with the perfect books; to the teachers and librarians, igniting a life-long love of stories; to the readers themselves, the reason for it *all*—all are here to create and find the best possible books for children and teens. These friendships make the tougher times in publishing—the rejections, the setbacks, the times when the words don't flow—bearable. I'm proud and honored to be a part of such an industry.

RICKI SCHULTZ (rickischultz.com) is an Ohio-based freelance writer and recovering high school English teacher. She writes young adult fiction and, as coordinator of The Write-Brained Network (writebrainednetwork.com), she enjoys connecting with other writers.

MEET THE SCBWI REGIONAL ADVISORS

....

by Chuck Sambuchino

If you want to write or illustrate books for kids, the number one piece of advice you're going to hear is "Join the SCBWI." I'd bet money on it.

SCBWI stands for the Society of Children's Book Writers & Illustrators, and is a worldwide organization that links together those who want to create content for kids. There are many regional chapters in the United States, and plenty internationally, as well. The group holds meetings, has annual conferences (both regional and national) and provides both a support system as well as a wealth of online resources.

But all that said, perhaps the SCBWI—and your nearest chapter especially—still seems a little vague and out of focus. You may wonder: What's the group like? What are their events like? Is my closest group small or big? To get to the bottom of these frequently asked questions—and to better put a face on these great regional chapters all around the world—I went straight to the people in charge for a little "getting to know you" chit-chat.

I conducted interviews with dozens of SCBWI coordinators (called "regional advisors," or "RA" for short) all around the world. Everyone you meet below is either an advisor or co-advisor for his or her regional group. Keep in mind that these are short interviews, and there is much more to learn about each organization and what they offer each month/year, so check out their websites by simply Googling "SCBWI" and "(regional area)."

So without further ado, meet the great volunteers who keep SCBWI going on a regional level!

MARY CRONK FARRELL: EASTERN WASHINGTON & NORTHERN IDAHO

TELL US ABOUT YOUR RECURRING WRITERS' CONFERENCE. The Inland Northwest is far-flung and sparsely populated, which is why our annual conference in September is so important.

It not only gives our members a chance to come together, make friends and learn craft—but it also serves to bring the publishing industry *to us*. We bring in at least one editor and one agent each year. This helps our members learn about the business, connect with professionals in the business and gain a sense of themselves as professionals.

WHAT MAKES YOU DO WHAT YOU DO? It is a tremendous amount of work and responsibility to run a region. I've been the RA now for just over one year and we have had some really exciting events such as a day-long "Plot Intensive" with editor Cheryl Klein, and a "Social Media Intensive" with Greg Pincus.

WHAT'S YOUR SINGLE BEST PIECE OF ADVICE FOR A NEW WRITER OR ILLUSTRATOR? Read books or go online to learn about the business of publishing. Educate yourself and read the kind of books you want to write or illustrate.

MICHELE CORRIEL: MONTANA

TELL US ABOUT YOUR RECURRING WRITERS' CONFERENCE. We put on at least one fall event. It can either be a conference or a retreat. It is really the only time all the members of the region can get together and network in person. It's also a great service to the region because being way out in Montana (a very large state with a small population), we create a wonderful opportunity for our members to meet and get critiques from big house editors and agents.

WHAT MAKES YOU DO WHAT YOU DO? I took over the position 11 years ago. A few members "encouraged" me to take it on and I found the experience to be very rewarding. It's great to hear about success stories. It's also a nice way to keep informed of the market, since I get so many questions and have to do research. (I'm a sucker for research!)

HOW WOULD YOU DESCRIBE THE MAKEUP OF YOUR CHAPTER? Our chapter is one of the smaller ones in the states. I think I've met all of my members or at least try to e-mail with them, if they can't make it to one of our events. It's a very supportive group, and when one member gets published everyone feels like they have a stake in it.

WHAT'S YOUR SINGLE BEST PIECE OF ADVICE FOR A NEW WRITER OR ILLUSTRATOR? READ! READ, READ, READ!

QUINETTE COOK: MINNESOTA

TELL US ABOUT YOUR RECURRING WRITERS' CONFERENCE. The yearly conference includes authors, illustrators, agents and editors. The session topics are varied and appeal to pre-published and published writers/illustrators. We offer portfolio and manuscript critiques. The feedback we receive is always positive and we have a number of member success stories as a result of these conferences.

WHAT MAKES YOU DO WHAT YOU DO? First, I love children's literature. The stories we write change lives. Second, SCBWI is one big fantastic family. When I joined, I was amazed at how welcoming everyone was to me. And they still are!

HOW WOULD YOU DESCRIBE THE MAKEUP OF YOUR CHAPTER? We have approximately 400+ members. We have recently added monthly "mixers" to get members and prospective members together for fun socializing.

WHAT'S YOUR SINGLE BEST PIECE OF ADVICE FOR A NEW WRITER OR ILLUSTRATOR? Read books. Read more books. Read even more books.

NANCY CASTALDO: EASTERN NEW YORK

TELL US ABOUT YOUR RECURRING WRITERS' CONFERENCE. We have changed from having a yearly full-day conference to hosting it every other year and making it longer. Last year our speakers included a literary author, bookseller, award-winning author, award-winning illustrator, editors, and an agent. Our membership also loves the critiques we offer by editors, agents and speakers.

WHAT MAKES YOU DO WHAT YOU DO? I love being part of the SCBWI family. I don't say that lightly. It really is a family. Warm, caring and supportive.

HOW WOULD YOU DESCRIBE THE MAKEUP OF YOUR CHAPTER? Our region was spun out of the Upstate New York region five years ago and has grown since then. We now host four regional Shoptalk meetings per month that are free and open to anyone interested in the industry. Eastern New York is a unique region, close enough to New York City, yet some areas are very remote. We have a fantastic group of both published and yet-to-be published members, eager to improve their craft and network.

WHAT'S YOUR SINGLE BEST PIECE OF ADVICE FOR A NEW WRITER OR ILLUSTRATOR? Get familiar with the SCBWI website. Usually, when someone e-mails me a question the answer can be found right on the website. There are terrific market resources, but for beginning writers and illustrators, there is also all the information needed to get your work ready for submission.

VICKI SANSUM: HOUSTON, TX

TELL US ABOUT YOUR RECURRING WRITERS' CONFERENCE. We put on one large conference every year as well as small workshops. For the annual conference, we bring in editors, agents, art directors and best-selling authors and illustrators to speak. This gives our members an opportunity to have critiques with these experts, network and to hear what's going on the world of children's publishing.

WHAT MAKES YOU DO WHAT YOU DO? I love being part of SCBWI. The organization is one of the most supportive groups I've ever been a part of. It doesn't matter if you're at the beginning of your writing or illustrating career or if you're already published, SCBWI is there to help you succeed.

HOW WOULD YOU DESCRIBE THE MAKEUP OF YOUR CHAPTER? We have a large group because we're in a big city. At every monthly meeting, we have lots of new people join us and attendance at our annual conference has skyrocketed over the past five years. We're a fun, welcoming group who take our state motto, *Friendship*, to heart.

WHAT'S YOUR SINGLE BEST PIECE OF ADVICE FOR A NEW WRITER OR ILLUSTRATOR? Join a good critique group.

DAN SEKARSKI: SWITZERLAND

HOW WOULD YOU DESCRIBE THE MAKEUP OF YOUR CHAPTER? We are a very small group of about 10 scattered throughout Switzerland. We don't put on any big regional activities here but function more as comrades in arms. We are quite distant from each other and generally meet twice a year to exchange views and keep in touch. Our communication is generally done by e-mail. We are all usually quite busy with individual and personal projects and attend the sessions of the other large regions in France, Germany or Italy.

WHAT'S YOUR SINGLE BEST PIECE OF ADVICE FOR A NEW WRITER OR ILLUSTRATOR? I don't believe much in magic formulas for writing, illustrating or publishing books. If you want to be a writer, by simple definition, you simply have to *write*. If you want to be an "author," you have to finish what you are writing and put it in a reasonable form to be shared by someone else. If you want to be popular and make money, it helps to be talented, hard working and fortunate. But you can't do that if you don't first write! Take care and have some fun out there! It will all fall into place one day.

JO S. KITTINGER: SOUTHERN BREEZE (AL, GA, MS)

TELL US ABOUT YOUR RECURRING WRITERS' CONFERENCE. Southern Breeze hosts two major conferences each year: "Writing and Illustrating for Kids" (WIK) and "Springmingle." Our fall WIK conference offers 28 workshops for attendees to choose from over 4 workshop breakouts, allowing attendees to target their interests. There is something for everyone. Our Springmingle conference is slanted to a more professional level. The networking and knowledge gained at these events is incredible. Attendance can open doors to closed publishing houses.

WHAT MAKES YOU DO WHAT YOU DO? I am passionate about the SCBWI and its value for authors and illustrators. I would have given up long before publication if not for SCBWI. Every time a member gets their first publication or their fifth, I get to celebrate with them.

How would you describe the makeup of your chapter? Southern Breeze SCBWI has grown tremendously in talent and published authors. Southern hospitality can be felt at all our events and is, in fact, in our DNA! Sweet tea and sweet advice are shared around the table. I've often heard Lin Oliver, (executive director of SCBWI) say that people often feel like they've "found their tribe" when discovering SCBWI. And I think that our region embraces that atmosphere. We're serious about the business of creating wonderful books for kids, but welcoming to others who are like-minded.

WHAT'S THE SINGLE BEST PIECE OF ADVICE FOR A NEW WRITER OR ILLUSTRATOR? Your book doesn't just have to be good, it has to be original. Most first books have very common themes—self esteem, bullying, manners. Dig deep for something fresh.

ANGELA CERRITO: ASSISTANT INTERNATIONAL ADVISOR

TELL US ABOUT YOUR RECURRING WRITERS' CONFERENCE. SCBWI presents a showcase at the Bologna Book Fair in Bologna, Italy every other year. The SCBWI Showcase displays books from members around the world. Both regions and individuals may present their work. There is an illustration display portfolio showcasing the breadth of SCBWI Illustrators worldwide. And, for the first time ever in 2012, we presented a live creative project: The SCBWI Bologna Scrawl Crawl (scbwibologna.blogspot.com).

WHAT MAKES YOU DO WHAT YOU DO? For each SCBWI Bologna event, SCBWI Regional Advisors, Assistant Advisors, Illustrator Coordinators and other members work together to make the showcase possible. Each time we present in Bologna, I see the rewards for our members, books being published into new languages, illustrators making new contacts or even landing their first book deals. The very best aspect of SCBWI in Bologna is that we are a community of writers and illustrators who help and support each other. Throughout the fair members can sign up for portfolio reviews, first page critiques and consultations with industry professionals.

WHAT'S THE SINGLE BEST TIP OF ADVICE FOR A NEW WRITER OR ILLUSTRATOR? When you first start writing and illustrating, success may or may not come quickly. It is important to find out what you enjoy most about the process and build from there.

KRISTI VALIANT: INDIANA

TELL US ABOUT YOUR RECURRING WRITERS' CONFERENCE. For 2013, we're joining with a number of other regions to host a huge Midwest conference. We feel our yearly conference is important to our writers and illustrators so they can learn from and be inspired by top professionals in the children's book publishing world.

WHAT MAKES YOU DO WHAT YOU DO? It is a lot of work, but I love organizing events that are helpful and inspiring. SCBWI greatly helped and continues to help me with my career, and I love volunteering to help others with their dreams.

WHAT'S THE SINGLE BEST PIECE OF ADVICE FOR A NEW WRITER OR ILLUSTRATOR? Picture book writers: Read over 30 recently-published picture books in one sitting at a bookstore or library and separate them into 3 piles: 1) don't want to read again, 2) want to read again, 3) want to buy. Analyze the piles. Which pile does your WIP manuscript belong in?

BEAULAH PEDREGOSA TAGUIWALO: PHILIPPINES

TELL US ABOUT YOUR RECURRING WRITERS' CONFERENCE. Since 2007, we've been holding an annual Children's Book Seminar in Iloilo City on the island of Panay. It is probably the only children's book event with activities for writing stories not only in English and Filipino, but also in Hiligaynon, the language spoken by people from Iloilo City and the neighboring province of Negros Occidental, and Kinaray-a, the endangered mother tongue of people in the rest of Panay island.

WHAT MAKES YOU DO WHAT YOU DO? Next to designing, illustrating, and writing a children's book, the most enjoyable thing I can think of doing on any given day is studying the work of other children's book creators, getting to know them, and thinking of ways to work together or help each other. I get to do all these by being an SCBWI chapter advisor.

HOW WOULD YOU DESCRIBE THE MAKEUP OF YOUR CHAPTER? Our chapter is small, friendly, and open to people of all nationalities who are passionate about and willing to discuss children's books of all kinds: local, foreign, delightful, disturbing, puzzling, surprising, with or without a moral lesson, has a happy or unhappy ending, perfect, defective, whatever. Our events are well-organized and professionally planned and run.

WHAT'S YOUR SINGLE BEST PIECE OF ADVICE FOR A NEW WRITER OR ILLUSTRATOR? Take your favorite children's book, list all the reasons why you like it, whether they make sense or not, then write, illustrate, design, and/or produce a book like it to get a first-hand, personal experience of what it feels like and what it takes.

HOLLY THOMPSON: TOKYO

TELL US ABOUT YOUR RECURRING WRITERS' CONFERENCE. We try to have a major all-day agent, editor or art director event every year. Most of our members don't have the chance to attend SCBWI events outside of our region, so these events are a chance for members to learn face to face from overseas (often U.S.) insiders in children's publishing markets. We also hold regular monthly events—speaker presentations, workshops, creative exchanges, networking nights, and sketch and word crawls.

WHAT MAKES YOU DO WHAT YOU DO? It is a lot of work, but there are enormous rewards— the constant interaction with writers, illustrators and translators at all stages of their careers, and the incredible family-like support from SCBWI headquarters and regional advisors around the world.

HOW WOULD YOU DESCRIBE THE MAKEUP OF YOUR CHAPTER? Diverse! Fun! We are writers, mostly in English, hailing from different countries; illustrators of all sorts of backgrounds and languages; and translators, Japanese to English, of children's content. SCBWI Tokyo is a steadily growing region, and we hope that editors, agents and art directors will contact us whenever they are traveling to Asia. We sometimes partner with SCBWI Hong Kong to share speakers, and a number of our members now participate annually in the Asian Festival of Children's Content in Singapore. We also like to know when authors or illustrators are visiting international or [Department of Defense] schools in Japan; sometimes we arrange SCBWI Tokyo events during their visits.

WHAT'S YOUR SINGLE BEST PIECE OF ADVICE FOR A NEW WRITER OR ILLUSTRATOR? Spare yourself years of mistakes; learn from your mentors in SCBWI.

SUSANNE GERVAY: AUSTRALIA AND NEW ZEALAND

TELL US ABOUT YOUR RECURRING WRITERS' CONFERENCE. Across Australia and New Zealand we hold boutique writers' mini-conferences with publishers, editors, book sellers, authors and illustrators every three months in Melbourne, Brisbane, Perth, Sydney and Auckland. In addition we hold ad-hoc smaller events in South Australia, Tasmania, regional Western Australia and regional Queensland. There is a major annual regional conference at Rottnest Island off the coast of Western Australia near Perth. It is a magical retreat/conference where the delegates stay in beach huts, bicycle around the island where they can illustrate beautiful coves or take time to write. The biennial conference in Sydney is a residential one held at the headquarters of SCBWI Australia and New Zealand at the Hughenden Boutique Hotel. It is a huge event with most Australian publishers participating. Authors and illustrators get the opportunity to pitch and some authors and illustrators have been published from these conferences.

WHAT MAKES YOU DO WHAT YOU DO? I love the community of children's writers and illustrators. The Australian and New Zealand community is especially sharing and there are great friendships made.

WHAT'S YOUR SINGLE BEST PIECE OF ADVICE FOR A NEW WRITER OR ILLUSTRATOR? Establish a writers' and/or illustrators' critique group that you trust. Share your work and develop your craft.

JUDY GOLDMAN: MEXICO

TELL US ABOUT YOUR RECURRING WRITERS' CONFERENCE. With the help of my then co-regional advisor, we did put on a couple of conferences years ago. But, since I can't do that anymore, what I do with Sally Cutting (the regional advisor of Spain) is bring out *La cometa*, a Spanish-language electronic bulletin that includes news about SCBWI major conferences as well as contests for writers and illustrators taking place in the U.S., Latin America, and Spain; news about kidlit in general as well as any other information we think will benefit our readers. Back issues are available on the SCBWI website.

WHAT MAKES YOU DO WHAT YOU DO? I guess a passion for what we do and being completely convinced about the benefits of belonging to the SCBWI, whether you're starting out or already have several books published. Also, working with such lovely people in the main office (Lin Oliver, Steve Mooser, Sara Rutenberg, Chelsea Mooser, and Sara Baker, to name a few).

HOW WOULD YOU DESCRIBE THE MAKEUP OF YOUR CHAPTER? My chapter is very small and spread out in a big country. Most of us have a good grasp of English or are expats.

WHAT'S YOUR SINGLE BEST PIECE OF ADVICE FOR A NEW WRITER OR ILLUSTRATOR? Read, read, read—and revise, revise, revise.

ALAN STACY: NORTH CENTRAL/NORTHEAST TEXAS

TELL US ABOUT YOUR RECURRING WRITERS' CONFERENCE. We have scaled down our larger events due to costs, location and a hundred other logistics. We have conducted "Agent/Editor Days" over the past five years (large conferences in 2007 and 2011) in lieu of a larger conference—and these have been extremely successful in that the entire focus has been providing writers with professional reviews of their manuscripts. Simple, no frills, one-day event, limited attendance.

WHAT MAKES YOU DO WHAT YOU DO? I personally get so much more out of the organization by shepherding and guiding newcomers into our group as others did for me when I first joined.

HOW WOULD YOU DESCRIBE THE MAKEUP OF YOUR CHAPTER? Growing. There's an emphasis on the professional aspect but also making more attempts to provide informal gatherings outside of the monthly meetings in order for the members to get better acquainted.

WHAT'S THE SINGLE BEST PIECE OF ADVICE FOR A NEW WRITER OR ILLUSTRATOR? Learn the power of the "P" words: passion, persistence, professionalism, patience, people. And "submit intelligently" means learning what the industry wants.

PATRICIA NEWMAN: NORTH/CENTRAL CALIFORNIA

TELL US ABOUT YOUR RECURRING WRITERS' CONFERENCE. Our region is far-flung—33 northern California counties. The Spring Spirit Conference is a way for us to come together as a region, celebrate our successes, learn from each other as well as the speakers, and develop new friendships, critique groups, and partnerships.

WHAT MAKES YOU DO WHAT YOU DO? I'm a volunteer at heart. I started in college and kept going, helping to launch an educational foundation for public schools in San Diego; raising money for a neighborhood playground in San Diego; hundreds of hours in the California public schools for my children; and now SCBWI and another non-profit formed to build a performing arts center in our school district. I believe in giving back to my community—whether it's my neighborhood or my professional association. But you're right, SCBWI requires hundreds of hours each year. The reason I come back is the people—not only the folks at headquarters and the other RAs, but our members who work so hard to improve their craft and to help us run the region.

HOW WOULD YOU DESCRIBE THE MAKEUP OF YOUR CHAPTER? We currently boast about 400 members, but geographically we're spread all over. We are connected electronically on Facebook, through a listserve, and via our regional page on the SCBWI website. Our members are supportive and friendly, willing to take risks, and willing to share what works and doesn't work. Most of all, our members are professional.

WHAT'S THE SINGLE BEST PIECE OF ADVICE FOR A NEW WRITER OR ILLUSTRATOR? If you write picture books, pick apart the vocabulary and sentence structure. Identify poetic elements. Study how the character arc is structured and how the conflict builds and is then resolved. Then apply the answers to your own work.

ROBIN KOONTZ: OREGON

TELL US ABOUT YOUR RECURRING WRITERS' CONFERENCE. We have had two major events per year—a spring conference and a fall retreat. The conferences are excellent opportunities for both writers and illustrators in the region to network and share knowledge, experience and information. They are also opportunities to meet and hear from editors, agents, art directors, authors and illustrators who are actively publishing.

WHAT MAKES YOU DO WHAT YOU DO? I like to help people in this business and hope that they, in turn, will give something back. It doesn't always work out that way, but when it does, it makes my job feel worthwhile.

HOW WOULD YOU DESCRIBE THE MAKEUP OF YOUR CHAPTER? The Oregon region has about 430 members. Only about 25 percent reside in the Portland area; the rest of us are scattered all over the state. We're known for being a very friendly, easygoing and giving region. We're proud that most of our published members do not disappear, but rather join our faculty and chip in to help others.

WHAT'S YOUR SINGLE BEST PIECE OF ADVICE FOR A NEW WRITER OR ILLUSTRATOR? Never give up on yourself. If you keep writing, your writing will improve and you will get published.

LESLIE HELAKOSKI: MICHIGAN

TELL US ABOUT YOUR RECURRING WRITERS' CONFERENCE. We hold two main conferences a year—one fall weekend event and one single day spring event plus small events sprinkled throughout the year. I look forward to these events every year! ANY information gained in the pursuit of writing for children is worthwhile. Our events bring in industry pros and are balanced with enthusiastic and supportive writers and illustrators. We are a support group for the kidlit industry.

WHAT MAKES YOU DO WHAT YOU DO? SCBWI helped me become published and I wanted to help keep that kind of thing going for other hopefuls.

HOW WOULD YOU DESCRIBE THE MAKEUP OF YOUR CHAPTER? We are a mid-sized, multi-faceted group.

WHAT'S YOUR SINGLE BEST PIECE OF ADVICE FOR A NEW WRITER OR ILLUSTRATOR? Read more books. I think it takes years of reading and looking at images to understand the depth of a good book or illustration.

CHRIS EBOCH: NEW MEXICO

TELL US ABOUT YOUR RECURRING WRITERS' CONFERENCE. We have several major events each year, such as a one-day intensive with a single speaker, a weekend sleepover retreat, and a conference with a combination of editors, agents and an art director. It's a great way for our local members to make personal contact with publishing professionals such as editors and agents.

WHAT MAKES YOU DO WHAT YOU DO? When I moved to New Mexico, volunteering was a way for me to meet new people and get involved with the writing community, through an organization I knew and loved. Seeing people blossom within the SCBWI community makes it worthwhile.

HOW WOULD YOU DESCRIBE THE MAKEUP OF YOUR CHAPTER? With about 200 members, we are considered a midsize chapter. Fortunately, the majority of members are clustered in the Albuquerque/Santa Fe area where we have our large events, though we do serve outlying regions including El Paso, Texas, with small monthly meetings. Members range from multi-published professionals to newcomers wondering what to do with their first idea. The community welcomes everyone, and many friendships have developed.

WHAT'S YOUR SINGLE BEST PIECE OF ADVICE FOR A NEW WRITER OR ILLUSTRATOR? Rushing toward publication usually leads to disappointment, so enjoy the journey, rather than focusing on the end goal.

KIM BAKER: WESTERN WASHINGTON

TELL US ABOUT YOUR RECURRING WRITERS' CONFERENCE. We put on a few events a year, but our annual conference is the largest. With over 400 attendees, it's a favorite for regional members and out-of-towners alike. We always try to have a mix of wonderful faculty and sessions that cater to attendees with a wide variety of interests and experience. We aim to have something for everyone, and to cover new ground every year. We have a mix of editors, agents, art directors, authors and illustrators presenting annually, but we've also brought in publicists, social media experts, librarians, booksellers—it's a great opportunity to cover relevant topics to our industry. And the camaraderie that you feel when you come together with like-minded people—there's nothing else like it.

WHAT MAKES YOU DO WHAT YOU DO? I know that I would never have found my way to publication without the SCBWI and I want to give back to honor that. Plus, I just love our community!

HOW WOULD YOU DESCRIBE THE MAKEUP OF YOUR CHAPTER? SCBWI Western Washington is one of the largest regions and we continue to see steady growth. We have a very strong community of savvy authors and illustrators with newbies joining all the time. We're fortunate that most of our published members tend to stay involved with the community. We want to offer resources for the brand new writers and the published alike, and we always try to strike the balance between professional, friendly and fun.

WHAT'S YOUR SINGLE BEST TIP OF ADVICE FOR A NEW WRITER OR ILLUSTRATOR? If you're going to do it, DO IT. Commit yourself to learning the craft, finding your voice, writing, getting feedback, revising, kicking apprehension out of the way and submitting.

SHANNON MORGAN: SOUTHWEST TEXAS

TELL US ABOUT YOUR RECURRING WRITERS' CONFERENCE. Our chapter offers an annual regional conference for writers and illustrators. We want our members to meet acquiring editors and literary agents—hearing firsthand advice and market information from those professionals, and getting inspired to tackle that dream project.

WHAT MAKES YOU DO WHAT YOU DO? My favorite aspect of serving as a regional advisor is being in a position to bring great learning opportunities to our chapter members. I focus on craft development because I believe that honing our crafts as illustrators and writers is one of the few aspects of our careers we can control.

HOW WOULD YOU DESCRIBE THE MAKEUP OF YOUR CHAPTER? Southwest Texas is a small chapter (about 100 members) that has begun to grow recently. Our members are curious, friendly, generous and eager to learn how publishing is changing.

WHAT'S YOUR SINGLE BEST PIECE OF ADVICE FOR A NEW WRITER OR ILLUSTRATOR? Do your homework. By that, I mean two things: (1) work to develop your craft, committing to continual improvement through drafting, analysis, critique and revision, and (2) get to know the publishing industry, understanding that it's first and foremost a business, that its models are changing, and that the professionals working in publishing have different goals and requirements to serve their portion of a voracious worldwide readership.

CLAUDIA PEARSON: SOUTHERN BREEZE (AL, GA, MS)

WHAT MAKES YOU DO WHAT YOU DO? I love working with people and am fascinated by the role children's literature plays in shaping our society. It is much more important than most adults think. It is also a more complicated business than most people think, and I enjoy interacting with professionals in the field. With all the changes coming to publishing, this is an exciting time to be involved.

WHAT'S YOUR SINGLE BEST PIECE OF ADVICE FOR A NEW WRITER OR ILLUSTRATOR? Learn about the business of publishing books for children, and remember it is a business.

CARLA SHANK: OKINAWA

TELL US ABOUT YOUR RECURRING WRITERS' CONFERENCE. No conference, but occasionally we do have speakers. We have had visits from Jen McVeity from Australia, Bobi Martin from Arizona, and Jan Brett was here for two years in a row! These community presentations take a tremendous amount of planning. It is worthwhile because we have the opportunity to learn from published authors all the refinement and skills needed to get our stories ready for publication.

WHAT MAKES YOU DO WHAT YOU DO? It is so rewarding to help writers learn the ins and outs of publishing. I like to be in the midst of writers where stories are born. I like the collegiality. There are surprising changes in the world of publishing happening daily and I want to keep up with the trends.

HOW WOULD YOU DESCRIBE THE MAKEUP OF YOUR CHAPTER? We are in the processing of reorganizing our chapter, and are anxious to meet new writers in the community.

WHAT'S YOUR SINGLE BEST PIECE OF ADVICE FOR A NEW WRITER OR ILLUSTRATOR? Learn the business end of publishing, since you already have the creative end covered—e.g. how to get an agent, how to do the best query to promote your work, how to do your taxes and so on. Learn the steps to the printed page with your name on the cover!

LINDA RODRIGUEZ BERNFELD: FLORIDA

TELL US ABOUT YOUR RECURRING WRITERS' CONFERENCE. I put on two major events. We have our three-day Florida Regional Conference in January and we have our Mid-Year Workshop in June in Disney World. We have been lucky enough to bring in terrific and well-known writers as well as top editors and agents to our January conference. The January conference and the June workshop have very different formats. Our conferences generally draw 175-200 people—so they are big enough that we can bring in 8-10 speakers but small enough so that people don't feel overwhelmed.

WHAT MAKES YOU DO WHAT YOU DO? Not only do I love organizing events, I get great joy in knowing that in an indirect way, I've helped a lot of people, many of them close friends, become published. It makes me so happy when someone e-mails me to tell me they signed with an agent they met at one of my conferences or that they revised a book based on what they learned at the June workshop and then they were able to go and sell that book.

HOW WOULD YOU DESCRIBE THE MAKEUP OF YOUR CHAPTER? Our group is fun and friendly but also hardworking. My membership is in the 800 plus range but we're very spread out so when we do come together in January and June, it's like a reunion. But I think the Florida members go out of their way to welcome new people. We want everyone to feel comfortable.

WHAT'S YOUR SINGLE BEST PIECE OF ADVICE FOR A NEW WRITER OR ILLUSTRATOR? Read, read, read and then go and read to kids. It makes you see books in very different way. You'll understand why publishers are asking for shorter picture books.

KRISTIN AKER HOWELL: SAN FRANCISCO SOUTH

TELL US ABOUT YOUR RECURRING WRITERS' CONFERENCE. We host a yearly Golden Gate Conference at Asilomar. Next year (2013) will mark our 30th. People come back year after year for inspiration and connection. We eat all our meals together, hear presentations, have critiques, beach walks and parties by the fire for two and a half days. It's a great opportunity to get to know other professionals in the industry.

HOW WOULD YOU DESCRIBE THE MAKEUP OF YOUR CHAPTER? I'd describe San Francisco South as a creative, curious and ambitious chapter. Our region includes Silicon Valley, so naturally we have a lot of interest and proficiency in technology.

WHAT'S YOUR SINGLE BEST PIECE OF ADVICE FOR A NEW WRITER OR ILLUSTRATOR? Read more.

ALICE MCGINTY: ILLINOIS

TELL US ABOUT YOUR RECURRING WRITERS' CONFERENCE. Our events offer an educational opportunity to learn from editors, authors and agents. It also gives them an opportunity to learn from each other and with each other.

WHAT MAKES YOU DO WHAT YOU DO? I got great benefits as a participant in events and knew how helpful it was and also liked the group of people who held positions of responsibility in Illinois SCBWI and wanted to be a part of leadership.

HOW WOULD YOU DESCRIBE THE MAKEUP OF YOUR CHAPTER? Our chapter is very established, large and supportive. We are both professional and friendly.

WHAT'S YOUR SINGLE BEST PIECE OF ADVICE FOR A NEW WRITER OR ILLUSTRATOR? Use books as teachers—study what is being published.

SYDNEY SALTER HUSSEMAN: UTAH/SOUTHERN IDAHO

TELL US ABOUT YOUR RECURRING WRITERS' CONFERENCE. We put on yearly events in Boise and Salt Lake City, along with other smaller events. I like to think that we bring New York out west for our events, offering our members important opportunities to network and learn from industry professionals.

WHAT MAKES YOU DO WHAT YOU DO? I love the writing community that SCBWI has created, not only in my region, but all over the world. Helping to make that happen is an incredible opportunity—and worth all the hours. I've also enjoyed watching my members' publishing dreams come true, especially when a talented writer signs with an agent from one of my events, or when someone gets a critique from an editor that later turns into a manuscript sale.

HOW WOULD YOU DESCRIBE THE MAKEUP OF YOUR CHAPTER? We're a small, cozy region, separated by miles of desert between our main population centers. We have passionate writers and illustrators dedicated to honing their craft so we do lots of carpooling between states!

WHAT'S YOUR SINGLE BEST PIECE OF ADVICE FOR A NEW WRITER OR ILLUSTRATOR? Learn to love revision.

SALLY RILEY: SOUTHERN NEW ENGLAND

TELL US ABOUT YOUR RECURRING WRITERS' CONFERENCE. We have one very large annual spring conference for all six New England states. The three RAs join in to help the conference directors for this event. In addition, we have several annual (recurring) smaller events (workshops, retreats, etc.) in our individual regions. The advantage of the larger conference (over 500 attendees), is that we can offer a wealth of inspiring keynote speakers, educational workshops and social events for networking.

WHAT MAKES YOU DO WHAT YOU DO? I have found it to be very exciting and rewarding. I love interacting with the other regional leaders. This networking is inspiring, not only for my job as RA, but for my writing as well. All in all, I have found I get a great deal more than I give.

HOW WOULD YOU DESCRIBE THE MAKEUP OF YOUR CHAPTER? New England is so large in size and number of members (we have one-tenth of all SCBWI members worldwide), that we've been sub-divided into 3 regions: Southern New England (RI and CT), Central New England (MA), and Northern New England (ME, NH, and VT). We have a great number of very experienced and generous writers and illustrators, willing to share their expertise with others.

WHAT'S YOUR SINGLE BEST PIECE OF ADVICE FOR A NEW WRITER OR ILLUSTRATOR? Find a critique group (in person or online) in order to get feedback on your writing and/or illustrating. Judging your own work is very difficult, and a critique group is one of the best ways to improve your craft.

VICTORIA A. SELVAGGIO: NORTHERN OHIO

TELL US ABOUT YOUR RECURRING WRITERS' CONFERENCE. It's a wonderful opportunity for those just beginning in the publishing industry and also for those who have already been successful. Our conference allows participants the availability to network with editors/agents/art directors/published authors and illustrators throughout the conference. We also have monthly events and critique meetings.

WHAT MAKES YOU DO WHAT YOU DO? I do it because I've seen firsthand through my own experiences, how valuable this organization is. I'm passionate about helping others. Also, having the opportunities to meet the people I've met, the opportunities to learn the information I've learned, and to see the result in my own writing excel—it's priceless.

HOW WOULD YOU DESCRIBE THE MAKEUP OF YOUR CHAPTER? We are growing with about 300 members. We have meetings that can be business-minded but we are always friendly, fun and open to experiencing activities that teach, motivate and inspire—while not providing extra stress.

WHAT'S YOUR SINGLE BEST PIECE OF ADVICE FOR A NEW WRITER OR ILLUSTRATOR? Be prepared to work long, hard hours—but remember that connecting with your reader through your manuscript/illustration is the single best reward you can ever wish for.

PAT EASTON: WESTERN PENNSYLVANIA

TELL US ABOUT YOUR RECURRING WRITERS' CONFERENCE. We have a conference in November, and a weekend-long retreat in April. We work hard to make sure we are serving the needs of our members, bringing in top writers and/or illustrators, editors, agents and other business professionals.

WHAT MAKES YOU DO WHAT YOU DO? I have been RA for 20 years, and every year I am proud to be part of such a great organization. Children's writers and illustrators, our editors and the agents as well as children's librarians and teachers create a nurturing, focused community dedicated to children, which as far as I'm concerned, makes them the best people in the world.

HOW WOULD YOU DESCRIBE THE MAKEUP OF YOUR CHAPTER? We have a mid-sized group of close to 300. We have many published writers and illustrators who seem to delight in helping our newcomers, so I'd call us very friendly and fun.

WHAT'S YOUR SINGLE BEST PIECE OF ADVICE FOR A NEW WRITER OR ILLUSTRATOR? Join a critique group. Not only will you get good feedback on your work but you'll also learn to be a better critic and ultimately a better self-critic.

MICHELLE PARKER-ROCK (2011 SCBWI MEMBER OF THE YEAR): ARIZONA

TELL US ABOUT YOUR RECURRING WRITERS' CONFERENCE. We put on an annual conference that includes publishers, editors, art directors, agents, marketers, authors, illustrators and other folks in our amazing business. The networking possibilities are a big draw. In fact, the conference actually makes it possible for our participants to have their work evaluated by folks they probably would not have had the chance to meet and it affords them the opportunity to submit their work for a period of time following the event to houses and agencies that might otherwise be closed to them.

WHAT MAKES YOU DO WHAT YOU DO? I love children's literature. SCBWI is also vital as an advisor for its members and as a group that unites writers, illustrators, publishers, editors, agents, librarians, and others around the world who are involved with creating children's literature and a wide variety of content for young people. What's not to love?

HOW WOULD YOU DESCRIBE THE MAKEUP OF YOUR CHAPTER? SCBWI Arizona is a medium-sized steadily growing region that is business-minded, supportive, informative and heart-felt. (And we're fun and friendly, too!)

WHAT'S YOUR SINGLE BEST PIECE OF ADVICE FOR A NEW WRITER OR ILLUSTRATOR? Join and become active in SCBWI.

CHUCK SAMBUCHINO (chucksambuchino.com, @chucksambuchino on Twitter) edits the *Guide to Literary Agents* (guidetoliteraryagents.com/blog) as well as the *Children's Writer's & Illustrator's Market*. His pop-humor books include *How to Survive a Garden Gnome Attack* (film rights optioned by Sony) and *Red Dog / Blue Dog: When Pooches Get Political* (reddog-bluedog.com). Chuck's other writing books include *Formatting & Submitting Your Manuscript, 3rd. Ed.,* as well as *Create Your Writer Platform* (fall 2012). Besides that, he is a husband, guitarist, dog owner, and cookie addict.

GLOSSARY OF INDUSTRY TERMS

AAR. Association of Authors' Representatives.

ABA. American Booksellers Association.

ABC. Association of Booksellers for Children.

ADVANCE. A sum of money a publisher pays a writer or illustrator prior to the publication of a book. It is usually paid in installments, such as one half on signing the contract, one half on delivery of a complete and satisfactory manuscript. The advance is paid against the royalty money that will be earned by the book.

ALA. American Library Association.

ALL RIGHTS. The rights contracted to a publisher permitting the use of material anywhere and in any form, including movie and book club sales, without additional payment to the creator.

ANTHOLOGY. A collection of selected writings by various authors or gatherings of works by one author.

ANTHROPOMORPHIZATION. The act of attributing human form and personality to things not human (such as animals).

ASAP. As soon as possible.

ASSIGNMENT. An editor or art director asks a writer, illustrator or photographer to produce a specific piece for an agreed-upon fee.

B&W. Black and white.

BACKLIST. A publisher's list of books not published during the current season but still in print.

BEA. BookExpo America.

BIENNIALLY. Occurring once every 2 years.

BIMONTHLY. Occurring once every 2 months.

BIWEEKLY. Occurring once every 2 weeks.

BOOK PACKAGER. A company that draws all elements of a book together, from the initial concept to writing and marketing strategies, then sells the book package to a book publisher and/or movie producer. Also known as book producer or book developer.

BOOK PROPOSAL. Package submitted to a publisher for consideration usually consisting of a synopsis and outline as well as sample chapters.

BUSINESS-SIZE ENVELOPE. Also known as a #10 envelope. The standard size used in sending business correspondence.

CAMERA-READY. Refers to art that is completely prepared for copy camera platemaking.

CAPTION. A description of the subject matter of an illustration or photograph; photo captions include persons' names where appropriate. Also called cutline.

CBC. Children's Book Council.

CLEAN-COPY. A manuscript free of errors and needing no editing; it is ready for typesetting.

CLIPS. Samples, usually from newspapers or magazines, of a writer's published work.

CONCEPT BOOKS. Books that deal with ideas, concepts and large-scale problems, promoting an understanding of what's happening in a child's world. Most prevalent are alphabet and counting books, but also includes books dealing with specific concerns facing young people (such as divorce, birth of a sibling, friendship or moving).

CONTRACT. A written agreement stating the rights to be purchased by an editor, art director or producer and the amount of payment the writer, illustrator or photographer will receive for that sale. (See the article "Running Your Business.")

CONTRIBUTOR'S COPIES. The magazine issues sent to an author, illustrator or photographer in which her work appears.

CO-OP PUBLISHER. A publisher that shares production costs with an author but, unlike subsidy publishers, handles all marketing and distribution. An author receives a high percentage of royalties until her initial investment is recouped, then standard royalties. (*Children's Writer's & Illustrator's Market* does not include co-op publishers.)

COPY. The actual written material of a manuscript.

COPYEDITING. Editing a manuscript for grammar usage, spelling, punctuation and general style.

COPYRIGHT. A means to legally protect an author's/illustrator's/photographer's work. This can be shown by writing the creator's name and the year of the work's creation.

COVER LETTER. A brief letter, accompanying a complete manuscript, especially useful if responding to an editor's request for a manuscript. May also accompany a book proposal.

CUTLINE. See caption.

DIVISION. An unincorporated branch of a company.

DUMMY. A loose mock-up of a book showing placement of text and artwork.

ELECTRONIC SUBMISSION. A submission of material by e-mail or Web form.

FINAL DRAFT. The last version of a polished manuscript ready for submission to an editor.

FIRST NORTH AMERICAN SERIAL RIGHTS. The right to publish material in a periodical for the first time, in the U.S. or Canada. (See the article "Running Your Business.")

F&GS. Folded and gathered sheets. An early, not-yet-bound copy of a picture book.

FLAT FEE. A one-time payment.

GALLEYS. The first typeset version of a manuscript that has not yet been divided into pages.

GENRE. A formulaic type of fiction, such as horror, mystery, romance, fantasy, suspense, thriller, science fiction or Western.

GLOSSY. A photograph with a shiny surface as opposed to one with a non-shiny matte finish.

GOUACHE. Opaque watercolor with an appreciable film thickness and an actual paint layer.

HALFTONE. Reproduction of a continuous tone illustration with the image formed by dots produced by a camera lens screen.

HARD COPY. The printed copy of a computer's output.

HARDWARE. Refers to all the mechanically-integrated components of a computer that are not software—circuit boards, transistors and the machines that are the actual computer.

HI-LO. High interest, low reading level.

HOME PAGE. The first page of a website.

IBBY. International Board on Books for Young People.

IMPRINT. Name applied to a publisher's specific line of books.

INTERNET. A worldwide network of computers that offers access to a wide variety of electronic resources.

IRA. International Reading Association.

IRC. International Reply Coupon. Sold at the post office to enclose with text or artwork sent to a recipient outside your own country to cover postage costs when replying or returning work.

KEYLINE. Identification of the positions of illustrations and copy for the printer.

LAYOUT. Arrangement of illustrations, photographs, text and headlines for printed material.

LINE DRAWING. Illustration done with pencil or ink using no wash or other shading.

MASS MARKET BOOKS. Paperback books directed toward an extremely large audience sold in supermarkets, drugstores, airports, newsstands, online retailers and bookstores.

MECHANICALS. Paste-up or preparation of work for printing.

MIDDLE GRADE OR MID-GRADE. See middle reader.

MIDDLE READER. The general classification of books written for readers approximately ages 9–12. Often called middle grade or mid-grade.

MS (MSS). Manuscript(s).

MULTIPLE SUBMISSIONS. See simultaneous submissions.

NCTE. National Council of Teachers of English.

ONE-TIME RIGHTS. Permission to publish a story in periodical or book form one time only. (See the article "Running Your Business.")

OUTLINE. A summary of a book's contents; often in the form of chapter headings with a descriptive sentence or two under each heading to show the scope of the book.

PACKAGE SALE. The sale of a manuscript and illustrations/photos as a "package" paid for with one check.

PAYMENT ON ACCEPTANCE. The writer, artist or photographer is paid for her work at the time the editor or art director decides to buy it.

PAYMENT ON PUBLICATION. The writer, artist or photographer is paid for her work when it is published.

PICTURE BOOK. A type of book aimed at preschoolers to 8-year-olds that tells a story using a combination of text and artwork, or artwork only.

PRINT. An impression pulled from an original plate, stone, block, screen or negative; also a positive made from a photographic negative.

PROOFREADING. Reading text to correct typographical errors.

QUERY. A letter to an editor or agent designed to capture interest in an article or book you have written or propose to write. (See the article "Before Your First Sale.")

READING FEE. Money charged by some agents and publishers to read a submitted manuscript. (*Children's Writer's & Illustrator's Market* does not include agencies that charge reading fees.)

REPRINT RIGHTS. Permission to print an already published work whose first rights have been sold to another magazine or book publisher. (See the article "Running Your Business.")

RESPONSE TIME. The average length of time it takes an editor or art director to accept or reject a query or submission, and inform the creator of the decision.

RIGHTS. The bundle of permissions offered to an editor or art director in exchange for printing a manuscript, artwork or photographs. (See the article "Running Your Business.")

ROUGH DRAFT. A manuscript that has not been checked for errors in grammar, punctuation, spelling or content.

ROUGHS. Preliminary sketches or drawings.

ROYALTY. An agreed percentage paid by a publisher to a writer, illustrator or photographer for each copy of her work sold.

SAE. Self-addressed envelope.

SASE. Self-addressed, stamped envelope.

SCBWI. The Society of Children's Book Writers and Illustrators.

SECOND SERIAL RIGHTS. Permission for the reprinting of a work in another periodical after its first publication in book or magazine form. (See the article "Running Your Business.")

SEMIANNUAL. Occurring every 6 months or twice a year.

SEMIMONTHLY. Occurring twice a month.

SEMIWEEKLY. Occurring twice a week.

SERIAL RIGHTS. The rights given by an author to a publisher to print a piece in one or more periodicals. (See the article "Running Your Business.")

SIMULTANEOUS SUBMISSIONS. Queries or proposals sent to several publishers at the same time. Also called multiple submissions. (See the article "Before Your First Sale.")

SLANT. The approach to a story or piece of artwork that will appeal to readers of a particular publication.

SLUSH PILE. Editors' term for their collections of unsolicited manuscripts.

SOFTWARE. Programs and related documentation for use with a computer.

SOLICITED MANUSCRIPT. Material that an editor has asked for or agreed to consider before being sent by a writer.

SPAR. Society of Photographers and Artists Representatives.

SPECULATION (SPEC). Creating a piece with no assurance from an editor or art director that it will be purchased or any reimbursements for material or labor paid.

SUBSIDIARY RIGHTS. All rights other than book publishing rights included in a book contract, such as paperback, book club and movie rights. (See the article "Running Your Business.")

SUBSIDY PUBLISHER. A book publisher that charges the author for the cost of typesetting, printing and promoting a book. Also called a vanity publisher. (Note: *Children's Writer's & Illustrator's Market* does not include subsidy publishers.)

SYNOPSIS. A brief summary of a story or novel. Usually a page to a page and a half, singlespaced, if part of a book proposal.

TABLOID. Publication printed on an ordinary newspaper page turned sideways and folded in half.

TEARSHEET. Page from a magazine or newspaper containing your printed art, story, article, poem or photo.

THUMBNAIL. A rough layout in miniature.

TRADE BOOKS. Books sold in bookstores and through online retailers, aimed at a smaller audience than mass market books, and printed in smaller quantities by publishers.

TRANSPARENCIES. Positive color slides; not color prints.

UNSOLICITED MANUSCRIPT. Material sent without an editor's, art director's or agent's request.

VANITY PUBLISHER. See subsidy publisher.

WORK-FOR-HIRE. An arrangement between a writer, illustrator or photographer and a company under which the company retains complete control of the work's copyright. (See the article "Running Your Business.")

YA. See young adult.

YOUNG ADULT. The general classification of books written for readers approximately ages 12–16. Often referred to as YA.

YOUNG READER. The general classification of books written for readers approximately ages 5–8.

NEW AGENT SPOTLIGHTS

Learn about new reps seeking clients.

....

by Chuck Sambuchino

//

One of the most common recurring work blog items I get complimented on (besides my headshot, which my wife has called "semi-dashing … almost") is my "New Agent Alerts," a series where I spotlight new/newer literary reps who are open to queries and looking for clients right now.

This is due to the fact that newer agents are golden opportunities for aspiring authors because they are actively building their client list. They're hungry to sign new clients and start the ball rolling with submissions to editors and books sold. Whereas an established agent with 40 clients may have little to no time to consider new writers' work let alone help them shape it, a newer agent may be willing to sign a promising writer whose work is not a guaranteed huge payday.

THE CONS AND PROS OF NEWER AGENTS

At writing conferences, a frequent question I get is "Is it OK to sign with a new agent?" The question comes about because people value experience, and wonder about the skill of someone who's new to the scene. The concern is an interesting one, so let me try to list out the downsides and upsides to choosing a rep who's in her first few years agenting.

The cons

- They are likely less experienced in contract negotiations.
- They likely know fewer editors at this point than a rep who's been in business a while, meaning there is a less likely chance they can help you get published. This is a big, justified point—and writers' foremost concern.
- They are likely in a weaker position to demand a high advance for you.

- New agents come and some go. This means if your agent is in business for a year or two and doesn't find the success for which they hoped, they could bail on the biz altogether. That leaves you without a home. If you sign with an agent who's been in business for 14 years, however, chances are they won't quit tomorrow.

The pros

- They are actively building their client list—and that means they are anxious to sign new writers and lock in those first several sales.
- They are usually willing to give your work a longer look. They may be willing to work with you on a project to get it ready for submission, whereas a more established agent has lots of clients and no time—meaning they have no spare moments to help you with shaping your novel or proposal.
- With fewer clients under their wing, you should get more attention than you would with an established rep.
- If they've found their calling and don't seem like they're giving up any time soon (and keep in mind, most do continue on as agents), you could have a decades-long relationship that pays off with lots of books.
- Just as they may have little going for them, they also have little going against them. An established agent once told me that a new agent is in a unique position because they have no duds under their belt. Their slate is clean.

HOW CAN YOU DECIDE FOR YOURSELF?

1. FACTOR IN IF THEY'RE PART OF A LARGER AGENCY. Agents share contacts and resources. If your agent is the new girl at an agency with five people, those other four agents will help her (and you) with submissions. In other words, she's new, but not alone.

2. LEARN WHERE THE AGENT CAME FROM. Has she been an apprentice at the agency for two years? Was she an editor for seven years and just switched to agenting? If they already have a few years in publishing under their belt, they're not as green as you may think. Agents don't become agents overnight.

3. ASK WHERE SHE WILL SUBMIT THE WORK. This is a big one. If you fear the agent lacks proper contacts to move your work, ask straight out: "What editors do you see us submitting this book to, and have you sold to them before?" The question tests their plan for where to send the manuscript and get it in print.

4. ASK THEM "WHY SHOULD I SIGN WITH YOU?" This is another straight-up question that gets right to the point. If she's new and has little/no sales at that point, she can't respond with "I sell tons of books and I make it rain cash money!! Dolla dolla bills, y'all!!!" She can't rely on her track record to entice you. So what's her sales pitch? Weigh her enthusiasm, her plan for the book, her promises of hard work and anything else she tells you. In the publishing business, you want communication and enthusiasm from agents (and editors). Both are invaluable. What's the point of signing with a huge agent when they don't return your e-mails and consider your book last on their list of priorities for the day?

5. IF YOU'RE NOT SOLD, YOU CAN ALWAYS SAY NO. It's as simple as that. Always query new/newer agents because, at the end of the day, just because they offer representation doesn't mean you have to accept.

NEW AGENT SPOTLIGHTS ("AGENTS & ART REPS" SECTION)

Peppered throughout this book's large number of agency listings (in the "Agents & Art Reps" listings section) are sporadic "New Agent Alert" sidebars. Look them over to see if these newer reps would be a good fit for your work. Always read personal information and submission guidelines carefully. Don't let an agent reject you because you submitted work incorrectly. Wherever possible, we have included a website address for their agency, as well as their Twitter handle for those reps that tweet.

Also please note that as of when this book went to press in 2012, all these agents were still active and looking for writers. That said, I cannot guarantee every one is still in their respective position when you read this, nor that they have kept their query inboxes open. I urge you to visit agency websites and double check before you query. (This is always a good idea in any case.) Good luck!

CHUCK SAMBUCHINO (chucksambuchino.com, @chucksambuchino on Twitter) edits the *Guide to Literary Agents* (guidetoliteraryagents.com/blog) as well as the *Children's Writer's & Illustrator's Market*. His pop-humor books include *How to Survive a Garden Gnome Attack* (film rights optioned by Sony) and *Red Dog / Blue Dog: When Pooches Get Political* (reddog-bluedog.com). Chuck's other writing books include *Formatting & Submitting Your Manuscript, 3rd. Ed.,* as well as *Create Your Writer Platform* (fall 2012). Besides that, he is a husband, guitarist, dog owner, and cookie addict.

YOUR WRITING CALENDAR

The best way for writers to achieve success is by setting goals. Goals are usually met by writers who give themselves or are given deadlines. Something about having an actual date to hit helps create a sense of urgency in most writers (and editors for that matter). This writing calendar is a great place to keep your important deadlines.

Also, this writing calendar is a good tool for recording upcoming writing events you'd like to attend or contests you'd like to enter. Or use this calendar to block out valuable time for yourself—to just write.

Of course, you can use this calendar to record other special events, especially if you have a habit of remembering to write but of forgetting birthdays or anniversaries. After all, this calendar is now yours. Do with it what you will.

AUGUST 2012

SUN	MON	TUE	WED	THURS	FRI	SAT
			1	2	3	4
5	6	7	8	9	10	11
12	13	14	15	16	17	18
19	20	21	22	23	24	25
26	27	28	29	30	31	

Think big. Establish large, long-term goals.

SEPTEMBER 2012

SUN	MON	TUE	WED	THU	FRI	SAT
						1
2	3	4	5	6	7	8
9	10	11	12	13	14	15
16	17	18	19	20	21	22
23	24	25	26	27	28	29
30						

Break down what steps you need to take to accomplish these long-term goals.

_____

_____

_____

_____

_____

OCTOBER 2012

SUN	MON	TUE	WED	THU	FRI	SAT
	1	2	3	4	5	6
7	8	9	10	11	12	13
14	15	16	17	18	19	20
21	22	23	24	25	26	27
28	29	30	31			

Set monthly writing goals for things such as word count or queries to submit.

NOVEMBER 2012

SUN	MON	TUE	WED	THU	FRI	SAT
				1	2	3
4	5	6	7	8	9	10
11	12	13	14	15	16	17
18	19	20	21	22	23	24
25	26	27	28	29	30	

Write a novel during November as part of NaNoWriMo!

DECEMBER 2012

SUN	MON	TUE	WED	THU	FRI	SAT
						1
2	3	4	5	6	7	8
9	10	11	12	13	14	15
16	17	18	19	20	21	22
23	24	25	26	27	28	29
30	31					

Take the first steps to revise what you wrote during NaNoWriMo.

JANUARY 2013

SUN	MON	TUE	WED	THU	FRI	SAT
		1	2	3	4	5
6	7	8	9	10	11	12
13	14	15	16	17	18	19
20	21	22	23	24	25	26
27	28	29	30	31		

Evaluate your 2011 accomplishments and make 2012 goals.

_____

_____

_____

_____

_____

FEBRUARY 2013

SUN	MON	TUE	WED	THU	FRI	SAT
					1	2
3	4	5	6	7	8	9
10	11	12	13	14	15	16
17	18	19	20	21	22	23
24	25	26	27	28		

Make an effort to find writing friends and peers who can help you edit your work.

MARCH 2013

SUN	MON	TUE	WED	THU	FRI	SAT
					1	2
3	4	5	6	7	8	9
10	11	12	13	14	15	16
17	18	19	20	21	22	23
24	25	26	27	28	29	30
31						

Join a writing organization (perhaps a chapter of SCBWI) or small, local writers group.

APRIL 2013

SUN	MON	TUE	WED	THU	FRI	SAT
	1	2	3	4	5	6
7	8	9	10	11	12	13
14	15	16	17	18	19	20
21	22	23	24	25	26	27
28	29	30				

Try writing poetry for National Poetry Month.

MAY 2013

SUN	MON	TUE	WED	THU	FRI	SAT
			1	2	3	4
5	6	7	8	9	10	11
12	13	14	15	16	17	18
19	20	21	22	23	24	25
26	27	28	29	30	31	

Plan to attend a writing conference this summer. Have work(s) ready to pitch.

JUNE 2013

SUN	MON	TUE	WED	THU	FRI	SAT
						1
2	3	4	5	6	7	8
9	10	11	12	13	14	15
16	17	18	19	20	21	22
23	24	25	26	27	28	29
30						

When your work is revised, start the query process. Query 6-10 markets at first.

JULY 2013

SUN	MON	TUE	WED	THU	FRI	SAT
	1	2	3	4	5	6
7	8	9	10	11	12	13
14	15	16	17	18	19	20
21	22	23	24	25	26	27
28	29	30	31			

Evaluate the submission process. If you're hitting a wall, tweak your query and first pages.

_____

_____

_____

_____

_____

AUGUST 2013

SUN	MON	TUE	WED	THU	FRI	SAT
				1	2	3
4	5	6	7	8	9	10
11	12	13	14	15	16	17
18	19	20	21	22	23	24
25	26	27	28	29	30	31

Get involved in social media. Set goals. Start a blog now, and join Twitter next month.

SEPTEMBER 2013

SUN	MON	TUE	WED	THU	FRI	SAT
1	2	3	4	5	6	7
8	9	10	11	12	13	14
15	16	17	18	19	20	21
22	23	24	25	26	27	28
29	30					

Keep a comprehensive file of all your writing ideas, from book concepts to character quirks.

_____

_____

_____

_____

_____

OCTOBER 2013

SUN	MON	TUE	WED	THU	FRI	SAT
		1	2	3	4	5
6	7	8	9	10	11	12
13	14	15	16	17	18	19
20	21	22	23	24	25	26
27	28	29	30	31		

Remember to back up all your writing on disc or through e-mail.

NOVEMBER 2013

SUN	MON	TUE	WED	THU	FRI	SAT
					1	2
3	4	5	6	7	8	9
10	11	12	13	14	15	16
17	18	19	20	21	22	23
24	25	26	27	28	29	30

Good writers read. Set a goal of reading at least two books a month.

DECEMBER 2013

SUN	MON	TUE	WED	THU	FRI	SAT
1	2	3	4	5	6	7
8	9	10	11	12	13	14
15	16	17	18	19	20	21
22	23	24	25	26	27	28
29	30	31				

Reward yourself for good work. Celebrate successes, big and small.

BOOK PUBLISHERS

///

There's no magic formula for getting published. It's a matter of getting the right manuscript on the right editor's desk at the right time. Before you submit it's important to learn publishers' needs, see what kind of books they're producing and decide which publishers your work is best suited for. *Children's Writer's & Illustrator's Market* is but one tool in this process. (Those just starting out, turn to Quick Tips for Writers & Illustrators.)

To help you narrow down the list of possible publishers for your work, we've included several indexes at the back of this book. The **Subject Index** lists book and magazine publishers according to their fiction and nonfiction needs or interests. The **Age-Level Index** indicates which age groups publishers cater to. The **Photography Index** indicates which markets buy photography for children's publications. The **Poetry Index** lists publishers accepting poetry.

If you write contemporary fiction for young adults, for example, and you're trying to place a book manuscript, go first to the Subject Index. Locate the fiction categories under Book Publishers and copy the list under Contemporary. Then go to the Age-Level Index and highlight the publishers on the Contemporary list that are included under the Young Adults heading. Read the listings for the highlighted publishers to see if your work matches their needs.

Remember, *Children's Writer's & Illustrator's Market* should not be your only source for researching publishers. Here are a few other sources of information:

- The Society of Children's Book Writers and Illustrators (SCBWI) offers members an annual market survey of children's book publishers for the cost of postage or free online at scbwi.org. (SCBWI membership information can also be found at scbwi.org.)

- The Children's Book Council website (cbcbooks.org) gives information on member publishers.
- If a publisher interests you, send a SASE for submission guidelines or check publishers' websites for guidelines *before* submitting. To quickly find guidelines online, visit the Colossal Directory of Children's Publishers at www.signaleader.com.
- Check publishers' websites. Many include their complete catalogs that you can browse. Web addresses are included in many publishers' listings.
- Spend time at your local bookstore to see who's publishing what. While you're there, browse through *Publishers Weekly* and *The Horn Book*.

SUBSIDY & SELF-PUBLISHING

Some determined writers who receive rejections from royalty publishers may look to subsidy and co-op publishers as an option for getting their work into print. These publishers ask writers to pay all or part of the costs of producing a book. We strongly advise writers and illustrators to work only with publishers who pay them. For this reason, we've adopted a policy not to include any subsidy or co-op publishers in *Children's Writer's & Illustrator's Market* (or any other Writer's Digest Books market books).

If you're interested in publishing your book just to share it with friends and relatives, self-publishing is a viable option, but it involves time, energy, and money. You oversee all book production details. Check with a local printer for advice and information on cost or check online for print-on-demand publishing options (which are often more affordable).

Whatever path you choose, keep in mind that the market is flooded with submissions, so it's important for you to hone your craft and submit the best work possible. Competition from thousands of other writers and illustrators makes it more important than ever to research publishers before submitting—read their guidelines, look at their catalogs, check out a few of their titles and visit their websites.

ABBEVILLE FAMILY

Abbeville Press, 137 Varick St., New York NY 10013. (212)366-5585. **Fax:** (212)366-6966. **E-mail:** cvance@abbeville.com. **Website:** www.abbeville.com. **Contact:** Cynthia Vance, ms/art acquisitions/director. Publishes 8 titles/year. 10% of books from first-time authors.

○ *Not accepting unsolicited mss.*

FICTION Picture books: animal, anthology, concept, contemporary, fantasy, folktales, health, hi-lo, history, humor, multicultural, nature/environment, poetry, science fiction, special needs, sports, suspense. Average word length 300-1,000 words.

HOW TO CONTACT Please refer to website for submission policy. If you wish to have your ms or materials returned, SASE with proper postage must be included.

ILLUSTRATION Works with approx 2-4 illustrators/year. Uses color artwork only.

PHOTOGRAPHY Buys stock and assigns work.

ABRAMS BOOKS FOR YOUNG READERS

115 W. 18th St., 6th Floor, New York NY 10011. **Website:** www.abramsyoungreaders.com.

○ Abrams no longer accepts unsolicited manuscripts or queries. Abrams title *365 Penguins*, by Jean-Luc Fromental, illustrated by Joelle Joliuet, won a Boston Globe-Horn Book Picture Book Honor Award in 2007. Abrams also publishes Laurent De Brunhoff, Graeme Base, and Laura Numeroff, among others.

NONFICTION For nonfiction picture books (20 pages maximum), submit entire ms. For books over 20 pages, submit table of contents, sample chapter, and chapter-by-chapter synopsis. "If other books already exist on the subject, provide the title, author, publisher, and year of copyright for competing books and explain how your work differs."

ILLUSTRATION Illustrations only: Do not submit original material; copies only. Contact: Chad Beckerman, art director.

○ ABSEY & CO.

23011 Northcrest Dr., Spring TX 77389. (281)257-2340. **E-mail:** abseyandco@aol.com; info@absey.biz. **Website:** www.absey.biz. **Contact:** Edward Wilson, editor-in-chief. "We accept mainstream fiction and nonfiction, poetry, educational books, especially those dealing in language arts. We do not accept e-mail submissions of manuscripts. Submit: A brief cover letter; a chapter by chapter outline; an author's information sheet (please focus on relevant qualifications and previous publishing experience); two or three sample chapters; SASE."

HOW TO CONTACT Responds to mss in 6-9 months.

TIPS Absey publishes a few titles every year. We like the author and the illustrator working together to create something magical. Authors and illustrators have input into every phase of production."

Ⓐ ○ ACTION PUBLISHING

P.O. Box 391, Glendale CA 91209. (323)478-1667. **Fax:** (323)478-1767. **Website:** www.actionpublishing.com.

○ *Acquires titles primarily through agents. Guidelines for unsolicited mss available online.*

FICTION Picture book: fantasy. Middle readers: adventure. Recently published The Family of Ree series, by Scott E. Sutton.

ILLUSTRATION Works with 2-4 illustrators/year. Reviews illustration packages from artists. Send samples. Send promotional literature. Responds only if interested. Samples returned with SASE or kept on file if interested and OK with illustrator.

PHOTOGRAPHY Buys stock and assigns work. "We use photos on an as-needed basis. Mainly publicity, advertising and copy work." Uses 35mm or 4×5 transparencies. Submit cover letter and promo piece.

TERMS Pays authors royalty based on wholesale price. Offers advances against royalties.

TIPS "We use a small number of photos. Promo is kept on file for reference if potential interest. If you are sending a book proposal, send query letter first with web link to sample photos if available."

ALADDIN/PULSE

1230 Avenue of the Americas, 4th Floor, New York NY 10020. (212)698-2707. **Fax:** (212)698-7337. **Website:** www.simonsays.com. **Contact:** Bethany Buck, vice president/publisher (Aladdin/Pulse); Liesa Abrams, executive editor (Aladdin); Emily Lawrence, associate editor (Aladdin); Alyson Heller, assistant editor (Aladdin); Jennifer Klonsky, editorial director (Pulse); Anica Rissi, executive editor (Pulse); Annette Pollert, associate editor (Pulse). Aladdin publishes picture books, beginning readers, chapter books, middle grade and tween fiction and nonfiction, and graphic novels and nonfiction in hardcover and paperback, with an emphasis on commercial, kid-friendly titles. Pulse publishes original teen series, single-title fiction, and select nonfiction, in hardcover and paperback. Publishes hardcover/paperback imprints of Simon & Schuster Children's Publishing Children's Division.

🔲 *Does not accept unsolicited mss.*

HOW TO CONTACT Accepts query letters with proposals (Aladdin); accepts query letters (Pulse).

AMERICAN PRESS

60 State St., Suite 700, Boston MA 02109. (617)247-0022. **E-mail:** americanpress@flash.net. **Website:** www.americanpresspublishers.com. Publishes college textbooks. Publishes 25 titles/year. 50% of books from first-time authors. 90% from unagented writers.

🔲 "Ms proposals are welcome in all subjects and disciplines."

NONFICTION "We prefer that our authors actually teach courses for which the manuscripts are designed." **HOW TO CONTACT** Query, or submit outline with tentative TOC. *No complete mss.* 350 queries received/year. 100 mss received/year. Responds in 3 months to queries. Publishes book 9 months after acceotance. **TERMS** Pays 5-15% royalty on wholesale price.

AMULET BOOKS

Abrams Books for Young Readers, 115 W. 18th St., New York NY 10001. **Website:** www.amuletbooks.com. **Contact:** Susan Van Metre, vice president/publisher; Tamar Brazis, editorial director; Cecily Kaiser, publishing director. 10% of books from first-time authors.

🔲 *Does not accept unsolicited fiction mss or queries.*

FICTION Middle readers: adventure, contemporary, fantasy, history, science fiction, sports. Young adults/teens: adventure, contemporary, fantasy, history, science fiction, sports, suspense. Recently published *Diary of a Wimpy Kid*, by Jeff Kinney; *The Sisters Grimm*, by Michael Buckley (mid-grade series); *ttyl*, by Lauren Myracle (YA novel); *Heart of a Samurai*, by Margi Preus (Newberry Honor Award winner).

ILLUSTRATION Works with 10-12 illustrators/year. Uses both color and b&w. Query with samples. Contact: Chad Beckerman, creative director. Samples filed.

PHOTOGRAPHY Buys stock images and assigns work.

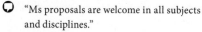

AVALON BOOKS

Thomas Bouregy & Co., Inc., 1202 Lexington Ave., Suite 283, New York NY 10028. (212)598-0222. **Fax:** (212)979-1862. **E-mail:** editorial@avalonbooks.com; avalon@avalonbooks.com. **Website:** www.avalonbooks.com. Publishes hardcover originals. Publishes 60 titles/year.

FICTION "We publish contemporary romances, historical romances, mysteries and westerns. Time period and setting are the author's preference. The historical romances will maintain the high level of reading expected by our readers. The books shall be wholesome fiction, without graphic sex, violence or strong language."

HOW TO CONTACT "We do accept unagented material. We no longer accept e-mail queries. When submitting, include a query letter, a 2-3 page (and no longer) synopsis of the entire ms, and the first three chapters. All submissions must be typed and double spaced. If we think that your novel might be suitable for our list, we will contact you and request that you submit the entire manuscript. Please note that any unsolicited full mss will not be returned. There is no need to send your partial to any specific editor at Avalon. The editors read all the genres that are listed above. Address your letter to The Editors." Responds in 2-3 months to queries. Publishes a book 12-18 months after acceptance.

TERMS Pays 10% royalty. Pays $1,000 advance. Guidelines available online.

TIPS "Avalon Books are geared and marketed for librarians to purchase and distribute."

AVON BOOKS/BOOKS FOR YOUNG READERS

HarperCollins Children's Books, 10 E. 53rd St., New York NY 10022. (212)207-7000. **Website:** www.harperchildrens.com.

🔲 *Avon is not accepting unagented submissions.*

AZRO PRESS

PMB 342, 1704 Llano St. B, Santa Fe NM 87505. (505)989-3272. **Fax:** (505)989-3832. **E-mail:** books@azropress.com; book@cybermesa.com. **Website:** www.azropress.com. **Contact:** Gae Eisenhardt.

🔲 *"Azro Press no longer accepts unsolicited submissions."*

FICTION Picture books: animal, history, humor, nature/environment. Young readers: adventure, animal, hi-lo, history, humor. Average word length: picture books—1,200; young readers—2,000-2,500.

NONFICTION Picture books: animal, geography, history. Young readers: geography, history.

ILLUSTRATION Accepts material from international illustrators. Works with 3 illustrators/year. Uses color and b&w artwork. Reviews ms/illustration packages. Reviews work for future assignments.

TERMS Pays authors royalty of 5-10% based on wholesale price. Pays illustrators by the project ($2,000) or royalty of 5%. Catalog available for #10 SASE and 3 first-class stamps or online.

TIPS "We only consider mss with Southwestern settings and themes, written and illustrated by people who live in the Southwest."

⊕ BAILIWICK PRESS

309 East Mulberry St., Fort Collins CO 80524. (970) 672-4878. **Fax:** (970) 672-4731. **E-mail:** info@bailiwickpress.com. **Website:** www.bailiwickpress.com. "We're a micro-press that produces books and other products that inspire and tell great stories. Our motto is 'books with something to say.' We are now considering submissions, agented and unagented, for children's and young adult fiction. We're looking for smart, funny, and layered writing that kids will clamor for. Illustrated fiction is desired but not required. (Illustrators are also invited to send samples.) Make us laugh out loud, ooh and aah, and cry, 'Eureka!'"

HOW TO CONTACT "Please read the Aldo Zelnick series to determine if we might be on the same page, then fill out our submission form. Please do not send submissions via snail mail. You must complete the online submission form to be considered. If, after completing and submitting the form, you also need to send us an e-mail attachment (such as sample illustrations or excerpts of graphics), you may e-mail them to info@bailiwickpress.com."

ILLUSTRATION Illustrated fiction desired but not required. Send samples.

TIPS "Remember, we're only looking for hysterically funny writing that complements our existing books."

BALZER & BRAY

HarperCollins Children's Books, 10 E. 53rd St., New York NY 10022. **Website:** www.harpercollinschildrens.com. Publishes 10 titles/year.

FICTION Picture books, young readers: adventure, animal, anthology, concept, contemporary, fantasy, history, humor, multicultural, nature/environment, poetry, science fiction, special needs, sports, suspense. Middle readers, young adults/teens: adventure, animal, anthology, contemporary, fantasy, history, humor, multicultural, nature/environment, poetry, science fiction, special needs, sports, suspense.

NONFICTION All levels: animal, biography, concept, cooking, history, multicultural, music/dance, nature/environment, science, self-help, social issues, special needs, sports. "We will publish very few non-fiction titles, maybe 1-2 per year."

HOW TO CONTACT Publishes book 18 months after acceptance.

ILLUSTRATION Works with 10 illustrators/year. Uses both color and b&w. Illustrations only: Send tearsheets to be kept on file. **Contact:** Editor. Responds only if interested. Samples are not returned.

PHOTOGRAPHY Works on assignment only.

TERMS Offers advances. Pays illustrators by the project.

◑ BARRONS EDUCATIONAL SERIES, INC.

250 Wireless Blvd., Hauppauge NY 11788. (800)645-3723. **Fax:** (631)434-3723. **E-mail:** fbrown@barronseduc.com. **Website:** www.barronseduc.com. **Contact:** Wayne R. Barr, manuscript acquisitions.

FICTION Picture books: animal, concept, multicultural, nature/environment. Young readers: adventure, multicultural, nature/environment, fantasy, suspense/mystery. Middle readers: adventure, fantasy, multicultural, nature/environment, problem novels, suspense/mystery. Young adults: problem novels. "Stories with an educational element are appealing."

NONFICTION Picture books: concept, reference. Young readers: biography, how-to, reference, self-help, social issues. Middle readers: hi-lo, how-to, reference, self-help, social issues. Young adults: reference, self-help, social issues, sports.

HOW TO CONTACT Query by mail. Submit outline/synopsis and sample chapters. "Submissions must be accompanied by SASE for response." Responds in 8 months. Publishes book 1 year after acceptance.

ILLUSTRATION Works with 20 illustrators/year. Reviews ms/illustration packages from artists. Query first; 3 chapters of ms with 1 piece of final art, remainder roughs. Illustrations only: Submit tearsheets or slides plus résumé.

TERMS Pays authors royalty of 10-12% based on net price or buys ms outright for $2,000 minimum. Pays illustrators by the project based on retail price. Catalog available for 9×12 SASE. Guidelines available for 9×12 SASE.

TIPS Writers: "We publish pre-school storybooks, concept books and middle grade and YA chapter books. No romance novels. Mss with an educational element are preferred." Illustrators: "We are happy to receive a sample illustration to keep on file for future consideration. Periodic notes reminding us of your work are acceptable." Children's book themes "are becoming much more contemporary and relevant to a child's day-to-day activities, fewer talking animals. We are interested in fiction (ages 7-11 and ages 12-16) dealing with modern problems."

BEHRMAN HOUSE, INC.

11 Edison Place, Springfield NJ 07081. (800)221-2755 or (973)379-7200. **Fax:** (973)379-7280. **Website:** www.behrmanhouse.com. Publishes books on all aspects of Judaism: history, cultural, textbooks, holidays. "Behrman House publishes quality books of Jewish content—history, Bible, philosophy, holidays, ethics—for children and adults." 12% of books from first-time authors.

NONFICTION All levels: Judaism, Jewish educational textbooks. Length: young reader—1,200; middle reader—2,000; young adult—4,000. Recently published *I Kid's Mensch Handbook*, by Scott E. Blumenthal; *Shalom Ivrit 3*, by Nili Ziv.

HOW TO CONTACT Prefers submissions in digital format. Send Word document to Rina Maimon, rina@behrmanhouse.com. Submit outline/synopsis, table of contents, and sample chapters or complete ms. Responds in 1 month to queries; 2 months to mss. Publishes book 18 months after acceptance.

ILLUSTRATION Works with 6 children's illustrators/year. Reviews ms/illustration packages from artists. "Query first." Illustrations only: Query with samples; send unsolicited art samples by mail. Responds to queries in 1 month; mss in 2 months.

PHOTOGRAPHY Purchases photos from freelancers. Buys stock and assigns work. Uses photos of families involved in Jewish activities. Uses color and b&w prints. Photographers should query with samples. Send unsolicited photos by mail. Submit portfolio for review.

TERMS Pays authors royalty of 3-10% based on retail price or buys ms outright for $1,000-5,000. Offers advance. Pays illustrators by the project (range: $500-5,000). Book catalog free on request.

TIPS Looking for "religious school texts" with Judaic themes or general trade Judaica.

Ⓐ Ⓞ BENCHMARK BOOKS

99 White Plains Rd., Tarrytown NY 10591. (914)332-8888. **Fax:** (914)332-1082. **E-mail:** mbisson@marshallcavendish.com. **Website:** www.marshallcavendish.us. **Contact:** Michelle Bisson, manuscript acquisitions. Publishes 300 titles/year.

> *Benchmark Books is not accepting any unsolicited mss at this time. Will consider agented mss.* "We look for interesting treatments of only nonfiction subjects related to elementary, middle school and high school curriculum."

NONFICTION Most nonfiction topics should be curriculum related. Average word length: 4,000-20,000. All books published as part of a series. Recently published Barbarians!, Amazing Machines, Perspectives On.

HOW TO CONTACT "Please read our catalog or view our website before submitting proposals. We only publish series. We do not publish individual titles." Submit outline/synopsis and 1 or more sample chapters. Responds to queries/mss in 3 months. Publishes a book 2 years after acceptance.

PHOTOGRAPHY Buys stock and assigns work.

TERMS Buys work outright. Sends galleys to authors. Book catalog available online. All imprints included in a single catalog.

Ⓐ THE BERKLEY PUBLISHING GROUP

Website: www.us.penguingroup.com/. **Contact:** Leslie Gelbman, president and publisher. The Berkley Publishing Group publishes a variety of general nonfiction and fiction including the traditional categories of romance, mystery and science fiction. Publishes paperback and mass market originals and reprints. Publishes 500 titles/year.

> "Due to the high volume of manuscripts received, most Penguin Group (USA) Inc. imprints do not normally accept unsolicited manuscripts. The preferred and standard method for having manuscripts considered for publication by a major publisher is to submit them through an established literary agent."

FICTION No occult fiction.

NONFICTION No memoirs or personal stories.

HOW TO CONTACT *Prefers agented submissions.*

BETHANY HOUSE

Baker Publishing Group, 6030 E. Fulton Rd., Ada MI 49301. (616)676-9185. **Fax:** (616)676-9573. **Website:** www.bethanyhouse.com. "Bethany House specializes in books that communicate Biblical truth and assist people in both spiritual and practical areas of life. While we do not accept unsolicited queries or proposals via telephone or e-mail, we will consider 1-page queries sent by fax and directed to adult nonfiction, adult fiction, or young adult/children." Publishes hardcover and trade paperback originals, mass market paperback reprints. Publishes 90-100 titles/year. 2% of books from first-time authors. 50% from unagented writers.

⊘ *All unsolicited mss returned unopened.*

HOW TO CONTACT Responds in 3 months to queries. Publishes a book 1 year after acceptance.

TERMS Pays royalty on net price. Pays advance. Book catalog for 9 x 12 envelope and 5 first-class stamps. Guidelines available online.

TIPS "Bethany House Publishers' publishing program relates Biblical truth to all areas of life—whether in the framework of a well-told story, of a challenging book for spiritual growth, or of a Bible reference work. We are seeking high-quality fiction and nonfiction that will inspire and challenge our audience."

○ BIRDSONG BOOKS

1322 Bayview Rd., Middletown DE 19709. (302)378-7274. **Fax:** (302)378-0339. **E-mail:** birdsong@birdsongbooks.com. **Website:** www.birdsongbooks.com. **Contact:** Nancy Carol Willis, president. "Birdsong Books seeks to spark the delight of discovering our wild neighbors and natural habitats. We believe knowledge and understanding of nature fosters caring and a desire to protect the Earth and all living things. Our emphasis is on North American animals and habitats, rather than people."

NONFICTION Picture books, young readers: activity books, animal, nature/environment. Average word length: picture books—800-1,000 plus content for 2-4 pages of back matter. Recently published *The Animals' Winter Sleep*, by Lynda-Graham Barber (age 3-6, nonfiction picture book); *Red Knot: A Shorebird's Incredible Journey*, by Nancy Carol Willis (age 6-9, nonfiction picture book); *Raccoon Moon*, by Nancy Carol Willis (ages 5-8, natural science picture book); *The*

Robins In Your Backyard, by Nancy Carol Willis (ages 4-7, nonfiction picture book).

HOW TO CONTACT Submit complete ms package with SASE. Responds to mss in 3 months. Publishes book 2-3 years after acceptance.

ILLUSTRATION Accepts material from residents of U.S. Works with 1 illustrator/year. Reviews ms/illustration packages from artists. Send ms with dummy (plus samples/tearsheets for style). Illustrations only: Query with brochure, résumé, samples, SASE, or tearsheets. Responds only if interested. Samples returned with SASE.

PHOTOGRAPHY Uses North American animals and habitats (currently wading birds—herons, egrets, and the like). Submit cover letter, résumé, promo piece, stock photo list.

TIPS "We are a small independent press actively seeking manuscripts that fit our narrowly defined niche. We are only interested in nonfiction, natural science picture books or educational activity books about North American animals and habitats. We are not interested in fiction stories based on actual events. Our books include several pages of back matter suitable for early elementary classrooms. Mailed submissions with SASE only. No e-mail submissions or phone calls, please. Cover letters should sell author/illustrator and book idea."

BLACK ROSE WRITING

E-mail: creator@blackrosewriting.com. **Website:** www.blackrosewriting.com. **Contact:** Reagan Rothe. "We publish only one genre—our genre. Black Rose Writing is an independent publishing house that believes in developing a personal relationship with our authors. We don't see them as clients or just another number on a page, but rather as people who we are willing to do whatever it takes to make them satisfied with their publishing choice. We are seeking growth in an array of different genres and searching for new publicity venues for our authors everyday. Black Rose Writing doesn't promise our authors the world, leading them to become overwhelmed by the competitive and difficult venture. We are honest with our authors, and we give them the insight to generate solid leads without wasting their time. Black Rose Writing works with our authors along many lines of promotion, (examples: showcasing your titles at festivals, scheduling book events, and sending out press releases and review copies) and provides a broad distribution that covers many book buyers and allows interested parties access to our titles easily. We want to make our authors' journeys into the publishing world a success and eliminate the fear of a toilsome and lengthy experience." Publishes majority trade paperback, occasional hard cover or children's book. Publishes 75+ titles/year.

○ Online store: www.blackrosewriting books.com

FICTION Considers all genre fiction.

NONFICTION War, biography, autobiography.

HOW TO CONTACT Query via e-mail. Submit synopsis and author bio. Please allow 3-4 weeks for response. Query via e-mail. Submit synopsis and author bio. Please allow 3-4 weeks for response. Responds in 1-2 months to mss.

TERMS Please check submission guidelines before contacting by e-mail.

TIPS "Please query via email first with synopsis and author information. Allow 3-4 weeks for response. Always spell-check and send an edited ms. Do not forward your initial contact e-mails."

Ⓐ BLOOMSBURY CHILDREN'S BOOKS

175 Fifth Ave., New York NY 10010. (646)307-5151. **E-mail:** bloomsbury.kids@bloomsburyusa.com. **Web-site:** www.bloomsburykids.com. Publishes 60 titles/year. 25% of books from first-time authors.

○ No phone calls or e-mails.

FICTION Picture books: adventure, animal, contemporary, fantasy, folktales, history, humor, multicultural, poetry, suspense/mystery. Young readers: adventure, animal, anthology, concept, contemporary, fantasy, folktales, history, humor, multicultural, suspense/mystery. Middle readers: adventure, animal, contemporary, fantasy, folktales, history, humor, multicultural, poetry, problem novels. Young adults: adventure, animal, anthology, contemporary, fantasy, folktales, history, humor, multicultural, problem novels, science fiction, sports, suspense/mystery.

HOW TO CONTACT Query. Submit clips, first 3 chapters. Responds in 6 months to queries; 6 months to ms. Considers unsolicited submissions, but responds only if interested.

TERMS Pays royalty. Pays advance. Book catalog available online. Guidelines available online.

TIPS "All Bloomsbury Children's Books submissions are considered on an individual basis. Bloomsbury Children's Books will no longer respond to unsolicited manuscripts or art submissions. Please include a telephone and e-mail address where we may contact you if we are interested in your work. Do not send a self-addressed stamped envelope. We regret the inconvenience, but unfortunately, we are too under-staffed to maintain a correspondence with authors. There is no need to send art with a picture book manuscript. Artists should submit art with a picture book manuscript. We do not return art samples. Please do not send us original art! Please note that we do accept simultaneous submissions, but please be courteous and inform us if another house has made an offer on your work. Do not send originals or your only copy of anything. We are not liable for artwork or manuscript submissions. Please address all submissions to the attention of 'Manuscript Submissions'. Please make sure that everything is stapled, paper-clipped, or rubber-banded together. We do not accept e-mail or CD/DVD submissions. Be sure your work is appropriate for us. Familiarize yourself with our list by going to bookstores or libraries."

○ BRIGHT RING PUBLISHING, INC.

P.O. Box 31338, Bellingham WA 98228. (360)592-9201. **Fax:** (360)592-4503. **E-mail:** maryann@brightring.com. **Website:** www.brightring.com. **Contact:** MaryAnn Kohl, editor.

○ *Bright Ring is no longer accepting ms or illustration submissions.*

CALKINS CREEK

Boyds Mills Press, 815 Church St., Honesdale PA 18431. **Website:** www.calkinscreekbooks.com. "We aim to publish books that are a well-written blend of creative writing and extensive research, which emphasize important events, people, and places in U.S. history."

FICTION All levels: history. Recently published *Healing Water*, by Joyce Moyer Hostetter (ages 10 and up, historical fiction); *The Shakeress*, by Kimberly Heuston (ages 12 and up, historical fiction).

NONFICTION All levels: history. Recently published *Farmer George Plants a Nation*, by Peggy Thomas (ages 8 and up, nonfiction picture book); *Robert H. Jackson*, by Gail Jarrow (ages 10 and up, historical biography).

HOW TO CONTACT Submit outline/synopsis and 3 sample chapters.

ILLUSTRATION Accepts material from international illustrators. Works with 25 (for all Boyds Mills Press imprints) illustrators/year. Uses both color and b&w. Reviews ms/illustration packages. For ms/illustration packages: Submit ms with 2 pieces of final art. Submit ms/illustration packages to address above, label package "Manuscript Submission." Reviews work for future assignments. If interested in illustrating future titles, query with samples. Submit samples to address above. Label package "Art Sample Submission."

PHOTOGRAPHY Buys stock images and assigns work. Submit photos to: address above, label package "Art Sample Submission." Uses color or b&w 8×10 prints. For first contact, send promo piece (color or b&w).

TERMS Pays authors royalty or work purchased outright. Guidelines available on website.

TIPS "Read through our recently published titles and review our catalog. When selecting titles to publish, our emphasis will be on important events, people, and places in U.S. history. Writers are encouraged to submit a detailed bibliography, including secondary and primary sources, and expert reviews with their submissions."

CANDLEWICK PRESS

99 Dover St., Somerville MA 02144. (617)661-3330. **Fax:** (617)661-0565. **E-mail:** bigbear@candlewick. com. **Website:** www.candlewick.com. **Contact:** Deb Wayshak, executive editor (fiction); Joan Powers, editor-at-large (picture books); Liz Bicknell, editorial director/associate publisher (poetry, picture books, fiction); Mary Lee Donovan, executive editor (picture books, nonfiction/fiction); Hilary Van Dusen, senior editor (nonfiction/fiction); Sarah Ketchersid, senior editor (board, toddler); Joan Powers, editor-at-large. "Candlewick Press publishes high-quality, illustrated children's books for ages infant through young adult. We are a truly child-centered publisher." Candlewick title *Good Masters! Sweet Ladies!: Voices from a Medieval Village*, by Amy Schlits, illustrated by Robert Byrd, won the John Newbery Medal in 2008. Their title *Twelve Rounds to Glory: The Story of Muhammad Ali*, by Charles R. Smith, Jr., illustrated by Bryan Collier, won a Coretta Scott King Author Honor Award in 2008. Their title *The Astonishing Life of Octavian Nothing*, by M.T. Anderson, won the Boston Globe-Horn Book Award in 2007. Publishes hardcover and trade paperback originals, and reprints. Publishes 200 titles/year. 5% of books from first-time authors.

○ *Candlewick Press is currently not accepting queries or unsolicited mss.*

FICTION Picture books: animal, concept, contemporary, fantasy, history, humor, multicultural, nature/environment, poetry. Middle readers, young adults: contemporary, fantasy, history, humor, multicultural, poetry, science fiction, sports, suspense/mystery.

NONFICTION Picture books: concept, biography, geography, nature/environment. Young readers: biography, geography, nature/environment.

HOW TO CONTACT "We do not accept editorial queries or submissions online. If you are an author or illustrator and would like us to consider your work, please read our submissions policy (online) to learn more."

ILLUSTRATION Works with approx. 40 illustrators/year. "We prefer to see a range of styles from artists along with samples showing strong characters (human or animals) in various settings with various emotions."

TERMS Pays authors royalty of 2½-10% based on retail price. Offers advance.

TIPS *"We no longer accept unsolicited mss. See our website for further information about us."*

CAROLRHODA BOOKS, INC.

1251 Washington Ave. N., Minneapolis MN 55401. **Website:** www.lernerbooks.com. "We will continue to seek targeted solicitations at specific reading levels and in specific subject areas. The company will list these targeted solicitations on our website and in national newsletters, such as the SCBWI Bulletin."

○ *Lerner Publishing Group no longer accepts unsolicited mss to any of their imprints except Kar-Ben Publishing.*

ILLUSTRATION Send samples with résumé.

PHOTOGRAPHY "With your submission, please include descriptive information about your image collection and your usage rates."

CARTWHEEL BOOKS

557 Broadway, New York NY 10012. **Website:** www. scholastic.com. **Contact:** Rotem Moscovich, editor; Jeffrey Salane, editor; Daniel Moreton, executive art director. Publishes 100 titles/year.

○ *Cartwheel Books is no longer accepting unsolicited mss. All unsolicited materials will be returned unread.*

FICTION Picture books, young readers: seasonal/holiday, humor, family/love. Average word length: picture books—100-500; easy readers—100-1,500.

NONFICTION Picture books, young readers: seasonal/curricular topics involving animals (polar animals, ocean animals, hibernation), nature (fall leaves, life cycles, weather, solar system), history (first Thanksgiving, MLK Jr., George Washington, Columbus). "Most of our nonfiction is either written on assignment or is within a series. We do not want to see any arts/crafts or cooking." Average word length: picture books—100-1,500; young readers—100-2,000.

HOW TO CONTACT For previously published or agented authors, submit complete ms. SASE required with all submissions. Responds in 6 months to mss. Publishes a book 2 years after acceptance.

ILLUSTRATION Works with 30 illustrators/year. Reviews illustration packages from artists. Illustrations only: Query with samples; arrange personal portfolio review; send promo sheet, tearsheets to be kept on file. Contact: Creative Director. Responds in 6 months. Samples returned with SASE; samples filed. Please do not send original artwork.

PHOTOGRAPHY Buys stock and assigns work. Uses photos of kids, families, vehicles, toys, animals. Submit published samples, color promo piece.

TERMS Pays advance against royalty or flat fee.

TIPS "With each Cartwheel list, we seek a pleasing balance of board books and novelty books, hardcover picture books and gift books, nonfiction, paperback storybooks and easy readers. Cartwheel seeks to acquire projects that speak to young children and their world: new and exciting novelty formats, fresh seasonal and holiday stories, curriculum/concept-based titles, and books for beginning readers. Our books are inviting and appealing, clearly marketable, and have inherent educational and social value. We strive to provide the earliest readers with relevant and exciting books that will ultimately lead to a lifetime of reading, learning, and wondering. Know what types of books we do. Check out bookstores or catalogs first to see where your work would fit best, and why."

○○◐◑ MARSHALL CAVENDISH CHILDREN'S BOOKS

99 White Plains Rd., Tarrytown NY 10591. (914)332-8888. **Fax:** (914)332-1082. **Website:** www.marshall-cavendish.us. **Contact:** Margery Cuyler, publisher. "Marshall Cavendish is an international publisher that publishes books, directories, magazines and digital platforms. Our philosophy of enriching life through knowledge transcends boundaries of geography and culture. In line with this vision, our products reach across the globe in 13 languages, and our publishing network spans Asia and the USA. Our brands have garnered international awards for educational excellence, and they include Marshall Cavendish Reference, Marshall Cavendish Benchmark, Marshall Cavendish Children, Marshall Cavendish Education and Marshall Cavendish Editions. Several have also achieved household-name status in the international market. We ceaselessly explore new avenues to convey our products to the world, with our extensive variety of genres, languages and formats. In addition, our strategy of business expansion has ensured that the reach and benefits of Marshall Cavendish's products extend across the globe, especially into previously uncharted markets in China and Eastern Europe. Our aspiration to further the desire for lifelong learning and self-development continues to guide our efforts." Publishes 60-70 titles/year.

Marshall Cavendish is no longer accepting unsolicited mss. However, the company will continue to consider agented mss.

TERMS Pays authors/illustrators advance and royalties.

○ CHARLESBRIDGE

85 Main St., Watertown MA 02472. (617)926-0329. **Fax:** (800)926-5775. **E-mail:** tradeeditorial@charlesbridge.com. **Website:** www.charlesbridge.com. Publishes 60% nonfiction, 40% fiction picture books and early chapter books. Publishes nature, science, multicultural, social studies, and fiction picture books and transitional "bridge books" (books ranging from early readers to middle grade chapter books).

FICTION Picture books and chapter books: "Strong, realistic stories with enduring themes." Considers the following categories: adventure, concept, contemporary, health, history, humor, multicultural, nature/environment, special needs, sports, suspense/mystery. Recently published *The Searcher and Old Tree*, by David McPhail; *Good Dog, Aggie*, by Lori Ries; *The Perfect Sword*, by Scott Goto; *Not So Tall for Six*, by Dianna Hutts Aston; *Wiggle and Waggle*, by Caroline Arnold; *Rickshaw Girl*, by Mitali Perkins.

NONFICTION Picture books and chapter books: animal, biography, careers, concept, geography, health, history, multicultural, music/dance, nature/environment, religion, science, social issues, special needs, hobbies, sports. Average word length: picture books—1,000.

HOW TO CONTACT Send mss as exclusive submission for 3 months. Responds only to mss of interest. Full mss only; no queries. Please do not include a self-addressed stamped envelope. "Exclusive submission" should be written on all envelopes and cover letters.

ILLUSTRATION Works with 5-10 illustrators/year. Uses color artwork only. Illustrations only: Query with samples; provide résumé, tearsheets to be kept on file. "Send no original artwork, please." Responds only if interested. Samples returned with SASE; samples filed. Originals returned at job's completion.

TERMS Pays authors and illustrators in royalties or work purchased outright. Guidelines available for SASE.

TIPS "Charlesbridge publishes picture books and transitional 'bridge books.' We look for fresh and engaging voices and directions in both fiction and nonfiction."

⊕ CHELSEA HOUSE, AN INFOBASE LEARNING COMPANY

132 W. 31st St., 17th Floor, New York NY 10001. (800)322-8755. **Fax:** (917)339-0326. **E-mail:** editorial@factsonfile.com. **Website:** www.chelseahouse.com. **Contact:** Laurie Likoff, editorial director; Justine Ciovacco, managing editor. "Chelsea Clubhouse, our elementary imprint, presents easy-to-read, full-color books for young readers in grades 2 through 5. All books are parts of series. We do not publish stand-alone books. Most series topics are developed by in-house editors, but suggestions are welcome. We prefer authors with a degree or solid experience in science or a history niche. Authors may query with résumé and list of publications." Publishes 300 titles/year. 10% of books from first-time authors.

◐ CHICAGO REVIEW PRESS

814 N. Franklin St., Chicago IL 60610. (312)337-0747. **Fax:** (312)337-5110. **E-mail:** frontdesk@chicagoreviewpress.com. **Website:** www.chicagoreviewpress.com. **Contact:** Cynthia Sherry, publisher; Allison Felus, managing editor. "Chicago Review Press publishes high-quality, nonfiction, educational activity books that extend the learning process through hands-on projects and accurate and interesting text. We look for activity books that are as much fun as they are constructive and informative."

◯ *Chicago Review Press does not publish fiction.*

NONFICTION Young readers, middle readers and young adults: activity books, arts/crafts, multicultural, history, nature/environment, science. "We're interested in hands-on, educational books; anything else probably will be rejected." Length: 144-160 pages. Recently published *Amazing Rubber Band Cars*, by Michael Rigsby (ages 9 and up); *Don't Touch That!*, by Jeff Day, M.D. (ages 7-9); and *Abraham Lincoln for Kids*, by Janis Herbert (ages 9 and up).

HOW TO CONTACT Enclose cover letter and no more than a table of contents and 1-2 sample chapters; prefers not to receive e-mail queries. Responds to queries/mss in 2 months. Publishes a book 1-2 years after acceptance.

ILLUSTRATION Works with 6 illustrators/year. Uses primarily b&w artwork. Reviews ms/illustration packages from artists. Submit 1-2 chapters of ms with corresponding pieces of final art. Illustrations only: Query with samples, résumé. Responds only if interested. Samples returned with SASE.

PHOTOGRAPHY Buys photos from freelancers ("but not often"). Buys stock and assigns work. Wants "instructive photos. We consult our files when we know what we're looking for on a book-by-book basis." Uses b&w prints.

TERMS Pays authors royalty of 7-12% based on retail price. Offers advances of $3,000-6,000. Pays illustrators by the project (range varies considerably). Pays photographers by the project (range varies considerably). Book catalog available for $3. Manuscript guidelines available for $3.

TIPS "We're looking for original activity books for small children and the adults caring for them—new themes and enticing projects to occupy kids' imaginations and promote their sense of personal creativity. We like activity books that are as much fun as they are constructive. Please write for guidelines so you'll know what we're looking for."

CHILDREN'S BRAINS ARE YUMMY (CBAY) BOOKS

P.O. Box 92411, Austin TX 78709. (512)789-1004. **Fax:** (512)473-7710. **E-mail:** madeline@cbaybooks.com; submissions@cbaybooks.com. **Website:** www.cbaybooks.com. **Contact:** Madeline Smoot, publisher. "CBAY Books currently focuses on quality fantasy and science fiction books for the middle grade and teen markets. We do welcome books that mix genres—a fantasy mystery for example—but since our press currently has a narrow focus, all submissions need to have fantasy or science fiction elements to fit in with our list. Starting in 2011, CBAY Books is accepting queries for teen books for original ebook publication. These books can be of any subgenre including mystery, fantasy, science fiction, historical, creative nonfiction, spiritual. Howeber, we are currently interested primarily in speculative fiction." Publishes 8 titles/year. 30% of books from first-time authors. 0% from unagented writers.

◯ *Currently considers only submissions for teen books.*

HOW TO CONTACT Accepts international material. All submissions must be electronic. Queries should be sent to submissions@cbaybooks.com and include cover letter and first 3,000 words. "We will not open anything with an attachment." Submit outline/synopsis and 3 sample chapters. Responds in 3 months to mss.
ILLUSTRATION Accepts international material. Works with 0-1 illustrators/year. Uses color artwork only. Reviews artwork. Send manuscripts with dummy. Send résumé and tearsheets. Send samples to Madeline Smoot. Responds to queries only if interested.
PHOTOGRAPHY Buy stock images.
TERMS Pays authors royalty 10%-15% based on wholesale price. Offers advances against royalties. Average amount $500. Brochure and guidelines available online at website.
TIPS "CBAY Books only accepts unsolicited submissions from authors at specific times for specific genres. Please check the website to see if we are accepting books at this time. Manuscripts received when submissions are closed are not read."

CHILD WELFARE LEAGUE OF AMERICA

1726 M St. NW, Suite 500, Washington D.C. 20036. (202)688-4200. **Fax:** (202)833-1689. **E-mail:** books@cwla.org. **Website:** www.cwla.org/pubs. CWLA is a privately supported, nonprofit, membership-based organization committed to preserving, protecting, and promoting the well-being of all children and their families. Publishes hardcover and trade paperback originals.
HOW TO CONTACT Submit complete ms and proposal with outline, table of contents, sample chapter, intended audience, and SASE.

TERMS Book catalog and ms guidelines online
TIPS "We are looking for positive, kid-friendly books for ages 3-9. We are looking for books that have a positive message—a feel-good book."

◯ CHRISTIAN ED. WAREHOUSE

2020 State Rd., Camp Hill PA 17011. (800)854-1531. **E-mail:** crogers@cehouse.com. **Website:** www.christianedwarehouse.com. "Christian Ed. Publishers is an independent, nondenominational, evangelical company founded over 50 years ago to produce Christ-centered curriculum materials based on the Word of God for thousands of churches of different denominations throughout the world. Our mission is to introduce children, teens, and adults to a personal faith in Jesus Christ, and to help them grow in their faith and service to the Lord. We publish materials that teach moral and spiritual values while training individuals for a lifetime of Christian service. Currently emphasizing Bible curriculum for preschool-preteen ages, including program and student books and take-home papers—all handled by our assigned freelance writers only. Do not send unsolicited manuscripts. Ask for a writer's application."

◯ Publishes 110 Bible curriculum titles/year.

FICTION Young readers: contemporary. Middle readers: adventure, contemporary, suspense/mystery. "All fiction is on assignment only."
NONFICTION Publishes Bible curriculum and take-home papers for all ages. Recently published *All-Stars for Jesus*, by Lucinda Rollings and Laura Gray, illustrated by Aline Heiser (Bible club curriculum for grades 4-6); *Honeybees Classroom Activity Sheets*, by Janet Miller and Wanda Pelfrey, illustrated by Ron Widman (Bible club curriculum for grades 2-3).
HOW TO CONTACT Responds in 1 month. Publishes assignments 1 year after acceptance.
ILLUSTRATION Works with 2-3 illustrators/year. Query by e-mail. Responds in 1 month. Samples returned with SASE.
TERMS Work purchased outright from authors for 3¢/word. Pays illustrators $18-20/page. Book catalog available for 9×12 SAE and 4 first-class stamps. Ms and art guidelines available for SASE or via e-mail.
TIPS "Read our guidelines carefully before submitting. Do not send unsolicited manuscripts. All writing and illustrating is done on assignment only and must be age-appropriate (preschool-6th grade). Ask for a writer's application."

CHRONICLE BOOKS

680 Second St., San Francisco CA 94107. **Website:** www.chroniclekids.com. (415)537-4200. **E-mail:** frontdesk@chroniclebooks.com

FICTION Picture books, young readers, middle readers, young adults: "We are open to a very wide range of topics." Recently published *Wave,* by Suzy Lee (all ages, picture book); *Ivy and Bean* (series), by Annie Barrows, illustrated by Sophie Blackall (ages 6-10, chapter book).

NONFICTION Picture books, young readers, middle readers, young adults: "We are open to a very wide range of topics." Recently published *Delicious: The Life & Art of Wayne Thiebaud*, by Susan Rubin (ages 9-14, middle grade).

HOW TO CONTACT Submit complete ms (picture books); submit query letter, outline/synopsis and 3 sample chapters (for older readers). Responds in 6 months if interested. Considers simultaneous submissions, "please indicate in letter." Will not consider submissions by fax, e-mail or disk. Do not include SASE; do not send original materials. No submissions will be returned; to confirm receipt, include a SASP.

ILLUSTRATION Works with 40-50 illustrators/year. Wants "unusual art, graphically strong, something that will stand out on the shelves. Fine art, not mass market." Reviews ms/illustration packages from artists. "Indicate if project *must* be considered jointly, or if editor may consider text and art separately." Illustrations only: Submit samples of artist's work (not necessarily from book, but in the envisioned style). Slides, tearsheets and color photocopies OK. (No original art.) Dummies helpful. Résumé helpful. Samples suited to our needs are filed for future reference. Samples not suited to our needs will be recycled. Queries and project proposals responded to in same time frame as author query/proposals."

PHOTOGRAPHY Purchases photos from freelancers. Works on assignment only.

TERMS Generally pays authors in royalties based on retail price, "though we do occasionally work on a flat fee basis." Advance varies. Illustrators paid royalty based on retail price or flat fee. Book catalog for 9×12 SAE and 8 first-class stamps. Ms guidelines for #10 SASE.

TIPS "Chronicle Books publishes an eclectic mixture of traditional and innovative children's books. Our aim is to publish books that inspire young readers to learn and grow creatively while helping them discover the joy of reading. We're looking for quirky, bold artwork and subject matter. We are interested in taking on projects that have a unique bent to them—be it subject matter, writing style, or illustrative technique. As a small list, we are looking for books that will lend us a distinctive flavor. We are also interested in growing our fiction program for older readers, including chapter books, middle grade, and young adult projects."

CLARION BOOKS

Houghton Mifflin Co., 215 Park Ave. S., New York NY 10003. **Website:** www.houghtonmifflinbooks.com; www.hmhco.com. "Clarion Books publishes picture books, nonfiction, and fiction for infants through grade 12. Avoid telling your stories in verse unless you are a professional poet." Publishes hardcover originals for children. Publishes 50 titles/year.

> "We are no longer responding to your unsolicited submission unless we are interested in publishing it. Please do not include a SASE. Submissions will be recycled, and you will not hear from us regarding the status of your submission unless we are interested. We regret that we cannot respond personally to each submission, but we do consider each and every submission we receive."

FICTION Submit complete ms. "Clarion is highly selective in the areas of historical fiction, fantasy, and science fiction. A novel must be superlatively written in order to find a place on the list. Mss that arrive without an SASE of adequate size will not be responded to or returned. Accepts fiction translations."

NONFICTION No unsolicited mss. Query with synopsis, sample chapters and SASE.

HOW TO CONTACT "Please submit exclusively to one HMH imprint." See Houghton Mifflin Harcourt Books for Children. Submit to only one Clarion ediotr. Responds in 3 months. Publishes book 2 years after accepted.

ILLUSTRATION Submit color copies or tearsheets. Do not submit original artwork or slides. "Illustrations that feature children or animals are helpful, but feel free to submit other subject matter." Pays illustrators royalty; flat fee for jacket illustration.

TERMS Pays 5-10% royalty on retail price. Pays minimum of $4,000 advance. Guidelines for #10 SASE or online.

TIPS "Looks for freshness, enthusiasm—in short, life."

CLEAR LIGHT PUBLISHERS

823 Don Diego, Santa Fe NM 87505. (505)989-9590. **Fax:** (505)989-9519. **E-mail:** market@clearlightbooks.com. **Website:** www.clearlightbooks.com/. **Contact:** Harmon Houghton, publisher. "Clear Light publishes books that accurately depict the positive side of human experience and inspire the spirit." Publishes hardcover and trade paperback originals. Publishes 20-24 titles/year. 10% of books from first-time authors. 50% from unagented writers.

NONFICTION Middle readers and young adults: multicultural, American Indian culture, religion and history; Southwestern Americana; Eastern philosophy and religion only.

HOW TO CONTACT Submit complete ms with book proposal and SASE. Guidelines available online. "No e-mail submissions. Authors supply art. Mss not considered without art or artist's renderings." 100 queries received/year. Responds in 3 months to queries. Publishes a book 1 year after acceptance.

ILLUSTRATION Reviews ms/illustration packages from artists. "No originals please." Submit ms with dummy and SASE.

TERMS Pays 10% royalty on wholesale price. Offers advance, a percent of gross potential. Book catalog free. Guidelines available online.

CONCORDIA PUBLISHING HOUSE

3558 S. Jefferson St.., St. Louis MO 63118. (314)268-1000. **Fax:** (314)268-1329. **E-mail:** publicity@cph.org. **Website:** www.cph.org. **Contact:** Rev. Paul T. McCain, publisher and executive director of editorial. "Concordia Publishing House produces quality resources that communicate and nurture the Christian faith and ministry of people of all ages, lay and professional. These resources include curriculum, worship aids, books, and religious supplies. We publish approximately 30 quality children's books each year. We boldly provide Gospel resources that are Christ-centered, Bible-based and faithful to our Lutheran heritage." Publishes hardcover and trade paperback originals.

Concordia is currently not considering children's books.

TERMS Pays authors royalties based on retail price or work purchased outright ($750-2,000). Ms guidelines for 1 first-class stamp and a #10 envelope.

TIPS "Do not send finished artwork with the manuscript. If sketches will help in the presentation of the manuscript, they may be sent. If stories are taken from the Bible, they should follow the Biblical account closely. Liberties should not be taken in fantasizing Biblical stories."

COTEAU BOOKS LTD.

2517 Victoria Ave., Regina, SK S4P 0T2 Canada. (306)777-0170. **E-mail:** coteau@coteaubooks.com. **Website:** www.coteaubooks.com. "Coteau Books publishes the finest Canadian fiction, poetry, drama and children's literature, with an emphasis on western writers." Publishes 14-16 titles/year. 25% of books from first-time authors.

Coteau Books publishes Canadian writers and illustrators only; mss from the U.S. are returned unopened.

FICTION Young readers, middle readers, young adults: adventure, contemporary, fantasy, history, humor, multicultural, nature/environment, science fiction, suspense/mystery. "No didactic, message pieces, nothing religious, no horror. No picture books." Recently published *Run Like Jäger*, by Karen Bass (ages 15 and up); *Longhorns & Outlaws*, by Linda Aksomitis (ages 9 and up); *Graveyard of the Sea*, by Penny Draper (ages 9 and up).

NONFICTION Young readers, middle readers, young adult/teen: biography, history, multicultural, nature/environment, social issues.

HOW TO CONTACT Children's/teen novels accepted from May 1 to August 31. Submit complete ms or 3-4 sample chapters, author bio. Responds to mss in 4 months. Publishes book 1-2 years after acceptance.

ILLUSTRATION Works with 1-4 illustrators/year. Illustrations only: Submit nonreturnable samples. Responds only if interested. Samples returned with SASE; samples filed. Send contact information and URL of online portfolio to: production@coteaubooks.com.

PHOTOGRAPHY "Very occasionally buys photos from freelancers." Buys stock and assigns work.

TERMS Pays authors royalty based on retail price. Book catalog free upon request with 9×12 SASE.

THE CREATIVE COMPANY

P.O. Box 227, Mankato MN 56002. (800)445-6209. **Fax:** (507)388-2746. **E-mail:** info@thecreativecompany.us. **Website:** www.thecreativecompany.us. **Contact:** Aaron Frisch. The Creative Company has two imprints: Creative Editions (picture books), and Creative Education (nonfiction series). Publishes 140 titles/year.

○ *"We are currently not accepting fiction submissions."*

NONFICTION Picture books, young readers, young adults: animal, arts/crafts, biography, careers, geography, health, history, hobbies, multicultural, music/dance, nature/environment, religion, science, social issues, special needs, sports. Average word length: young readers—500; young adults—6,000. Recently published *Empire State Building*, by Kate Riggs (age 7, young reader); *The Assassination of Archduke Ferdinand*, by Valerie Bodden (age 14, young adult/teen).

HOW TO CONTACT Submit outline/synopsis and 2 sample chapters, along with division of titles within the series. Responds in 3 months to queries/mss. Publishes a book 2 years after acceptance.

PHOTOGRAPHY Buys stock. Contact: Tricia Kleist, photo editor. Model/property releases not required; captions required. Uses b&w prints. Submit cover letter, promo piece. Ms and photographer guidelines available for SAE.

TERMS Guidelines available for SAE.

TIPS "We are accepting nonfiction series submissions only. Fiction submissions will not be reviewed or returned. Nonfiction submissions should be presented in series (4, 6, or 8) rather than single."

CRICKET BOOKS

Imprint of Carus Publishing, 70 E. Lake St., Suite 300, Chicago IL 60601. (603)924-7209. **Fax:** (603)924-7380. **Website:** www.cricketmag.com. Cricket Books publishes picture books, chapter books, and middle-grade novels. Publishes hardcover originals. Publishes 5 titles/year.

○ *Currently not accepting queries or mss. Check website for submissions details and updates.*

HOW TO CONTACT Publishes ms 18 months after acceptance.

ILLUSTRATION Works with 4 illustrators/year. Uses color and b&w. Illustration only: Please send artwork submissions via e-mail to: mail@cicadamag.com. Make sure "portfolio samples—cricket books" is the subject line of the e-mail. The file should be 72 dpi RGB jpg format. **Contact:** John Sandford. Responds only if interested.

TERMS Pays up to 10% royalty on retail price. Average advance: $1,500 and up.

TIPS "Take a look at the recent titles to see what sort of materials we're interested in, especially for non-fiction. Please note that we aren't doing the sort of strictly educational nonfiction that other publishers specialize in."

CROSSWAY BOOKS

A division of Good News Publishing, 1300 Crescent St., Wheaton IL 60187. (630)682-4300. **Fax:** (630)682-4785. **E-mail:** info@crossway.org; submissions@crossway.org. **Website:** www.crosswaybooks.org. **Contact:** Jill Carter, editorial administrator. "Crossway Books lists titles written from an evangelical Christian perspective." Member ECPA. Distributes titles through Christian bookstores and catalogs. Promotes titles through magazine ads, catalogs. Publishes 85 titles/year.

○ *Does not accept unsolicited mss.*

HOW TO CONTACT "Send us an e-mail query and, if your idea fits within our acquisitions guidelines, we'll invite a proposal." Publishes ms 18 months after acceptance.

TERMS Pays negotiable royalty.

DARBY CREEK PUBLISHING

Lerner Publishing Group, 1251 Washington Ave. N, Minneapolis MN 55401. (612)332-3344. **Fax:** (612)332-7615. **Website:** www.darbycreekpublishing.com. **Contact:** Andrew Karre, editorial director. "Darby Creek publishes series fiction titles for emerging, striving and reluctant readers ages 7 to 18 (grades 2-12). From beginning chapter books to intermediate fiction and page-turning YA titles, Darby Creek books engage readers with strong characters and formats they'll want to pursue." Darby Creek does not publish picture books. Publishes children's chapter books, middle readers, young adult. Mostly series. Publishes 25 titles/year.

○ "We are currently not accepting any submissions. If that changes, we will provide all children's writing publications with our new info."

FICTION Middle readers, young adult. Recently published: the Surviving Southside series, by various authors; the Agent Amelia series, by Michael Broad; the Mallory McDonald series, by Laurie B. Friedman; and the Alien Agent series, by Pamela F. Service.

NONFICTION Middle readers: biography, history, science, sports. Recently published *Albino Animals*, by Kelly Milner Halls, illustrated by Rick Spears; *Mir-*

acle: The True Story of the Wreck of the Sea Venture, by Gail Karwoski.

ILLUSTRATION Illustrations only: Send photocopies and résumé with publishing history. "Indicate which samples we may keep on file and include SASE and appropriate packing materials for any samples you wish to have returned."

TERMS Offers advance-against-royalty contracts.

DELACORTE PRESS

1745 Broadway, Mail Drop 9-2, New York NY 10019. (212)782-9000. **Website:** www.randomhouse.com/kids. Publishes middlegrade and young adult fiction in hard cover, trade paperback, mass market and digest formats. Publishes middle-grade and young adult fiction in hardcover, trade paperback, mass market and digest formats.

○ All other query letters or ms submissions must be submitted through an agent or at the request of an editor. No e-mail queries.

Ⓐ DELACORTE PRESS BOOKS FOR YOUNG READERS

(212)782-9000. **Website:** www.randomhouse.com/kids; www.randomhouse.com/teens. Distinguished literary fiction and commercial fiction for the middle grade and young adult categories.

○ Not currently accepting unsolicited mss.

Ⓐ DIAL BOOKS FOR YOUNG READERS

Imprint of Penguin Group USA, 345 Hudson St., New York NY 10014. (212)366-2000. **Website:** www.penguin.com/youngreaders. **Contact:** Lauri Hornik, president and publisher. "Dial Books for Young Readers publishes quality picture books for ages 18 months-6 years; lively, believable novels for middle readers and young adults; and occasional nonfiction for middle readers and young adults." Publishes hardcover originals. Publishes 50 titles/year. 20% of books from first-time authors.

FICTION Especially looking for lively and well-written novels for middle grade and young adult children involving a convincing plot and believable characters. The subject matter or theme should not already be overworked in previously published books. The approach must not be demeaning to any minority group, nor should the roles of female characters (or others) be stereotyped, though we don't think books should be didactic, or in any way message-y. No topics inap-

propriate for the juvenile, young adult, and middle grade audiences. No plays.

ILLUSTRATION Address submissions to Dial Design.

HOW TO CONTACT "We accept entire picture book manuscripts and a maximum of 10 pages for longer works (novels, easy-to-reads). When submitting a portion of a longer work, please provide an accompanying cover letter that briefly describes your manuscript's plot, genre (i.e. easy-to-read, middle grade or YA novel), the intended age group, and your publishing credits, if any." Accepts unsolicited queries. "Due to the overwhelming number of unsolicited manuscripts we receive, we at Dial Books for Young Readers have had to change our submissions policy. As of August 1, 2005, Dial will no longer respond to your unsolicited submission unless interested in publishing it. Please do not include SASE with your submission. You will not hear from Dial regarding the status of your submission unless we are interested, in which case you can expect a reply from us within four months." 5,000 queries received/year. Responds in 4-6 months to queries.

TERMS Pays royalty. Pays varies advance. Book catalog for 9×12 envelope and 4 first-class stamps.

TIPS "Our readers are anywhere from preschool age to teenage. Picture books must have strong plots, lots of action, unusual premises, or universal themes treated with freshness and originality. Humor works well in these books. A very well-thought-out and intelligently presented book has the best chance of being taken on. Genre isn't as much of a factor as presentation."

DISKUS PUBLISHING

E-mail: editor@diskuspublishing.com. **Website:** www.diskuspublishing.com. **Contact:** Ruth Soloman, inspirational and children's editor; Holly Janey, submissions editor. Publishes e-books. Publishes 50 titles/year.

○ *"Currently DiskUs Publishing is closed for submissions. We will reopen for submissions in the near future. We get thousands of submissions each month and our editors need time to get through the current ones. Keep checking our website for updates on the status of our submissions reopen date."*

FICTION Adventure, children's/juvenile, ethnic (general), family saga, fantasy (space fantasy), historical, horror, humor, juvenile, literary, mainstream/contemporary, military/war, multicultural (general), mystery, psychic/supernatural, religious, romance, science fiction, short story collections, suspense, thriller/espionage, western, young adult. "We are actively seeking confessions for our Diskus Confessions line, as well as short stories for our Quick Pick line. We only accept e-mailed submissions for these lines."

HOW TO CONTACT Submit publishing history, bio, estimated word count and genre. Submit complete ms. Publishes ms 6-8 months after acceotance.

TERMS Pays 40% royalty. Book catalog for SASE. Guidelines for SASE or online.

Ⓐ◐ DISNEY HYPERION BOOKS FOR CHILDREN

Website: www.hyperionbooksforchildren.com.

○ *Does not accept unsolicited mss or queries.*

FICTION Picture books, early readers, middle readers, young adults: adventure, animal, anthology (short stories), contemporary, fantasy, history, humor, multicultural, poetry, science fiction, sports, suspense/mystery. Middle readers, young adults: commercial fiction.

NONFICTION Narrative nonfiction for elementary schoolers.

HOW TO CONTACT *All submissions must come via an agent.*

ILLUSTRATION Works with 100 illustrators/year. "Picture books are fully illustrated throughout. All others depend on individual project." Illustrations only: Submit résumé, business card, promotional literature or tearsheets to be kept on file. Responds only if interested. Original artwork returned at job's completion.

PHOTOGRAPHY Works on assignment only. Provide résumé, business card, promotional literature or tearsheets to be kept on file.

DIVERSION PRESS

E-mail: diversionpress@yahoo.com. **Website:** www.diversionpress.com. Publishes hardcover, trade and mass market paperback originals. Publishes 5-10 titles/year. 75% of books from first-time authors. 100% from unagented writers.

○ Query via e-mail. Does not accept unsolicited mss.

FICTION "We will happily consider any children's or young adult books if they are illustrated. If your story has potential to become a series, please address that in your proposal. Fiction short stories and poetry will be considered for our anthology series. See website for details on how to submit your ms."

NONFICTION "The editors have doctoral degrees and are interested in a broad range of academic works. We are also interested in how-to, slice of life, and other nonfiction areas." Does not review works that are sexually explicit or religious, or that put children in a bad light.

HOW TO CONTACT Send query/proposal first. Mss accepted by request only. Responds in 2 weeks to queries. Responds in 1 month to proposals. Publishes ms 1-2 years after acceptance.

TERMS Pays 10% royalty on wholesale price. Guidelines available online

TIPS "Read our website and blog prior to submitting. We like short, concise queries. Tell us why your book is different, not like other books. Give us a realistic idea of what you will do to market your book—that you will actually do. We will ask for more information if we are interested."

Ⓐ DK PUBLISHING

375 Hudson St., New York NY 10014. **Website:** www.dk.com. "DK publishes photographically illustrated nonfiction for children of all ages."

○ *DK Publishing does not accept unagented mss or proposals.*

DNA PRESS & NARTEA PUBLISHING

DNA Press, P.O. Box 9311, Glendale CA 91226. **E-mail:** editors@dnapress.com. **Website:** www.dnapress.com. Book publisher for young adults, children, and adults. Publishes books in electronic format only. Publishes 10 titles/year. 90% of books from first-time authors. 100% from unagented writers.

FICTION All books should be oriented to explain science even if they do not fall 100% under the category of science fiction.

NONFICTION "We publish business, real estate and investment books."

HOW TO CONTACT Submit book proposal via e-mail. Guidelines for proposals available online. 500 queries received/year. 400 mss received/year. Responds in 3 months to mss. Publishes book 8 months after acceptance.

TERMS Pays 10-15% royalty. Book catalog and ms guidelines free.

TIPS Quick response, great relationships, high commission/royalty.

Ⓐ DOG-EARED PUBLICATIONS

P.O. Box 620863, Middletown WI 53562. (888)831-3777 or (608)831-1410. **Fax:** (608)831-1410. **E-mail:** field@dog-eared.com. **Website:** www.dog-eared.com. **Contact:** Nancy Field, publisher. "The home of Dog-Eared Publications is a perfect place to create children's nature books! Perched on a hilltop in Middleton, Wisconsin, we are surrounded by wild meadows and oak forests where deer, wild turkeys, and even bobcats leave their marks."

NONFICTION Middle readers: activity books, animal, nature/environment, science. Average word length: varies. Recently published *Discovering Black Bears*, by Margaret Anderson, Nancy J. Field and Karen Stephenson, illustrated by Michael Maydak (middle readers, activity book); *Leapfrogging Through Wetlands*, by Margaret J. Anderson, Nancy Field and Karen Stephenson, illustrated by Michael Maydak (middle readers, activity book); *Ancient Forests*, by Margaret Anderson, Nancy Field and Karen Stephenson, illustrated by Sharon Torvik (middle readers, activity book).

HOW TO CONTACT Submit ms with cover letter describing intended age of audience, previous publications and background. "If a SASE is not included, we will not respond."

ILLUSTRATION Works with 2-3 illustrators/year. Reviews ms/illustration packages from artists. Submit query and a few art samples. "We are only interested in biologically accurate nature art and accurate human illustrations. Cartoons do not interest us." Responds only if interested. Samples not returned; samples filed. "Interested in realistic nature art!"

TERMS Pays author royalty based on wholesale price. Offers advance. Brochure available for SASE and 1 first-class stamp or on website.

DREAMLAND BOOKS INC.

P.O.Box 1714, Minnetonka MN 55345. (612)281-4704. **E-mail:** dreamlandbooks@inbox.com. **Website:** www.dreamlandbooksinc.com.

FICTION "We are currently not accepting children's story submissions. However, if you have a master or doctoral degree in creative writing, literature, or like field and already have at least one non-vanity book published, we welcome query letters." Considers flash stories (500 words maximum) for issues of the Cellar Door Poetry journal. Submit ms.

POETRY Considers all forms and subjects for issues of the Cellar Door Poetry journal. Does not publish work that promotes pornography or violence. "If you are a new poet, this might especially be a great opportunity for you to get published."

ILLUSTRATION Considers art submissions for both books and Cellar Door Poetry. "We will not consider work by artists who have pornographic, demonic, or violent images in their portfolio. We prefer working with artists who have entirely child-friendly art."

HOW TO CONTACT Submit mss by e-mail. Often comments on rejected poems.

DUTTON CHILDREN'S BOOKS

Penguin Group (USA), Inc., 375 Hudson St., New York NY 10014. **E-mail:** duttonpublicity@us.penguingroup.com. **Website:** www.penguin.com/youngreaders. **Contact:** Lauri Hornik, president and publisher. Estab. 1852. Dutton Children's Books publishes fiction and nonfiction for readers ranging from preschoolers to young adults on a variety of subjects. Publishes hardcover originals as well as novelty formats. Dutton Children's Books has a diverse, general-interest list that includes picture books, and fiction for all ages and occasional retail-appropriate nonfiction. 15% of books from first-time authors.

Ⓠ "Cultivating the creative talents of authors and illustrators and publishing books with purpose and heart continue to be the mission and joy at Dutton."

FICTION Dutton Children's Books has a diverse, general interest list that includes picture books; easy-to-read books; and fiction for all ages, from first chapter books to young adult readers. Recently published *Skippyjon Jones, Lost in Space*, by Judy Schachner (picture book); *Thirteen*, by Lauren Myracle (middle grade novel); *Paper Towns*, by John Green (young adult novel); and *If I Stay*, by Gayle Forman (young adult novel).

NONFICTION Query with SASE.

HOW TO CONTACT Query letter only; include SASE.

TERMS Pays royalty on retail price. Offers advance. Pays royalty on retail price. Pays advance.

Ⓒ EDCON PUBLISHING GROUP

30 Montauk Blvd., Oakdale NY 11769. (631)567-7227. **Fax:** (631)567-8745. **E-mail:** edcon@edconpublishing.com. **Website:** www.edconpublishing.com.

Ⓠ Looking for educational games and non-fiction work in the areas of math, science, reading and social studies.

NONFICTION Grades 1-12, though primarily 6-12 remedial.

HOW TO CONTACT Submit outline/synopsis and 1 sample chapter. Submission kept on file unless return is requested. Include SASE for return. Publishes book 6 months after acceptance.

ILLUSTRATION Buys b&w and color illustrations and is currently seeking computerized graphic art. Send postcards, samples, links to edcon@edconepublishing.com. Mailed submissions kept on file, not returned.

TERMS Pays illustrators by the project ($100-500). Work purchased outright from authors for up to $1,000. Catalog available online.

EDUPRESS, INC.

P.O. Box 8610, Madison WI 53708. (800)694-5827 or (920)563-9571 ext. 332. **Fax:** (920)563-7395. **E-mail:** edupress@highsmith.com; LBowie@highsmith.com. **Website:** www.edupressinc.com. **Contact:** Liz Bowie. Edupress, Inc., publishes supplemental curriculum resources for Pre K through 6th grade. Currently emphasizing reading and math materials, as well as science and social studies.

> "Our mission is to create products that make kids want to go to school!"

NONFICTION "Edupress is currently looking for unique, quality supplemental resources for social studies, science, language arts, math and early learning, as well as teacher resources based on educational thoery. Products should be geared toward standards-based learning."

HOW TO CONTACT Submit complete ms, outline and sample pages, or detailed proposal via mail or e-mail with "Manuscript Submission" as the subject line. Mss longer than 5 pages should be sent via mail. Include cover letter with résumé, synopsis and targeted grade range. "Please provide us with a 'Key Market Statement' describing why you wrote/designed the product. Please list competitive products in the field with special emphasis on product apart from its competitors." Responds in 2-4 months to queries and mss. Publishes ms 1-2 years after acceptance.

ILLUSTRATION Query with samples. Contact: Cathy Baker, product development manager. Responds only if interested. Samples returned with SASE.

PHOTOGRAPHY Buys stock.

TERMS Work purchased outright from authors. Catalog available on website.

TIPS "We are looking for unique, research-based, quality supplemental materials for Pre-K through eighth grade. We publish all subject areas in many different formats, including games. Our materials are intended for classroom and home schooling use."

EERDMANS BOOKS FOR YOUNG READERS

2140 Oak Industrial Dr. NE, Grand Rapids MI 49505. (616)459-459. **Fax:** (616)459-6540. **E-mail:** youngreaders@eerdmans.com; gbrown@eerdmans.com. **Website:** www.eerdmans.com/youngreaders. **Contact:** Gayle Brown, art director. "We are seeking books that encourage independent thinking, problem-solving, creativity, acceptance, kindness. Books that encourage moral values without being didactic or preachy. "Board books, picture books, middle reader fiction, young adult fiction, nonfiction, illustrated storybooks. A submission stands out when it's obvious that someone put time into it—the publisher's name and address are spelled correctly, the package is neat, and all of our submission requirements have been followed precisely. We look for short, concise cover letters that explain why the ms fits with our list, and/or how the ms fills an important need in the world of children's literature. Send ms submissions to acquisitions editor. We regret that due to the volume of material we receive, we cannot comment on mss we are unable to accept."

> "We seek to engage young minds with words and pictures that inform and delight, inspire and entertain. From board books for babies to picture books, nonfiction, and novels for children and young adults, our goal is to produce quality literature for a new generation of readers. We believe in books!"

FICTION Picture books: animal, contemporary, folktales, history, humor, multicultural, nature/environment, poetry, religion, special needs, social issues, sports, suspense. Young readers: animal, contemporary, fantasy, folktales, history, humor, multicultural, poetry, religion, special needs, social issues, sports, suspense. Middle readers: adventure, contemporary, fantasy, history, humor, multicultural, nature/environment, problem novels, religion, social issues, sports, suspense. Young adults/teens: adventure, contemporary, fantasy, folktales, history, humor, multicultural, nature/environment, problem novels, religion, sports, suspense. Average word length: picture books—1,000; middle readers—15,000; young adult—45,000. "Right now we are not acquiring books that revolve around a holiday. (No Christmas, Thanksgiving, Easter, Halloween, Fourth of July, Hanukkah books.) We do not publish retold or original fairy tales, nor do we publish books about witches or ghosts or vampires." For picture books, submit entire ms. For novels, submit entire ms or query with synopsis and at least 3 sample chapters.

NONFICTION Middle readers: biography, history, multicultural, nature/environment, religion, social issues. Young adults/teens: biography, history, multicultural, nature/environment, religion, social issues. Average word length: middle readers—35,000; young adult books—35,000.

HOW TO CONTACT 6,000 mss received/year. Responds to mss in 3-4 months. Publishes middle reader and YA books 1 year after acceptance; publishes picture books in 2-3 years. Does not respond to submissions or queries via e-mail or fax.

ILLUSTRATION Accepts material from international illustrators. Works with 10-12 illustrators/year. Uses color artwork primarily. Reviews work for future assignments. If interested in illustrating future titles, send promo sheet. Samples not returned. Samples filed.

TERMS Pays 5-7% royalty on retail.

TIPS "Find out who Eerdmans is before submitting a manuscript. Look at our website, request a catalog, and check out our books. While we no longer require submissions to be exclusive, we do ask that you inform us if you are simultaneously submitting elsewhere."

EGMONT USA

443 Park Ave. S, New York NY 10016. (212)685-0102. **E-mail:** info@egmontusa.com; egmont@egmontusa.com. **Website:** www.egmontusa.com. Specializes in trade books. Publishes 5 picture books/year; 5 young readers/year; 20 middle readers/year; 20 young adult/year. "Egmont USA publishes quality commercial fiction. We are committed to editorial excellence and to providing first-rate care for our authors. Our motto is that we turn writers into authors and children into passionate readers." 25% of books from first-time authors.

> *"Unfortunately, Egmont USA is not currently able to accept unsolicited submissions; we only accept submissions from literary agents."*

FICTION Picture books: animal, concept, contemporary, humor, multicultural. Young readers: adventure, animal, contemporary, humor, multicultural. Middle readers: adventure, animal, contemporary, fantasy, humor, multicultural, problem novels, science fiction, special needs. Young adults/teens: adventure, animal, contemporary, humor, multicultural, problem novels, science fiction, special needs.

HOW TO CONTACT Publishes book 18 months after acceptance.

ILLUSTRATION Only interested in agented in material. Works with 5 illustrators/year. Uses both color and b&w.

TERMS Pays authors royalties based on retail price.

⊕ ENETE ENTERPRISES

E-mail: EneteEnterprises@gmail.com. **Website:** www.EneteEnterprises.com. **Contact:** Shannon Enete, editor. Publishes hardcover originals, trade paperback originals, mass market paperback originals, electronic originals. Publishes 6 titles/year. 95% of books from first-time authors. 100% from unagented writers.

FICTION "We are looking for new fiction that could grow into a series of books."

NONFICTION "Actively seeking books about healthcare/medicine. More specifically: back care, emergency medicine, international medicine, healthcare, insurance, EMT or paramedic, or alternative medicine."

HOW TO CONTACT Submit query, proposal, or ms by e-mail. Receives 55 queries/year; 20 ms/year. Responds to queries/proposals in 1 month; mss in 1-3 months. Publishes book 3-6 months after acceptance.

TERMS Pays royalties of 1-15%. Guidelines available on website.

TIPS "Send me your best work. Do not rush a draft."

ENSLOW PUBLISHERS INC.

Box 398, 40 Industrial Rd., Berkeley Heights NJ 07922. (908)771-2504. **Fax:** (908)771-0925. **E-mail:** info@enslow.com. **Website:** www.enslow.com. **Contact:** Brian D. Enslow, vice president. Publishes 200 titles/year. 30% of books from first-time authors.

> Enslow Imprint MyReportLinks.com Books produces books on animals, states, presidents, continents, countries, and a variety of other topics for middle readers and young adults, and offers links to online sources of information on topics covered in books.

NONFICTION Young readers, middle readers, young adults: animal, arts/crafts, biography, careers, geography, health, history, multicultural, nature/environment, science, social issues, sports. Middle readers, young adults: hi-lo. "Enslow is moving into the elementary (grades 3-4) level and is looking for authors who can write biography and suggest other nonfiction themes at this level." Average word length: young readers—2,000; middle readers—5,000; young adult—18,000. Published *It's About Time! Science Projects*, by Robert Gardner (grades 3-6, science); *Georgia O'Keeffe: Legendary American Painter*, by Jodie A. Shull (grades 6-12, biography); *California: A MyReportLinks.com Book*, by Jeff Savaga (grades 5-8, social studies/history).

HOW TO CONTACT Send for guidelines. Query via e-mail at customerservice@enslow.com. Responds to queries and mss in 2 weeks. Publishes book 18 months after acceptance.

ILLUSTRATION Submit résumé, business card, or tearsheets to be kept on file. Responds only if interested. Samples returned with SASE only.

TERMS Pays illustrators by the project. Pays photographers by the project or per photo. Sends galleys to authors. Pays authors royalties or work purchased outright. Book catalog/ms guidelines available for $3, along with an 8½×11 SASE and $2 postage.

FACTS ON FILE

132 W. 31st St., New York NY 10001. (800)322-8755. **Fax:** (800)678-3633. **E-mail:** editorial@factsonfile.com. **Website:** www.factsonfile.com. **Contact:** Laurie Likoff, editorial director; Andrew Gyory, editor-in-chief. "We produce high-quality reference materials for the school library market and the general nonfiction trade." Publishes 25-30 young adult titles/year. 5% of books by first-time authors; 25% of books from agented writers; additional titles through book packagers, co-publishers and unagented writers.

NONFICTION Middle readers, young adults: animal, biography, careers, geography, health, history, multicultural, nature/environment, reference, religion, science, social issues and sports.

HOW TO CONTACT Submit outline/synopsis and sample chapters. Responds to queries in 10 weeks. Publishes book 1 year after acceptance.

TERMS Book catalog free on request. Submission guidelines for SASE or online.

TIPS "Most projects have high reference value and fit into a series format."

FARRAR, STRAUS & GIROUX

175 Fifth Ave., New York NY 10010. (212)741-6900. **Fax:** (212)633-2427. **E-mail:** childrens.editorial@fs

gbooks.com. **Website:** www.fsgkidsbooks.com. Farrar title *How I Learned Geography*, by Uri Shulevitz, won a Caldecott Honor Medal in 2009. Farrar/Frances Foster title *The Wall: Growing Up Behind the Iron Curtain*, by Peter Sís, won a Caldecott Honor Medal in 2008. Farrar/Melanie Kroupa title *Rex Zero and the End of the World*, by Tim Wynne-Jones, won a Boston Globe-Horn Book Fiction and Poetry Honor Award in 2007. Farrar/Frances Foster title *Dreamquake: Book Two of the Dreamhunter Duet*, by Elizabeth Knox, won a Michael L. Printz Honor Award in 2008.

> As of January 2010, Farrar Straus & Giroux does not accept unsolicited manuscripts. "We recommend finding a literary agent to represent you and your work."

FICTION All levels: all categories. "Original and well-written material for all ages." Recently published *The Cabinet of Wonders*, by Marie Rutkoski; *Last Night*, by Hyewon Yum.

NONFICTION All levels: all categories. "We publish only literary nonfiction."

ILLUSTRATION Works with 30-60 illustrators/year. Reviews ms/illustration packages from artists. Submit ms with 1 example of final art, remainder roughs. Do not send originals. Illustrations only: Query with tearsheets. Responds if interested in 3 months. Samples returned with SASE; samples sometimes filed.

TERMS Book catalog available for 9×12 SASE with $1.95 postage. Ms guidelines online.

TIPS "Study our catalog before submitting. We will see illustrators' portfolios by appointment. Don't ask for criticism and/or advice—due to the volume of submissions we receive, it's just not possible. Never send originals. Always enclose SASE."

FITZHENRY & WHITESIDE LTD.

195 Allstate Pkwy., Markham ON L3R 4T8, Canada. (905)477-9700. **E-mail:** fitzkids@fitzhenry.ca; godwit@fitzhenry.ca; charkin@fitzhenry.ca. **Website:** www.fitzhenry.ca. **Contact:** Sharon Fitzhenry, president; Cathy Sandusky, education sales manager; Christie Harkin, submissions editor. Emphasis on Canadian authors and illustrators, subject or perspective. Publishes 15 titles/year. 10% of books from first-time authors.

> "We are no longer accepting mss for board books, narrative poetry, seasonal stories or books designed to be a series. Nor are we

interested in mss written to convey a lesson or a moral."

HOW TO CONTACT Publishes book 1-2 years after acceptance.

FICTION Picture books (500-850 words), middle grade (25,000-35,00 words), young adult (40,000-50,000 words).

NONFICTION Picture books (ages 5 and up), school curriculum related middle grade, school curriculum related young adult.

ILLUSTRATION Works with approximately 10 illustrators/year. Reviews ms/illustration packages from artists. Submit outline and sample illustration (copy). Illustrations only: Query with samples and promo sheet. Samples not returned unless requested.

PHOTOGRAPHY Buys photos from freelancers. Buys stock and assigns work. Captions required. Uses b&w 8×10 prints; 35mm and 4×5 transparencies, 300+ dpi digital images. Submit stock photo list and promo piece.

TERMS Pays authors 8-10% royalty with escalations. Offers "respectable" advances for picture books, split 50/50 between author and illustrator. Pays illustrators by project and royalty. Pays photographers per photo.

TIPS "We respond to quality."

○ FIVE STAR PUBLICATIONS, INC.

P.O. Box 6698, Chandler AZ 85246. (480)940-8182. **Fax:** (480)940-8787. **E-mail:** info@fivestarpublications.com. **Website:** www.fivestarpublications.com. Publishes 7 middle readers/year. **Contact:** Linda Radke, president. "Helps produce and market award-winning books."

○ "Five Star Publications publishes and promotes award-winning fiction, nonfiction, cookbooks, children's literature and professional guides. More information about Five Star Publications, Inc., a 25-year leader in the book publishing/book marketing industry, is available online at our website." Other websites: www.LittleFivestar.com, www.FiveStarLegends.com; www.FiveStarSleuths.com; www.SixPointsPress.com.

ILLUSTRATION Works with 3 illustrators/year. Reviews ms/illustration packages from artists. Query. Illustrations only: Query with samples. Responds only if interested. Samples filed.

PHOTOGRAPHY Buys stock and assigns work. Works on assignment only. Submit letter.

TIPS Features the Purple Dragonfly Book Awards and Royal Dragonfly Book Awards, which were conceived and designed with children in mind. "Not only do we want to recognize and honor accomplished authors in the field of children's literature, but we also want to highlight and reward up-and-coming newly published authors, as well as younger published writers. In our efforts to include everyone, the awards are divided into distinct subject categories, ranging from books on the environment and cooking to books on sports and family issues. (Please see the complete categories list on the entry form on our website.)"

FLUX

Llewellyn Worldwide, Ltd., Llewellyn Worldwide, Ltd., 2143 Wooddale Dr., Woodbury, MN 55125. (877)639-9753. **Fax:** (651)291-1908. **Website:** www.fluxnow.com. **Contact:** Brian Farrey, acquisitions editor. "Flux seeks to publish authors who see YA as a point of view, not a reading level. We look for books that try to capture a slice of teenage experience, whether in real or imagined worlds." Publishes 21 titles/year. 50% of books from first-time authors.

○ *Does not accept unsolicited mss.*

FICTION Young adults: adventure, contemporary, fantasy, history, humor, problem novels, religion, science fiction, sports, suspense. Average word length: 50,000.

TERMS Pays royalties of 10-15% based on wholesale price. Book catalog and guidelines available on website.

TIPS "Read contemporary teen books. Be aware of what else is out there. If you don't read teen books, you probably shouldn't write them. Know your audience. Write incredibly well. Do not condescend."

FORT ROSS INC.

26 Arthur Place, Yonkers NY 10701. (914)375-6448. **E-mail:** fortross@optonline.net. **Website:** www.fortrossinc.com. Buys and sells rights for more than 500 titles per year, mostly in Russian and in Russia. Genres include children adapted classics, adventure, fantasy, horror, romance, science fiction, biography, history and self-help. **Contact:** Dr. Kartsev, executive director. "Generally, we publish Russia-related books in English or Russian. Sometimes we publish various fiction and nonfiction books in collaboration with Eastern European publishers in translation. We are looking mainly for well-established authors." Publishes paperback originals. 100 queries received/year;

100 mss received/year. Pays 6-8% royalty on wholesale price or makes outright purchase of $500-1,500; negotiable advance. Publishes in hardcover and paperback originals. Publishes Ernest Hemingway, A *Moveable Feast*: The Restored Edition (in Russian).

HOW TO CONTACT Responds in 1 month to queries and proposals; 3 months to mss. 12 months

FREE SPIRIT PUBLISHING, INC.

217 Fifth Ave. N, Suite 200, Minneapolis MN 55401. (612)338-2068. **Fax:** (612)337-5050. **E-mail:** acquisitions@freespirit.com. **Website:** www.freespirit.com. "We believe passionately in empowering kids to learn to think for themselves and make their own good choices." Publishes trade paperback originals and reprints. Publishes 12-18 titles/year. 5% of books from first-time authors. 75% from unagented writers.

> Free Spirit does not accept fiction, poetry or storybook submissions.

NONFICTION Seeks nonfiction proposals in the following categories: early childhood (board books and picture books), self-help for kids and teens, gifted and talented, learning differences, parenting, teaching. Complete guidelines available online. "Many of our authors are educators, mental health professionals, and youth workers involved in helping kids and teens." No fiction or picture storybooks, poetry, single biographies or autobiographies, books with mythical or animal characters, or books with religious or New Age content.

HOW TO CONTACT Submit book proposal via mail. Proposals should include cover letter stating qualifications, intent, and intended audience and market analysis (how your book stands out from the field), along with outline, 2 sample chapters, résumé, and SASE. For early childhood submissions, submit entire ms. "Please review catalog and author guidelines (both available online) before submitting proposal." Reponds to queries in 4-6 months. "If you'd like material returned, enclose a SASE with sufficient postage."

ILLUSTRATION Works with 5 illustrators/year. Submit samples to creative director for consideration. If appropriate, samples will be kept on file and artist will be contacted if a suitable project comes up. Enclose SASE if you'd like materials returned.

PHOTOGRAPHY Uses stock photos. Does not accept photography submissions.

TERMS Pays advance. Book catalog and ms guidelines online.

TIPS "Our books are issue-oriented, jargon-free, and solution-focused. Our audience is children, teens, teachers, parents and youth counselors. We are especially concerned with kids' social and emotional well-being and look for books with ready-to-use strategies for coping with today's issues at home or in school—written in everyday language. We are not looking for academic or religious materials, or books that analyze problems with the nation's school systems. Instead, we want books that offer practical, positive advice so kids can help themselves, and parents and teachers can help kids succeed."

FREESTONE/PEACHTREE, JR.

1700 Chattahoochee Ave., Atlanta GA 30318. (404)876-8761. **Fax:** (404)875-2578. **E-mail:** hello@ peachtree-online.com. **Website:** www.peachtree-online.com. **Contact:** Helen Harriss, acquisitions. Publishes 4-8 titles/year.

> Freestone and Peachtree, Jr. are imprints of Peachtree Publishers. No e-mail or fax queries or submissions, please.

FICTION Middle readers: adventure, animal, history, nature/environment, sports. Young adults: fiction, history, biography, mystery, adventure. Does not want to see science fiction, religion, or romance. Recent publications for comparison are: *This Girl is Different*, by J.J. Johnson (ages 12-16, young adult), *The Cheshire Cheese Cat*, by Carmen Agra Deedy and Randall Wright, illustrated by Barry Moser (ages 8 and up, middle reader), and *Grow*, by Juanita Havill, illustrated by Stanislawa Kodman (middle reader, ages 8-12).

NONFICTION Picture books, young readers, middle readers, young adults: history, sports. Picture books: animal, health, multicultural, nature/environment, science, social issues, special needs.

HOW TO CONTACT Submit 3 sample chapters by postal mail only. No query necessary. Responds in 6 months-1 year. Publishes book 1-2 years after acceptance.

ILLUSTRATION Works with 10-20 illustrators/year. Responds only if interested. Samples not returned; samples filed. Originals returned at job's completion.

TERMS Pays authors royalty. Pays illustrators by the project or royalty. Pays photographers by the project or per photo.

FRONT STREET

Website: www.frontstreetbooks.com. Imprint of Boyds Mills Press, 815 Church Street, Honesdale PA 18431.

Website: www.frontstreetbooks.com. Publishes 20-25 titles/year. "We are an independent publisher of books for children and young adults." Publishes hardcover originals and trade paperback reprints. Books: coated paper; offset printing; case binding; 4-color illustrations. Averages 15 fiction titles/year. Distributes titles through independent sales reps, wholesalers, and via order line directly from Front Street. Promotes titles through sales and professional conferences, sales reps, reviews, catalogs, website, and direct marketing. 2,000 queries received/year. 5,000 mss received/year.

FICTION Picture books, middle grade, young adult. For picture books, submit entire ms. For longer books, submit cover letter, synopsis and first 3 chapters. Label package "Manuscript Submissions." Recently published *I'm Being Stalked by a Moonshadow*, by Doug MacLeod; *Runaround*, by Helen Hemphill; *Baby*, by Joseph Monninger.

HOW TO CONTACT Include SASE with submissions if you want them returned. "We try to respond within three months."

ILLUSTRATION Reviews artwork/photos with ms. Send photocopies. Keeps illustration samples on file. Label package "Art Sample Submission."

TERMS Pays royalty on retail price. Pays advance. Book catalog available online. Guidelines available online.

TIPS "Read through our recently published titles and review our website. Check to see what's on the market and in our catalog before submitting your story. Feel free to query us if you're not sure."

FULCRUM PUBLISHING

4690 Table Mountain Dr., Suite 100, Golden CO 80403. (303)277-1623. **Fax:** (303)279-7111. **E-mail:** info@fulcrum-books.com; acquisitions@fulcrum books.com. **Website:** www.fulcrum-books.com. **Contact:** T. Baker, acquisitions editor.

NONFICTION Middle and early readers: Western history, nature/ environment, Native American.

HOW TO CONTACT Submit proposal to acquisitions@fulcrumbooks.com. Does not accept submissions via postal mail or fax. Proposals should include synopsis, 2-3 sample chapters, biographical informations, description of intended audience, market assessment, list of competing titles, what you can do to market your book. Responds in 3 months. "Publisher does not send response letters unless we are interested in publishing."

PHOTOGRAPHY Works on assignment only.

TERMS Pays authors royalty based on wholesale price. Offers advances. Catalog available for SASE. Ms guidelines available online at website.

TIPS "Research our line first. We look for books that appeal to the school market and trade. "

GAUTHIER PUBLICATIONS, INC.

Frog Legs Ink, P.O. Box 806241, Saint Clair Shores MI 48080. **Fax:** (586)279-1515. **E-mail:** info@gauthi erpublications.com; submissions@gauthierpublica tions.com. **Website:** www.eatabook.com. Hardcover originals and trade paperback originals. Publishes 10 titles/year. 50% of books from first-time authors. 50% from unagented writers.

> Frog Legs Ink (imprint) is always looking for new writers and illustrators.

FICTION "We are particularly interested in mystery, thriller, graphic novels, horror and young adult areas for the upcoming year. We do, however, consider most subjects if they are intriguing and well written."

HOW TO CONTACT Query with SASE. "Please do not send full ms unless we ask for it. If we are interested we will request a few sample chapters and an outline. Since we do take the time to read and consider each piece, response can take up to 8 weeks. Mailed submissions without SASE included are destroyed if we are not interested."

ILLUSTRATION "Please send a résumé with professional experience and credentials along with copies or tear-sheets of work. Do not send originals. We will contact you if we will be keeping your work on file or if it seems appropriate for a current project. If you do not send a SASE, your materials will be destroyed if we do not have a place for them. Response can take up to 1 month."

TERMS Pays 5-10% royalty on retail price. Guidelines available for SASE, or online at website www.gauthi erpublications.com, or by email at: submissions@ gauthierpublications.com.

GIBBS SMITH

P.O. Box 667, Layton UT 84041. (801)544-9800. **Fax:** (801)544-8853. **E-mail:** info@gibbs-smith.com. **Website:** www.gibbs-smith.com. Publishes 3 titles/year. 50% of books from first-time authors. 50% from unagented writers.

> Gibbs Smith is currently not accepting fiction or picture books.

NONFICTION Middle readers: activity. Length: 15,000 words maximum.

HOW TO CONTACT Considers unsolicited mss only through online submission form. Nonfiction: Submit an outline and writing samples for activity books. Responds in 3 months. Publishes ms 1-2 years after acceptance.

ILLUSTRATION Works with 2 illustrators/year. Reviews ms/illustration packages from artists. Query. Submit ms with 3-5 pieces of final art. Provide résumé, promo sheet, slides (duplicate slides, not originals). Responds only if interested. Samples returned with SASE; samples filed.

TERMS Pays authors royalty of 2% based on retail price or work purchased outright ($500 minimum). Offers advances (average amount: $2,000). Pays illustrators by the project or royalty of 2% based on retail price. Sends galleys to authors; color proofs to illustrators. Original artwork returned at job's completion. Book catalog available for 9×12 SAE and $2.30 postage. Ms guidelines available by e-mail.

TIPS "We target ages 5-11. We do not publish young adult novels or chapter books."

DAVID R. GODINE, PUBLISHER

15 Court Square, Suite 320 Boston MA 02108. (617)451-9600. **Fax:** (617)350-0250. **E-mail:** info@godine.com. **Website:** www.godine.com. "We publish books that matter for people who care."

 This publisher is no longer considering unsolicited mss of any type.

FICTION Picture books: adventure, animal, contemporary, folktales, nature/environment. Young readers: adventure, animal, contemporary, folk or fairy tales, history, nature/environment. Middle readers: adventure, animal, contemporary, folk or fairy tales, history, mystery, nature/environment. Young adults/teens: adventure, animal, contemporary, history, mystery, nature/environment. Recently published *Little Red Riding Hood*, by Andrea Wisnewski (picture book); *The Merchant of Noises*, by Anna Rozen, illustrated by François Avril.

NONFICTION Picture books: alphabet, animal, nature/environment. Young readers: activity books, animal, history, music/dance, nature/environment. Middle readers: activity books, animal, biography, history, music/dance, nature/environment. Young adults: biography, history, music/dance, nature/environment.

POETRY Young readers, middle readers, young adults/teens.

HOW TO CONTACT Only interested in agented material.

ILLUSTRATION Only interested in agented material. Works with 1-3 illustrators/year. "Please do not send original artwork unless solicited. Almost all of the children's books we accept for publication come to us with the author and illustrator already paired up. Therefore, we rarely use freelance illustrators." Samples returned with SASE.

TIPS "E-mail submissions are not accepted. Always enclose a SASE. Keep in mind that we do not accept unsolicited mss and that we rarely use freelance illustrators."

GOLDEN BOOKS

Website: www.randomhouse.com/golden.

FICTION Publishes board books, novelty books, picture books, workbooks, series (mass market and trade).

HOW TO CONTACT *Does not accept unsolicited submissions.*

GRAPHIA

222 Berkeley St., Boston MA 02116. (617)351-5000. **E-mail:** Childrens_Publicity@hmhpub.com; erica_zappy@hmco.com. **Website:** www.graphiabooks.com. "Graphia publishes quality paperbacks for today's teen readers, ages 14 and up. From fiction to nonfiction, poetry to graphic novels, Graphia runs the gamut, all unified by the quality of writing that is the hallmark of this imprint."

FICTION Young adults: adventure, contemporary, fantasy, history, humor, multicultural. Recently published: *The Off Season*, by Catherine Murdock; *Come in from the Cold*, by Marsha Qualey; *Breaking Up is Hard to Do*, with stories by Niki Burnham, Terri Clark, Ellen Hopkins, and Lynda Sandoval; *Zahrah the Windseeker,* by Nnedi Okorafot-Mbachu.

NONFICTION Young adults: biography, history, multicultural, nature/environment, science, social issues.

POETRY Young adults.

HOW TO CONTACT Query. Responds to queries in 3 months.

ILLUSTRATION Do not send original artwork or slides. Send color photocopies, tearsheets or photos to Art Dept. Include SASE if you would like your samples mailed back to you.

○ GREAT SOURCE EDUCATION GROUP

Houghton Mifflin Harcourt, Editorial Department, 181 Ballardvale St., Wilmington MA 01887. **Website:** www.greatsource.com. Great Source's main publishing efforts are instructional and focus on the school market. For all materials, the reading level must be appropriate to the skill level of the students and the nature of the materials.

NONFICTION Material must be appealing to students, proven classroom-effective, and consistent with current research.

TERMS Guidelines available online.

GREENHAVEN PRESS

27500 Drake Rd., Farmington Hills MI 48331. **Website:** www.gale.com/greenhaven. Publishes 220 young adult academic reference titles/year. 50% of books by first-time authors. "Greenhaven continues to print quality nonfiction anthologies for libraries and classrooms. Our well known Opposing Viewpoints series is highly respected by students and librarians in need of material on controversial social issues. Greenhaven accepts no unsolicited manuscripts." Send query, résumé, and list of published works by e-mail. Work purchased outright from authors; write-for-hire, flat fee.

NONFICTION Young adults (high school): controversial issues, social issues, history, literature, science, environment, health. Recently published (series): Issues That Concern You; Writing the Critical Essay: An Opening Viewpoints Guide; Introducing Issues with Opposing Viewpoints; Social Issues in Literature; and Perspectives on Diseases and Disorders.

GREENWILLOW BOOKS

HarperCollins Publishers, 1350 Avenue of the Americas, New York NY 10019. (212)207-7000. **Website:** www.harperchildrens.com. **Contact:** Virginia Duncan, vice president/publisher; Paul Zakris, art director. Greenwillow Books publishes quality picture books and fiction for young readers of all ages, and nonfiction primarily for children under seven years of age. "We hope that at the heart of each book there is honesty, emotion and depth—conveyed by an author or an artist who has something that is worth saying to children and who says it in a way that is worth reading."

○ *Currently not accepting unsolicited mail, mss or queries.*

FICTION Picture books, novels. Recent titles: *The Train of States*, by Peter Sís; *If Not for the Cat*, by Jack Prelutsky, illustrated by Ted Rand; *Happy Haunting, Amelia Bedelia*, by Herman Parish, illustrated by Lynn Sweat. Publishes hardcover originals and reprints.

NONFICTION Primarily for children under 7 years of age.

TERMS Pays authors royalty. Offers advances. Pays illustrators royalty or by the project. Sends galleys to authors.

○ GROSSET & DUNLAP PUBLISHERS

Penguin Putnam Inc., 345 Hudson St., New York NY 10014. **Website:** www.penguingroup.com. **Contact:** Francesco Sedita, vice president/publisher. Grosset & Dunlap publishes children's books that show children that reading is fun, with books that speak to their interests, and that are affordable so that children can build a home library of their own. "Grosset & Dunlap publishes high-interest, affordable books for children ages 0-10 years." Publishes hardcover (few) and mass market paperback originals. Publishes 140 titles/year.

FICTION All book formats except for picture books. Submit a summary and the first chapter or two for longer works. Recently published series: Frankly Frannie; George Brown, Class Clown; Bedeviled; Hank Zipzer; Camp Confidential; Katie Kazoo; Magic Kitten; Magic Puppy; The Hardy Boys; Nancy Drew; The Little Engine That Could. Licensed series: Angelina Ballerina; Disney's Club Penguin; Charlie & Lola; Star Wars: The Clone Wars; WWE; Disney's Classic Pooh; Max & Ruby; The Penguins of Madagascar; Batman: The Brave and the Bold; Strawberry Shortcake.

HOW TO CONTACT "We do not accept e-mail submissions." Responds in 4 months if interested.

TERMS Pays royalty. Pays advance.

NONFICTION Nonfiction that is particularly topical or of wide interest in the mass market; new concepts for novelty format for preschoolers; and very well-written easy readers on topics that appeal to primary graders have the best chance of selling to our firm.

○ GROUNDWOOD BOOKS

110 Spadina Ave. Suite 801, Toronto ON M5V 2K4, Canada. (416)321-2241. **Fax:** (416)321-3033. **Website:** www.groundwoodbooks.com. Publishes 10 picture books/year; 3 young readers/year; 5 middle readers/year; 5 young adult titles/year, approximately 2 nonfiction titles/year. 10% of books from first-time authors.

FICTION All ages: novels. "We do not generally publish stories with an obvious moral or message, or genre fiction such as thrillers or mysteries." Recently published *Harvey*, by Herve Bouchard, illustrated by Janice Nadeau; *Queen of Hearts*, by Martha Brooks (YA); *Between Sisters*, by Adwoa Badoe (YA); *No Safe Place*, by Deborah Ellis (YA).

HOW TO CONTACT Currently not accepting unsolicited submissions for picture books. Submit synopsis and sample chapters. "We accept multiple submissions as long as this is indicated in the ms." Responds to mss in 4-6 months.

ILLUSTRATION Works with 20 illustrators/year. Reviews ms/illustration packages from artists. Illustrations only: Send résumé, promo sheet, slides, color or b&w copies, and tearsheets. Guidelines available online. Responds only if interested. Samples not returned.

TERMS Offers advances.

TIPS "Try to familiarize yourself with our list before submitting to judge whether or not your work is appropriate for Groundwood. Visit our website for guidelines."

ⓐ HARPERTEEN

10 E. 53rd St., New York NY 10022. (202)207-7000. **Fax:** (212)261-6668. **E-mail:** harperteen@harpercollins.com. **Website:** www.harpercollins.com. HarperTeen is a teen imprint that publishes hardcovers, paperback reprints and paperback originals. Publishes 100 titles/year.

> *HarperCollins Children's Books is not accepting unsolicited and/or unagented mss or queries.* Unfortunately the volume of these submissions is so large that they cannot receive the attention they deserve. Such submissions will not be reviewed or returned.

ⓒ HAYES SCHOOL PUBLISHING CO. INC.

321 Pennwood Ave., Wilkinsburg PA 15221. (412)371-2373. **Fax:** (800)543-8771. **E-mail:** chayes@hayespub.com. **Website:** www.hayespub.com. **Contact:** Clair N. Hayes. Produces folders, workbooks, stickers, certificates. Wants to see supplementary teaching aids for grades K-12. Interested in all subject areas. Will consider simultaneous and electronic submissions. Guidelines available for SASE or via e-mail. Query with description or complete ms. Responds in 6 weeks. SASE for return of submissions.

ILLUSTRATION Works with 3-4 illustrators/year. Responds in 6 weeks. Samples returned with SASE;

samples filed. Originals not returned at job's completion.

TERMS Work purchased outright. Purchases all rights.

HOLIDAY HOUSE INC.

425 Madison Ave., New York NY 10017. (212)688-0085. **Fax:** (212)421-6134. **Website:** www.holidayhouse.com. 20% of books from first-time authors. 80% from unagented writers.

NONFICTION All levels, but more picture books than middle-grade nonfiction titles: animal, biography, concept, contemporary, geography, historical, math, multicultural, music/dance, nature/environment, religion, science, social issues.

HOW TO CONTACT Send complete ms to the acquisitions editor via US mail. "We do not accept certified or registered mail. We respond only to manuscripts that meet our current needs."

ILLUSTRATION Works with 35 illustrators/year. Reviews ms illustration packages from artists. Send ms with dummy. Do not submit original artwork or slides. Color photocopies or printed samples are preferred. Responds only if interested. Samples filed.

TERMS Book catalog and guidelines available for SASE.

TIPS "We need books with strong stories, writing and art. We do not publish board books or novelties. No easy readers."

⓰ HOUGHTON MIFFLIN HARCOURT

222 Berkeley St., Boston MA 02116. (617)351-5000. **E-mail:** Childrens_Publicity@hmhpub.com. **Website:** www.houghtonmifflinbooks.com. "We do not accept manuscripts that are handwritten or submitted on computer disk. You do not have to furnish illustrations, but if you wish, copies of a few comprehensive sketches or duplicate copies of original art will suffice." Publishes hardcover originals and trade paperback reprints and originals. Publishes 60 titles/year.

> Houghton title *Kakapo Rescue* won the 2011 Sibert Medal. *Dark Emperor and Other Poems of the Night,* by Joyce Sidman, illustrated by Rick Allen was a 2011 Newbery Honor Book.

FICTION All levels: all categories except religion. "We do not rule out any theme, though we do not publish specifically religious material." Recently published *Red Sings from Treetops: A Year in Colors*, by

Joyce Sidman, illustrated by Pamela Zagarenski (ages 5-8, picture book/poetry); *The Entomological Tales of Augustus T. Percival: Petronella Saves Nearly Everyone* (middle grade); *Cashay* (ages 12 and up, YA novel).

NONFICTION All categories except religion. Recently published *Down, Down, Down; A Journey to the Bottom of the Sea*, by Steve Jenkins (ages 5-8, picture); *The Frog Scientist*, by Pamela S. Turner, photographs by Andy Comins (ages 10 and up).

HOW TO CONTACT "Please submit exclusively to one HMH imprint." Responds in 4 months only if interested. Do not send SASE.

ILLUSTRATION Works with 60 illustrators/year. Reviews ms/illustration packages or illustrations only from artists: Query with samples (colored photocopies are fine); provide tearsheets. Responds in 4 months if interested. Samples returned with SASE; samples filed if interested. Address art submissions to: Art Department, Children's Trade Books.

HOUGHTON MIFFLIN HARCOURT BOOKS FOR CHILDREN

Imprint of Houghton Mifflin Trade & Reference Division, 222 Berkeley St., Boston MA 02116. (617)351-5000. **Fax:** (617)351-1111. **E-mail:** children's_books@hmco.com. **Website:** www.houghtonmifflinbooks.com. Houghton Mifflin Harcourt gives shape to ideas that educate, inform, and above all, delight. Faxed or e-mailed manuscripts and proposals are not considered. Complete submission guidelines available on website. Publishes hardcover originals and trade paperback originals and reprints. Publishes 100 titles/year. 10% of books from first-time authors. 60% from unagented writers.

💬 Does not respond to or return mss unless interested.

FICTION Submit complete ms.

NONFICTION Query with synopsis, sample chapters, and SASE. Interested in innovative books and subjects about which the author is passionate.

HOW TO CONTACT "Please submit to only one HMH imprint." 5,000 queries received/year. 14,000 mss received/year. Responds in 3 months to queries. Publishes ms 2 years after acceptance.

TERMS Pays 5-10% royalty on retail price. Pays variable advance. Guidelines available online.

HOUGHTON MIFFLIN HARCOURT CHILDREN'S BOOKS

215 Park Ave. S, New York NY 10003. **Website:** www.hmhbooks.com. Publishes hardcover originals and trade paperback reprints. 20% of books from first-time authors.

💬 *"We are no longer responding to your unsolicited submissions."*

TERMS Pays authors and illustrators royalty based on retail price. Pays photographers by the project. Sends galleys to authors; dummies to illustrators. Original artwork returned at job's completion.

HUNTER HOUSE PUBLISHERS

P.O. Box 2914, Alameda CA 94501. (510)865-5282. **Fax:** (510)865-4295. **E-mail:** acquisitions@hunterhouse.com. **Website:** www.hunterhouse.com. Visit website for submission guidelines. Submit overview and chapter-by-chapter synopsis, sample chapters, and statistics on subject area, support organizations or networks, personal bio, and marketing ideas. "Testimonials from professionals or well-known authors are helpful, especially for health books."

NONFICTION Books are fitness/diet/exercise and activity games/social skills/classroom management-oriented. Does *not* want to see books for young children, fiction, illustrated picture books, memoir or autobiography. Published SmartFun activity book series (currently about 20 books): each has 101 games that encourage imagination, social interaction, and self-expression in children (generally between ages 3-15). Widely used in homes, schools, day-care centers, clubs, and camps. Each activity includes set-up, age range, difficulty level, materials list and a time suggestion.

HOW TO CONTACT Submit proposal with overview, outline, biographical informations and marketing considerations. Accepts simultaneous and e-mail solutions. Responds to queries in 1-3 months; mss in 3-6 months. Publishes ms 18 months after acceptance.

TERMS Payment varies. Sends galleys to authors. Book catalog available. But most updated information is on website; ms guidelines for standard SAE and 1 first-class stamp.

TIPS "Looking for children's activity books focused on education, teamwork, skill-building, etc. The children's books we publish are for a select, therapeutic audience. No fiction! Please, no fiction."

IDEALS CHILDREN'S BOOKS AND CANDYCANE PRESS

Website: www.idealsbooks.com.

FICTION Picture books: animal, concept, history, religion. Board books: animal, history, nature/environment, religion. Average word length: picture books—1,500; board books—200.

IDEALS PUBLICATIONS INC.

2630 Elm Hill Pike, Suite 100, Nashville TN 37214. (615)781-1451. **E-mail:** kwest@guideposts.org. **Website:** www.idealsbooks.com. "Ideals Publications publishes 20 to 25 new children's titles a year, primarily for 2- to 8-year-olds. Our backlist includes more than 400 titles, and we publish picture books, activity books, board books, and novelty and sound books covering a wide array of topics, such as Bible stories, holidays, early learning, history, family relationships, and values. Our bestselling titles include *The Story of Christmas*, *The Story of Easter*, *Seaman's Journal*, *How Do I Love You ?*, *My Daddy and I*, and *The Story of Jesus*. Through our dedication to publishing high-quality and engaging books, we never forget our obligation to our littlest readers to help create those special moments with books."

FICTION Subjects include holiday, inspirational, and patriotic themes; relationships and values; and general fiction. Mss should be no longer than 800 words. CandyCane Press publishes board books and novelty books for children ages 2 to 5. Subject matter is similar to Ideals Children's Books, with a focus on younger children. Mss should be no longer than 250 words.

HOW TO CONTACT Send complete ms with SASE. Do not query. Do not submit art or photographs with ms. Responds in 3 months.

ILLUSTRATION Submit tearsheets or color photocopies. Samples filed. Responds if interested.

PHOTOGRAPHY Submit tearsheets. Does not consider unpublished photographers. Responds if interested.

ILLUMINATION ARTS

P.O. Box 1865, Bellevue WA 98009. (425)968-5097. **Fax:** (425)968-5634. **Website:** www.illumin.com. **Contact:** Ruth Thompson, editorial director.

> ⊙ *Currently not accepting new submissions. Check website for updates.*

FICTION Length: Prefers under 1,000, but will consider up to 1,500 words. Recently published *God's Promise*, by Maureen Moss, illustrated by Gerald Purnell; *Roonie B. Moonie: Lost and Alone*, by Janan Cain.

TERMS Pays authors and illustrators royalty based on wholesale price. Book fliers available for SASE.

TIPS "Read our books or visit website to see what our books are like. Follow submission guidelines found on website. Be patient. We are unable to track unsolicited submissions."

IMPACT PUBLISHERS, INC.

P.O. Box 6016 Atascadero CA 93423. (805)466-5917. **E-mail:** submissions@impactpublishers.com; publisher@impactpublishers.com. **Website:** www.impactpublishers.com. Imprints: Little Imp Books, Rebuilding Books, The Practical Therapist Series. "Our purpose is to make the best human services expertise available to the widest possible audience. We publish only popular psychology and self-help materials written in everyday language by professionals with advanced degrees and significant experience in the human services." Publishes 3-5 titles/year. 20% of books from first-time authors.

NONFICTION Young readers, middle readers, young adults: self-help. Recently published *Jigsaw Puzzle Family: The Stepkids' Guide to Fitting It Together*, by Cynthia MacGregor (ages 8-12, children's/divorce/emotions).

HOW TO CONTACT Submit proposal with résumé, outline and sample chapters. Complete guidelines available online. Submit via postal mail or e-mail, but not both.

ILLUSTRATION Currently not seeking illustration submissions.

TERMS Pays authors royalty of 10-12%. Offers advances. Pays illustrators by the project. Book catalog available for #10 SAE with 2 first-class stamps; ms guidelines available for SASE. All imprints included in a single catalog. Responds to queries/mss in 3 months.

TIPS "Please do not submit fiction, poetry or narratives."

JEWISH LIGHTS PUBLISHING

LongHill Partners, Inc., Sunset Farm Offices, Rt. 4, P.O. Box 237, Woodstock VT 05091. (802)457-4000. **Fax:** (802)457-4004. **E-mail:** editorial@jewishlights.com; sales@jewishlights.com. **Website:** www.jewishlights.com. **Contact:** Tim Holtz, art acquisitions. "Jewish Lights publishes books for people of all faiths and all backgrounds who yearn for books that attract, engage, educate and spiritually inspire. Our authors are at the forefront of spiritual thought and deal with the quest for the self and for meaning in life by drawing on the Jewish wisdom tradition. Our books cover topics including history, spirituality, life cycle, children, self-help, recovery, theology and philosophy. We do not publish autobiography, biography, fiction, haggadot, poetry or cookbooks. At this point we plan to do only two books for children annually, and one will be for younger children (ages 4-10)." Publishes hardcover and trade paperback originals, trade paperback reprints. Publishes 30 titles/year. 50% of books from first-time authors. 75% from unagented writers.

FICTION Picture books, young readers, middle readers: spirituality. "We are not interested in anything other than spirituality." Recently published *God's Paintbrush*, by Sandy Eisenberg Sasso, illustrated by Annette Compton (ages 4-9).

NONFICTION Picture book, young readers, middle readers: activity books, spirituality. Recently published *When a Grandparent Dies: A Kid's Own Remembering Workbook for Dealing with Shiva and the Year Beyond*, by Nechama Liss-Levinson, Ph.D. (ages 7-11); *Tough Questions Jews Ask: A Young Adult's Guide to Building a Jewish Life*, by Rabbi Edward Feinstein (ages 12 and up). "We do not publish haggadot, biography, poetry, or cookbooks."

HOW TO CONTACT Query with outline/synopsis, 2 sample chapters and marketing plan; submit complete ms for picture books. Include SASE. Responds in 6 months to queries. Publishes ms 1 year after acceptance.

TERMS Pays authors royalty of 10% of revenue received; 15% royalty for subsequent printings. Book catalog and ms guidelines online.

TIPS "We publish books for all faiths and backgrounds that also reflect the Jewish wisdom tradition. Explain in your cover letter why you're submitting your project to us in particular. Make sure you know what we publish."

JOURNEYFORTH

Imprint of BJU Press, 1700 Wade Hampton Blvd., Greenville SC 29614. (864)242-5100, ext. 4350. **Fax:** (864)298-0268. **E-mail:** nlohr@bju.edu. **Website:** www.journeyforth.com. **Contact:** Nancy Lohr. "Small independent publisher of trustworthy novels and biographies for readers pre-school through high school from a conservative Christian perspective, Christian living books, and Bible studies for adults." Specializes in trade books. Publishes paperback originals. Publishes 1 picture book/year; 2 young readers/year; 4 middle readers/year; 4 young adult titles/year. 10% of books by first-time authors. 8% from unagented writers.

FICTION Young readers, middle readers, young adults: adventure, animal, contemporary, fantasy, folktales, history, humor, multicultural, nature/environment, problem novels, suspense/mystery. Average word length: Ages 6-8—8,000-10,000; ages 9-12—30,000-50,000; young adult/teens—40,000-60,000. Our fiction is all based on a moral and Christian worldview.

HOW TO CONTACT Submit outline/synopsis and 5 sample chapters. "Do not send stories with magical elements. We are not currently accepting picture books. We do not publish: romance, science fiction, poetry, short stories and drama." Responds in 3 months. Publishes book 12-15 months after acceptance. Will consider previously published work.

ILLUSTRATION Works with 2-4 illustrators/year. Query with samples. Send promo sheet; will review website portfolio if applicable. Responds only if interested. Samples returned with SASE; samples filed.

TERMS Pays authors royalty based on wholesale price. Pays illustrators by the project. Originals returned to artist at job's completion. Pays royalty. Book catalog available free. Guidelines available online at www.bjupress.com/books/freelance.php.

TIPS "We aim to produce well-written books for readers of varying abilities and interests and fully consistent with biblical worldview. Review our backlist to be sure your work is a good fit. Study the publisher's guidelines. No picture books and no submissions by e-mail."

KAMEHAMEHA PUBLISHING

567 S. King St., Suite 118, Honolulu HI 96813. **E-mail:** publishing@ksbe.edu. **Website:** www.Kamehameha Publishing.org. "Kamehameha Schools Press publishes in the areas of Hawaiian history, Hawaiian culture, Hawaiian language and Hawaiian studies."

FICTION Young reader, middle readers, young adults: biography, history, multicultural, Hawaiian folklore.

NONFICTION Young reader, middle readers, young adults: biography, history, multicultural, Hawaiian folklore.

HOW TO CONTACT Responds in 3 months to queries and mss. Publishes ms 2 years after acceptance.

ILLUSTRATION Uses color and b&w artwork. Illustrations only: Query with samples. Responds only if interested. Samples not returned.

TERMS Work purchased outright from authors or by royalty agreement. Call or write for book catalog.

TIPS "Writers and illustrators must be knowledgeable in Hawaiian history/culture and be able to show credentials to validate their proficiency. Greatly prefer to work with writers/illustrators available in the Honolulu area."

Ⓐ ⓒ ⊙ KANE/MILLER BOOK PUBLISHERS

Kane/Miller: A Division of EDC Publishing, 4901 Morena Blvd., Suite 213, San Diego CA 92117. (858)456-0540. **Fax:** (858)456-9641. **E-mail:** info@kanemiller.com. **E-mail:** submissions@kanemiller.com. **Website:** www.kanemiller.com. "Kane/Miller Book Publishers is a division of EDC Publishing, specializing in award-winning children's books from around the world. Our books bring the children of the world closer to each other, sharing stories and ideas, while exploring cultural differences and similarities. Although we continue to look for books from other countries, we are now actively seeking works that convey cultures and communities within the US. We are looking for picture book fiction and nonfiction on those subjects that may be defined as particularly American: sports such as baseball, historical events, American biographies, American folk tales, etc. We are committed to expanding our early and middle grade fiction list. We're interested in great stories with engaging characters in all genres (mystery, fantasy, adventure, historical, etc.) and, as with picture books, especially those with particularly American subjects."

> "We like to think that a child reading a Kane/Miller book will see parallels between his own life and what might be the unfamiliar setting and characters of the story. And that by seeing how a character who is somehow or in some way dissimilar—an outsider—finds a way to fit comfortably into a culture or community or situation while maintaining a healthy sense of self and self-dignity, she might be empowered to do the same."

FICTION Picture books: concept, contemporary, health, humor, multicultural. Young readers: contemporary, multicultural, suspense. Middle readers: contemporary, humor, multicultural, suspense.

HOW TO CONTACT All submissions sent via USPS should be sent to: Editorial Department. Please do not send anything requiring a signature. Work submitted

for consideration may also be sent via e-mail. Please send either the complete picture book ms, the published book (with a summary and outline in English, if that is not the language of origin) or a synopsis of the work and two sample chapters. Do not send originals. Responds in 3 months.

ILLUSTRATION Illustrators may send color copies, tear sheets, or other non-returnable illustration samples. If you have a website with additional samples of your work, please include the web address. Please do not send original artwork, or samples on CD.

TIPS "A SASE must be included if you send your submission via USPS; otherwise you will not receive a reply. If we wish to follow up, we will notify you."

KAR-BEN PUBLISHING

11430 Strand Dr. No. 2, Rockville MD 20852. (301)984-8733. **Fax:** (301)881-9195. **E-mail:** Editorial@Karben.com. **Website:** www.karben.com. Publishes hardcover, trade paperback and electronic originals. Publishes 10-15 titles/year. 20% of books from first-time authors. 70% from unagented writers.

FICTION "We seek picture book mss of about 1,000 words on Jewish-themed topics for children." Picture books: adventure, concept, folktales, history, humor, multicultural, religion, special needs; must be on a Jewish theme. Average word length: picture books—1,000. Recently published *Engineer Ari and the Rosh Hashanah Ride*, by Deborah Bodin Cohen, illustrated by Shahar Kober; and *The Wedding That Saved a Town*, by Yale Strom, illustrated by Jenya Prosmitsky.

NONFICTION "In addition to traditional Jewish-themed stories about Jewish holidays, history, folktales and other subjects, we especially seek stories that reflect the rich diversity of the contemporary Jewish community." Picture books, young readers: activity books, arts/crafts, biography, careers, concept, cooking, history, how-to, multicultural, religion, social issues, special needs; must be of Jewish interest. No textbooks, games, or educational materials.

HOW TO CONTACT Submit full ms. 800 mss received/year. Responds in 6 weeks. Most mss published within 2 years. Do not submit art with ms.

ILLUSTRATION Query with samples. Color photocopies and tearsheets preferred.

TERMS Pays 3-5% royalty on NET price. Pays $500-2,500 advance. Book catalog available online; free upon request. Guidelines available online.

TIPS "Authors: Do a literature search to make sure similar title doesn't already exist. Illustrators: Look at our online catalog for a sense of what we like—bright colors and lively composition."

KIDS CAN PRESS

25 Dockside Dr., Toronto ON M5A 0B5, Canada. (416)479-7000. **Fax:** (416)960-5437. **E-mail:** info@kidscan.com; kkalmar@kidscan.com. **Website:** www.kidscanpress.com. U.S. address: 2250 Military Rd., Tonawanda, NY 14150.

Kids Can Press is currently accepting unsolicited mss from Canadian adult authors only.

FICTION Picture books, young readers: adventure, animal, concept, contemporary, folktales, history, humor, multicultural, nature/environment, special needs, sports, suspense/mystery. "We do not accept young adult fiction or fantasy novels for any age." Average word length: picture books—1,000-2,000; young readers—750-1,500; middle readers 10,000-15,000. Recently published *Rosie & Buttercup* by Chieri Ugaki, illustrated by Shephane Jorisch (picture book); *The Landing* by John Ibbitson (novel); *Scaredy Squirrel* by Melanie Watt, illustrated by Melanie Watt (picture book).

NONFICTION Picture books: activity books, animal, arts/crafts, biography, careers, concept, health, history, hobbies, how-to, multicultural, nature/environment, science, social issues, special needs, sports. Young readers: activity books, animal, arts/crafts, biography, careers, concept, history, hobbies, how-to, multicultural. Middle readers: cooking, music/dance. Average word length: picture books—500-1,250; young readers—750-2,000; middle readers—5,000-15,000. Recently published *The Kids Book of Canadian Geography*, by Briony Penn, illustrated by Heather Collins (informational activity); *It's Moving Day!*, by Pamela Hickman, illustrated by Geraldo Valerio (animal/nature); *Everywear*, by Ellen Warwick, illustrated by Bernice Lum (craft book).

HOW TO CONTACT Submit outline/synopsis and 2 to 3 sample chapters. For picture books submit complete ms. Responds in 6 months only if interesed. Publishes book 18-24 months after acceptance.

ILLUSTRATION Works with 40 illustrators/year. Reviews ms/illustration packages from artists. Send color copies of illustration portfolio, cover letter outlining other experience. Send tearsheets, color photocopies. Responds only if interested.

KNOPF, DELACORTE, DELL BOOKS FOR YOUNG READERS

1745 Broadway, New York NY 10019. (212)782-9000. **Website:** www.randomhouse.com/kids. Imprint of Random House Children's Books, Division of Random House, Inc.

Knopf/Crown Books for Young Readers is seeking submissions, but Bantam Delacorte Dell is not. No e-mail samples are accepted. No calls accepted. See listings for Random House/Golden Books for Young Readers Group, Delacorte and Doubleday Books for Young Readers, Alfred A. Knopf and Crown Books for Young Readers, and Wendy Lamb Books.

FICTION Picture books: submit ms with cover letter. Novels: submit cover letter, synopsis and 25 pages. Do not include SASE.

HOW TO CONTACT Responds in 6 months if interested.

KRBY CREATIONS, LLC

P.O. Box 327, Bay Head NJ 08742. (732)691-3010. **Fax:** (815)846-0636. **E-mail:** info@KRBYCreations.com. **Website:** www.KRBYCreations.com.

FICTION Recently published picture books include *The Snowman in the Moon*, by Stephen Heigh; *Mulch the Lawnmower*, by Scott Nelson; *My Imagination*, by Katrina Estes-Hill.

HOW TO CONTACT Writers *must* request guidelines by e-mail prior to submitting mss. See website. Submissions without annotation found in guidelines will not be considered. Responds to queries in 1 week; mss in 3 months. Publishes book 1 year after acceptance.

ILLUSTRATION Send samples with cover letter and résumé. "Include your expectations of compensation/advances in your cover letter."

TERMS Pays authors royalty of 6-15% based on wholesale price. Catalog on website. Offers guidelines by e-mail.

TIPS "Submit as professionally as possible; make your vision clear to us about what you are trying to capture. Know your market/audience and identify it in your proposal. Tell us what is new/unique with your idea."

KREGEL PUBLICATIONS

Kregel, Inc., P.O. Box 2607, Grand Rapids MI 49501. (616)451-4775. **Fax:** (616)451-9330. **E-mail:** kregel books@kregel.com. **Website:** www.kregelpublica tions.com. **Contact:** Dennis R. Hillman, publisher. "Our mission as an evangelical Christian publisher is to provide—with integrity and excellence—trusted, Biblically based resources that challenge and encourage individuals in their Christian lives. Works in theology and Biblical studies should reflect the historic, orthodox Protestant tradition." Publishes hardcover and trade paperback originals and reprints. Publishes 90 titles/year. 20% of books from first-time authors.

> *Kregel Publications no longer accepts unsolicited submissions.*

FICTION Fiction should be geared toward the evangelical Christian market. Wants books with fast-paced, contemporary storylines presenting a strong Christian message in an engaging, entertaining style.
NONFICTION "We serve evangelical Christian readers and those in career Christian service."
HOW TO CONTACT Publishes ms 16 months after acceptance.
TERMS Pays royalty on wholesale price. Pays negotiable advance. Guidelines available online.
TIPS "Our audience consists of conservative, evangelical Christians, including pastors and ministry students."

WENDY LAMB BOOKS

Imprint of Random House Children's Books/Random House, Inc., 1745 Broadway, New York NY 10019. (212)782-9000. **Fax:** (212)782-9452. **E-mail:** wlamb@ randomhouse.com; cmeckler@randomhouse.com. **Website:** www.randomhouse.com. Publishes hardcover originals.

> Literary fiction and nonfiction for readers 8-15.

FICTION Recently published *When You Reach Me*, by Rebecca Stead; *Love, Aubrey*, by Suzanne LaFleur; *Eyes of the Emperor*, by Graham Salisbury; *A Brief Chapter in My Impossible Life*, by Dana Reinhardt; *What They Found: Love on 145th Street*, by Walter Dean Myers; *Eleven*, by Patricia Reilly Giff. Other WLB authors include Christopher Paul Curtis, Gary Paulsen, Donna Jo Napoli, Peter Dickinson, Marthe Jocelyn, Graham McNamee.
HOW TO CONTACT "Query letter with SASE for reply. A query letter should briefly describe the book you have written, the intended age group, and your

brief biography and publishing credits, if any. If you like, you may send no more than 10 pages of the ms."
TERMS Pays royalty. Guidelines for SASE.
TIPS "Please note that we do not publish picture books. Please send the first 10 pages of your ms (or until the end of the first chapter) along with a cover letter, synopsis, and SASE. Before you submit, please take a look at some of our recent titles to get an idea of what we publish."

Ⓐ LAUREL-LEAF

Imprint of Random House Children's Books/Random House, Inc. 1745 Broadway, New York NY 10019. (212)782-9000. **Fax:** (212)782-9452. **Website:** www. randomhouse.com/teens.

> Quality reprint paperback imprint for young adult paperback books. *Does not accept unsolicited mss.*

ILLUSTRATION "Artwork for picture books, middle grade, young adult novels and nonfiction. Please send samples (postcards). No e-mail submissions."

LEE & LOW BOOKS

95 Madison Ave., Suite #1205, New York NY 10016. (212)779-4400. **E-mail:** general@leeandlow.com. **Website:** www.leeandlow.com. **Contact:** Louise May, editor-in-chief (multicultural children's fiction/nonfiction). "Our goals are to meet a growing need for books that address children of color, and to present literature that all children can identify with. We only consider multicultural children's books. Currently emphasizing material for 5-12 year olds. Sponsors a yearly New Voices Award for first-time picture book authors of color. Contest rules online at website or for SASE." Publishes hardcover originals and trade paperback reprints. Publishes 12-14 titles/year. 20% of books from first-time authors. 50% from unagented writers.
FICTION Picture books, young readers: anthology, contemporary, history, multicultural, poetry. Picture book, middle reader: contemporary, history, multicultural, nature/environment, poetry, sports. Average word length: picture books—1,000-1,500 words. Recently published *Gracias~Thanks*, by Pat Mora; *Balarama*, by Ted and Betsy Lewin; *Yasmin's Hammer*, by Ann Malaspina; *Only One Year*, by Andrea Cheng (chapter book). "We do not publish folklore or animal stories."
NONFICTION Picture books: concept. Picture books, middle readers: biography, history, multicul-

tural, science and sports. Average word length: picture books-1,500-3,000. Recently published *Seeds of Change*, by Jen Cullerton Johnson; *Sharing Our Homeland*, by Trish Marx.

HOW TO CONTACT For picture books, submit complete ms. For middle grade mss of more than 10,000 words, query with synopsis/outline. Receives 100 queries/year; 1,200 mss/year. Responds in 6 months to mss if interested. Publishes book 2 years after acceptance.

ILLUSTRATION Works with 12-14 illustrators/year. Uses color artwork only. Reviews ms/illustration packages from artists. "We are especially interested in samples that feature children/people of color and that show an ability to illustrate the same character consistently over many scenes." Illustrations only: Query with samples, résumé, promo sheet and tearsheets. Responds only if interested. Samples returned with SASE; samples sometimes filed. Original artwork returned at job's completion.

PHOTOGRAPHY Buys photos from freelancers. Works on assignment only. Model/property releases required. Submit cover letter, résumé, promo piece and book dummy.

TERMS Pays net royalty. Pays authors advances against royalty. Pays illustrators advance against royalty. Photographers paid advance against royalty. Book catalog available online. Guidelines available online or by written request with SASE.

TIPS "Check our website to see the kinds of books we publish. Do not send mss that don't fit our mission."

LEGACY PRESS

P.O. Box 261129, San Diego CA 92196. (800)323-7337. **E-mail:** editor@rainbowpublishers.com. **Website:** www.rainbowpublishers.com; www.legacypresskids.com. Publishes 4 young readers/year; 4 middle readers/year; 4 young adult titles/year. 50% of books by first-time authors. "Our mission is to publish Bible-based, teacher resource materials that contribute to and inspire spiritual growth and development in kids ages 2-12."

NONFICTION Young readers, middle readers, young adult/teens: activity books, arts/crafts, how-to, reference, religion.

HOW TO CONTACT Submit book proposal with 2-5 chapters. Guidelines available online. Responds to queries in 6 weeks, mss in 3 months.

ILLUSTRATION Submit samples by mail. "Note that we only contract with illustrators who work with

Quark, Illustrator or Photoshop software (Mac OS preferred), so please indicate which software and operating system you use."

TERMS For authors work purchased outright (range: $500 and up). Pays illustrators by the project (range: $300 and up). Sends galleys to authors.

TIPS "Our Rainbow imprint publishes reproducible books for teachers of children in Christian ministries, including crafts, activities, games and puzzles. Our Legacy imprint publishes titles for children such as devotionals, fiction and Christian living. Please write for guidelines and study the market before submitting material."

LERNER PUBLISHING GROUP

1251 Washing Ave. N, Minneapolis MN 55401. (800)328-4929. **E-mail:** editorial@karben.com; dwallek@igigraphics.com. **Website:** www.karben.com; www.lernerbooks.com. Primarily publishes books for children ages 7-18. List includes titles in geography, natural and physical science, current events, ancient and modern history, high interest, sports, world cultures, and numerous biography series.

> ○ Lerner Publishing Group no longer accepts submissions in any of their imprints except for Kar-Ben Publishing."

HOW TO CONTACT "We will continue to seek targeted solicitations at specific reading levels and in specific subject areas. The company will list these targeted solicitations on our website and in national newsletters, such as the SCBWI *Bulletin*."

○● ARTHUR A. LEVINE BOOKS

Scholastic, Inc., 557 Broadway, New York NY 10012. (212)343-4436. **Fax:** (212)343-4890. **E-mail:** arthuralevinebooks@scholastic.com; eclement@scholastic.com; arthuralevinebooks@gmail.com. **Website:** www.arthuralevinebooks.com. **Contact:** Arthur A. Levine, editorial director; Cheryl Klein, senior editor. Imprint of Scholastic, Inc. "Arthur A. Levine is looking for distinctive literature, for children and young adults, for whatever's extraordinary." Publishes hardback and soft cover prints and reprints. Averages 18-20 total titles/year.

> ○ "As we have recently switched to an online submissions review, we will no longer be accepting paper queries through the mail."

FICTION Recently published *Bobby Vs. Girls (Accidentally)*, by Lisa Yee (chapter book); *The Perfect Gift*, by Mary Newell DePalma, (picture book); *Moribito II: Guardian of the Darkness*, by Nahoko Uehashi, trans. by Cathy Hirano (novel); *The Memory Bank*, by Carolyn Coman (chapter book); *Plain Kate*, by Erin Bow (novel); *Marcelo In The Real World*, by Francisco X Stork; *Lips Touch*, by Laini Taylor, illustrations by Jim Di Bartolo.

NONFICTION Recently published *Peaceful Heroes*, by Jonah Winter, illustrated by Sean Addy (picture book); *The Fabulous Feud of Gilbert and Sullivan*, by Jonah Winter, illustrated by Richard Egielski (picture book).

POETRY Query with 5 sample pages.

HOW TO CONTACT Query via e-mail to arthuralevinebooks@gmail.com. For novels, include 2 sample chapters. For nonfiction or poetry, include 5 sample pages. For picture books, include complete ms. Attach samples/mss as separate Word documents. In subject line, indicate the format/age group of your submission (e.g., "Picture Book Query"). Responds in 1 month to queries; 5 months to mss. Publishes a book 18 months after acceptance.

ILLUSTRATION Query by e-mail. Include 3 sample illustrations as attachment. Include links to online portfolios.

Ⓐ LITTLE, BROWN AND CO. BOOKS FOR YOUNG READERS

Hachette Book Group USA, 237 Park Ave., New York NY 10017. (212)364-1100. **Fax:** (212)364-0925. **E-mail:** pamela.gruber@hbgusa.com. **Website:** www.lb-kids.com; www.lb-teens.com. "Little, Brown and Co. Children's Publishing publishes all formats including board books, picture books, middle grade fiction, and nonfiction YA titles. We are looking for strong writing and presentation, but no predetermined topics." *Only interested in solicited agented material.* Publishes 100-150 titles/year.

FICTION Picture books: humor, adventure, animal, contemporary, history, multicultural, folktales. Young adults: contemporary, humor, multicultural, suspense/mystery, chick lit. Multicultural needs include "any material by, for and about minorities." Average word length: picture books—1,000; young readers—6,000; middle readers—15,000- 50,000; young adults—50,000 and up.

NONFICTION "Writers should avoid looking for the 'issue' they think publishers want to see, choosing instead topics they know best and are most enthusiastic about/inspired by." Middle readers, young adults: arts/crafts, history, multicultural, nature, self help, social issues, sports, science. Average word length: middle readers—15,000-25,000; young adults—20,000-40,000. Recently published *American Dreaming*, by Laban Carrick Hill; *Exploratopia*, by the Exploratorium; *Yeah! Yeah! Yeah!: The Beatles, Beatlemania, and the Music that Changed the World*, by Bob Spitz.

HOW TO CONTACT *Agented submissions only.* Responds in 1 month to queries; 2 months to proposals and mss. Publishes ms 2 years after acceptance.

ILLUSTRATION Does not accept unsolicited submissions of art.

PHOTOGRAPHY Works on assignment only. Model/property releases required; captions required. Publishes photo essays and photo concept books. Uses 35mm transparencies. Photographers should provide résumé, promo sheets or tearsheets to be kept on file.

TERMS Pays authors royalties based on retail price. Pays illustrators and photographers by the project or royalty based on retail price. Sends galleys to authors; dummies to illustrators. Pays negotiable advance.

TIPS "In order to break into the field, authors and illustrators should research their competition and try to come up with something outstandingly different."

Ⓒ LOLLIPOP POWER BOOKS

120 Morris Street, Durham NC 27701. (919)560-2738. **Fax:** (919)560-2759. **E-mail:** carolinawrenpress@earthlink.net; andreaselch@earthlink.net. **Website:** www.carolinawrenpress.org. Currently not accepting unsolicited submissions. "Please check our website to see if we have re-opened submissions."

"In the past, Carolina Wren Press and Lollipop Power specialized in children's books that counter stereotypes or debunk myths about race, gender, sexual orientation, etc. We are also interested in books that deal with health or mental health issues—one of our biggest sellers is *Puzzles* (about a young girl coping with Sickle Cell Disease) and we are currently promoting *Peace Comes to Ajani*, about anger management. Many of our children's titles are bilingual (English/Spanish). Please note, however, that as of 2009, we are no longer holding open submission periods for children's literature."

TERMS Pays authors royalty of 10% minimum based on retail price or work purchased outright from authors (range: $500-2,000). Pays illustrators by the project (range: $500-2,000). Catalog available on website.

MAGICAL CHILD

Shades of White, 301 Tenth Ave., Crystal City MO 63019. **E-mail:** acquisitions@magicalchildbooks. com. **Website:** www.magicalchildbooks.com. "The Neo-Pagan Earth Religions Community is the fastest growing demographic in the spiritual landscape, and Pagan parents are crying out for books appropriate for the Pagan kids. It is our plan to fill this small, but growing need."

   ○ As of 2012, magical child is no longer accepting submissions.

FICTION Picture Books: adventure, contemporary, nature/environment. Young readers: adventure, contemporary, nature/environment. Middle readers: adventure, contemporary, nature/environment, submit only stories appropriate for Earth Religions *not* Native American. Average word length: picture books—500-800; young readers—500-4,500; middle readers—11,200-28,000. Recently published *Aidan's First Full Moon Circle*, by W. Lyon Martin (ages 5-8, picture book); *An Ordinary Girl, A Magical Child*, by W. Lyon Martin (ages 5-8, chapter book); *Smoky and the Feast of Mabon*, by Catherynne M. Valente (ages 4-8, picture book).

NONFICTION Middle Readers: biography, history (Earth religions only for both). Average word length: middle readers—11,200-28,000.

HOW TO CONTACT Responds in 3 weeks to queries; 3-6 months to mss.

ILLUSTRATION Works with 1-2 illustrators/year. Uses color artwork only. Reviews ms/illustrations packages from artists. Send manuscript with dummy. Illustrations only: send résumé, client list, tearsheets. Contact: Art Director. Samples returned with SASE; samples filed if interested.

TERMS Pays authors royalty based on retail price. Offers advances. Pays illustrators royalty based on wholesale price.

TIPS "Visit our submissions guidelines on the website. Follow the information provided there. We expect our authors to take an active role in promoting their books. If you can't do that, please don't submit your manuscript. *No calls, please.* Our list is *very* specific. Please do not send us manuscripts outside of our requested needs."

MAGINATION PRESS

750 First Street NE, Washington DC 20002. (202)336-5000. **Fax:** (202)336-5624. **E-mail:** rteeter@apa.org. **Website:** www.apa.org/pubs/magination/index.aspx. **Contact:** Kristine Enderle, managing editor. Magination Press is an imprint of the American Psychological Association. "We publish books dealing with the psycho/therapeutic resolution of children's problems and psychological issues with a strong self-help component." Submit complete ms. Materials returned only with SASE. Publishes 12 titles/year. 75% of books from first-time authors.

FICTION All levels: psychological and social issues, self-help, health, parenting concerns and special needs. Picture books, middle school readers. Recently published *Nobody's Perfect: A Story for Children about Perfection*, by Ellen Flanagan Burns, illustrated by Erica Pelton Villnave (ages 8-12); *Murphy's Three Homes: A Story for Children in Foster Care*, by Jan Levinson Gilman, illustrated by Kathy O'Malley (ages 4-8).

NONFICTION All levels: psychological and social issues, self-help, health, multicultural, special needs. Recently published *Putting on the Brakes: Understanding and Taking Control of Your ADD or ADHD* (ages 8-13), by Patricia Quinn and Judith M. Stern, illustrated by Joe Lee.

HOW TO CONTACT Submit complete ms, plus summary, description of audience and market, and résumé. "Be sure to specify in your summary the psychological issue or situation you are addressing." Complete guidelines online. Responds in 6 months. Publishes book 18-24 months after acceptance.

ILLUSTRATION Works with 10-15 illustrators/year. Reviews ms/illustration packages. Will review artwork for future assignments. Responds only if interested, or immediately if SASE or response card is included. "We keep samples on file."

✎ MASKEW MILLER LONGMAN

(27)(21)531-8103. **E-mail:** antheavariend@mml.co.za. **Website:** www.mml.co.za. "The Maskew Miller Longman Group has over 100 years of publishing experience in southern Africa, with staff and offices in countries throughout southern, central and east Africa. As partners to government in the educational arena, we develop local materials for local needs. We are one of the leading educational publishers in Africa. We tap into global expertise: whether it be in education, technology or customer services, we benefit from being part of Pearson Education, which is the largest educational publisher in the world and which produces the best and most up-to-date learning material available. We publish in more than 50 languages, including all of South Africa's official languages as well as French, Portuguese, and numerous African languages in each of the countries in which we operate." Publishes teacher references and dictionaries for educational markets. Interested in all genres (poetry/ novels/short stories/plays) of African language literature, as well as material for the Young Africa and They Fought for Freedom series in English.

◯ MASTER BOOKS

P.O. Box 726, Green Forest AR 72638. (870)438-5288. **Fax:** (870)438-5120. **E-mail:** submissions@ newleafpress.net; nlp@newleafpress.net; amanda@newleafpress.net. **Website:** www.master books.net. **Contact:** Craig Forman, acquisitions editor. Publishes 3 middle readers/year; 2 young adult nonfiction titles/year; 15 adult trade books/year. 10% of books from first-time authors.

NONFICTION Picture books: activity books, animal, nature/environment, creation. Young readers, middle readers, young adults: activity books, animal, biography Christian, nature/environment, science, creation. Recently published *Passport to the World* (middle readers); *Demolishing Supposed Bible Contradictions*, compiled by Ken Ham (adult series).

HOW TO CONTACT Submit book proposal with proposal form to be found online. Do not submit ms unless it is requested. Responds in 3 months. Publishes book 1 year after acceptance.

TERMS Pays authors royalty of 3-15% based on wholesale price. Book catalog available upon request. Guidelines available on website.

TIPS "All of our children's books are creation-based, including topics from the Book of Genesis. We look also for home school educational material that would be supplementary to a home school curriculum."

◯ MARGARET K. MCELDERRY BOOKS

Imprint of Simon & Schuster Children's Publishing Division, Simon & Schuster, 1230 Sixth Ave., New York NY 10020. (212)698-7200. **Website:** www.si monsayskids.com. **Contact:** Justin Chanda, vice president; Karen Wojtyla, editorial director; Ruta Rimas, associate editor; Emily Fabre, assistant editor. "Mar-

garet K. McElderry Books publishes hardcover and paperback trade books for children from preschool age through young adult. This list includes picture books, middle grade and teen fiction, poetry, and fantasy. The style and subject matter of the books we publish is almost unlimited. We do not publish textbooks, coloring and activity books, greeting cards, magazines, pamphlets, or religious publications." Publishes 30 titles/year. 15% of books from first-time authors. 50% from unagented writers.

◯ *Does not accept unsolicited mss.*

FICTION We will consider any category. Results depend on the quality of the imagination, the artwork, and the writing. Average word length: picture books—500; young readers—2,000; middle readers—10,000-20,000; young adults—45,000-50,000. Recently Published: *Monster Mess*, by Margery Cuyler, illustrated by S. D. Schindler (picture book); *The Joy of Spooking: Fiendish Deeds*, by P. J. Bracegirdle (chapter book); *Identical*, by Ellen Hopkins (teen); *Where is Home, Little Pip?*, by Karma Wilson; illustrated by Jane Chapman (picture book); *Doctor Ted*, by Andrea Beaty, illustrated by Pascal Lemaitre (picture book); *To Be Mona*, by Kelly Easton (teen).

NONFICTION Looks for originality of ideas, clarity and felicity of expression, well-organized plot and strong characterization (fiction) or clear exposition (nonfiction); quality.

TERMS Pays authors royalty based on retail price. Pays illustrator royalty of by the project. Pays photographers by the project. Original artwork returned at job's completion. Offers $5,000-8,000 advance for new authors. Guidelines for SASE.

TIPS "Read! The children's book field is competitive. See what's been done and what's out there before submitting. We look for high quality: an originality of ideas, clarity and felicity of expression, a well organized plot, and strong character-driven stories. We're looking for strong, original fiction, especially mysteries and middle grade humor. We are always interested in picture books for the youngest age reader. Study our titles."

MEADOWBROOK PRESS

6110 Blue Circle Dr., Minnesota MN 55343. (800)338-2232). **Fax:** (952)930-1940. **E-mail:** info@meadow brookpress.com. **Website:** www.meadowbrookpress. com. Publishes trade paperback originals and reprints. 20% of books from first-time authors.

NONFICTION Publishes activity books, arts/crafts, how-to. Average word length: varies. Recently published *The Siblings' Busy Book* by Heather Kempskie & Lisa Hanson (activity book). No academic or biography.

POETRY Recently published *I Hope I Don't Strike Out*, by Bruce Lansky. "Meadowbrook Press is currently looking for your funniest poems to be considered for our future poetry anthologies. Our primary target audience is children age 6-12. Be sure to read our books or visit our popular children's poetry website www.gigglepoetry.com to get a feel for our style." Length: 24 lines maximum.

HOW TO CONTACT Query or submit outline with sample chapter. 1,500 queries received/year. Responds only if interested to queries. Publishes book 2 years after acceptance.

ILLUSTRATION Works with 4 illustrators/year. Submit 2-3 nonreturnable samples. Responds only if interested. Samples filed.

PHOTOGRAPHY Buys photos from freelancers. Buys stock. Model/property releases required.

TERMS Pays 7 1/2% royalty. Pays $50-100/poem plus 1 contributor's copy. Pays small advance. Book catalog for SASE. Guidelines available online.

TIPS "Always send for guidelines before submitting material. Always submit nonreturnable copies; we do not respond to queries or submissions unless interested."

MERIWETHER PUBLISHING LTD.

885 Elkton Dr., Colorado Springs CO 80907. (719)594-9916. **Fax:** (719)594-9916. **E-mail:** editor@meriwether.com. **Website:** www.meriwetherpublishing.com. **Contact:** Ted Zapel; Rhonda Wray. "Our niche is drama. Our books cover a wide variety of theatre subjects from play anthologies to theatrecraft. We publish books of monologues, duologues, short one-act plays, scenes for students, acting textbooks, how-to speech and theatre textbooks, and improvisation and theatre games. Our Christian books cover worship on such topics as clown ministry, storytelling, banner-making, drama ministry, children's worship and more. We also publish anthologies of Christian sketches. We do not publish works of fiction or devotionals." 75% of books from first-time authors.

FICTION Middle readers, young adults: anthology, contemporary, humor, religion. "We publish plays, not prose fiction. Our emphasis is comedy plays instead of educational themes."

NONFICTION Middle readers: activity books, how-to, religion, textbooks. Young adults: activity books, drama/theater arts, how-to church activities, religion. Average length: 250 pages. Recently published *Acting for Life*, by Jack Frakes; *Scenes Keep Happening*, by Mary Krell-Oishi; *Service with a Smile*, by Daniel Wray.

HOW TO CONTACT For drama, submit ms. For books, query or submit sample chapters or outline. Responds in 2 months. Publishes book 6-12 months after acceptance.

ILLUSTRATION "We do our illustration in house."

TERMS Pays authors royalty of 10% based on retail or wholesale price.

TIPS "We are currently interested in finding unique treatments for theater arts subjects: scene books, how-to books, musical comedy scripts, monologues and short comedy plays for teens."

MILKWEED EDITIONS

1011 Washington Ave. S., Suite 300, Minneapolis MN 55415. (612)332-3192. **Fax:** (612)215-2550. **E-mail:** submissions@milkweed.org. **Website:** www.milkweed.org. "Milkweed Editions publishes with the intention of making a humane impact on society, in the belief that literature is a transformative art uniquely able to convey the essential experiences of the human heart and spirit. To that end, Milkweed Editions publishes distinctive voices of literary merit in handsomely designed, visually dynamic books, exploring the ethical, cultural, and aesthetic issues that free societies need continually to address." Publishes hardcover, trade paperback, and electronic originals; trade paperback and electronic reprints. Publishes 3-4 middle reader titles/year. 25% of books from first-time authors. 75% from unagented writers.

"Please consider our previous publications when considering submissions."

FICTION Novels for adults and for readers 8-13. High literary quality. Adult readers: literary fiction, nonfiction, poetry, essays. Middle readers/young adult: adventure, contemporary, fantasy, multicultural, nature/environment, suspense/mystery. Does not want to see folktales, health, hi-lo, mystery, picture books, poetry, religion, romance, science, sports. Average length: middle readers/young adult—90-200 pages. Recently published *The Linden Tree*, by Ellie Mathews (contemporary); *The Cat*, by Jutta Richter (contemporary/translation).

HOW TO CONTACT Accepts mss only January-March and July-September. Query with SASE, submit completed ms. Responds in 6 months to queries, proposals, and mss. Publishes book in 18 months.

TERMS Pays authors variable royalty based on retail price. Offers advance against royalties. Pays varied advance from $500-10,000. Book catalog available online at website. Guidelines available online at website www.milkweed.org/content/blogcategory.

TIPS "We are looking for excellent writing with the intent of making a humane impact on society. Please read submission guidelines before submitting and acquaint yourself with our books in terms of style and quality before submitting. Many factors influence our selection process, so don't get discouraged."

☺ THE MILLBROOK PRESS

Lerner Publishing Group, 1251 Washington Ave. N, Minneapolis MN 55401. **Website:** www.lernerbooks.com. **Contact:** Carol Hinz, editorial director. "Millbrook Press publishes informative picture books, illustrated nonfiction titles, and inspiring photo-driven titles for grades K–5. Our authors approach curricular topics with a fresh point of view. Our fact-filled books engage readers with fun yet accessible writing, high-quality photographs, and a wide variety of illustration styles. We cover subjects ranging from the parts of speech and other language arts skills; to history, science, and math; to art, sports, crafts, and other interests. Millbrook Press is the home of the bestselling Words Are CATegorical® series and Bob Raczka's Art Adventures."

> *"We do not accept unsolicited manuscripts from authors.* Occasionally, we may put out a call for submissions, which will be announced on our website."

MITCHELL LANE PUBLISHERS INC.

P.O. Box 196, Hockessin DE 19707. (302)234-9426. **Fax:** (866)834-4164. **E-mail:** barbaramitchell@mitchelllane.com. **Website:** www.mitchelllane.com. **Contact:** Barbara Mitchell, publisher. Publishes hardcover and library bound originals. Publishes 80 titles/year. 0% of books from first-time authors. 90% from unagented writers.

NONFICTION Young readers, middle readers, young adults: biography, nonfiction, and curriculum-related subjects. Average word length: 4,000-50,000 words. Recently published *Katy Perry* and *Prince William*

(both Blue Banner Biographies); *Justin Bieber* (A Robbie Reader); Earth Science Projects for Kids series; Your Land and My Land: Middle East series; and World Crafts and Recipes series.

HOW TO CONTACT Submit cover letter, résumé and unedited writing sample. *All unsolicited mss discarded.* 100 queries received/year. 5 mss received/year. Responds only if interested to queries.

ILLUSTRATION Works with 2-3 illustrators/year. Reviews ms/illustration packages from artists. Query. Illustration only: Query with samples; send résumé, portfolio, slides, tearsheets. Responds only if interested. Samples not returned; samples filed.

PHOTOGRAPHY Buys stock images. Needs photos of famous and prominent minority figures. Captions required. Uses color prints or digital images. Submit cover letter, résumé, published samples, stock photo list.

TERMS Work purchased outright from authors (range: $350-2,000). Pays illustrators by the project (range: $40-400). Book catalog available free.

TIPS "We hire writers on a 'work-for-hire' basis to complete book projects we assign. Send résumé and writing samples that do not need to be returned."

MODERN PUBLISHING

155 E. 55th St., New York NY 10022. (212)826-0850. **Fax:** (212)759-9069. **Website:** www.modernpublishing.com. "Modern Publishing is a privately owned mass-market children's book publisher specializing in coloring and activity books, hardcover and paperback picture storybooks, puzzle and crossword collections, educational workbooks, board books, beginning readers, novelty and holiday books and other genres in various trim sizes and formats. Our titles feature both time-tested favorites and the hottest new licensed characters; generic characters; and characters from our Honey Bear imprint. Our titles are geared for children from infancy through 10 years of age. Modern Publishing's history spans 40 years offering the highest quality book products at unbeatable prices. Our distribution includes chain drug stores, mass market, trade outlets, educational and specialty stores in the U.S. and Canada, including book clubs and fairs, for all of the 250+ titles we publish yearly. We also offer full creative services to develop and print proprietary book products and premium promotional items."

> "Modern Publishing is currently focusing on licensed properties and coloring and

activity books. We are no longer considering submissions that don't fall within those categories."

ILLUSTRATION "Please send all art sample and concepts along with the Web address of your portfolio and an outline of your skills, experience, and the electronic formats with which you work."

Ⓐ MOODY PUBLISHERS

Moody Bible Institute, 820 N. LaSalle Blvd., Chicago IL 60610. (800)678-8812. **Fax:** (312)329-4157. **E-mail:** mpcustomerservice@moody.edu. **Website:** www.moodypublishers.org. "The mission of Moody Publishers is to educate and edify the Christian and to evangelize the non-Christian by ethically publishing conservative, evangelical Christian literature and other media for all ages around the world, and to help provide resources for Moody Bible Institute in its training of future Christian leaders." Publishes hardcover, trade, and mass market paperback originals. Publishes 60 titles/year. 1% of books from first-time authors. 80% from unagented writers.

⊖ Moody Publishers does not accept unsolicited mss of nonfiction or children's fiction.

◎ MOOSE ENTERPRISE BOOK & THEATRE PLAY PUBLISHING

684 Walls Rd., Sault Ste. Marie ON P6A 5K6, Canada. (705) 779-3331. **Fax:** (705) 779-3331. **E-mail:** mooseenterprises@on.aibn.com;ealcid@moose-hidebooks.com. **Website:** www.moosehidebooks.com. **Contact:** Edmond Alcid, editor. Editorial philosophy: "To assist the new writers of moral standards."

FICTION Middle readers, young adults: adventure, fantasy, humor, suspense/mystery, story poetry. Recently published *Realm of the Golden Feather,* by C.R. Ginter (ages 12 and up, fantasy); *Tell Me a Story,* short story collection by various authors (ages 9-11, humor/adventure); *Spirits of Lost Lake,* by James Walters (ages 12 and up, adventure); *Rusty Butt—Treasure of the Ocean Mist,* by R.E. Forester.

NONFICTION Middle readers, young adults: biography, history, multicultural.

HOW TO CONTACT Submit 2-3 chapters and biographical information. "Do not include reviews, awards, or past accomplishments. We judge an author and their work by the story before us." Include SASE.

Responds to queries in 1 month; mss in 3 months. Publishes book 1 year after acceptance.

ILLUSTRATION Uses primarily b&w artwork for interiors, cover artwork in color. Illustrations only: Query with samples. Responds in 1 month, if interested. Samples returned with SASE; samples filed.

TERMS Pays royalties. Ms guidelines available for SASE or online.

TIPS "Do not copy trends; be yourself—give me something new, something different."

NEW CANAAN PUBLISHING COMPANY LLC

2384 N. Hwy 341, Rossville GA 30741. (423)285-8672. **Fax:** (678)306-1471. **E-mail:** djm@newcanaanpublishing.com. **Website:** www.newcanaanpublishing.com. "We seek books with strong educational or traditional moral content and books with Christian themes." Publishes 1 picture book/year; 1 young reader/year; 1 middle reader/year; 1 young adult title/year. 50% of books from first-time authors.

⊖ New Canaan no longer reviews unsolicited mss.

FICTION All levels: adventure, history, religion (Christian only), suspense/mystery. Picture books: Christian themes. Average word length: picture books—1,000-3,000; young readers—8,000-30,000; middle readers—8,000-40,000; young adults—15,000-50,000.

NONFICTION All levels: religion (Christian only), textbooks. Average word length: picture books—1,000-3,000; young readers—8,000-30,000; middle readers—8,000-40,000; young adults—15,000-50,000.

ILLUSTRATION Works with 1-2 illustrators/year. Reviews ms/illustration packages from artists. Query or send ms with dummy.

TERMS Pays authors royalty of 7-12% based on wholesale price. Royalty may be shared with illustrator where relevant. Pays illustrators royalty of 4-6% as share of total royalties. Guidelines available on website.

TIPS "We are small, so please be patient."

NOMAD PRESS

2456 Christian St., White River Junction VT 05001. (802)649-1995. **Fax:** (802)649-2667. **E-mail:** rachel@nomadpress.net; info@nomadpress.net. **Website:** www.nomadpress.net. **Contact:** Alex Kahan, publisher. "We produce nonfiction children's activity books that bring a particular science or cultural topic into sharp focus. Nomad Press does not accept unsolicited manuscripts. If authors are interested in contributing to our children's series, please send a writing résumé that includes relevant experience/expertise and publishing credits."

○ Nomad Press does not accept picture books or fiction.

NONFICTION Middle readers: activity books, history, science. Average word length: middle readers—30,000. Recently published *Explore Transportation!*, by Marylou Morano Kjelle (ages 6-9); *Discover the Oceans,* by Lauri Berkenkamp (ages 8-12); *Amazing Biome Project*, by Donna Latham (ages 9-12); *Explore Colonial America!*, by Verna Fisher (ages 6-9); *Discover the Desert*, by Kathy Ceceri (ages 8-12).

HOW TO CONTACT Responds to queries in 3-4 weeks. Publishes book 1 year after acceptance.

TERMS Pays authors royalty based on retail price or work purchased outright. Offers advance against royalties. Catalog available on website.

TIPS "We publish a very specific kind of nonfiction children's activity book. Please keep this in mind when querying or submitting."

○ ONSTAGE PUBLISHING

190 Lime Quarry Rd., Suite 106-J, Madison AL 35758. (256)461-0661. **E-mail:** info@onstagepublishing.net. **Website:** www.onstagepublishing.com.

○ "To everyone who has submitted a ms, we are currently about 6 months behind. We should get back on track eventually. Please feel free to submit your ms to other houses. OnStage Publishing understands that authors work very hard to produce the finished ms and we do not have to have exclusive submission rights. Please let us know if you sell your ms. Meanwhile, keep writing and we'll keep reading for our next acquisitions."

FICTION Middle readers: adventure, contemporary, fantasy, history, nature/environment, science fiction, suspense/mystery. Young adults: adventure, contemporary, fantasy, history, humor, science fiction, suspense/mystery. Average word length: chapter books—3,000-9,000 words; middle readers—10,000-40,000 words; young adults—40,000-60,000 words. Recently published *China Clipper* by Jamie Dodson (an adventure for boys ages 12+); *Huntsville, 1892: Clara* (a chapter book

for grades 3-5). "We do not produce picture books." Under 100 pages—submit complete ms. Over 100 pages—submit summary, first 3 chapters and description of intended audience.

NONFICTION Ages 8 and up. Query.

HOW TO CONTACT Accepts submissions and queries by postal mail and e-mail. Do not include attachments in e-mail. Responds in 6 months.

ILLUSTRATION Reviews ms/illustration packages from artists. Submit with 3 pieces of final art. Samples not returned.

TERMS Pays authors/illustrators/photographers advance plus royalties.

TIPS "Study our titles and get a sense of the kind of books we publish, so that you know whether your project is likely to be right for us."

ORCHARD BOOKS

557 Broadway, New York NY 10012. (212)343-6215. **E-mail:** mcroland@scholastic.com. **Website:** www. scholastic.com. **Contact:** Ken Geist, vice president/editorial director; David Saylor, vice president/creative director. Publishes 20 titles/year. 10% of books from first-time authors.

○ *Orchard is not accepting unsolicited manuscripts.*

FICTION All levels: animal, contemporary, history, humor, multicultural, poetry. Recently published *Bulldog's Big Day*, by Kate McMullan and Pascal Lemaitre; *Story County: Here We Come!*, by Derek Anderson; *Robin Hood and the Golden Arrow,* by Robert San Souci and E.B. Lewis; *Eight Days,* by Edwidge Danticat and Alix Delinois; *If You're a Monster and You Know It*, by Rebecca Emberley and Ed Emberley; *One Drowsy Dragon,* by Ethan Long; *Max Spaniel: Funny Lunch,* by David Catrow; *Firehouse!*, by Mark Teague; *Farm,* by Elisha Cooper, *Princess Pigtoria and the Pea*, by Pamela Duncan Edwards and Henry Cole; *While the World Is Sleeping*, by Pamela Duncan Edwards and Daniel Kirk; *One More Hug for Madison*, by Caroline Jayne Church.

HOW TO CONTACT Art director reviews ms/illustration portfolios. Submit tearsheets or photocopies. Responds to art samples in 1 month. Samples returned with SASE.

TERMS Most commonly offers an advance against list royalties.

TIPS "Read some of our books to determine first whether your manuscript is suited to our list."

OUR CHILD PRESS

P.O. Box 4379, Philadelphia PA 19118. **Phone/fax:** (610)308-8988. **E-mail:** info@ourchildpress.com. **Website:** www.ourchildpress.com. **Contact:** Carol Perrott, president. 90% of books from first-time authors.

FICTION All levels: adoption, multicultural, special needs. Published *Like Me*, written by Dawn Martelli, illustrated by Jennifer Heyd Wharton; *Is That Your Sister?*, by Catherine and Sherry Bunin; *Oliver: A Story About Adoption*, by Lois Wickstrom.

HOW TO CONTACT Responds to queries/mss in 6 months. Publishes a book 6-12 months after acceptance.

ILLUSTRATION Works with 1-5 illustrators/year. Reviews ms/illustration packages from artists. Manuscript/illustration packages and illustration only: Query first. Submit résumé, tearsheets and photocopies. Responds to art samples in 2 months. Samples returned with SASE; samples kept on file.

TERMS Pays authors royalty of 5-10% based on wholesale price. Pays illustrators royalty of 5-10% based on wholesale price. Book catalog for business-size SAE and 67 cents.

○ OUR SUNDAY VISITOR, INC.

200 Noll Plaza, Huntington IN 46750. **E-mail:** booksed@osv.com. **Website:** www.osv.com. **Contact:** Beth McNamara, editor; Tyler Ottinger, design manager. "We are a Catholic publishing company seeking to educate and deepen our readers in their faith. Currently emphasizing devotional, inspirational, Catholic identity, apologetics, and catechetics." Publishes paperback and hardbound originals. Publishes 40-50 titles/year.

> ○ Our Sunday Visitor, Inc. is publishing only those children's books that are specifically Catholic. See website for submission guidelines."

NONFICTION Prefers to see well-developed proposals as first submission with annotated outline and definition of intended market; Catholic viewpoints on family, prayer, and devotional books, and Catholic heritage books. Picture books, middle readers, young readers, young adults. Recently published *Little Acts of Grace*, by Rosemarie Gortler and Donna Piscitelli, illustrated by Mimi Sternhagen.

HOW TO CONTACT Submit outline/synopsis and 1-2 sample chapters. Responds in 2 months. Publishes ms 1-2 years after acceptance.

TERMS Pays authors royalty of 10-12% net. Pays illustrators by the project (range: $25-1,500). Book catalog for 9×12 envelope and first-class stamps; ms guidelines available online.

TIPS "Stay in accordance with our guidelines."

RICHARD C. OWEN PUBLISHERS, INC.

P.O. Box 585, Katonah NY 10536. (914)232-3903; (800)262-0787. **E-mail:** richardowen@rcowen.com. **Website:** www.rcowen.com. **Contact:** Richard Owen, publisher. "We publish child-focused books, with inherent instructional value, about characters and situations with which five-, six-, and seven-year-old children can identify—books that can be read for meaning, entertainment, enjoyment and information. We include multicultural stories that present minorities in a positive and natural way. Our stories show the diversity in America." Not interested in lesson plans, or books of activities for literature studies or other content areas. Submit complete ms and cover letter.

> ○ "Due to high volume and long production time, we are currently limiting to nonfiction submissions only."

NONFICTION "Our books are for kindergarten, first- and second-grade children to read on their own. The stories are very brief—under 1,000 words—yet well structured and crafted with memorable characters, language, and plots." Picture books, young readers: animals, careers, history, how-to, music/dance, geography, multicultural, nature/environment, science, sports. Multicultural needs include: "Good stories respectful of all heritages, races, cultural—African-American, Hispanic, American Indian." Wants lively stories. No "encyclopedic" type of information stories. Recently published *The Coral Reef*.

HOW TO CONTACT Submit ms or proposal. Include bibliography. Responds to mss in 1 year. Publishes a book 2-3 years after acceptance.

ILLUSTRATION Works with 20 illustrators/year. Uses color artwork only. Illustration only: Send color copies/reproductions or photos of art or provide tearsheets; do not send slides or originals. Include SASE and cover letter. Responds only if interested; samples filed.

TERMS Pays authors royalty of 5% based on net price or outright purchase (range: $25-500). Offers no advances. Pays illustrators by the project (range: $100-2,000) or per photo (range: $100-150). Book catalog available with SASE. Ms guidelines with SASE or online.

TIPS "We don't respond to queries or e-mails. Please do not fax or e-mail us. Because our books are so brief, it is better to send an entire manuscript. We publish story books with inherent educational value for young readers—books they can read with enjoyment and success. We believe students become enthusiastic, independent, life-long learners when supported and guided by skillful teachers using good books. The professional development work we do and the books we publish support these beliefs."

PACIFIC PRESS

1350 N. Kings Rd., Nampa ID 83653. (208)465-2500. **Fax:** (208)465-2531. **E-mail:** scocad@pacificpress.com. **E-mail:** booksubmissions@pacificpress.com;. **Website:** www.pacificpress.com. **Contact:** Scott Cady, acquisitions; Gerald Monks, creative director. Pacific Press brings the Bible and Christian lifestyle to children. Publishes 1 picture book/year; 2 young readers/year; 2 middle readers/year. Publishes 5 titles/year. 5% of books from first-time authors.

FICTION Picture books, young readers, middle readers, young adults: religious subjects only. No fantasy. Average word length: picture books—100; young readers—1,000; middle readers—15,000; young adults—40,000. Recently published *Octopus Encounter*, by Sally Streib; *Shepherd Warrior*, by Bradley Booth.

NONFICTION Picture books, young readers, middle readers, young adults: religion. Average word length: picture books—100; young readers—1,000; middle readers—15,000; young adults—40,000. Recently published *A Child's Steps to Jesus* (3 vols), by Linda Carlyle; *Escape*, by Sandy Zaugg; *What We Believe*, by Seth Pierce.

HOW TO CONTACT Responds to queries in 3 months; mss in 1 year. Publishes a book 6-12 months after acceptance.

ILLUSTRATION Works with 2-6 illustrators/year. Uses color artwork only. Query. Responds only if interested. Samples returned with SASE.

PHOTOGRAPHY Buys stock and assigns work. Model/property releases required.

TERMS Pays author royalty of 6-15% based on wholesale price. Offers advances (average amount: $1,500). Pays illustrators royalty of 6-15% based on wholesale price. Pays photographers 6-15% based on wholesale price. Catalog available on website. Ms guidelines for SASE.

TIPS Pacific Press is owned by the Seventh-day Adventist Church. The Press rejects all material that is not Bible-based.

PAUL DRY BOOKS

1616 Walnut St., Suite 808, Philadelphia PA 19103. (215)231-9939. **Fax:** (215)231-9942. **E-mail:** pdry@pauldrybooks.com; editor@pauldrybooks.com. **Website:** www.pauldrybooks.com. "We publish fiction, both novels and short stories, and nonfiction, biography, memoirs, history, and essays, covering subjects from Homer to Chekhov, bird watching to jazz music, New York City to shogunate Japan." Hardcover and trade paperback originals, trade paperback reprints.

○ "Take a few minutes to familiarize yourself with the books we publish. Then if you think your book would be a good fit in our line, we invite you to submit the following: A 1- or 2-page summary of the work. Be sure to tell us how many pages or words the full book will be; a sample of 20 to 30 pages; your bio. A brief description of how you think the book (and you, the author) could be marketed."

TIPS Book catalog available online.

PAULINE BOOKS & MEDIA

50 St. Paula's Ave., Boston MA 02130. (617)522-8911. **Fax:** (617)541-9805. **E-mail:** design@paulinemedia.com; editorial@paulinemedia.com. **Website:** www.paulinesa.org. "Submissions are evaluated on adherence to Gospel values, harmony with the Catholic tradition, relevance of topic, and quality of writing." Publishes trade paperback originals and reprints. Publishes 40 titles/year. 15% of books from first-time authors. 5% from unagented writers.

FICTION Children's fiction only. "We are now accepting submissions for easy-to-read and middle reader chapter fiction. Please see our writers' guidelines."

NONFICTION Picture books, young readers, middle readers: religion. Average word length: picture books—500-1,000; young readers—8,000-10,000; middle readers—15,000-25,000. Recently published *God Made Wonderful Me!*, by Genny Monchamp; *Adventures of Saint Paul*, by Oldřich Selucký; *Anna Mei: Cartoon Girl*, by Carol A. Grund; *Goodness Graces! Ten Short Stories about the Sacraments*, by Diana R. Jenkins. No biography/autobiography, poetry, or strictly nonreligious works considered.

HOW TO CONTACT Submit proposal package, including outline, 1-2 sample chapters, cover letter, synopsis, intended audience and proposed length. Encourages electronic submissions. Responds in 3 months to queries, proposals and mss. Publishes a book 11 months after acceptance.

ILLUSTRATION Works with 10-15 illustrators/year. Uses color and black-and-white artwork. Illustrations only: Send résumé and 4-5 color samples. Samples and résumés will be kept on file unless return is requested and SASE provided.

TERMS Payment varies by project, but generally consists of royalties with advance. Flat fees sometimes considered for smaller works. Book catalog available online. Guidelines available online and by e-mail.

TIPS "Manuscripts may or may not be explicitly catechetical, but we seek those that reflect a positive worldview, good moral values, awareness and appreciation of diversity, and respect for all people. All material must be relevant to the lives of young readers and must conform to Catholic teaching and practice."

PAULIST PRESS

997 Macarthur Blvd., Mahwah NJ 07430. (201)825-7300. **Fax:** (201)825-8345. **E-mail:** info@paulistpress.com; dcrilly@paulistpress.com. **Website:** www.paulistpress.com. **Contact:** Rev. Mark-David Janus, editorial director; Donna Crilly, editorial. "Paulist Press publishes ecumenical theology, Roman Catholic studies, and books on scripture, liturgy, spirituality, church history, and philosophy, as well as works on faith and culture. Our publishing is oriented toward adult-level nonfiction. We do not publish poetry." Publishes hardcover and electronic originals and electronic reprints. Publishes 12 children's titles/year. 50% of books from first-time authors.

FICTION Submit cover letter, résumé, ms, SASE. Accepts unsolicited mss, but most titles have been commissioned.

NONFICTION Picture book; beginning readers: books of blessings, prayer books, Catholic guidebooks; middle grade; young adult: biographies of saints and modern heroes. Submit cover letter, résumé, ms, SASE. Accepts unsolicited mss, but most titles have been commissioned.

HOW TO CONTACT Receives 250 submissions/year. Responds in 2 months to queries and proposals; 2-3 months on mss. Publishes a book 12-18 months after acceptance.

TERMS Advance payment is $500, payable on publication. Illustrators sometimes receive a flat fee when all we need are spot illustrations. Pays advance. Book catalog available online. Guidelines available online and by e-mail.

TIPS "Our typical reader is probably Roman Catholic and wants the content to be educational about Catholic thought and practice, or else the reader is a spiritual seeker who looks for discovery of God and the spiritual values that churches offer but without the church connection."

PEACE HILL PRESS

Affiliate of W.W. Norton, 18021 The Glebe Ln., Charles City VA 23030. (804)829-5043. **Fax:** (804)829-5704. **E-mail:** info@peacehillpress.com. **Website:** www.peacehillpress.com. **Contact:** Peter Buffington, acquisitions editor. Publishes hardcover and trade paperback originals. Publishes 4-8 titles/year. "We are a small, family-run company, working together to produce the best materials for classical education."

NONFICTION History and language arts.

HOW TO CONTACT Submit proposal package, outline, 1 sample chapter. Publishes a book 18 months after acceptance.

TERMS Pays 6-10% royalty on retail price. Pays $500-1,000 advance.

PEACHTREE PUBLISHERS, LTD.

1700 Chattahoochee Ave., Atlanta GA 30318. (404)876-8761. **Fax:** (404)875-2578. **E-mail:** hello@peachtree-online.com; jackson@peachtree-online.com. **Website:** www.peachtree-online.com. **Contact:** Helen Harriss, acquisitions editor; Loraine Joyner, art director; Melanie McMahon Ives, production manager. Publishes 30-35 titles/year.

FICTION Picture books, young readers: adventure, animal, concept, history, nature/environment. Middle readers: adventure, animal, history, nature/environment, sports. Young adults: fiction, mystery, adventure. Does not want to see science fiction, romance.

NONFICTION Picture books: animal, history, nature/environment. Young readers, middle readers, young adults: animal, biography, nature/environment. Does not want to see religion.

HOW TO CONTACT Submit complete ms (for picture books) or 3 sample chapters (for longer works) by postal mail only. Submit complete ms or 3 sample chapters by postal mail only. Responds to queries and mss in 6-7 months. Publishes book 1-2 years after acceptance.

ILLUSTRATION Works with 8-10 illustrators/year. Illustrations only: Query production manager or art director with samples, résumé, slides, color copies to keep on file. Responds only if interested. Samples returned with SASE; samples filed.

◎ 🕮 PELICAN PUBLISHING COMPANY

1000 Burmaster St., Gretna LA 70053. (504)368-1175. **Fax:** (504)368-1195. **E-mail:** editorial@pelicanpub. com. **Website:** www.pelicanpub.com. **Contact:** Nina Kooij, editor-in-chief. "We believe ideas have consequences. One of the consequences is that they lead to a best-selling book. We publish books to improve and uplift the reader. Currently emphasizing business and history titles." Publishes 20 young readers/year; 3 middle readers/year. "Our children's books (illustrated and otherwise) include history, biography, holiday, and regional. Pelican's mission is to publish books of quality and permanence that enrich the lives of those who read them." Publishes hardcover, trade paperback and mass market paperback originals and reprints. Publishes 70 titles/year. 15% of books from first-time authors. 95% from unagented writers.

FICTION "We publish maybe one novel a year, usually by an author we already have. Almost all proposals are returned." Young readers: history, holiday, science, multicultural and regional. Middle readers: Louisiana history. Multicultural needs include stories about African-Americans, Irish-Americans, Jews, Asian-Americans, and Hispanics. Does not want animal stories, general Christmas stories, "day at school" or "accept yourself" stories. Maximum word length: young readers—1,100; middle readers—40,000. Recently published *The Oklahoma Land Run* by Una Belle Townsend (ages 5-8, historical/regional). No young adult, romance, science fiction, fantasy, gothic, mystery, erotica, confession, horror, sex, or violence. Also no psychological novels.

NONFICTION "We look for authors who can promote successfully. We require that a query be made first. This greatly expedites the review process and can save the writer additional postage expenses." Currently seeking historical picture books. Young readers: biography, history, holiday, multicultural. Middle readers: Louisiana history, holiday, regional. Recently published *Batty about Texas*, by J. Jaye Smith (ages 5-8, science/regional). No multiple queries or submissions.

HOW TO CONTACT Submit complete ms, biographical information and SASE. Does not consider simultaneous submissions or submissions via email. Responds in 1 month to queries; 3 months to mss. Publishes a book 9-18 months after acceptance.

ILLUSTRATION Works with 20 illustrators/year. "Our children's books are generally full color with both whimsical and realistic, human and animal charaters. Our young adult books require black and white line work in a mostly realistic style." Reviews ms/illustration packages from artists. Query first. Illustrations only: Query with samples (no originals). Responds only if interested. Samples returned with SASE; samples kept on file.

TERMS Pays authors in royalties; buys ms outright "rarely." Illustrators paid by "various arrangements." Advance considered. Book catalog and ms guidelines online.

TIPS "We do extremely well with cookbooks, popular histories, and business. We will continue to build in these areas. The writer must have a clear sense of the market and knowledge of the competition. A query letter should describe the project briefly, give the author's writing and professional credentials, and promotional ideas."

PHILOMEL BOOKS

Imprint of Penguin Group (USA), Inc., 375 Hudson St., New York NY 10014. (212)366-2000. **Website:** www.us.penguingroup.com. **Contact:** Michael Green, president/publisher; Annie Beth Ericsson, junior designer. "We look for beautifully written, engaging manuscripts for children and young adults." Publishes hardcover originals. Publishes 8-10 titles/year. 5% of books from first-time authors. 20% from unagented writers.

FICTION All levels: adventure, animal, boys, contemporary, fantasy, folktales, historical fiction, humor, sports, multicultural. Middle readers, young adults: problem novels, science fiction, suspense/mystery. No concept picture books, mass-market "character" books, or series. Average word length: picture books—1,000; young readers—1,500; middle readers—14,000; young adult—20,000. No series or activity books. No generic, mass-market oriented fiction.

NONFICTION Picture books.

HOW TO CONTACT Submit complete picture book ms or 10 sample pages.

ILLUSTRATION Works with 8-10 illustrators/year. Reviews ms/illustration packages from artists. Query with art sample first. Illustrations only: Query with samples. Send résumé and tearsheets. Responds to art samples in 1 month. Original artwork returned at job's completion. Samples returned with SASE or kept on file.

TERMS Pays authors in royalties. Average advance payment "varies." Illustrators paid by advance and in royalties. Pays negotiable advance. Book catalog for 9×12 envelope and 4 first-class stamps. Guidelines for #10 SASE.

TIPS Wants "unique fiction or nonfiction with a strong voice and lasting quality. Discover your own voice and own story and persevere." Looks for "something unusual, original, well written. Fine art or illustrative art that feels unique. The genre (fantasy, contemporary, or historical fiction) is not so important as the story itself and the spirited life the story allows its main character."

○ PIANO PRESS

P.O. Box 85, Del Mar CA 92014. (619)884-1401. **Fax:** (858)755-1104. **E-mail:** pianopress@pianopress.com. **Website:** www.pianopress.com. **Contact:** Elizabeth C. Axford, editor. "We publish music-related books, either fiction or nonfiction, coloring books, songbooks, and poetry."

○ Piano Press considers submissions via e-mail only.

FICTION Picture books, young readers, middle readers, young adults: folktales, multicultural, poetry, music. Average word length: picture books—1,500-2,000. Recently published *Strum a Song of Angels*, by Linda Oatman High and Elizabeth C. Axford; *Music and Me*, by Kimberly White and Elizabeth C. Axford.

NONFICTION Picture books, young readers, middle readers, young adults: multicultural, music/dance. Average word length: picture books—1,500-2,000. Recently published *The Musical ABC*, by Dr. Phyllis J. Perry and Elizabeth C. Axford; *Merry Christmas Happy Hanukkah—A Multilingual Songbook & CD*, by Elizabeth C. Axford.

HOW TO CONTACT Query via e-mail only. Do not send mss or attachments. Responds to queries in 3 months; mss in 6 months. Publishes book 1 year after acceptance.

ILLUSTRATION Works with 1 or 2 illustrators/year. Reviews ms/illustration packages from artists. Query.

Illustrations only: Query with samples. Provide link to website if applicable. Responds in 3 months. Samples returned with SASE; samples filed.

PHOTOGRAPHY Buys stock and assigns work. Looking for music-related, multicultural. Model/property releases required. Uses glossy or flat, color or b&w prints. Submit cover letter, résumé, client list, published samples, stock photo list.

TERMS Pays authors, illustrators, and photographers royalty of 5-10% based on retail price. Book catalog available for #10 SASE and 2 first-class stamps.

TIPS "We are looking for music-related material only for any juvenile market. Please do not send non-music-related materials. Query first before submitting anything."

PINEAPPLE PRESS, INC.

P.O. Box 3889, Sarasota FL 34230. (941)739-2219. **Fax:** (941)739-2296. **E-mail:** info@pineapplepress.com. **Website:** www.pineapplepress.com. **Contact:** June Cussen, executive editor. "Our only children's books are on Florida topics for Florida schools." Publishes hardcover and trade paperback originals. Publishes 25 titles/year. 50% of books from first-time authors. 95% from unagented writers.

FICTION Picture books, young readers, middle readers, young adults: animal, folktales, history, nature/environment. Recently published *The Treasure of Amelia Island*, by M.C. Finotti (ages 8-12).

NONFICTION Picture books: animal, history, nature/environmental, science. Young readers, middle readers, young adults: animal, biography, geography, history, nature/environment, science. Recently published *Those Magical Manatees*, by Jan Lee Wicker and *Those Beautiful Butterflies,* by Sarah Cussen. "We will consider most nonfiction topics when related to Florida."

HOW TO CONTACT Query with outline/synopsis, sample chapters and SASE. For nonfiction, include market analysis. 1,000 queries received/year. 500 mss received/year. Responds to queries/samples/mss in 2 months. Publishes a book 1 year after acceptance.

ILLUSTRATION Works with 2 illustrators/year. Reviews ms/illustration packages from artists. Query with nonreturnable samples. Contact: June Cussen, executive editor. Illustrations only: Query with brochure, nonreturnable samples, photocopies, résumé. Responds only if interested. Samples returned with SASE, but prefers nonreturnable; samples filed.

TERMS Pays authors royalty of 10-15%. Book catalog for 9×12 SAE with $1.25 postage. Guidelines available online.

TIPS "Quality first novels will be published, though we usually only do one or two novels per year and they must be set in Florida. We regard the author/editor relationship as a trusting relationship with communication open both ways. Learn all you can about the publishing process and about how to promote your book once it is published. A query on a novel without a brief sample seems useless."

PIÑATA BOOKS

Imprint of Arte Público Press, University of Houston, 4902 Gulf Freeway, Bldg 19, Room 100, Houston TX 77204-2004. (713)743-2845. **Fax:** (713)743-2847. **E-mail:** submapp@uh.edu. **Website:** www.artepublicopress.com. **Contact:** Nicolas Kanellos, director. "Piñata Books is dedicated to the publication of children's and young adult literature focusing on U.S. Hispanic culture by U.S. Hispanic authors. Arte Publico's mission is the publication, promotion and dissemination of Latino literature for a variety of national and regional audiences, from early childhood to adult, through the complete gamut of delivery systems, including personal performance as well as print and electronic media." Publishes hardcover and trade paperback originals. Publishes 10-15 titles/year. 80% of books from first-time authors.

○ Accepts material from U.S./Hispanic authors only (living abroad OK). Mss, queries, synopses, etc., are accepted in either English or Spanish.

FICTION Recently published *We Are Cousins/ Somos primos,* by Diane Gonzales Bertrand (picture book)*; Butterflies on Carmen Street/Mariposas en la calle Carmen,* by Monica Brown (picture book)*; Windows into My World: Latino Youth Write Their Lives* (young adult); *Trino's Choice,* by Diane Gonzales Bertrand (ages 11 and up); *Delicious Hullabaloo/Pachanga Deliciosa,* by Pat Mora (picture book); and *The Year of Our Revolution,* by Judith Ortiz Cofer (young adult).

NONFICTION Recently published *Cesar Chavez: The Struggle for Justice/Cesar Chavez: La lucha por la justicia,* by Richard Griswold del Castillo, illustrated by Anthony Accardo (ages 7 and up).

HOW TO CONTACT Submit sample chapters or complete ms via online submission form. Responds in 2-3 month to queries; 4-6 months to mss. Publishes book 2 years after acceptance.

ILLUSTRATION Works with 6 illustrators/year. Uses color artwork only. Reviews ms/illustration packages from artists. Submit samples via online submission form. Responds only if interested. Samples filed.

TERMS Pays 10% royalty on wholesale price. Pays $1,000-3,000 advance. Book catalog and ms guidelines available via website or with #10 SASE.

PLUM BLOSSOM BOOKS

Parallax Press, P.O. Box 7355, Berkeley CA 94707. (510)525-0101. **Fax:** (510)525-7129. **E-mail:** rachel@parallax.org. **Website:** www.parallax.org. **Contact:** Rachel Neumann, senior editor. "Plum Blossom Books publishes stories for children of all ages that focus on mindfulness in daily life, Buddhism, and social justice." 30% of books from first-time authors.

FICTION Picture books: adventure, contemporary, folktales, multicultural, nature/environment, religion. Young readers: adventure, contemporary, folktales, multicultural, nature/environment, religion. Middle readers: multicultural, nature/environment, religion. Young adults/teens: nature/environment, religion. Recently published *The Hermit and the Well*, by Thich Nhat Hanh, illustrated by Vo-Dinh Mai (ages 4-8, hardcover); *Each Breath a Smile*, by Sister Thuc Nghiem and Thich Nhat Hanh, illustrated by Thi Hop and Nguyen Dong (ages 2-5, paperback picture book); *Meow Said the Mouse*, by Beatrice Barbey, illustrated by Philippe Ames (ages 5-8, picture and activity book).

NONFICTION All levels: nature/environment, religion (Buddhist), Buddhist counting books.

HOW TO CONTACT Responds to queries in 1-2 weeks; mss in 1 month. Publishes book 9-12 months after acceptance.

ILLUSTRATION Accepts material from international illustrators. Works with 3 illustrators/year. Uses both color and b&w. Reviews ms/illustration packages. For ms/illustration packages: Query. Send ms with dummy. Reviews work for future assignments. If interested in illustrating future titles, query with samples. Responds in 4 weeks. Samples returned with SASE. Samples filed.

PHOTOGRAPHY Buys stock images and assigns work. **Contact:** Rachel Neumann. Uses b&w prints. For first contact, send cover letter and published samples.

TERMS Pays authors 20% based on wholesale price. Pays illustrators by the project. Catalog available for SASE. Writers' guidelines on website and for SASE.

TIPS "Read our books before approaching us. We are very specifically looking for mindfulness and Buddhist messages in high-quality stories where the Buddhist message is implied rather than stated outright."

PRICE STERN SLOAN, INC.

345 Hudson St., New York NY 10014. (212)366-2000. **Website:** www.us.penguingroup.com/youngreaders. **Contact:** Francesco Sedita, vice-president/publisher. "Price Stern Sloan publishes quirky mass market novelty series for childrens as well as licensed movie tie-in books."

○ Price Stern Sloan does not accept e-mail submissions.

FICTION Publishes picture books and novelty/board books including Mad Libs Movie and Television Tie-ins, and unauthorized biographies. "We publish unique novelty formats and fun, colorful paperbacks and activity books. We also publish the Book with Audio Series *Wee Sing* and *Baby Loves Jazz*." Recently published: *Baby Loves Jazz* board book with CD Series; new formats in the classic *Mr. Men/Little Miss* series.

NONFICTION Recently published: movie/TV tie-in titles: *Speed Racers, Journey 3D*. Unauthorized biographies: *Mad for Miley* and *Jammin' with the Jonas Brothers*.

HOW TO CONTACT Submit summary and sample chapters.

TERMS Book catalog available for 9×12 SASE and 5 first-class stamps. Ms guidelines available for SASE.

TIPS "Price Stern Sloan publishes unique, fun titles."

PUFFIN BOOKS

Imprint of Penguin Group (USA), Inc., 345 Hudson St., New York NY 10014. (212)366-2000. **Website:** www.penguinputnam.com. **Contact:** Kristin Gilson, editorial director. "Puffin Books publishes high-end trade paperbacks and paperback reprints for preschool children, beginning and middle readers, and young adults." Publishes trade paperback originals and reprints. Publishes 225 titles/year. 1% of books from first-time authors. 5% from unagented writers.

FICTION Young adult novels, middle grade and easy-to-read grades 1-3: fantasy and science fiction, graphic novels, classics. Recently Published *Three Cups of Tea:*

Young Readers Edition, by Greg Mortenson and David Oliver Relin, adapted for young readers by Sarah Thomson; *The Big Field*, by Mike Lupica; *Geek Charming*, by Robin Palmer. No picture books.

NONFICTION Biography, illustrated books. "Women in history books interest us."

HOW TO CONTACT Submit 30 pages maximum. No unsolicited mss for picture books will be considered. Receives 600 queries and mss/year. Responds in 5 months. Publishes book 1 year after acceptance.

ILLUSTRATION Reviews artwork. Send color copies.

PHOTOGRAPHY Reviews photos. Send color copies.

TERMS Royalty varies. Pays varies advance. Book catalog for 9×12 SAE with 7 first-class stamps.

TIPS "Our audience ranges from little children 'first books' to young adult (ages 14-16). An original idea has the best luck."

PUSH

Scholastic, 557 Broadway, New York NY 10012. **E-mail:** david@thisispush.com. **Website:** www.thisispush.com. **Contact:** David Levithan, editor. PUSH publishes new voices in teen literature. Publishes 6-9 titles/year. 50% of books from first-time authors.

○ PUSH does not accept unsolicited mss or queries, only agented or referred fiction/memoir.

FICTION Young adults: contemporary, multicultural, poetry. Recently published *Splintering*, by Eireann Corrigan; *Never Mind the Goldbergs*, by Matthue Roth; *Perfect World*, by Brian James.

NONFICTION Young adults: memoir, poetry memoir.

POETRY Young adults: poetry memoir. Recently published *Talking in the Dark*, by Billy Merrell; *You Remind Me of You*, by Eireann Corrigan.

HOW TO CONTACT *Does not accept unsolicited mss.*

TIPS "We only publish first-time writers (and then their subsequent books), so authors who have published previously should not consider PUSH. Also, for young writers in grades 7-12, we run the PUSH Novel Contest with the Scholastic Art & Writing Awards. Every year it begins in October and ends in March. Rules can be found on our website."

RAINBOW PUBLISHERS

P.O. Box 261129, San Diego CA 92196. (858)277-1167. **E-mail:** editor@rainbowpublishers.com; info@rainbowpublishers.com. **Website:** www.rainbowpublishers.com; www.legacypresskids.com. "Our mission is to publish Bible-based, teacher resource materials that contribute to and inspire spiritual growth and development in kids ages 2-12."

NONFICTION Young readers, middle readers, young adult/teens: activity books, arts/crafts, how-to, reference, religion.

HOW TO CONTACT Submit table of contents, 2-5 chapters and SASE. Responds in 2 months.

ILLUSTRATION Works with 25 illustrators/year. Reviews ms/illustration packages from artists. Submit ms with 2-5 pieces of final art. Illustrations only: Query with samples. "Note that we contract only with illustrators who work in Illustrator or Photoshop software (Mac OS preferred), so please indicate which software and operating system you use." Responds in 2 months. Samples returned with SASE; samples filed.

TERMS Pays illustrators by the project (range: $300 and up). For authors work purchased outright (range: $500 and up).

TIPS "Our Rainbow imprint publishes reproducible books for teachers of children in Christian ministries, including crafts, activities, games and puzzles. Our Legacy imprint publishes titles for children such as devotionals, fiction and Christian living. Please write for guidelines and study the market before submitting material."

RAINTOWN PRESS

1111 E. Burnside St. No. 309, Portland OR 97214. (503)962-9612. **E-mail:** submissions@raintownpress. com. **Website:** www.raintownpress.com. **Contact:** Misty V'Marie, acquisitions editor; Ellery Harvey, art director. Publishes 1-4 middle readers; 1-4 young adult titles/year. 100% of books from first-time authors. "We are Portland, Oregon's first independent press dedicated to publishing literature for middle grade and young adult readers. We hope to give rise to their voice, speaking directly to the spirit they embody through our books and other endeavors. The gray days we endure in the Pacific Northwest are custom-made for reading a good book—or in our case, making one. The rain inspires, challenges, and motivates us. To that end, we say: Let it drizzle. We will soon publish picture books."

○ RainTown Press will not be accepting submissions until February 2013. Please check online for updates.

FICTION Middle readers/young adult/teens: Wants adventure, animal, contemporary, fantasy, folktales, graphic novels, health, hi-lo, history, humor, multicultural, nature/environment, problem novels, sci-fi, special needs, sports. Length: middle readers—45,00 words minimum; young adult—60,000 words minimum. Does not consider novellas. Catalog available on website.

HOW TO CONTACT Query with synopsis, first fifty pages, list of comparative titles and description of your online media presence, if any. Prefers electronic submissions. See online submission guide for detailed instructions. Responds in 3 months. Publishes ms 1 year after acceptance.

ILLUSTRATION Reviews ms/illustration packages from artists (will review packages for future titles); uses both color and b&w. Submit query, link to online portfolio. Originals not returned. Does not show dummies to illustrators.

PHOTOGRAPHY Buys stock images and assigned work. Model/property releases required with submissions. Photo captions required. Use high-res digital materials. Send cover letter, client list, portolio (online preferred).

TERMS Pays 8-15% royalty on net sales. Does not pay advance. Catalog available on website. Imprints included in a single catalog. Guidelines available on website for writers, artists, and photographers.

TIPS "The middle grade and YA markets have sometimes very stringent conventions for subject matter, theme, etc. It's most helpful if an author knows his/her genre inside and out. Read, read, read books that have successfully been published for your genre. This will ultimately make your writing more marketable. Also, follow a publisher's submission guidelines to a tee. We try to set writers up for success. Send us what we're looking for."

ⓐ RANDOM HOUSE CHILDREN'S BOOKS

Random House, Inc., 1745 Broadway, New York NY 10019. (212)782-9000. **Website:** www.random house.com. "Producing books for preschool children through young adult readers, in all formats from board to activity books to picture books and novels, Random House Children's Books brings together world-famous franchise characters, multimillion-copy series and top-flight, award-winning authors and illustrators."

FICTION "Random House publishes a select list of first chapter books and novels, with an emphasis on fantasy and historical fiction." Chapter books, middle-grade readers, young adult.

HOW TO CONTACT Accepts unsolicited submissions for certain imprints only. Guidelines available online.

ILLUSTRATION The Random House publishing divisions hire their freelancers directly. To contact the appropriate person, send a cover letter and résumé to the department head at the publisher as follows: "Department Head" (e.g., Art Director, Production Director), "Publisher/Imprint" (e.g., Knopf, Doubleday, etc.), 1745 Broadway New York, NY 10019. Works with 100-150 freelancers/year. Works on assignment only. Send query letter with résumé, tearsheets and printed samples; no originals. Samples are filed. Negotiates rights purchased. Assigns 5 freelance design jobs/year. Pays by the project.

TIPS "We look for original, unique stories. Do something that hasn't been done before."

◑◐ RANDOM HOUSE-GOLDEN BOOKS FOR YOUNG READERS GROUP

Contact: Mallory Loehr, vice president/publishing director; Chris Angelilli, vice president/editor-in-chief; Cathy Goldsmith, associate publisher/art director. "Random House Books aims to create books that nurture the hearts and minds of children, providing and promoting quality books and a rich variety of media that entertain and educate readers from 6 months to 12 years." 2% of books from first-time authors.

○ Random House-Golden Books does not accept unsolicited manuscripts, only agented material. They reserve the right not to return unsolicited material.

TERMS Pays authors in royalties; sometimes buys mss outright. Book catalog free on request.

RAVEN TREE PRESS

A Division of Delta Publishing Company, 1400 Miller Pkwy., McHenry IL 60050. (877)256-0579. **Fax:** (800)909-9901. **E-mail:** raven@deltapublishing.com; acquisitions@deltapublishing.com. **Website:** www.raventreepress.com. "We publish entertaining and educational picture books in a variety of formats. Bilingual (English/Spanish), English-only, Spanish-only, and wordless editions. Publishes hardcover and trade paperback originals. Publishes 8-10 titles/year.

50% of books from first-time authors. 90% from unagented writers.

○ "Raven Tree Press is unable to accept unsolicited manuscripts or illustration submissions at this time. Please try back again soon."

HOW TO CONTACT "Submission guidelines available online. Do not query or send mss without first checking submission guidelines on our website for most current information." 1,500 mss received/year. Responds in 2 months to mss.

TERMS Pays royalty. Pays variable advance. Book catalog available online. Guidelines available online.

TIPS "Submit only based on guidelines. No e-mail or snail mail queries please. Word count is a definite issue, since we are bilingual."

RAZORBILL

Penguin Group, 345 Hudson St., New York NY 10014. (212)414-3448. **Fax:** (212)414-3343. **E-mail:** laura.schechter@us.penguingroup.com; Ben.Schrank@us.penguingroup.com. **Website:** www.razorbillbooks.com. **Contact:** Gillian Levinson, assistant edtor. "This division of Penguin Young Readers is looking for the best and the most original of commercial contemporary fiction titles for middle grade and YA readers. A select quantity of nonfiction titles will also be considered." Publishes 30 titles/year.

FICTION Middle readers: adventure, contemporary, graphic novels, fantasy, humor, problem novels. Young adults/teens: adventure, contemporary, fantasy, graphic novels, humor, multicultural, suspense, paranormal, science fiction, dystopian, literary, romance. Average word length: middle readers—40,000; young adult—60,000. Recently published *Thirteen Reasons Why*, by Jay Asher (ages 14 and up, a NY Times Bestseller); Vampire Academy series by Richelle Mead (ages 12 and up; NY Times Best-selling series); *The Teen Vogue Handbook* (ages 12 and up; a NY Times Bestseller); and *I Am a Genius of Unspeakable Evil and I Want to Be Your Class President*, by Josh Lieb (ages 12 and up; a NY Times Bestseller).

NONFICTION Middle readers and young adults/teens: concept.

HOW TO CONTACT Submit outline/synopsis and 30 pages maximum, along with query and SASE. Responds to queries/mss in 1-3 months. Publishes book 1-2 after acceptance.

TERMS Offers advance against royalties.

TIPS "New writers will have the best chance of acceptance and publication with original, contemporary material that boasts a distinctive voice and well-articulated world. Check out www.razorbillbooks.com to get a better idea of what we're looking for."

⟳ RENAISSANCE HOUSE

465 Westview Ave., Englewood NJ 07631. (800)547-5113. **E-mail:** raquel@renaissancehouse.net. **Website:** www.renaissancehouse.net. Publishes biographies, folktales, coffee table books, instructional, textbooks, adventure, picture books, juvenile and young adult. "We are a book packaging publisher specializing in the creation and development of educational and commercial materials in English, Spanish and French." Children's, educational, multicultural, and textbooks, advertising rep. Represents 80 illustrators. 95% of artwork handled is children's book illustration. Currently open to illustrators and photographers seeking representation. Open to both new and established illustrators.

FICTION Picture books: animal, folktales, multicultural. Young readers: animal, anthology, folktales, multicultural. Middle readers, young adult/teens: anthology, folktales, multicultural, nature/environment.

HOW TO CONTACT Submit outline/synopsis. Will consider e-mail submissions. Responds to queries/mss in 2 months. Publishes ms 1 year after acceptance.

ILLUSTRATION Works with 25 illustrators/year. Uses color artwork only. Reviews ms/illustration packages from artists. Send ms with dummy. Contact: Sam Laredo. Illustrations only: Send tearsheets. Contact: Raquel Benatar. Responds in 3 weeks. Samples not returned; samples filed.

Ⓐ ROARING BROOK PRESS

175 Fifth Ave., New York NY 10010. (646)307-5151. **E-mail:** david.langva@roaringbrookpress.com. **E-mail:** press.inquiries@macmillanusa.com. **Website:** http://us.macmillan.com/roaringbrook.aspx. **Contact:** David Langva. Roaring Brook Press is an imprint of Macmillan, a group of companies that includes Henry Holt and Farrar, Straus & Giroux. Roaring Brook title *First the Egg*, by Laura Vaccaro Seeger, won a Caldecott Honor Medal and a Theodor Seuss Geisel Honor in 2008. Their title *Dog and Bear: Two Friends, Three Stories*, also by Laura Vaccaro Seeger, won the Boston Globe-Horn Book Picture Book Award in 2007.

> 💬 Roaring Brook is not accepting unsolicited mss.

FICTION Picture books, young readers, middle readers, young adults: adventure, animal, contemporary, fantasy, history, humor, multicultural, nature/environment, poetry, religion, science fiction, sports, suspense/mystery. Recently published *Happy Birthday, Bad Kitty*, by Nick Bruel; *Cookie*, by Jacqueline Wilson.

NONFICTION Picture books, young readers, middle readers, young adults: adventure, animal, contemporary, fantasy, history, humor, multicultural, nature/environment, poetry, religion, science fiction, sports, suspense/mystery.

HOW TO CONTACT *Not accepting unsolicited mss or queries.*

ILLUSTRATION Works with 25 illustrators/year. Illustrations only: Query with samples. Do not send original art; copies only through the mail. Samples returned with SASE.

TERMS Pays authors royalty based on retail price.

TIPS "You should find a reputable agent and have him/her submit your work."

SASQUATCH BOOKS

1904 Third Ave., Suite 710, Seattle WA 98104. (206)467-4307. **Fax:** (206)467-4301. **E-mail:** ttabor@sasquatch books.com. **Website:** www.sasquatchbooks.com. **Contact:** Gary Luke, editorial director; Terence Maikels, acquisitions editor; Heidi Lenze, acquisitions editor. "Sasquatch Books publishes books for and from the Pacific Northwest, Alaska, and California. Sasquatch Books' publishing program is a veritable celebration of regionally written words. Undeterred by political or geographical borders, Sasquatch defines its region as the magnificent area that stretches from the Brooks Range to the Gulf of California and from the Rocky Mountains to the Pacific Ocean. Our top-selling Best Places® travel guides serve the most popular destinations and locations of the West. We also publish widely in the areas of food and wine, gardening, nature, photography, children's books, and regional history, all facets of the literature of place. With more than 200 books brimming with insider information on the West, we offer an energetic eye on the lifestyle, landscape, and worldview of our region. Considers queries and proposals from authors and agents for new projects that fit into our West Coast regional publishing program. We can evaluate query letters, proposals, and complete mss." Publishes regional hardcover and trade paperback originals. Publishes 30 titles/year. 20% of books from first-time authors. 75% from unagented writers.

○ "When you submit to Sasquatch Books, please remember that the editors want to know about you *and* your project, along with a sense of who will want to read your book."

FICTION Young readers: adventure, animal, concept, contemporary, humor, nature/environment. Recently published *Amazing Alaska*, by Deb Vanasse, illustrated by Karen Lewis; *Sourdough Man*, by Cherie Stihler, illustrated by Barbara Lavallee.

NONFICTION "We are seeking quality nonfiction works about the Pacific Northwest and West Coast regions (including Alaska to California). The literature of place includes how-to and where-to as well as history and narrative nonfiction." Picture books: activity books, animal, concept, nature/environment. Recently published *Larry Gets Lost in New York City*, written and illustrated by John Skewes (picture book); *Searching for Sasqatch*, by Nathaniel Lachenmeyer, illustrated by Vicki Bradley (picture book).

HOW TO CONTACT Submit query, proposal or ms, with SASE. Send submissions to The Editors. E-mailed submissions and queries are not recommended. Please include return postage if you want your materials back. Responds to queries in 3 months. Publishes book 6-9 months after acceptance.

ILLUSTRATION Accepts material from international illustrators. Works with 5 illustrators/year. Uses both color and b&w. Reviews ms/illustration packages. For ms/illustration packages: Query. Submit ms/illustration packages to The Editors. Reviews work for future assignments. If interested in illustrating future titles, query with samples. Samples returned with SASE. Samples filed.

TERMS Pays royalty on cover price. Pays wide range advance. Book catalog for 9×12 envelope and 2 first-class stamps. Guidelines available online.

TIPS "We sell books through a range of channels in addition to the book trade. Our primary audience consists of active, literate residents of the West Coast."

○ SCHOLASTIC INC.

557 Broadway, New York NY 10012. (212)343-6100. **Website:** www.scholastic.com. Scholastic Trade Books is an award-winning publisher of original children's books. Scholastic publishes more than 600 new hardcover, paperback and novelty books each year. The list includes the phenomenally successful pub-lishing properties Harry Potter®, Goosebumps®, The 39 Clues™, I Spy™, and The Hunger Games; bestselling and award-winning authors and illustrators, including Blue Balliett, Jim Benton, Meg Cabot, Suzanne Collins, Christopher Paul Curtis, Ann M. Martin, Dav Pilkey, J.K. Rowling, Pam Muñoz Ryan, Brian Selznick, David Shannon, Mark Teague, and Walter Wick, among others; as well as licensed properties such as Star Wars® and Rainbow Magic®.

○ Accepts agented submissions only.

○ SCHOLASTIC LIBRARY PUBLISHING

90 Old Sherman Turnpike, Danbury CT 06810. (203)797-3500. **Fax:** (203)797-3197. **Website:** www.scholastic.com/aboutscholastic/librarypublishing.htm. **Contact:** Phil Friedman, vice president/publisher; Kate Nunn, editor-in-chief; Marie O'Neil, art director. "Scholastic Library is a leading publisher of reference, educational, and children's books. We provide parents, teachers, and librarians with the tools they need to enlighten children to the pleasure of learning and prepare them for the road ahead. Publishes informational (nonfiction) for K-12; picture books for young readers, grades 1-3." Publishes hardcover and trade paperback originals.

○ *Accepts agented submissions only.*

FICTION Publishes 1 picture book series, Rookie Readers, for grades 1-2. Does not accept unsolicited mss.

NONFICTION Photo-illustrated books for all levels: animal, arts/crafts, biography, careers, concept, geography, health, history, hobbies, how-to, multicultural, nature/environment, science, social issues, special needs, sports. Average word length: young readers—2,000; middle readers—8,000; young adult—15,000.

HOW TO CONTACT *Agented submissions only.*

ILLUSTRATION Works with 15-20 illustrators/year. Uses color artwork and line drawings. Illustrations only: Query with samples or arrange personal portfolio review. Responds only if interested. Samples returned with SASE. Samples filed. Do not send originals. No phone or e-mail inquiries; contact only by mail.

TERMS Pays authors royalty based on net or work purchased outright. Pays illustrators at competitive rates.

○ SCHOLASTIC PRESS

Imprint of Scholastic, Inc., 557 Broadway, New York NY 10012. (212)343-6100. **Fax:** (212)343-4713. **Web-**

site: www.scholastic.com. **Contact:** Liz Szabla, editorial director, Scholastic Press. Scholastic Press publishes fresh, literary picture book fiction and nonfiction; fresh, literary nonseries or nongenre-oriented middle grade and young adult fiction. Currently emphasizing subtly handled treatments of key relationships in children's lives; unusual approaches to commonly dry subjects, such as biography, math, history, or science. De-emphasizing fairy tales (or retellings), board books, genre, or series fiction (mystery, fantasy, etc.). Publishes hardcover originals. Publishes 60 titles/year. 1% of books from first-time authors.

FICTION Looking for strong picture books, young chapter books, appealing middle grade novels (ages 8-11) and interesting and well-written young adult novels. Wants fresh, exciting picture books and novels—inspiring, new talent. Published *Chasing Vermeer*, by Blue Balliet; *Here Today*, by Ann M. Martin; *Detective LaRue*, by Mark Teague.

HOW TO CONTACT *Agented submissions and previously published authors only.* 2,500 queries received/year. Responds in 3 months to queries; 6-8 months to mss. Publishes book 2 years after acceptance.

ILLUSTRATION Works with 30 illustrators/year. Uses both b&w and color artwork. Illustrations only: Query with samples; send tearsheets. Responds only if interested. Samples returned with SASE. Original artwork returned at job's completion.

TERMS Pays royalty on retail price. Pays variable advance.

TIPS "Read *currently* published children's books. Revise, rewrite, rework and find your own voice, style and subject. We are looking for authors with a strong and unique voice who can tell a great story and have the ability to evoke genuine emotion. Children's publishers are becoming more selective, looking for irresistible talent and fairly broad appeal, yet still very willing to take risks, just to keep the game interesting."

SCIENCE & HUMANITIES PRESS

P.O. Box 7151, Chesterfield MO 63006. (636)394-4950. **E-mail:** banis@sciencehumanitiespress.com. **Website:** www.sciencehumanitiespress.com. **Contact:** Dr. Bud Banis, publisher. Publishes trade paperback originals and reprints, and electronic originals and reprints. Publishes 20-30 titles/year. 25% of books from first-time authors. 100% from unagented writers.

FICTION Adventure, historical, humor, literary, mainstream/contemporary, military/war, mystery, regional, romance, science fiction, short story collections, spiritual, sports, suspense, western, young adult. "We prefer books with a theme that gives a market focus."

NONFICTION "Submissions are best as brief descriptions by e-mail, including some description of the author's background/credentials, and thoughts on approach to nontraditional or specialized markets. Why is the book important and who would buy it? Prefer description by e-mail. Need not be a large format proposal."

HOW TO CONTACT Does not accept unsolicited mss without a SASE. "We prefer that you send proposals by e-mail with a brief description, marketing concept, and possibly a sample of the writing." 1,000 queries received/year. 50 mss received/year. Responds in 2 months to queries and proposals; 3 months to mss. Publishes ms 1 year after acceptance.

TERMS Pays 8% royalty on retail price. Book catalog available online. Guidelines available online.

TIPS "Our expertise is electronic publishing for continuous short-run-in-house production."

SECOND STORY PRESS

20 Maud St., Suite 401, Toronto, Ontario M5V 2M5, Canada. (416)537-7850. **Fax:** (416)537-0588. **E-mail:** info@secondstorypress.ca; marketing@secondstorypress.com. **Website:** www.secondstorypress.ca. "We are a Canadian feminist press publishing books of special interest to girls and women."

FICTION Considers non-sexist, non-racist, and nonviolent stories, as well as historical fiction, chapter books, picture books. Recently published *Lilly and the Paper Man*, by Rebecca Upjohn; *Mom and Mum Are Getting Married!*, by Ken Setterington.

NONFICTION Picture books: biography. Recently published *Hiding Edith: A True Story*, by Kathy Kacer (a new addition to our Holocaust Remembrance Series for Young Readers).

HOW TO CONTACT Submit complete ms or submit outline and sample chapters by postal mail only. No electronic submissions or queries.

TIPS Will consider material from US authors but focuses on residents of Canada.

SEEDLING CONTINENTAL PRESS

520 E. Bainbridge St., Elizabethtown PA 17022. **E-mail:** bspencer@continentalpress.com. **Website:** www.continentalpress.com. **Contact:** Megan Bergonzi. Publishes books for classroom use only for the

beginning reader in English. "Natural language and predictable text are requisite. Patterned text is acceptable, but must have a unique story line. Poetry, books in rhyme and full-length picture books are not being accepted. Illustrations are not necessary."

FICTION Young readers: adventure, animal, folktales, humor, multicultural, nature/environment. Does not accept texts longer than 16 pages or over 300 words. Average word length: young readers—100.

NONFICTION Young readers: animal, arts/crafts, biography, careers, concept, multicultural, nature/environment, science. Does not accept texts longer than 16 pages or over 300 words. Average word length: young readers—100.

HOW TO CONTACT Submit complete ms. "Submissions should include an 8-, 12-, or 16-page format, including the title page. No other format is reviewed. Plase do not submit queries, manuscript summaries, or confirmation postcards." Responds to mss in 6 months. Publishes book 1-2 years after acceptance.

ILLUSTRATION Works with 8-10 illustrators/year. Uses color and b&w artwork. Reviews ms/illustration packages from artists. Submit ms with dummy. Illustrations only: Color copies or line art. Responds only if interested. Samples returned with SASE only; samples filed if interested.

PHOTOGRAPHY Buys photos from freelancers. Works on assignment only. Model/property releases required. Uses color prints and 35mm transparencies. Submit cover letter and color promo piece.

TERMS Work purchased outright from authors.

TIPS "See our website. Follow writers' guidelines carefully and test your story with children and educators."

SHEN'S BOOKS

1547 Palos Verdes Mall No. 291, Walnut Creek CA 94597. (925)262-8108. **Fax:** (888)269-9092. **E-mail:** info@shens.com. **Website:** www.shens.com. **Contact:** Renee Ting, president.

FICTION "We are currently only considering picture book manuscripts of fewer than 2500 words. Stories must reflect the culture of an Asian country or that of Asian-Americans. Stories involving multiple ethnicities and tolerance will be considered as long as at least one culture depicted is Asian." Recently published *Grandfather's Story Cloth*, by Linda Gerdner, illustrated by Stuart Loughridge (ages 4-8); *The Wakame Gatherers*, by Holly Thompson, illus-

trated by Kazumi Wilds (ages 4-8); *Romina's Rangoli*, by Malathi Michelle Iyengar, illustrated by Jennifer Wanardi (ages 4-8); *The Day the Dragon Danced*, by Kay Haugaard, illustrated by Carolyn Reed Barritt (ages 4-8).

NONFICTION Picture books, young readers: multicultural. Recently published *Chinese History Stories* edited by Renee Ting; *Selvakumar Knew Better*, by Virginia Kroll, illustrated by Xiaojun Li (ages 4-8).

HOW TO CONTACT Responds to queries in 1-2 weeks; mss in 6-12 months. Publishes book 1-2 years after acceptance.

ILLUSTRATION Accepts material from international illustrators. Works with 2 illustrators/year. Uses color artwork only. Reviews ms/illustration packages. For ms/illustration packages: Send ms with dummy. Submit ms/illustration packages to Renee Ting, president. Reviews work for future assignments. If interested in illustrating future titles, query with samples. Submit samples to Renee Ting, president. Samples not returned. Samples filed.

PHOTOGRAPHY Works on assignment only. Submit photos to Renee Ting, president.

TERMS Authors' pay negotiated by project. Catalog available on website.

TIPS "Be familiar with our catalog before submitting."

SILVERLAND PRESS

E-mail: editor@silverlandpress.com. **Website:** www.silverlandpress.com. **Contact:** Karen Friesen, editor.

Silverland Press grew from the desire to encourage and celebrate writers and the commitment to publish fiction that challenges readers' perspectives and tells a gripping story. We publish children's and young adult stories in many different genres.

FICTION Young adult: urban fantasy, mystery, romance, science fiction, fantasy. "We accept manuscripts between 40,000 words and 75,000 words targeting a young adult audience. At the current time we are especially interested in acquiring children's and young adult stories of all lengths where the work is part of a series."

HOW TO CONTACT Submit via e-mail. In the subject line of the e-mail include the word "submission" and the title of the ms. Include a brief description of your story, word count, publishing history (if any), mailing address, and if ms is agented or not.

SIMON & SCHUSTER BOOKS FOR YOUNG READERS

Imprint of Simon & Schuster Children's Publishing, 1230 Avenue of the Americas, New York NY 10020. (212)698-7000. **Fax:** (212)698-2796. **Website:** www.simonsayskids.com. "Simon and Schuster Books For Young Readers is the Flagship imprint of the S&S Children's Division. We are committed to publishing a wide range of contemporary, commercial, award-winning fiction and nonfiction that spans every age of children's publishing. BFYR is constantly looking to the future, supporting our foundation authors and franchises, but always with an eye for breaking new ground with every publication. We publish high-quality fiction and nonfiction for a variety of age groups and a variety of markets. Above all, we strive to publish books that we are passionate about." Publishes hardcover originals. Publishes 75 titles/year.

　　○ *No unsolicited mss.* All unsolicited mss returned unopened. Queries are accepted via mail.

FICTION "We're looking for picture books centered on a strong, fully-developed protagonist who grows or changes during the course of the story; YA novels that are challenging and psychologically complex; also imaginative and humorous middle-grade fiction."

NONFICTION Picture books: concept. All levels: narrative, current events, biography, history. "We're looking for picture books or middle grade nonfiction that have a retail potential. No photo essays." Recently published Insiders Series (picture book nonfiction, all ages).

HOW TO CONTACT Query with SASE only. Responds in 2 months to queries and mss. Publishes ms 2-4 years after acceptance.

ILLUSTRATION Works with 70 illustrators/year. Do not submit original artwork. Does not accept unsolicited or unagented illustration submissions.

TERMS Pays variable royalty on retail price. Guidelines for #10 SASE.

TIPS "Our imprint's slogan is 'Reading You'll Remember.' We aim to publish books that are fresh, accessible and family-oriented; we want them to have an impact on the reader."

ⓐ SIMON & SCHUSTER CHILDREN'S PUBLISHING

Simon & Schuster, Inc., 1230 Avenue of the Americas, New York NY 10020. (212)698-7000. **Website:** www.simonsayskids.com. Publishes hardcover and paperback fiction, nonfiction, trade, library, mass market titles, and novelty books for preschool through young adult readers. Publishes 650 titles/year.

　　○ *No unsolicited mss.*

SKINNER HOUSE BOOKS

The Unitarian Universalist Association, 25 Beacon St., Boston MA 02108. (617)742-2100 ext. 603. **Fax:** (617)742-7025. **E-mail:** bookproposals@uua.org; skinnerhouse@uua.org. **Website:** www.uua.org/skinner. **Contact:** Betsy Martin. "We publish titles in Unitarian Universalist faith, liberal religion, history, biography, worship, and issues of social justice. Most of our children's titles are intended for religious education or worship use. They reflect Unitarian Universalist values. We also publish inspirational titles of poetic prose and meditations. Writers should know that Unitarian Universalism is a liberal religious denomination committed to progressive ideals. Currently emphasizing social justice concerns." Publishes trade paperback originals and reprints. Publishes 10-20 titles/year. 50% of books from first-time authors. 100% from unagented writers.

FICTION All levels: anthology, multicultural, nature/environment, religion. Recently published *A Child's Book of Blessings and Prayers*, by Eliza Blanchard (ages 4-8, picture book); *Meet Jesus: The Life and Lessons of a Beloved Teacher*, by Lynn Gunney (ages 5-8, picture book); *Magic Wanda's Travel Emporium*, by Joshua Searle-White (ages 9 and up, stories).

NONFICTION All levels: activity books, multicultural, music/dance, nature/environment, religion. *Unitarian Universalism Is a Really Long Name*, by Jennifer Dant (picture book, resource that answers children's questions about Unitarian Universalism, ages 5-9).

HOW TO CONTACT Query or submit outline/synopsis and 2 sample chapters. Responds to queries in 3 weeks. Publishes book 1 year after acceptance.

ILLUSTRATION Works with 2 illustrators/year. Uses both color and b&w. Reviews ms/illustration packages from artists. Query. Contact: Suzanne Morgan, design director. Responds only if interested. Samples returned with SASE.

PHOTOGRAPHY Buys stock images and assigns work. Contact: Suzanne Morgan, design director. Uses inspirational types of photos. Model/property releases required; captions required. Uses color, b&w. Submit cover letter, résumé.

TERMS Book catalog for 6×9 SAE with 3 first-class stamps. Guidelines available online.

TIPS "From outside our denomination, we are interested in mss that will be of help or interest to liberal churches, Sunday School classes, parents, ministers, and volunteers. Inspirational/spiritual and children's titles must reflect liberal Unitarian Universalist values."

SMALLFELLOW PRESS

9454 Wilshire Blvd. Suite 550, Beverly CA 90212. E-mail: asls@pacbell.net; tallfellow@pacbell.net. Website: www.smallfellow.com. Contact: Larry Sloan, Leonard Stern.

- *Smallfellow no longer accepts ms/art submissions.*

SOUNDPRINTS/STUDIO MOUSE

Palm Publishing, 50 Washington St., 12th Floor, Noralk CT 06854. (800)228-7839. **Fax:** (203)864-1776. **E-mail:** soundprints@soundprints.com. **Website:** www.soundprints.com.

FICTION Picture books, young readers: adventure, animal, fantasy, history, multicultural, nature/environment, sports. Recently published *Smithsonian Alphabet of Earth*, by Barbie Heit Schwaeber, and illustrated by Sally Vitsky (preschool-2nd grade, hardcover and paperback available with audio CD plus bonus audiobook and e-book downloads); *First Look at Insects*, by Laura Gates Galvin, illustrated by Charlotte Oh.

HOW TO CONTACT Query or submit complete ms. Responds to queries and mss in 6 months. Publishes book 1-2 years after acceptance.

ILLUSTRATION Illustration: Works with 3-7 illustrators/year. Uses color artwork only. Send tearsheets with contact information, "especially Web address if applicable." Samples not returned; samples filed.

PHOTOGRAPHY Buys stock and assign work. Model/property release and captions required. Send color promo sheet.

TERMS Catalog available on website. Guidelines for SASE.

SPINNER BOOKS

University Games, 2030 Harrison St., San Francisco CA 94110. (415)503-1600. **Fax:** (415)503-0085. **E-mail:** info@ugames.com. **Website:** www.ugames.com. "Spinners Books publishes books of puzzles, games and trivia."

NONFICTION Picture books: games & puzzles. Recently published *20 Questions*, by Bob Moog (adult); *20 Questions for Kids*, by Bob Moog (young adult).

HOW TO CONTACT *Only interested in agented material.* Query. Responds to queries in 3 months; mss in 2 months only if interested. Publishes book 6 months after acceptance.

ILLUSTRATION Only interested in agented material. Uses both color and b&w. Illustrations only: Query with samples. Responds in 3 months only if interested. Samples not returned.

STANDARD PUBLISHING

8805 Governor's Hill Dr., Suite 400, Cincinnati OH 45249. (800)543-1353. **E-mail:** customerservice@standardpub.com. **E-mail:** adultministry@standardpub.com; ministrytochildren@standardpub.com; ministrytoyouth@standardpub.com. **Website:** www.standardpub.com. Publishes resources that meet church and family needs in the area of children's ministry.

TERMS Guidelines and current publishing objectives available online.

STERLING PUBLISHING CO., INC.

387 Park Ave. S., 10th Floor, New York NY 10016. (212)532-7160. **Fax:** (212)981-0508. **E-mail:** ragis@sterlingpublishing.com; customerservice@sterlingpublishing.com. **Website:** www.sterlingpublishing.com/kids. "Sterling publishes highly illustrated, accessible, hands-on, practical books for adults and children." Publishes hardcover and paperback originals and reprints. 15% of books from first-time authors.

- "Our mission is to publish high-quality books that educate, entertain, and enrich the lives of our readers."

FICTION Picture books. "We do not publish fictional chapter books or novels."

NONFICTION "Our nonfiction list primarily focuses on activity-based subjects, such as crafts, activities, puzzles, and science experiments. We also have a small focus on history and biographies."

HOW TO CONTACT Submit outline, publishing history, 1 sample chapter (typed and double-spaced), SASE. Explain your idea. Send sample illustrations where applicable. For children's books, please submit full mss. "We do not accept electronic (e-mail) submissions. Be sure to include information about yourself with particular regard to your skills and qualifications in the subject area of your submission.

It is helpful for us to know your publishing history—whether or not you've written other books and, if so, the name of the publisher and whether those books are currently in print."

ILLUSTRATION Works with 50 illustrators/year. Reviews ms/illustration packages from artists. Illustrations only: Send promo sheet. Contact: Karen Nelson, creative director. Responds in 6 weeks. Samples returned with SASE; samples filed.

PHOTOGRAPHY Buys stock and assigns work. Contact: Karen Nelson.

TERMS Pays royalty or work purchased outright. Offers advances (average amount: $2,000). Catalog available on website. Guidelines available online.

TIPS "We are primarily a nonfiction activities-based publisher. We have a picture book list, but we do not publish chapter books or novels. Our list is not trend-driven. We focus on titles that will backlist well. "

STONE ARCH BOOKS

7825 Telegraph Rd., Bloomington MN 55438. (952)224-0514. **Fax:** (952)933-2410. **E-mail:** author. sub@capstonepub.com; il.sub@capstonepub.com. **Website:** www.stonearchbooks.com. **Contact:** Michael Dahl, editorial director; Heather Kindseth, art director.

FICTION Young readers, middle readers, young adults: adventure, contemporary, fantasy, humor, light humor, mystery, science fiction, sports, suspense. Average word length: young readers—1,000-3,000; middle readers and early young adults—5,000-10,000.

HOW TO CONTACT Send résumé and sample chapters via e-mail to author.sub@capstonepub.com. Do not send attachments.

ILLUSTRATION Works with 35 illustrators/year. Uses both color and b&w. Send résumé and samples via e-mail to il.sub@capstonepub.com. Do not send attachments.

TERMS Work purchased outright from authors. Catalog available on website.

TIPS "A high-interest topic or activity is one that a young person would spend their free time on without adult direction or suggestion."

STOREY PUBLISHING

210 MASS MoCA Way, North Adams MA 01247. (800)793-9396. **Fax:** (413)346-2196. **E-mail:** webmaster@storey.com. **Website:** www.storey.com. **Contact:** Deborah Balmuth, editorial director (building, sewing, gift). "The mission of Storey Publishing is to serve our customers by publishing practical information that encourages personal independence in harmony with the environment. We seek to do this in a positive atmosphere that promotes editorial quality, team spirit, and profitability. The books we select to carry out this mission include titles on gardening, small-scale farming, building, cooking, homebrewing, crafts, part-time business, home improvement, woodworking, animals, nature, natural living, personal care, and country living. We are always pleased to review new proposals, which we try to process expeditiously. We offer both work-for-hire and standard royalty contracts." Publishes hardcover and trade paperback originals and reprints. Publishes 40 titles/year. 25% of books from first-time authors. 60% from unagented writers.

HOW TO CONTACT Guidelines for book proposals available online. 600 queries received/year. 150 mss received/year. Responds in 1 month to queries; 3 months to proposals/mss. Publishes book 2 years after acceptance.

TERMS We offer both work-for-hire and standard royalty contracts. Pays advance. Book catalog available free. Guidelines available online at website.

SYLVAN DELL PUBLISHING

612 Johnnie Dodds, Suite A2, Mt. Pleasant SC 29464. (843)971-6722. **Fax:** (843)216-3804. **E-mail:** don nagerman@sylvandellpublishing.com. **Website:** www.sylvandellpublishing.com. **Contact:** Donna German, editor. "The picture books we publish are usually, but not always, fictional stories that relate to animals, nature, the environment, and science. All books should subtly convey an educational theme through a warm story that is fun to read and that will grab a child's attention. Each book has a 3-5 page *For Creative Minds* section to reinforce the educational component. This section will have a craft and/or game as well as 'fun facts' to be shared by the parent, teacher, or other adult. Authors do not need to supply this information. Mss. should be less than 1,500 words and meet all of the following 4 criteria: fun to read—mostly fiction with nonfiction facts woven into the story; national or regional in scope; ties into early elementary school curriculum; marketable through a niche market such as a zoo, aquarium, or museum gift shop." Publishes hardcover, trade paperback, and electronic originals. Publishes 10 titles/year. 50% of books from first-time authors. 100% from unagented writers.

FICTION Picture books: animal, folktales, nature/environment, math-related. Word length—picture books: no more than 1,500. Recently published *Whistling Wings*, by first-time author Laura Goering, illustrated by Laura Jacques; *Sort it Out!*, by Barbara Mariconda, illustrated by Sherry Rogers; *Saturn for my Birthday*, by first-time author John McGranaghan, illustrated by Wendy Edelson.

NONFICTION Recently published *River Beds: Sleeping in the World's Rivers*, by Gail Langer Karwoski, illustrated by Connie McLennan."We are not looking for mss. about: pets (dogs or cats in particular); new babies; local or state-specific; magic; biographies; history-related; ABC books; poetry; series; young adult books or novels; holiday-related books. We do not consider mss. that have been previously published in any way, including e-books or self-published."

HOW TO CONTACT Accepts electronic submissions only. Snail mail submissions are discarded without being opened. 2,000 mss received/year. Acknowledges receipt of ms submission within one week. Publishes book 18 months after acceptance. May hold onto mss of interest for 1 year until acceptance.

ILLUSTRATION Works with 10 illustrators/year. Prefers to work with illustrators from the US and Canada. Uses color artwork only. Submit Web link or 2-3 electronic images. Contact: Donna German. "I generally keep submissions on file until I match the manuscripts to illustration needs."

TERMS Pays 6-8% royalty on wholesale price. Pays small advance. Book catalog and guidelines available online.

TIPS "Please make sure that you have looked at our website to read our complete submission guidelines and to see if we are looking for a particular subject. Manuscripts must meet all four of our stated criteria. We look for fairly realistic, bright and colorful art—no cartoons. We want the children excited about the books. We envision the books being used at home and in the classroom."

SYNERGEBOOKS

948 New Highway 7, Columbia TN 38401. (931)223-5900. **E-mail:** synergebooks@aol.com. **Website:** www.synergebooks.com. **Contact:** Debra Staples, publisher/acquisitions editor. "SynergEbooks is first and foremost a digital publisher, so most of our marketing budget goes to those formats. Authors are required to direct-sell a minimum of 100 digital copies of a title before it's accepted for print." Publishes trade paperback and electronic originals. Publishes 40-60 titles/year. 95% of books from first-time authors. 99.9% from unagented writers.

FICTION "We no longer put any of our children's books into print."

NONFICTION "Please browse our site to become familiar with the genres we publish."

HOW TO CONTACT "First, be sure to check to see if we are open for submissions. We do not keep submissions that are sent in during the time we are closed." Query by e-mail and include first 3 chapters (.doc, docx, or .rtf format only) as an attachment. Detailed submission guidelines available at www.synergebooks.com/subguide.html. 250 queries received/year. 250 mss received/year.

TERMS Pays 15-40% royalty; makes outright purchase. Book catalog available online at www.synergebooks.com/paperbacks.html. Guidelines available online at www.synergebooks.com/subguide.html.

TIPS "At SynergEbooks, we work with the author to promote their work."

TANGLEWOOD BOOKS

P.O. Box 3009, Terre Haute IN 47803. **E-mail:** khamlin@tanglewoodbooks.com; ptierney@tanglewoodbooks.com. **Website:** www.tanglewoodbooks.com. **Contact:** Kairi Hamlin, acquisitions editor; Peggy Tierney, publisher. "Tanglewood Press strives to publish entertaining, kid-centric books." Publishes 10 titles/year. 20% of books from first-time authors.

FICTION Picture books: adventure, animal, concept, contemporary, fantasy, humor; middle readers; young adult. Average word length: picture books—800. Recently published *68 Knots*, by Michael Robert Evans (young adult); *The Mice of Bistrot des Sept Frères*, written and illustrated by Marie LeTourneau; *Chester Raccoon and the Acorn Full of Memories*, by Audrey Penn, illustrated by Barbara Gibson.

NONFICTION Occasionally publishes nonfiction. "We would be most likely to consider a manuscript on some interesting history—whether of an event, an era, or a person not well known or covered elsewhere."

HOW TO CONTACT Submit via e-mail to khamin@tanglewoodbooks.com. Include complete picture book ms or query letter and sample chapters. Responds to mss in 18 months. Publishes book 2 years after acceptance.

ILLUSTRATION Accepts material from international illustrators. Works with 3-4 illustrators/year. Uses both color and b&w. Reviews ms/illustration packages. For ms/illustration packages: Send ms with sample illustrations. Submit ms/illustration packages to Peggy Tierney, publisher. If interested in illustrating future titles, query with samples. Submit samples to Peggy Tierney, publisher. Samples not returned. Samples filed.

TERMS Illustrators paid by the project for covers and small illustrations; royalty of 3-5% for picture books. Author sees galleys for review. Illustrators see dummies for review. Originals returned to artist at job's completion.

TIPS "Please see lengthy 'Submissions' page on our website."

THIRD WORLD PRESS

P.O. Box 19730, Chicago IL 60619. (773)651-0700. **Fax:** (773)651-7286. **E-mail:** twpress3@aol.com; gwenmtwp@aol.com. **Website:** www.twpbooks.com. **Contact:** Bennett J. Johnson. "We look for the maximum effect of creative expression and cultural enlightenment in all of the written genres, including fiction, nonfiction, poetry, drama, young adult, and children's books that may not have an outlet otherwise. Third World Press welcomes the opportunity to review solicited and unsolicited manuscripts that explore African-centered life and thought through the genres listed. Publishes hardcover and trade paperback originals and reprints. Publishes 20 titles/year. 20% of books from first-time authors. 80% from unagented writers.

○ Third World Press is open to submissions in July only.

HOW TO CONTACT Query with SASE. Submit outline, clips, 5 sample chapters. 200-300 queries received/year. 200 mss received/year. Responds in 6 months to queries. Responds in 5 months to mss. Publishes ms 18 months after acceptance.

TERMS Compensation based upon royalties. Individual arrangement with author depending on the book, etc. Guidelines for #10 SASE.

○ THISTLEDOWN PRESS LTD.

118 20th Street W., Saskatoon, Saskatchewan S7M 0W6, Canada. (306)244-1722. **Fax:** (306)244-1762. **E-mail:** editorial@thistledownpress.com **Website:** www.thistledownpress.com. **Contact:** Allan Forrie, publisher.

○ "Thistledown originates books by Canadian authors only, although we have co-published titles by authors outside Canada. We do not publish children's picture books."

FICTION Young adults: adventure, anthology, contemporary, fantasy, humor, poetry, romance, science fiction, suspense/mystery, short stories. Average word length: young adults—40,000. Recently published *Up All Night*, edited by R.P. MacIntyre (young adult, anthology); *Offside*, by Cathy Beveridge (young adult, novel); *Cheeseburger Subversive*, by Richard Scarsbrook; *The Alchemist's Daughter*, by Eileen Kernaghan.

HOW TO CONTACT Submit outline/synopsis, sample chapters, marketing plans and SASE. *Does not accept mss.* Do not query by e-mail. Responds to queries in 4 months. Publishes book 1 year after acceptance.

ILLUSTRATION Prefers agented illustrators but "not mandatory." Works with few illustrators. Illustrations only: Query with samples, promo sheet, slides, tearsheets. Responds only if interested. Samples returned with SASE; samples filed.

TERMS Pays authors royalty of 10-12% based on net dollar sales. Pays illustrators and photographers by the project (range: $250-750). Book catalog free on request. Guidelines available for #10 envelope and IRC.

TIPS "Send cover letter including publishing history and SASE."

○ TIGHTROPE BOOKS

17 Greyton Crescent, Toronto, Ontario M6E 2G1, Canada. (647)348-4460. **E-mail:** info@tightropebooks.com. **Website:** www.tightropebooks.com. **Contact:** Shirarose Wilensky, editor. Publishes hardcover and trade paperback originals. Publishes 12 titles/year. 70% of books from first-time authors. 100% from unagented writers.

○ "Due to a large backlog, Tightrope Books is temporarily suspending unsolicited submissions." Check website for updates.

HOW TO CONTACT Query with SASE. Submit proposal package, including: synopsis, 1 sample chapter and completed ms. Responds if interested. Publishes book 1 year after acceptance.

TERMS Pays 5-15% royalty on retail price. Pays advance of $200-300. Catalog and guidelines free on request and online.

TIPS "Audience is young, urban, literary, educated, unconventional."

TILBURY HOUSE

Harpswell Press, Inc., 103 Brunswick Ave., Gardiner ME 04345. (800)582-1899. **Fax:** (207)582-8227. **E-mail:** tilbury@tilburyhouse.com. **Website:** www.tilburyhouse.com. **Contact:** Audrey Maynard, children's book editor; Jennifer Bunting, publisher. Publishes 10 titles/year.

FICTION Picture books: multicultural, nature/environment. Special needs include books that teach children about tolerance and honoring diversity. Recently published *One of Us*, by Peggy Moss; *Moon Watchers: Shirin's Ramadan Miracle*, by Reza Jalali; and *The Lunch Thief*, by Anne Bromely, illustrated by Robert Casilla. "We don't publish 'general' children's books about animals, fables, or fantasy."

NONFICTION Regional adult biography/history/maritime/nature, and children's picture books that deal with issues, such as bullying, multiculturalism, etc.

HOW TO CONTACT Submit complete ms for children's books. Responds to mss in 2 months. Publishes ms 1 year after acceptance.

ILLUSTRATION Works with 2-3 illustrators/year. Illustrations only: Query with samples. Responds in 1 month. Samples returned with SASE. Original artwork returned at job's completion.

PHOTOGRAPHY Buys photos from freelancers. Works on assignment only.

TERMS Pays royalty based on wholesale price. Book catalog available free. Guidelines available online.

TIPS "We are always interested in stories that will encourage children to understand the natural world and the environment, as well as stories with social justice themes. We really like stories that engage children to become problem solvers as well as those that promote respect, tolerance and compassion. We do not publish books with personified animal characters; historical fiction; chapter books; fantasy."

TOR BOOKS

Tom Doherty Associates, LLC. 175 Fifth Ave., New York NY 10010. **Website:** www.tor-forge.com. **Contact:** Juliet Pederson, publishing coordinator. Publishes Publishes 5-10 middle readers/year; 5-10 young adult titles/year. titles/year.

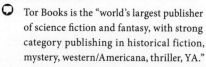 Tor Books is the "world's largest publisher of science fiction and fantasy, with strong category publishing in historical fiction, mystery, western/Americana, thriller, YA."

FICTION Average word length: middle readers—30,000; young adults—60,000-100,000.

NONFICTION Middle readers and young adult: geography, history, how-to, multicultural, nature/environment, science, social issues. Does not want to see religion, cooking. Average word length: middle readers—25,000-35,000; young adults—70,000. Published *Strange Unsolved Mysteries*, by Phyllis Raybin Emert; *Stargazer's Guide to the Galaxy*, by Q.L. Pearce (ages 8-12, guide to constellations, illustrated).

HOW TO CONTACT Submit outline/synopsis, first three chapters and SASE. "We do not accept queries."

TERMS Pays author royalty. Pays illustrators by the project. Book catalog available for 9×12 SAE and 3 first-class stamps. See website for latest submission guidelines.

TIPS "Know the house you are submitting to, familiarize yourself with the types of books they are publishing. Get an agent. Allow him/her to direct you to publishers who are most appropriate. It saves time and effort."

ⓐ TYNDALE HOUSE PUBLISHERS, INC.

351 Executive Dr., Carol Stream IL 60188. (800)323-9400. **Fax:** (800)684-0247. **Website:** www.tyndale.com. **Contact:** Katara Washington Patton, acquisitions; Talinda Iverson, art acquisitions. "Tyndale House publishes practical, user-friendly Christian books for the home and family." Publishes hardcover and trade paperback originals and mass paperback reprints. Publishes 15 titles/year.

FICTION "Christian truths must be woven into the story organically. No short story collections. Youth books: character building stories with Christian perspective. Especially interested in ages 10-14. We primarily publish Christian historical romances, with occasional contemporary, suspense, or standalones."

HOW TO CONTACT *Agented submissions only. No unsolicited mss.*

ILLUSTRATION Uses full-color for book covers, b&w or color spot illustrations for some nonfiction. Illustrations only: Query with photocopies (color or b&w) of samples, résumé.

PHOTOGRAPHY Buys photos from freelancers. Works on assignment only.

TERMS Pays negotiable royalty. Pays negotiable advance. Guidelines for 9×12 SAE and $2.40 for postage or visit website.

TIPS "All accepted mss will appeal to Evangelical Christian children and parents."

⊕ UNTREED READS PUBLISHING

506 Kansas St., San Francisco CA 94107. (415)621-0465. **Fax:** (415)621-0465. **E-mail:** general@untreedreads.com; submissions@untreedreads.com. **Website:** www.untreedreads.com. **Contact:** Jay A. Hartman, editor-in-chief (fiction—all genres). Publishes electronic originals and reprints. Publishes 35 titles/year. 80% of books from first-time authors. 75% from unagented writers.

FICTION "We look forward to long-term relationships with our authors. We encourage works that are either already a series or could develop into a series. We are one of the few publishers publishing short stories and are happy to be a resource for these good works. We welcome short story collections. Also, we look forward to publishing children's books, cookbooks, and other works that have been known for illustrations in print as the technology in the multiple e-readers improves. We hope to be a large platform for diverse content and authors. We seek mainstream content, but if you're an author or have content that doesn't seem to always 'fit' into traditional market we'd like to hear from you." No erotica, picture books, poetry, poetry in translation, or romance.

NONFICTION "We are very interested in developing our textbook market. E-readers don't currently support graphs, tables, images, etc. as well as print books; however, we plan to be trendsetters in this as the technology in the e-readers improves. Also we are eager to increase our number of business books. We always look for series or works that could develop into a series."

HOW TO CONTACT Check online to see if Untreed Reads is currently accepting submissions. "Please note that any submissions received between our reading seasons will not be retained or read." Receives 50 submissions/year. Responds in 1/2 month on queries, 1 month on proposals, and 1 1/2 months on mss.

TERMS Pays 50-60% royalty on retail price. Catalog and guidelines available online at website.

TIPS "For our fiction titles we lean toward a literary audience. For nonfiction titles, we want to be a platform for business people, entrepreneurs, and speakers to become well known in their fields of expertise. However, for both fiction and nonfiction we want to appeal to many audiences."

⊕ URJ PRESS

633 Third Ave., 7th Floor, New York NY 10017. (212)650-4120. **Fax:** (212)650-4119. **E-mail:** press@urj.org. **Website:** www.urjpress.com. **Contact:** Michael H. Goldber, publisher/editor-in-chief. "URJ publishes textbooks for the religious classroom, children's tradebooks and scholarly work of Jewish education import—no adult fiction and no YA fiction." Publishes hardcover and trade paperback originals. Publishes 22 titles/year. 70% of books from first-time authors. 90% from unagented writers.

○ *URJ Press publishes books related to Judaism.*

FICTION Picture books: religion. Average word length: picture books—1,500. Recently published *The Purim Costume*, by Peninnah Schran, illustrated by Tammy L. Keiser (ages 4-8, picture book); *A Year of Jewish Stories: 52 Tales for Children and Their Families*, by Grace Ragues Maisel and Samantha Shubert, illustrated by Tammy L. Keiser (ages 4-12, picture book).

NONFICTION Picture books, young readers, middle readers: religion. Average word length: picture books—1,500. Recently published *The Seven Spices: Stories and Recipes Inspired by the Food of the Bible*, by Matt Biers-Ariel, illustrated by Tama Goodman (story and recipe book).

HOW TO CONTACT Submit book proposal form (available online) via postal mail or fax. 500 queries received/year. 400 mss received/year. Responds to queries/mss in 4 months. Publishes book 18-24 months after acceptance.

ILLUSTRATION Works with 5 illustrators/year. Reviews ms/illustration packages from artists. Send ms with dummy. Illustrations only: Send portfolio to be kept on file. Responds in 2 months. Samples returned with SASE. Looking specifically for Jewish themes.

PHOTOGRAPHY Buys stock and assigns work. Uses photos with Jewish content. Prefers modern settings. Submit cover letter and promo piece.

TERMS Pays 3-5% royalty on retail price. Makes outright purchase of 500-2,000. Pays $500-2,000 advance. Book catalog and ms guidelines free or on website.

TIPS "Look at some of our books. Have an understanding of the Reform Judaism community. In addition to bookstores, we sell to Jewish congregations and Hebrew day schools."

⊘ VIKING CHILDREN'S BOOKS

345 Hudson St., New York NY 10014. **E-mail:** avery studiopublicity@us.penguingroup.com. **Website:** www.penguingroup.com. **Contact:** Catherine Frank, executive editor. "Viking Children's Books is known for humorous, quirky picture books, in addition

to more traditional fiction. We publish the highest quality fiction, nonfiction, and picture books for preschoolers through young adults." Publishes hardcover originals. Publishes 70 titles/year.

○ *Does not accept unsolicited submissions.*

FICTION All levels: adventure, animal, contemporary, fantasy, history, humor, multicultural, nature/environment, poetry, problem novels, romance, science fiction, sports, suspense/mystery. Recently published *Llama Llama Misses Mama*, by Anna Dewdney (ages 2 up, picture book); *Wintergirls*, by Laurie Halse Anderson (ages 12 and up); *Good Luck Bear*, by Greg Foley (ages 2 up); *Along for the Ride*, by Sarah Dessen (ages 12 up).

NONFICTION All levels: biography, concept, history, multicultural, music/dance, nature/environment, science, and sports. Recently published *Harper Lee*, by Kerry Madden (ages 11 and up, biography); *Knucklehead*, by Jon Scieszka (ages 7 and up, autobiography); *Marching for Freedom,* by Elizabeth Partridge (ages 11 and up, nonfiction).

HOW TO CONTACT *Accepts agented mss only.* Responds to queries/mss in 6 months. Publishes book 1-2 years after acceptance.

ILLUSTRATION Works with 30 illustrators/year. Responds to artist's queries/submissions only if interested. Samples returned with SASE only or samples filed. Originals returned at job's completion.

TERMS Pays 2-10% royalty on retail price or flat fee. Pays negotiable advance.

TIPS No "cartoony" or mass-market submissions for picture books.

WALKER & COMPANY

175 Fifth Ave., New York NY 10010. **E-mail:** Emily.Easton@bloomsburyusa.com; childrenspublicityusa@bloomsbury.com; teensusa@bloomsbury.com. **Website:** www.bloomsburykids.com and www.bloomsburyteens.com. **Contact:** Emily Easton, publishing director; Stacy Cantor Abrams, editor; Mary Kate Castellani, associate editor. Publishes 45 titles/year. 5% of books from first-time authors. 15% from unagented writers.

FICTION Picture books: adventure, history, humor. Middle readers: coming-of-age, adventure, contemporary, history, humor, multicultural. Young adults: adventure, contemporary, romance, humor, historical fiction, suspense/mystery, paranormal. Recently published fiction: *Ribbit Rabbit*, by Candace Ryan and

Mike Lowery (ages 3-5, picture book); *Grandma's Gift*, by Eric Velasquez (ages 4-8, picture book); *Sugar and Ice*, by Kate Messner (8-12, middle grade novel); *Rules of Attraction*, by Simone Elkeles; and *Haunting Violet*, by Alyx Harvey (ages 14 and up).

NONFICTION Recently published nonfiction: *Poop Happened: A History of the World from the Bottom Up*, by Sarah Albee, illustrated by Robert Leighton, (ages 8-12, middle grade nonfiction); *Saving Audie*, by Dorothy Patent and William Muñoz (ages 6-9, picture book nonfiction); *101 Ways to Become a Superhero*, by Richard Horne (ages 12 and up, teen nonfiction).

HOW TO CONTACT Submit outline/synopsis and sample chapters; complete ms for picture books.

ILLUSTRATION Works with 20-25 illustrators/year. Editorial department reviews ms/illustration packages from artists. Query or submit ms with 4-8 samples. Illustrations only: tearsheets. "Please do not send original artwork."

TERMS Pays authors royalty of 5-10%; pays illustrators royalty or flat fee. Offers advance payment against royalties. Writers' guidelines available for SASE.

TIPS Writers: "Make sure you study our catalog before submitting. We are a small house with a tightly focused list. Illustrators: Have a well-rounded portfolio with different styles." Does not want to see folktales, ABC books, early readers, paperback series. "Walker and Company is committed to introducing talented new authors and illustrators to the children's book field."

○ WEIGL PUBLISHERS INC.

350 Fifth Ave. 59th Floor, New York NY 10118. (866)649-3445. **Fax:** (866)449-3445. **E-mail:** linda@weigl.com. **Website:** www.weigl.com. **Contact:** Heather Kissock, acquisitions. Publishes 25 young readers/year; 40 middle readers/year; 20 young adult titles/year. "Our mission is to provide innovative high-quality learning resources for schools and libraries worldwide at a competitive price." Publishes 85 titles/year. 15% of books from first-time authors.

NONFICTION Young readers: animal, biography, geography, history, multicultural, nature/environment, science. Middle readers: animal, biography, geography, history, multicultural, nature/environment, science, social issues, sports. Young adults: biography, careers, geography, history, multicultural, nature/environment, social issues. Average word length: young readers—100 words/page; middle readers—200 words/page; young adults—300 words/page. Recently published Amazing Animals (ages 9 and up, science series); U.S. Sites and Symbols (ages 8 and up, social studies series); Science Q&A (ages 9 and up, social studies series).

HOW TO CONTACT Query by e-mail only. Publishes book 6-9 months after acceptance.

ILLUSTRATION Pays illustrators by the project. Book catalog available for 9×11 SASE. Catalog available on website.

PHOTOGRAPHY Pays per photo.

TERMS Book catalog available for 9×11 SASE. Catalog available on website.

WHITE MANE KIDS

73 W. Burd St., P.O. Box 708, Shippensburg PA 17257. (717)532-2237. **Fax:** (717)532-6110. **E-mail:** marketing@whitemane.com. **Website:** www.whitemane.com. **Contact:** Harold Collier, acquisitions editor.

FICTION Middle readers, young adults: history (primarily American Civil War). Average word length: middle readers—30,000. Does not publish picture books. Recently published *The Witness Tree and the Shadow of the Noose: Mystery, Lies, and Spies in Manassas*, by K.E.M. Johnston, and *Drumbeat: The Story of a Civil War Drummer Boy*, by Robert J. Trout (grades 5 and up).

NONFICTION Middle readers, young adults: history. Average word length: middle readers—30,000. Does not publish picture books. Recently published *Hey, History Isn't Boring Anymore! A Creative Approach to Teaching the Civil War*, by Kelly Ann Butterbaugh (young adult).

HOW TO CONTACT "Download and print out the Proposal Guidelines form. Fill out the form and mail it along with the title of the manuscript, statement of purpose, marketing ideas, a sample dust jacket paragraph, general manuscript information, and how you were referred to White Mane." Responds in 3 months. Publishes book 18 months after acceptance.

ILLUSTRATION Works with 4 illustrators/year. Illustrations used for cover art only. Responds only if interested. Samples returned with SASE.

PHOTOGRAPHY Buys stock and assigns work. Submit cover letter and portfolio.

TERMS Pays authors royalty of 7-10%. Pays illustrators and photographers by the project. Book catalog and writers' guidelines available for SASE.

TIPS "Make your work historically accurate. We are interested in historically accurate fiction and nonfiction for middle and young adult readers. We do *not* publish picture books. Our primary focus is the American Civil War and some American Revolution topics."

WHITE MANE PUBLISHING COMPANY INC.

73 W. Burd St., P.O. Box 708, Shippensburg PA 17257. (717)532-2237; (888)948-6263. **Fax:** (717)532-6110. **E-mail:** marketing@whitemane.com. **Website:** www.whitemane.com.

HOW TO CONTACT "Download and print out the Proposal Guidelines form. Fill out the form and mail it along with the title of the manuscript, statement of purpose, marketing ideas, a sample dust jacket paragraph, general manuscript information, and how you were referred to White Mane."

○ ○ ALBERT WHITMAN & COMPANY

250 S. Northwest Hwy., Suite 320, Park Ridge IL 60068. (800)255-7675. **Fax:** (847)581-0039. **E-mail:** mail@awhitmanco.com. **Website:** www.albertwhitman.com. "Albert Whitman & Company publishes books for the trade, library, and school library market. We have an open submissions policy. We are interested in reviewing the following types of projects: picture book manuscripts for ages 2-8; novels and chapter books for ages 8-12; young adult novels; nonfiction for ages 3-12 and young adults." Best known for the classic series The Boxcar Children®. "Albert Whitman publishes good books for children on a variety of topics: holidays, special needs (such as diabetes), and problems like divorce. The majority of our titles are picture books with less than 1,500 words. De-emphasizing bedtime stories." Publishes in original hardcover, paperback, board books. Publishes 40 titles/year. 10% of books from first-time authors. 50% from unagented writers.

FICTION Picture books, young readers, middle readers: adventure, concept (to help children deal with problems), fantasy, history, humor, multicultural, suspense. Middle readers: problem novels, suspense/mystery. "We are interested in contemporary multicultural stories, stories with holiday themes, and exciting distinctive novels. We publish a wide variety of topics and are interested in stories that help children deal with their problems and concerns. Does not want to see "religion-oriented, ABCs, pop-up, romance, counting."

NONFICTION Picture books, young readers, middle readers: animal, arts/crafts, health, history, hobbies, multicultural, music/dance, nature/environment, science, sports, special needs. Does not want to see "religion, any books that have to be written in, or fictionalized biographies.

HOW TO CONTACT Submit complete picture book ms or query with outline and sample chapters. Include cover letter. Responds (only if interested) in 3 months to queries; 4 months to proposals and mss. Publishes a book 18 months after acceptance.

ILLUSTRATION *"We are not accepting illustration samples at this time. Submissions will not be returned."*

PHOTOGRAPHY Publishes books illustrated with photos, but not stock photos—desires photos all taken for project. "Our books are for children and cover many topics; photos must be taken to match text. Books often show a child in a particular situation (e.g. kids being home-schooled, a sister whose brother is born prematurely)." Photographers should query with samples; send unsolicited photos by mail.

TERMS On retail price: Pays 10% royalty for novels; 5% for picture books. Pays advance. Catalog available for 9×12 SASE and 3 first-class stamps. Guidelines available on website.

TIPS "In both picture books and nonfiction, we are seeking stories showing life in other cultures and the variety of multicultural life in the U.S. We also want fiction and nonfiction about mentally or physically challenged children; some recent topics have been autism, stuttering, and diabetes. Look up some of our books first to be sure your submission is appropriate for Albert Whitman & Co. We publish trade books that are especially interesting to schools and libraries. We recommend you study our website before submitting your work."

WILLIAMSON BOOKS

2630 Elm Hill Pike, Suite 100, Nashville TN 37214. **E-mail:** kwest@guideposts.org. **Website:** www.idealspublications.com. Publishes "very successful nonfiction series (Kids Can! series) on subjects such as history, science, arts/crafts, geography, diversity, multiculturalism. Little Hands series (ages 2-6), Kaleidoscope Kids series (age 7 and up) and Quick Starts for Kids! series (ages 8 and up). Our goal is to help every child fulfill his/her potential and experience personal growth."

NONFICTION Hands-on active learning books, animals, African-American, arts/crafts, Asian, biography, diversity, careers, geography, health, history, hobbies, how-to, math, multicultural, music/dance, nature/environment, Native American, science, writing and journaling. Does not want to see textbooks, picture books, fiction. "Looking for all things African-American, Asian-American, Hispanic, Latino, and Native American including crafts and traditions, as well as their history, biographies, and personal retrospectives of growing up in the U.S. for grades pre K-8th. We are looking for books in which learning and doing are inseparable." Recently published *Keeping Our Earth Green; Leap Into Space; China.*

HOW TO CONTACT Submit compete ms with SASE. Responds in 3 months. Publishes book 1 year after acceptance.

ILLUSTRATION Works with at least 2 illustrators and 2 designers/year. "We're interested in expanding our illustrator and design freelancers." Uses primarily 2-color and 4-color artwork. Responds only if interested. Samples returned with SASE; samples filed.

PHOTOGRAPHY Buys photos from freelancers; uses archival art and photos.

TERMS Pays authors advance against future royalties based on wholesale price or purchases outright. Pays illustrators by the project. Pays photographers per photo. Guidelines available for SASE.

TIPS "Please do not send any fiction or picture books of any kind—those should go to Ideals Children's Books. Look at our books to see what we do. We're interested in interactive learning books with a creative approach packed with interesting information, written for young readers ages 3-7 and 8-14. In nonfiction children's publishing, we are looking for authors with a depth of knowledge shared with children through a warm, embracing style. Our publishing philosophy is based on the idea that all children can succeed and have positive learning experiences. Children's lasting learning experiences involve their participation."

WINDRIVER PUBLISHING, INC.

72 N. WindRiver Rd., Silverton ID 83867. (208)752-1836. **Fax:** (208)752-1876. **E-mail:** info@windriverpublishing.com. **Website:** www.windriverpublishing.com. **Contact:** E. Keith Howick, Jr., president; Gail Howick, vice president/editor-in-chief. "Authors who wish to submit book proposals for review must do so according to our Submissions Guidelines, which can be found on our website, along with an on-line submission form, which is our preferred submission

method. *We do not accept submissions of any kind by e-mail.*" Publishes hardcover originals and reprints, trade paperback originals, and mass market originals. Publishes 8 titles/year. 95% of books from first-time authors. 90% from unagented writers.

⬭ WindRiver Publishing is not currently accepting submissions.

HOW TO CONTACT *Does not accept unsolicited mss.* 1,000 queries received/year. 300 mss received/year. Responds in 1-2 months to queries; 4-6 months to proposals/mss. Publishes book 1 year after acceptance.
TERMS Book catalog available online. Guidelines available online.
TIPS "We do not accept manuscripts containing graphic or gratuitous profanity, sex, or violence. See online instructions for details."

PAULA WISEMAN BOOKS

1230 Sixth Ave., New York NY 10020. (212)698-7000. **Fax:** (212)698-2796. **E-mail:** paula.wiseman@simonandschuster.com; Alexandra.Penfold@simonandschuster.com. **Website:** www.kids.simonandschuster.com. **Contact:** Paula Wiseman, vice president/publisher; Alexandra Penfold, editor. Publishes 20 titles/year. 10% of books from first-time authors.
FICTION Considers all categories. Average word length: picture books—500; others standard length. Recently published *Which Puppy?*, by Kate Feiffer, illustrated by Jules Feiffer.
NONFICTION Picture books: animal, biography, concept, history, nature/environment. Young readers: animal, biography, history, multicultural, nature/environment, sports. Average word length: picture books—500; others standard length.
HOW TO CONTACT *Does not accept unsolicited or unagented mss.*
ILLUSTRATION Works with 15 illustrators/year. *Does not accept unsolicited or unagented illustrations or submissions.*

WIZARDS OF THE COAST BOOKS FOR YOUNG READERS

P.O. Box 707, Renton WA 98057. (425)254-2287; (800)324-6496. **E-mail:** nina.hess@wizards.com. **Website:** www.wizards.com. **Contact:** Nina Hess. Wizards of the Coast publishes only science fiction and fantasy shared-world titles. Currently emphasizing solid fantasy writers. De-emphasizing gothic fiction. Dragonlance; Forgotten Realms; Magic: The Gathering; Eberron. Wizards of the Coast publishes

games as well, including Dungeons & Dragons® role-playing game. Publishes hardcover and trade paperback originals and trade paperback reprints. Publishes 10 titles/year. 5% of books from first-time authors.
FICTION Young readers, middle readers, young adults: fantasy only. Average word length: middle readers—30,000-40,000; young adults—60,000-75,000. Recently published *A Practical Guide to Dragon Riding*, by Lisa Trumbauer (ages 6 and up); *The Stowaway*, by R.A. Salvatore and Geno Salvatore (10 and up), *Red Dragon Codex*, by R. Henham (ages 8-12).
HOW TO CONTACT Query with samples. Publishes book 9-24 months after acceptance.
ILLUSTRATION Works with 4 illustrators/year. Query. Illustrations only: Query with samples, résumé.
TERMS Pays authors 4-6% based on retail price. Pays illustrators by project. Offers advances (average amount: $4,000). Catalog available on website. Ms guidelines available on website.
TIPS Editorial staff attended or plans to attend ALA conference.

WORDSONG

Boyds Mills Press, 815 Church St., Honesdale PA 18431. **Fax:** (570)253-0179. **E-mail:** submissions@boydsmillspress.com; eagarrow@boydsmillspress.com. **Website:** www.wordsongpoetry.com. "The only imprint in children's publishing in America dedicated to poetry, Wordsong captures the vibrant, unexpected, emotional connections between text and young readers. Our books range from the silly to the serious and are infused with the wordplay and imagery that allow readers to view the world in new and thoughtful ways."
POETRY Submit book-length collection of original poems. Do not query.
HOW TO CONTACT Responds to mss in 3 months.
ILLUSTRATION Works with 7 illustrators/year. Reviews ms/illustration packages from artists. Submit complete ms with 1 or 2 pieces of art. Illustrations only: Query with samples best suited to the art (postcard, 8½ × 11, etc.). Label package "Art Sample Submission." Responds only if interested. Samples returned with SASE.
PHOTOGRAPHY Assigns work.
TERMS Pays authors royalty or work purchased outright.
TIPS "Collections of original poetry, not anthologies, are our biggest need at this time. Keep in mind that

the strongest collections demonstrate a facility with multiple poetic forms and offer fresh images and insights. Check to see what's already on the market and on our website before submitting."

○ WORLD BOOK, INC.

233 N. Michigan Ave. Suite 2000, Chicago IL 60601. (312)729-5800. **Fax:** (312)729-5600. **Website:** www. worldbook.com. **Contact:** Paul A. Kobasa, editor-in-chief. "World Book, Inc. (publisher of The World Book Encyclopedia), publishes reference sources and nonfiction series for children and young adults in the areas of science, mathematics, English-language skills, basic academic and social skills, social studies, history, and health and fitness. We publish print and non-print material appropriate for children ages 3-14. WB does not publish fiction, poetry, or wordless picture books."

NONFICTION Young readers: animal, arts/crafts, careers, concept, geography, health, reference. Middle readers: animal, arts/crafts, careers, geography, health, history, hobbies, how-to, nature/environment, reference, science. Young adult: arts/crafts, careers, geography, health, history, hobbies, how-to, nature/environment, reference, science.

HOW TO CONTACT Submit outline/synopsis only; no mss. Responds to queries in 2 months. Publishes book 18 months after acceptance.

ILLUSTRATION Works with 10-30 illustrators/year. Illustrations only: Query with samples. Responds only if interested. Samples returned with SASE; samples filed "if extra copies and if interested."

PHOTOGRAPHY Buys stock and assigns work. Needs broad spectrum; editorial concept, specific natural, physical and social science spectrum. Model/property releases required; captions required. Submit cover letter, résumé, promo piece (color and b&w).

TERMS Payment negotiated on project-by-project basis.

ZUMAYA PUBLICATIONS, LLC

3209 S. Interstate 35, #1086, Austin TX 78741. **E-mail:** submissions@zumayapublications.com. **E-mail:** submissions@zumayapublications.com. **Website:** www. zumayapublications.com. **Contact:** Elizabeth Burton, executive editor. Publishes trade paperback and electronic originals and reprints. Publishes 20-25 titles/year. 75% of books from first-time authors. 98% from unagented writers.

FICTION "We are currently oversupplied with speculative fiction and are reviewing submissions in SF, fantasy and paranormal suspense by invitation only. We are much in need of GLBT and YA/middle grade, historical and western, New Age/inspirational (no overtly Christian materials, please), non-category romance, thrillers. As with nonfiction, we encourage people to review what we've already published so as to avoid sending us more of the same, at least, insofar as the plot is concerned. While we're always looking for good specific mysteries, we want original concepts rather than slightly altered versions of what we've already published." Length: juvenile—40,000 words minimum.

NONFICTION "The easiest way to figure out what I'm looking for is to look at what we've already done. Our main nonfiction interests are in collections of true ghost stories, ones that have been investigated or thoroughly documented, memoirs that address specific regions and eras and books on the craft of writing. That doesn't mean we won't consider something else."

HOW TO CONTACT Electronic query only. 1,000 queries received/year. 100 mss received/year. Responds in 6 months to queries and proposals; 9 months to mss. Publishes book 2 years after acceptance.

TERMS Guidelines available online.

TIPS "We're catering to readers who may have loved last year's best seller but not enough to want to read 10 more just like it. Have something different. If it does not fit standard pigeonholes, that's a plus. On the other hand, it has to have an audience. And if you're not prepared to work with us on promotion and marketing, it would be better to look elsewhere."

CANADIAN & INTERNATIONAL BOOK PUBLISHERS

//

While the United States is considered the largest market in children's publishing, the children's publishing world is by no means strictly dominated by the U.S. After all, the most prestigious children's book extravaganza in the world occurs each year in Bologna, Italy, at the Bologna Children's Book Fair and some of the world's most beloved characters were born in the United Kingdom (e.g., Winnie-the-Pooh and Mr. Potter).

In this section you'll find book publishers from English-speaking countries around the world, including Canada, Australia, New Zealand and the United Kingdom. The listings in this section look just like the U.S. Book Publishers section; and the publishers listed are dedicated to the same goal—publishing great books for children.

Like always, be sure to study each listing and research each publisher carefully before submitting material. Determine whether a publisher is open to U.S. or international submissions, as many publishers accept submissions only from residents of their own country. Some publishers accept illustration samples from foreign artists, but do not accept manuscripts from foreign writers. Illustrators do have a slight edge in this category as many illustrators generate commissions from all around the globe. Visit publishers' websites to be certain they publish the sort of work you do. Visit online bookstores to see if publishers' books are available there. Write or e-mail to request catalogs and submission guidelines.

When mailing requests or submissions out of the United States, remember that U.S. postal stamps are useless on your SASE. Always include International Reply Coupons (IRCs) with your SAE. Each IRC is good for postage for one letter. So if you want the publisher to return your manuscript or send a catalog, be sure to enclose enough IRCs to pay the postage. For more help visit the United States Postal Service website at usps.com/global. Visit timeanddate.com/worldclock and American Computer Resources, Inc.'s International Calling

Code Directory at the-acr.com/codes/cntrycd.htm before calling or faxing internationally to make sure you're calling at a reasonable time and using the correct numbers.

As in the rest of *Children's Writer's & Illustrator's Market,* the maple leaf ☺ symbol identifies Canadian markets. Look for the International ☻ symbol throughout *Children's Writer's & Illustrator's Market* as well. Several of the Society of Children's Book Writers and Illustrator's (SCBWI) international conferences are listed in the Conferences & Workshops section along with other events in locations around the globe. Look for more information about SCBWI's international chapters on the organization's website, scbwi.org. You'll also find international listings in Magazines and Young Writer's & Illustrator's Markets. See Useful Online Resources for sites that offer additional international information.

☼ ANNICK PRESS, LTD.

15 Patricia Ave., Toronto, Ontario M2M 1H9, Canada. (416)221-4802. **Fax:** (416)221-8400. **E-mail:** annickpress@annickpress.com. **Website:** www.annickpress.com. **Contact:** Rick Wilks, director; Colleen MacMillan, associate publisher; Sheryl Shapiro, creative director. "Annick Press maintains a commitment to high quality books that entertain and challenge. Our publications share fantasy and stimulate imagination, while encouraging children to trust their judgment and abilities." Publishes 5 picture books/year; 6 young readers/year; 8 middle readers/year; 9 young adult titles/year. Publishes picture books, juvenile and YA fiction and nonfiction; specializes in trade books. Publishes 25 titles/year. 20% of books from first-time authors. 80-85% from unagented writers.

○ *Does not accept unsolicited mss.*

FICTION Publisher of children's books. Publishes hardcover and trade paperback originals. Average print order: 9,000. First novel print order: 7,000. Plans 18 first novels this year. Averages 25 total titles/year. Distributes titles through Firefly Books Ltd. Juvenile, young adult. Recently published *The Apprentice's Masterpiece: A Story of Medieval Spain*, by Melanie Little, ages 12 and up; Chicken, Pig, Cow series, written and illustrated by Ruth Ohi, ages 2-5; Single Voices series, Melanie Little, Editor, ages 14 and up; *Crusades*, by Laura Scandiffio, illustrated by John Mantha, ages 9-11. Not accepting picture books at this time.

NONFICTION Recently published *Pharaohs and Foot Soldiers: One Hundred Ancient Egyptian Jobs you Might Have Desired or Dreaded*, by Kristin Butcher, illustrations by Martha Newbigging, ages 9-12; *The Bite of the Mango*, by Mariatu Kamara with Susan McClelland, ages 14 and up; *Adventures on the Ancient Silk Road*, by Priscilla Galloway with Dawn Hunter, ages 10 and up; *The Chinese Thought of it: Amazing Inventions and Innovations,* by Ting-xing Ye, ages 9-11.

HOW TO CONTACT 5,000 queries received/year. 3,000 mss received/year. Publishes a book 2 years after acceptance.

TERMS Pays authors royalty of 5-12% based on retail price. Offers advances (average amount: $3,000). Pays illustrators royalty of 5% minimum. Book catalog and guidelines available online

☼ BOREALIS PRESS, LTD.

8 Mohawk Crescent, Napean, Ontario K2H 7G6, Canada. (613)829-0150. **Fax:** (613)829-7783. **E-mail:** drt@borealispress.com. **Website:** www.borealispress.com. Our mission is to publish work that will be of lasting interest in the Canadian book market. Currently emphasizing Canadian fiction, nonfiction, drama, poetry. De-emphasizing children's books. Publishes hardcover and paperback originals and reprints. Publishes 20 titles/year. 80% of books from first-time authors. 95% from unagented writers.

FICTION Only material Canadian in content and dealing with significant aspects of the human situation.

NONFICTION Only material Canadian in content. Looks for style in tone and language, reader interest, and maturity of outlook.

HOW TO CONTACT Query with SASE. Submit clips, 1-2 sample chapters. *No unsolicited mss.* Responds in 2 months to queries; 4 months to mss. Publishes book 18 months after acceptance.

TERMS Pays 10% royalty on net receipts; plus 3 free author's copies. Book catalog available online. Guidelines available online.

☼ THE BRUCEDALE PRESS

P.O. Box 2259, Port Elgin, Ontario N0H 2C0, Canada. (519)832-6025. **E-mail:** brucedale@bmts.com. **Website:** www.bmts.com/~brucedale. The Brucedale Press publishes books and other materials of regional interest and merit, as well as literary, historical, and/or pictorial works. Publishes hardcover and trade paperback originals. Publishes 3 titles/year. 75% of books from first-time authors. 100% from unagented writers.

○ *Accepts works by Canadian authors only. Submissions accepted in September and March only.*

HOW TO CONTACT 50 queries received/year. 30 mss received/year. Publishes book 1 year after acceptance.

TERMS Pays royalty. Book catalog for #10 SASE (Canadian postage or IRC) or online. Guidelines available online.

TIPS Our focus is very regional. In reading submissions, I look for quality writing with a strong connection to the Queen's Bush area of Ontario. All authors should visit our website, get a catalog, and read our books before submitting.

🐝 BUSTER BOOKS

16 Lion Yard, Tremadoc Rd., London SW4 7NQ, United Kingdom. 020 7720 8643. **Fax:** 022 7720 8953. **E-mail:** enquiries@michaelomarabooks.com. **Website:** www.mombooks.com. "We are dedicated to providing irresistible and fun books for children of all ages. We typically publish black-and-white nonfiction for children aged 8-12 novelty titles-including doodle books."

HOW TO CONTACT Prefers synopsis and sample text over complete ms.

TIPS "We do not accept fiction submissions. Please do not send original artwork as we cannot guarantee its safety." Visit website before submitting.

🐝 CHILD'S PLAY (INTERNATIONAL) LTD.

Children's Play International, Ashworth Rd. Bridgemead, Swindon, Wiltshire SN5 7YD, United Kingdom. **E-mail:** allday@childs-play.com; neil@childs-play.com; office@childs-play.com. **Website:** www.childs-play.com. **Contact:** Sue Baker, Neil Burden, manuscript acquisitions. Specializes in nonfiction, fiction, educational material, multicultural material. Produces 30 picture books/year; 10 young readers/year; 2 middle readers/year. "A child's early years are more important than any other. This is when children learn most about the world around them and the language they need to survive and grow. Child's Play aims to create exactly the right material for this all-important time." Publishes 45 titles/year. 20% of books from first-time authors.

FICTION Picture books: adventure, animal, concept, contemporary, folktales, multicultural, nature/environment. Young readers: adventure, animal, anthology, concept, contemporary, folktales, humor, multicultural, nature/environment, poetry. Average word length: picture books—1,500; young readers—2,000. Recently published *Snug*, by Carol Thompson (ages 0-2, picture book); *The Lost Stars*, by Hannah Cumming (ages 4-8 yrs, picture book); *Uuggh!*, by Claudia Boldt (ages 4-8 yrs, picture book); *First Time Doctor/Dentist/Hospital/Vet*, by Jess Stockham (ages 2-5 yrs, picture book); New Baby Series, by Rachel Fuller (ages 1-3, board book).

NONFICTION Picture books: activity books, animal, concept, multicultural, music/dance, nature/environment, science. Young readers: activity books, animal, concept, multicultural, music/dance, nature/environment, science. Average word length: picture books—2,000; young readers—3,000. Recently published *Roly Poly Discovery,* by Kees Moerbeek (ages 3+ years, novelty).

HOW TO CONTACT Responds to queries in 10 weeks; mss in 15 weeks. Publishes book 2 years after acceptance.

ILLUSTRATION Accepts material from international illustrators. Works with 10 illustrators/year. Uses color artwork only. Reviews ms/illustration packages. For ms/illustration packages: Query or submit ms/illustration packages to Sue Baker, editor. Reviews work for future assignments. If interested in illustrating future titles, query with samples, CD, website address. Submit samples to Annie Kubler, art director. Responds in 10 weeks. Samples not returned. Samples filed.

TIPS "Look at our website to see the kind of work we do before sending. Do not send cartoons. We do not publish novels. We do publish lots of books with pictures of babies/toddlers."

🐝 CHRISTIAN FOCUS PUBLICATIONS

Geanies House, Tain Ross-shire IV20 1TW, United Kingdom. 44 (0) 1862 871 011. **Fax:** 44 (0) 1862 871 699. **E-mail:** info@christianfocus.com. **Website:** www.christianfocus.com. **Contact:** Catherine Mackenzie, publisher. Specializes in Christian material, nonfiction, fiction, educational material. Publishes 22-32 titles/year. 2% of books from first-time authors.

FICTION Picture books, young readers, adventure, history, religion. Middle readers: adventure, problem novels, religion. Young adult/teens: adventure, history, problem novels, religion. Average word length: young readers—5,000; middle readers—max 10,000; young adult/teen—max 20,000. Recently published *Back Leg of a Goat*, by Penny Reeve, illustrated by Fred Apps (middle reader Christian/world issues); *Trees in the Pavement,* by Jennifer Grosser (teen fiction/Christian/Islamic and multicultural issues); *The Duke's Daughter*, by Lachlan Mackenzie; illustrated by Jeff Anderson (young reader folk tale/Christian).

NONFICTION All levels: activity books, biography, history, religion, science. Average word length: picture books—5,000; young readers—5,000; middle readers—5,000-10,000; young adult/teens—10,000-20,000. Recently published *Moses the Child-Kept by God*, by Carine Mackenzie, illustrated by Graham Kennedy (young reader, Bible story); *Hearts and Hands-History Lives vol. 4*, by Mindy Withrow, cover illustration by

Jonathan Williams (teen, church history); *Little Hands Life of Jesus,* by Carine Mackenzie, illustrated by Rafaella Cosco (picture book, Bible stories about Jesus).
HOW TO CONTACT Query or submit outline/synopsis and 3 sample chapters. Will consider electronic submissions and previously published work. Query or submit outline/synopsis and 3 sample chapters. Will consider electronic submissions and previously published work. Responds to queries in 2 weeks; mss in 3 months. Publishes book 1 year after acceptance.
ILLUSTRATION Works on 15-20 potential projects. "Some artists are chosen to do more than one. Some projects just require a cover illustration, some require full color spreads, others black and white line art." **Contact:** Catherine Mackenzie, children's editor. Responds in 2 weeks only if interested. Samples are not returned.
PHOTOGRAPHY "We only purchase royalty free photos from particular photographic associations. However portfolios can be presented to our designer." **Contact:** Daniel van Straaten. Photographers should send cover letter, résumé, published samples, client list, portfolio.
TIPS "Be aware of the international market as regards to writing style/topics as well as illustration styles. Our company sells rights to European as well as Asian countries. Fiction sales are not as good as they were. Christian fiction for youngsters is not a product that is performing well in comparison to nonfiction such as Christian biography/Bible stories/church history, etc."

COTEAU BOOKS

(306)777-0170. **Fax:** (306)522-5152. **E-mail:** coteau@ coteaubooks.com. **Website:** www.coteaubooks.com. **Contact:** Geoffrey Ursell, publisher. "Our mission is to publish the finest in Canadian fiction, nonfiction, poetry, drama, and children's literature, with an emphasis on Saskatchewan and prairie writers. De-emphasizing science fiction, picture books." Publishes trade paperback originals and reprints Publishes 16 titles/year. 25% of books from first-time authors. 90% from unagented writers.
FICTION *Canadian authors only.* No science fiction. No children's picture books.
NONFICTION *Canadian authors only.*
HOW TO CONTACT Submit bio, complete ms, SASE. Submit bio, 3-4 sample chapters, SASE. 200 queries received/year. 200 mss received/year. Responds in 3 months to queries and manuscripts

TERMS Pays 10% royalty on retail price. 12 months Book catalog available free Guidelines available online
TIPS "Look at past publications to get an idea of our editorial program. We do not publish romance, horror, or picture books but are interested in juvenile and teen fiction from Canadian authors. Submissions, even queries, must be made in hard copy only. We do not accept simultaneous/multiple submissions. Check our website for new submission timing guidelines."

COTEAU BOOKS LTD.

2517 Victoria Ave., Regina, Saskatchewan S4P 0T2, Canada. (306)777-0170. **E-mail:** coteau@coteaubooks.com. **Website:** www.coteaubooks.com. "Coteau Books publishes the finest Canadian fiction, poetry, drama and children's literature, with an emphasis on western writers." Publishes 14-16 titles/year. 25% of books from first-time authors.

Coteau Books publishes Canadian writers and illustrators only; mss from the U.S. are returned unopened.

FICTION Teen, young readers, middle readers, young adults: adventure, contemporary, fantasy, history, humor, multicultural, nature/environment, science fiction, suspense/mystery. "No didactic, message pieces, nothing religious, no horror. No picture books." Recently published *New: Run Like Jäger,* by Karen Bass (ages 15 and up); *Longhorns & Outlaws,* by Linda Aksomitis (ages 9 and up); *Graveyard of the Sea,* by Penny Draper (ages 9 and up).
NONFICTION Young readers, middle readers, young adult/teen: biography, history, multicultural, nature/environment, social issues.
HOW TO CONTACT Fiction accepted from Jan. 1 to April 30; Children's/Teen novels from May 1 to August 31. Submit complete ms or 3-4 sample chapters, author bio. Nonfiction accepted year round. Submit complete ms or 3-4 sample chapters, author bio. Responds to mss in 4 months. Publishes book 1-2 years after acceptance.
ILLUSTRATION Works with 1-4 illustrators/year. Illustrations only: Submit nonreturnable samples. Responds only if interested. Samples returned with SASE; samples filed.
PHOTOGRAPHY "Very occasionally buys photos from freelancers." Buys stock and assigns work.
TERMS Pays authors royalty based on retail price. Book catalog free upon request with 9×12 SASE.

DUNDURN PRESS, LTD.

3 Church St., Suite 500, Toronto, Ontario M5E 1M2, Canada. (416)214-5544. **E-mail:** info@dundurn.com. **E-mail:** submissions@dundurn.com. **Website:** www.dundurn.com. **Contact:** Kirk Howard, president and publisher. Dundurn publishes books by Canadian authors. Publishes hardcover and trade paperback originals and reprints. 25% of books from first-time authors. 50% from unagented writers.

> "We do not publish children's books for readers under 7 years of age. This includes picture books."

FICTION No romance, science fiction, or experimental.
HOW TO CONTACT Submit sample chapters, synopsis, author fee, SASE/IRCs, or submit complete ms. Accepts submissions via postal mail only. Submit cover letter, synopsis, cv, sample chapters, SASE/IRC, or submit complete ms. Accepts submissions via postal mail only. 600 queries received/year. Responds in 3 months to queries. Publishes book 1 year after acceptance.
TERMS Guidelines available online.

DAVID FICKLING BOOKS

31 Beamont St., Oxford OX1 2NP, United Kingdom. (018)65-339000. **Fax:** (018)65-339009. **E-mail:** DFickling@randomhouse.co.uk; tburgess@randomhouse.co.uk. **Website:** www.avidficklingbooks.co.uk. Publishes 12 titles/year.
FICTION Considers all categories. Recently published *Once Upon a Time in the North*, by Phillip Pullman; *The Curious Incident of the Dog in the Night-time*, by Mark Haddon; *The Boy in the Striped Pyjamas*, by John Boyne.
HOW TO CONTACT Submit 3 sample chapters. Responds to mss in 3 months.
ILLUSTRATION Reviews ms/illustration packages from artists. Illustrations only: query with samples.
PHOTOGRAPHY Submit cover letter, résumé, promo pieces.

FITZHENRY & WHITESIDE LTD.

195 Allstate Pkwy., Markham, Ontario L3R 4T8, Canada. (905)477-9700. **Fax:** (905)477-9179. **E-mail:** fitzkids@fitzhenry.ca; godwit@fitzhenry.ca; charkin@fitzhenry.ca. **Website:** www.fitzhenry.ca/. **Contact:** Sharon Fitzhenry, president; Cathy Sandusky, children's publisher; Christie Harkin, submissions editor. Emphasis on Canadian authors and illustrators, subject or perspective. Publishes 15 titles/year. 10% of books from first-time authors.
HOW TO CONTACT Publishes book 1-2 years after acceptance.
ILLUSTRATION Works with approximately 10 illustrators/year. Reviews ms/illustration packages from artists. Submit outline and sample illustration (copy). Illustrations only: Query with samples and promo sheet. Samples not returned unless requested.
PHOTOGRAPHY Buys photos from freelancers. Buys stock and assigns work. Captions required. Uses b&w 8×10 prints; 35mm and 4×5 transparencies, 300+ dpi digital images. Submit stock photo list and promo piece.
TERMS Pays authors 8-10% royalty with escalations. Offers "respectable" advances for picture books, split 50/50 between author and illustrator. Pays illustrators by project and royalty. Pays photographers per photo.
TIPS "We respond to quality."

FRANCES LINCOLN CHILDREN'S BOOKS

Frances Lincoln, 4 Torriano Mew, Torriano Ave., London NW5 2RZ, United Kingdom. 00442072844009. **E-mail:** flcb@franceslincoln.com. **Website:** www.franceslincoln.com. "Our company was founded by Frances Lincoln in 1977. We published our first books two years later, and we have been creating illustrated books of the highest quality ever since, with special emphasis on gardening, walking and the outdoors, art, architecture, design and landscape. In 1983, we started to publish illustrated books for children. Since then we have won many awards and prizes with both fiction and nonfiction children's books." Publishes 100 titles/year. 6% of books from first-time authors.
FICTION Picture books, young readers, middle readers, young adults: adventure, animal, anthology, fantasy, folktales, health, history, humor, multicultural, nature/environment, special needs, sports. Average word length: picture books—1,000; young readers—9,788; middle readers— 20,653; young adults— 35,407. Recently published *The Sniper*, by James Riordan (young adult/teen novel); *Amazons! Women Warriors of the World*, by Sally Pomme Clayton, illustrated by Sophie Herxheimer (picture book); *Young Inferno*, by

John Agard, illustrated by Satoshi Kitamura (graphic novel/picture book).

NONFICTION Picture books, young readers, middle readers, young adult: activity books, animal, biography, careers, cooking, graphic novels, history, multicultural, nature/environment, religion, social issues, special needs. Average word length: picture books—1,000; middle readers—29,768. Recently published *Tail-End Charlie*, by Mick Manning and Brita Granstroöm (picture book); *Our World of Water*, by Beatrice Hollyer, with photographers by Oxfam (picture book); *Look! Drawing the Line in Art*, by Gillian Wolfe (picture book).

HOW TO CONTACT Query by e-mail. Query by e-mail. Responds to mss in minimum of 6 weeks. Publishes book 18 months after acceptance.

ILLUSTRATION Works with approx 56 illustrators/year. Uses both color and b&w. Reviews ms/illustration packages from artist. Sample illustrations. Illustrations only: Query with samples. Responds only if interested. Samples are returned with SASE. Samples are kept on file only if interested.

PHOTOGRAPHY Buys stock images and assign work. Uses children, multicultural photos. Submit cover letter, published samples, or portfolio.

GROUNDWOOD BOOKS

110 Spadina Ave. Suite 801, Toronto, Ontario M5V 2K4, Canada. (416)363-4343. **Fax:** (416)363-1071. **E-mail:** nfroman@groundwoodbooks.com. **Website:** www.groundwoodbooks.com. Groundwood Books. Publishes 10 picture books/year; 3 young readers/year; 5 middle readers/year; 5 young adult titles/year, approximately 2 nonfiction titles/year. 10% of books from first-time authors.

FICTION Recently published *Harvey*, by Herva Bouchard and Janice Nadeau; *A Queen of Hearts*, by Martha Brooks (Y/A); *Between Sisters*, by Adwoa Badoe (Y/A); *No Safe Place*, by Deborah Ellis (Y/A).

NONFICTION *Technology (A Groundwork Guide)*, by Wayen Grady picture books recently published: *No*, by Claudia Rueda; *Hello Baby* board books, photographs by Jorge Uzon; *Roslyn Rutabaga and the Biggest Hole on Earth!*, by Marie-Louise Gay; *Doggy Slippers*, by Jorge Luján, illustrated by Isol; *Arroz con leche / Rice Pudding* (un poema para cocinar / a cooking poem), by Jorge Argueta, illustrated by Fernando Vilela; *Canadian Railroad Trilogy*, by Gordon Lightfoot, illustrated by Ian Wallace; *Book of Big Brothers*, by Cary Fagan, illustrated by Luc

Melanson; *Viola Desmond Won't Be Budged*, by Jody Nyasha Warner, illustrated by Richard Rudnicki.

HOW TO CONTACT Submit synopsis and sample chapters. Responds to mss in 6-8 months.

ILLUSTRATION Works with 20 illustrators/year. Reviews ms/illustration packages from artists. Illustrations only: Send résumé, promo sheet, slides, color or b&w copies, and tearsheets. Responds only if interested. Samples not returned.

TERMS Offers advances.

TIPS "Try to familiarize yourself with our list before submitting to judge whether or not your work is appropriate for Groundwood. Visit our website for guidelines (http://www.groundwoodbooks.com/gw_guidelines.cgm)."

HINKLER

45-55 Fairchild St., Heatherton, Victoria 3202, Australia. (61)(3)9552-1333. **Fax:** (61)(3)9558-2566. **E-mail:** enquiries@hinkler.com.au; Stevie.Brockley@hinkler.com.au. **Website:** www.hinklerbooks.com. **Contact:** Stephen Ungar, CEO/publisher. "Packaged entertainment affordable to every family."

KIDS CAN PRESS

25 Dockside Dr., Toronto, Ontario M5A 0B5, Canada. (416)479-7000. **Fax:** (416)960-5437. **E-mail:** info@kidscan.com; kkalmar@kidscan.com. **Website:** www.kidscanpress.com. U.S. address: 2250 Military Rd., Tonawanda, NY 14150.

Kids Can Press is currently accepting unsolicited mss from Canadian adult authors only.

FICTION Picture books, young readers: concepts. We do not accept young adult fiction or fantasy novels for any age. Adventure, animal, contemporary, folktales, history, humor, multicultural, nature/environment, special needs, sports, suspense/mystery. Average word length: picture books 1,000-2,000; young readers 750-1,500; middle readers 10,000-15,000; young adults over 15,000. Recently published *Rosie & Buttercup* by Chieri Ugaki, illustrated by Shephane Jorisch (picture book); *The Landing* by John Ibbitson (novel); *Scaredy Squirrel* by Melanie Watt, illustrated by Melanie Watt (picture book).

NONFICTION Picture books: activity books, animal, arts/crafts, biography, careers, concept, health, history, hobbies, how-to, multicultural, nature/environment, science, social issues, special needs, sports. Young readers: activity books, animal, arts/crafts, biography, careers, concept, history, hobbies, how-to, multicultural. Middle readers: cooking, music/dance. Average word length: picture books 500-1,250; young readers 750-2,000; middle readers 5,000-15,000. Recently published *The Kids' Book of Canadian Geography*, by Jane Drake and Ann Love, illustrated by Heather Collins (informational activity); *Science, Nature, Environment*; *Moving Day*, by Pamela Hickman, illustrated by Geraldo Valerio (animal/nature); *Everywear*, by Ellen Warwick, illustrated by Bernice Lum (craft book).

HOW TO CONTACT Submit outline/synopsis and 2-3 sample chapters. For picture books submit complete ms. Submit outline/synopsis and 2-3 sample chapters. For picture books submit complete ms. Responds in 6 months only if interesed. Publishes book 18-24 months after acceptance.

ILLUSTRATION Works with 40 illustrators/year. Reviews ms/illustration packages from artists. Send color copies of illustration portfolio, cover letter outlining other experience. Contact: Art Director. Illustrations only: Send tearsheets, color photocopies. Responds only if interested.

🐨 KOALA BOOKS

P.O. Box 626, Mascot, New South Wales 1460, Australia. (61)(02)9667-2997. **Fax:** (61)(02)9667-2881. **Website:** www.koalabooks.com.au. "Koala Books is an independent wholly Australian-owned children's book publishing house. Our strength is providing quality books for children at competitive prices."

HOW TO CONTACT Submit complete ms, blurb, brief author bio, list of published works, SASE. Submit complete ms, blurb, brief author bio, list of published works, SASE. Responds to mss in 3 months.

ILLUSTRATION Accepts material from residents of Australia only. Illustrations only: Send cover letter, brief bio, list of published works and samples (color photographs or photocopies) in A4 folder suitable for filing." Contact: children's designer. Responds only if interested. Samples not returned; samples filed.

TERMS Pays authors royalty of 10% based on retail price or work purchased outright occasionally.

TIPS "Take a look at our website to get an idea of the kinds of books we publish. A few hours research in a quality children's bookshop would be helpful when choosing a publisher."

🐯 LITTLE TIGER PRESS

1 The Coda Centre, 189 Munster Rd., London SW6 6AW, United Kingdom. 44)20-7385 6333. **E-mail:** info@littletiger.co.uk; jcollins@littletiger.co.uk. **Website:** www.littletigerpress.com.

FICTION Picture books: animal, concept, contemporary, humor. Average word length: picture books—750 words or less. Recently published *Gruff the Grump*, by Steve Smallman and Cee Biscoe (ages 3-7, picture book); *One Special Day*, by M. Christina Butler and Tina Macnaughton (ages 3-7, touch-and-feel, picture book).

ILLUSTRATION Digital submissions preferred please send in digital samples as pdf or jpeg attachments to artsubmissions@littletiger.co.uk. Files should be flattened and no bigger than 1mb per attachment. Include name and contact details on any attachments. For printed submissions please send in printed color samples as A4 printouts. Do not send in original artwork as we cannot be held responsible for unsolicited original artwork being lost or damaged in the post. We aim to acknowledge unsolicited material and to return material if so requested within three months. Please include S.A.E. if return of material is requested.

TIPS "Every reasonable care is taken of the mss and samples we receive, but we cannot accept responsibility for any loss or damage. Try to read or look at as many books on the Little Tiger Press list before sending in your material. Refer to our website www.littletigerpress.com for further details."

☯ MANOR HOUSE PUBLISHING, INC.

452 Cottingham Crescent, Ancaster, Ontario L9G 3V6, Canada. **E-mail:** mbdavie@manor-house.biz. **Website:** www.manor-house.biz. **Contact:** Mike Davie, president (novels, poetry, and nonfiction). Publishes hardcover, trade paperback, and mass market paperback originals reprints. Publishes 5-6 titles/year. 90% of books from first-time authors. 90% from un-agented writers.

FICTION Stories should have Canadian settings and characters should be Canadian, but content should have universal appeal to wide audience.

NONFICTION "We are a Canadian publisher, so mss should be Canadian in content and aimed as much as possible at a wide, general audience. At this point in time, we are only publishing books by Canadian citizens residing in Canada."

HOW TO CONTACT Query via e-mail. Submit proposal package, clips, bio, 3 sample chapters. Submit complete ms. Query via e-mail. Submit proposal package, outline, bio, 3 sample chapters. Submit complete ms. 30 queries received/year; 20 mss received/year. Queries and mss to be sent by e-mail only. "We will respond in 30 days if interested-if not, there is no response. Do not follow up unless asked to do so." Publishes book 1 year after acceptance.

TERMS Pays 10% royalty on retail price. Book catalog available online. Guidelines available via e-mail.

TIPS "Our audience includes everyone-the general public/mass audience. Self-edit your work first, make sure it is well written with strong Canadian content."

MANTRA LINGUA

Global House, 303 Ballards Ln., London N12 8NP, United Kingdom. (44)(208)445-5123. **E-mail:** jean@mantralingua.com. **Website:** www.mantralingua.com.

> Mantra Lingua publishes dual-language books in English and more that 42 languages. They also publish talking books and resources with their Talking Pen technology, which brings sound and interactivity to their products. They will consider good contemporary stories, myths and folklore for picture books only.

FICTION Picture books, young readers, middle readers: folktales, multicultural stories, myths. Average word length: picture books—1,000-1,500; young readers—1,000-1,500. Recently published *Keeping Up With Cheetah*, by Lindsay Camp, illustrated by Jill Newton (ages 3-7); *Lion Fables*, by Heriette Barkow, illustrated by Jago Ormerod (ages 6-10).

HOW TO CONTACT Submit outline/synopsis (250 words) via postal mail. Incluse SASE for returns.

ILLUSTRATION Uses 2D animations for CD-ROMs. Query with samples. Responds only if interested. Samples not returned; samples filed.

MOOSE ENTERPRISE BOOK & THEATRE PLAY PUBLISHING

684 Walls Rd., Sault Ste. Marie, Ontario P6A 5K6, Canada. (705) 779-3331. **Fax:** (705) 779-3331. **E-mail:** mooseenterprises@on.aibn.com. **Website:** www.moosehidebooks.com. **Contact:** Edmond Alcid. Editorial philosophy: "To assist the new writers of moral standards."

> This publisher does not offer payment for stories published in its anthologies and/or book collections. Be sure to send a SASE for guidelines.

FICTION Middle readers, young adults: adventure, fantasy, humor, suspense/mystery, story poetry. Recently published *Realm of the Golden Feather*, by C.R. Ginter (ages 12 and up, fantasy); *Tell Me a Story*, short story collection by various authors (ages 9-11, humor/adventure); *Spirits of Lost Lake*, by James Walters (ages 12 and up, adventure); *Rusty Butt-Treasure of the Ocean Mist*, by R.E. Forester.

NONFICTION Middle readers, young adults: biography, history, multicultural.

HOW TO CONTACT Query. Query. Responds to queries in 1 month; mss in 3 months. Publishes book 1 year after acceptance.

ILLUSTRATION Uses primarily b&w artwork for interiors, cover artwork in color. Illustrations only: Query with samples. Responds in 1 month, if interested. Samples returned with SASE; samples filed.

TERMS Pays royalties. Ms guidelines available for SASE.

TIPS "Do not copy trends; be yourself—give me something new, something different."

ORCA BOOK PUBLISHERS

P.O. Box 5626, Stn. B, Victoria, British Columbia V8R 6S4, Canada. **Fax:** (877)408-1551. **E-mail:** orca@orcabook.com. **Website:** www.orcabook.com. **Contact:** Christi Howes, editor (picture books); Sarah Harvey, editor (young readers); Andrew Wooldridge, editor (juvenile and teen fiction); Bob Tyrrell, publisher (YA, teen). Publishes hardcover and trade paperback originals, and mass market paperback originals and reprints. Publishes 30 titles/year. 20% of books from first-time authors. 75% from unagented writers.

> Only publishes Canadian authors.

FICTION Picture books: animals, contemporary, history, nature/environment. Middle readers: contemporary, history, fantasy, nature/environment, problem novels, graphic novels. Young adults: adventure, contemporary, hi-lo (Orca Soundings), history, multicultural, nature/environment, problem novels, suspense/mystery, graphic novels. Average word length: picture books—500-1,500; middle readers—20,000-35,000; young adult—25,000-45,000; Orca Soundings—13,000-15,000; Orca Currents—13,000-15,000. Published *Tall in the Saddle*, by Anne Carter, illustrated by David McPhail (ages 4-8, picture book); *Me* *and Mr. Mah*, by Andrea Spalding, illustrated by Janet Wilson (ages 5 and up, picture book); *Alone at Ninety Foot*, by Katherine Holubitsky (young adult). No romance, science fiction.

NONFICTION Only publishes Canadian authors.

HOW TO CONTACT Query with SASE. Submit proposal package, outline, clips, 2-5 sample chapters, SASE. Query with SASE. 2,500 queries received/year. 1,000 mss received/year. Responds in 1 month to queries; 2 months to proposals and mss. Publishes book 12-18 months after acceptance.

ILLUSTRATION Works with 8-10 illustrators/year. Reviews ms/illustration packages from artists. Submit ms with 3-4 pieces of final art. "Reproductions only, no original art please." Illustrations only: Query with samples; provide reésumeé, slides. Responds in 2 months. Samples returned with SASE; samples filed.

TERMS Pays 10% royalty. Book catalog for 8½x11 SASE. Guidelines available online.

TIPS "Our audience is students in grades K-12. Know our books, and know the market."

PEMMICAN PUBLICATIONS, INC.

150 Henry Ave., Winnipeg, Manitoba R3B 0J7, Canada. (204)589-6346. **Fax:** (204)589-2063. **E-mail:** pemmican@pemmican.mb.ca. **Website:** www.pemmican-publications.ca. **Contact:** Randal McIlroy, managing editor (Metis culture & heritage). "Pemmican Publications is a Metis publishing house, with a mandate to publish books by Metis authors and illustrators and with an emphasis on culturally relevant stories. We encourage writers to learn a little about Pemmican before sending samples. Pemmican publishes titles in the following genres: Adult Fiction, which includes novels, story collections and anthologies; nonfiction, with an emphasis on social history and biography reflecting Metis experience; children's and young adult titles; aboriginal languages, including Michif and Cree." Publishes trade paperback originals and reprints. Publishes 5-6 titles/year. 50% of books from first-time authors. 100% from unagented writers.

FICTION All mss must be Metis culture and heritage related.

NONFICTION All mss must be Metis culture and heritage related.

HOW TO CONTACT Submit proposal package including outline and 3 sample chapters. Submit proposal package including outline and 3 sample chapters. 120 queries received/year. 120 mss received/year.

Responds to queries, proposals, and mss in 3 months. Publishes book 1-2 years after acceptance.

TERMS Pays 10% royalty on retail price. Book catalog available free with SASE. Guidelines available online.

TIPS "Our mandate is to promote Metis authors, illustrators and stories. No agent is necessary."

PICCADILLY PRESS

5 Castle Rd., London NW1 8PR, United Kingdom. (44)(207)267-4492. **Fax:** (44)(207)267-4493. **E-mail:** books@piccadillypress.co.uk. **Website:** www.piccadillypress.co.uk. "Piccadilly Press is the perfect choice for variety of reading for everyone aged 2-16! We're an independent publisher, celebrating 26 years of specialising in teen fiction and nonfiction, childrens fiction, picture books and parenting books by highly acclaimed authors and illustrators and fresh new talents too.We hope you enjoy reading the books as much as we enjoy publishing them."

FICTION Picture books: animal, contemporary, fantasy, nature/environment. Young adults: contemporary, humor, problem novels. Average word length: picture books—500-1,000; young adults—25,000-35,000. Recently published *Fifty Fifty*, by S.L. Powell (young adult); *Camden Town Tales: The Celeb Next Door*, by Hilary Freeman (young adult); *Letters From an Alien Schoolboy*, by Ros Asquit (Children Age 6+); *Grub in Love*, by Abi Burlingham and Sarah Warburton (picture book).

NONFICTION Young adults: self help (humorous). Average word length: young adults—25,000-35,000. *Everything You Wanted to Ask About..Periods*, by Tricia Kreitman, Dr. Fiona Findlay & Dr. Rosemary Jones.

HOW TO CONTACT Submit complete ms for picture books or submit outline/synopsis and 2 sample chapters for YA. Enclose a brief cover letter and SASE for reply. Submit outline/synopsis and 2 sample chapters. Responds to mss in 6 weeks.

ILLUSTRATION Illustrations only: Query with samples (do not send originals).

TIPS "Take a look in bookshops to see if there are many other books of a similar nature to yours—this is what your book will be competing against, so make sure there is something truly unique about your story. Looking at what else is available will give you ideas as to what topics are popular, but reading a little of them will also give you a sense of the right styles, language and length appropriate for the age-group."

🌑 MATHEW PRICE LTD.

Albany Court, Albury, Thame, Oxfordshire OX9 2LP, United Kingdom. **E-mail:** info@mathewprice.com. **E-mail:** submissions@mathewprice.com. **Website:** www.mathewprice.com. U.S. address: 12300 Ford St., Suite 455, Dallas, TX. 75234. **Contact:** Mathew Price, chairman. "Mathew Price Ltd. works to bring to market talented authors and artists profitably by publishing books for children that lift the hearts of people young and old all over the world." Publishes 2-3 picture books/year; 2 young readers/year; 1-2 gift book/year.

🗨 Looking especially for stories for 2- to 4-year-olds and fiction for young adults, especially fantasy.

HOW TO CONTACT *Will accept e-mail submissions only.*

ILLUSTRATION Accepts material from artists in other countries. Uses color artwork only. Reviews ms/illustration packages from artists sent by e-mail only. Illustrations only: send PDFs or JPEGs by e-mail.

TIPS "Study the market; keep a copy of all your work."

🌑 QED PUBLISHING

The Quarto Group, 226 City Rd., London EC1V 2TT, United Kingdom. +44 (0)20 7812 8633. **Fax:** +44 (0)20 7253 4370. **E-mail:** zetad@quarto.com. **Website:** www.quarto.com. **Contact:** Zeta Davies, associate publisher. Publishes 70 titles/year.

FICTION Average word length: picture books—500; young readers—3,000; middle readers—3,500. Recently published *The Tickety Tale Teller*, by Maureen Haselhurst, illustrated by Barbara Vagnozzi (ages 4+); *The Thief of Bracken Farm*, by Emma Barnes, illustrated by Hannah Wood (ages 4+); *The Big Fuzzy*, by Caroline Castle, illustrated by Daniel Howarth (ages 4+).

NONFICTION Picture books: animal, arts/crafts, biography, geography, reference, science. Young readers: activity books, animal, arts/crafts, biography, geography, reference, science. Middle readers: activity books, animal, arts/crafts, biography, geography, science. Average word length: picture books—500; young readers—3,000; middle readers—3,500. Recently published *Exploring the Earth*, by Peter Grego (ages 7 and up); *The Ancient Egyptians*, by Fiona Mac-

donald (ages 7+, science); *The Great Big Book of Pirates*, by John Malam (ages 7+, history).

HOW TO CONTACT Query.

ILLUSTRATION Accepts material from international illustrators. Works with 25 illustrators/year. For ms/illustration packages: Submit ms with 2 pieces of final art. Reviews work for future assignments. Submit samples to Amanda Askew, editor. Responds in 2 weeks. Samples filed.

PHOTOGRAPHY Buys stock images and assigns work. Submit photos to Zeta Davies, creative director. Uses step-by-step photos. For first contact, send CD of work or online URL.

TIPS "Be persistent."

⊙ RAINCOAST BOOK DISTRIBUTION, LTD.

2440 Viking Way, Richmond, British Columbia V6V 1N2, Canada. (604)448-7100. **Fax:** (604)270-7161. **E-mail:** info@raincoast.com. **Website:** www.raincoast.com. Publishes hardcover and trade paperback originals and reprints. Publishes 60 titles/year. 10% of books from first-time authors. 40% from unagented writers.

FICTION *No unsolicited mss.*

NONFICTION *No unsolicited mss.*

HOW TO CONTACT Query with SASE. 3,000 queries received/year. Publishes book within 2 years of acceptance.

TERMS Pays 8-12% royalty on retail price. Pays $1,000-6,000 advance. Book catalog for #10 SASE.

Ⓐ 🌑 RANDOM HOUSE CHILDREN'S BOOKS

61-63 Uxbridge Rd., London W5 5SA, United Kingdom. (44)(208)231-6000. **Fax:** (44)(208)231-6737. **E-mail:** enquiries@randomhouse.co.uk; lduffy@randomhouse.co.uk. **Website:** www.kidsatrandomhouse.co.uk. **Contact:** Philippa Dickinson, managing director. Publishes 250 titles/year.

🗨 *Only interested in agented material.*

FICTION Picture books: adventure, animal, anthology, contemporary, fantasy, folktales, humor, multicultural, nature/environment, poetry, suspense/mystery. Young readers: adventure, animal, anthology, contemporary, fantasy, folktales, humor, multicultural, nature/environment, poetry, sports, suspense/mystery. Middle readers: adventure, animal, anthology, contemporary, fantasy, folktales, humor, multicultural, nature/environment, problem novels, romance, sports, suspense/mystery. Young adults: adventure, contemporary, fantasy, humor, multicultural, nature/environment, problem novels, romance, science fiction, suspense/mystery. Average word length: picture books—800; young readers—1,500-6,000; middle readers—10,000-15,000; young adults—20,000-45,000.

ILLUSTRATION Works with 50 illustrators/year. Reviews ms/illustration packages from artists. Query with samples. Contact: Margaret Hope. Samples are returned with SASE (IRC).

PHOTOGRAPHY Buys photos from freelancers. Contact: Margaret Hope. Photo captions required. Uses color or b&w prints. Submit cover letter, published samples.

TERMS Pays authors royalty. Offers advances.

TIPS "Although Random House is a big publisher, each imprint only publishes a small number of books each year. Our lists for the next few years are already full. Any book we take on from a previously unpublished author has to be truly exceptional. Mss should be sent to us via literary agents."

⊘ RONSDALE PRESS

3350 W. 21st Ave., Vancouver, British Columbia V6S 1G7, Canada. (604)738-4688. **Fax:** (604)731-4548. **E-mail:** rons dale@shaw.ca. **Website:** http://ronsdalepress.com. **Contact:** Ronald B. Hatch, director (fiction, poetry, social commentary); Veronica Hatch, managing director (children's literature). "Ronsdale Press is a Canadian literary publishing house that publishes 12 books each year, three of which are children's titles. Of particular interest are books involving children exploring and discovering new aspects of Canadian history." Publishes trade paperback originals. Publishes 12 titles/year. 40% of books from first-time authors. 95% from unagented writers.

⊘ *Canadian authors only.*

FICTION Young adults: Canadian novels. Average word length: middle readers and young adults—50,000. Recently published *Red Goodwin*, by John Wilson (ages 10-14); *Tragic Links*, by Cathy Beveridge (ages 10-14); *Dark Times*, edited by Ann Walsh (anthology of short stories, ages 10 and up); *Submarine Outlaw*, by Phillip Roy; *The Way Lies North*, by Jean Rae Baxter (ages 10-14).

NONFICTION Middle readers, young adults: animal, biography, history, multicultural, social issues. Av-

erage word length: young readers—90; middle readers-90. "We publish a number of books for children and young adults in the age 8 to 15 range. We are especially interested in YA historical novels. We regret that we can no longer publish picture books."

HOW TO CONTACT Submit complete ms. Submit complete ms. 300 queries received/year. 800 mss received/year. Responds to queries in 2 weeks; mss in 2 months. Publishes book 1 year after acceptance.

ILLUSTRATION Works with 2 illustrators/year. Reviews ms/illustration packages from artists. Requires only cover art. Responds in 2 weeks. Samples returned with SASE. Originals returned to artist at job's completion.

TERMS Pays 10% royalty on retail price. Book catalog for #10 SASE. Guidelines available online.

TIPS "Ronsdale Press is a literary publishing house, based in Vancouver, and dedicated to publishing books from across Canada, books that give Canadians new insights into themselves and their country. We aim to publish the best Canadian writers."

⊘ SECOND STORY PRESS

20 Maud St., Suite 401, Toronto, Ontario M5V 2M5, Canada. (416)537-7850. **Fax:** (416)537-0588. **E-mail:** info@secondstorypress.ca; marketing@secondstorypress.com. **Website:** www.secondstorypress.ca.

FICTION Considers non-sexist, non-racist, and non-violent stories, as well as historical fiction, chapter books, picture books. Recently published *Lilly and the Paper Man*, by Rebecca Upjohn; *Mom and Mum Are Getting Married!*, by Ken Setterington.

NONFICTION Picture books: biography. Recently published *Hiding Edith: A True Story*, by Kathy Kacer (a new addition to our Holocaust remembrance series for young readers).

HOW TO CONTACT *Accepts appropriate material from residents of Canada only.* Submit complete ms or submit outline and sample chapters by postal mail only. No electronic submissions or queries.

⊘ TAFELBERG PUBLISHERS

Imprint of NB Publishers, P.O. Box 879, Cape Town 8000, South Africa. (27)(21)406-3033. **Fax:** (27)(21)406-3812. **E-mail:** nb@nb.co.za. **Website:** www.tafelberg.com. **Contact:** Danita van Romburgh, editorial secretary; Louise Steyn, publisher. General publisher best known for Afrikaans fiction, authoritative political works, children's/youth literature, and a variety of illustrated and nonillustrated nonfiction. Publishes 10 titles/year.

FICTION Picture books, young readers: animal, anthology, contemporary, fantasy, folktales, hi-lo, humor, multicultural, nature/environment, scient fiction, special needs. Middle readers, young adults: animal (middle reader only), contemporary, fantasy, hi-lo, humor, multicultural, nature/environment, problem novels, science fiction, special needs, sports, suspense/mystery. Average word length: picture books—1,500-7,500; young readers—25,000; middle readers—15,000; young adults—40,000. Recently published *Because Pula Means Rain*, by Jenny Robson (ages 12-15, realism); *BreinBliksem*, by Fanie Viljoen (ages 13-18, realism); *SuperZero*, by Darrel Bristow-Bovey (ages 9-12, realism/humor).

HOW TO CONTACT Query or submit complete ms. Submit complete ms. Responds to queries in 2 weeks; mss in 6 months. Publishes book 1 year after acceptance.

ILLUSTRATION Works with 2-3 illustrators/year. Reviews ms/illustration packages from artists. Send ms with dummy or e-mail and jpegs. Contact: Louise Steyn, publisher. Illustrations only: Query with brochure, photocopies, résumé, URL, JPEGs. Responds only if interested. Samples not returned.

TERMS Pays authors royalty of 15-18% based on wholesale price.

TIPS "Writers: Story needs to have a South African or African style. Illustrators: I'd like to look, but the chances of getting commissioned are slim. The market is small and difficult. Do not expect huge advances. Editorial staff attended or plans to attend the following conferences: IBBY, Frankfurt, SCBWI Bologna."

☺ THISTLEDOWN PRESS LTD.

118 20th Street West, Saskatoon, Saskatchewan S7M 0W6, Canada. (306)244-1722. **Fax:** (306)244-1762. **Website:** www.thistledownpress.com. **Contact:** Allan Forrie, publisher.

> ☺ "Thistledown originates books by Canadian authors only, although we have co-published titles by authors outside Canada. We do not publish children's picture books."

FICTION Middle readers, young adults: adventure, anthology, contemporary, fantasy, humor, poetry, romance, science fiction, suspense/mystery, short stories. Average word length: young adults—40,000. Recently published *Up All Night*, edited by R.P. Ma-

cIntyre (young adult, anthology); *Offside*, by Cathy Beveridge (young adult, novel); *Cheeseburger Subversive*, by Richard Scarsbrook; *The Alchemist's Daughter*, by Eileen Kernaghan.

HOW TO CONTACT Submit outline/synopsis and sample chapters. *Does not accept mss.* Do not query by e-mail. Responds to queries in 4 months. Publishes book 1 year after acceptance.

ILLUSTRATION Prefers agented illustrators but "not mandatory." Works with few illustrators. Illustrations only: Query with samples, promo sheet, slides, tearsheets. Responds only if interested. Samples returned with SASE; samples filed.

TERMS Pays authors royalty of 10-12% based on net dollar sales. Pays illustrators and photographers by the project (range: $250-750). Book catalog free on request. Guidelines available for #10 envelope and IRC.

TIPS "Send cover letter including publishing history and SASE."

☺ TRADEWIND BOOKS

(604)662-4405. **E-mail:** tradewindbooks@mail.lycos.com. **Website:** www.tradewindbooks.com. **Contact:** Michael Katz, publisher; Carol Frank, art director; R. David Stephens, senior editor. "Tradewind Books publishes juvenile picture books and young adult novels. Requires that submissions include evidence that author has read at least 3 titles published by Tradewind Books." Publishes hardcover and trade paperback originals. Publishes 5 titles/year. 15% of books from first-time authors. 50% from unagented writers.

FICTION Picture books: adventure, multicultural, folktales. Average word length: 900 words. Recently published *City Kids*, by X.J. Kennedy and illustrated by Phillpe Beha; *Roxy* by PJ Reece; *Viva Zapata!* by Emilie Smith and illustrated by Stefan Czernecki.

HOW TO CONTACT Send complete ms for picture books. *YA novels by Canadian authors only. Chapter books by US authors considered.* Responds to mss in 2 months. Publishes book 3 years after acceptance.

ILLUSTRATION Works with 3-4 illustrators/year. Reviews ms/illustration packages from artists. Send illustrated ms as dummy. Illustrations only: Query with samples. Responds only if interested. Samples returned with SASE; samples filed.

TERMS Pays 7% royalty on retail price. Pays variable advance. Book catalog and ms guidelines online.

🌀 USBORNE PUBLISHING

83-85 Saffron Hill, London EC1N 8RT, United Kingdom. (44)(020)7430-2800. **Fax:** (44)(020)7430-1562. **E-mail:** mail@usborne.co.uk; pippas@usborne.co.uk; alicep@usborne.co.uk; Graeme@usborne.co.uk. **Website:** www.usborne.com. "Usborne Publishing is a multiple-award winning, world-wide children's publishing company specializing in superbly researched and produced information books with a unique appeal to young readers."

FICTION Young readers, middle readers: adventure, contemporary, fantasy, history, humor, multicultural, nature/environment, science fiction, suspense/mystery, strong concept-based or character-led series. Average word length: young readers—5,000-10,000; middle readers—25,000-50,000. Recently published Secret Mermaid series by Sue Mongredien (ages 7 and up); *School Friends*, by Ann Bryant (ages 9 and up).

ILLUSTRATION Works with 100 illustrators per year. Illustrations only: Query with samples. Samples not returned; samples filed.

PHOTOGRAPHY Contact: Usborne Art Department. Submit samples.

TERMS Pays authors royalty.

TIPS "Do not send any original work and, sorry, but we cannot guarantee a reply."

🌀 WEIGL EDUCATIONAL PUBLISHERS LTD.

6325 10th St., SE, Calgary, Alberta T2H 2Z9, Canada. (403)233-7747. **Fax:** (403)233-7769. **E-mail:** linda@weigl.com. **Website:** www.weigl.ca. "Textbook publisher catering to juvenile and young adult audience (K-12)." Makes outright purchase. Responds ASAP to queries. Query with SASE. Publishes hardcover originals and reprints, school library softcover. Publishes 104 titles/year. 100% from unagented writers.

TERMS Book catalog available for free.

🌀 WHITECAP BOOKS, LTD.

(640)980-9852. **Fax:** (604)980-8197. **E-mail:** whitecap@whitecap.ca. **Website:** www.whitecap.ca. "Whitecap Books is a general trade publisher with a focus on food and wine titles. Although we are interested in reviewing unsolicited ms submissions, please note that we only accept submissions that meet the needs of our current publishing program. Please see some of most recent releases to get an idea of the kinds of titles we are interested in." Publishes hardcover and trade paperback originals. Publishes 40 titles/year. 20% of books from first-time authors. 90% from unagented writers.

FICTION No children's picture books or adult fiction.

NONFICTION Young children's and middle reader's nonfiction focusing mainly on nature, wildlife and animals. "Writers should take the time to research our list and read the submission guidelines on our website. This is especially important for children's writers and cookbook authors. We will only consider submissions that fall into these categories: cookbooks, wine and spirits, regional travel, home and garden, Canadian history, North American natural history, juvenile series-based fiction." "At this time, we are not accepting the following categories: self-help or inspirational books, political, social commentary, or issue books, general how-to books, biographies or memoirs, business and finance, art and architecture, religion and spirituality."

HOW TO CONTACT See guidelines. Submit cover letter, synopsis, SASE via ground mail. See guidelines online at website. 500 queries received/year; 1,000 mss received/year. Responds in 2-3 months to proposals. Publishes book 1 year after acceptance.

ILLUSTRATION Works with 1-2 illustrators/year. Uses color artwork only. Reviews ms/illustration packages from artists. Query. Contact: Rights and Acquisitions. Illustrations only: Send postcard sample with tearsheets. Contact: Michelle Mayne, art director. Responds only if interested.

PHOTOGRAPHY Only accepts digital photography. Submit stock photo list. Buys stock and assigns work. Model/property releases required.

TERMS Pays royalty. Pays negotiated advance. Catalog and guidelines available online at website.

TIPS "We want well-written, well-researched material that presents a fresh approach to a particular topic."

MAGAZINES

///

Children's magazines are a great place for unpublished writers and illustrators to break into the market. Writers, illustrators and photographers alike may find it easier to get book assignments if they have tearsheets from magazines. Having magazine work under your belt shows you're professional and have experience working with editors and art directors and meeting deadlines.

But magazines aren't merely a breaking-in point. Writing, illustration and photo assignments for magazines let you see your work in print quickly, and the magazine market can offer steady work and regular paychecks (a number of them pay on acceptance). Book authors and illustrators may have to wait a year or two before receiving royalties from a project. The magazine market is also a good place to use research material that didn't make it into a book project you're working on. You may even work on a magazine idea that blossoms into a book project.

TARGETING YOUR SUBMISSIONS

It's important to know the topics typically covered by different children's magazines. To help you match your work with the right publications, we've included several indexes in the back of this book. The **Subject Index** lists both book and magazine publishers by the fiction and nonfiction subjects they're seeking.

If you're a writer, use the Subject Index in conjunction with the **Age-Level Index** to narrow your list of markets. Targeting the correct age group with your submission is an important consideration. Many rejection slips are sent because a writer has not targeted a manuscript to the correct age. Few magazines are aimed at children of all ages, so you must be certain your manuscript is written for the audience level of the particular magazine you're submitting to. Magazines for children (just as magazines for adults) may also target a specific gender.

If you're a poet, refer to the **Poetry Index** to find which magazines publish poems.

Each magazine has a different editorial philosophy. Language usage also varies between periodicals, as does the length of feature articles and the use of artwork and photographs. Reading magazines *before* submitting is the best way to determine if your material is appropriate. Also, because magazines targeted to specific age groups have a natural turnover in readership every few years, old topics (with a new slant) can be recycled.

If you're a photographer, the **Photography Index** lists children's magazines that use photos from freelancers. Using it in combination with the subject index can narrow your search. For instance, if you photograph sports, compare the Magazine list in the Photography Index with the list under Sports in the Subject Index. Highlight the markets that appear on both lists, then read those listings to decide which magazines might be best for your work.

Since many kids' magazines sell subscriptions through direct mail or schools, you may not be able to find a particular publication at bookstores or newsstands. Check your local library, or send for copies of the magazines you're interested in. Most magazines in this section have sample copies available and will send them for a SASE or small fee.

Also, many magazines have submission guidelines and theme lists available for a SASE. Check magazines' websites, too. Many offer excerpts of articles, submission guidelines, and theme lists and will give you a feel for the editorial focus of the publication.

Watch for the Canadian ☼ and International ◑ symbols. These publications' needs and requirements may differ from their U.S. counterparts.

ADVOCATE, PKA'S PUBLICATION

1881 Little Westkill Rd., Prattsville NY 12468. (518)299-3103. **E-mail:** advoad@localnet.com. **Website:** www.facebook.com/AdvocatePKAPublications. **Contact:** Patricia Keller, publisher. "*Advocate, PKA's Publication*, published bimonthly, is an advertiser-supported tabloid using original, previously unpublished works, such as feature stories, essays, 'think' pieces, letters to the editor, profiles, humor, fiction, poetry, puzzles, cartoons, or line drawings. Advocates for good writers and quality writings. *Advocate*'s submitters are talented people of all ages who do not earn their livings as writers. We wish to promote the arts and to give those we publish the opportunity to be published." Estab. 1987. Circ. 7,000.

○ Gaited Horse Association newsletter is included in this publication. Horse-oriented stories, poetry, art and photos are currently needed.

FICTION Middle readers, young adults/teens, adults: adventure, animal, contemporary, fantasy, folktales, health, humorous, nature/environment, problem-solving, romance, science fiction, sports, suspense/mystery. Looks for "well written, entertaining work, whether fiction or nonfiction." Buys approximately 42 mss/year. Prose pieces should not exceed 1,500 words. Wants to see more humorous material, nature/environment and romantic comedy. "Nothing religious, pornographic, violent, erotic, pro-drug or anti-environment." Send complete ms.

NONFICTION Middle readers, young adults/teens: animal, arts/crafts, biography, careers, concept, cooking, fashion, games/puzzles, geography, history, hobbies, how-to, humorous, interview/profile, nature/environment, problem-solving, science, social issues, sports, travel. Buys 10 mss/year. Prose pieces should not exceed 1,500 words. Send complete ms.

POETRY Wants "nearly any kind of poetry, any length." No religious or pornographic. Occasionally comments on rejected poems.

HOW TO CONTACT Responds to queries in 6 weeks; mss in 2 months. Publishes ms 2-18 months after acceptance.

ILLUSTRATION Uses b&w artwork only. Uses cartoons. Reviews ms/illustration packages from artists. Submit a photo print (b&w or color), an excellent copy of work (no larger than 8×10) or original. Prints in black and white but accepts color work that converts well to gray scale. Illustrations only: "Send previously unpublished art with SASE, please." Responds in 2 months. Samples returned with SASE; samples not filed. Credit line given.

PHOTOS Buys photos from freelancers. Model/property releases required. Uses color and b&w prints (no slides). Send unsolicited photos by mail with SASE. Responds in 2 months. Wants nature, artistic and humorous photos.

TERMS Acquires first rights for mss, artwork and photographs. Pays on publication with 2 contributor's copies.

TIPS Subscription: $18.50 (6 issues). Sample: $5 (includes guidelines). "Please, no simultaneous submissions, work that has appeared on the Internet, pornography, overt religiosity, anti-environmentalism or gratuitous violence. Artists and photographers should keep in mind that we are a b&w paper. Please do not send postcards. Use envelope with SASE."

AMERICAN CAREERS

Career Communications, Inc., 6701 W. 64th St., Overland Park KS 66202. (800)669-7795. **E-mail:** ccinfor@carcom.com. **Website:** www.carcom.com; www.americancareersonline.com. **Contact:** Mary Pitchford; Jerry Kanabel, art director. "*American Careers* provides career, salary, and education information to middle school and high school students. Self-tests help them relate their interests and abilities to future careers." Estab. 1989. Circ. 500,000.

NONFICTION Query by mail only with published clips. Length: 300-1,000 words. Pays $100-450.

HOW TO CONTACT Accepts queries by mail.

PHOTOS State availability. Captions, identification of subjects, model releases required. Negotiates payment individually.

TERMS Buys all rights. Makes work-for-hire assignments. Byline given. Pays 1 month after acceptance. No kill fee. 10% freelance written. Sample copy for $4. Guidelines for #10 SASE.

TIPS "Letters of introduction or query letters with samples and résumés are ways we get to know writers. Samples should include how-to articles and career-related articles. Articles written for teenagers also would make good samples. Short feature articles on careers, career-related how-to articles, and self-assessment tools (10-20 point quizzes with scoring information) are primarily what we publish."

AMERICAN CHEERLEADER

Macfadden Performing Arts Media LLC, 110 William St., 23rd Floor, New York NY 10038. (646)459-4800.

Fax: (646)459-4900. **E-mail:** mwalker@american cheerleader.com; acmail@americancheerleader.com. **Website:** www.americancheerleader.com. **Contact:** Joanna Schwartz, publisher; Sheila Noone, editor-in-chief. Bimonthly magazine covering high school, college, and competitive cheerleading. "We try to keep a young, informative voice for all articles—'for cheerleaders, by cheerleaders.'" Estab. 1995. Circ. 200,000.

NONFICTION Young adults: biography, interview/profile (sports personalities), careers, fashion, beauty, health, how-to (cheering techniques, routines, pep songs, etc.), problem-solving, sports, cheerleading-specific material. "We're looking for authors who know cheerleading." Buys 20 mss/year. Query with published clips; provide résumé, business card, tearsheets to be kept on file. Length: 750-2,000 words. Pays $100-250 for assigned articles. Pays $100 maximum for unsolicited articles.

HOW TO CONTACT Editorial lead time 3 months. Responds in 4 weeks to queries. Responds in 2 months to mss. Publishes mss an average of 4 months after acceptance. Accepts queries by mail, e-mail, online submission form.

ILLUSTRATION Reviews ms/illustration packages from artists. Illustrations only: Query with samples; arrange portfolio review. Responds only if interested. Samples filed. Originals not returned at job's completion. Credit line given.

PHOTOS State availability. Model releases required. Reviews transparencies, 5x7 prints. Offers $50/photo.

TERMS Buys all rights. Byline given. Pays on publication. Offers 25% kill fee. 30% freelance written. Sample copy for $2.95. Guidelines free.

TIPS "We invite proposals from freelance writers who are involved in or have been involved in cheerleading—i.e., coaches, sponsors, or cheerleaders. Our writing style is upbeat and 'sporty' to catch and hold the attention of our teenaged readers. Articles should be broken down into lots of sidebars, bulleted lists, Q&As, etc."

ASK

Carus Publlishing, 70 E. Lake St., Suite 300, Chicago IL 60601. **E-mail:** ask@caruspub.com. **Website:** www. cricketmag.com. **Contact:** Liz Huyck, editor. Magazine published 9 times/year. "*Ask* is a magazine of arts and sciences for curious kids who like to find out how the world works." Estab. 2002.

NONFICTION Needs young readers, middle readers: science, engineering, invention, machines, archaeol-ogy, animals, nature/environment, history, history of science. "*Ask* commissions all articles but welcomes queries from authors on subjects relating to upcoming themes. Particularly looking for odd, unusual, and interesting stories likely to interest science-oriented kids." Writers interested in working for *Ask* should send a résumé and two writing samples (including at least 200 words unedited) for consideration. Average word length: 150-1,600.

ILLUSTRATION Buys 10 illustrations/issue; 60 illustrations/year. Works on assignment only. For illustrations, send query with samples.

PHOTOS Send query with samples.

TERMS Byline given. See www.cricketmag.com/19-Submission-Guidelines-for-ASK-magazine-for-children-ages-6-9 for current issue theme list and calendar.

AUSTRALASIANJOURNAL OF EARLY CHILDHOOD

Early Childhood Australia, P.O. Box 86, Deakin West ACT 2600, Australia. (61)(2)6242-1800. **Fax:** (61)(2)6242-1818. **E-mail:** publishing@earlychildhood.org.au. **Website:** www.earlychildhoodaustralia.org.au. **Contact:** Chris Jones, publishing manager. Non-profit early childhood advocacy organization, acting in the interests of young children from birth to 8 years of age, their families and those in the early childhood field. Specialist publisher of early childhood magazines, journals and booklets.

NONFICTION Needs essays. Send complete ms. Length: Magazine articles, 600-1,000 words; research-based papers, 3,000-6,500 words; submissions for booklets, approximately 5,000 words.

TERMS Guidelines available online.

BABYBUG

Carus Publishing, 70 East Lake St., Chicago IL 60601. **E-mail:** babybug@caruspub.com. **Website:** www.cricketmag.com. **Contact:** Alice Letvin, editorial director; Suzanne Beck, managing art director. "*Babybug* is 'the listening and looking board-book magazine for infants and toddlers,' intended to be read aloud by a loving adult to foster a love of books and reading in young children ages 6 months-3 years. *Babybug* is 6×7, 24 pages long, printed in large type on high-quality cardboard stock with rounded corners and no staples." Estab. 1994. Circ. 45,000.

FICTION Looking for very simple and concrete stories. Rhythmic, rhyming. Length: 4-6 short sentences.

NONFICTION Must use very basic words and concepts.

POETRY Submit no more than 5 poems at a time. Lines/poem: 8 lines maximum. Considers previously published poems. Acquires North American publication rights for previously published poems; acquires all rights for unpublished poems.

HOW TO CONTACT Submit complete ms, SASE. Responds in 6 months.

ILLUSTRATION Uses color artwork only. Works on assignment only. Reviews ms/illustration packages from artists. "The manuscripts will be evaluated for quality of concept and text before the art is considered." Contact: Suzanne Beck. Illustrations only: Send tearsheets or photo prints/photocopies with SASE. "Submissions without SASE will be discarded." Responds in 3 months. Samples filed.

PHOTOS Pays $500/spread; $250/page.

TERMS Pays $25 minimum for mss. Byline given. 50% freelance written. Guidelines available online or for SASE.

TIPS "Imagine having to read your story or poem—out loud—50 times or more! That's what parents will have to do. Babies and toddlers demand, 'Read it again!' Your material must hold up under repetition. And humor is much appreciated by all."

BOYS' LIFE

Boy Scouts of America, P.O. Box 152079, 1325 West Walnut Hill Ln., Irving TX 75015. (972)580-2366. **Fax:** (972)580-2079. **Website:** www.boyslife.org. **Contact:** Paula Murphy, senior editor; Clay Swartz, associate editor; Michael Goldman, managing editor; Aaron Derr, senior writer. *Boys' Life* is a monthly 4-color general interest magazine for boys 7-18, most of whom are Cub Scouts, Boy Scouts or Venturers. Estab. 1911. Circ. 1.1 million.

FICTION All fiction is assigned.

NONFICTION Scouting activities and general interests (nature, Earth, health, cars, sports, science, computers, space and aviation, entertainment, history, music, animals, how-to's, etc.). All articles are commissioned. Query with SASE. No phone queries. Average word length for articles: 500-1,500 words, including sidebars and boxes. Average word length for columns: 300-750. Pays $400-$1,500.

HOW TO CONTACT Responds to queries/mss in 2 months. Publishes approximately one year after acceptance. Accepts queries by mail only.

ILLUSTRATION Buys 10-12 illustrations/issue; 100-125 illustrations/year. Works on assignment only. Reviews ms/illustration packages from artists. "Query first." Illustrations only: Send tearsheets. Responds to art samples only if interested. Samples returned with SASE. Original artwork returned at job's completion. Works on assignment only.

PHOTOS Photo guidelines free with SASE. Boy Scouts of America Magazine Division also publishes *Scouting* magazine. "Most photographs are from specific assignments that freelance photojournalists shoot for *Boys' Life*. Interested in all photographers, but do not send unsolicited images." Pays $500 base editorial day rate against placement fees, plus expenses.

TERMS Buys one-time rights. Byline given. Pays on acceptance. 75% freelance written. Prefers to work with published/established writers; works with small number of new/unpublished writers each year. Sample copies for $3.95 plus 9x12 SASE. Guidelines available with SASE and online.

TIPS "We strongly recommend reading at least 12 issues of the magazine before submitting queries. We are a good market for any writer willing to do the necessary homework. Write for a boy you know who is 12. Our readers demand punchy writing in relatively short, straightforward sentences. The editors demand well-reported articles that demonstrate high standards of journalism. We follow the Associated Press manual of style and usage. Learn and read our publications before submitting anything."

BOYS' QUEST

P.O. Box 227, Bluffton OH 45817-0227. (419)358-4610, ext. 101. **Fax:** (419)358-8020. **Website:** http://funforkidzmagazines.com/. **Contact:** Marilyn Edwards, editor. Bimonthly magazine. "*Boys' Quest* is a magazine created for boys from 5 to 14 years, with youngsters 8, 9 and 10 the specific target age. Our point of view is that every young boy deserves the right to be a young boy for a number of years before he becomes a young adult." Estab. 1995. Circ. 10,000.

FICTION Picture-oriented material, young readers, middle readers: adventure, animal, history, humorous, multicultural, nature/environment, problem-solving, sports. Does not want to see violence, teenage themes. Buys 30 mss/year. Query or send complete ms (preferred). Send SASE with correct postage. No faxed or e-mailed material. Length: 200-500 words.

NONFICTION Needs nonfiction pieces that are accompanied by clear photos. Articles accompanied by photos with high resolution are far more likely to be accepted than those that need illustrations. Query or send complete ms (preferred). Send SASE with correct postage. No faxed or e-mailed material. Length: 500 words.

POETRY Reviews poetry. Limit submissions to 6 poems. Length: 21 lines maximum.

HOW TO CONTACT Responds to queries in 2 weeks; mss in 2 weeks (if rejected); 6 weeks (if scheduled). Accepts queries by mail.

ILLUSTRATION Buys 10 illustrations/issue; 60-70 illustrations/year. Uses b&w artwork only. Works on assignment only. Reviews ms/illustration packages from artists. Illustrations only: Query with samples, tearsheets, SASE. Responds in 1 month only if interested. Samples returned with SASE; samples filed. Credit line given.

PHOTOS Photos used for support of nonfiction. "Excellent photographs included with a nonfiction story are considered very seriously." Model/property releases required. Uses b&w, 5x7 or 3x5 prints. Query with samples; send unsolicited photos by mail. Responds in 3 weeks. "We use a number of photos, printed in b&w, inside the magazine. These photos support the articles." $5/photo.

TERMS Buys first North American serial rights for mss. Byline given. Pays on publication. Guidelines and open themes available for SASE, or visit www.funforkidz.com and click on "Writers" at the bottom of the homepage.

TIPS "First be familiar with our magazines. We are looking for lively writing, most of it from a young boy's point of view—with the boy or boys directly involved in an activity that is both wholesome and unusual. We need nonfiction with photos and fiction stories—around 500 words—puzzles, poems, cooking, carpentry projects, jokes and riddles. We will entertain simultaneous submissions as long as that fact is noted on the ms."

BREAD FOR GOD'S CHILDREN

P.O. Box 1017, Arcadia FL 34265. (863)494-6214. **Fax:** (863)993-0154. **E-mail:** bread@breadministries.org. **Website:** www.breadministries.org. **Contact:** Judith M. Gibbs, editor. An interdenominational Christian teaching publication published 6-8 times/year written to aid children and youth in leading a Christian life. Estab. 1972. Circ. 10,000 (U.S. & Canada).

FICTION "We are looking for writers who have a solid knowledge of Biblical principles and are concerned for the youth of today living by those principles. Our stories must be well written, with the story itself getting the message across—no preaching, moralizing, or tag endings." Young readers, middle readers, young adult/teen: adventure, religious, problem-solving, sports. Looks for "teaching stories that portray Christian lifestyles without preaching." Buys approximately 10-15 mss/year. Send complete ms. Length: young children—600-800 words; older children—900-1,500 words.

NONFICTION All levels: how-to. "We do not want anything detrimental to solid family values. Most topics will fit if they are slanted to our basic needs." Buys 3-4 mss/year. Length: 500-800 words.

HOW TO CONTACT Responds to mss in 6 months. Publishes ms an average of 6 months after acceptance. Accepts queries by mail.

ILLUSTRATION "The only illustrations we purchase are those occasional good ones accompanying an accepted story."

TERMS Pays on publication. Pays $30-50 for stories; $30 for articles. Buys first rights. Byline given. No kill fee. 10% freelance written. Sample copies for 9×12 SAE and 5 first-class stamps. Guidelines for #10 SASE.

TIPS "We want stories or articles that illustrate overcoming obstacles by faith and living solid, Christian lives. Know our publication and what we have used in the past. Know the readership and publisher's guidelines. Stories should teach the value of morality and honesty without preaching. Edit carefully for content and grammar."

☺ ☺ BRILLIANT STAR

1233 Central St., Evanston IL 60201. (847)853-2354. **Fax:** (847)256-1372. **E-mail:** brilliant@usbnc.org; sengle@usbnc.org. **Website:** www.brilliantstarmagazine.org. **Contact:** Susan Engle, associate editor; Amethel Parel-Sewell, art director; Aaron Kreader, graphic designer. "*Brilliant Star* presents Bahá'í history and principles through fiction, nonfiction, activities, interviews, puzzles, cartoons, games, music, and art. Universal values of good character, such as kindness, courage, creativity, and helpfulness, are incorporated into the magazine." Estab. 1969.

FICTION Middle readers: contemporary, fantasy, folktale, multicultural, nature/environment, problem-solving, religious. Submit complete ms. Length: 700-1,400 words.

NONFICTION Middle readers: arts/crafts, games/ puzzles, geography, how-to, humorous, multicultural, nature/environment, religion, social issues. Buys 6 mss/year. Query. Length: 300-700 words.

POETRY "We only publish poetry written by children at the moment."

ILLUSTRATION Reviews ms/illustration packages from artists. Illustrations only: Query with samples. Contact: Aaron Kreader, graphic designer. Responds only if interested. Samples kept on file. Credit line given.

PHOTOS Buys photos with accompanying ms only. Model/property release required; captions required. Responds only if interested.

TERMS Buys first rights and reprint rights for mss, artwork, and photos. Byline given. Pays 2 contributor's copies. Guidelines available for SASE or via e-mail.

TIPS "*Brilliant Star*'s content is developed with a focus on children in their 'tween' years, ages 8-12. This is a period of intense emotional, physical, and psychological development. Familiarize yourself with the interests and challenges of children in this age range. Protagonists in our fiction are usually in the upper part of our age range: 10-12 years old. They solve their problems without adult intervention. We appreciate seeing a sense of humor but not related to bodily functions or put-downs. Keep your language and concepts age-appropriate. Use short words, sentences, and paragraphs. Activities and games may be submitted in rough or final form. Send us a description of your activity along with short, simple instructions. We avoid long, complicated activities that require adult supervision. If you think they will be helpful, please try to provide step-by-step rough sketches of the instructions. You may also submit photographs to illustrate the activity."

☻ CADET QUEST MAGAZINE

P.O. Box 7259, Grand Rapids MI 49510-7259. (616)241-5616. **Fax:** (616)241-5558. **E-mail:** submissions@calvinistcadets.org. **Website:** www.calvinistcadets.org. **Contact:** G. Richard Broene, editor; Robert deJonge, art director. Magazine published 7 times/year. "*Cadet Quest Magazine* shows boys 9-14 how God is at work in their lives and in the world around them." Estab. 1958. Circ. 7,500.

   ○   Accepts submissions by mail, or by e-mail (must include ms in text of e-mail). Will not open attachments.

FICTION Middle readers, boys/early teens: adventure, humorous, multicultural, problem-solving, religious, sports. Buys 14 mss/year. Average word length: 900-1,500. Considerable fiction is used. Fast-moving stories that appeal to a boy's sense of adventure or sense of humor are welcome. Needs adventure, religious. spiritual, sports, comics. Avoid preachiness. Avoid simplistic answers to complicated problems. Avoid long dialogue and little action. No fantasy, science fiction, fashion, horror or erotica. Send complete ms. Pays 4-6¢/word, and 1 contributor's copy.

NONFICTION Needs how-to, humor, inspirational, interview, personal experience. informational. Send complete ms. Length: 500-1,500 words. Pays 4-6¢/ word, and 1 contributor's copy.

HOW TO CONTACT Responds in 2 months to mss. Publishes ms an average of 4-11 months after acceptance.

ILLUSTRATION Buys 2 illustrations/issue; buys 12 illustrations/year. Works on assignment only. Reviews ms/illustration packages from artists.

PHOTOS Pays $20-30 for photos purchased with ms.

TERMS Buys first North American serial rights, buys one-time rights, buys second serial (reprint) rights, buys simultaneous rights. Rights purchased vary with author and material. Byline given. Pays on acceptance. No kill fee. 40% freelance written. Works with a small number of new/unpublished writers each year. Sample copy for 9x12 SASE. Guidelines for #10 SASE.

TIPS "Best time to submit stories/articles is early in the year (February-April). Also remember readers are boys ages 9-14. Stories must reflect or add to the theme of the issue and be from a Christian perspective."

◎ CALLIOPE

Cobblestone Publishing Co., 30 Grove St., Suite C, Peterborough NH 03458-1454. (603)924-7209. **Fax:** (603)924-7380. **E-mail:** cfbakeriii@meganet.net. **Website:** www.cobblestonepub.com. **Contact:** Rosalie Baker and Charles Baker, co-editors; Lou Waryncia, editorial director; Ann Dillon, art director. Magazine published 9 times/year covering world history (East and West) through 1800 AD for 8 to 14-year-old kids. Articles must relate to the issue's theme. Lively, original approaches to the subject are the primary concerns of the editors in choosing material. Estab. 1990. Circ. 13,000.

   ○   "A query must consist of the following to be

considered: a brief cover letter stating subject and word length of the proposed article; a detailed one-page outline explaining the information to be presented in the article; a bibliography of materials the author intends to use in preparing the article; a SASE. Writers new to *Calliope* should send a writing sample with query. In all correspondence, please include your complete address as well as a telephone number where you can be reached. A writer may send as many queries for one issue as he or she wishes, but each query must have a separate cover letter, outline and bibliography as well as a SASE. Telephone and e-mail queries are not accepted. Handwritten queries will not be considered. Queries may be submitted at any time, but queries sent well in advance of deadline may not be answered for several months."

FICTION Middle readers and young adults: adventure, folktales/retold legends, plays, history, biographical fiction. Material must relate to forthcoming themes. Length: 800 words maximum. Pays 20-25¢/word

NONFICTION Needs essays, general interest, historical, how-to, crafts/woodworking, humor, interview, personal experience, photo feature, recipe, technical, travel. Query with writing sample, 1-page outline, bibliography, SASE. 700-800/feature articles; 300-600 words/supplemental nonfiction. Pays 20-25¢/word.

HOW TO CONTACT If interested, responds 5 months before publication date. Accepts queries by mail.

ILLUSTRATION Illustrations only: Send tearsheets, photocopies. Original work returned upon job's completion (upon written request).

PHOTOS Buys photos from freelancers. Uses b&w/color prints, 35mm transparencies and 300 dpi digital images. "If you have photographs pertaining to any upcoming theme, please contact the editor by mail or fax, or send them with your query. You may also send images on speculation." Model/property release preferred. Reviews b&w prints, color slides. Reviews photos with or without accompanying manuscript. Pays $15-100/b&w; $25-100/color. "Please note that fees for non-professional quality photographs are negotiated. Cover fees are set on an individual basis for one-time use, plus promotional use. All cover images are color. Prices set by museums, societies, stock photography houses, etc., are paid or negotiated. Pho-

tographs that are promotional in nature (e.g., from tourist agencies, organizations, special events, etc.) are usually submitted at no charge." Pays on publication. Credit line given.

TERMS Byline given. Pays on publication. Kill fee. 50% freelance written. Sample copy for $5.95, $2 shipping and handling, and 10x13 SASE. Guidelines available online.

TIPS "Authors are urged to use primary resources and up-to-date scholarly resources in their bibliography. In all correspondence, please include your complete address and a telephone number where you can be reached."

CARUS PUBLISHING COMPANY

70 E. Lake St., Suite 300, Chicago IL 60601. **Website:** www.cricketmag.com. "We do not accept e-mailed submissions. Manuscripts must be typed and accompanied by a SASE so that we may respond to your submission. Manuscripts without an accompanying SASE will not be considered. Unfortunately, we are unable to return mss. Please do not send us your only copy. When submitting poetry, please send us no more than 6 poems at a time. Be sure to include phone and e-mail contact information. Please allow us up to 8 months for careful consideration of your submission. No phone calls, please."

See listings for *Babybug, Cicada, Click, Cricket, Ladybug, Muse, Spider* and *ASK*. Carus Publishing owns Cobblestone Publishing, publisher of *AppleSeeds, Calliope, Cobblestone, Dig, Faces* and *Odyssey*.

CATHOLIC FORESTER

Catholic Order of Foresters, 355 Shuman Blvd., P.O. Box 3012, Naperville IL 60566-7012. (800)552-0145. **Fax:** (630)983-3384. **E-mail:** magazine@catholicforester.org. **Website:** www.catholicforester.org. **Contact:** Patricia Baron, associate editor; Danielle Marsh, art director. Quarterly magazine for members of the Catholic Order of Foresters, a fraternal insurance benefit society. "*Catholic Forester* is a quarterly magazine filled with product features, member stories, and articles affirming fraternalism, unity, friendship, and true Christian charity among members. Although a portion of each issue is devoted to the organization and its members, a few freelance pieces are published in most issues. These articles cover varied topics to create a balanced issue for the purpose of informing, educating, and entertaining our readers." Estab. 1883. Circ. 137,000.

FICTION Needs humorous, religious, inspirational. Length: 500-1,500 words. Pays 50¢/word.

NONFICTION Needs health and wellness, money management and budgeting, parenting and family life, interesting travels, insurance, nostalgia, humor, inspirational, religious. Will consider previously published work. Send complete ms by mail, fax, or e-mail. Rejected material will not be returned without accompanying SASE. Length: 500-1,500 words. Pays 50¢/word.

HOW TO CONTACT Editorial lead time 6 months. Responds in 3 months to mss.

ILLUSTRATION Buys 2-4 illustrations/issue. Uses color artwork only.

PHOTOS State availability. Negotiates payment individually.

TERMS Buys first North American serial rights for mss, one-time rights for art. Pays on acceptance. 20% freelance written. Sample copy for 9x12 SAE and 4 first-class stamps. Guidelines available online.

TIPS "Our audience includes a broad age spectrum, ranging from youth to seniors. A good children's story with a positive lesson or message would rate high on our list."

○ CHEMMATTERS

1155 16th St., NW, Washington DC 20036. (202)872-6164. **Fax:** (202)833-7732. **E-mail:** chemmatters@acs.org. **Website:** www.acs.org/chemmatters. **Contact:** Pat Pages, editor; Cornithia Harris, art director. Covers content found in a standard high school chemistry textbook. Estab. 1983.

NONFICTION Query with published clips. Pays $500-1,000 for article. Additional payment for ms/illustration packages and for photos accompanying articles.

HOW TO CONTACT Responds to queries/mss in 2 weeks. Publishes ms 6 months after acceptance. Accepts queries by mail, e-mail.

ILLUSTRATION Buys 3 illustrations/issue; 12 illustrations/year. Uses color artwork only. Works on assignment only. Reviews ms/illustration packages from artists. Query. Illustrations only: Query with promo sheet, résumé. Responds in 2 weeks. Samples returned with SASE; samples not filed. Credit line given.

PHOTOS Looking for photos of high school students engaged in science-related activities. Model/property release required; captions required. Uses color prints, but prefers high-resolution PDFs. Query with samples. Responds in 2 weeks.

TERMS Minimally buys first North American serial rights, but prefers to buy all rights, reprint rights, electronic rights for mss. Buys all rights for artwork; nonexclusive first rights for photos. Pays on acceptance. Sample copies free for 10×13 SASE and 3 first-class stamps. Writers' guidelines free for SASE (available as e-mail attachment upon request).

TIPS "Be aware of the content covered in a standard high school chemistry textbook. Choose themes and topics that are timely, interesting, fun, *and* that relate to the content and concepts of the first-year chemistry course. Articles should describe real people involved with real science. Best articles feature young people making a difference or solving a problem."

CICADA MAGAZINE

Cricket Magazine Group, 70 E. Lake St., Suite 300, Chicago IL 60601. (312)701-1720. **Fax:** (312)701-1728. **E-mail:** dvetter@caruspub.com. **Website:** www.cicadamag.com. **Contact:** Marianne Carus, editor-in-chief; Deborah Vetter, executive editor; John Sandford, art director. Bimonthly literary magazine for ages 14 and up. Publishes original short stories, poems, and first-person essays written for teens and young adults. *Cicada* publishes fiction and poetry with a genuine teen sensibility, aimed at the high school and college-age market. The editors are looking for stories and poems that are thought-provoking but entertaining. Estab. 1998. Circ. 10,000.

FICTION Young adults: adventure, contemporary, fantasy, historical, humor/satire, multicultural, nature/environment, romance, science fiction, sports, suspense/mystery, novellas (1/issue). Buys up to 42 mss/year. The main protagonist should be at least 14 and preferably older. Stories should have a genuine teen sensibility and be aimed at readers in high school or college. Length: 5,000 words maximum (up to 15,000 words/novellas). Pays up to 25¢/word.

NONFICTION Needs essays, personal experience. book reviews. Young adults: first-person coming-of-age experiences that are relevant to teens and young adults (example: life in the Peace Corps). Buys up to 6 mss/year. Submit complete ms, SASE. Length: 5,000 words maximum; 300-500 words/book reviews. Pays up to 25¢/word.

POETRY Reviews serious, humorous, free verse, rhyming (if done well) poetry. Limit submissions to 5 poems. Length: 25 lines maximum. Pays up to $3/line on publication.

HOW TO CONTACT Responds in 2 months to mss.

ILLUSTRATION Buys 20 illustrations/issue; 120 illustrations/year. Uses color artwork for cover; b&w for interior. Works on assignment only. Reviews ms/illustration packages from artists. "To submit samples, e-mail a link to your online portfolio to: dvetter@cicadamag.com. You may also e-mail a sample up to a maximum attachment size of 50 KB. We will keep your samples on file and contact you if we find an assignment that suits your style."

PHOTOS Wants documentary photos (clear shots that illustrate specific artifacts, persons, locations, phenomena, etc., cited in the text) and "art" shots of teens in photo montage/lighting effects, etc. Send photocopies/tearsheets of artwork.

TERMS Byline given. Pays on publication. 80% freelance written. Guidelines available online.

TIPS "Quality writing, good literary style, genuine teen sensibility, depth, humor, good character development, avoidance of stereotypes. Read several issues to familarize yourself with our style."

COBBLESTONE

A Division of Carus Publishing, 30 Grove St., Suite C, Peterborough NH 03458. (800)821-0115. **Fax:** (603)924-7380. **E-mail:** customerservice@caruspub.com. **Website:** www.cobblestonepub.com. Covers material for ages 9-14. "We are interested in articles of historical accuracy and lively, original approaches to the subject at hand. Our magazine is aimed at youths from ages 9 to 14. Writers are encouraged to study recent *Cobblestone* back issues for content and style. (Sample issues are available for $6.95 plus $2.00 shipping and handling. Sample issues will not be sent without prepayment.) All material must relate to the theme of a specific upcoming issue in order to be considered. To be considered, a query must accompany each individual idea (however, you can mail them all together) and must include the following: a brief cover letter stating the subject and word length of the proposed article, a detailed one-page outline explaining the information to be presented in the article, an extensive bibliography of materials the author intends to use in preparing the article, a SASE. Authors are urged to use primary resources and up-to-date scholarly resources in their bibliography. Writers new to *Cobblestone* should send a writing sample with the query. If you would like to know if your query has been received, please also include a stamped postcard that requests acknowledgment of receipt. In all correspondence, please include your complete address as well as a telephone number where you can be reached. A writer may send as many queries for one issue as he or she wishes, but each query must have a separate cover letter, outline, bibliography, and SASE. All queries must be typed. Please do not send unsolicited mss—queries only! Prefers to work with published/established writers. Each issue presents a particular theme, making it exciting as well as informative. Half of all subscriptions are for schools. All material must relate to monthly theme." Circ. 15,000.

◑ "*Cobblestone* stands apart from other children's magazines by offering a solid look at one subject and stressing strong editorial content, color photographs throughout, and original illustrations." *Cobblestone* themes and deadlines are available on website or with SASE."

FICTION Needs adventure, historical, biographical, retold legends, folktales, multicultural. Query. Length: 800 words maximum. Pays 20-25¢/word.

NONFICTION Needs historical, humor, interview, personal experience, photo feature, travel, crafts, recipes, activities. Query with writing sample, 1-page outline, bibliography, SASE. 800 words/feature articles; 300-600 words/supplemental nonfiction; up to 700 words maximum/activities. Pays 20-25¢/word.

POETRY Serious and light verse considered. Must have clear, objective imagery. 100 lines maximum. Pays on an individual basis. Acquires all rights.

HOW TO CONTACT Accepts queries by mail, fax.

ILLUSTRATION Reviews ms/illustration packages from artists. Query. Illustrations only: Send photocopies, tearsheets, or other nonreturnable samples. "Illustrators should consult issues of *Cobblestone* to familiarize themselves with our needs." Responds to art samples in 1 month. Samples are not returned; samples filed. Original artwork returned at job's completion (upon written request). Credit line given. Illustrators: "Submit color samples, not too juvenile. Study past issues to know what we look for. The illustration we use is generally for stories, recipes and activities."

PHOTOS Captions, identification of subjects required, model release. Reviews contact sheets, transparencies, prints. Pays on publication. Credit line given. Pays $15-100/b&w; $25-100/color. "Please note that fees for non-professional quality photographs are negotiated."

TERMS Byline given. Pays on publication. Offers 50% kill fee. 50% freelance written. Guidelines available on website or with SASE; sample copy for $6.95, $2 shipping/handling, 10x13 SASE.

TIPS "Review theme lists and past issues to see what we're looking for."

CRICKET

Carus Publishing Co., 700 E. Lake St., Suite 300, Chicago IL 60601. (312)701-1720, ext. 10. **Website:** www.cricketmag.com. **Contact:** Marianne Carus, editor-in-chief; Lonnie Plecha, executive editor; Karen Kohn, senior art director. Monthly magazine for children ages 9-14. "*Cricket* is looking for more fiction and nonfiction for the older end of its 9-14 age range, as well as contemporary stories set in other countries. It also seeks humorous stories and mysteries (not detective spoofs), fantasy and original fairy tales, stand-alone excerpts from unpublished novels, and well-written/researched science articles." Estab. 1973. Circ. 73,000.

FICTION Middle readers, young adults/teens: contemporary, fantasy, folk and fairy tales, history, humorous, science fiction, suspense/mystery. Buys 70 mss/year. Recently published work by Aaron Shepard, Arnold Adoff and Nancy Springer. No didactic, sex, religious, or horror stories. Submit complete ms. Length: 200-2,000 words. Pays 25¢/word maximum, and 6 contributor's copies; $2.50 charge for extras.

NONFICTION Middle readers, young adults/teens: adventure, architecture, archaeology, biography, foreign culture, games/puzzles, geography, natural history, science and technology, social science, sports, travel. Multicultural needs include articles on customs and cultures. Requests bibliography with submissions. Buys 30 mss/year. Submit complete ms, SASE. Length: 200-1,500 words. Pays 25¢/word maximum.

POETRY Reviews poems. Limit submission to 5 poems or less. Serious, humorous, nonsense rhymes. 50 lines maximum. Pays $3/line maximum.

HOW TO CONTACT Responds in 4-6 months to mss. Accepts queries by mail.

ILLUSTRATION Buys 22 illustrations (7 separate commissions)/issue; 198 illustrations/year. Preferred theme for style: "stylized realism; strong people, especially kids; good action illustration; whimsical and humorous. All media, generally full color." Reviews ms/illustration packages from artists, "but reserves option to re-illustrate." Send complete ms with sample and query. Illustrations only: Provide link to website or tearsheets and good quality photocopies to be kept on file. SASE required for response/return of samples.

PHOTOS Purchases photos with accompanying ms only. Model/property releases required. Uses 300 dpi digital files, color glossy prints. Commissions all art separately from the text. Tearsheets/photocopies of both color and b&w work are considered. Accepts artwork done in pencil, pen and ink, watercolor, acrylic, oil, pastels, scratchboard, and woodcut. Does not want work that is overly caricatured or cartoony. It is especially helpful to see pieces showing young people, animals, action scenes, and several scenes from a narrative showing a character in different situations and emotional states.

TERMS Byline given. Pays on publication. Guidelines available online.

TIPS Writers: "Read copies of back issues and current issues. Adhere to specified word limits. Would currently like to see more fantasy and science fiction." Illustrators: "Send only your best work and be able to reproduce that quality in assignments. Put name and address on *all* samples. Know a publication before you submit."

DIG

30 Grove St., Suite C, Peterborough NH 03450. (603)924-7209. **Fax:** (603)924-7380. **E-mail:** cfbakeriii@meganet.net. **Website:** www.cobblestonepub.com. **Contact:** Rosalie Baker, editor; Lou Waryncia, editorial director; Ann Dillon, art director. An archaeology magazine for kids ages 8-14. Publishes entertaining and educational stories about discoveries, artifacts, archaeologists. Estab. 1999.

Dig was purchased by Cobblestone Publishing, a division of Carus Publishing.

FICTION Query. Guidelines available online. Multiple queries accepted, may not be answered for many months.

NONFICTION Query. "A query must consist of all of the following to be considered: a brief cover letter stating the subject and word length of the proposed article, a detailed one-page outline explaining the information to be presented in the article, a bibliography of materials the author intends to use in preparing the article, and a SASE. Writers new to *Dig* should send a writing sample with query." Multiple queries accepted, may not be answered for many months.

ILLUSTRATION Buys 10-15 illustrations/issue; 60-75 illustrations/year. Prefers color artwork. Works on assignment only. Reviews ms/illustration packages from artists. Query. Illustrations only: Query with samples. Arrange portfolio review. Send tearsheets. Responds in 2 months only if interested. Samples not returned; samples filed. Credit line given.

PHOTOS Uses anything related to archaeology, history, artifacts, and current archaeological events that relate to kids. Uses color prints and 35mm transparencies and 300 dpi digital images. Provide résumé, promotional literature or tearsheets to be kept on file. Responds only if interested.

TERMS Buys all rights for mss. Buys one-time rights for photos. Pays on publication.

TIPS "We are looking for writers who can communicate archaeological concepts in a conversational, interesting, informative and *accurate* style for kids. Writers should have some idea where photography can be located to support their articles."

DRAMATICS MAGAZINE

Educational Theatre Association, 2343 Auburn Ave., Cincinnati OH 45219. (513)421-3900. **E-mail:** dcorathers@schooltheatre.org. **Website:** www.edta. org. **Contact:** Don Corathers, editor. "*Dramatics* is for students (mainly high school age) and teachers of theater. Mix includes how-to (tech theater, acting, directing, etc.), informational, interview, photo feature, humorous, profile, technical. We want our student readers to grow as theater artists and become a more discerning and appreciative audience. Material is directed to both theater students and their teachers, with strong student slant." Pays $100-500 for plays; $50-500 for articles; up to $100 for illustrations. Estab. 1929. Circ. 35,000.

FICTION Young adults—drama (one-act and full-length plays). "We prefer unpublished scripts that have been produced at least once." Does not want to see plays that show no understanding of the conventions of the theater. No plays for children, no Christmas or didactic "message" plays. Submit complete ms. Buys 5-9 plays/year. Emerging playwrights have better chances with résumé of credits. Length: 750-3,000 words.

NONFICTION Young adults: arts/crafts, careers, how-to, interview/profile, multicultural (all theater-related). "We try to portray the theater community in all its diversity." Submit complete ms. Length: 750-3,000 words.

HOW TO CONTACT Publishes ms 3 months after acceptance.

ILLUSTRATION Buys 0-2 illustrations/year. Works on assignment only. Arrange portfolio review; send résumé, promo sheets and tearsheets. Responds only if interested. Samples returned with SASE; samples not filed. Credit line given.

PHOTOS Buys photos with accompanying ms only. Looking for "good-quality production or candid photography to accompany article. We very occasionally publish photo essays." Model/property release and captions required. Prefers hi-res JPG files. Will consider prints or transparencies. Query with résumé of credits. Responds only if interested.

TERMS Byline given. Pays on acceptance. Sample copy available for 9x12 SASE with 4-ounce first-class postage. Guidelines available for SASE.

TIPS "Obtain our writers' guidelines and look at recent back issues. The best way to break in is to know our audience—drama students, teachers, and others interested in theater—and write for them. Writers who have some practical experience in theater, especially in technical areas, have an advantage, but we'll work with anybody who has a good idea. Some freelancers have become regular contributors."

⊜ EXPLORE

Website: www.pearsonplaces.com.au/places/magazines_place/explore.aspx.

> ◌ As of 2012, *Explore* is no longer accompanied by a print magazine. *Explore* continues to publish articles on its website.

NONFICTION Young readers, middle readers: animal, arts/crafts, biography, careers, cooking, health, history, hobbies, how-to, interview/profile, math, multicultural, nature/environment, problem-solving, science, social issues, sports, travel. Average word length: 200-600. Byline given.

HOW TO CONTACT Responds to queries in 1 month; mss in 3 months.

TERMS Pays on publication.

TIPS *Explore* is a theme-based publication. Check the website to see upcoming themes and deadlines.

FACES

Cobblestone Publishing, 30 Grove St., Suite C, Peterborough NH 03458. (603)924-7209; (800)821-0115. **Fax:** (603)924-7380. **E-mail:** customerservice@caruspub.com; facesmag@yahoo.com **Website:** www.cobblestonepub.com. "Published monthly throughout the year, *Faces* covers world culture for ages 9-14. It stands apart from other children's magazines by offering a solid look at one subject and stressing strong editorial content, color photographs throughout, and original illustrations. *Faces* offers an equal balance of feature articles and activities, as well as folktales and legends." Estab. 1984. Circ. 15,000.

FICTION Needs ethnic, historical, retold legends/folktales, original plays. Length: 800 words maximum. Pays 20-25¢/word.

NONFICTION Needs historical, humor, interview, personal experience, photo feature, travel, recipes, activities, crafts. Query with writing sample, 1-page outline, bibliography, SASE. Length: 800 words/feature articles; 300-600/supplemental nonfiction; up to 700 words/activities. Pays 20-25¢/word.

HOW TO CONTACT Accepts queries by mail, e-mail (facesmag@yahoo.com).

ILLUSTRATION Buys 3 illustrations/issue; buys 27 illustrations/year. Preferred theme or style: Material that is meticulously researched (most articles are written by professional anthropologists); simple, direct style preferred, but not too juvenile. Works on assignment only. Roughs required. Reviews ms/illustration packages from artists. Illustrations only: Send samples of b&w work. "Illustrators should consult issues of *Faces* to familiarize themselves with our needs. The illustration we use is generally for retold legends, recipes and activities." Responds to art samples only if interested. Samples returned with SASE. Original artwork returned at job's completion (upon written request). Credit line given.

PHOTOS Wants photos relating to forthcoming themes. "Contact the editor by mail or fax, or send photos with your query. You may also send images on speculation." Captions, identification of subjects, model releases required. Reviews contact sheets, transparencies, prints. Pays $15-100/b&w; $25-100/color; cover fees are negotiated.

TERMS Buys all rights for mss; one-time rights for photos. Byline given. Pays on publication. Offers 50% kill fee. 90-100% freelance written. Sample copy for

$6.95, $2 shipping and handling, 10x13 SASE. Guidelines with SASE or online.

TIPS "Writers are encouraged to study past issues of the magazine to become familiar with our style and content. Writers with anthropological and/or travel experience are particularly encouraged; *Faces* is about world cultures. All feature articles, recipes and activities are freelance contributions. Study past issues to know what we look for."

THE FRIEND MAGAZINE

The Church of Jesus Christ of Latter-day Saints, 50 E. North Temple St., Salt Lake City UT 84150. (801)240-2210. **E-mail:** friend@ldschurch.org. **Website:** www.lds.org. **Contact:** Mark Robison, art director. Monthly magazine for 3-12 year olds. Estab. 1971. Circ. 275,000.

NONFICTION Needs historical, humor, inspirational, religious, adventure, ethnic, nature, family- and gospel-oriented puzzles, games, and cartoons. Submit complete ms. Length: 600 words maximum.

POETRY "We are looking for easy-to-illustrate poems with catchy cadences. Poems should convey a sense of joy and reflect gospel teachings. Also brief poems that will appeal to preschoolers." Length: 20 lines maximum.

HOW TO CONTACT Responds in 2 months to mss.

ILLUSTRATION Illustrations only: Query with samples; arrange personal interview to show portfolio; provide résumé and tearsheets for files.

PHOTOS "We are looking for short photo essays (200–300 words) about individual children. These stories should focus on something interesting the child has done, such as a hobby or service project. These stories should be written in first person from the child's point of view. Please send 6–10 usable photos that illustrate the story. If your story is chosen for publication, we may contact you to request additional photos."

TERMS Pays on acceptance. Buys all rights for mss. Pays $100-150 (400 words and up) for stories; $30 for poems; $20 minimum for activities and games. Contributors are encouraged to send for sample copy for $1.50, 9×12 SASE and 4 first class stamps. Free writers' guidelines. Buys all rights for mss. Pays on acceptance.

TIPS "*The Friend* is published by The Church of Jesus Christ of Latter-day Saints for boys and girls up to 11 years of age. All submissions are carefully read by the *Friend* staff, and those not accepted are returned within 2 months for SASE. Submit seasonal material at least one year in advance. Query letters and simultaneous submissions are not encouraged. Authors may request rights to have their work reprinted after their manuscript is published."

FUN FOR KIDZ

P.O. Box 227, Bluffton OH 45817-0227. (419)358-4610. **Fax:** (419)358-8020. **Website:** www.funforkidz.com. **Contact:** Marilyn Edwards, articles editor. *"Fun for Kidz* is a magazine created for boys and girls ages 5-14, with youngsters 8, 9, and 10 the specific target age. The magazine is designed as an activity publication to be enjoyed by both boys and girls on the alternative months of *Hopscotch* and *Boys' Quest* magazines." Estab. 2002.

> *Fun for Kidz* is theme oriented. Send SASE for theme list and writers' guidelines or visit www. funforkidz.com and click on "Writers" at the bottom of the homepage.

FICTION Picture-oriented material, young readers, middle readers: adventure, animal, history, humorous, problem-solving, multicultural, nature/environment, sports. Length: 300-700 words.

NONFICTION Picture-oriented material, young readers, middle readers: animal, arts/crafts, cooking, games/puzzles, history, hobbies, how-to, humorous, problem-solving, sports, carpentry projects. Submit complete ms. Length: 300-700 words.

POETRY Pays $10 minimum.

HOW TO CONTACT Responds in 2 weeks to queries; 6 weeks to mss. Accepts queries by mail.

ILLUSTRATION Works on assignment mostly. "We are anxious to find artists capable of illustrating stories and features. Our inside art is pen and ink." Query with samples. Samples kept on file.

PHOTOS "We use a number of b&w photos inside the magazine; most support the articles used."

TERMS Buys first North American serial rights. Byline given. Pays on acceptance.

TIPS "Our point of view is that every child deserves the right to be a child for a number of years before he or she becomes a young adult. As a result, *Fun for Kidz* looks for activities that deal with timeless topics, such as pets, nature, hobbies, science, games, sports, careers, simple cooking, and anything else likely to interest a child."

GIRLS' LIFE

Monarch Publishing, 4529 Harford Rd., Baltimore MD 21214. (410)426-9600. **Fax:** (410)254-0991. **E-mail:** jessica@girlslife.com. **Website:** www.girlslife.

com. **Contact:** Karen Bokram, founding editor; Jessica D'Argenio Waller, senior editor. Bimonthly magazine covering girls ages 9-15. Estab. 1994. Circ. 400,000.

FICTION "We accept short fiction. They should be stand-alone stories and are generally 2,500-3,500 words." Query by mail or e-mail with detailed story idea. Submit complete ms on spec only.

NONFICTION Needs book excerpts, essays, general interest, how-to, humor, inspirational, interview, new product, travel. "Features and articles should speak to young women ages 10-15 looking for new ideas about relationships, family, friends, school, etc. with fresh, savvy advice. Front-of-the-book columns and quizzes are a good place to start." Query by mail or e-mail with published clips. Submit complete ms on spec only. Length: 700-2,000 words. Pays $350/regular column; $500/feature.

HOW TO CONTACT Editorial lead time 4 months. Responds in 3 months to queries. Publishes ms an average of 3 months after acceptance. Accepts queries by mail, e-mail.

PHOTOS State availability with submission if applicable. Reviews contact sheets, negatives, transparencies. Negotiates payment individually. Captions, identification of subjects, model releases required.

TERMS Buys all rights. Byline given. Pays on publication. Sample copy for $5 or online. Guidelines available online.

TIPS "Send thought-out queries with published writing samples and detailed résumé. Have fresh ideas and a voice that speaks to our audience—not down to them. And check out a copy of the magazine or visit girlslife.com before submitting."

GREEN TEACHER

Green Teacher, 95 Robert St., Toronto ON M5S 2K5, Canada. (416)960-1244. **Fax:** (416)925-3474. **E-mail:** info@greenteacher.com. **Website:** www.greenteacher.com. **Contact:** Gail Littlejohn, article editor; Tim Grant, photo editor. *"Green Teacher* is a magazine that helps youth educators enhance environmental and global education inside and outside of schools." Estab. 1991. Circ. 15,000.

NONFICTION Multicultural, nature, environment. Query. Length: 750-2,500 words.

HOW TO CONTACT Responds to queries in 1 month. Publishes ms 8 months after acceptance. Accepts queries by mail, e-mail.

ILLUSTRATION Buys 3 illustrations/issue from free-lancers; 10 illustrations/year from freelancers. Black & white artwork only. Works on assignment only. Reviews ms/illustration packages from artists. Query with samples; tearsheets. Responds only if interested. Samples not returned. Samples filed. Credit line given.

PHOTOS Purchases photos both separately and with accompanying mss. "Activity photos, environmental photos." Uses b&w prints. Query with samples. Responds only of interested.

TERMS Pays on acceptance.

GUIDE

55 W. Oak Ridge Dr., Hagerstown MD 21740. (301)393-4037. **Fax:** (301)393-4055. **E-mail:** guide@rhpa.org. **Website:** www.guidemagazine.org. **Contact:** Randy Fishell, editor; Brandon Reese, designer. "*Guide* is a Christian story magazine for young people ages 10-14. The 32-page, 4-color publication is published weekly by the Review and Herald Publishing Association. Our mission is to show readers, through stories that illustrate Bible truth, how to walk with God now and forever." Estab. 1953.

NONFICTION "Each issue includes 3-4 true stories. *Guide* does not publish fiction, poetry, or articles (devotionals, how-to, profiles, etc.). However, we sometimes accept quizzes and other unique nonstory formats. Each piece should include a clear spiritual element." Length: 1,000-1,200 words. Pays 7-10¢/word.

HOW TO CONTACT Responds in 6 weeks to mss. Accepts queries by mail, e-mail.

TERMS Byline given. Pays on acceptance. Sample copy free with 6x9 SAE and 2 first-class stamps. Guidelines available on website.

TIPS "Children's magazines want mystery, action, discovery, suspense, and humor—no matter what the topic. For us, truth is stronger than fiction."

HIGHLIGHTS FOR CHILDREN

803 Church St., Honesdale PA 18431. (570)253-1080. **Fax:** (570)251-7847. **Website:** www.highlights.com. **Contact:** Christine French Cully, editor-in-chief; Cindy Faber Smith, art director. Monthly magazine for children up to age 12. "This book of wholesome fun is dedicated to helping children grow in basic skills and knowledge, in creativeness, in ability to think and reason, in sensitivity to others, in high ideals, and in worthy ways of living—for children are the world's most important people. We publish stories for beginning and advanced readers. Up to 500 words for beginners

(ages 3-7), up to 800 words for advanced (ages 8-12)." Estab. 1946. Circ. 2.5 million.

FICTION Meaningful stories appealing to both girls and boys, up to age 12. Vivid, full of action. Engaging plot, strong characterization, lively language. Prefers stories in which a child protagonist solves a dilemma through his or her own resources. Seeks stories that the child ages 8-12 will eagerly read, and the child ages 2-7 will like to hear when read aloud (500-800 words). Stories require interesting plots and a number of illustration possiblities. Also needs rebuses (picture stories 120 words or under), stories with urban settings, stories for beginning readers (100-500 words), sports and humorous stories, adventures, holiday stories and mysteries. "We also would like to see more material of 1-page length (300 words), both fiction and factual." Needs adventure, fantasy, historical, humorous, animal, contemporary, folktales, multicultural, problem-solving, sports. No war, crime or violence. Send complete ms. Pays $150 minimum plus 2 contributor's copies.

NONFICTION "Generally we prefer to see a manuscript rather than a query. However, we will review queries regarding nonfiction." Length: 800 words maximum. Pays $25 for craft ideas and puzzles; $25 for fingerplays; $150 and up for articles.

POETRY Lines/poem: 16 maximum ("most poems are shorter"). Considers simultaneous submissions ("please indicate"); no previously published poetry. No e-mail submissions. "Submit typed manuscript with very brief cover letter."

HOW TO CONTACT Accepts queries by mail. Responds in 2 months. Occasionally comments on submissions "if manusript has merit or author seems to have potential for our market."

ILLUSTRATION Buys 25-30 illustrations/issue. Preferred theme or style: Realistic, some stylization. Works on assignment only. Reviews ms/illustration packages from artists. Illustrations only: Photocopies, promo sheet, tearsheets, or slides. Résumé optional. Portfolio only if requested. Responds to art samples in 2 months. Samples returned with SASE; samples filed. Credit line given.

PHOTOS Reviews color 35mm slides, photos, or electronic files. Photo essays: "5-8 images that collectively tell a story. Brief captions should be supplied."

TERMS Always sends prepublication galleys. Pays 2 contributor's copies; "money varies." Acquires all rights. Pays on acceptance. 80% freelance written.

Sample copy free. Guidelines available for SASE or on website in "About Us" area.

TIPS "Know the magazine's style before submitting. Send for guidelines and sample issue if necessary." Writers: "At *Highlights* we're paying closer attention to acquiring more nonfiction for young readers than we have in the past." Illustrators: "Fresh, imaginative work encouraged. Flexibility in working relationships a plus. Illustrators presenting their work need not confine themselves to just children's illustrations as long as work can translate to our needs. We also use animal illustrations, real and imaginary. We need crafts, puzzles and any activity that will stimulate children mentally and creatively. We are always looking for imaginative cover subjects. Know our publication's standards and content by reading sample issues, not just the guidelines. Avoid tired themes, or put a fresh twist on an old theme so that its style is fun and lively. We'd like to see stories with subtle messages, but the fun of the story should come first. Write what inspires you, not what you think the market needs. We are pleased that many authors of children's literature report that their first published work was in the pages of *Highlights*. It is not our policy to consider fiction on the strength of the reputation of the author. We judge each submission on its own merits. With factual material, however, we do prefer that writers be authorities in their field or people with first-hand experience. In this manner we can avoid the encyclopedic article that merely restates information readily available elsewhere. We don't make assignments. Query with simple letter to establish whether the nonfiction subject is likely to be of interest. A beginning writer should first become familiar with the type of material that *Highlights* publishes. Include special qualifications, if any, of author. Write for the child, not the editor. Write in a voice that children understand and relate to. Speak to today's kids, avoiding didactic, overt messages. Even though our general principles haven't changed over the years, we are contemporary in our approach to issues. Avoid worn themes."

HIGHLIGHTS HIGH FIVE

807 Church St., Honesdale PA 18431. **Fax:** (570)251-7847. **Website:** www.highlights.com/high-five. **Contact:** Kathleen Hayes, editor. "*Highlights High Five* was created to help you encourage your young child's development—and have fun together at the same time. Based on sound educational principles and widely ac-cepted child-development theories, each monthly issue brings a 40-page, high-quality mix of read-aloud stories and age appropriate activities that will help you set your child firmly on the path to becoming a lifelong learner. Stories for younger readers should have 170 words or less and should appeal to children ages 2-6." Estab. 2009.

HOW TO CONTACT At this time, accepts very few mss. Most articles are commissioned or written in-house. *Highlights Magazine* does accept freelance writing. See guidelines on the website. Accepts queries by mail.

TIPS "Writers may find it helpful to read several issues of *High Five*."

HOPSCOTCH

P.O. Box 227, Bluffton OH 45817. (419)358-4610. **Fax:** (419)358-8020. **E-mail:** customerservice@funforkidz.com. **Website:** www.hopscotchmagazine.com. **Contact:** Marilyn Edwards, editor. "For girls from ages 5-14, featuring traditional subjects—pets, games, hobbies, nature, science, sports, etc.—with an emphasis on articles that show girls actively involved in unusual and/or worthwhile activities." Estab. 1989. Circ. 14,000.

FICTION Needs picture-oriented material, young readers, middle readers: adventure, animal, history, humorous, nature/environment, sports, suspense/mystery. Does not want to see stories dealing with dating, sex, fashion, hard rock music. Submit complete ms. Length: 500 words maximum.

NONFICTION Needs picture-oriented material, young readers, middle readers: animal, arts/crafts, biography, cooking, games/puzzles, geography, hobbies, how-to, humorous, math, nature/environment, science. "Need more nonfiction with quality photos about a *Hopscotch*-age girl involved in a worthwhile activity." Query or submit complete ms. Length: 400-700 words.

POETRY Needs poems that complement the issue theme.

HOW TO CONTACT Responds in 2 weeks to queries; 5 weeks to mss.

ILLUSTRATION Buys approximately 10 illustrations/issue; buys 60-70 articles/year. "Generally, the illustrations are assigned after we have purchased a piece (usually fiction). Occasionally, we will use a painting—in any given medium—for the cover, and these are usually seasonal." Uses b&w artwork only for inside; color for cover. Reviews ms/illustration packages from artists. Query first or send complete ms with final art. Illustrations only: Send résumé, portfolio, client list and tearsheets. Responds to art samples only if interested and SASE in 1 month. Samples returned with SASE. Credit line given.

PHOTOS Purchases photos with accompanying ms only, except for cover photo. Looking for photos to accompany articles. Model/property releases required. Uses 5×7, b&w prints; 35mm transparencies. Black & white photos should go with ms. Should show girl or girls ages 5-14.

TERMS Byline given. Pays on publication.

TIPS "Remember we publish only 6 issues a year, which means our editorial needs are extremely limited. Please look at our guidelines and our magazine. Remember, we use far more nonfiction than fiction. Guidelines and current theme list can be downloaded from our website. If decent photos accompany the piece, it stands an even better chance of being accepted. We believe it is the responsibility of the contributor to come up with photos. Please remember, our readers are 5-14 years—most are 8-10—and your text should reflect that. Many magazines try to entertain first and educate second. We try to do the reverse. Our magazine is more simplistic, like a book to be read from cover to cover. We are looking for wholesome, non-dated material."

☺ HORSEPOWER

P.O. Box 670, Aurora ON L4G 4J9, Canada. 800)505-7428. **Fax:** (905)841-1530. **E-mail:** info@horse-canada.com. **Website:** www.horse-canada.com. **Contact:** Amy Harris, managing editor. Bimonthly 16-page magazine, bound into *Horse-Canada*, a bimonthly family horse magazine. "*Horsepower* offers how-to articles and stories relating to horse care for kids ages 6-16, with a focus on safety." Estab. 1988. Circ. 17,000.

☺ *Horsepower no longer accepts fiction.*

NONFICTION Middle readers, young adults: arts/crafts, biography, careers, fashion, games/puzzles, health, history, hobbies, how-to, humorous, interview/profile, problem-solving, travel. Buys 6-10 mss/year. Submit complete ms. Length: 500-1,200 words.

HOW TO CONTACT Responds to mss in 3 months.

ILLUSTRATION Buys 3 illustrations/year. Reviews ms/illustration packages from artists. Contact: Editor. Query with samples. Responds only if interested.

Samples returned with SASE; samples kept on file. Credit line given.

PHOTOS Looks for photos of kids and horses, instructional/educational, relating to riding or horse care. Uses color matte or glossy prints. Query with samples. Responds only if interested. Accepts TIFF or JPEG, 300 dpi, disk or e-mail. Children on horseback must be wearing riding helmets or photos cannot be published.

TERMS Buys one-time rights for mss. Pays on publication. Guidelines available for SASE.

TIPS "Articles must be easy to understand, yet detailed and accurate. How-to or other educational features must be written by, or in conjunction with, a riding/teaching professional. Note: Preference will be given to Canadian writers and photographers due to Canadian content laws. Non-Canadian contributors accepted on a very limited basis."

HUNGER MOUNTAIN

Vermont College of Fine Arts, 36 College St., Montpelier VT 05602. (802)828-8517. **E-mail:** hungermtn@vermontcollege.edu. **Website:** www.hungermtn.org. Monthly online publication and annual perfect-bound journal covering high quality fiction, poetry, creative nonfiction, craft essays, writing for children, and artwork. Accepts high quality work from unknown, emerging or successful writers. No genre fiction, drama or academic articles, please. Estab. 2002.

FICTION Needs adventure, high quality short stories and short shorts. No genre fiction, meaning science fiction, fantasy, horror, erotic, etc. Length: 10,000 words maximum. Pays $25-100.

NONFICTION Prose for children and young adults is acceptable. Payment varies.

POETRY No light verse, humor/quirky/catchy verse, greeting card verse. Submit at least 3 poems at a time.

HOW TO CONTACT Responds in 4 months to mss. Publishes ms an average of 1 year after acceptance. "Submit online or by mail. Please see www.hungermtn.org for complete guidelines before submitting."

PHOTOS Send photos. Reviews contact sheets, transparencies, prints, GIF/JPEG files. Slides preferred. Negotiates payment individually.

TERMS Buys first worldwide serial rights. Byline given. Pays on publication. No kill fee. Sample copy for $10. Writers' guidelines online.

TIPS "Manuscripts must be typed, prose double-spaced. No multiple-genre submissions. Fresh viewpoints and human interest are very important, as is originality. We are committed to publishing an outstanding journal of the arts. Do not send entire novels or short story collections. Do not send previously published work."

IMAGINATION CAFÉ

Imagination Café, P.O. Box 1536, Valparaiso IN 46384. (219)510-4467. **Email:** submissions@imagination-cafe.com; editor@imagination-cafe.com. **Website:** www.imagination-cafe.com. **Contact:** Rosanne Tolin, editor. "*Imagination Café* is dedicated to empowering kids and tweens by encouraging curiosity in the world around them, as well as exploration of their talents and aspirations. *Imagination Café*'s mission is to offer children tools to discover their passions by providing them with reliable information, resources and safe opportunities for self-expression. *Imagination Café* publishes general interest articles with an emphasis on career exploration for kids. There is also material on school, science, history, and sports. Plus, celebrity briefs, recipes, animals, and other general interest pieces." Estab. 2006.

FICTION Length: 1,000 words maximum. "Avoid the 'adult saves the day' trap. Kid protagonists only, please."

NONFICTION Prefers mss over queries. Guidelines available online.

TERMS Buys electronic and non-exclusive print rights.

TIPS "*Imagination Café* is not a beginner's market. Most of our contributors are published writers. Please study the website before submitting, and make sure your writing is clearly directed to a kid audience, no adults. That means informative, interesting text written in a clear, concise, even clever manner that suitable for the online reader. Have fun with it and be sure include web-friendly, relevant links and sidebars."

INSIGHT

The Review and Herald Publishing Association, 55 W. Oak Ridge Dr., Hagerstown MD 21740. (301)393-4038. **E-mail:** insight@rhpa.org. **Website:** www.insightmagazine.org. Weekly magazine covering spiritual life of teenagers. *Insight* publishes true dramatic stories, interviews, and community and mission service features that relate directly to the lives of Christian teenagers, particularly those with a Seventh-day Adventist background. Estab. 1970. Circ. 16,000.

'Big Deal' appears in *Insight* often, covering a topic of importance to teens. Each feature contains: an opening story involving real teens (can be written in first-person), Scripture Picture (a sidebar that discusses what the Bible says about the topic) and another sidebar (optional) that adds more perspective and help.

NONFICTION Needs how-to, teen relationships and experiences, humor, interview, personal experience, photo feature, religious. Send complete ms. Length: 500-1,500 words. Pays $25-150 for assigned articles. Pays $25-125 for unsolicited articles.

HOW TO CONTACT Editorial lead time 6 months. Responds in 1 month to mss. Publishes ms an average of 4 months after acceptance. Accepts queries by mail, e-mail, fax.

PHOTOS State availability. Model releases required. Reviews contact sheets, negatives, transparencies, prints. Negotiates payment individually.

TERMS Buys first rights, buys second serial (reprint) rights. Byline given. Pays on publication. No kill fee. 80% freelance written Sample copy for $2 and #10 SASE. Guidelines available online.

TIPS "Skim two months of *Insight*. Write about your teen experiences. Use informed, contemporary style and vocabulary. Follow Jesus' life and example."

JACK AND JILL

U.S. Kids, 1100 Waterway Blvd., Indianapolis IN 46206-0567. (317)634-1100. **E-mail:** editor@saturdayeveningpost.com. **Website:** www.jackandjillmag.org. Bimonthly magazine published 6 times/year for children ages 8-12. "Write entertaining and imaginative stories for kids, not just about them. Writers should understand what is funny to kids, what's important to them, what excites them. Don't write from an adult 'kids are so cute' perspective. We're also looking for health and healthful lifestyle stories and articles, but don't be preachy." Estab. 1938. Circ. 200,000.

"Please do not send artwork. We prefer to work with profesional illustrators of our own choosing."

FICTION Young readers and middle readers: adventure, contemporary, folktales, health, history, humorous, nature, sports. Buys 30-35 mss/year. Submit complete ms. Queries not accepted. Length: 600-800 words. Pays 30¢/word.

NONFICTION Young readers, middle readers: animal, arts, crafts, cooking, games, puzzles, history, hobbies, how-to, humorous, interviews, profile, nature, science, sports. Buys 8-10 mss/year. Submit complete ms. Queries not accepted. Length: 700 words maximum. Pays 30¢/word.

POETRY Wants light-hearted poetry appropriate for the age group. Length: 30 lines maximum. Pays $25-50.

HOW TO CONTACT Manuscripts must be typewritten with contact information in upper right-hand corner of each page. SASE required. Responds to mss in 3 months. Publishes ms an average of 8 months after acceptance.

PHOTOS Does not purchase single photos. Buys photo features: 10 photos maximum. Buys high-quality photos that accompany ms. Captions and model releases required.

TERMS Buys all rights for mss; one-time rights for photos. Byline given. Pays on publication. 50% freelance written. Guidelines available online.

TIPS "We are constantly looking for new writers who can tell good stories with interesting slants—stories that are not full of out-dated and time-worn expressions. We like to see stories about kids who are smart and capable, but not sarcastic or smug. Problem-solving skills, personal responsibility, and integrity are good topics for us. Obtain current issues of the magazine and study them to determine our present needs and editorial style."

JUNIOR BASEBALL

(203)210-5726. **E-mail:** publisher@juniorbaseball. com. **Website:** www.juniorbaseball.com. **Contact:** Jim Beecher, publisher. Bimonthly magazine covering youth baseball. Focused on youth baseball players ages 7-17 (including high school) and their parents/coaches. Edited to various reading levels, depending upon age/skill level of feature. Estab. 1996. Circ. 20,000.

NONFICTION Needs how-to, skills, tips, features, how to play better baseball, etc.; interview, with major league players; only on assignment, personal experience, from coach or parent perspective. Query. Length: 500-1,000 words. Pays $50-100.

HOW TO CONTACT Editorial lead time 3 months. Responds in 2 weeks to queries; 1 month to mss. Publishes ms an average of 4 months after acceptance.

PHOTOS Photos can be e-mailed in 300 dpi JPEGs. State availability. Captions, identification of subjects required. Reviews 35mm transparencies, 3 x 5 prints. Offers $10-100/photo; negotiates payment individually.

TERMS Buys all rights. Byline given. Pays on publication. No kill fee. 25% freelance written. Sample copy for $5 and online.

TIPS "Must be well-versed in baseball. Have a child who is very involved in the sport, or have extensive hands-on experience in coaching baseball, at the youth, high school or higher level. We can always use accurate, authoritative skills information, and good photos to accompany is a big advantage. This magazine is read by experts. No fiction, poems, games, puzzles, etc." Does not want first-person articles about your child.

THE KERF

College of the Redwoods, 883 W. Washington Blvd., Crescent City CA 95531. (707) 476-4370. **E-mail:** ken-letko@redwoods.edu. **Website:** www.redwoods.edu/Departments/english/poets&writers/clm.htm. **Contact:** Ken Letko, editor. *The Kerf*, published annually in fall, features "poetry that speaks to the environment and humanity." Wants "poetry that exhibits an environmental consciousness." Considers poetry by children and teens. Has published poetry by Ruth Daigon, Alice D'Alessio, James Grabill, George Keithley, and Paul Willis. *The Kerf* is 54 pages, digest-sized, printed via Docutech, saddle-stapled, with CS2 coverstock. Receives about 1,000 poems/year, accepts up to 3%. Press run is 400 (150 shelf sales); 100 distributed free to contributors and writing centers. Sample: $5. Make checks payable to College of the Redwoods. Estab. 1995.

POETRY Submit up to 5 poems (7 pages maximum) at a time. No previously published poems or simultaneous submissions. Reads submissions January 15-March 31 only.

KEYS FOR KIDS

P.O. Box 1001, Grand Rapids MI 49501-1001. (616)647-4500. **Fax:** (616)647-4950. **E-mail:** hazel@cbhministries.org. **Website:** www.cbhministries.org. **Contact:** Hazel Marett, fiction editor. "CBH Ministries is an international Christian ministry based on the Gospel of Jesus Christ, which produces and distributes excellent media resources to evangelize and disciple kids and their families." Estab. 1982.

FICTION Buys 60 mss/year. Needs religious. "Tell a story (not a Bible story) with a spiritual application." Submit complete ms. Length: 400 words. Pays $25 for stories.

TERMS Buy reprint rights or first rights for mss. Pays on acceptance. Sample copy for 6x9 SAE and 3 first-class stamps. Guidelines for SASE.

TIPS "Be sure to follow guidelines after studying sample copy of the publication."

KIDZ CHAT

8805 Governor's Hill Dr., Suite 400, Cincinnati OH 45249. (513)931-4050. **Fax:** (877)867-5751. **E-mail:** mredford@standardpub.com. **Website:** www.standardpub.com. **Contact:** Marjorie Redford, editor. Circ. 55,000.

○ *Kidz Chat* has decided to reuse much of the material that was a part of the first publication cycle. They will not be sending out theme lists, sample copies or writers' guidelines or accepting any unsolicited material because of this policy.

◐ LADYBUG

Carus Publishing Co., 700 E. Lake St., Suite 300, Chicago IL 60601. (312)701-1720. **Website:** www.cricketmag.com. **Contact:** Marianne Carus, editor-in-chief; Suzanne Beck, managing art director. *LADYBUG,* published monthly, is a reading and listening magazine for young children (ages 2-6). "We look for quality literature and nonfiction." Subscription: $35.97/year (12 issues). Sample: $5; sample pages available on website. Estab. 1990. Circ. 125,000.

FICTION Picture-oriented material: adventure, animal, fantasy, folktales, humorous, multicultural, nature/environment, problem-solving, science fiction, sports, suspense/mystery. "Open to any easy fiction stories." Buys 50 mss/year. Submit complete ms, include SASE. Length: 800 words maximum. Pays 25¢/word ($25 minimum).

NONFICTION Picture-oriented material: activities, animal, arts/crafts, concept, cooking, humorous, math, nature/environment, problem-solving, science. Send complete ms, SASE. Length: 400 words maximum. Pays 25¢/word ($25 minimum).

POETRY Wants poetry that is "rhythmic, rhyming; serious, humorous, active." 20 lines maximum. Pays $3/line ($25 minimum).

HOW TO CONTACT Responds in 6 months to mss.

ILLUSTRATION Buys 12 illustrations/issue; 145 illustrations/year. Prefers "bright colors; all media, but uses watercolor and acrylics most often; same size as magazine is preferred but not required." To be considered for future assignments: Submit promo sheet, slides, tearsheets, color and b&w photocopies. Responds to art samples in 3 months. Submissions without SASE will be discarded.

PHOTOS Pays $500/spread; $250/page.

TERMS Byline given. Pays on publication. Guidelines available online.

TIPS "Reread manuscript before sending. Keep within specified word limits. Study back issues before submitting to learn about the types of material we're looking for. Writing style is paramount. We look for rich, evocative language and a sense of joy or wonder. Remember that you're writing for preschoolers—be age-appropriate, but not condescending or preachy. A story must hold enjoyment for both parent and child through repeated read-aloud sessions. Remember that people come in all colors, sizes, physical conditions, and have special needs. Be inclusive!"

LEADING EDGE

E-mail: editor@leadingedgemagazine.com; fiction@leadingedgemagazine.com; art@leadingedgemagazine.com **Website:** www.leadingedgemagazine.com. Semiannual magazine covering science fiction and fantasy. "We strive to encourage developing and established talent and provide high quality speculative fiction to our readers." Does not accept mss with sex, excessive violence, or profanity. "*Leading Edge* is a magazine dedicated to new and upcoming talent in the field of science fiction and fantasy." Has published fiction by Orson Scott Card, Brandon Sanderson and Dave Wolverton. Has published poetry by Michael Collings, Tracy Ray, Susan Spilecki and Bob Cook. Estab. 1980. Circ. 200.

○ Accepts unsolicited submissions. Does not accept simultaneous submissions.

FICTION Needs fantasy, science fiction. Send complete ms with cover letter and SASE. Include estimated word count. Length: 15,000 words maximum. Pays $10-50.

POETRY "Publishes 2-4 poems per issue. Poetry should reflect both literary value and popular appeal and should deal with science fiction- or fantasy-related themes." Submit 1 or more poems at a time. No e-mail submissions. Cover letter is preferred. Include name, address, phone number, length of poem, title, and type of poem at the top of each page. Please include SASE with every submission." Pays $10 for first 4 pages; $1.50/each subsequent page.

HOW TO CONTACT Responds in 2-4 months to mss. Publishes ms an average of 2-4 months after acceptance.

ILLUSTRATION Buys 24 illustrations/issue; 48 illustrations/year. Uses b&w artwork only. Works on assignment only. Contact: Art Director. Illustrations only: Send postcard sample with portfolio, samples, URL. Responds only if interested.Samples filed. Credit line given.

TERMS Buys first North American serial rights. Byline given. Pays on publication. No kill fee. 90% freelance written. Sample copy for $5.95. Guidelines available online at website.

TIPS "Buy a sample issue to know what is currently selling in our magazine. Also, make sure to follow the writers' guidelines when submitting."

LIVE WIRE

8805 Governor's Hill Drive, Suite 400, Cincinnati OH 45249. (513)931-4050. **Fax:** (877)867-5751. **E-mail:** mredford@standardpub.com. **Website:** www.standardpub.com. Estab. 1949.

○   *Live Wire* has decided to reuse much of the material that was a part of the first publication cycle. They will not be sending out theme lists, sample copies, or writers' guidelines or accepting any unsolicited material because of this policy.

THE LOUISVILLE REVIEW

Spalding University, 851 S. Fourth St., Louisville KY 40203. (502)873-4398. **Fax:** (502)992-2409. **E-mail:** louisvillereview@spalding.edu. **Website:** www.louisvillereview.org. **Contact:** Kathleen Driskell, associate editor. *The Louisville Review*, published twice/year, prints all kinds of poetry. Has a section devoted to poetry by children and teens (grades K-12) called The Children's Corner. Has published poetry by Wendy Bishop, Gary Fincke, Michael Burkard, and Sandra Kohler. *The Louisville Review* is 150 pages, digest-sized, flat-spined. Receives about 700 submissions/year, accepts about 10%. Single copy: $8; subscription: $14/year, $27/2 years, $40/3 years (foreign subscribers add $6/year for s&h). Sample: $5. Estab. 1976.

POETRY Considers simultaneous submissions; no previously published poems. Accepts submissions via online manager; please see website for more information. "Poetry by children must include permission of parent to publish if accepted. Address those submissions to The Children's Corner." Reads submissions year round. Time between acceptance and publication is up to 4 months. Submissions are read by 3 readers. Guidelines available on website. Responds in 4-6 months. Pays in contributor's copies.

HOW TO CONTACT Use online submission manager or submit via mail with SASE.

⊕ LYRICAL PASSION POETRY E-ZINE

P.O. Box 17331, Arlington VA 22216. **E-mail:** LPPEzineSubmissions@gmail.com. **Website:** www.lyrical-passionpoetry.yolasite.com. **Contact:** Raquel D. Bailey, founding editor. Founded by award-winning poet Raquel D. Bailey, Lyrical Passion Poetry E-Zine is an attractive monthly online literary magazine specializing in Japanese short form poetry. Publishes quality artwork, well-crafted short fiction and poetry in English by emerging and established writers. Literature of lasting literary value will be considered. Welcomes the traditional to the experimental. Poetry works written in German will be considered if accompanied by translations. Offers annual short fiction and poetry contests. Estab. 2007. Circ. 500 online visitors/month.

FICTION Cover letter preferred. Fiction should be typed, double-spaced.

POETRY Multiple submissions are permitted but no more than 3 submissions in a 6-month period. Submissions from minors should be accompanied by a cover letter from parent with written consent for their child's submission to be published on the website with their child's first initial and last name accompanied by their age at the time of submission. Does not want: dark, cliché, limerick, erotica, extremely explicit, violent or depressing literature. Free verse poetry length: 1-40 lines.

HOW TO CONTACT Responds in 2 months. Publishes ms 1 month after acceptance. Accepts queries by e-mail.

TERMS Acquires first-time rights, electronic rights: must be the first literary venue to publish online or in any electronic format. Rights revert to poets upon publication. Guidelines and upcoming themes available on website.

MUSE

Cricket Magazine Group, 700 E. Lake St., Suite 300, Chicago IL 60601. **E-mail:** muse@caruspub.com. **Website:** www.cricketmag.com. "The goal of *Muse* is to give as many children as possible access to the most important ideas and concepts underlying the principal areas of human knowledge. Articles should meet the highest possible standards of clarity and transparency aided, wherever possible, by a tone of skepticism, humor, and irreverence." All articles are commissioned. To be considered for assignments, experienced science writers may send a résumé and 3 published clips. Estab. 1996. Circ. 40,000.

🗨 *Muse is not accepting unsolicited mss or queries.*

NONFICTION Middle readers, young adult: animal, arts, history, math, nature/environment, problem-solving, science, social issues.

ILLUSTRATION Works on assignment only. Credit line given. "Send prints or tearsheets, but please, no portfolios or original art, and above all, *do not send samples that need to be returned.*"

PHOTOS Needs vary. Query with samples to photo editor.

NATIONAL GEOGRAPHIC KIDS

National Geographic Society, 1145 17th St. NW, Washington DC 20036. **E-mail:** chughes@ngs.org; asilen@ngs.org; jsumner@ngs.org. **Website:** www.kids.national geographic.com. **Contact:** Catherine Hughes, science editor; Andrea Silen, associate editor; Jay Sumner, photo director. Magazine published 10 times/year. "It's our mission to excite kids about their world. We are the children's magazine that makes learning fun." Estab. 1975. Circ. 1.3 million.

NONFICTION Needs general interest, humor, interview, technical, travel. animals, human interest, science, technology, entertainment, archaeology, pets. Query with published clips and résumé. Length: 100-1,000 words. Pays $1/word for assigned articles.

HOW TO CONTACT Publishes ms an average of 6 months after acceptance. Accepts queries by mail.

PHOTOS State availability. Captions, identification of subjects, model releases required. Reviews contact sheets, negatives, transparencies, prints. Negotiates payment individually.

TERMS Buys all rights. Makes work-for-hire assignments. Byline given. Pays on acceptance. Offers 10% kill fee. 70% freelance written. Sample copy for #10 SASE. Guidelines free.

TIPS "Submit relevant clips. Writers must have demonstrated experience writing for kids. Read the magazine before submitting. Send query and clips via snail mail—materials will not be returned. No SASE required unless sample copy is requested."

NATURE FRIEND MAGAZINE

4253 Woodcock Lane, Dayton VA 22821. (540)867-0764. **E-mail:** info@naturefriendmagazine.com; editor@naturefriendmagazine.com; photos@nature friendmagazine.com. **Website:** www.dogwoodrid geoutdoors.com; www.naturefriendmagazine.com. **Contact:** Kevin Shank, publisher. Monthly magazine covering nature. Picture-oriented material, conversational, no talking animal stories. No evolutionary material. "*Nature Friend* includes stories, puzzles, science experiments, nature experiments—all submissions need to honor God as creator." Estab. 1983. Circ. 13,000.

NONFICTION Needs how-to, nature, science experiments (for ages 8-12), photo features, articles about interesting/unusual animals. Send complete ms. Length: 250-900 words. Pays 5¢/word.

HOW TO CONTACT Editorial lead time 4 months. Responds in 6 months to mss.

PHOTOS Send photos. Captions, identification of subjects required. Reviews prints. Offers $20-75/photo

TERMS Buys first rights, buys one-time rights. Byline given. Pays on publication. No kill fee. 80% freelance written. Sample copy and writers' guidelines for $5 postage paid.

TIPS "We want to bring joy and knowledge to children by opening the world of God's creation to them. We endeavor to create a sense of awe about nature's creator and a respect for His creation. I'd like to see more submissions on hands-on things to do with a nature theme (not collecting rocks or leaves—real stuff). Also looking for good stories that are accompanied by good photography."

NEW MOON

New Moon Publishing, P.O. Box 161287, Duluth MN 55816. (218)728-5507. **Fax:** (218)728-0314. **E-mail:** girl@newmoon.org. **Website:** www.newmoon.org. Bimonthly magazine covering girls ages 8-14, edited by girls aged 8–14. "In general, all material should be pro-girl and feature girls and women as the primary focus. *New Moon* is for every girl who wants her voice heard and her dreams taken seriously. *New Moon* celebrates girls, explores the passage from girl to woman, and builds healthy resistance to gender inequities. The *New Moon* girl is true to herself and *New Moon* helps her as she pursues her unique path in life, moving confidently into the world." Estab. 1992. Circ. 30,000.

🗨 *New Moon accepts submissions from girls and women only.*

FICTION All girl-centered. Needs adventure, fantasy, historical, humorous, slice-of-life vignettes.

Send complete ms. Length: 900-1,600 words. Pays 6-12¢/word.

NONFICTION Publishes nonfiction by adults in Herstory and Women's Work departments only. Needs essays, general interest, humor, inspirational, interview, opinion, personal experience, written by girls, photo feature, religious, travel, multicultural/girls from other countries. Send complete ms. Length: 600 words. Pays 6-12¢/word.

POETRY No poetry by adults.

HOW TO CONTACT Responds in 2 months to mss. Publishes ms an average of 6 months after acceptance. Accepts queries by mail, e-mail, fax.

ILLUSTRATION Buys 6-12 illustrations/year from freelancers. *New Moon* seeks 4-color cover illustrations. Reviews ms/illustrations packages from artists. Query. Submit ms with rough sketches. Illustration only: Query; send portfolio and tearsheets. Samples not returned; samples filed. Responds in 6 months only if interested. Credit line given.

PHOTOS State availability. Captions, identification of subjects required. Negotiates payment individually

TERMS Buys all rights. Byline given. Pays on publication. 25% freelance written. Sample copy for $7 or online. Guidelines for SASE or online.

TIPS "We'd like to see more girl-written feature articles that relate to a theme. These can be about anything the girl has done personally, or she can write about something she's studied. Please read *New Moon* before submitting to get a sense of our style. Writers and artists who comprehend our goals have the best chance of publication. We love creative articles—both nonfiction and fiction—that are not condescending to our readers. Keep articles to suggested word lengths; avoid stereotypes. Refer to our guidelines and upcoming themes."

ON COURSE

1445 Boonville Ave., Springfield MO 65802-1894. (417)862-2781. **Fax:** (417)862-1693. **E-mail:** oncourse@ag.org; josborn@ag.org. **Website:** www.oncourse.ag.org. **Contact:** Amber Weigand-Buckley, editor; Josh Carter, art director. *On Course* is a magazine to empower students to grow in a real-life relationship with Christ. Works on assignment basis only. Résumés and writing samples will be considered for inclusion in Writers File to receive story assignments. Estab. 1991.

 ◯ *On Course* no longer uses illustrations, only photos.

FICTION Young adults: Christian discipleship, contemporary, humorous, multicultural, problem-solving, sports. Length: 800 words.

NONFICTION Young adults: careers, interview/profile, multicultural, religion, social issues, college life, Christian discipleship.

PHOTOS Buys photos from freelancers. "Teen life, church life, college life; unposed; often used for illustrative purposes." Model/property releases required. Uses color glossy prints and 35mm or 214×214 transparencies. Query with samples; send business card, promotional literature, tearsheets or catalog. Responds only if interested.

TERMS Buys first or reprint rights for mss. Byline given. Pays on acceptance. Sample copy free for 9x11 SASE. Writers' guidelines for SASE.

POCKETS

The Upper Room, P.O. Box 340004, 1908 Grand Ave., Nashville TN 37203-0004. (800)972-0433. **Fax:** (615)340-7275. **E-mail:** pockets@upperroom.org. **Website:** http://pockets.upperroom.org. **Contact:** Lynn W. Gilliam, editor. Magazine published 11 times/year. "*Pockets* is a Christian devotional magazine for children ages 8-12. All submissions should address the broad theme of the magazine. Each issue is built around one theme with material which can be used by children in a variety of ways. Scripture stories, fiction, poetry, prayers, art, graphics, puzzles and activities are included. Submissions do not need to be overtly religious. They should help children experience a Christian lifestyle that is not always a neatly-wrapped moral package, but is open to the continuing revelation of God's will. Seasonal material, both secular and liturgical, is desired." Estab. 1981.

 ◯ Does not accept e-mail or fax submissions.

FICTION adventure, ethnic/multicultural, historical (general), religious/inspirational, slice-of-life vignettes. No violence, science fiction, romance, fantasy, or talking animal stories. Send complete ms with SASE. Length: 600-1,000 words. Pays 14¢/word.

NONFICTION Picture-oriented, young readers, middle readers: cooking, games/puzzles. "*Pockets* seeks biographical sketches of persons, famous or unknown, whose lives reflect their Christian commitment, written in a way that appeals to children." Does not accept how-to articles. "Nonfiction reads like a story." Multicultural needs include: stories that feature children of various racial/ethnic groups and do so in a way that is true to those depicted. Buys 10 mss/year. Length: 400-1,000 words. Pays 14¢/word.

POETRY Considers poetry by children. Length: 4-20 lines. Pays $25 minimum.

HOW TO CONTACT Responds in 8 weeks to mss. Publishes ms an average of 1 year after acceptance.

ILLUSTRATION Buys 25-35 illustrations/issue. Preferred theme or style: varied; both 4-color. Works on assignment only. Illustrations only: Send promo sheet, tearsheets.

PHOTOS Send 4-6 close-up photos of children actively involved in peacemakers at work activities. Send photos, contact sheets, prints, or digital images. Must be 300 dpi. Pays $25/photo.

TERMS Buys first North American serial rights. Byline given. Pays on acceptance. No kill fee. 60% freelance written. Each issue reflects a specific theme. Sample copy available with a 9x12 SASE with 4 first-class stamps attached to envelope. Guidelines on website.

TIPS "Theme stories, role models, and retold scripture stories are most open to freelancers. Poetry is also open. It is very helpful if writers read our writers' guidelines and themes on our website."

RAINBOW RUMPUS

P.O. Box 6881, Minneapolis MN 55406. (612)721-6442. **E-mail:** fictionandpoetry@rainbowrumpus. org; editor@rainbowrumpus.org. **Website:** www. rainbowrumpus.org. **Contact:** Beth Wallace, editor-in-chief. "*Rainbow Rumpus* is the world's only online literary magazine for children and youth with lesbian, gay, bisexual, and transgender (LGBT) parents. We are creating a new genre of children's and young adult fiction. Please carefully read and observe the guidelines on our website. Stories should be written from the point of view of children or teens with LGBT parents or other family members, or who are connected to the LGBT community. Stories for 4- to 12-year-old children should be approximately 800 to 2,500 words in length. Stories for 13- to 18-year-olds may be as long as 5,000 words. Stories featuring families of color, bisexual parents, transgender parents, family members with disabilities, and mixed-race families are particularly welcome. *Rainbow Rumpus* pays $75 per story on publication. We purchase first North American online rights. All fiction and poetry submissions should be sent to our editor-in-chief via our contact page. Be sure to select the 'Submissions'

category. A staff member will be in touch with you shortly to obtain a copy of your manuscript." Estab. 2005. Circ. 250 visits/day.

FICTION All levels: adventure, animal, contemporary, fantasy, folktales, history, humorous, multicultural, nature/environment, problem solving, science fiction, sports, suspense/mystery. Buys 24 mss/year. Submit complete ms via e-mail with the word "Submission" in the subject line. Length: 800-5,000 words. Pays $75/story.

NONFICTION Needs interview, profile, social issues. Query. Length: 800-5,000 words. Pays $75/story.

ILLUSTRATION Buys 1 illustration/issue. Uses both b&w and color artwork. Reviews ms/illustration packages from artists: Query. Illustrations only: Query with samples. Contact: Beth Wallace, Editor in Chief. Samples not returned; samples filed depending on the level of interest. Credit line given.

TERMS Buys first rights for mss; may request print anthology and audio or recording rights. Byline given. Pays on publication. Writers' guidelines available on website.

TIPS Emerging writers encouraged to submit. You do not need to be a member of the LGBT community to participate.

READ

1 Reader's Digest Rd.,P.O. Box 120023, Pleasantville NY 10570. **Website:** www.weeklyreader.com.

○ *READ* no longer accepts unsolicited mss. Those that are sent will not be read, responded to, or returned.

RED LIGHTS

2740 Andrea Drive, Allentown PA 18103-4602. (212)875-9342. **E-mail:** mhazelton@rcn.com; marilynhazelton@rcn.com. **Contact:** Marilyn Hazelton, editor. *red lights*, published semiannually in January and June, is devoted to English-language tanka and tanka sequences. Has published poetry by Sanford Goldstein, Michael McClintock, Laura Maffei, Linda Jeannette Ward, Jane Reichhold, and Michael Dylan Welch. *red lights* is 36-40 pages, saddle-stapled, with Japanese textured paper cover; copies are numbered. Single copy: $8; subscription: $16 U.S., $18 USD Canada, $20 USD foreign. Make checks payable to "red lights" in the U.S. Estab. 2004.

POETRY Wants "print-only tanka, mainly 'free-form' but also strictly syllabic 5-7-5-7-7; will consider tanka sequences and tan-renga."

TIPS "Each issue features a '*red lights* featured tanka' on the theme of 'red lights.' Poet whose poem is selected receives 1 contributor's copy."

SCIENCE WEEKLY

P.O. Box 70638, Chevy Chase MD 20813. (301)680-8804. **Fax:** (301)680-9240. **E-mail:** scienceweekly@erols.com. **Website:** www.scienceweekly.com. **Contact:** Dr. Claude Mayberry, publisher. *Science Weekly* uses freelance writers to develop and write an entire issue on a single science topic. Send résumé only, not submissions. Authors preferred within the greater D.C./Virginia/Maryland area. *Science Weekly* works on assignment only. Estab. 1984. Circ. 200,000.

Submit résumé only.

NONFICTION Young readers, middle readers (K-6th grade): science/math education, education, problem-solving.

TERMS Pays on publication. Sample copy free with SAE and 3 first-class stamps.

Ⓐ SEVENTEEN MAGAZINE

300 W. 57th St., 17th Floor, New York NY 10019. (917)934-6500. **Fax:** (917)934-6574. **E-mail:** mail@seventeen.com. **Website:** www.seventeen.com. Monthly magazine. "We reach 14.5 million girls each month. Over the past five decades, *Seventeen* has helped shape teenage life in America. We represent an important rite of passage, helping to define, socialize and empower young women. We create notions of beauty and style, proclaim what's hot in popular culture and identify social issues." Estab. 1944.

Seventeen no longer accepts fiction submissions.

NONFICTION Young adults: careers, cooking, hobbies, how-to, humorous, interview/profile, multicultural, social issues. Buys 7-12 mss/year. Length: 200-2,000 words.

ILLUSTRATION *Only interested in agented material.* Buys 10 illustrations/issue; 120 illustrations/year. Works on assignment only. Reviews ms/illustration packages. Illustrations only: Query with samples. Responds only if interested. Samples not returned; samples filed. Credit line given.

PHOTOS Looking for photos to match current stories. Model/property releases required; captions required. Uses color, 8×10 prints; 35mm, 4×5 or 8×10 transparencies. Query with samples or résumé of credits, or submit portfolio for review. Responds only if interested.

TERMS Buys first North American serial rights, first rights, or all rights for mss. Buys exclusive rights for 3 months. Byline sometimes given. Pays on publication. Writers' guidelines for SASE.

TIPS Send for guidelines before submitting.

SHARING THE VICTORY

Fellowship of Christian Athletes, 8701 Leeds Rd., Kansas City MO 64129. (816)921-0909. **Fax:** (816)921-8755. **E-mail:** stv@fca.org. **Website:** www.fca.org. **Contact:** Jill Ewert, managing editor; Matt Casner, creative director. Published 6 times/year. "We seek to serve as a ministry tool of the Fellowship of Christian Athletes by informing, inspiring and involving coaches, athletes and all whom they influence, that they may make an impact for Jesus Christ." Estab. 1959. Circ. 80,000.

NONFICTION Needs inspirational, interview (with name athletes and coaches solid in their faith), personal experience, photo feature. "Articles should be accompanied by at least three quality photos." Query. Considers electronic sumbissions via e-mail. Length: 1,000-2,000 words. Pays $150-400 for assigned and unsolicited articles.

HOW TO CONTACT Responds to queries/mss in 3 months. Publishes ms an average of 4 months after acceptance.

PHOTOS Purchases photos separately. Looking for photos of sports action. Uses color prints and high resolution electronic files of 300 dpi or higher. State availability. Reviews contact sheets. Payment based on size of photo.

TERMS Buys first rights and second serial (reprint) rights. Byline given. Pays on publication. No kill fee. 50% freelance written. Prefers to work with published/established writers, but works with a growing number of new/unpublished writers each year. Sample copy for $2 and 9x12 SASE with 3 first-class stamps. Guidelines available online.

TIPS "Profiles and interviews of particular interest to coed athletes, primarily high school and college age. Our graphics and editorial content appeal to youth. The area most open to freelancers is profiles on or interviews with well-known athletes or coaches (male, female, minorities) who have been or are involved in some capacity with FCA."

SHINE BRIGHTLY

GEMS Girls' Clubs, P.O. Box 7259, Grand Rapids MI 49510. (616)241-5616. **Fax:** (616)241-5558. **E-mail:** shinebrightly@gemsgc.org. **Website:** www.gemsgc.org.

Contact: Jan Boone, exectuive director; Kelli Ponstein, managing editor. Monthly magazine (with combined June/July/August summer issue). "Our purpose is to lead girls into a living relationship with Jesus Christ and to help them see how God is at work in their lives and the world around them. Puzzles, crafts, stories, and articles for girls ages 9-14." Estab. 1970. Circ. 17,000.

FICTION Does not want "unrealistic stories and those with trite, easy endings. We are interested in manuscripts that show how girls can change the world." Needs adventure, experiences girls could have in their hometowns or places they might realistically visit, ethnic, historical, humorous, mystery, religious, romance, slice-of-life vignettes, suspense. Believable only, nothing too preachy. Submit complete ms in body of e-mail. No attachments. Length: 700-900 words. Pays up to $35, plus 2 copies.

NONFICTION Needs adventure, humor, inspirational, mystery, seasonal and holiday, interview, personal experience, photo feature, religious, travel. Avoid the testimony approach. Submit complete ms in body of e-mail. No attachments. Length: 100-800 words. Pays up to $35, plus 2 copies.

POETRY Limited need for poetry. Pays $5-15.

HOW TO CONTACT Responds in 2 months to mss. Publishes ms an average of 1 year after acceptance.

ILLUSTRATION Samples returned with SASE. Credit line given.

PHOTOS Purchased with or without ms. Appreciates multicultural subjects. Reviews 5x7 or 8x10 clear color glossy prints. Pays $25-50 on publication.

TERMS Buys first North American serial rights, buys second serial (reprint) rights, buys simultaneous rights. Byline given. Pays on publication. No kill fee. 80% freelance written. Works with new and published/established writers. Sample copy with 9x12 SASE with 3 first class stamps and $1. Guidelines available online.

TIPS Writers: "Please check our website before submitting. We have a specific style and theme that deals with how girls can impact the world. The stories should be current, deal with pre-adolescent problems and joys, and help girls see God at work in their lives through humor as well as problem-solving." Prefers not to see anything on the adult level, secular material, or violence. Writers frequently oversimplify the articles and often write with a Pollyanna attitude. An author should be able to see his/her writing style as exciting and appealing to girls ages 9-14. The style can be fun, but also teach a truth. Subjects should be current and important to *SHINE brightly* readers. Use our theme update as a guide. We would like to receive material with a multicultural slant."

SKIPPING STONES: A MULTICULTURAL LITERARY MAGAZINE

P.O. Box 3939, Eugene OR 97403-0939. (541)342-4956. **E-mail:** editor@skippingstones.org. **Website:** www.skippingstones.org. **Contact:** Arun Toké, editor. "*Skipping Stones* is an award-winning multicultural, nonprofit magazine designed to promote cooperation, creativity and celebration of cultural and ecological richness. We encourage submissions by children of color, minorities and under-represented populations. We want material meant for children and young adults/teenagers with multicultural or ecological awareness themes. Think, live and write as if you were a child, tween or teen. Wants material that gives insight to cultural celebrations, lifestyle, customs and traditions, glimpse of daily life in other countries and cultures. Photos, songs, artwork are most welcome if they illustrate/highlight the points. Translations are invited if your submission is in a language other than English." Estab. 1988. Circ. 2,200 print, plus Web.

FICTION Middle readers, young adult/teens: contemporary, meaningful, humorous. All levels: folktales, multicultural, nature/environment. Multicultural needs include: bilingual or multilingual pieces; use of words from other languages; settings in other countries, cultures or multi-ethnic communities. Needs adventure, ethnic, historical, humorous, multicultural, international, social issues. Send complete ms. Length: 1,000 words maximum. Pays with contributor's copies.

NONFICTION Needs essays, general interest, humor, inspirational, interview, opinion, personal experience, photo feature, travel. All levels: animal, biography, cooking, games/puzzles, history, humorous, interview/profile, multicultural, nature/environment, creative problem-solving, religion and cultural celebrations, sports, travel, social and international awareness. Does not want to see preaching, violence or abusive language; no suspense or romance stories. Send complete ms. Length: 1,000 words maximum.

POETRY No poems by authors over 18 years old. Length: 30 lines maximum.

HOW TO CONTACT Editorial lead time 3-4 months. Responds only if interested. Send nonreturnable samples. Publishes ms an average of 4-8 months after acceptance. Accepts queries by mail, e-mail.

ILLUSTRATION Prefers illustrations by teenagers and young adults. Will consider all illustration packages. Manuscript/illustration packages: Query; submit complete ms with final art; submit tearsheets. Responds in 4 months. Credit line given.

PHOTOS Black & white photos preferred, but color photos with good contrast are welcome. Needs: youth 7-17, international, nature, celebrations, photo essays (10-15 prints). Send photos. Captions required. Reviews 4x6 or 5x7 prints, low-res JPEG files. Offers no additional payment for photos.

TERMS Buys first North American serial rights, nonexclusive reprint, and electronic rights. Byline given. No kill fee. 80% freelance written. Sample copy for $6. Writers' guidelines online or for SASE.

TIPS "Be original and innovative. Use multicultural, nature, or cross-cultural themes. Multilingual submissions are welcome." Adults are encouraged to submit creative informational stories rather than pure fiction.

SPARKLE

GEMS Girls' Clubs, P.O. Box 7259, Grand Rapids MI 49510. (616)241-5616. **Fax:** (616)241-5558. **E-mail:** kelli@gemsgc.org. **Website:** www.gemsgc.org. **Contact:** Kelli Ponstein, editor; Sara DeRidder, art director/photo editor. Bimonthly magazine for girls ages 6-9. "Our mission is to prepare young girls to live out their faith and become world-changers. We strive to help girls make a difference in the world. We look at the application of scripture to everyday life. We strive to delight the reader and cause the reader to evalute her own life in light of the truth presented. Finally, we strive to teach practical life skills." Estab. 2002. Circ. 5,000.

FICTION Young readers: adventure, animal, contemporary, fantasy, folktale, health, history, humorous, multicultural, music and musicians, nature/environment, problem-solving, religious, recipes, service projects, sports, suspense/mystery, interacting with family and friends. Send complete ms. Length: 100-400 words. Pays $35 maximum.

NONFICTION Young readers: animal, arts/crafts, biography, careers, cooking, concept, games/puzzles, geography, health, history, hobbies, how-to, interview/profile, math, multicultural, nature/environment, problem-solving, quizzes, science, social issues, sports, travel, personal experience, inspirational, music/drama/art. Looking for inspirational biographies, stories from Zambia, and ideas on how to live a green

lifestyle. Send complete ms. Length: 100-400 words. Pays $35 maximum.

POETRY Prefers rhyming. "We do not wish to see anything that is too difficult for a first grader to read. We wish it to remain light. The style can be fun, but also teach a truth." No violence or secular material.

HOW TO CONTACT Editorial lead time 3 months. Responds in 3 weeks to queries. Responds in 3 months to mss. Accepts queries by mail, e-mail.

ILLUSTRATION Buys 1-2 illustrations/issue; 8-10 illustrations/year. Uses color artwork only. Works on assignment only. Reviews ms/illustration packages from artists. Send ms with dummy. Illustrations only: send promo sheet. Responds in 3 weeks only if interested. Samples returned with SASE; samples filed. Credit line given.

PHOTOS Send photos. Identification of subjects required. Reviews at least 5x7 clear color glossy prints, GIF/JPEG files on CD. Offers $25-50/photo.

TERMS Buys first North American serial rights, buys first rights, buys one-time rights, buys second serial (reprint) rights, buys simultaneous rights. Byline given. Pays on publication. Offers $20 kill fee. 80% freelance written. Sample copy for 9x13 SASE, 3 first-class stamps, and $1 for coverage/publication cost. Writers' guidelines for #10 SASE or online.

TIPS "Keep it simple. We are writing to 1st-3rd graders. It must be simple yet interesting. Manuscripts should build girls up in Christian character but not be preachy. They are just learning about God and how He wants them to live. Manuscripts should be delightful as well as educational and inspirational.Writers should keep stories simple but not write with a 'Pollyanna' attitude. Authors should see their writing style as exciting and appealing to girls ages 6-9. Subjects should be current and important to *Sparkle* readers. Use our theme as a guide. We would like to receive material with a multicultural slant."

SPIDER

Cricket Magazine Group, 70 East Lake St., Suite 300, Chicago IL 60601. (312)701-1720. **Fax:** (312)701-1728. **Website:** www.cricketmag.com. **Contact:** Marianne Carus, editor-in-chief; Suzanne Beck, managing art director. Monthly reading and activity magazine for children ages 6 to 9. "*Spider* introduces children to the highest quality stories, poems, illustrations, articles, and activities. It was created to foster in beginning readers a love of reading and discovery that will last a lifetime. We're looking for writers who respect children's intelligence." Estab. 1994. Circ. 70,000.

FICTION Stories should be easy to read. Recently published work by Polly Horvath, Andrea Cheng and Beth Wagner Brust. Needs fantasy, humorous, science fiction. folk tales, fairy tales, fables, myths. No romance, horror, religious. Submit complete ms and SASE. Length: 300-1,000 words. Pays 25¢/word maximum.

NONFICTION Submit complete ms, bibliography, SASE. Length: 300-800 words. Pays 25¢/word maximum.

POETRY Length: 20 lines maximum. Pays $3/line maximum.

HOW TO CONTACT Responds in 6 months to mss.

ILLUSTRATION Buys 5-10 illustrations/issue; 45-90 illustrations/year. Uses color artwork only. "We prefer that you work on flexible or strippable stock, no larger than 20×22 (image area 19×21). This will allow us to put the art directly on the drum of our separator's laser scanner. Art on disk CMYK, 300 dpi. We use more realism than cartoon-style art." Works on assignment only. Reviews ms/illustration packages from artists. Illustrations only: Send promo sheet and tearsheets. Responds in 3 months. Samples returned with SASE; samples filed. Credit line given.

PHOTOS Buys photos from freelancers. Buys photos with accompanying ms only. Model/property releases and captions required. Uses 35mm, 214×214 transparencies or digital files. Send unsolicited photos by mail; provide résumé and tearsheets. Responds in 3 months. For art samples, it is especially helpful to see pieces showing children, animals, action scenes, and several scenes from a narrative showing a character in different situations. Send photocopies/tearsheets. Also considers photo essays (prefers color, but b&w is also accepted). Captions, identification of subjects, model releases required. Reviews contact sheets, transparencies, 8×10 prints.

TERMS Byline given. Pays on publication. 85% freelance written. Guidelines available online.

TIPS "We'd like to see more of the following: engaging nonfiction, fillers, and 'takeout page' activities; folktales, fairy tales, science fiction, and humorous stories. Most importantly, do not write down to children."

🎧 STONE SOUP

Children's Art Foundation, P.O. Box 83, Santa Cruz CA 95063-0083. (831)426-5557. **Fax:** (831)426-1161.

E-mail: editor@stonesoup.com. **Website:** www.stonesoup.com. **Contact:** Ms. Gerry Mandel, editor. Bimonthly magazine of writing and art by children ages 13 and under, including fiction, poetry, book reviews, and illustrations. *Stone Soup* is 48 pages, 7x10, professionally printed in color on heavy stock, saddle-stapled, with coated cover with full-color illustration. Receives 5,000 poetry submissions/year, accepts about 12. Press run is 15,000. Subscription: membership in the Children's Art Foundation includes a subscription, $37/year. *Stone Soup*, published 6 times/year, showcases writing and art by children ages 13 and under. "We have a preference for writing and art based on real-life experiences; no formula stories or poems. We publish only writing by children ages 13 and under. We do not publish writing by adults." Estab. 1973. Circ. 15,000.

💬 "Stories and poems from past issues are available online."

FICTION Needs adventure, ethnic, experimental, fantasy, historical, humorous, mystery, science fiction, slice-of-life vignettes, suspense. "We do not like assignments or formula stories of any kind." Send complete ms; no SASE. Length: 150-2,500 words. Pays $40, a certificate, and 2 contributor's copies.

NONFICTION Needs historical, personal experience, book reviews. Submit complete ms; no SASE. Pays $40, a certificate and 2 contributor's copies.

POETRY *Stone Soup*, published 6 times/year, showcases writing and art by children ages 13 and under. Wants free verse poetry. Does not want rhyming poetry, haiku, or cinquain. Pays $40/poem, a certificate and 2 contributor's copies.

HOW TO CONTACT Publishes ms an average of 4 months after acceptance.

ILLUSTRATION Considers ms/illustration packages. Illustrations only: Works on assignment only. Send 3 samples of artwork. "We are especially interested in artists who can draw or paint complete scenes in color. At least one of your samples should include people." Pays $25/illustration.

TERMS Buys all rights. Pays on publication. 100% freelance written. Sample copy by phone only. Guidelines available online.

TIPS "All writing we publish is by young people ages 13 and under. We do not publish any writing by adults. We can't emphasize enough how important it is to read a couple of issues of the magazine. You can read stories and poems from past issues online. We have a strong preference for writing on subjects that mean a lot to the author. If you feel strongly about something that happened to you or something you observed, use that feeling as the basis for your story or poem. Stories should have good descriptions, realistic dialogue, and a point to make. In a poem, each word must be chosen carefully. Your poem should present a view of your subject and a way of using words that are special and all your own."

TURTLE MAGAZINE FOR PRESCHOOL KIDS

U.S. Kids, 1100 Waterway Blvd., P.O. Box 567, Indianapolis IN 46206-0567. (317)634-1100. **Fax:** (317)684-8094. **Website:** www.turtlemag.org. **Contact:** Terry Harshman, editor; Bart Rivers, art director. *Turtle* uses read-aloud stories, especially suitable for bedtime or naptime reading, for children ages 2-5. Also uses poems, simple science experiments, easy recipes and health-related articles. Circ. 300,000.

FICTION Picture-oriented material: health-related, medical, history, humorous, multicultural, nature/environment, problem-solving, sports, recipes, simple science experiments. Avoid stories in which the characters indulge in unhealthy activities. Submit complete ms. *Queries are not accepted.* Length: 150-300 words. Pays $70 minimum and 10 contributor's copies.

NONFICTION Picture-oriented material: cooking, health, sports, simple science. "We use very simple experiments illustrating basic science concepts. These should be pretested. We also publish simple, healthful recipes." Submit complete ms. *Queries are not accepted.* Length: 250 words maximum. Pays $70 minimum and 10 contributor's copies.

POETRY "We're especially looking for short poems (4-8 lines) and slightly longer action rhymes to foster creative movement in preschoolers. We also use short verse on our inside front cover and back cover." Pays $25 minimum.

HOW TO CONTACT Send complete mss. Responds to mss in 3 months.

TERMS Pays on publication. Byline given. No kill fee. Buys all rights for mss. Writers' guidelines free with SASE and on website. Sample copy $3.95.

TIPS "Our need for health-related material, especially features that encourage fitness, is ongoing. Health subjects must be age-appropriate. When writing about them, think creatively and lighten up! Always keep in mind that in order for a story or article to educate preschoolers, it first must be entertaining—warm and engaging, exciting, or genuinely funny. Here the trend is toward leaner, lighter writing. There will be a growing need for interactive activities. Writers might want to consider developing an activity to accompany their concise manuscripts."

YOUNG RIDER

P.O. Box 8237, Lexington KY 40533. (859)260-9800. **Fax:** (859)260-9814. **E-mail:** yreditor@bowtieinc.com. **Website:** www.youngrider.com. **Contact:** Lesley Ward, editor. The magazine for horse and pony lovers. "*Young Rider* magazine teaches young people, in an easy-to-read and entertaining way, how to look after their horses properly, and how to improve their riding skills safely." Estab. 1994.

FICTION Young adults. "We would prefer funny stories, with a bit of conflict, which will appeal to the 13-year-old age group. They should be written in the third person, and about kids." Buys 4-5 short stories/year. Length: 800-1,000 words. Pays $150.

NONFICTION Young adults: animal, careers, health (horse), riding. Query with published clips. Length: 1,000 words maximum.

HOW TO CONTACT Rsponds to queries in 2 weeks. Publishes ms 6-12 months after acceptance.

ILLUSTRATION Buys 2 illustrations/issue; 10 illustrations/year. Works on assignment only. Reviews ms/illustration packages from artists. Query. Contact: Lesley Ward, editor. Illustrations only: Query with samples. Contact: Lesley Ward, editor. Responds in 2 weeks. Samples returned with SASE. Credit line given.

PHOTOS Buys photos with accompanying ms only. Uses high-res digital images only—in focus, good light. Model/property release required; captions required. Query with samples. Responds in 2 weeks.

TERMS Buys first North American serial rights for mss, artwork, photos. Byline given. Pays on publication. Sample copy for $3.50. Guidelines for SASE.

TIPS "Fiction must be in third person. Read magazine before sending in a query. No 'true story from when I was a youngster.' No moralistic stories. Fiction must be up-to-date and humorous, teen-oriented. Need horsy interest or celebrity rider features. No practical or how-to articles—all done in-house."

AGENTS & ART REPS

//

This section features listings of literary agents and art reps who either specialize in, or represent a good percentage of, children's writers and/or illustrators. While there are a number of children's publishers who are open to non-agented material, using the services of an agent or rep can be beneficial to a writer or artist. Agents and reps can get your work seen by editors and art directors more quickly. They are familiar with the market and have insights into which editors and art directors would be most interested in your work. Also, they negotiate contracts and will likely be able to get you a better deal than you could get on your own.

Agents and reps make their income by taking a percentage of what writers and illustrators receive from publishers. The standard percentage for agents is 10 to 15 percent; art reps generally take 25 to 30 percent. We have not included any agencies in this section that charge reading fees.

WHAT TO SEND

When putting together a package for an agent or rep, follow the guidelines given in their listings. Most agents open to submissions prefer initially to receive a query letter describing your work. For novels and longer works, some agents ask for an outline and a number of sample chapters, but you should send these only if you're asked to do so. Never fax or e-mail query letters or sample chapters to agents without their permission. Just as with publishers, agents receive a large volume of submissions. It may take them a long time to reply, so you may want to query several agents at one time. It's best, however, to have a complete manuscript considered by only one agent at a time. Always include a self-addressed, stamped envelope (SASE).

For initial contact with art reps, send a brief query letter and self-promo pieces, following the guidelines given in the listings. If you don't have a flier or brochure, send photocopies. Always include a SASE.

For those who both write and illustrate, some agents listed will consider the work of author/illustrators. Read through the listings for details.

As you consider approaching agents and reps with your work, keep in mind that they are very choosy about whom they take on to represent. Your work must be high quality and presented professionally to make an impression on them. For more information on approaching agents and additional listings, see *Guide to Literary Agents* (Writer's Digest Books). For additional listings of art reps see *Artist's & Graphic Designer's Market* (Writer's Digest Books).

TARGET YOUR AGENTS

If you are looking for a literary agent, a comprehensive, free resource to use is the **Guide to Literary Agents Blog** (guidetoliteraryagents.com/blog), part of the Writer's Digest blog family. The blog includes new agent alerts, agent interviews, "How I Got My Agent" stories from writers, lots of guest columns from published authors, writers' conference spotlights, examples of successful queries, examples of synopsis content, and more.

JUDITH ENGRACIA (LIZA DAWSON ASSOCIATES)

lizadawsonassociates.com/

ABOUT JUDITH: She is a new literary agent building her client list at Liza Dawson Associates. She also runs the OmNomNom Books blog. She was interviewed on the Literary Rambles blog as well as the Random Thoughts Blog.

SHE IS SEEKING: literary fiction, urban fantasy, paranormal romance, thrillers, mysteries, young adult, and middle grade.

HOW TO SUBMIT: Her e-mail is not up online yet, but if it follows the others at the agency, it would logically be queryjudith@LizaDawsonAssociates.com. OR–you could simply submit via snail mail, include a SASE, and address it to her specifically: Liza Dawson Associates, 350 Seventh Avenue, Suite 2003, New York, NY 10001 Send a query only as first contact.

AGENTS

ADAMS LITERARY

7845 Colony Rd., C4 #215, Charlotte NC 28226. (704)542-1440. **Fax:** (704)542-1450. **E-mail:** info@adamsliterary.com. **E-mail:** submissions@adamsliterary.com. **Website:** www.adamsliterary.com. **Contact:** Tracey Adams, Josh Adams, Quinlan Lee.

REPRESENTS Represents "The finest children's book authors and artists."

TERMS Agent receives 15% commission on domestic sales; 20% on foreign sales. Offers written contract.

HOW TO CONTACT Contact through online form on website only. Send e-mail if that is not operating correctly. "All submissions and queries must be made through the online form on our website. We will not review—and will promptly recycle—any unsolicited submissions or queries we receive by post. Before submitting your work for consideration, please carefully review our complete guidelines. While we have an established client list, we do seek new talent—and we accept submissions from both published and aspiring authors and artists."

TIPS "Guidelines are posted (and frequently updated) on our website."

BOOKSTOP LITERARY AGENCY

67 Meadow View Rd., Orinda CA 94563. **E-mail:** kendra@bookstopliterary.com; info@bookstopliterary.com. **Website:** www.bookstopliterary.com.

REPRESENTS "Special interest in Hispanic, Asian American, and African American writers; quirky picture books; clever adventure/mystery novels; and authentic and emotional young adult voices."

TERMS Agent receives 15% commission on domestic sales. Offers written contract, binding for 1 year.

HOW TO CONTACT Please send: cover letter, entire ms for picture books; first 30 pages of novels; proposal, and sample chapters OK for nonfiction. E-mail submissions: Paste cover letter and first 10 pages of manuscript into body of e-mail, send to info@bookstopliterary.com. Send sample illustrations only if you are an illustrator.

CURTIS BROWN, LTD.

(212)473-5400. **E-mail:** gknowlton@cbltd.com. **Website:** www.curtisbrown.com. **Contact:** Ginger Knowlton. Alternate address: Peter Ginsberg, president at

NEW AGENT SPOTLIGHT

STEPHEN BARR (WRITERS HOUSE)
Writershouse.com

ABOUT STEPHEN: Stephen landed at Writers House in 2008, became its biggest fan about four seconds later, and started taking on his own clients in 2010. He spent the first 21 years of his life in Southern California and was inspired to become involved in publishing after seeing Robert Downey Jr.'s portrayal of Terry Crabtree in *Wonder Boys*. He loves working with writers and editing their manuscripts to get them ready for submission. He was recently profiled in the *New York Times*.

HE IS SEEKING: "I'm a pretty omnivorous agent—I've got a permanent hankering for unexpected memoirs with itchy voices, narrative nonfiction that tackles hard-to-tackle issues, wry and rarely paranormal young adult, laugh-until-you-squirt-milk-out-of-your-nose middle grade, sweet and wacky (but still logical) picture books from author/illustrators, and fiction that rewards the reader line-by-line and gets to know at least one character really, really well (recent favorites include *Jeff in Venice*, *The Lazarus Project*, *Diary of a Bad Year*, and *Horns*, which was awesome). I'm also willing to be a sucker for smart, unconventional thrillers, mysteries that bend reality, ghost stories that blow reality to hell, fictional or not-so-fictional portrayals of abnormal psychology, and humor that's more than just an infinitely repeated gag in sheep's clothing."

HOW TO CONTACT: "Send a friendly, honest e-query, anchored by the first five or 10 pages of the manuscript. Send submissions to sbarr@writershouse.com with the word 'Query' in the subject line."

CBSF, 1750 Montgomery St., San Francisco CA 94111. (415)954-8566.
RECENT SALES This agency prefers not to share information on specific sales.
TERMS Agent receives 15% commission on domestic sales; 20% on foreign sales. Offers written contract. 75 days notice must be given to terminate contract. Offers written contract. Charges for some postage (overseas, etc.).
HOW TO CONTACT Prefers to read materials exclusively. *No unsolicited mss.* Query with SASE. If a picture book, send only one picture book ms. Considers simultaneous queries, "but please tell us." Returns material only with SASE. Obtains most new clients through recommendations from others, solicitations, conferences.

BROWNE & MILLER LITERARY ASSOCIATES, LLC
410 S. Michigan Ave. Suite 460, Chicago IL 60605. (312)922-3063. **Fax:** (312)922-1905. **E-mail:** mail@browneandmiller.com; Lauren@browneandmiller.com. **Website:** www.browneandmiller.com.

REPRESENTS Considers primarily YA fiction, fiction, young adult. "We love great writing and have a wonderful list of authors writing YA in particular." Not looking for picture books, middle grade.

RECENT SALES Sold 10 books for young readers in the last year.

TERMS Agent receives 15% commission on domestic sales; 20% on foreign sales. Offers written contract, binding for 2 years. 30 days notice must be given to terminate contract.

HOW TO CONTACT Query with SASE. Accepts queries by e-mail. Obtains clients through recommendations from others.

TIPS "We are very hands-on and do much editorial work with our clients. We are passionate about the books we represent and work hard to help clients reach their publishing goals."

PEMA BROWNE LTD.

11 Tena Place, Valley Cottage NY 10989. (845)268-0029. **Website:** www.pemabrowneltd.com. **Contact:** Pema Browne.

○ Looking for "professional and unique" talent.

REPRESENTS Specializes in general commercial.

RECENT SALES *The Daring Ms. Quimby*, by Suzanne Whitaker (Holiday House).

TERMS Rep receives 30% illustration commission; 20% author commission. Exclusive area representation is required. For promotional purposes, talent must provide color mailers to distribute. Representative pays mailing costs on promotion mailings.

HOW TO CONTACT For first contact, send query letter, direct mail flier/brochure and SASE. If interested will ask to mail appropriate materials for review. Portfolios should include tearsheets and transparencies or good color photocopies, plus SASE. Accepts queries by mail only. Obtains new talent through recommendations and interviews (portfolio review). Current clients include HarperCollins, Holiday House, Bantam Doubleday Dell, Nelson/Word, Hyperion, Putnam. Client list available upon request.

TIPS "We are doing more publishing—all types—less advertising." Looks for "continuity of illustration and dedication to work."

ANDREA BROWN LITERARY AGENCY, INC.

1076 Eagle Dr., Salinas CA 93905. (831)422-5925. **Fax:** (831)422-5915. **E-mail:** andrea@andreabrownlit.com; caryn@andreabrownlit.com. **Website:** www.andreabrownlit.com. **Contact:** Andrea Brown, president.

REPRESENTS Specializes in "all kinds of children's books—illustrators and authors."98% juvenile books. Considers: Nonfiction (animals, anthropology/archaeology, art/architecture/design, biography/autobiography, current affairs, ethnic/cultural interests, history, how-to, nature/environment, photography, popular culture, science/technology, sociology, sports); fiction (historical, science fiction); picture books, young adult.

RECENT SALES *Chloe*, by Catherine Ryan Hyde (Knopf); Sasha Cohen autobiography (HarperCollins); *The Five Ancestors*, by Jeff Stone (Random House); *Thirteen Reasons Why*, by Jay Asher (Penguin); *Identical*, by Ellen Hopkins (S&S)

TERMS Agent receives 15% commission on domestic sales. Agent receives 20% commission on foreign sales. Offers written contract.

HOW TO CONTACT For picture books, submit complete ms, SASE. For fiction, submit short synopsis, SASE, first 3 chapters. For nonfiction, submit proposal, 1-2 sample chapters. For illustrations, submit 4-5 color samples (no originals). "We only accept queries via e-mail. No attachments, with the exception of jpeg illustrations from illustrators." Visit the agents' bios on our website and choose only one agent to whom you will submit your e-query. Send a short e-mail query letter to that agent with QUERY in the subject field. Obtains most new clients through referrals from editors, clients and agents. Check website for guidelines and information.

LIZA DAWSON ASSOCIATES

350 Seventh Ave., Suite 2003, New York NY 10001. (212)465-9071. **Fax:** (212)947-0460. **E-mail:** queryliza@lizadawsonassociates.com. **Website:** www.lizadawsonassociates.com. **Contact:** Anna Olswanger.

REPRESENTS "This agency specializes in readable literary fiction, thrillers, mainstream historicals, women's fiction, academics, historians, business, journalists and psychology."

TERMS Agent receives 15% commission on domestic sales. Agent receives 20% commission on foreign sales. Offers written contract. Charges clients for photocopying and overseas postage.

HOW TO CONTACT Query with first 5 pages. Query by e-mail only. No phone calls. Obtains most new clients through recommendations from others, conferences.

DUNHAM LITERARY, INC.

156 Fifth Ave., Suite 625, New York NY 10010-7002. (212)929-0994. **E-mail:** query@dunhamlit.com. **Website:** www.dunhamlit.com. **Contact:** Jennie Dunham.
RECENT SALES Sold 30 books for young readers in the last year. *Peter Pan*, by Robert Sabuda (Little Simon); *Flamingos on the Roof*, by Calef Brown (Houghton); *Adele and Simon in America*, by Barbara McClintock (Farrar, Straus & Giroux); *Caught Between the Pages*, by Marlene Carvell (Dutton); *Waiting For Normal*, by Leslie Connor (HarperCollins), *The Gollywhopper Games*, by Jody Feldman (Greenwillow); *America the Beautiful*, by Robert Sabuda; *Dahlia*, by Barbara McClintock; *Living Dead Girl*, by Tod Goldberg; *In My Mother's House*, by Margaret McMulla; *Black Hawk Down*, by Mark Bowden; *Look Back All the Green Valley*, by Fred Chappell; *Under a Wing*, by Reeve Lindbergh; *I Am Madame X*, by Gioia Diliberto.
TERMS Agent receives 15% commission on domestic sales. Agent receives 20% commission on foreign sales.
HOW TO CONTACT Query with SASE. Obtains most new clients through recommendations from others, solicitations.

● DWYER & O'GRADY, INC.

P.O. Box 790, Cedar Key FL 32625-0790. (352)543-9307. **Fax:** (603)375-5373. **Website:** www.dwyerogrady.com. **Contact:** Elizabeth O'Grady, Jeffrey Dwyer.

"We are not accepting new clients at this time."

REPRESENTS "This agency represents only writers and illustrators of children's books."
TERMS Agent receives 15% commission on domestic sales. Agent receives 20% commission on foreign sales. Offers written contract; 1-month notice must be given to terminate contract. This agency charges clients for photocopying of longer mss or mutually agreed-upon marketing expenses.
HOW TO CONTACT Do not send unsolicited material. Check website to see if policy changes. Obtains most new clients through recommendations from others, direct approach by agent to writer whose work they've read.
TIPS "This agency previously had an address in New Hampshire. Mail all materials to the new Florida address."

DYSTEL & GODERICH LITERARY MANAGEMENT

1 Union Square W., Suite 904, New York NY 10003. (212)627-9100. **Fax:** (212)627-9313. **E-mail:** mbourret@dystel.com. **Website:** www.dystel.com. **Contact:** Michael Bourret; Jim McCarthy.
REPRESENTS This agency specializes in cookbooks and commercial and literary fiction and nonfiction. "We are actively seeking fiction for all ages, in all genres. We're especially interested in quality young adult fiction, from realistic to paranormal, and all kinds of middle grade, from funny boy books to more sentimental fare. Though we are open to author/illustrators, we are not looking for picture book mss. And, while we would like to see more YA memoir, nonfiction is not something we usually handle." No plays, screenplays, or poetry.
TERMS Agent receives 15% commission on domestic sales. Agent receives 19% commission on foreign sales. Offers written contract.
HOW TO CONTACT Query with SASE. Please include the first 3 chapters in the body of the e-mail. E-mail queries preferred (Michael Bourret only accepts email queries); will accept mail. See website for full guidelines. Obtains most new clients through recommendations from others, solicitations, conferences.
TIPS "DGLM prides itself on being a full-service agency. We're involved in every stage of the publishing process, from offering substantial editing on mss and proposals, to coming up with book ideas for authors looking for their next project, negotiating contracts and collecting monies for our clients. We follow a book from its inception through its sale to a publisher, its publication, and beyond. Our commitment to our writers does not, by any means, end when we have collected our commission. This is one of the many things that makes us unique in a very competitive business."

○ EDUCATIONAL DESIGN SERVICES LLC

5750 Bou Ave, Suite 1508, N. Bethesda MD 20852. **E-mail:** blinder@educationaldesignservices.com. **Website:** www.educationaldesignservices.com. **Contact:** B. Linder.
REPRESENTS "We specialize in educational materials to be used in classrooms (in class sets), for staff development or in teacher education classes." Actively seeking educational, text materials. Not looking for picture books, story books, fiction; no illustrators.

CLAIRE DUNNINGTON
(VICKY BIJUR LITERARY AGENCY)

Vickybijuragency.com
@VBLA

ABOUT CLAIRE: Claire Dunnington has a BA in Expository Writing from Brown University and an MFA from Columbia University in Nonfiction.

SHE IS SEEKING: young adult fiction, and, in particular, strong realistic YA fiction and literary middle grade fiction. (For reference, some authors she enjoyed when she was growing up were Phyllis Reynolds Naylor, Louis Sachar, Jerry Spinelli, Noel Streatfeild, Zilpha Keatley Snyder, and Virginia Euwer Wolff.) She is happy to consider dystopian and futuristic YA, but is much less interested in vampires, werewolves, ghosts, and the like.

HOW TO SUBMIT: "Our general query e-mail is assistant@vickybijuragency.com (for general queries, as Vicky represents nonfiction, literary fiction, commercial fiction, and mystery), but authors with YA fiction can query me directly at claire@vickybijuragency.com. A prospective author should send a query letter including a brief synopsis and the first chapter of the manuscript. This should be pasted as text in the body of the e-mail, rather than attached."

RECENT SALES *How to Solve Word Problems in Mathematics*, by Wayne (McGraw-Hill*); Preparing for the 8*th *Grade Test in Social Studies*, by Farran-Paci (Amsco); *Minority Report*, by Gunn-Singh (Scarecrow Education); *No Parent Left Behind,* by Petrosino & Spiegel (Rowman & Littlefield*); Teaching Test-taking Skills* (R&L Education); *10 Languages You'll Need Most in the Classroom*, by Sundem, Krieger, Pickiewicz (Corwin Press*); Kids, Classrooms & Capital Hill*, by Flynn (R&L Education).

TERMS Agent receives 15% commission on domestic sales; 25% on foreign sales. Offers written contract, binding until any party opts out. Terminate contract through certified letter.

HOW TO CONTACT Query by e-mail or with SASE or send outline and 1 sample chapter. Considers simultaneous queries and submissions if so indicated. Returns material only with SASE. Obtains clients through recommendations from others, queries/solicitations, or through conferences.

ETHAN ELLENBERG LITERARY AGENCY

548 Broadway, #5-E, New York NY 10012. (212)431-4554. **Fax:** (212)941-4652. **E-mail:** agent@ethanellenberg.com. **Website:** http://ethanellenberg.com. **Contact:** Ethan Ellenberg.

REPRESENTS "This agency specializes in commercial fiction—especially thrillers, romance/women's, and specialized nonfiction. We also do a lot of children's books. Actively seeking commercial fiction as noted above—romance/fiction for women, science fiction and fantasy, thrillers, suspense and mysteries. Our other two main areas of interest are children's books and narrative nonfiction. We are actively seeking clients, follow the directions on our website." Does not want to receive poetry, short stories, or screenplays.

NEW AGENT SPOTLIGHT

BROOKS SHERMAN
(FINEPRINT LITERARY MANAGEMENT)
Fineprintlit.com
@byobrooks

ABOUT BROOKS: Brooks Sherman is thrilled to be living once more in Brooklyn, after a two-year stint with the Peace Corps in bucolic West Africa and a one-year stint in the savage jungles of Hollywood. He joined FinePrint Literary Management as an intern in 2010 and now, as an associate agent, is actively seeking a range of both fiction and nonfiction projects.

HE IS SEEKING: On the adult side, literary and upmarket fiction running the gamut from contemporary (with an eye toward multicultural or satirical) to speculative (particularly urban/contemporary fantasy, horror/dark fantasy, and slipstream). Brooks also has a weakness for historical fiction and a burgeoning interest in crime fiction. For nonfiction, he is particularly interested in works that focus on current events, history, and pop science/sociology. On the children's side, he is looking to build a list of boy-focused middle grade novels (all subgenres, but particularly fantasy adventure and contemporary), and is open to young adult fiction of all types except paranormal romance.

Brooks is specifically seeking projects that balance strong voice with gripping plot lines; he particularly enjoys flawed (but sympathetic) protagonists and stories that organically blur the lines between genres. Stories that make him laugh earn extra points. Recent favorites include *Whiteman* by Tony D'Souza, *The Time Traveler's Wife* by Audrey Niffenegger, the Monstrumologist series by Rick Yancey, *The Thieves of Manhattan* by Adam Langer, and *Horns* by Joe Hill.

HOW TO CONTACT: Send queries to brooks@fineprintlit.com.

TERMS Agent receives 15% commission on domestic sales. Agent receives 10% commission on foreign sales. Offers written contract. Charges clients (with their consent) for direct expenses limited to photocopying and postage.

HOW TO CONTACT For fiction, send introductory letter, outline, first 3 chapters, SASE. For nonfiction, send query letter, proposal, 1 sample chapter, SASE.

For children's books, send introductory letter, up to 3 picture book mss, outline, first 3 chapters, SASE.

TIPS We do consider new material from unsolicited authors. Write a good, clear letter with a succinct description of your book. We prefer the first 3 chapters when we consider fiction. For all submissions, you must include a SASE or the material will be discarded. It's always hard to break in, but talent will find a home. Check our website for complete submission guidelines. We continue to see natural storytellers and nonfiction writers with important books.

THE ELAINE P. ENGLISH LITERARY AGENCY

4710 41st St. NW, Suite D, Washington DC 20016. (202)362-5190. **Fax:** (202)362-5192. **E-mail:** queries@elaineenglish.com. **E-mail:** elaine@elaineenglish.com. **Website:** www.elaineenglish.com/literary.php. **Contact:** Elaine English, Lindsey Skouras.

REPRESENTS Actively seeking women's fiction, including single-title romances, and young adult fiction. Does not want to receive any science fiction, time travel, or picture books.

RECENT SALES Have been to Sourcebooks, Tor, Harlequin.

TERMS Agent receives 15% commission on domestic sales. Agent receives 20% commission on foreign sales. Offers written contract; 30-day notice must be given to terminate contract. Charges only for shipping expenses; generally taken from proceeds.

HOW TO CONTACT Generally prefers e-queries sent to queries@elaineenglish.com. If requested, submit synopsis, first 3 chapters, SASE. Please check website for further details. Obtains most new clients through recommendations from others, conferences, submissions.

FLANNERY LITERARY

1140 Wickfield Ct., Naperville IL 60563. (630)428-2682. **Fax:** (630)428-2683. **E-mail:** FlanLit@aol.com. **Contact:** Jennifer Flannery.

REPRESENTS This agency specializes in children's and young adult fiction and nonfiction. It also accepts picture books. 100% juvenile books.

TERMS Agent receives 15% commission on domestic sales. Agent receives 20% commission on foreign sales. Offers written contract, binding for life of book in print; 1-month notice must be given to terminate contract.

HOW TO CONTACT Query with SASE. No e-mail submissions or queries. Obtains new clients through referrals and queries.

TIPS "Write an engrossing, succinct query describing your work. We are always looking for a fresh new voice."

BARRY GOLDBLATT LITERARY LLC

320 Seventh Ave. #266, Brooklyn NY 11215. (718)832-8787. **Fax:** (718)832-5558. **E-mail:** query@bgliterary.com. **Contact:** Barry Goldblatt.

REPRESENTS "Please see our website for specific submission guidelines and information on agents' particular tastes."

RECENT SALES The Infernal Devices trilogy, by Cassandra Clare; *Clappy as a Ham*, by Michael Ian Black; *Pearl*, by Jo Knowles; *The Book of Blood and Shadows*, by Robin Wasserman; *Summerton*, by Karen Healey; *The Diviners*, by Libba Bray.

TERMS Agent receives 15% commission on domestic sales; 20% on foreign and dramatic sales. Offers written contract. 60 days notice must be given to terminate contract.

HOW TO CONTACT Obtains clients through referrals, queries, and conferences.

TIPS "We're a group of hands-on agents, with wide ranging interests. Get us hooked with a great query letter, then convince us with an unforgettable manuscript."

⊕ DOUG GRAD LITERARY AGENCY, INC.

156 Prospect Park West, Brooklyn NY 11215. (718)788-6067. **E-mail:** doug.grad@dgliterary.com. **E-mail:** query@dgliterary.com. **Website:** www.dgliterary.com. **Contact:** Doug Grad.

RECENT SALES *Drink the Tea*, by Thomas Kaufman (St. Martin's); *15 Minutes: The Impossible Math of Nuclear War*, by L. Douglas Keeney (St. Martin's).

HOW TO CONTACT Query by e-mail first at query@dgliterary.com. No sample material unless requested.

ASHLEY GRAYSON LITERARY AGENCY

1342 W. 18th St., San Pedro CA 90732. **Fax:** (310)514-1148. **E-mail:** graysonagent@earthlink.net. **Website:** www.graysonagency.com/blog.

REPRESENTS "We prefer to work with published (traditional print), established authors. We will give first consideration to authors who come recommended to us by our clients or other publishing professionals. We accept a very small number of new, previously unpublished authors. The agency is temporarily closed to queries from writers who are not published at book length (self published or print-on-demand do not count). There are only three exceptions to this policy: (1) Unpublished authors who have received an offer from a reputable publisher, who need an agent before beginning contract negotiations; (2) Authors who are recommended by a published author, editor or agent who has read the work in question; (3) Authors whom we have met at conferences and from whom we have requested submissions. Authors who are recognized within their field or area may still query with proposals. We are seeking more mysteries and thrillers."

RECENT SALES Sold 25+ books last year. *Juliet Dove, Queen of Love*, by Bruce Coville (Harcourt); *Alosha*, by Christopher Pike (TOR); *Sleeping Freshmen Never Lie*, by David Lubar (Dutton); *Ball Don't Lie*, by Matt de la Peña (Delacorte); *Wiley & Grampa's Creature Features*, by Kirk Scroggs (10-book series, Little Brown); *Snitch*, by Allison van Diepen (Simon Pulse). Also represents: J.B. Cheaney (Knopf), Bruce Wetter (Atheneum).

TERMS Agent receives 15% commission on domestic sales. Agent receives 20% commission on foreign sales.

HOW TO CONTACT As of early 2008, the agency was only open to fiction authors with publishing credits (no self-published). For nonfiction, only writers with great platforms will be considered.

TIPS "We do request revisions as they are required. We are long-time agents, professional and known in the business. We perform professionally for our clients and we ask the same of them."

THE GREENHOUSE LITERARY AGENCY

11308 Lapham Dr., Oakton VA 22124. **E-mail:** submissions@greenhouseliterary.com. **Website:** www.greenhouseliterary.com. **Contact:** Sarah Davies.

"It's very important to me to have a strong, long-term relationship with clients. Having been 25 years in the publishing industry, I know the business from the inside and have excellent contacts in both the US and UK. I work hard to find every client the very best publisher and deal for their writing. My editorial background means I can work creatively with authors where necessary; I aim to submit high-quality manuscripts to publishers while respecting the role of the editor who will have their own publishing vision."

REPRESENTS "We exclusively represent authors writing fiction for children and teens. The agency has offices in both the USA and UK, and Sarah Davies (who is British) personally represents authors to both markets. The agency's commission structure reflects this—taking 15% for sales to both US and UK, thus treating both as 'domestic' market.'" All genres of children's and YA fiction—ages 5+. Does not want to receive nonfiction, poetry, picture books (text or illustration) or work aimed at adults; short stories, educational or religious/inspirational work, pre-school/novelty material, or screenplays.

RECENT SALES *Princess for Hire*, by Lindsey Leavitt (Hyperion); *What Happened on Fox Street*, by Tricia Springstubb (Harpercollins); *The Replacement*, by Brenna Yovanoff (Razorbill); *Just Add Magic*, by Cindy Callaghan (Aladdin).

TERMS Agent receives 15% commission on domestic sales. Agent receives 25% commission on foreign sales. Offers written contract. This agency charges very occasionally for copies for submission to film agents or foreign publishers.

HOW TO CONTACT E-mail queries only; short letter containing a brief outline, biography and any writing 'credentials'. Up to the first five pages of text may be pasted into the e-mail. All submissions are answered. Obtains most new clients through recommendations from others, solicitations, conferences.

TIPS "Before submitting material, authors should read the Greenhouse's 'Top 10 Tips for Authors of Children's Fiction,' which can be found on our website."

HERMAN AGENCY

350 Central Park West, New York NY 10025. (212)749-4907. **E-mail:** Ronnie@HermanAgencyInc.com. **Website:** www.hermanagencyinc.com. Literary and artistic agency. Member of SCBWI, Graphic Artists' Guild and Authors' Guild. Some of the illustrators represented: Joy Allen, Seymour Chwast, Troy Cummings, Barry Gott, Jago, Gideon Kendall, Ana Martin Larranaga, Mike Lester, John Nez, Michael Rex, Richard Torrey, Deborah Zemke. Some of the authors represented: Martha Alderson, Larry Brimner. Martha Brockenbrough, Shelley Corielli, Ralph Fletcher, Janet Gurtler, Deloris Jordan, Robin Mellon, Anastasia Suen. Currently not accepting new clients unless they have been successfully published by major trade publishing houses.

TERMS Receives 25% commission for illustration assignments; 15% for ms assignments. Artists pay 75% of costs for promotional material, about $200 a year. Offers written contract. Advertising costs are split: 75% paid by illustrator; 25% paid by rep.

HOW TO CONTACT Exclusive representation required. For first contact, e-mail only. Responds in 4-6 weeks. For first contact, artists or author/artists should e-mail a link to their website with bio and list of published books as well as new picture book manuscript or dummy to Ronnie or Katia. We will contact you in a month only if your samples are right for us. For first contact, authors of middle-grade or YA

STEPHANIE SUN (WEED LITERARY)

weedliterary.com/
@sooheesun

ABOUT STEPHANIE: Stephanie Sun of Weed Literary is a graduate of Boston College, and she joined the agency in 2009 after working at Bedford/St. Martin's, Tor/Forge, and Trident Media Group.

SHE IS SEEKING: Her interests are diverse and she enjoys reading commercial fiction (middle grade, young adult, debut, and upmarket fiction), commercial nonfiction (narrative nonfiction and memoir) and books dealing with sports or pop culture (blog, food, and music). "Weed Literary does not handle the following: picture books, mysteries, thrillers, romance, military."

HOW TO CONTACT: "We prefer queries to be e-mailed to Stephanie@weedliterary.com. Please keep letters to one page and do not send attachments unless they are requested. If you prefer snail mail, please send, along with an SASE for our reply, to: Weed Literary, LLC, 27 West 20th Street, New York, NY 10011."

should e-mail bio, list of published books and first 10 pages to Jill Corcoran. Jill will contact you within a month if she is interested in seeing more of your manuscript. Finds illustrators and authors through recommendations from others, conferences, queries/solicitations. Submit via e-mail to one of the agents listed above. See website for specific agents' specialties. **TIPS** "Check our website to see if you belong with our agency."

JANKLOW & NESBIT ASSOCIATES

445 Park Ave., New York NY 10022. (212)421-1700. **Fax:** (212)980-3671. **E-mail:** info@janklow.com. **Website:** janklowandnesbit.com. **Contact:** Julie Just, literary agent. **REPRESENTS** *Does not want to receive unsolicited submissions or queries.* **HOW TO CONTACT** Query with samples. Considers electronic submissions. Yes Obtains most new clients through recommendations from others. **TIPS** "Please send a short query with sample chapters or artwork."

BARBARA S. KOUTS, LITERARY AGENT

P.O. Box 560, Bellport NY 11713. (631)286-1278. **Fax:** (631) 286-1538. **Contact:** Barbara S. Kouts. **REPRESENTS** This agency specializes in children's books. **RECENT SALES** *Code Talker*, by Joseph Bruchac (Dial); *The Penderwicks*, by Jeanne Birdsall (Knopf); *Froggy's Baby Sister*, by Jonathan London (Viking). **TERMS** Agent receives 10% commission on domestic sales. Agent receives 20% commission on foreign sales. This agency charges clients for photocopying. **HOW TO CONTACT** Query with SASE. Accepts queries by mail only. Obtains most new clients through recommendations from others, solicitations, conferences. **TIPS** "Write, do not call. Be professional in your writing."

GINA MACCOBY LITERARY AGENCY

P.O. Box 60, Chappaqua NY 10514. (914)238-5630. **E-mail:** query@maccobylit.com; gmaccoby@aol.com. **Contact:** Gina Maccoby. **RECENT SALES** This agency sold 21 titles last year.

NEW AGENT SPOTLIGHT

KATHLEEN RUSHALL
(MARSAL LYON LITERARY AGENCY)

marsallyonliteraryagency.com/
@KatRushall

ABOUT KATHLEEN: She is a new literary agent building her client list at Waterside Productions (and now Marsal Lyon Literary). Kathleen entered the publishing world with an internship at the Sandra Dijkstra Literary Agency, and from there she started at Waterside Productions in 2009 as a literary assistant. She has her MA in English with a specialization in children's literature.

SHE IS SEEKING: young adult and middle grade fiction across the board (historical fiction, science fiction, mystery, humor, fantasy, romance, thriller, and horror), picture books, and adult nonfiction (business, parenting, how-to, women's interest, humor, health, crafts).

HOW TO SUBMIT: You can send your electronic submissions to her at kathleen@ marsallyonliteraryagency.com. For fiction submissions, please write the word "QUERY" in the subject line, and include your query letter with the first 10 pages of your work in the body of your e-mail. For nonfiction submissions, please e-mail her your query letter and your complete proposal as an attachment.

TERMS Agent receives 15% commission on domestic sales. Agent receives 25% commission on foreign sales. Charges clients for photocopying. May recover certain costs, such as legal fees or the cost of shipping books by air to Europe or Japan.
HOW TO CONTACT Query with SASE. If querying by e-mail, put "query" in subject line. Obtains most new clients through recommendations from clients and publishers.

MCINTOSH & OTIS, INC.
353 Lexington Ave., New York NY 10016. (212)687-7400. **Fax:** (212)687-6894. **E-mail:** info@mcintoshandotis.com. **Website:** www.mcintoshandotis.net. **Contact:** Edward Necarsulmer IV.
REPRESENTS Actively seeking "books with memorable characters, distinctive voice, and a great plot." Not looking for educational, activity books, coloring books.

TERMS Agent receives 15% commission on domestic sales; 20% on foreign sales.
HOW TO CONTACT Query with SASE Exclusive submission only. Obtains clients through recommendations from others, editors, conferences and queries.
TIPS "No e-mail or phone calls!"

⊕ THE MCVEIGH AGENCY
345 W 21st St., New York NY 10011-3035. **E-mail:** queries@themcveighagency.com. **Website:** www.themcveighagency.com. **Contact:** Linda Epstein.

○ "I am a very hands-on, old-school agent who likes to edit mss as much as I like to negotiate deals. My favorite agents were always what I called 'honest sharks,' out to get the best deal for their client, always looking ahead, but always conducted business in such a way that everyone came away as happy as possible. In short—they had integrity and determination to represent their clients to the best of their abilities, and that's what I aspire to. I'm an experienced editor who knows virtually everyone in the field, having worked at almost every major publishing house. My knowledge of how to line edit a manuscript combined with my contacts allows me to help both new and established talent publish their works."

REPRESENTS Actively seeking genre mashups, a book that combines two common but disparate themes and combines them to comic or dramatic effect. As far as middle grade and young adult, this agency seeks everything, but especially scary books, historical steampunk, and books that would appeal to children of color.

TERMS Agent receives 15% on domestic sales; 15% on foreign sales. Offers written contract. 30 days notice must be given for termination of contract.

HOW TO CONTACT E-query. In the subject line of your e-mail, please write "Query," then the type of manuscript (e.g. YA, MG, PB, adult, nonfiction), and then the title of your book. The body of your e-mail should consist of your query letter, followed by the first 20 pages of your ms (for fiction) or your full proposal (for nonfiction). Please do not add your ms as an attachment. If the agency is interested in reading more, they'll request that you e-mail the full ms. Obtains new clients through recommendations from others, queries/solicitations, conferences.

ERIN MURPHY LITERARY AGENCY

2700 Woodlands Village, #300-458, Flagstaff AZ 86001. (928)525-2056. **Fax:** (928)525-2480. **Website:** http://emliterary.com. **Contact:** Erin Murphy, president; Ammi-Joan Paquette, associate agent.

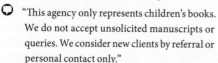 "This agency only represents children's books. We do not accept unsolicited manuscripts or queries. We consider new clients by referral or personal contact only."

REPRESENTS Specializes in children's books only.

TERMS Agent receives 15% commission on domestic sales; 25% on foreign sales. Offers written contract. 30 days notice must be given to terminate contract.

MUSE LITERARY MANAGEMENT

189 Waverly Place, #4, New York NY 10014-3135. (212)925-3721. **E-mail:** museliterarymgmt@aol.com.

Website: www.museliterary.com/. **Contact:** Deborah Carter.

REPRESENTS Specializes in ms development, the sale and administration of print, performance, and foreign rights to literary works, and post-publication publicity and appearances. Actively seeking "writers with formal training who bring compelling voices and a unique outlook to their mss. Those who submit should be receptive to editorial feedback and willing to revise during the submission process in order to remain competitive." Does not want "mss that have been worked over by book doctors (collaborative projects OK, but writers must have chops); category romance, chick lit, sci-fi, fantasy, horror, stories about cats and dogs, vampires or serial killers, fiction or nonfiction with religious or spiritual subject matter."

TERMS Agent receives 15% commission on domestic sales. Agent receives 20% commission on foreign sales. One-year contract offered when writer and agent agree that the ms is ready for submission; mss in development are not bound by contract. Sometimes charges for postage and photocopying. All expenses are preapproved by the client.

HOW TO CONTACT Query with SASE. Query via e-mail (no attachments). Discards unwanted queries. Obtains most new clients through recommendations from others, conferences.

TIPS "I give editorial feedback and work on revisions on spec. Agency agreement is offered when the writer and I feel the manuscript is ready for submission to publishers. Writers should also be open to doing revisions with editors who express serious interest in their work, prior to any offer of a publishing contract. All aspects of career strategy are discussed with writers, and all decisions are ultimately theirs. I make multiple and simultaneous submissions when looking for rights opportunities, and share all correspondence. All agreements are signed by the writers. Reimbursement for expenses is subject to client's approval, limited to photocopying (usually press clips) and postage. I always submit fresh manuscripts to publishers printed in my office with no charge to the writer."

JEAN V. NAGGAR LITERARY AGENCY, INC.

216 E. 75th St., Suite 1E, New York NY 10021. (212)794-1082. **E-mail:** jweltz@jvnla.com; jvnla@jvnla.com. **E-mail:** jweltz@jvnla.com; jregel@jvnla.com; atasman@jvnla.com; atasman@jvnla.com. **Website:** www.jvnla.com. **Contact:** Jean Naggar.

REPRESENTS This agency specializes in mainstream fiction, nonfiction and literary fiction with commercial potential.

RECENT SALES *Night Navigation*, by Ginnah Howard; *After Hours at the Almost Home*, by Tara Yelen; *An Entirely Synthetic Fish: A Biography of Rainbow Trout*, by Anders Halverson; *The Patron Saint of Butterflies*, by Cecilia Galante; *Wondrous Strange*, by Lesley Livingston; *6 Sick Hipsters*, by Rayo Casablanca; *The Last Bridge*, by Teri Coyne; *Gypsy Goodbye*, by Nancy Springer; *Commuters*, by Emily Tedrowe; *The Language of Secrets*, by Dianne Dixon; *Smiling to Freedom*, by Martin Benoit Stiles; *The Tale of Halcyon Crane*, by Wendy Webb; *Fugitive*, by Phillip Margolin; *BlackBerry Girl*, by Aidan Donnelley Rowley; *Wild Girls*, by Pat Murphy.

TERMS Agent receives 15% commission on domestic sales. Agent receives 20% commission on foreign sales. Offers written contract. Charges for overseas mailing, messenger services, book purchases, long-distance telephone, photocopying—all deductible from royalties received.

HOW TO CONTACT Query via e-mail. Prefers to read materials exclusively. No fax queries. Obtains most new clients through recommendations from others.

TIPS "Use a professional presentation. Because of the avalanche of unsolicited queries that flood the agency every week, we have had to modify our policy. We will now only guarantee to read and respond to queries from writers who come recommended by someone we know. Our areas are general fiction and nonfiction—no children's books by unpublished writers, no multimedia, no screenplays, no formula fiction, and no mysteries by unpublished writers. We recommend patience and fortitude: the courage to be true to your own vision, the fortitude to finish a novel and polish it again and again before sending it out, and the patience to accept rejection gracefully and wait for the stars to align themselves appropriately for success."

ALISON J. PICARD, LITERARY AGENT

Phone/Fax: (508)477-7192. **E-mail:** ajpicard@aol.com. **Contact:** Alison Picard.

REPRESENTS "Many of my clients have come to me from big agencies, where they felt overlooked or ignored. I communicate freely with my clients and offer a lot of career advice, suggestions for revising manuscripts, etc. If I believe in a project, I will sub-

mit it to a dozen or more publishers, unlike some agents who give up after four or five rejections." No science fiction/fantasy, westerns, poetry, plays or articles.

RECENT SALES *Zitface*, by Emily Ormand (Marshall Cavendish); *Totally Together*, by Stephanie O'Dea (Running Press); *The Ultimate Slow Cooker Cookbook*, by Stephanie O'Dea (Hyperion); Two Untitled Cookingbooks, by Erin Chase (St. Martin's Press); *A Journal of the Flood Year*, by David Ely (Portobello Books-United Kingdom, L'Ancora, — Italy); *A Mighty Wall*, by John Foley (Llewellyn/Flux); *Jelly's Gold*, by David Housewright (St. Martin's Press).

TERMS Agent receives 15% commission on domestic sales. Agent receives 20% commission on foreign sales. Offers written contract, binding for 1 year; 1-week notice must be given to terminate contract.

HOW TO CONTACT Query with SASE. Obtains most new clients through recommendations from others, solicitations.

TIPS "Please don't send material without sending a query first via mail or e-mail. I don't accept phone or fax queries. Always enclose an SASE with a query."

PROSPECT AGENCY

551 Valley Road, PMB 377, Upper Montclair NJ 02043. (718)788-3217. **Fax:** (718)360-9582. **E-mail:** esk@ prospectagency.com. **Website:** www.prospectagency.com. **Contact:** Emily Sylvan Kim, Becca Stumpf, Rachel Orr, Teresa Keitlinski.

All submissions are elcetronic; "mss and queries that are not a good fit for our agency are rejected via e-mail."

REPRESENTS Handles nonfiction, fiction, picture books, middle grade, young adult. "We're looking for strong, unique voices and unforgettable stories and characters."

RECENT SALES Sold 15 books for young readers in the last year. (Also represents adult fiction.) Recent sales include: *Ollie and Claire* (Philomel), *Vicious* (Bloomsbury), *Tempest Rising* (Walker Books), *Where do Diggers Sleep at Night* (Random House Children's), *A DJ Called Tomorrow* (Little,Brown), The *Princesses of Iowa* (Candlewick).

TERMS Agent receives 15% on domestic sales; 20% on foreign sales sold directly; and 25% on sales using a subagent. Offers written contract.

HOW TO CONTACT Send outline and 3 sample chapters. Accepts queries through website only. "We

BECKY VINTER (FINEPRINT LITERARY MANAGEMENT)
Fineprintlit.com
@BVinter

ABOUT BECKY: Becky Vinter began her career in publishing at the Feminist Press in 2006, before moving to NAL/Penguin, where she edited commercial women's fiction. She joined FinePrint Literary Management in 2011 and is currently looking for a range of both fiction and nonfiction projects. Becky grew up in London and earned her BA in English Literature from the University of Leeds. She now lives in Brooklyn.

SHE IS SEEKING: Becky likes the whole spectrum of women's fiction, from literary to "book club" to romance and mysteries. She is also in the market for YA fiction with strong female protagonists. In nonfiction, she likes well-crafted narrative nonfiction, including memoir, current events, travel, pop science, wellness, yoga and food.

HOW TO SUBMIT: Please send queries to becky@fineprintlit.com.

AGENTS & ART REPS

do not accept submissions to multiple Prospect agents (please submit to only 1 agent at Prospect Agency)." Obtains new clients through conferences, recommendations, queries, and some scouting.

WENDY SCHMALZ AGENCY

P.O. Box 831, Hudson NY 12534. (518)672-7697. E-mail: wendy@schmalzagency.com. **Website:** www. schmalzagency.com. **Contact:** Wendy Schmalz.

 Prior to opening her agency, Wendy Schmalz was an agent for 23 years at Harold Ober Associates.

REPRESENTS Actively seeking young adult novels, middle grade novels. Obtains clients through recommendations from others. Not looking for picture books, science fiction or fantasy.

TERMS Agent receives 15% commission on domestic sales; 20% on foreign sales; 25% for Asian sales.

HOW TO CONTACT Query with SASE. Accepts queries by e-mail. Obtains clients through recommendations from others.

SUSAN SCHULMAN LITERARY AGENCY

454 W. 44th St., New York NY 10036. (212)713-1633. **Fax:** (212)581-8830. **E-mail:** schulmanqueries@yahoo.com. **Contact:** Susan Schulman.

REPRESENTS "We specialize in books for, by and about women and women's issues including nonfiction self-help books, fiction and theater projects. We also handle the film, television and allied rights for several agencies as well as foreign rights for several publishing houses." Actively seeking new nonfiction. Considers plays. Does not want to receive poetry, television scripts or concepts for television.

RECENT SALES Sold 50 titles in the last year.

TERMS Agent receives 15% commission on domestic sales. Agent receives 20% commission on foreign sales. Offers written contract; 30-day notice must be given to terminate contract.

HOW TO CONTACT Query with SASE. Submit outline, synopsis, author bio, 3 sample chapters. Obtains most new clients through recommendations from others, solicitations, conferences.

NEW AGENT SPOTLIGHT

JESSIE CAMMACK
(JABBERWOCKY LITERARY AGENCY)

awfulagent.com

ABOUT JESSIE: Jessie Cammack is the digital rights manager for JABberwocky. She grew up in Los Angeles and moved to New York in 2005 to attend Columbia University, where she earned a degree in (mostly 19th century) English literature and (mostly 20th century) American history. While she was in college, she worked at Borders Books (the late Santa Monica store as well as the Columbus Circle store) and at The Overlook Press. She started at JABberwocky in fall 2009, and is actively building her client list.

SHE IS SEEKING: epic fantasy, YA science fiction, literary fiction. "I rarely rep nonfiction, but if I do, it's generally fairly serious history about a subject in which I am very interested. Recent examples I've read include Jennifer Homans's exhaustive history of ballet, *Apollo's Angels*, and Kate Cambor's rather novelistic triple biography, *Gilded Youth*."

HOW TO CONTACT: The agency's webpage says they are closed to queries, but Jessie told me that they will soon reopen, and regardless, she herself is open to queries right now. Send all queries via snail mail: JABberwocky Literary Agency, PO Box 4558, Sunnyside, NY 11104-0558. Send a one-page query with SASE if you want a reply. "Including a synopsis or a few sample pages is optional and acceptable." E-queries will not be read.

TIPS "Keep writing!" Schulman describes her agency as "professional boutique, long-standing, eclectic."

SERENDIPITY LITERARY AGENCY, LLC

305 Gates Ave., Brooklyn NY 11216. (718)230-7689. **Fax:** (718)230-7829. **E-mail:** rbrooks@serendipitylit. com; info@serendipitylit.com. **Website:** www.serendipitylit.com. **Contact:** Regina Brooks.

○ "I adore working with first-time authors whose books challenge the readers emotionally; tears and laughter. I also represent award-winning illustrators."

REPRESENTS African-American nonfiction, commercial fiction, young adult novels with an urban flair and juvenile books. No stage plays, screenplays or poetry.

RECENT SALES *A Wreath for Emmitt Till*, by Marilyn Nelson (Houghton Mifflin); *A Song for Present Existence*, by Marilyn Nelson and Tonya Hegamin (Scholastic); *Ruby and the Booker Boys*, by Derrick Barnes (Scholastic); *Brenda Buckley's Universe and Everything In It*, by Sundee Frazier (Delacorte Books for Young Readers); *Wait Until the Black Girl Sings*, by Bil Wright (Scholastic); *First Semester*, by Cecil R. Cross II (KimaniTru/ Harlequin).

TERMS Agent receives 15% commission on domestic sales. Agent receives 20% commission on foreign sales. Offers written contract; 2-month notice must be given to terminate contract. Charges clients for office fees, which are taken from any advance.

HOW TO CONTACT Prefers to read materials exclusively. For nonfiction, submit proposal, outline, 1 sample chapter (electronically), SASE. Write the field on the back of the envelope. For adult fiction, please send a query letter that includes basic information that describes your project. Your query letter should include the title, premise, and length of the manuscript. See our guidelines onine. Write the genre of your book on the back of your envelope. Based on your initial query letter and synopsis, our office may request sample chapters, or your ms in its entirety. Obtains most new clients through conferences, referrals.

TIPS "See *Writing Great Books for Young Adults.* Looking for high concept ideas with big hooks."

THE SPIELER AGENCY

27 W. 20 St., Suite 305, New York NY 10011. **E-mail:** thespieleragency@gmail.com. **Contact:** Katya Balter, acquisitions.

TERMS Agent receives 15% commission on domestic sales. Charges clients for messenger bills, photocopying, postage.

HOW TO CONTACT Accepts electronic submissions, or send query letter and sample chapters. Returns materials only with SASE; otherwise materials are discarded when rejected. Obtains most new clients through recommendations, and listing in *Guide to Literary Agents.*

TIPS "Check www.publishersmarketplace.com/members/spielerlit."

STIMOLA LITERARY STUDIO, INC.

308 Livingston Ct., Edgewater NJ 07020. **Fax: /Phone:** (201)945-9353. **E-mail:** info@stimolaliterarystudio.com. **Website:** www.stimolaliterarystudio.com. **Contact:** Rosemary B. Stimola.

⚪ Prior to opening her agency Rosemary Stimola was an independent children's bookseller.

REPRESENTS Actively seeking remarkable young adult fiction and debut picture book author/illustrators. No institutional books.

RECENT SALES Sold 40 books for young readers in the last year. Among these, *A Touch Mortal,* by Leah Clifford (Greenwillow/Harper Collins); *Black Hole Sun,* by David Gill (Greenwillow/Harper Collins); *Dot,*

by Patricia Intriago (FSG/Macmillan); *Inside Out and Back Again,* by Thanhha Lai (Harper Collins); *The Fox Inheritance,* by Mary Pearson (Henry Holt/Macmillan); *Henry Aaron's Dream,* by Matt Tavares (Candlewick Press); *Throat,* by R.A. Nelson (Knopf/RH).

TERMS Agent receives 15% commission on domestic sales. Agent receives 20% (if subagents are employed) commission on foreign sales. Offers written contract, binding for all children's projects. 60 days notice must be given to terminate contract. Charges $85 one-time fee per project to cover expenses.

HOW TO CONTACT Query via e-mail. "No attachments, please!" Yes While unsolicited queries are welcome, most clients come through editor, agent, client referrals.

TIPS Agent is hands-on, no-nonsense. May request revisions. Does not edit but may offer suggestions for improvement. Well-respected by clients and editors. "A firm but reasonable deal negotiator."

⊕ THE STRINGER LITERARY AGENCY, LLC

E-mail: stringerlit@comcast.net. **Website:** www.stringerlit.com. **Contact:** Marlene Stringer.

REPRESENTS This agency specializes in fiction. Does not want to receive picture books, plays, short stories or poetry.

RECENT SALES *Out for Blood* and *Stolen,* by Alyxandra Harvey (Walker Books); *Change of Heart,* by Shari Maurer (WestSide Books); *I Stole Johnny Depp's Alien Girlfriend,* by Gary Ghislain (Chronicle Books); *The Land of Hope & Glory Trilogy,* by Geoffrey Wilson (Hodder); *..And On The Piano, Nicky Hopkins!,* by Julian Dawson (Plus One Press); *Poison Kissed,* by Erica Hayes (St. Martin's); *Possum Summer,* by Jen K. Blom (Holiday House).

HOW TO CONTACT Electronic submissions only.

TIPS "If your manuscript falls between categories, or you are not sure of the category, query and we'll let you know if we'd like to take a look. We strive to respond as quickly as possible. If you have not received a response in the time period indicated, please re-query."

ANN TOBIAS: A LITERARY AGENCY FOR CHILDREN'S BOOKS

520 E. 84th St., Apt. 4L, New York NY 10028. **E-mail:** AnnTobias84@hotmail.com. **Contact:** Ann Tobias.

REPRESENTS This agency specializes in books for children.

TERMS Agent receives 15% commission on domestic sales. Agent receives 20% commission on foreign sales. This agency charges clients for photocopying, overnight mail, foreign postage, foreign telephone.

HOW TO CONTACT For all age groups and genres: Send a one-page letter of inquiry accompanied by a one-page writing sample, double-spaced. No attachments will be opened. Obtains most new clients through recommendations from editors.

TIPS "Read at least 200 children's books in the age group and genre in which you hope to be published. Follow this by reading another 100 children's books in other age groups and genres so you will have a feel for the field as a whole."

S©OTT TREIMEL NY

434 Lafayette St., New York NY 10003. (212)505-8353. **E-mail:** general@scotttreimelny.com. **Website:** ScottTreimelNY.blogspot.com; www.ScottTreimelNY.com. **Contact:** John M. Cusick.

REPRESENTS This agency specializes in tightly focused segments of the trade and institutional markets. Career clients.

RECENT SALES *The Hunchback Assignments*, by Arthur Slade (Random House, HarperCollins Canada; HarperCollins Australia); *Shotgun Serenade*, by Gail Giles (Little, Brown); *Laundry Day*, by Maurie Manning (Clarion); *The P.S. Brothers*, by Maribeth Boelts (Harcourt); *The First Five Fourths*, by Pat Hughes (Viking); *Old Robert and the Troubadour Cats*, by Barbara Joosse (Philomel); *Ends*, by David Ward (Abrams); *Dear Canada*, by Barbara Haworth-Attard (Scholastic); *Soccer Dreams*, by Maribeth Boelts (Candlewick); *Lucky Me*, by Richard Scrimger (Tundra); *Play, Louie, Play*, by Muriel Harris Weinstein (Bloomsbury).

TERMS Agent receives 15% commission on domestic sales. Agent receives 20% commission on foreign sales. Offers verbal or written contract. Charges clients for photocopying, express postage, messengers, and books needed to sell foreign, film and other rights.

HOW TO CONTACT Submissions accepted only via website.

TIPS "We look for dedicated authors and illustrators able to sustain longtime careers in our increasingly competitive field. I want fresh, not derivative story concepts with overly familiar characters. We look for gripping stories, characters, pacing, and themes. We remain mindful of an authentic (to the age) point-of-view, and look for original voices. We spend significant time hunting for the best new work, and do launch debut talent each year. It

is best *not* to send mss with lengthy submission histories already."

WRITERS HOUSE

21 W. 26th St., New York NY 10010. (212)685-2400. **Fax:** (212)685-1781. **E-mail:** mmejias@writershouse.com; smalk@writershouse.com. **Website:** www.writershouse.com. **Contact:** Michael Mejias.

REPRESENTS This agency specializes in all types of popular fiction and nonfiction. Does not want to receive scholarly, professional, poetry, plays, or screenplays.

TERMS Agent receives 15% commission on domestic sales. Agent receives 20% commission on foreign sales. Offers written contract, binding for 1 year. Agency charges fees for copying mss/proposals and overseas airmail of books.

HOW TO CONTACT Query with SASE. Please send us a query letter of no more than 2 pages, which includes your credentials, an explanation of what makes your book unique and special, and a synopsis. (If submitting to Steven Malk: Writers House, 7660 Fay Ave., #338H, La Jolla, CA 92037) Obtains most new clients through recommendations from authors and editors.

TIPS "Do not send mss. Write a compelling letter. If you do, we'll ask to see your work. Follow submission guidelines and please do not simultaneously submit your work to more than one Writers House agent."

WRITERS HOUSE (STEVEN MALK)

7660 Fay Ave., #338H, La Jolla CA 92037. **E-mail:** smalk@writershouse.com. (West Coast Office), 7660 Fay Ave., #338H, La Jolla, CA 92037. **Contact:** Steven Malk. e-mail: smalk@WritersHouse.com 21 W. 26th St. New York NY 10010. (212)685-2400; (212)685-1781

⟳ See Writers House listing above for more information.

REPRESENTS Children's Nonfiction, fiction, picture books, middle-grade novels, young adult, illustrators.

ART REPS

ART FACTORY

925 Elm Grove Rd., Elm Grove WI 53122. (262)785-1940. **Fax:** (262)785-1611. **E-mail:** tstocki@artfactoryltd.com. **Website:** www.artfactoryillustrators.com. **Contact:** Tom Stocki.

REPRESENTS Currently open to illustrators seeking representation. Open to both new and established illustrators.

KAT SALAZAR
(LARSEN POMADA LITERARY AGENTS)
larsenpomada.com
@KatLovesBooks

ABOUT KAT: Kat Salazar joined Larsen Pomada Literary Agents in February 2011 as an intern for the agency working directly for agency co-founder Elizabeth Pomada. Previously she worked for University of Washington Press as a Marketing Assistant and held internships at University of California Press, HarperOne of HarperCollins, and Wales Literary Agency. Currently, she is the Publishing Assistant at Red Wheel/Weiser/Conari Press as well as the agency's newest Associate Agent and the San Francisco Writers Conference Social Media Coordinator. Kat earned a BA degree from University of Washington, double majoring in English: Literature and Communications: Journalism. For more about Kat you can follow her on Twitter at @KatLovesBooks or read her blog: KatLovesBooks.blogspot.com.

SHE IS SEEKING: Kat is actively looking for young adult, middle grade, and children's picture books. For adult audiences, she is interested in literary fiction and urban fantasy.

HOW TO SUBMIT: Please query her with the first 10 pages of your manuscript and a 1-2-page synopsis copied and pasted into the body of an e-mail to QueryKatSalazar@gmail.com.

TERMS Receives 25-30% commission. Offers written contract. Advertising costs are split: 75% paid by illustrators; 25% paid by rep.

HOW TO CONTACT For first contact, send query letter, tearsheets. Responds only if interested. Calls to schedule an appointment. Portfolio should include tearsheets. Finds illustrators through queries/solicitations.

TIPS "Have a unique style."

CAROL BANCROFT & FRIENDS

P.O. Box 2030, Danbury CT 06813. (203)730-8270 or (800)720-7020. **Fax:** (203)730-8275. **E-mail:** cb_friends8270@sbcglobal.net or cbfriends@sbcglobal.net; artists@carolbancroft.com. **Website:** www.carolbancroft.com. **Contact:** Joy Elton Tricarico, owner; Carol Bancroft, founder.

REPRESENTS Specializes in illustration for children's publishing-text and trade; any children's-related material.

TERMS Rep receives 25% commission. Advertising costs are split: 75% paid by talent; 25% paid by representative.

HOW TO CONTACT E-mail 2-3 samples with your address or mail 6-10 samples, along with a SASE, to the P.O. box address. For promotional purposes, artists must provide "laser copies (not slides), tearsheets, promo pieces, good color photocopies, etc.; 6 pieces or more is best; narrative scenes and children interacting."

NEW AGENT SPOTLIGHT

SARA SCIUTO (FULL CIRCLE LITERARY)

fullcircleliterary.com/
@sarasciuto

ABOUT SARA: A recent graduate of University of California San Diego, Sara Sciuto also completed literature coursework at NYU. Before joining Full Circle, she gained valuable experience working on film and foreign rights with the Taryn Fagerness Agency. Her great passions in life are travel and good food—and good books, of course, but that goes without saying! While she's always cultivating new obsessions, her latest are photography and sailing.

SHE IS SEEKING: Sara is actively building her list with a focus on middle grade and young adult, in particular, dystopian, science fiction, fantasy, and unique paranormal. She also enjoys contemporary stories with a strong, authentic voice (but no chick-lit, please). She has a particular soft spot for anything in the Deep South (sweet contemporary to dark paranormal), gritty contemporary, utilitarian dystopias or dystopian thrillers, anything with international locales or period settings (think flappers or "Mad Men"), and anything with artistic themes. Sara is also looking for standout picture books, especially those with a quirky or humorous narrative. She's also considering select nonfiction in the areas of craft, design, how-to, lifestyle, and pop culture. Currently, she is not considering any adult fiction (all genres).

HOW TO SUBMIT: "We only accept electronic submissions. Send a 1-page query letter (in the body of the e-mail, no attachments please) including a description of your book, writing credentials and author highlights. Put 'Query For Sara' in the subject line. Following your query, please include the first 10 pages or complete picture book manuscript text within the body of the email. For nonfiction, include a proposal with one sample chapter. Please send your queries to: submissions@fullcircleliterary.com. (Queries sent to any other Full Circle Literary e-mail address will not be read or opened.) Due to the overwhelming number of submissions we receive, we are only able to respond if we are interested in your project. If interested, within 6-8 weeks we will contact you to request additional materials (such as sample chapters or a complete manuscript)."

TIPS "We look for artists who can draw animals and people with imagination and energy, depicting engaging characters with action in situational settings."

PEMA BROWNE LTD.

71 Pine Rd., Woodbourne NY 12788. (845)268-0029. **E-mail:** ppbltd@optonline.net. **Website:** www.pemabrowneltd.com. **Contact:** Pema Browne.

○ Looking for "professional and unique" talent.

REPRESENTS Specializes in general commercial.
RECENT SALES *The Daring Miss Quimby*, by Suzanne Whitaker, illustrated by Catherine Stock (Holiday House).
TERMS Rep receives 30% illustration commission; 20% author commission. Exclusive area representation is required. For promotional purposes, talent must provide color mailers to distribute. Representative pays mailing costs on promotion mailings.
HOW TO CONTACT For first contact, send query letter, direct mail flier/brochure and SASE. If interested will ask to mail appropriate materials for review. Portfolios should include tearsheets and transparencies or good color photocopies, plus SASE. Accepts queries by mail only. Obtains new talent through recommendations and interviews (portfolio review). Current clients include HarperCollins, Holiday House, Bantam Doubleday Dell, Nelson/Word, Hyperion, Putnam. Client list available upon request.
TIPS "We are doing more publishing—all types—less advertising." Looks for "continuity of illustration and dedication to work."

CATUGEAU: ARTIST AGENT, LLC

3009 Margaret Jones Ln., Williamsburg VA 23185. (757)221-0666. **Website:** www.CATugeau.com. **Contact:** Christina Tugeau, owner/agent.

○ Accepting limited new artists from North America only.

REPRESENTS Actively seeking illustrations only (and book ideas from agency artists).
TERMS Receives 25% commission.
HOW TO CONTACT For first contact, e-mail samples and live website link, with note. No CDs. "Artists responsible for providing samples for portfolios, promotional books and mailings." Finds illustrators through recommendations from others, conferences, personal search.
TIPS "Do research, read articles on CAT website, study picture books at bookstores, promote yourself

a bit to learn the industry. Be professional. Know what you do best, and be prepared to give rep what they need to present you! Do have e-mail and scanning capabilities, too."

○ CORNELL & McCARTHY LLC

2-D Cross Highway, Westport CT 06880. (203)454-4210. **Fax:** (203)454-4258. **E-mail:** contact@cmartreps.com. **Website:** www.cmartreps.com. **Contact:** Merial Cornell.

REPRESENTS Specializes in children's books: trade, mass market, educational. Obtains new talent through recommendations, solicitation, conferences.
TERMS Agent receives 25% commission. Advertising costs are split: 75% paid by talent; 25% paid by representative.
HOW TO CONTACT For first contact, send query letter, direct mail flier/brochure, tearsheets, photocopies and SASE or e-mail. For promotional purposes, talent must provide 10-12 strong portfolio pieces relating to children's publishing.
TIPS "Work hard on your portfolio."

CREATIVE FREELANCERS, INC.

P.O. Box 366, Tallevast FL 34270. (800)398-9544. **E-mail:** creative@illustratorsonline.com. **Website:** www.illustratorsonline.com. **Contact:** Marilyn Howard.
REPRESENTS Specializes in children's books, advertising, architectural, conceptual. Markets include: advertising agencies; corporations/client direct; design firms; editorial/magazines; paper products/greeting cards; publishing/books; sales/promotion firms.
TERMS Rep receives 30% commission. Exclusive area representation is preferred. Advertising costs are split: 75% paid by talent; 25% paid by representative.
HOW TO CONTACT For first contact, send tearsheets, low-res JPEGs or "whatever best shows work." Responds back only if interested. For promotional purposes, talent must provide scans of artwork.
TIPS Looks for experience, professionalism and consistency of style. Obtains new talent through "word of mouth and website."

DIMENSION

13420 Morgan Ave. S., Burnsville MN 55337. (952)201-3981. **E-mail:** jkoltes@dimensioncreative.com; jkoltes@visi.com. **Website:** www.dimensioncreative.com. **Contact:** Joanne Koltes.
REPRESENTS Advertises in *Picturebook* and *Minnesota Creative*.

HOW TO CONTACT Contact with samples via e-mail. Responds only if interested.

THOROGOOD KIDS/GOOD ILLUSTRATION

11-15 Betterton St., Covent Garden, London WC2H 9BP United Kingdom. (347)627-0243. **E-mail:** draw@ goodillustration.com. **Website:** www.goodillustration.com.

HOW TO CONTACT "For first contact, send tearsheets, photocopies, SASE, direct mail flyer/brochure. After initial contact, we will contact the illustrator if we want to see the portfolio. Portfolio should include tearsheets, photocopies. Finds illustrators through queries/solicitations, conferences." Accepts illustration, illustration/ms packages.

TIPS "Be unique and research your market. Talent will win out!"

PAT HACKETT/ARTIST REP

7014 N. Mercer Way, Mercer Island WA 98040-2130. (206)447-1600. **Fax:** (206)447-0739. **E-mail:** pat@ pathackett.com. **Website:** www.pathackett.com. **Contact:** Pat Hackett.

REPRESENTS Looking for illustrators with unique, strong, salable style. Currently open to illustrators seeking representation. Open to both new and established illustrators.

TERMS Receives 25-33% commission. Advertising costs are split: 75% paid by illustrators; 25% paid by rep.

HOW TO CONTACT For first contact, send query letter, tearsheets, SASE, direct mail flyer/brochure, or e-mail. Responds only if interested. Wait for response.

LEVY CREATIVE MANAGEMENT

245 E. 63rd St., Suite 1622, New York NY 10065. (212)687-6463. **Fax:** (212)661-4839. **E-mail:** info@ levycreative.com. **Website:** www.levycreative.com. **Contact:** Sari S. Schorr.

REPRESENTS Currently open to illustrators seeking representation. Open to both new and established illustrators.

TERMS Offers written contract. Advertising costs are split: 75% paid by illustrators; 25% paid by rep.

HOW TO CONTACT For first contact, send tearsheets, photocopies, SASE. See submission guidelines on website. Portfolio should include professionally presented materials. Finds illustrators through recommendations from others, word of mouth, competitions.

MB ARTISTS

775 Sixth Ave., No. 6, New York NY 10001. (212)689-7830. **E-mail:** mela@mbartists.com. **Website:** www.mbartists.com. **Contact:** Mela Bolinao.

REPRESENTS Specializes in illustration for juvenile markets. Markets include: advertising agencies; editorial/magazines; publishing/books, board games, stationary, etc.

RECENT SALES *Peanut Butter and Homework Sandwiches*, illustrated by Jack E. Davis (Putnam); *Pirates Go to School*, illustrated by John Manders (Scholastic); *The Adventures of Granny Clearwater,* illustrated by by Laura Huliska Beith (Henry Holt); *Grandma Calls Me Gigglepie*, illustrated by Hiroe Nakata (Robin Corey Books); *Twelve Haunted Rooms of Halloween*, illustrated by Macky Pamintuan (Sterling).

TERMS Rep receives 25% commission. No geographic restrictions. Advertising costs are split: 75% paid by talent; 25% paid by representative.

HOW TO CONTACT For first contact, send query letter, direct mail flier/brochure, website address, tearsheets, slides, photographs or color copies and SASE or send website link to mela@mbartists.com. Portfolio should include at least 12 images appropriate for the juvenile market.

THE NEIS GROUP

14600 Sawyer Ranch Rd., Dripping Springs TX 78620. (616)450-1533. **E-mail:** jneis@neisgroup.com. **Website:** www.neisgroup.com. **Contact:** Judy Neis.

REPRESENTS Currently open to illustrators seeking representation. Looking for established illustrators only.

TERMS Receives 25% commission.

HOW TO CONTACT For first contact, send bio, tearsheets, direct mail flier/brochure. After initial contact, drop off portfolio of nonreturnables. Portfolio should include tearsheets, photocopies. Prefers "portfolios on disc, color printouts and e-mail capabilities whenever possible." Obtains new talent through recommendations from others and queries/solicitations.

WANDA NOWAK/CREATIVE ILLUSTRATORS AGENCY

231 E. 76th St., 5D, New York NY 10021. (212)535-0438. **Fax:** (212)535-1629. **E-mail:** wanda@wandanow.com. **Website:** www.wandanow.com.

REPRESENTS Actively seeking "unique, individual style."

NEW AGENT SPOTLIGHT

CARLIE WEBBER (THE JANE ROTROSEN AGENCY)

janerotrosen.com/
@carliebeth

ABOUT CARLIE: Carlie Webber refused to major in English in college because no one would let her read Stephen King or R.L. Stine for class. She took her love of young adult and genre fiction to the University of Pittsburgh, where she obtained a Master of Library and Information Science, and worked as a YA librarian and reviewer for publications including Kirkus Reviews. Wishing to explore her interest in the business side of books, she decided to switch from librarianship to publishing and enrolled in the Columbia Publishing Course. Now she is building her agenting career on her favorite genres.

SHE IS SEEKING: young adult (any and all genres), horror, mystery, thriller, suspense, contemporary romance, humor, literary fiction, women's fiction. "More specific examples from my submissions wishlist: anything set in the grunge era; GLBTQ for YA; high-concept YA; genre mashups, like paranormal romantic suspense.

HOW TO SUBMIT: Send an e-mail with a query, a synopsis, and either the first 30 pages or three chapters, whichever is more, to cwebber@janerotrosen.com, and please put the word "Query" in the subject line.

TERMS Receives 30% commission. Exclusive representation required. Offers written contract. Advertising costs are split: 70% paid by illustrators; 30% paid by rep. Advertises in *Workbook, American Illustrators*.
HOW TO CONTACT For first contact, send e-mail with PDF. Finds illustrators through recommendations from others, sourcebooks, exhibitions.
TIPS "Develop your own style. Send a little illustrated story, which will prove you can carry a character in different situations with facial expressions, etc."

LIZ SANDERS AGENCY

2415 E. Hangman Creek Ln., Spokane WA 99224-8514. (509)993-6400. **E-mail:** liz@lizsanders.com; artsubmissions@lizsanders.com. **Website:** www.lizsanders.com. **Contact:** Liz Sanders, owner.
REPRESENTS Markets include publishing, licensed properties, entertainment and advertising. Currently open to illustrators seeking representation. Open to both new and established illustrators.
TERMS Receives 30% commission against pro bono mailing program. Offers written contract.
HOW TO CONTACT For first contact, send tearsheets, direct mail flier/brochure, color copies, non-returnable or e-mail to artsubmissions@lizsanders.com. Obtains new talent through recommendations from industry contacts, conferences and queries/solicitations, Literary Market Place.

S.I. INTERNATIONAL

43 E. 19th St., 2nd Floor, New York NY 10003. (212)254-4996. **Fax:** (212)995-0911. **E-mail:** information@si-i.com; hspiers@si-i.com. **Website:** www.si-i.com. **Contact:** Donald Bruckstein, artist relations.
REPRESENTS Specializes in license characters, educational publishing and children's illustration, digital

NEW AGENT SPOTLIGHT

ERIN HARRIS (SKOLNICK LITERARY)

skolnickagency.com

ABOUT ERIN: Erin Harris is an agent at the Irene Skolnick Literary Agency. She represents (among others): David Yezzi, executive editor of *The New Criterion* and author of the forthcoming biography *Anthony Hecht: The Poet and the Age* (St. Martin's Press); Rosalie Knecht, the English language translator of César Aira's *The Seamstress and the Wind* (New Directions); Bryan Furuness, author of the forthcoming novel *The Lost Episodes of Revie Bryson* (Dzanc); and Carla Power, a *Time Magazine* contributor and former *Newsweek* correspondent. A graduate of the MFA program in creative writing at The New School, Erin received her B.A. in English from Trinity College (Hartford, CT), where she was Presidential Fellow of the English Department and inducted into Phi Beta Kappa.

SHE IS SEEKING: literary novels with compelling plots and international settings; literary thrillers and mysteries (she'd love to find the next Tana French!); noirs (especially starring headstrong female protagonists); and YA and middle grade novels that transport her to magical places.

HOW TO SUBMIT: You can query Erin via e-mail at submissions@skolnickagency.com. Your query should include: a description of your manuscript, your contact information, and your author bio. In the author bio, be sure to inform her of any previous publications, awards, professional and/or academic affiliations, and media appearances. In addition, please paste the first 10 pages of your manuscript into the body of your e-mail. She will not open attachments unless they have been requested.

art and design, mass market paperbacks. Markets include design firms; publishing/books; sales/promotion firms; licensing firms; digital art and design firms. Looking for artists "who have the ability to do children's illustration and to do license characters either digitally or reflectively."
TERMS Rep receives 25-30% commission. Advertising costs are split: 70% paid by talent; 30% paid by rep. "Contact agency for details. Must have mailer."

HOW TO CONTACT For first contact, send query letter, tearsheets. After initial contact, write for appointment to show portfolio of tearsheets, slides.

GWEN WALTERS ARTIST REPRESENTATIVE

1801 S. Flagler Dr., No. 1202, West Palm Beach FL 33401. (561)805-7739. **E-mail:** artincgw@gmail.com. **Website:** www.gwenwaltersartrep.com. **Contact:** Gwen Walters.

REPRESENTS Currently open to illustrators seeking representation. Looking for established illustrators only.

RECENT SALES Sells to "All major book publishers."

TERMS Receives 30% commission. Artist needs to supply all promo material. Offers written contract.

HOW TO CONTACT For first contact, send tearsheets. Finds illustrators through recommendations from others.

TIPS "You need to pound the pavement for a couple of years to get some experience under your belt. Don't forget to sign all artwork. So many artists forget to stamp their samples."

WENDYLYNN & CO.

504 Wilson Rd., Annapolis MD 21401. (410)224-2729. **E-mail:** wendy@wendylynn.com; janice@wendylynn.com. **Website:** www.wendylynn.com. **Contact:** Wendy Mays; Janice Onken.

REPRESENTS Currently open to considering illustrators seeking representation. Open to both new and established illustrators. Not interested in cartoon style illustration.

TERMS Receives 25% commission. Exclusive representation required. Offers written contract. Requires participation in a children's illustrators website that artist pays for annually. Agent pays 100% of all other promotion.

HOW TO CONTACT For first contact, e-mail 4-5 JPEG samples and link to website. Responds if interested. Portfolio should include a minimum of 20 strong images. Finds illustrators through recommendations from others and from portfolio reviews.

TIPS "Work on making your characters consistent and vibrant, showing movement and emotion. Be able to scan your artwork and send digital files. Create an interesting and user-friendly website of your illustrations."

CLUBS & ORGANIZATIONS

Contacts made through organizations such as the ones listed in this section can be quite beneficial for children's writers and illustrators. Professional organizations provide numerous educational, business, and legal services in the form of newsletters, workshops, or seminars. Organizations can provide tips about how to be a more successful writer or artist, as well as what types of business cards to keep, health and life insurance coverage to carry, and competitions to consider.

An added benefit of belonging to an organization is the opportunity to network with those who have similar interests, creating a support system. As in any business, knowing the right people can often help your career, and important contacts can be made through your peers. Membership in a writer's or artist's organization also shows publishers you're serious about your craft. This provides no guarantee your work will be published, but it gives you an added dimension of credibility and professionalism.

Some of the organizations listed here welcome anyone with an interest, while others are only open to published writers and professional artists. Organizations such as the Society of Children's Book Writers and Illustrators (SCBWI, scbwi.org) have varying levels of membership. SCBWI offers associate membership to those with no publishing credits, and full membership to those who have had work for children published. International organizations such as SCBWI also have regional chapters throughout the U.S. and the world. Write or call for more information regarding any group that interests you, or check the websites of the many organizations that list them. Be sure to get information about local chapters, membership qualifications, and services offered.

AMERICAN ALLIANCE FOR THEATRE & EDUCATION

7979 Old Georgetown Rd., 10th Floor, Bethesda MD 20814. (301)951-7977. **E-mail:** info@aate.com. **Website:** www.aate.com. Purpose of organization: to promote standards of excellence in theatre and drama education. "We achieve this by assimilating quality practices in theatre and theatre education, connecting artists, educators, researchers and scholars with each other, and by providing opportunities for our members to learn, exchange and diversify their work, their audiences and their perspectives." Membership cost: $115 annually for individuals in U.S. and Canada, $220 annually for organizations, $60 annually for students, and $70 annually for retired people, $310 annually for University Departmental memberships; add $30 outside Canada and U.S. Holds annual conference (July or August). Contests held for unpublished play reading project and annual awards in various categories. Awards plaque and stickers for published playbooks. Publishes list of unpublished plays deemed worthy of performance and stages readings at conference. Contact national office at number above or see website for contact information for Playwriting Network Chairpersons.

AMERICAN SOCIETY OF JOURNALISTS AND AUTHORS

1501 Broadway, Suite 302, New York NY 10036. **Website:** www.asja.org. Qualifications for membership: "Need to be a professional freelance nonfiction writer. Refer to website for further qualifications." Membership cost: Application fee—$50; annual dues—$195. Group sponsors national conferences. Professional seminars online and in person around the country. Workshops/conferences open to nonmembers. Publishes a newsletter for members that provides confidential information for nonfiction writers. **Contact:** Alexandra Owens, executive director.

ARIZONA AUTHORS ASSOCIATION

6145 West Echo Lane, Glendale AZ 85302. (623)847-9343. **E-mail:** info@azauthors.com. **Website:** www.azauthors.com. Purpose of organization: to offer professional, educational and social opportunities to writers and authors, and serve as a network. Members must be authors, writers working toward publication, agents, publishers, publicists, printers, illustrators, etc. Membership cost: $45/year writers; $30/year students; $60/year other professionals in publishing industry. Holds regular workshops and meetings. Publishes bimonthly newsletter and *Arizona Literary Magazine*. Sponsors Annual Literary Contest in poetry, essays, short stories, novels, and published books with cash prizes and awards bestowed at a public banquet. Winning entries are also published or advertised in the *Arizona Literary Magazine*. First and second place winners in poetry, essay and short story categories are entered in the Pushcart Prize. Winners in published categories receive free listings by www.fivestarpublications.com. Send SASE or view website for guidelines. **Contact:** Toby Heathcotte, president.

THE AUTHORS GUILD, INC.

31 E. 32nd St., 7th Floor, New York NY 10016. (212)564-5904. **Fax:** (212)564-5363. **E-mail:** staff@authorsguild.org. **Website:** www.authorsguild.org. Purpose of organization: to offer services and materials intended to help authors with the business and legal aspects of their work, including contract problems, copyright matters, freedom of expression and taxation. Guild has 8,000 members. Qualifications for membership: Must be book author published by an established American publisher within 7 years or any author who has had 3 works (fiction or nonfiction) published by a magazine or magazines of general circulation in the last 18 months. Associate membership also available. Annual dues: $90. Different levels of membership include: associate membership with all rights except voting available to an author who has a firm contract offer or is currently negotiating a royalty contract from an established American publisher. "The Guild offers free contract reviews to its members. The Guild conducts several symposia each year at which experts provide information, offer advice and answer questions on subjects of interest and concern to authors. Typical subjects have been the rights of privacy and publicity, libel, wills and estates, taxation, copyright, editors and editing, the art of interviewing, standards of criticism and book reviewing. Transcripts of these symposia are published and circulated to members. The *Authors Guild Bulletin*, a quarterly journal, contains articles on matters of interest to writers, reports of Guild activities, contract surveys, advice on problem clauses in contracts, transcripts of Guild and League symposia and information on a variety of professional topics. Subscription included in the cost of the annual dues." **Contact:** Paul Aiken, executive director.

☉ CANADIAN SOCIETY OF CHILDREN'S AUTHORS, ILLUSTRATORS AND PERFORMERS

104-40 Orchard View Blvd., Toronto ON M4R 1B9 Canada. (416)515-1559. **E-mail:** office@canscaip.org. **Website:** www.canscaip.org. Purpose of organization: development of Canadian children's culture and support for authors, illustrators and performers working in this field. Qualifications for membership: Members—professionals who have been published (not self-published) or have paid public performances/records/tapes to their credit. Friends—share interest in field of children's culture. Membership cost: $85 (Members dues), $45 (Friends dues). Sponsors workshops/conferences. Manuscript evaluation services; publishes newsletter: includes profiles of members; news round-up of members' activities countrywide; market news; news on awards, grants, etc; columns related to professional concerns. **Contact:** Lena Coakley, administrative director.

LEWIS CARROLL SOCIETY OF NORTH AMERICA

11935 Beltsville Dr., Beltsville MD 20705. **E-mail:** secretary@lewiscarroll.org. **Website:** www.lewiscarroll.org. "We are an organization of Carroll admirers of all ages and interests and a center for Carroll studies." Qualifications for membership: "An interest in Lewis Carroll and a simple love for Alice (or the Snark for that matter)." Membership cost: $35 (regular membership), $50 (foreign membership), $100 (sustaining membership). The Society meets twice a year—in spring and in fall; locations vary. Publishes a semi-annual journal, *Knight Letter*, and maintains an active publishing program. **Contact:** Clare Imholtz, secretary.

THE CHILDREN'S BOOK COUNCIL, INC.

54 W. 39th St., 14th Floor, New York NY 10018. (212)966-1990. **Fax:** (212)966-2073. **E-mail:** cbc.info@cbcbooks.org. **Website:** www.cbcbooks.org. Purpose of organization: A nonprofit trade association of children's and young adult publishers and packagers, CBC promotes the enjoyment of books for children and young adults and works with national and international organizations to that end. The CBC has sponsored Children's Book Week since 1945 and Young People's Poetry Week since 1999. Qualifications for membership: trade publishers and packagers of children's and young adult books and related literary materials are eligible for membership. Publishers wishing to join should contact the CBC for dues information. Sponsors workshops and seminars for publishing company personnel. Children's Book Week poster and downloadable bookmark available, information at www.bookweekonline.com. **Contact:** Robin Adelson, executive director.

FLORIDA FREELANCE WRITERS ASSOCIATION

P.O. Box A, North Stratford NH 03590. (603)922-8338. **E-mail:** FFWA@writers-editors.com. **Website:** www.ffwamembers.com; www.writers-editors.com. Purpose of organization: To provide a link between Florida writers and buyers of the written word; to help writers run more effective editorial businesses. Qualifications for membership: "None. We provide a variety of services and information, some for beginners and some for established pros." Membership cost: $90/year. Publishes a newsletter focusing on market news, business news, how-to tips for the serious writer. Annual Directory of Florida Markets included in FFWA newsletter section and electronic download. Publishes annual *Guide to CNW/Florida Writers*, which is distributed to editors around the country. Sponsors contest: annual deadline March 15. Guidelines on website. Categories: juvenile, adult nonfiction, adult fiction and poetry. Awards include cash for top prizes, certificate for others. Contest open to nonmembers. **Contact:** Dana K. Cassell, executive director.

GRAPHIC ARTISTS GUILD

32 Broadway, Suite 1114, New York NY 10004. (212)791-3400. **Fax:** 212-791-0333. **E-mail:** admin@gag.org; Patricia@gag.org. **Website:** www.graphicartistsguild.org. Purpose of organization: "To promote and protect the economic interests of member artists. It is committed to improving conditions for all creators of graphic arts and raising standards for the entire industry." Qualification for full membership: 50% of income derived from the creation of graphic artwork. Associate members include those in allied fields and students. Initiation fee: $30. Full memberships: $200; student membership: $75/year. Associate membership: $170/year. Publishes *Graphic Artists Guild Handbook: Pricing and Ethical Guidelines* (members receive a copy as part of their membership). **Contact:** Patricia McKiernan, executive director.

HORROR WRITERS ASSOCIATION

244 5th Avenue, Suite 2767, New York NY 10001. **E-mail:** hwa@horror.org. **Website:** www.horror.org.

Purpose of organization: To encourage public interest in horror and dark fantasy and to provide networking and career tools for members. Qualifications for membership: Complete membership rules online at www.horror.org/memrule.htm. At least one low-level sale is required to join as an affiliate. Non-writing professionals who can show income from a horror-related field may join as an associate (booksellers, editors, agents, librarians, etc.). To qualify for full active membership, you must be a published, professional writer of horror. Membership cost: $65 annually. Holds annual Stoker Awards Weekend and HWA Business Meeting. Publishes monthly newsletter focusing on market news, industry news, HWA business for members. Sponsors awards. Gives the Bram Stoker Awards for superior achievement in horror annually. Awards include a handmade Stoker trophy designed by sculptor Stephen Kirk. Awards open to nonmembers. **Contact:** John Little, office manager.

INTERNATIONAL READING ASSOCIATION

800 Barksdale Rd., P.O. Box 8139, Newark DE 19714-8139. (302)731-1600 ext. 293. **Fax:** (302)731-1057. **E-mail:** pubinfo@reading.org. **Website:** www.reading.org. Purpose of organization: "Formed in 1956, the International Reading Association seeks to promote high levels of literacy for all by improving the quality of reading instruction through studying the reading process and teaching techniques; serving as a clearinghouse for the dissemination of reading research through conferences, journals, and other publications; and actively encouraging the lifetime reading habit. Its goals include professional development, advocacy, partnerships, research, and global literacy development." **Open to students.** Sponsors annual convention. Publishes a newsletter called "Reading Today." Sponsors a number of awards and fellowships. Visit the IRA website for more information on membership, conventions and awards.

INTERNATIONAL WOMEN'S WRITING GUILD

P.O. Box 810, Gracie Station, New York NY 10028. (212)737-7536. **Fax:** (212)737-9469. **E-mail:** iwwg@iwwg.org; dirhahn@iwwg.org. **Website:** www.iwwg.org. IWWG is "a network for the personal and professional empowerment of women through writing." Qualifications: Open to any woman connected to the written word regardless of professional portfolio. Membership cost: $55/65 annually. "IWWG sponsors

several annual conferences a year in all areas of the U.S. The major conference is held in June of each year at Yale University in New Haven, Connecticut. It is a week-long conference attracting 350 women internationally." Also publishes a 32-page newsletter, *Network*, 4 times/year; offers dental and vision insurance at group rates, referrals to literary agents. **Contact:** Hannelore Hahn, founder/executive editor.

☺ LEAGUE OF CANADIAN POETS

920 Yonge St., Suite 608, Toronto ON M4W 3C7 Canada. (416)504-1657. **Fax:** (416)504-0096. **Website:** www.poets.ca. The L.C.P. is a national organization of published Canadian poets. Our constitutional objectives are to advance poetry in Canada and to promote the professional interests of the members. Qualifications for membership: full—publication of at least 1 book of poetry by a professional publisher; associate membership—an active interest in poetry, demonstrated by several magazine/periodical publication credits; student—an active interest in poetry, 12 sample poems required; supporting—any friend of poetry. Membership fees: full—$175/year, associate—$60, student—$20, supporting—$100. Holds an Annual General Meeting every spring; some events open to nonmembers. "We also organize reading programs in schools and public venues. We publish a newsletter that includes information on poetry/poetics in Canada and beyond. Also publish the books *Poetry Markets for Canadians*; *Who's Who in the League of Canadian Poets*; *Poets in the Classroom* (teaching guide), and online publications. The Gerald Lampert Memorial Award for the best first book of poetry published in Canada in the preceding year and The Pat Lowther Memorial Award for the best book of poetry by a Canadian woman published in the preceding year. Deadline for awards: November 1. Visit www.poets.ca for more details. Sponsors youth poetry competition. Visit www.youngpoets.ca for details. **Contact:** Joanna Poblocka, executive director; Joe Blades, president.

LITERARY MANAGERS AND DRAMATURGS OF THE AMERICAS

P.O. Box 36. 20985 P.A.C.C., New York NY 10129. **E-mail:** lmda@lmda.org. **Website:** www.lmda.org. LMDA is a not-for-profit service organization for the professions of literary management and dramaturgy. Student Membership: $25/year. Open to students in dramaturgy, performing arts and literature programs, or related disciplines. Proof of student status required.

Includes national conference, New Dramaturg activities, local symposia, job phone and select membership meetings. Active Membership: $60/year. Open to full-time and part-time professionals working in the fields of literary management and dramaturgy. All privileges and services including voting rights and eligibility for office. Institutional Membership: $200/year. Open to theaters, universities, and other organizations. Includes all privileges and services except voting rights and eligibility for office. Publishes a newsletter featuring articles on literary management, dramaturgy, LMDA program updates and other articles of interest. Spotlight sponsor membership $500/year; Open to theatres, universities, and other organizations; includes all priviledges for up to six individual members, plus additional promotional benefits.

THE NATIONAL LEAGUE OF AMERICAN PEN WOMEN

Pen Arts Building, 1300 17th St. N.W., Washington D.C. 20036-1973. (202)785-1997. **Fax:** (202)452-8868. **E-mail:** nlapwl@verizon.net. **Website:** www.americanpenwomen.org. Purpose of organization: to promote professional work in art, letters, and music since 1897. Qualifications for membership: An applicant must show "proof of sale" in each chosen category—art, letters, and music. Levels of membership include: Active, Associate, International Affiliate, Members-at-Large, Honorary Members (in one or more of the following classifications: Art, Letters, and Music). Holds workshops/conferences. Publishes magazine 4 times/year titled *The Pen Woman*. Sponsors various contests in areas of Art, Letters, and Music. Awards made at Biennial Convention. Semiannual scholarships awarded to non-Pen Women for mature women. Awards include cash prizes—up to $1,000. Specialized contests open to nonmembers. **Contact:** Jean Elizabeth Holmes, president.

NATIONAL WRITERS ASSOCIATION

10904 S. Parker Rd., #508, Parker CO 80138. (303)841-0246. **Fax:** (303)841-2607. **E-mail:** natlwritersassn@hotmail.com. **Website:** www.nationalwriters.com. Purpose of organization: association for freelance writers. Qualifications for membership: associate membership—must be serious about writing; professional membership—must be published and paid writer (cite credentials). Membership cost: $65 associate; $85 professional; $35 student. Sponsors workshops/conferences: TV/screenwriting workshops,

NWAF Annual Conferences, Literary Clearinghouse, editing and critiquing services, local chapters, National Writer's School. Open to non-members. Publishes industry news of interest to freelance writers; how-to articles; market information; member news and networking opportunities. Nonmember subscription: $20. Sponsors poetry contest; short story contest; article contest; novel contest. Awards cash for top 3 winners; books and/or certificates for other winners; honorable mention certificate places 5-10. Contests open to nonmembers.

NATIONAL WRITERS UNION

256 W. 38th St., Suite 703, New York NY 10018. (212)254-0279. **Fax:** (212)-254-0673. **E-mail:** nwu@nwu.org. **Website:** www.nwu.org. Purpose of organization: Advocacy for freelance writers. Qualifications for membership: "Membership in the NWU is open to all qualified writers, and no one shall be barred or in any manner prejudiced within the Union on account of race, age, sex, sexual orientation, disability, national origin, religion or ideology. You are eligible for membership if you have published a book, a play, three articles, five poems, one short story or an equivalent amount of newsletter, publicity, technical, commercial, government or institutional copy. You are also eligible for membership if you have written an equal amount of unpublished material and you are actively writing and attempting to publish your work" Membership cost: annual writing income less than $5,000—$120/year; $5,001-15,000—$195/year; $15,001-30,000—$265/year; $30,001-$45,000—$315/year; $45,001 and up—$340/year. Holds workshops throughout the country. Members only section on website offers rich resources for freelance writers. Skilled contract advice and grievance help for members.

PEN AMERICAN CENTER

588 Broadway, Suite 303, New York NY 10012. (212)334-1660. **Fax:** (212)334-2181. **E-mail:** pen@pen.org. **Website:** www.pen.org. Purpose of organization: "An association of writers working to advance literature, to defend free expression, and to foster international literary fellowship." Qualifications for membership: "The standard qualification for a writer to become a member of PEN is publication of two or more books of a literary character, or one book generally acclaimed to be of exceptional distinction. Also eligible for membership: editors who have demonstrated

commitment to excellence in their profession (usually construed as five years' service in book editing); translators who have published at least two book-length literary translations; playwrights whose works have been produced professionally; and literary essayists whose publications are extensive even if they have not yet been issued as a book. Candidates for membership may be nominated by a PEN member or they may nominate themselves with the support of two references from the literary community or from a current PEN member. Membership dues are $100 per year and many PEN members contribute their time by serving on committees, conducting campaigns and writing letters in connection with freedom-of-expression cases, contributing to the PEN journal, participating in PEN public events, helping to bring literature into underserved communities, and judging PEN literary awards. PEN members receive a subscription to the PEN journal, the PEN Annual Report, and have access to medical insurance at group rates. Members living in the New York metropolitan and tri-state area, or near the Branches, are invited to PEN events throughout the year. Membership in PEN American Center includes reciprocal privileges in PEN American Center branches and in foreign PEN Centers for those traveling abroad. Application forms are available on the Web at www.pen.org. Associate Membership is open to everyone who supports PEN's mission, and your annual dues ($40; $20 for students) provides crucial support to PEN's programs. When you join as an Associate Member, not only will you receive a subscription to the PEN journal, *PEN America* (http://pen.org/page.php/prmID/150), and notices of all PEN events but you are also invited to participate in the work of PEN. PEN American Center is the largest of the 141 centers of PEN International, the world's oldest human rights organization and the oldest international literary organization. PEN International was founded in 1921 to dispel national, ethnic, and racial hatreds and to promote understanding among all countries. PEN American Center, founded a year later, works to advance literature, to defend free expression, and to foster international literary fellowship. The Center has a membership of 3,400 distinguished writers, editors, and translators. In addition to defending writers in prison or in danger of imprisonment for their work, PEN American Center sponsors public literary programs and forums on current issues, sends prominent authors to inner-city schools to encourage

reading and writing, administers literary prizes, promotes international literature that might otherwise go unread in the United States, and offers grants and loans to writers facing financial or medical emergencies. In carrying out this work, PEN American Center builds upon the achievements of such dedicated past members as W.H. Auden, James Baldwin, Willa Cather, Robert Frost, Langston Hughes, Thomas Mann, Arthur Miller, Marianne Moore, Susan Sontag, and John Steinbeck. The Children's Book Authors' Committee sponsors annual public events focusing on the art of writing for children and young adults and on the diversity of literature for juvenile readers. The PEN/Phyllis Naylor Working Writer Fellowship was established in 2001 to assist a North American author of fiction for children or young adults (**E-mail:** awards@pen.org). Visit www.pen.org for complete information." Sponsors several competitions per year. Monetary awards range from $2,000-35,000.

PUPPETEERS OF AMERICA, INC.

26 Howard Ave., New Haven CT 06519. (888)568-6235. **E-mail:** membership@puppeteers.org. **Website:** www.puppeteers.org. Purpose of organization: to promote the art and appreciation of puppetry as a means of communications and as a performing art. The Puppeteers of America boasts an international membership. Qualifications for membership: interest in the art form. Membership cost: single adult, $55; seniors (65+) and youth members (6-17 years of age), $35; full-time college student, $35; family, $75; couple, $65; senior couple, $55, company, $90. Membership discounts to festivals and puppetry store purchases, access to the Audio Visual Library & Consultants in many areas of puppetry. The *Puppetry Journal*, a quarterly periodical, provides a color photo gallery, news about puppeteers, puppet theaters, exhibitions, touring companies, technical tips, new products, new books, films, television, and events sponsored by the Chartered Guilds in each of the 8 P of A regions. Includes *Playboard, the P of A Newsletter*; subsciption to the *Puppetry Journal* only, $40 (libraries/ institutions only). **Contact:** Fred Thompson, membership officer.

SCIENCE FICTION AND FANTASY WRITERS OF AMERICA, INC.

P.O. Box 877, Chestertown MD 21620. **E-mail:** exec dir@sfwa.org. **Website:** www.sfwa.org. Purpose of organization: to encourage public interest in science fiction literature and provide organization format for writers/editors/artists within the genre. Qualifications for membership: at least 1 professional sale or other professional involvement within the field. Membership cost: annual active dues—$70; affiliate—$55; one-time installation fee of $10; dues year begins July 1. Different levels of membership include: active—requires 3 professional short stories or 1 novel published; associate—requires 1 professional sale; or affiliate—which requires some other professional involvement such as artist, editor, librarian, bookseller, teacher, etc. Workshops/conferences: annual awards banquet, usually in April or May. Open to nonmembers. Publishes quarterly journal, the *SFWA Bulletin*. Nonmember subscription: $18/year in U.S. Sponsors Nebula Awards for best published science fiction or fantasy in the categories of novel, novella, novelette and short story. Awards trophy. Also presents the Damon Knight Memorial Grand Master Award for lifetime achievement, and, beginning in 2006, the Andre Norton Award for outstanding young adult science fiction or fantasy book of the year. **Contact:** Jane Jewell, executive director.

SOCIETY OF CHILDREN'S BOOK WRITERS AND ILLUSTRATORS

8271 Beverly Blvd., Los Angeles CA 90048. (323)782-1010. **Fax:** (323)782-1892. **E-mail:** scbwi@scbwi.org. **Website:** www.scbwi.org. Purpose of organization: to assist writers and illustrators working or interested in the field. Qualifications for membership: an interest in children's literature and illustration. Membership cost: $70/year, plus one time $85 initiation fee. Different levels of membership include: P.A.L. membership—published by publisher listed in SCBWI Market Surveys; full membership—published authors/illustrators (includes self-published); associate membership—unpublished writers/illustrators. Holds 100 events (workshops/conferences) worldwide each year. National Conference open to nonmembers. Publishes bi-monthly magazine on writing and illustrating children's books. Sponsors annual awards and grants for writers and illustrators who are members. **Contact:** Stephen Mooser, president; Lin Oliver, executive director.

SOCIETY OF ILLUSTRATORS

128 E. 63rd St., New York NY 10065. (212)838-2560. **Fax:** (212)838-2561. **E-mail:** info@societyillustrators.org. **Website:** www.societyillustrators.org. "Our mission is to promote the art and appreciation of illus-

tration, its history and evolving nature through exhibitions, lectures and education." Annual dues for nonresident illustrator members (those living more than 125 air miles from SI's headquarters): $300. Dues for resident illustrator members: $500 per year; resident associate members: $500. "Artist members shall include those who make illustration their profession and earn at least 60% of their income from their illustration. Associate members are those who earn their living in the arts or who have made a substantial contribution to the art of illustration. This includes art directors, art buyers, creative supervisors, instructors, publishers and like categories. The candidate must complete and sign the application form, which requires a brief biography, a listing of schools attended, other training and a résumé of his or her professional career. Candidates for illustrators membership, in addition to the above requirements, must submit examples of their work." **Contact:** Anelle Miller, director.

SOCIETY OF MIDLAND AUTHORS

P.O. 10419, Chicago IL 60610-0419. **Website:** www.midlandauthors.com. Purpose of organization: create closer association among writers of the Middle West; stimulate creative literary effort; maintain collection of members' works; encourage interest in reading and literature by cooperating with other educational and cultural agencies. Qualifications for membership: membership by invitation only. Must be author or co-author of a book demonstrating literary style and published by a recognized publisher and be identified through residence with Illinois, Indiana, Iowa, Kansas, Michigan, Minnesota, Missouri, Nebraska, North Dakota, Ohio, South Dakota or Wisconsin. **Open to students** (if authors). Membership cost: $35/year dues. Different levels of membership include: regular—published book authors; associate, nonvoting—not published as above but having some connection with literature, such as librarians, teachers, publishers and editors. Program meetings held 5 times a year, featuring authors, publishers, editors or the like individually or on panels. Usually second Tuesday of October, November, February, March and April. Also holds annual awards dinner in May. Publishes a newsletter focusing on news of members and general items of interest to writers. Sponsors contests. "Annual awards in six categories, given at annual dinner in May. Monetary awards for books published that premiered professionally in previous calendar year. Send SASE to contact person for details."

Categories include adult fiction, adult nonfiction, juvenile fiction, juvenile nonfiction, poetry, biography. No picture books. Contest open to nonmembers. Deadline for contest: February 1. **Contact:** Robert Loerzel, president.

SOCIETY OF SOUTHWESTERN AUTHORS

Fax: (520)751-7877. **E-mail:** wporter202@aol.com. **Website:** www.ssa-az.org. Purpose of organization: to promote fellowship among professional and associate members of the writing profession, to recognize members' achievements, to stimulate further achievement, and to assist persons seeking to become professional writers. Qualifications for membership: Professional Membership: proof of publication of a book, articles, TV screenplay, etc. Associate Membership: proof of desire to write, and/or become a professional. Self-published authors may receive status of Professional Membership at the discretion of the board of directors. Membership cost: $30 initiation plus $30/year dues. The Society of Southwestern Authors sponsors an annual 2-day writers conference (all genres) held September 26-27; watch website ssa-az.org. SSA publishes a bimonthly newsletter, *The Write Word*, promoting members' published works, advice to fellow writers, and up-to-the-minute trends in publishing and marketing. Yearly writing contest open to all writers; short story, memoir, poetry, children's stories. Applications available in February—e-mail Mike Rom at Mike_Rom@hotmail.com; Subject Line: SSA Writer's Contest. **Contact:** Penny Porter.

○ TEXT & ACADEMIC AUTHORS ASSOCIATION (TAA)

9313 42nd St., Pinellas Park FL 33782. (727)563-0020. **E-mail:** richard.hull@taaonline.net; kim.pawlak@taaonline.net. **Website:** www.taaonline.net. TAA's overall mission is to enhance the quality of textbooks and other academic materials, such as journal articles, monographs and scholarly books, in all fields and disciplines. Qualifications for membership: all authors and prospective authors are welcome. Membership cost: $30 first year; graduated levels for following years. Workshops/conferences: June each year. Newsletter focuses on all areas of interest to textbook and academic authors. **Contact:** Richard T. Hall, executive director; Kim Pawlick, associate executive director.

THEATRE FOR YOUNG AUDIENCES/USA

2936 N. Southport Ave. 3rd Floor, Chicago IL 60657. **E-mail:** info@tyausa.org. **Website:** www.assitej-usa.

org. Purpose of organization: to promote theater for children and young people by linking professional theaters and artists together; sponsoring national, international and regional conferences and providing publications and information. Also serves as U.S. Center for International Association of the Theatre for Children and Young People. Different levels of memberships include: organizations, individuals, students, retirees, libraries. TYA Today includes original articles, reviews and works of criticism and theory, all of interest to theater practitioners (included with membership). Publishes *Marquee*, a directory that focuses on information on members in U.S.

VOLUNTEER LAWYERS FOR THE ARTS

1 E. 53rd St., 6th Floor, New York NY 10022. (212)319-2787, ext. 1. **Fax:** (212)752-6575. **E-mail:** epaul@vlany.org. **Website:** www.vlany.org. Purpose of organization: Volunteer Lawyers for the Arts is dedicated to providing free arts-related legal assistance to low-income artists and not-for-profit arts organizations in all creative fields. Over 1,000 attorneys in the New York area donate their time through VLA to artists and arts organizations unable to afford legal counsel. Everyone is welcome to use VLA's Art Law Line, a legal hotline for any artist or arts organization needing quick answers to arts-related questions. VLA also provides clinics, seminars and publications designed to educate artists on legal issues which affect their careers. Members receive discounts on publications and seminars as well as other benefits. Some of the many publications we carry are *All You Need to Know About the Music Business*; *Business and Legal Forms for Fine Artists*; *Contracts for the Film & Television Industry*, plus many more. **Contact:** Elena M. Paul, executive director.

WESTERN WRITERS OF AMERICA, INC.

1012 Mesa Vista Hall, MSCO6 3770, 1 University of NM, Albuquerque NM 87131. (505)277-5234. **E-mail:** wwa@unm.edu. **Website:** www.westernwriters.org. Open to students. Purpose of organization: to further all types of literature that pertains to the American West. Membership requirements: must be a published author of Western material. Membership cost: $75/year ($90 foreign). Different levels of membership include: Active and Associate—the two vary upon number of books or articles published. Holds annual conference. Publishes bimonthly magazine focusing on Western literature, market trends, book reviews, news of members, etc. Nonmembers may subscribe for $30 ($50 foreign). Sponsors youth writing contests. Spur Awards given annually for a variety of types of writing. Awards include plaque, certificate, publicity. Contest and Spur Awards open to nonmembers. **Contact:** Paul Andrew Hutton, executive director.

☼ WRITERS' FEDERATION OF NEW BRUNSWICK

P.O. Box 306, Moncton NB E1C 8L4 Canada. (506)459-7228. **E-mail:** wfnb@nb.aibn.com. **Website:** www.wfnb.ca. Purpose of organization: "to promote New Brunswick writing and to help writers at all stages of their development." Qualifications for membership: interest in writing. Membership cost: $40, basic annual membership; $20, high school students; $45, family membership; $50, institutional membership; $100, sustaining member; $250, patron; and $1,000, lifetime member. Holds workshops/conferences. Publishes a newsletter with articles concerning the craft of writing, member news, contests, markets, workshops and conference listings. Sponsors annual literary competition, $15 entry fee for members, $20 for nonmembers. Categories: fiction, nonfiction, poetry, children's literature—3 prizes per category of $150, $75, $50; Alfred Bailey Prize of $400 for poetry ms; The Richards Prize of $400 for short novel, collection of short stories or section of long novel; The Sheree Fitch Prize for writing by young people (14-18 years of age). Contest open to nonmembers (residents of Canada only). **Contact:** Lee Thompson, executive director.

☼ WRITERS' FEDERATION OF NOVA SCOTIA

1113 Marginal Rd., Halifax NS B3H 4P7 Canada. (902)423-8116. **Fax:** (902)422-0881. **E-mail:** talk@writers.ns.ca. **Website:** www.writers.ns.ca. Purpose of organization: "to foster creative writing and the profession of writing in Nova Scotia; to provide advice and assistance to writers at all stages of their careers; and to encourage greater public recognition of Nova Scotian writers and their achievements." Regional organization open to anybody who writes. Currently has 800+ members. Levels of membership/dues: $45 CAD annually ($20 CAD students). Offerings include resource library with over 2,500 titles, promotional services, workshop series, annual festivals, mentorship program. Publishes *Eastword*, a bimonthly newsletter containing "a plethora of information on who's doing what; markets and contests; and current writing events and issues." Members and nationally known writers give readings that are open to the public. Additional information available on website.

☼ WRITERS GUILD OF ALBERTA

11759 Groat Rd., Edmonton AB T5M 3K6 Canada. (780)422-8174. **Fax:** (780)422-2663. **E-mail:** mail@writersguild.ab.ca. **Website:** www.writersguild.ab.ca. Purpose of organization: to support, encourage and promote writers and writing, to safeguard the freedom to write and to read, and to advocate for the well-being of writers in Alberta. Currently has over 1,000 members. Offerings include retreats/conferences; monthly events; bimonthly magazine that includes articles on writing and a market section; weekly electronic bulletin with markets and event listings; and the Stephan G. Stephansson Award for Poetry (Alberta residents only). Membership cost: $60/year; $30 for seniors/students. Holds workshops/conferences. Publishes a newsletter focusing on markets, competitions, contemporary issues related to the literary arts (writing, publishing, censorship, royalties etc.). Sponsors annual Literary Awards in five categories (novel, nonfiction, children's literature, poetry, drama). Awards include $1,500, leather-bound book, promotion and publicity. Open to nonmembers.

CONFERENCES & WORKSHOPS

//

Writers and illustrators eager to expand their knowledge of the children's publishing industry should consider attending one of the many conferences and workshops held each year. Whether you're a novice or seasoned professional, conferences and workshops are great places to pick up information on a variety of topics and network with experts in the publishing industry, as well as with your peers.

Listings in this section provide details about what conference and workshop courses are offered, where and when they are held, and the costs. Some of the national writing and art organizations also offer regional workshops throughout the year. Write, call or visit websites for information.

Writers can find listings of more than 1,000 conferences (searchable by type, location and date) at The Writer's Digest/Shaw Guides Directory to Writers' Conferences, Seminars, and Workshops—writersdigestconference.com.

Members of the Society of Children's Book Writers and Illustrators can find information on conferences in national and local SCBWI newsletters. Nonmembers may attend SCBWI events as well. SCBWI conferences are listed in the beginning of this section under a separate subheading. For information on SCBWI's annual national conferences, contact them at (323)782-1010 or check their website for a complete calendar of national and regional events (scbwi.org).

CONFERENCES & WORKSHOPS CALENDAR

To help you plan your conference travel, here is a month-by-month calendar of conferences, workshops and retreats. The calendar lists conferences alphabetically by the month in which they occur.

JANUARY

Kindling Words East (Burlington VT)
San Diego State University Writers' Conference (San Diego CA)
SCBWI—Florida Regional Conference (Miami FL)
Winter Poetry & Prose Getaway in Cape May (Cape May NJ)

FEBRUARY

San Francisco Writers Conference (San Francisco CA)
SCBWI Annual Conference on Writing and Illustrating for Children (New York NY)
SCBWI—Norca (San Francisco/South) Retreat at Asilomar (Pacific Grove CA)
SCBWI—Southern Breeze Springmingle (Atlanta GA)
South Coast Writers Conference (Gold Beach OR)

MARCH

Big Sur Writing Workshop (Big Sur CA)
Florida Christian Writers Conference (Bradenton FL)
Virginia Festival of the Book (Charlottesville VA)
Whidbey Island Writers' Conference (Langley WA)
Tennessee Williams/New Orleans Literary Festival (New Orleans LA)

APRIL

AEC Conference on Southern Literature (Chattanooga TN)
Missouri Writers' Guild Annual State Conference (St. Charles MO)
Mount Hermon Christian Writers Conference (Mount Hermon CA)
SCBWI—Iowa Conference (Iowa City IA)
SCBWI—Oregon Spring Conference (Portland OR)
SCBWI—Western Washington State Annual Conference (Redmond WA)

MAY

Annual Spring Poetry Festival (New York NY)
Kindling Words West (Abiquiu NM)

Oklahoma Writers' Federation, Inc. Annual Conference (Oklahoma City OK)
Pima Writers' Workshop (Tucson AZ)
SCBWI—New England Annual Conference (New England)

JUNE

Aspen Summer Words Writing Retreat (Aspen CO)
Children's Writers & Illustrators Conference (Corte Madera CA)
Highland Summer Conference (Radford VA)
International Creative Writing Camp (Minot ND)
Iowa Summer Writing Festival (Iowa City IA)
Manhattanville Summer Writers' Week (Purchase NY)
SCBWI—Florida Mid-Year Writing Workshop (Boca Raton FL)
SCBWI—New Jersey Annual Summer Conference (Princeton NJ)
Southeastern Writer's Association—Annual Writer's Workshop (Athens GA)
UMKC/Writers Place Writers Workshops (Kansas City MO)
Wesleyan Writers Conference (Middletown CT)
Write! Canada (Guelph, Ontario, Canada)
Write-by-the-Lake Writer's Workshop & Retreat (Madison WI)
Write-to-Publish Conference (Wheaton IL)
Writers Retreat Workshop (Erlanger KY)

JULY

Duke University Youth Programs: Creative Writers' Workshop (Durham NC)
Hofstra University Summer Workshop (Hempstead NY)
Iowa Summer Writing Festival (Iowa City IA)
Maritime Writers' Workshop (Fredericton, New Brunswick, Canada)
Midwest Writers Workshop (Muncie IN)
Montrose Christian Writer's Conference (Montrose PA)
Pacific Northwest Children's Book Conference (Portland OR)
Pacific Northwest Writers Association Summer Writer's Conference (Seattle WA)
Robert Quackenbush's Children's Book Writing and Illustrating Workshop (New York NY)
Sage Hill Writing Experience (Saskatoon, Saskatchewan, Canada)
Saskatchewan Festival of Words and Workshops (Moose Jaw, Saskatchewan, Canada)
SCBWI—Florida Mid-Year Writing Workshop (Boca Raton FL)
Steamboat Springs Writers Conference (Steamboat Springs CO)

CONFERENCES & WORKSHOPS

AUGUST

Cape Cod Writer's Conference (Cape Cod MA)
Green Lake Christian Writers Conference (Green Lake WI)
The Manuscript Workshop in Vermont (Londonderry VT)
SCBWI Annual Conference on Writing and Illustrating for Children (Los Angeles CA)
Willamette Writers Annual Writers Conference (West Lim OR)

SEPTEMBER

League of Utah Writers' Roundup (Ogden UT)
SCBWI—Carolinas Annual Fall Conference (Durham NC)
SCBWI—Midsouth Fall Conference (Nashville TN)
SCBWI—Northern Ohio Annual Conference (Cleveland OH)
SCBWI—Rocky Mountain Events (Lakewood CO)

OCTOBER

East Texas Christian Writers Conference (Marshall TX)
Ozark Creative Writers, Inc. Conference (Eureka Springs AR)
The Pacific Coast Children's Writers Workshop (Aptos CA)
SCBWI—Michigan Fall Conference (Michigan)
SCBWI—Midatlantic Annual Fall Conference (Arlington VA)
SCBWI—Southern Breeze Writing and Illustrating for Kids (Birmingham AL)
SCBWI—Wisconsin Fall Retreat for Working Writers (Oconomowoc WI)
Surrey International Writer's Conference (Surrey, British Columbia, Canada)
Vancouver International Writers Festival (Vancouver, British Columbia, Canada)
Write on the Sound Writers Conference (Edmonds WA)

NOVEMBER

Jewish Children's Book Writers' Conference (New York NY)
LaJolla Writers Conference (LaJolla CA)
North Carolina Writers' Network Fall Conference (Durham NC)
Ohio Kentucky Indiana Children's Literature Conference (Highland Heights KY)
SCBWI—Eastern Pennsylvania Critique Fest (Lancaster PA)
SCBWI—Illinois Prairie Writers Day (Palatine IL)
SCBWI—Missouri Children's Writer's Conference (St. Charles MO)
SCBWI—Western Washington State Retreat (Washington)

DECEMBER

Big Sur Writing Workshop (Big Sur CA)

MULTIPLE OR SEASONAL EVENTS

The conference listings below include information on multiple or year-round events or events that are seasonal (held in fall or spring, for example). Please read the listings for more information on the dates and locations of these events and check the conferences' websites.

American Christian Writers Conference
BookExpo America/Writer's Digest Books Writers Conference (New York NY)
Booming Ground Online Writers Studio
Cat Writers' Association Annual Writers Conference
The DIY Book Festival
Duke University Youth Programs: Creative Writers' Workshop
Gotham Writers' Workshop (New York NY)
Highlights Foundation Founders Workshops (Honesdale PA)
Iowa Summer Writing Festival (Iowa City IA)
The Manuscript Workshop in Vermont (Londonderry VT)
Publishinggame.com Workshop
SCBWI—Arizona Events
SCBWI—Eastern Canada Annual Events
SCBWI—Dakotas
SCBWI—Iowa Conferences
SCBWI—Los Angeles Events
SCBWI—Metro New York Professional Series (New York NY)
SCBWI—Michigan Spring Conference
SCBWI—New Jersey First Page Sessions (Princeton NJ)
SCBWI—Pocono Mountains Retreat (Sterling PA)
SCBWI—Taiwan Events
SCBWI—Ventura/Santa Barbara Events
SCBWI—Western Washington State Retreats & Conference
SouthWest Writers Conferences
Sydney Children's Writers and Illustrators Network (Woollahra, New South Wales, Australia)
UMKC/Writers Place Writers Workshops (Kansas City MO)
Writers' League of Texas Workshop Series (Austin TX)
Writer's Digest Writers' Conferences (New York, NY and Los Angeles, CA)
The Writers' Retreat Writing Workshop at Castle Hill

SCBWI CONFERENCES

SCBWI; ANNUAL CONFERENCES ON WRITING AND ILLUSTRATING FOR CHILDREN

Website: www.scbwi.org. **Contact:** Lin Oliver, conference director. Writer and illustrator workshops geared toward all levels. **Open to students.** Covers all aspects of children's book and magazine publishing—the novel, illustration techniques, marketing, etc. Annual conferences held in August in Los Angeles and in New York in February. Cost of conference (LA): approximately $390; includes all 4 days and one banquet meal. Write for more information or visit website.

SCBWI–ARIZONA; EVENTS

P.O. Box 26384, Scottsdale AZ 85255-0123. **E-mail:** RegionalAdvisor@scbwi-az.org. **Website:** www. scbwi-az.org. **Contact:** Michelle Parker-Rock, regional advisor. SCBWI Arizona will offer a variety of workshops, retreats, intensives, conferences, meetings and other craft and industry-related events. Open to members and nonmembers, published and nonpublished. Registration to major events is usually limited. Pre-registration always required. Visit website, write, or e-mail for more information.

SCBWI BOLOGNA BIENNIAL CONFERENCE

E-mail: Angela@SCBWIBologna.org; Kathleen@SCBWIBologna.org. **Website:** www.scbwibologna. org. The SCBWI Showcase Booth at the Bologna Book Fair: It will feature authors and illustrators from SCBWI regions, SCBWI PAL members, and special author and illustrator events.

SCBWI–CANADA EAST

E-mail: araeast@scbwicanada.org; raeast@scbwicanada.org. **Website:** www.scbwicanada.org/east. **Contact:** Lizann Flatt, regional advisor. Writer and illustrator events geared toward all levels. Usually offers one event in spring and another in the fall. Check website Events pages for updated information.

SCBWI COLORADO/WYOMING (ROCKY MOUNTAIN); EVENTS

E-mail: denise@rmcscbwi.org; todd.tuell@rmcscbwi. org. **Website:** www.rmcscbwi.org. **Contact:** Todd Tuell and Denise Vega, co-regional advisors. SCBWI Rocky Mountain chapter (CO/WY) offers special events, schmoozes, meetings, and conferences throughout the year. Major events: Fall Conference (annually, September); Summer Retreat, "Big Sur in the Rockies" (bi- and triannually). More info on website.

SCBWI–DAKOTAS; SPRING CONFERENCE

2521 S. 40th St., Grand Forks ND 58201. **E-mail:** cdrylander@yahoo.com. **Website:** www.dakotas-scbwi.org. **Contact:** Chris Rylander, regional advisor. This is a conference for writers and illustrators of all levels. Previous conferences have included speakers Tim Gilner, S.T. Underdahl, Roxane Salonen, and Marilyn Kratz. Annual event held every spring. Check website for details.

SCBWI–DAKOTAS; WRITERS CONFERENCE IN CHILDREN'S LITERATURE

Grand Forks ND 58201. (701)720-0464. **E-mail:** cdrylaner@yahoo.com. **Website:** www.dakotas-scbwi.org. **Contact:** Chris Rylander, regional advisor. Conference sessions geared toward all levels. "Although the conference attendees are mostly writers, we encourage and welcome illustrators of every level." Open to students. "Our conference offers 3-4 children's authors, editors, publishers, illustrators, or agents. Past conferences have included Kent Brown (publisher, Boyds Mills Press); Alexandra Penfold (editor, Simon & Schuster); Jane Kurtz (author); Anastasia Suen (author); and Karen Ritz (illustrator). Conference held each fall. "Please call or e-mail to confirm dates. Writers and illustrators come from throughout the northern plains, including North Dakota, South Dakota, Montana, Minnesota, Iowa, and Canada." Writing facilities available: campus of University of North Dakota. Local art exhibits and/or concerts may coincide with conference. Cost of conference includes Friday evening reception and sessions, Saturday's sessions, and lunch. A manuscript may be submitted 1 month in advance for critique (extra charge). E-mail for more information.

SCBWI–EASTERN PENNSYLVANIA

Website: www.scbwiepa.org. This event is hosted by three regions, Eastern PA, Western PA and MD/DE/VA region. This event has the large conference opportunities with small retreat appeal. Watch website for more details, www.scbwiepa.org.

SCBWI–FLORIDA; MID-YEAR WRITING WORKSHOP

12973 SW 112 Ct., Miami FL 33186. (305)382-2677. **E-mail:** lindabernfeld@gmail.com. **Website:** www.

scbwiflorida.com. **Contact:** Linda Bernfeld, regional advisor. Annual 5-week workshop held June-July in Boca Raton, FL. Workshop is geared toward helping everyone hone their writing skills. Attendees choose one track and spend the day with industry leaders who share valuable information about that area of children's book writing. There are a minimum of 3 tracks, picture book, middle grade and young adult. The 4th and 5th tracks are variable, covering subjects such as poetry, non-fiction, humor or writing for magazines. E-mail for more information.

SCBWI—FLORIDA; REGIONAL CONFERENCE

12973 SW 112 Ct., Miami FL 33186. (305)382-2677. **E-mail:** lindabernfeld@gmail.com. **Website:** www.scbwiflorida.com. **Contact:** Linda Bernfeld, regional advisor. Annual conference held in January in Miami. Past keynote speakers have included Linda Sue Park, Richard Peck, Bruce Coville, Bruce Hale, Arthur A. Levine, Judy Blume, Kate DiCamillo. Cost of conference: approximately $225. The 3-day conference will have workshops Friday afternoon and a field trip to Books and Books Friday evening.

✚ SCBWI—ILLINOIS; PRAIRIE WRITERS DAY

E-mail: biermanlisa@hotmail.com. **Website:** www.scbwi-illinois.org. **Contact:** Lisa Bierman, regional advisor. Full day of guest speakers, editors/agents TBD. Ms critiques available as well as break-out sessions on career and craft. See website for complete description.

SCBWI—IOWA CONFERENCES

P.O. Box 1436, Bettendorf IA 52722-0024. **E-mail:** hecklit@aol.com. **Website:** www.scbwi-iowa.org/. **Contact:** Connie Heckert, regional advisor. Writer and illustrator workshops in all genres of children writing. The Iowa Region offers conferences of high quality events usually over a three-day period with registration options. Recent speakers included Allyn Johnston, Marla Frazee, Julie Romeis, Samantha McFerrin, Scott Treimel. Holds spring and fall events on a regional level, and network events across that state. Individual critiques and portfolio review offerings vary with the program and presenters. For more information e-mail or visit website.

SCBWI—LOS ANGELES; EVENTS

P.O. Box 1728, Pacific Palisades CA 90272. (310)573-7318. **Website:** www.scbwisocal.org. **Contact:** Sarah Laurenson, co-regional advisor; Edie Pagliasotti, co-regional advisor. SCBWI—Los Angeles hosts 6 major events each year: **Writer's Workshop** (winter)—half-day workshop featuring speaker demonstrating nuts and bolts techniques on the craft of writing for children; **Writer's Day** (spring)—a one-day conference featuring speakers, a professional forum, writing contests and awards; **Critiquenic** (summer)—a free informal critiquing session for writers and illustrators facilitated by published authors/illustrators, held after a picnic lunch; **Writers & Illustrator's Sunday Field Trip** (fall)—hands-on creative field trip for writers and illustrators; **Working Writer's Retreat** (fall)—a 3-day, 2-night retreat featuring an editor/agent, speakers, and intensive critiquing. **Illustrator's Day** (winter)—A one-day conference featuring speakers, juried art competition, contests, portfolio review/display. See calendar of events on website for more details and dates.

SCBWI—METRO NEW YORK; PROFESSIONAL SERIES

P.O. Box 1475, Cooper Station, New York NY 10276. (212)545-3719. **E-mail:** scbwi_metrony@yahoo.com. **Website:** http://metro.nyscbwi.org. **Contact:** Seta Toroyan, regional advisor. Writer and illustrator workshops geared toward all levels. The Metro New York Professional Series generally meets the second Tuesday of each month, from September to June, 7:30-9:30 p.m. Check website to confirm location, dates, times, and speakers. Cost of workshop: $15 for SCBWI members; $20 for nonmembers. "We feature an informal evening with coffee, cookies, and top editors, art directors, agents, publicity and marketing people, librarians, reviewers and more."

SCBWI—MICHIGAN; CONFERENCES

Website: www.Kidsbooklink.org. **Contact:** Monica Harris, co-regional advisor; Leslia Helakoski, co-regional advisor. One-day conference held in April/May and 3-day fall conference held in October. Workshops periodically. Speakers TBA. See website for details on all upcoming events.

SCBWI—MIDATLANTIC; ANNUAL FALL CONFERENCE

P.O. Box 3215, Reston VA 20195. **E-mail:** scbwimidatlantic@gmail.com. **Website:** www.SCBWI-MidAtlantic.org. **Contact:** Sydney Dunlap and Erin Teagan, conference co-chairs; Ellen Braaf, regional advisor. For updates and details visit website. Registration limited to 200. Conference fills quickly. Cost: $115 for SCBWI members; $145 for nonmembers. Includes continental breakfast. Lunch is on your own. (The food court at the Ballston Common Mall is two blocks away.)

SCBWI—MIDSOUTH FALL CONFERENCE

P.O. Box 396, Cordova TN 38088. **E-mail:** expressdog@bellsouth.net; cameron_s_e@yahoo.com. **Website:** www.scbwi-midsouth.org. **Contact:** Genetta Adair and Sharon Cameron, conference coordinators. Conference for writers and illustrators of all experience. 2012 conference was held September 14-16 in Nashville. In the past, workshops were offered on "Plotting Your Novel," "Understanding the Language of Editors," "Landing an Agent," "How to Prepare a Portfolio," "Negotiating a Contract," "The Basics for Beginners," and many others. Attendees are invited to bring a manuscript and/or art portfolio to share in the optional, no-charge critique group session. Illustrators are invited to bring color copies of their art (not originals) to be displayed in the illustrators' showcase. For an additional fee, attendees may schedule a 15-minute manuscript critique or portfolio critique by the editor, art director or other expert consultant. Annual conference held in September. Registration limited to 130 attendees. Cost to be determined. The 2010 Midsouth Fall Conference included Balzer & Bray editor Ruta Rimas; nonfiction book pakager and editor Lionel Bender from London, England; Andrea Brown agent Kelly Sonnack; ICM agent Tina Wexler; award-winning author Linda Sue Park and more.

SCBWI—MISSOURI; CHILDREN'S WRITER'S CONFERENCE

P.O. Box 76975, 103 CEAC, St. Peters MO 63376-0975. (636)922-8233. **Website:** www.moscbwi.org. **Contact:** Stephanie Bearce, regional advisor. **Open to students.** Speakers include editors, writers, agents, and other professionals. Topics vary from year to year, but each conference offers sessions for both writers and illustrators as well as for newcomers and published writers. Previous topics included: "What Happens When Your Manuscript is Accepted" by Dawn Weinstock, editor; "Writing—Hobby or Vocation?" by Chris Kelleher; "Mother Time Gives Advice: Perspectives from a 25 Year Veteran" by Judith Mathews, editor; "Don't Be a Starving Writer" by Vicki Berger Erwin, author; and "Words & Pictures: History in the Making," by author-illustrator Cheryl Harness. Annual conference held in early November.

For exact date, see SCBWI website or the events page of the Missouri SCBWI website. Registration limited to 75-90. Cost of conference includes one-day workshop (8 a.m. to 5 p.m.) plus lunch. Write for more information.

SCBWI—NEW ENGLAND; ANNUAL CONFERENCE

Nashua NH 03063. **E-mail:** northernnera@scbwi.org. **Website:** www.nescbwi.org. **Contact:** Anna Boll, regional advisor. Conference is for all levels of writers and illustrators. **Open to students.** "We offer many workshops at each conference, and often there is a multi-day format. Examples of subjects addressed: manuscript development, revision, marketing your work, productive school visits, picture book dummy formatting, adding texture to your illustrations, etc." Annual conference held in May. Registration limited to 450. Cost: TBD; includes pre-conference social, great keynote speaker, many workshop options, lunch, snacks, etc. Keynote speakers for 2012 conference were Sara Zarr, Kate Messner, Harry Bliss. "Details (additional speakers, theme, number of workshop choices, etc.) will be posted to our website as they become available. Registration will not start until March. Opportunities for one-on-one manuscript critiques and portfolio reviews will be available at the conference."

⊕ SCBWI—NEW JERSEY; ANNUAL SUMMER CONFERENCE

SCBWI-New Jersey: Society of Children's Book Writers & Illustrators, **Website:** www.newjerseyscbwi.com. **Contact:** Kathy Temean, regional advisor. This weekend conference is held in the beginning of June in Princeton, NJ. Multiple one-on-one critiques; "how to" workshops for every level; first page sessions; agent pitches and interaction with the faculty of editors, agents, art director and authors are some of the highlights of the weekend. On Friday attendees can sign up for writing intensives or register for illustrators' day with the art directors. Published authors attending the conference can sign up to participate in the bookfair to sell and autograph their books; illustrators have the opportunity to display their artwork. Attendees have the option to participate in group critiques after dinner on Saturday evening and attend a mix and mingle with the faculty on Friday night. Meals are included with the cost of admission. Conference is known for its high ratio of faculty to attendees and interaction opportunities.

SCBWI—NEW JERSEY; FIRST PAGE SESSIONS

E-mail: njscbwi@newjerseyscbwi.com; kathy@ newjerseyscbwi.com; laurie@newjerseyscbwi.com. **Website:** www.newjerseyscbwi.com. Held 4 times a year in Princeton, NJ. Two editors/agents give their first impression of a first page and let participants know if they would read more. These sessions are held late afternoon during the week and are limited to 30 people. Attendees can choose to have dinner with the editors after the session. Please visit www. newjerseyscbwi.com for more information.

SCBWI—NEW JERSEY; MENTORING WORKSHOPS

Website: www.newjerseyscbwi.com. **Contact:** Kathy Temean, regional advisor. These workshops have become very popular and fill quickly. Workshops provide an inspiring environment for writers to work on their manuscript and have personal contact with their mentor/editor. Each workshop consists of 14 writers and 2 editors or 28 people and 4 editors. Weekend workshops allow writers to spend 45 minutes, one-on-one, with their mentor to discuss their manuscript and career direction, first-page critiques, pitch sessions and other fun writing activities. One-day workshops consist of 20-minute, one-on-one critiques and Q&A session, plus first-page critiques. These workshops are held in the winter, spring, and fall each year in Princeton, NJ. Please visit www.newjerseyscbwi.com for more information.

SCBWI—NEW MEXICO; HANDSPRINGS: A CONFERENCE FOR CHILDREN'S WRITERS AND ILLUSTRATORS

PO Box 1084, Socorro NM **E-mail:** handsprings@ scbwi-nm.org. **Website:** www.scbwi-nm.org. **Contact:** Lois Bradley, registrar; Chris Eboch, regional advisor. Conference for beginner and intermediate writers and illustrators. Registration limited to 100. "Offers intensive craft-based workshops and large-group presentations." Cost: $110-150 for basic Saturday registration dependent on registration; $40-50 for private critiques (lowest prices are for SCBWI members). "The Friday evening party includes social time and mini book launches. Saturday features a full day of keynote speeches by visiting editors, agents and/or art directors; breakout

workshops on the craft and business of writing; and optional written critiques with the editors or written portfolio review by the art director."

SCBWI—NORCA (SAN FRANCISCO/ SOUTH); GOLDEN GATE CONFERENCE AT ASILOMAR

Website: www.scbwisf.org. **Contact:** Amy Laughlin and Kristin Howell, co-regional advisors. "We welcome published and 'not-yet-published' writers and illustrators. Lectures and workshops are geared toward professionals and those striving to become professional. Program topics cover aspects of writing or illustrating, and marketing, from picture books to young adult novels. Past speakers include editors, agents, art directors, Newbery Award-winning authors, and Caldecott Award-winning illustrators. Annual conference, generally held third or fourth weekend in February; Friday evening through Sunday lunch. Registration limited to approximately 140. Ms or portfolio review available. Most rooms shared with one other person. Additional charge for single when available. Desks available in most rooms. All rooms have private baths. Conference center is set in wooded campus on Asilomar Beach in Pacific Grove, California. Approximate cost: $465 for SCBWI members, $610 for nonmembers; includes shared room, 6 meals and all conference activities. Vegetarian meals available. Coming together for shared meals and activities builds a strong feeling of community among the speakers and conferees. Scholarships available to SCBWI members. Registration opens end of October/November. For more information, including exact costs and dates, visit our website."

SCBWI—NORTHERN OHIO; ANNUAL CONFERENCE

Website: www.nohscbwi.org. **Contact:** Victoria A. Selvaggio, regional advisor. Northern Ohio's conference is crafted for all levels of writers and illustrators of children's literature. "Our annual event will be held at the Sheraton Cleveland Airport Hotel. Conference costs will be posted on our website with registration information. SCBWI members receive a discount. Additional fees apply for late registration, critiques, or portfolio reviews. Cost includes an optional Friday evening Opening Banquet from 6-10 p.m. with a keynote speaker; Saturday event from 8:30 a.m. to 5 p.m. which includes breakfast snack, full-day conference with headliner presentations, general sessions, breakout workshops, lunch, panel discussion, bookstore, and autograph session. The Illustrator Showcase is open to all attendees at no additional cost. Grand door prize drawn at the end of the day Saturday, is free admission to the following year's conference. Further information, including Headliner Speakers will be posted on our website. All questions can be directed to vselvaggio@windstream.net."

SCBWI—OREGON CONFERENCES

E-mail: robink@scbwior.com. **Website:** www.scbwior.com. **Contact:** Robin Koontz, regional advisor. Writer and illustrator workshops and presentations geared toward all levels. "We invite editors, art directors, agents, attorneys, authors, illustrators and others in the business of writing and illustrating for children. Faculty members offer craft presentations, workshops, first-page sessions and individual critiques as well as informal networking opportunities. Critique group network opportunities for local group meetings and regional retreats; see website for details. Spring Conference: Held in the Portland area (2 day event the third Fri-Sat in May (one-day attendance is permitted). Cost for presentations and workshops: about $150; includes continental breakfast and lunch on Saturday. Critique fee: $35; attendees only. Friday intensive sessions cost about $100 for the day with professional tracks in writing and illustrating. Registration limited to 300 for the conference and 55 for the retreat. SCBWI Oregon is a regional chapter of the Society of Children's Book Writers and Illustrators. SCBWI Members receive a discount for all events. Oregon and S. Washington members get preference.

SCBWI—POCONO MOUNTAINS RETREAT

Website: www.scbwiepa.org. Held in the spring at Shawnee Inn, Shawnee on the Delaware, PA. Faculty addresses craft, web design, school visits, writing, illustration and publishing. Registration limited to 150. Cost of retreat: tuition $140, meals, room and board averages $250 for the weekend. For information, online registration and brochure, visit website.

SCBWI—SAN DIEGO; CHAPTER MEETINGS & WORKSHOPS

San Diego CA 92127. (619)713-5462. **E-mail:** ra-sd@sandiego-scbwi.org. **Website:** www.sandiego-scbwi.org. **Contact:** Janice M. Yuwiler, regional advisor. Writer and illustrator meetings and workshops geared

toward all levels. Topics vary but emphasize writing and illustrating for children. Check website, e-mail or call for more information. "The San Diego chapter holds meetings the second Saturday of each month from September to May at the University of San Diego from 2 to 4 p.m.; cost $7 (members), $9 (nonmembers). Check website for room, speaker and directions." Check website for 2013 meeting schedule. Published members share lessons learned and holiday book sale. 2012 conference held in February, Writer's Retreat in May. Check website for details. Season tickets include all regular chapter meetings during the season and newsletter issues for one calendar year as well as discounts on conferences/retreats. See the website for conference/workshop dates, times and prices. Chapter also helps members find critique groups for ongoing enhancement of skills.

SCBWI—SOUTHERN BREEZE; SPRINGMINGLE

P.O. Box 26282, Birmingham AL 35260. **Website:** www.southern-breeze.net. **Contact:** Jo Kittinger and Claudia Pearson, regional advisors. Writer and illustrator conference geared toward intermediate, advanced and professional levels. Speakers typically include agents, editors, authors, art directors, illustrators. Open to SCBWI members, non-members and college students. Annual conference held in Atlanta, Georgia. Usually held in late February. Registration limited. Cost of conference: approximately $225; Typically includes Friday dinner, Saturday lunch and Saturday banquet. Ms critiques and portfolio reviews available for additional fee. Pre-registration is necessary. Mail SASE to Southern Breeze or visit website.

SCBWI—SOUTHERN BREEZE; WRITING AND ILLUSTRATING FOR KIDS

P.O. Box 26282, Birmingham AL 35260. **E-mail:** sjkittinger@gmail.com. **Website:** www.southern-breeze.org. **Contact:** Jo Kittinger, regional advisor. Writer and illustrator workshops geared toward all levels. Open to SCBWI members, non-members and college students. All sessions pertain specifically to the production and support of quality children's literature. This one-day conference offers about 30 workshops on craft and the business of writing. Picture books, chapter books, novels covered. Entry and professional level topics addressed by published writers and illustrators, editors and agents. Annual conference. Fall conference is held the third weekend in October in the Birmingham, AL, metropolitan area. (Museums, shopping, zoo, gardens, universities and colleges are within a short driving distance.) All workshops are limited to 30 or fewer people. Pre-registration is necessary. Some workshops fill quickly. Cost of conference: approximately $110 for members, $135 for nonmembers, $120 for students; program includes keynote speaker, 4 workshops (selected from 30), lunch, and Friday night dessert party. Mss critiques and portfolio reviews are available for an additional fee; mss must be sent early. Registration is by mail ahead of time. Ms and portfolio reviews must be pre-paid and scheduled. Send a SASE to: Southern Breeze, P.O. Box 26282, Birmingham AL 35260 or visit website. Fall conference is always held in Birmingham, Alabama. Room block at a hotel near conference site (usually a school) is by individual reservation and offers a conference rate. Speakers include editors, agents, art directors, authors, and/or illustrators. WIK13 speakers to be announced.

SCBWI—VENTURA/SANTA BARBARA; FALL CONFERENCE

E-mail: alexisinca@aol.com. **Website:** www.scbwisocal.org/calendar.htm. **Contact:** Alexis O'Neill, regional advisor. Writers' conference geared toward all levels. Speakers include editors, authors, illustrators and agents. Fiction and nonfiction picture books, middle grade and YA novels, and magazine submissions addressed. Annual writing contest in all genres plus illustration display. For fees and other information e-mail or go to website.

SCBWI—WESTERN WASHINGTON STATE; CONFERENCE & RETREAT

Western Region of SCBWI, P.O. Box 156, Enumclaw WA 98022. **E-mail:** info@scbwi-washington.org. **Website:** www.scbwi-washington.org. **Contact:** Joni Sensel and Laurie Thompson, co-regional advisors. "The Western Washington region of SCBWI hosts an annual conference in April, a retreat in November, and monthly meetings and events throughout the year. Please visit the website for complete details."

SCBWI—WISCONSIN; FALL RETREAT FOR WORKING WRITERS

Website: www.scbwi-wi.com. **Contact:** Pam Beres. Writer and illustrator conference geared toward all levels. All our sessions pertain to children's writing/illustration. Faculty addresses writing/illustrating/

publishing. Annual conference held October. Go to our website for more information.

GENERAL CONFERENCES

AEC CONFERENCE ON SOUTHERN LITERATURE

Arts & Education Council (AEC), 3069 S. Broad St., Suite 2, Chattanooga TN 37408-3056. (423)267-1218 or (800)267-4232. **Fax:** (423)267-1018. **E-mail:** srobin son@artsedcouncil.org. **Website:** http://artsedcoun cil.org; http://southernlitconference.org. **Contact:** Susan Robinson. The 2013 conference will be held April 18-20 in Chattanooga, TN. "The AEC Conference stands out because of its unique collaboration with the Fellowship of Southern Writers, an organization founded by towering literary figures like Eudora Welty, Cleanth Brooks, Walker Percy and Robert Penn Warren to recognize and encourage literature in the South. The 2012 Conference marked 23 years since the Fellowship selected Chattanooga for its headquarters and chose to collaborate with the Conference on Southern Literature. Up to 50 members of the Fellowship will participate in this year's event, discussing hot topics and reading from their latest works. The Fellowship will also award nine literary prizes and induct eight new members, making this event the place to discover up-and-coming voices in Southern literature. The AEC Conference attracts over 1,000 readers and writers from all over the United States. It strives to maintain an informal atmosphere where conversations will thrive, inspired by a common passion for the written word. This conference started as one of 12 pilot agencies founded by a Ford Foundation grant. In 1983, the AEC organization changed its name to the Arts & Education Council to more accurately reflect its outreach in Chattanooga. The AEC is the only organization of the 12 still in existence. The AEC produces innovative events and programs that enrich the Chattanooga community, including the Conference on Southern Literature and its school literacy outreach, the Chattanooga Festival of Writers, Culture Fest, TheatreExpress, the Back Row Film Series, Independent Film Series, and current affairs television programs "Point of View" and "First View." In 2009, they reached 70,000 through these outreach initiatives.

ALGONKIAN FIVE DAY NOVEL CAMP

2020 Pennsylvania Ave. NW, Suite 443, Washington DC 20006. **E-mail:** algonkian@webdelsol.com. **Web-**

site: fwwriters.algonkianconferences.com. Conference duration: 5 days. Average attendance: 12 students maximum per workshop. "During 45+ hours of actual workshop time, students will engage in those rigorous narrative and complication/plot exercises necessary to produce a publishable manuscript. Genres we work with include general commercial fiction, literary fiction, serious and light women's fiction, mystery/cozy/thriller, SF/F, young adult, and memoir/narrative nonfiction. The three areas of workshop emphasis will be PREMISE, PLATFORM, and EXECUTION.

ACCOMMODATIONS "The Algonkian Park is located 30 miles from Washington, D.C., 12 miles from Dulles International Airport. All cottages feature central air and heat, fireplaces, decks with grills, equipped kitchens, cathedral ceilings, and expansive riverside views of the Potomac. Participants each have their own room in the cottage."

ADDITIONAL INFORMATION "The address of the Algonkian Park Management headquarters is 47001 Fairway Drive, Sterling, Virginia, and their phone number is 703-450-4655. If you have any questions about the cottages or facilities, ask for Lawan, the manager."

ANNUAL SPRING POETRY FESTIVAL

City College, 160 Convent Ave., New York NY 10031. (212)650-6356. **Website:** www1.ccny.cuny.edu/prospective/humanities/poetry. Writer workshops geared to all levels. **Open to students.** Annual poetry festival held in May. Registration limited to 325. Cost of workshops and festival: free. Write for more information. Site: Theater B of Aaron Davis Hall.

ASPEN SUMMER WORDS LITERARY FESTIVAL & WRITING RETREAT

Aspen Writers' Foundation, 110 E. Hallam St., #116, Aspen CO 81611. (970)925-3122. **Fax:** (970)925-5700. **E-mail:** info@aspenwriters.org. **Website:** www.aspenwriters.org. **Contact:** Natalie Lacy, programs coordinator. Estab. 1976. Annual conference held the fourth week of June. Conference duration: 5 days. Average attendance: 150 at writing retreat; 300+ at literary festival. Retreat for fiction, creative nonfiction, poetry, magazine writing, food writing, and literature. Festival includes author readings, craft talks, panel discussions with publishing industry insiders, professional consultations with editors and agents, and social gatherings. Retreat faculty members have included Andrea Barzi, Katherine Fausset, Anjali Singh, Joshua Kend-

all and Keith Flynn. Festival presenters have included Ngugi Wa Thiong'o, Henry Louis Gates, Jr., and Leila Aboulela.

COSTS Check website each year for updates. Offers a limited number of partial-tuition scholarships.

ACCOMMODATIONS Discount lodging at the conference site will be available. Free shuttle around town.

ADDITIONAL INFORMATION Workshops admission deadline is April 15. Manuscripts for juried workshops must be submitted by April 15 for review and selection. 10 page limit for workshop application manuscript. Deadline for agent/editor meeting registration is May 27th. Brochures available for SASE, by e-mail and phone request, and on website.

BACKSPACE WRITERS CONFERENCE & AGENT AUTHOR SEMINAR

P.O. Box 454, Washington MI 48094. (732)267-6449. **E-mail:** karendionne@bksp.org. **Website:** www.backspacewritersconference.com. **Contact:** Christopher Graham or Karen Dionne, co-founders. Conference duration: 3 days. Average attendance: 150-200. "We focus on all genres, from nonfiction to literary fiction and everything in between, covering all popular genres from mysteries, and thrillers to young adult and romance. Formal pitch sessions are a staple at most writers' conferences. However, in planning our Backspace events, we discovered that agents hate conducting pitch sessions almost as much as authors dread doing them. In fact, many of the agents we've talked to are happy to sit on a panel or conduct a workshop, but decline to participate in formal pitch sessions. The goal of the Backspace Agent-Author Seminars is to help authors connect with agents—lots of agents—thereby giving authors the opportunity to ask questions specific to their interests and concerns. We facilitate this through small group workshops of usually no more than 10 writers and 2 agents. Workshops concentrate on query letters and opening pages. That's why we've built so much free time into the program." Agents in attendance have included Donald Maass, Kristin Nelson, Janet Reid and Jeff Kleinman.

COSTS $200-700; offers member, group, and student discounts along with additional workshops that are priced separately.

ADDITIONAL INFORMATION See website for more information. Brochures available in January. Accepts inquiries by e-mail and phone. Agents and editors attend conference.

BALTIMORE WRITERS' CONFERENCE

PRWR Program, Linthicum Hall 218K, Towson University, 8000 York Rd., Towson MD 21252. (410)704-5196. **E-mail:** prwr@towson.edu. **Website:** www.towson.edu/writersconference. Estab. 1994. "Annual conference held in November at Towson University. Conference duration: 1 day. Average attendance: 150-200. Covers all areas of writing and getting published. Held at Towson University. Session topics include fiction, nonfiction, poetry, magazine and journals, agents and publishers. Sign up the day of the conference for quick critiques to improve your stories, essays, and poems."

COSTS $75-95 (includes all-day conference, lunch and reception). Student special rate of $35 before mid-October, $50 thereafter.

ACCOMMODATIONS Hotels are close by, if required.

ADDITIONAL INFORMATION Writers may register through the BWA website. Send inquiries via e-mail.

BIG SUR WRITING WORKSHOP

Henry Miller Library, Highway One, Big Sur CA 93920. (831)667-2574. **Website:** www.henrymiller.org; bigsurwriting.wordpress.com. **Contact:** Magnus Toren, executive director. Annual workshops are held in December and March focusing on children's and young adult writing. Workshop held in Big Sur Lodge in Pfeiffer State Park. Cost of workshop: $720; includes meals, lodging, workshop, Saturday evening reception; $600 if lodging not needed.

BLUE RIDGE "AUTUMN IN THE MOUNTAINS" NOVEL RETREAT

(800)588-7222. **E-mail:** ylehman@bellsouth.net. **Website:** www.lifeway.com/novelretreat. **Contact:** Yvonne Lehman, director. Estab. 2007. Annual retreat held in October at Ridgecrest/LifeWay Conference Center near Asheville NC. Retreat duration: Sunday through lunch on Thursday. Average attendance: 55. All areas of novel writing are included. For beginning and advanced novelists. Site: LifeWay/Ridgecrest Conference Center, 20 miles east of Asheville, NC. Faculty: Dr. Dennis Hensley, Dr. Angela Hunt, Ray Blackston, Jeff Gerke, Deborah Raney, Ann Tatlock, Yvonne Lehman. No editors or agents. Mornings: large group class. Afternoons: writing time and workshops. Evening: discussion and faculty panel.

COSTS Retreat Tuition: $315; Room: $89; Meals: $124.

ACCOMMODATIONS Mountain Laurel Hotel.

❍ BOOMING GROUND ONLINE WRITERS STUDIO

Buch E-462, 1866 Main Mall, UBC, Vancouver, British Columbia V6T 1Z1 Canada. **Fax:** (604)648-8848. **E-mail:** contact@boomingground.com. **Website:** www.booming ground.com. **Contact:** Jordan Hall, director. Writer mentorships geared toward beginner, intermediate, and advanced levels in novel, short fiction, poetry, nonfiction, and children's writing and more. **Open to students.** Online mentorship program—students work for 6 months with a mentor by e-mail, allowing up to 120-240 pages of material to be created. Program cost: $500 (Canadian).

BREAD LOAF WRITERS' CONFERENCE

Middlebury College, Middlebury VT 05753. (802)443-5286. **Fax:** (802)443-2087. **E-mail:** ncargill@middlebury.edu. **Website:** www.middlebury.edu/blwc. Estab. 1926. Annual conference held in late August. Conference duration: 11 days. Offers workshops for fiction, nonfiction, and poetry. Agents, editors, publicists, and grant specialists will be in attendance.

COSTS $2,345 (includes tuition, housing).

ACCOMMODATIONS Bread Loaf Campus in Ripton, Vermont.

ADDITIONAL INFORMATION 2011 Conference Dates: August 10-20. Location: mountain campus of Middlebury College. Average attendance: 230.

CAT WRITERS' ASSOCIATION ANNUAL WRITERS CONFERENCE

66 Adams Street, Jamestown NY 14701. (716)484-6155. **E-mail:** dogwriter@windstream.net. **Website:** www.catwriters.org. **Contact:** Susan M. Ewing, president. The Cat Writers' Association holds an annual conference at varying locations around the U.S. The agenda for the conference is filled with seminars, editor appointments, an autograph party, networking breakfast, reception and annual awards banquet, as well as the annual meeting of the association. See website for details.

CLARION WEST WRITERS WORKSHOP

P.O. Box 31264, Seattle WA 98103-1264. (206)322-9083. **E-mail:** info@clarionwest.org. **Website:** www.clarionwest.org. Contact us through our webform. **Contact:** Leslie Howle, workshop director. Clarion West is an intensive 6-week workshop for writers preparing for professional careers in science fiction and fantasy, held annually in Seattle WA. Usually goes from mid-June through end of July. Conference duration: 6 weeks. Average attendance: 18. Held near the University of Washington. Deadline for applications is March 1. Instructors are well-known writers and editors in the field.

COSTS $3,200 (for tuition, housing, most meals). Limited scholarships are available based on financial need.

ACCOMMODATIONS Workshop tuition, dormitory housing and most meals: $3,200. Students stay on-site in workshop housing at one of the University of Washington's sorority houses. "Students write their own stories every week while preparing critiques of all the other students' work for classroom sessions. This gives participants a more focused, professional approach to their writing. The core of the workshop remains speculative fiction, and short stories (not novels) are the focus." Conference information available in Fall. For brochure/guidelines send SASE, visit website, e-mail or call. Accepts inquiries by e-mail, phone, SASE. Limited scholarships are available, based on financial need. Students must submit 20-30 pages of ms with 4-page biography and $40 fee ($30 if received prior to Feb. 10) for applications sent by mail or e-mail to qualify for admission.

ADDITIONAL INFORMATION This is a critique-based workshop. Students are encouraged to write a story every week; the critique of student material produced at the workshop forms the principal activity of the workshop. Students and instructors critique mss as a group. Conference guidelines are available for a SASE. Visit the website for updates and complete details.

✚ COD WRITERS' CONFERENCE

P.O. Box 408, Osterville MA 02655. **E-mail:** writers@capecodwriterscenter.org. **Website:** www.capecod writerscenter.org. **Contact:** Nancy Rubin Stuart, artistic director. Cod Writer's Conference. Duration: Third week in August, 5 days. Offers workshops in fiction, commercial fiction, nonfiction, poetry, screen writing, digital communications, getting published, manuscript evaluation, mentoring sessions with faculty. Held at the Craigville Conference Center in a Cape Cod village overlooking Nantucket Sound.

COSTS Vary, average for one 5-day class and registration: $200.

CONFERENCE FOR WRITERS & ILLUSTRATORS OF CHILDREN'S BOOKS

51 Tamal Vista Blvd., Corte Madera CA 94925. (415)927-0960, ext. 239. **Fax:** (415)927-3069. **E-mail:** bpconferences@bookpassage.com. **Website:** www.bookpassage.com. **Contact:** Kathryn Petrocelli, con-

ference coordinator. Writer and illustrator conference geared toward beginner and intermediate levels. Sessions cover such topics as the nuts and bolts of writing and illustrating, publisher's spotlight, market trends, developing characters/finding voice in your writing, and the author/agent relationship. Four-day conference held each summer. Includes opening night dinner, 3 lunches and a closing reception.

THE DIY BOOK FESTIVAL

7095 Hollywood Blvd., Suite 864, Los Angeles CA 90028-0893. (323)665-8080. **Fax:** (323)372-3883. **E-mail:** diyconvention@aol.com. **Website:** www.diy convention.com. **Contact:** Bruce Haring, managing director. Writer and illustrator workshops geared toward beginner and intermediate levels. **Open to students.** Festival focuses on getting your book into print, book marketing and promotion. Annual workshop. Cost of workshop: $50; includes admission to event, entry to prize competition, lunch for some events. Check website for current dates and locations: www.diyconvention.com.

DUKE UNIVERSITY YOUTH PROGRAMS: CREATIVE WRITERS' WORKSHOP

Campus Box 90700, Room 201, The Bishop's House, Durham NC 27708. **Website:** www.learnmore.duke.edu/youth. **Open to students grades 10-11.** The Creative Writers' Workshop provides an intensive creative writing experience for advanced high school age writers who want to improve their skills in a community of writers. "The interactive format gives participants the opportunity to share their work in small groups, one-on-one with instructors, and receive feedback in a supportive environment. The review and critique process helps writers sharpen critical thinking skills and learn how to revise their work." Annual workshop. Every summer there is one 2-week residential session. Costs for 2012—$1,810 for residential campers; $1,170 for extended day campers. Visit website for more information. www.learnmore.duke.edu/youth.

FESTIVAL OF FAITH AND WRITING

Department of English, Calvin College, 1795 Knollcrest Circle SE, Grand Rapids MI 49546. (616)526-6770. **E-mail:** ffw@calvin.edu. **Website:** www.calvin.edu/festival. Estab. 1990. Biennial festival held in April. Conference duration: 3 days. The festival brings together writers, editors, publishers, musicians, artists, and readers to discuss and celebrate insightful writing that explores issues of faith. Focuses on fiction, nonfiction, memoir, poetry, drama, children's, young adult, academic, film, and songwriting. Past speakers have included Joyce Carol Oates, Salman Rushdie, Patricia Hampl and Michael Chabon. Agents and editors attend the festival.

COSTS Consult festival website.

ACCOMMODATIONS Shuttles are available to and from local hotels. Shuttles are also available for overflow parking lots. A list of hotels with special rates for conference attendees is available on the festival website. High school and college students can arrange on-campus lodging by e-mail.

ADDITIONAL INFORMATION Online registration opens in October. Accepts inquiries by e-mail and phone.

FISHTRAP, INC.

400 Grant Street, P.O. Box 38, Enterprise OR 97828-0038. (541)426-3623. **E-mail:** director@fishtrap.org. **Website:** www.fishtrap.org. **Contact:** Barbara Dills, interim director. In 21 years, Fishtrap has hosted over 200 published poets, novelists, journalists, songwriters and nonfiction writers as teachers and presenters. Although workshops are kept small, thousands of writers, teachers, students and booklovers from around the West have participated in Fishtrap events on a first come first served basis. Writer workshops geared toward beginner, intermediate, advanced and professional levels. Open to students, scholarships available. A series of writing workshops and a writers' gathering is held each July. During the school year Fishtrap brings writers into local schools and offers workshops for teachers and writers of children's and young adult books. Other programs include writing and K-12 teaching residencies, writers' retreats, and lectures. College credit available for many workshops. See website for full program descriptions and to get on the e-mail and mail lists.

FLATHEAD RIVER WRITERS CONFERENCE

P.O. Box 7711, Kalispeil MT 59904-7711. **E-mail:** answers@authorsoftheflathead.org. **Website:** www.authorsoftheflathead.org. Estab. 1990.

ACCOMMODATIONS Rooms are available at a discounted rate.

ADDITIONAL INFORMATION Come prepared to learn from renowned speakers and enjoy this spectacular area near Glacier National Park. Previous presenters jhave included agents Deborah Herman of The Jeff Herman Agency, Katharine Sands of the Sarah Jane Frey-

mann Literary Agency, children's book author Kathi Appelt, and best-selling memoir author Laura Munson. Watch our website for additional speakers and other details. Register early, as seating is limited.

GREATER LEHIGH VALLEY WRITERS GROUP "THE WRITE STUFF WRITERS CONFERENCE

3650 Nazareth Pike, PMB #136, Bethlehem PA 18020-1115. **E-mail:** writestuffchair@glvwg.org. **Website:** www.glvwg.org/. **Contact:** Donna Brennan, chair. Estab. 1993.

COSTS Members, $100 (includes Friday evening session and all Saturday workshops, 2 meals, and a chance to pitch to an editor or agent); non-members, $120. Late registration, $135. Pre-conference workshops require an additional fee.

ADDITIONAL INFORMATION "The Writer's Flash contest is judged by conference participants. Write 100 words or less in fiction, creative nonfiction, or poetry. Brochures available in January by SASE, or by phone, e-mail, or on website. Accepts inquiries by SASE, e-mail or phone. Agents and editors attend conference. For updated info refer to the website. Breakout rooms offer craft topics, business of publishing, editor and agent panels. Book fair with book signing by published authors and presenters."

GREEN LAKE CHRISTIAN WRITERS CONFERENCE

W2511 State Road 23, Green Lake Conference Center, Green Lake WI 54941-9599. (920)294-3323. **E-mail:** program@glcc.org. **Website:** www.glcc.org. Estab. 1948. Conference duration: 1 week. Attendees may be well-published or beginners, may write for secular and/or Christian markets. Leaders are experienced writing teachers. Attendees can spend 11.5 contact hours in the workshop of their choice: fiction, nonfiction, poetry, inspirational/devotional. Seminars include specific skills: marketing, humor, songwriting, writing for children, self-publishing, writing for churches, interviewing, memoir writing, the magazine market. Evening: panels of experts will answer questions. Social and leisure activities included. GLCC is in south central Wisconsin, has 1,000 acres, 2.5 miles of shoreline on Wisconsin's deepest lake, and offers a resort setting.

ACCOMMODATIONS Hotels, lodges and all meeting rooms are a/c. Affordable rates, excellent meals.

ADDITIONAL INFORMATION Brochure and scholarship info from website or contact Jan White (920-294-7327). To register, call 920-294-3323.

GREEN MOUNTAIN WRITERS CONFERENCE

47 Hazel St., Rutland VT 05701. (802)236-6133. E-mail: ydaley@sbcglobal.net. **Website:** www.vermont writers.com. **Contact:** Yvonne Daley, director. Estab. 1999. "Annual conference held in the summer. Covers fiction, creative nonfiction, poetry, journalism, nature writing, essay, memoir, personal narrative, and biography. Held at an old dance pavillion on on a remote pond in Tinmouth, Vermont. Speakers have included Stephen Sandy, Grace Paley, Ruth Stone, Howard Frank Mosher, and Chris Bohjalian."

COSTS $500 before July 1; $525 after July 1. Partial scholarships are available.

ACCOMMODATIONS "We have made arrangements with a major hotel in nearby Rutland and 3 area bed and breakfast inns for special accommodations and rates for conference participants. You must make your own reservations."

ADDITIONAL INFORMATION Participants' mss can be read and commented on at a cost. Sponsors contests. Conference publishes a literary magazine featuring work of participants. Brochures available in January on website or for SASE, e-mail. Accepts inquiries by SASE, e-mail, phone. Further information available on website, by e-mail or by phone.

HIGHLIGHTS FOUNDATION FOUNDERS WORKSHOPS

814 Court St., Honesdale PA 18437. (570)253-1172. **Fax:** (570)253-0179. **E-mail:** contact@highlights foundation.org. **Website:** www.highlightsfoundation. org/pages/current/FWsched_preview.html. **Contact:** Kent L. Brown, Jr. Estab. 2000. Conference duration: 3-7 days. Average attendance: limited to 10-14. Genre specific workshops and retreats on children's writing: fiction, nonfiction, poetry, promotions. "Our goal is to improve, over time, the quality of literature for children by educating future generations of children's authors." Highlights Founders' home in Boyds Mills, PA.

ACCOMMODATIONS Coordinates pickup at local airport. Offers overnight accommodations. Participants stay in guest cabins on the wooded grounds surrounding Highlights Founders' home adjacent to the house/conference center.

ADDITIONAL INFORMATION Some workshops require pre-workshop assignment. Brochure available for SASE, by e-mail, on website, by phone, by fax. Accepts inquiries by phone, fax, e-mail, SASE. Editors attend

conference. "Applications will be reviewed and accepted on a first-come, first-served basis; applicants must demonstrate specific experience in writing area of workshop they are applying for—writing samples are required for many of the workshops."

INDIANAPOLIS YOUTH LITERATURE CONFERENCE

(317)278-2375; (317)275-4100. **Website:** www.slis.iu pui.edu. Annual conference held in late January/early February featuring top writers in the field of children's literature. Registration limited to 300. Cost of conference: $75. Three plenary addresses, 2 workshops, book signing, reception and conference bookstore. The conference is geared toward three groups: teachers, librarians and writers/illustrators. Co-sponsors include the Indianapolis Marion County Public Library, Indiana State Library, and Kids Ink Children's Bookstore.

INTERNATIONAL CREATIVE WRITING CAMP

(701)838-8472. **Fax:** (701)838-1351. **E-mail:** info@in ternationalmusiccamp.com. **Website:** www.interna tionalmusiccamp.com. **Contact:** Dr. Timothy Wollenzien, camp director. Writer and illustrator workshops geared toward beginner, intermediate and advanced levels. **Open to students.** Sessions offered include those covering poems, plays, mystery stories, essays. Workshop annually in June. Registration limited to 40. The summer camp location at the International Peace Garden on the Border between Manitoba and North Dakota is an ideal site for creative thinking. Excellent food, housing and recreation facilities are available. Cost of workshop: Before May 1st—$355; after May 1st—$370. Write for more information.

IWWG ANNUAL SUMMER CONFERENCE

International Women's Writing Guild, P.O. Box 810, Gracie Station, New York NY 10028. (212)737-7536. **Fax:** (212)737-9469. **E-mail:** iwwg@iwwg.org. **Website:** www.iwwg.org. **Contact:** Hannelore Hahn, executive director. Writer and illustrator workshops geared toward all levels. Offers over 50 different workshops—some are for children's book writers and illustrators. Also sponsors other events throughout the U.S. Workshops held every summer for a week. Length of each session: 90 minutes; sessions take place for an entire week. Registration limited to 500. Write for more information.

JACKSON HOLE WRITERS CONFERENCE

PO Box 1974, Jackson WY 83001. (307)413-3332. E-mail: nicole@jacksonholewritersconference.com. Website: www.jacksonholewritersconference.com. Estab. 1991. Annual conference held in June. Conference duration: 4 days. Average attendance: 110. Covers fiction, creative nonfiction, and young adult and offers ms critiques from authors, agents, and editors. Agents in attendance will take pitches from writers. Paid manuscript critique programs are available.

COSTS $355-385, includes all workshops, speaking events, cocktail party, BBQ, and goodie bag with dining coupons. $75 spouse/guest registration; $50 ms evaluation; $75 extended ms evaluation. "You must register for conference to be eligible for ms evaluation."

ADDITIONAL INFORMATION Held at the Center for the Arts in Jackson, Wyoming, and online.

JOURNEY INTO THE IMAGINATION: A WEEKEND WRITING WORKSHOP

995 Chapman Rd., Yorktown NY 10598. (914)962-4432. E-mail: emily@emilyhanlon.com. Website: www.creativesoulworks.com. Contact: Emily Hanlon. PO Box 536 Estab. 2004. Annual. Held the last weekend in April. Average attendance: 15-20. "Purpose of workshop: fiction, memoir, short story, creativity, and the creative process." Site: Wisdom House Retreat Center in Litchfield, CT. "We stay in an old farmhouse on the retreat center grounds. Excellent food and lovely surroundings and accommodations. The core of this weekend's work is welcoming the unknown into your writing. We will go on a magical mystery tour to find and embrace new characters and to deepen our relationship to characters who already may people our stories. Bring something on which you are already working or simply bring along your Inner Writer, pen and a journal, and let the magic unfold!"

COSTS 3 nights—$625-825, dependent on choice of room. Early Registration extended to March 1.

ADDITIONAL INFORMATION For brochure, visit www.creativesoulworks.com/Journey_Into_the_Imagination_Wisdom_House_April2012.htm.

KENYON REVIEW WRITERS WORKSHOP

Kenyon College, Gambier OH 43022. (740)427-5207. Fax: (740)427-5417. E-mail: kenyonreview@kenyon.edu; writers@kenyonreview.org. Website: www.kenyonreview.org. Contact: Anna Duke Reach, director. Estab. 1990. Annual 8-day workshop held in June. Participants apply in poetry, fiction, or creative nonfic-

tion, and then participate in intensive daily workshops which focus on the generation and revision of significant new work. Held on the campus of Kenyon College in the rural village of Gambier, Ohio. Workshop leaders have included David Baker, Ron Carlson, Rebecca McClanahan and Meghan O'Rourke.

COSTS $1,995 includes tuition, room and board.

ACCOMMODATIONS The workshop operates a shuttle to and from Gambier and the airport in Columbus, Ohio. Offers overnight accommodations. Participants are housed in Kenyon College student housing. The cost is covered in the tuition.

ADDITIONAL INFORMATION Application includes a writing sample. Admission decisions are made on a rolling basis. Workshop information is available online at www.kenyonreview.org/workshops in November. For brochure send e-mail, visit website, call, fax. Accepts inquiries by SASE, e-mail, phone, fax.

KINDLING WORDS EAST

Website: www.kindlingwords.org. Annual retreat held in late January near Burlington, Vermont. A retreat with three strands: writer, illustrator and editor; professional level. Intensive workshops for each strand, and an open schedule for conversations and networking. Registration limited to approximately 70. Hosted by the 4-star Inn at Essex (room and board extra). Participants must be published by a CBC listed publisher, or if in publishing, occupy a professional position. Registration opens August 1 or as posted on the website, and fills quickly. Check website to see if spaces are available, to sign up to be notified when registration opens each year, or for more information.

KINDLING WORDS WEST

Website: www.KindlingWords.org. Annual retreat held in late May at a stunning and sacred location: Mable Dodge Luhan House, in Taos, NM. KWW is an artist's colony–style week with workshops by gifted teachers followed by a working retreat. Participants gather just before dinner to have white-space discussions; evenings include fireside readings, star gazing and songs. $400 tuition; room/board extra. Participants must be published by CBC-recognized publisher. Go to www.kindlingwords.org to view speakers and register.

LA JOLLA WRITERS CONFERENCE

P.O. Box 178122, San Diego CA 92177. (858)467-1978. E-mail: akuritz@san.rr.com. Website: www.lajollawritersconference.com. Contact: Jared Kuritz, director. "Annual conference held in October/November.

Conference duration: 3 days. Average attendance: 200. In addition to covering nearly every genre, we also take particular pride in educating our attendees on the business aspect of the book industry by having agents, editors, publishers, publicists, and distributors teach classes. Our conference offers 2 types of classes: lecture sessions that run for 50 minutes, and workshops that run for 110 minutes. Each block period is dedicated to either workshop or lecture-style classes. During each block period, there will be 6-8 classes on various topics from which you can choose. For most workshop classes, you are encouraged to bring written work for review. Literary agents from The Andrea Brown Literary Agency, The Dijkstra Agency, The McBride Agency and Full Circle Literary Group have participated in the past. Costs are available online."

LAS VEGAS WRITERS CONFERENCE

Henderson Writers' Group, 614 Mosswood Dr., Henderson NV 89015. (702)564-2488; or, toll-free, (866)869-7842. **E-mail:** marga614@mysticpublish ers.com. **Website:** www.lasvegaswritersconference. com. Annual. Held in April. Conference duration: 3 days. Average attendance: 150 maximum. "Join writing professionals, agents, industry experts, and your colleagues for 3 days in Las Vegas as they share their knowledge on all aspects of the writer's craft. While there are formal pitch sessions, panels, workshops, and seminars, the faculty is also available throughout the conference for informal discussions and advice. Plus, you're bound to meet a few new friends, too. Workshops, seminars, and expert panels will take you through writing in many genres including fiction, creative nonfiction, screenwriting, journalism, and business and technical writing. There will be many Q&A panels for you to ask the experts all your questions." Site: Sam's Town Hotel and Gambling Hall in Las Vegas.
COSTS $400 before December 31, $450 until conference, and $500 at the door. One day registration is $275.
ADDITIONAL INFORMATION Sponsors contest. Agents and editors participate in conference.

LEAGUE OF UTAH WRITERS' ANNUAL ROUNDUP

P.O. Box 18430, Kearns UT 84118. **E-mail:** writer scache435@gmail.com. **Website:** www.luwriters.org/ index.html. **Contact:** Tim Keller, president; Irene Hastings, president-elect; Dorothy Crofts, secretary. The

League of Utah Writers is a non-profit organization dedicated to offering friendship, education, and encouragement to the writers of Utah. New members are always welcome. Writer workshops geared toward beginner, intermediate or advanced. Annual conference.

MANHATTANVILLE SUMMER WRITERS' WEEK

2900 Purchase St., Purchase NY 10577. (914)323-5239. **Fax:** (914)323-3122. **E-mail:** sirabiank@mville.edu. **Website:** www.manhattanville.edu; www.mville.edu/ summerwritersweek. **Contact:** Karen Sirabian, program director. Writer workshops geared toward writers and aspiring writers. **Open to students.** Writers' week offers a special workshop for writers interested in children's/young adult writing. Workshop leaders have included Patricia Gauch, Richard Peck, Elizabeth Winthrop and Janet Lisle. Annual workshop held in June. Cost of workshop: $725 (non-credit); includes a full week of writing activities, 5-day workshop on children's literature; lectures; readings; sessions with editors and agents; etc. Workshop may be taken for 2 graduate credits. Write or e-mail for more information.

THE MANUSCRIPT WORKSHOP IN VERMONT

P.O. Box 529, Londonderry VT 05148. **E-mail:** aplbrk2@earthlink.net. **Website:** www.barbaraseul ing.com. **Contact:** Barbara Seuling, director. Writer workshop for all levels. Annual workshop estab. 1992. Generally held mid to late July and August and sometimes early September. The time is divided among instructive hands-on sessions in the mornings, writing time in the afternoons, and critiquing in the evenings. A guest speaker from the world of children's books may be a guest at the workshops. Cost of workshop: $750 per person; applicants are responsible for their accommodations and meals at the inn.

☺ MARITIME WRITERS' WORKSHOP

UNB College of Extended Learning, P.O. Box 4400, Fredericton, New Brunswick E3B 5A3 Canada. (506)458-7106. **E-mail:** bpaynter@unb.ca. **Website:** www.unb.ca/cel/programs/creative/maritime-writers/ index.html. **Contact:** Beth Paynter, coordinator. Workshops run 9 a.m.-4 p.m. daily, on topics such as life writing, ficiton, and how to get published. Group workshop plus individual conferences, public readings, etc. Registration limited. Cost: $125; students: $75.

MENDOCINO COAST WRITERS CONFERENCE

1211 Del Mar Dr., Fort Bragg CA 95437. (707)937-9983. **E-mail:** info@mcwc.org. **Website:** www.mcwc.org. Estab. 1988. Annual conference held in July. Average attendance: 80. Provides workshops for fiction, nonfiction, and poetry. Held at a small community college campus on the northern Pacific Coast. Workshop leaders have included Kim Addonizio, Lynne Barrett, John Dufresne, John Lescroart, Ben Percy, Luis Rodriguez, and Ellen Sussman. Agents and will be speaking and available for meetings with attendees.

COSTS $525+ (includes panels, meals, 2 socials with guest readers, 4 public events, 3 morning intensive workshops in 1 of 6 subjects, and a variety of afternoon panels and lectures)

ACCOMMODATIONS Information on overnight accommodations is made available.

ADDITIONAL INFORMATION Emphasis is on writers who are also good teachers. Brochures are online after in mid-February. Send inquiries via e-mail.

MIDWEST WRITERS WORKSHOP

Ball State University, Department of Journalism, Muncie IN 47306. (765)282-1055. **E-mail:** midwestwriters@yahoo.com. **Website:** www.midwestwriters.org. **Contact:** Jama Kehoe Bigger, director. Writer workshops geared toward intermediate level. Topics include most genres. Our faculty/speakers have included Joyce Carol Oates, George Plimpton, Clive Cussler, Haven Kimmel, James Alexander Thom, Wiliam Zinsser, Phillip Gulley, and children's writers Rebecca Kai Dotlich, April Pulley Sayre, Peter Welling, Claire Ewert and Michelle Medlock Adams. Workshop also includes agent pitch sessions, ms evaluation and a writing contest. Annual workshop held in late July. Registration tentatively limited to 125. Cost: $115-325. Most meals included. Offers scholarships. See website for more information.

MISSOURI WRITERS' GUILD ANNUAL STATE CONFERENCE

E-mail: mwgvpchair@gmail.com. **Website:** www.missouriwritersguild.org. **Contact:** Tricia Sanders, vice president/conference chairman. Writer and illustrator workshops geared to all levels. **Open to students.** Annual conference held early April or early May each year. Annual conference "gives writers the opportunity to hear outstanding speakers and to receive information on marketing, research, and writing techniques."

MONTROSE CHRISTIAN WRITERS' CONFERENCE

218 Locust St., Montrose PA 18801. (570)278-1001 or (800)598-5030. **Fax:** (570)278-3061. **E-mail:** info@montrosebible.org. **Website:** www.montrosebible.org. Estab. 1990. "Annual conference held in July. Offers workshops, editorial appointments, and professional critiques. We try to meet a cross-section of writing needs, for beginners and advanced, covering fiction, poetry, and writing for children. It is small enough to allow personal interaction between attendees and faculty. Speakers have included William Petersen, Mona Hodgson, Jim Fletcher, and Terri Gibbs."

ACCOMMODATIONS Will meet planes in Binghamton, NY and Scranton, PA. On-site accomodations: room and board $285-330/conference; $60-70/day including food (2009 rates). RV court available.

ADDITIONAL INFORMATION "Writers can send work ahead of time and have it critiqued for a small fee." The attendees are usually church related. The writing has a Christian emphasis. Conference information available in April. For brochure send SASE, visit website, e-mail, call or fax. Accepts inquiries by SASE, e-mail, fax, phone.

MOONDANCE INTERNATIONAL FILM FESTIVAL

970 Ninth St., Boulder CO 80302. (303)545-0202. **E-mail:** director@moondancefilmfestival.com. **Website:** www.moondancefilmfestival.com. **Contact:** Elizabeth English, executive director. Moondance Film Festival Workshop sessions include screenwriting, playwriting, short stories, filmmaking (feature, documentary, short, animation), TV and video filmmaking, writing for TV (MOW, sitcoms, drama), writing for animation, adaptation to screenplays (novels and short stories), how to get an agent, what agents want to see, and pitch panels. Check website for more information and registration forms. "The Moondance competition includes special categories for writers and filmmakers who create work for the children's market!" Entry forms and guidelines are on the website.

OHIO KENTUCKY INDIANA CHILDREN'S LITERATURE CONFERENCE

Northern Kentucky University, 405 Steely Library, Highland Heights KY 41099. (859)572-6620. **Fax:** (859) 572-5390. **E-mail:** smithjen@nku.edu. **Website:**

http://oki.nku.edu. **Contact:** Jennifer Smith, staff development coordinator. Writer and illustrator conference geared toward all levels. **Open to University.** Annual conference. Emphasizes multicultural literature for children and young adults. Conference held annually in November. Contact Jennifer Smith for more information. Cost of conference: $75; includes registration/attendance at all workshop sessions, *Tristate Authors and Illustrators of Children's Books Directory*, continental breakfast, lunch, author/illustrator signings. Manuscript critiques are available for an additional cost. E-mail or call for more information.

OKLAHOMA WRITERS' FEDERATION, INC. ANNUAL CONFERENCE

Website: www.owfi.org. **Contact:** Linda Apple, president. Writer workshops geared toward all levels. **Open to students.** "Forty seminars, with 30 speakers consisting of editors, literary agents and many bestselling authors. Topics range widely to include craft, marketing, and all genres of writing." Annual conference. held during the first weekend in May each year. Writing facilities available: book room, autograph party, two lunch workshops. Cost of writers conference: $150 before March 15; $175 after March 15; $70 for single days; $25 for lunch workshops. Full tuition includes 2-day conference (all events except lunch workshops) and 2 dinners plus one 10-minute appointment with an attending editor or agent of your choice (must be reserved in advance). "If writers would like to participate in the annual writing contest, they must become members of OWFI. You don't have to be a member to attend the conference." See website for more information.

OUTDOOR WRITERS ASSOCIATION OF AMERICA ANNUAL CONFERENCE

615 Oak St., Suite 201, Missoula MT 59801. (406)728-7434. **E-mail:** info@owaa.org; rginer@owaa.org. **Website:** http://owaa.org. **Contact:** Robin Giner, meeting planner. Writer workshops geared toward all levels. Annual 3-day conference. Craft improvement seminars; newsmaker sessions. 2012 conference was held in Chena Hot Springs-Fairbanks, Alaska. Cost of workshop: $390-450; includes attendance at all workshops and most meals. Attendees must have prior approval from executive director before attendance is permitted. Write for more information.

OZARK CREATIVE WRITERS, INC. CONFERENCE

P.O. Box 424, Eureka Springs AR 72632. **E-mail:** ozarkcreativewriters@gmail.com. **Website:** www.ozarkcreativewriters.org. Open to professional and amateur writers; workshops are geared to all levels and all forms of the creative process and literary arts. Sessions sometimes include songwriting, with presentations by best-selling authors, editors, and agents. The OCW Conference promotes writing by offering competitions in all genres. The annual event is held on the second full weekend in October at the Inn of the Ozarks, in the resort town of Eureka Springs, Arkansas. Approximately 200 attend each year; many also enter the creative writing competitions.

PACIFIC NORTHWEST CHILDREN'S BOOK CONFERENCE

P.O. Box 751, Portland OR 97207. (503)725-9786 or (800)547-8887. **Fax:** (503)725-5599. **E-mail:** snydere@pdx.edu. **Website:** www.ceed.pdx.edu/children/. **Contact:** Elizabeth Snyder. Focus on the craft of writing and illustrating for children while working with an outstanding faculty of acclaimed editors, authors, and illustrators. Daily afternoon faculty-led writing and illustration workshops. Acquire specific information on how to become a professional in the field of children's literature. Annual workshop for all levels. Cost depends on options selected, including: noncredit or 3 graduate credits or graduate credits; individual ms/portfolio reviews and room and board at Reed campus.

PACIFIC NORTHWEST WRITERS ASSOCIATION SUMMER WRITER'S CONFERENCE

PMB 2717, 1420 NW Gilman Blvd., Ste. 2, Issaquah WA 98027. (425)673-2665. **E-mail:** staff@pnwa.org. **Website:** www.pnwa.org. Writer conference geared toward beginner, intermediate, advanced and professional levels. Meet agents and editors. Learn craft from renowned authors. Uncover new marketing secrets. PNWA's 57th Annual Conference was held July 19-22, 2012.

PHILADELPHIA WRITERS' CONFERENCE

P.O. Box 7171, Elkins Park PA 19027-0171. (215) 619-7422. **E-mail:** dresente@mc3.edu. **Website:** www.pwcwriters.org. **Contact:** Dana Resente. Estab. 1949. Annual. Conference held June 8-10 for 2012. Average attendance: 160-200. Conference covers many forms of writing: novel, short story, genre fiction, nonfiction book, magazine writing, blogging, juvenile, poetry. **COSTS** Advance registration postmarked by April 15 is $205; after April 8 and walk-in registration is $225. The banquet and buffet are $40 each. Master classes are $50. **ACCOMMODATIONS** Holiday Inn, Independence Mall, Fourth and Arch Streets, Philadelphia, PA 19106-2170. "Hotel offers discount for early registration." **ADDITIONAL INFORMATION** Sponsors contest. "Length is generally 2,500 words for fiction or nonfiction. 1st Prize, in addition to cash and certificate, gets free tuition for following year." Also offers ms critique. Accepts inquiries by e-mail and SASE. Agents and editors attend conference. Visit us on the web for further agent and speaker details."

PIMA WRITERS' WORKSHOP

Pima College, 2202 W. Anklam Rd., Tucson AZ 85709. (520)206-6084. **Fax:** (520)206-6020. **E-mail:** mfiles@pima.edu. **Website:** www.pima.edu. **Contact:** Meg Files, director. Writer conference geared toward beginner, intermediate and advanced levels. **Open to students.** The conference features presentations and writing exercises on writing and publishing stories for children and young adults, among other genres. Annual conference. Workshop held in May. Cost: $100 (can include ms critique). Participants may attend for college credit. Meals and accommodations not included. Features a dozen authors, editors, and agents talking about writing and publishing fiction, nonfiction, poetry, and stories for children. Write for more information.

PUBLISHINGGAME.COM WORKSHOP

Newton MA 02459. (617)630-0945. **E-mail:** alyza@publishinggame.com. **Website:** www.publishinggame.com. **Contact:** Alyza Harris, coordinator. Writer workshops geared toward beginner, intermediate and advanced levels. Sessions will include: Find a Literary Agent, Self-Publish Your Children's Book, Book Promotion for Children's Books. Held every month in a different location. Please see http://www.publishinggame.com for current schedule. Registration limited to 18. Fills quickly! Cost of workshop: $195; includes information-packed course binder and light refreshments. E-mail for more information. Workshop now available as a 5-CD audio workshop. For information on getting more media attention for your novel, nonfiction or children's book, see Fern Reiss's complementary Expertizing workshop at www.expertizing.com.

ROBERT QUACKENBUSH'S CHILDREN'S BOOK WRITING AND ILLUSTRATING WORKSHOP

460 E. 79th St., New York NY 10075. (212)861-2761. **E-mail:** rqstudios@aol.com. **Website:** www.rquackenbush.com. A 4-day extensive workshop on writing and illustrating books for young readers held annually the second week in July at author/artist Robert Quackenbush's Manhattan studio for beginning and advanced writers and illustrators. The focus of this workshop is on creating manuscripts and/or illustrated book dummies from start to finish for picture books and beginning reader chapter books ready to submit to publishers. Also covered is writing fiction and nonfiction for middle grades and young adults, if that is the attendee's interest. In addition, attention is given to review of illustrator's portfolios, and new trends in illustration, including animation for films, are explored. During the 4 days, the workshop meets from 9 a.m to 4 p.m. including one hour for lunch. Registration is limited to 10. Some writing and/or art supplies are available at the studio and there is an art store nearby, if needed. There are also electrical outlets for attendees' laptop computers. Cost of workshop is $750. A $100 non-refundable deposit is required to enroll; balance is due three weeks prior the workshop. Attendees are responsible for arranging for their own hotel and meals. On request, suggestions are given for economical places to stay and eat. Recommended by Foder's Great American Learning Vacations, which says, "This unique workshop, held annually since 1982, provides the opportunity to work with Robert Quackenbush, a prolific author and illustrator of children's books with more than 200 fiction and nonfiction books for young readers to his credit, including mysteries, biographies and songbooks. The workshop attracts both professional and beginning writers and artists of different ages from all over the world." Brochure available. Class is for beginners and professionals. Critiques during workshop. Private consultations also available at an hourly rate. "Programs suited to your needs; individualized schedules can be designed. Write or phone to discuss your goals and you will receive a prompt reply." Also inquire about fall, winter and spring workshops that meet once a week for ten weeks each that are offered to artists and writers in the New York area. A list of recommended hotels and res-

CONFERENCES & WORKSHOPS

taurants is sent upon receipt of deposit to applicants living out of the area of New York City. Conference information available 1 year prior to conference. For brochure, send SASE, e-mail, visit website, call or fax. Accepts inquiries by fax, e-mail, phone, SASE.

ROCKY MOUNTAIN FICTION WRITERS COLORADO GOLD

Rocky Mountain Fiction Writers, P.O. Box 735, Conifer CO 80433. **E-mail:** conference@rmfw.org. **Website:** www.rmfw.org. Estab. 1982. Annual conference held in September. Conference duration: 3 days. Average attendance: 350. Themes include general novel-length fiction, genre fiction, contemporary romance, mystery, science fiction/fantasy, mainstream, and history. New since 2012: Friday morning master classes. Speakers have included Bernard Cornwell, Terry Brooks, Dorothy Cannell and Patricia Gardner Evans. Approximately 8 editors and 5 agents attend annually.
COSTS Costs available online.
ACCOMMODATIONS Special rates will be available at conference hotel.
ADDITIONAL INFORMATION Editor-conducted workshops are limited to 8 participants for critique, with auditing available. Pitch appointments available at no charge.

SANTA BARBARA WRITERS CONFERENCE

27 W. Anapamu St., Suite 305, Santa Barbara CA 93101. (805)568-1516. **E-mail:** info@sbwriters.com. **Website:** www.sbwriters.com. Estab. 1972. Annual conference held in June. Check website for specific dates. Average attendance: 200. Covers fiction, nonfiction, journalism, memoir, poetry, playwriting, screenwriting, travel writing, young adult, children's literature, humor, and marketing.
ACCOMMODATIONS Hyatt Santa Barbara.
ADDITIONAL INFORMATION Register online or contact for brochure and registration forms.

☺ SASKATCHEWAN FESTIVAL OF WORDS AND WORKSHOPS

217 Main St. N., Moose Jaw SK S6H 0W1 Canada. **E-mail:** word.festival@sasktel.net. **Website:** www.festivalofwords.com. **Contact:** Donna Lee Howes. Writer workshops geared toward beginner and intermediate levels. **Open to students.** Readings that include a wide spectrum of genres—fiction, creative nonfiction, poetry, songwriting, screenwriting, playwriting, dramatic reading with actors, graphic novels; Great Big Book Club Discussion with author; children's writing,

panels; independent film screening; slam poetry; interviews and performances. Annual festival. Workshop held third weekend in July. Cost of workshop varies from $10 for a single reading to $200 for a full pass (as of 2012). Trivia Night Fun ticket is extra. Visit website for more information.

NANCY SONDEL'S PACIFIC COAST CHILDREN'S WRITERS WORKSHOP

P.O. Box 244, Aptos CA 95001. **Website:** www.childrenswritersworkshop.com. "Our seminar serves semi-advanced through professional-level adult writers. A concurrent, intergenerational workshop is open to students age 14 and up, who give adults target-reader feedback. Intensive focus on craft as a marketing tool. Team-taught master classes (open clinics for ms critiques) explore such topics as 'Envision and Edit Your Whole Novel' and 'Story Architecture and Arcs.' Continuous close contact with faculty, who have included literary agent Andrea Brown and Dial Books senior editor Kate Harrison.**" Past seminars:** October 7-9, 2011 and October 5-7, 2012. Registration limited to 12 adults and 6 teens. For the most critique options, submit sample chapters and synopsis with e-application by mid May; open until filled. **Content:** Character-driven novels with protagonists ages 11 and older. Collegial format; 90 percent hands-on, with dialogues between seasoned faculty and savvy, congenial peers. "Our faculty critiques early as well as optional later chapters, plus synopses. Our pre-workshop anthology of peer manuscripts maximizes learning and networking. Several enrollees have landed contracts as a direct result of our seminar." **Details:** "Visit our website and e-mail us via the contact form."

SOUTHEASTERN WRITERS ASSOCIATION—ANNUAL WRITERS WORKSHOP

161 Woodstone, Athens GA 30605. **E-mail:** purple@southeasternwriters.com. **Website:** www.southeasternwriters.com. **Contact:** Amy Munnell & Sheila Hudson, presidents. **Open to all writers.** Contests with cash prizes. Instruction offered for novel and short fiction, nonfiction, writing for children, humor, inspirational writing, and poetry. Manuscript deadline April 1st, includes free evaluation conference(s) with instructor(s). Agent in residence. Annual 4-day workshop held in June. Cost of workshop: $395 for 4 days or $150-350 daily tuition. Accommodations: Offers overnight ac-

commodations on workshop site. Visit website for more information and cost of overnight accommodations. E-mail or send SASE for brochure.

○ SURREY INTERNATIONAL WRITERS CONFERENCE

SIWC c/o SD 36, Unit 400, 9260-140 Street, Surrey, British Columbia V3V 5Z4 Canada. **E-mail:** kathychung@siwc.ca. **Website:** www.siwc.ca. **Contact:** Kathy Chung, conference coordinator. Writing workshops geared toward beginner, intermediate and advanced levels. More than 70 workshops and panels, on all topics and genres. Blue Pencil and agent/editor pitch sessions included. Annual conference held every October. Different conference price packages available. Check our website for more information.

● SYDNEY CHILDREN'S WRITERS AND ILLUSTRATORS NETWORK

The Hughenden Boutique Hotel, 14 Queen St., Woollahra, New South Wales 2025 Australia . (61) 2 9363 4863. **Fax:** (61) 2 9362 0398. **Website:** www.sgervay.com. **Contact:** Susanne Gervay. Writer and illustrator network geared toward professionals. Topics emphasized include networking, information and expertise about Australian children's publishing industry. Network held the first Wednesday of every month, except for January, commencing at 10:30 a.m. Registration limited to 30. Writing facilities available: Internet and conference facilities. As a prerequisite must be published in a commercial or have a book contract. E-mail for more information. "This is a professional meeting which aims at an interchange of ideas and information between professional children's authors and illustrators. Editors and other invited guests speak from time to time."

TMCC (RENO) WRITERS' CONFERENCE

5270 Neil Rd., Reno NV 89502. (775)829-9010. **Fax:** (775)829-9032. **E-mail:** wdce@tmcc.edu. **Website:** wdce.tmcc.edu. Estab. 1991. Annual, held each April. Average attendance: 150. Conference focuses on strengthening mainstream/literary fiction and nonfiction works and how to market them to agents and publishers. Site: Truckee Meadows Community College in Reno, Nevada. "There is always an array of speakers and presenters with impressive literary credentials, including agents and editors." Speakers have included Chuck Sambuchino, Sheree Bykofsky, Andrea Brown, Dorothy Allison, Karen Joy Fowler, James D. Houston,

James N. Frey, Gary Short, Jane Hirschfield, Dorrianne Laux, and Kim Addonizio

COSTS $109 for a full-day seminar; $32 for a 10-minute one-on-one appointment with an agent or editor.

ACCOMMODATIONS The Silver Legacy, in downtown Reno, offers a special rate and shuttle service to the Reno/Tahoe International Airport, which is less than 20 minutes away.

ADDITIONAL INFORMATION "The conference is open to all writers, regardless of their level of experience. Brochures are available online and mailed in January. Send inquiries via e-mail."

TONY HILLERMAN WRITERS CONFERENCE

1063 Willow Way, Santa Fe NM 87505. (505)471-1565. **E-mail:** wordharvest@wordharvest.com. **Website:** www.wordharvest.com. **Contact:** Jean Schaumberg, co-director. Estab. 2004. Annual. Conference duration: 3 days. Average attendance: 100. Site: Hotel Santa Fe. Pre-conference workshop offers hands-on writing practice with a published author who is also a seasoned teacher. Other programs focus on perfecting the craft of writing and learning the business aspects of writing and publishing. "We'll honor the winner of the Tony Hillerman Prize for best first mystery at a dinner with a keynote speaker. A 'flash critique' session, open to any interested attendee, will add to the fun and information."

COSTS Previous year's costs: $395 pre-registration.

ACCOMMODATIONS Hotel Santa Fe; offers $115 single or double occupancy. Book online with the hotel.

ADDITIONAL INFORMATION Sponsors a $10,000 first mystery novel contest with St. Martin's Press and a mystery short story contest with *New Mexico Magazine*. Brochures available in July for SASE, by phone, e-mail, and on website. Accepts inquiries by SASE, phone, e-mail. Deadline for the Hillerman Mystery Competition is June 1; August 15 for the Hillerman Short Story contest.

UMKC WRITERS WORKSHOPS

5300 Rockhill Rd., Kansas City MO 64110. (816)235-2736. **Fax:** (816)235-5279. **E-mail:** wittfeldk@umkc. edu. **Website:** www.newletters.org/writingConferences.asp. **Contact:** Kathi Wittfeld. New Letters Writer's Conference and Mark Twain Writer's Workshop are geared toward intermediate, advanced and professional levels. Workshops open to students and community. Annual workshops. Workshops held in Summer. Cost of workshop varies. Write for more information.

WILLAMETTE WRITERS CONFERENCE

2108 Buck St., Portland OR 97068. (503)305-6729. **Fax:** (503)452-0372. **E-mail:** wilwrite@willamette writers.com. **Website:** www.willamettewriters.com. Estab. 1981. Annual conference held in August. Conference duration: 3 days. Average attendance: 600. "Williamette Writers is open to all writers, and we plan our conference accordingly. We offer workshops on all aspects of fiction, nonfiction, marketing, the creative process, screenwriting, etc. Also we invite top-notch inspirational speakers for keynote addresses. Recent theme was 'The Writers Way.' We always include at least 1 agent or editor panel and offer a variety of topics of interest to both fiction and nonfiction writers and screenwriters."

ADDITIONAL INFORMATION Brochure/guidelines are available for a catalog-sized SASE.

WRITE-BY-THE-LAKE WRITER'S WORKSHOP & RETREAT

21 N. Park St., 7th Floor, Madison WI 53715. (608)262-3447. **E-mail:** cdesmet@dcs.wisc.edu. **Website:** www.dcs.wisc.edu/lsa/writing. **Contact:** Christine DeSmet, coordinator. Writer workshops geared toward beginner, intermediate, and advanced levels. **Open to students** (1-3 graduate credits available in English). "One weeklong session is devoted to writing for children." Annual workshop held in mid-June. Registration limited to 15. Writing facilities available: computer labs. Cost of workshop: $345 before May 16; $395 after May 17. Cost includes instruction, welcome luncheon, and pastry/coffee each day. E-mail for more information. "Brochure goes online every January for the following June."

WRITERS' LEAGUE OF TEXAS WORKSHOPS AND SUMMER WRITING RETREAT

611 S. Congress Ave., Suite 130, Austin TX 78704. (512)499-8914. **Fax:** (512)499-0441. **E-mail:** wlt@ writersleague.org. **Website:** www.writersleague.org. **Contact:** Sara Kocek, program coordinator. "Classes and workshops provide practical advice and guidance on the craft of writing for writers at all stages of their career." Retreat: Annual Summer Writing Academy in Alpine, TX, is a weeklong writing intensive with five tracks. Special presentations: "The Secrets of the Agents" series of workshops with visiting literary agents. Classes and workshops topics include e-publishing, creative nonfiction, screenwriting, novel

writing, short fiction, journaling, manuscript revision, memoir writing, poetry, essays, freelance writing, publicity, author/book websites, and blogging. Instructors include Carol Dawson, Karleen Koen, Kirsten Cappy, Eric Butterman, Cyndi Hughes, Scott Wiggerman, Debra Monroe, Jennifer Ziegler, W.K. Stratton.

THE WRITERS RETREATS' NETWORK

Website: www.writersretreat.com. **Contact:** Micheline Cote. A worldwide selection of residential retreats opened year-round to writers—most of them offering on-site coaching and mentoring. The retreats cater to writers of all genres and offer on-site support such as mentoring, workshops, editing, and lodging; some of them offer scholarships. To start and operate a retreat in your area, visit our website and find out about the new handbook A Writers' Retreat: Starting from Scratch to Success!

WRITERS RETREAT WORKSHOP

Website: www.writersretreatworkshop.com. **Contact:** Jason Sitzes, director. Intensive workshops geared toward beginner, intermediate and advanced levels. Workshops are appropriate for writers of full length novels for children/YA. Also, for writers of all novels or narrative nonfiction. Annual workshop, held in Marydale Retreat Center, Erlanger, KY, in May/June. Registration limited to 32: beginners and advanced. Writing facilities available: private rooms with desks. Cost includes tuition, food and lodging for 9 nights, daily classes, writing space, time and assignments, consultation and instruction. One annual scholarship available: February deadline. Requirements: short synopsis required to determine appropriateness of novel for our nuts-and-bolts approach to getting the work in shape for publication. Write for more information. For complete updated details, visit www.writersretreatworkshop.com.

WRITING WORKSHOP AT CASTLE HILL

1 Depot Rd., P.O. Box 756, Truro MA 02666-0756. **E-mail:** cherie@castlehill.org. **Website:** www.castle hill.org. Poetry, fiction and memoir workshops geared toward intermediate and advanced levels. **Open to students.** Past workshops have incuded "Elements of Fiction," "Poetry in Plein Air," "Broadsides and Beyond: Poetry as Public Art," and "Finding the Me in Memoir." Faculty have included Anne Bernays, Elizabeth Bradfield, and Judy Huge. See website for dates and more information.

"What writers' conference would you recommend? Which one is the best to attend?"

We at WD get this question all the time. We're guessing that people decide they're going to "do it right" and hit up a big event—and they are just trying to make sure that they get some serious bang for their buck.

Now, to answer the question, let's just acknowledge immediately that there is no definitive answer. It will be different for everyone, so we must examine three things: 1) the different kinds of writers' events, 2) how money plays into a decision, and 3) what you want to get out of the event.

DIFFERENT TYPES OF EVENTS

General writers' conferences. These are just what you think they are—writers' conferences that are general in nature and geared toward all categories and levels of writers. There are hundreds of these nationwide every year, and a lot of the biggest fall under this category.

Writers' conferences with a specialized focus. There are plenty of these, too. These gatherings have a unique focus to them—and that usually means they are all about romance writing, or Christian writing, or children's/juvenile writing, or screenwriting (& TV), or mystery/thriller writing.

Writing retreats. Retreats are unique in that the focus is about craft and actually sitting down to write. There are usually no agents present, because that is not the purpose of the whole thing. You find a serene location somewhere and just try to focus and write. Lots of MFA profs, etc., teach these things, and there are even several overseas.

LET'S TALK MONEY...

Yes, money can and should play into your decision. Obviously, it's a lot easier to drive 20 miles to a conference and be able to come home each night to tuck the kids in than it is to fly to Alaska for four nights. And let's face it: A lot of events are expensive—and not every up-and-coming scribe can manage the required dough.

The first thing we recommend you do is look local. There are tons of events every year, so there's a good chance a conference may be near you. Try simply using Google and search "writers conference" and "(city)" or "(state)" and see what comes up. Example: Perhaps you live in Virginia? There are sizeable events in Newport News, Hampton Roads, Richmond and Roanoke. Then there's the regional SCBWI conference that varies locations between Virginia, DC and Maryland. That's a lot of nearby opportunities!

Check out the regional chapter sites for the SCBWI (children's writers). The large organization has many regional chapters, plenty of which put on an annual event.

If money is an issue, consider just attending part of a conference. A lot of conferences have various options that affect your fee—attending dinners, participating in pitch slams, access to special sessions, etc. Pay attention to any and all pricing options.

Lastly—and we don't know why more people don't take advantage of this—consider combining a conference and a vacation (or work trip). Two birds with one stone. Got a relative in San Diego or Atlanta? See them and hit a conference on the same trip to save travel costs. Plus, you can write off most of your expenses next April.

WHAT DO YOU WANT TO GET OUT OF THE EXPERIENCE?

This question, obviously, is key.

Perhaps if you want to just sit down and *write*—maybe finally start that novel—then an intensive retreat is just what you need.

If you're not sure what you need (perhaps you're creating a lot of different stories and writing projects), then a general conference sounds like a good bet.

If you're actively looking for writing critique partners and beta readers, then *aim local*—so you can meet other local writers and form a group that will pay off with valuable peer edits down the road.

If your work is polished and the only thing on your mind is pitching, then you're looking for an event that has not only a sizeable number of agents and editors attending—but more specifically, a good amount of professionals who seek the *genre/category you're writing*. If you attend a large conference and pay $600 to schmooze with 20 agents, it won't be of much help if only 1-2 will consider that picture book you've composed.

If you want *eyes on your work*, look for a conference that offers a personal critique of your writing. Some even offer a variety of critiques from pros, so you can different perspectives and opinions on your work.

If you want to visit someplace beautiful, you can certainly do that. Instructors will rarely turn down an invitation to instruct in Jackson Hole, WY (gorgeous! hiking!) or Las Vegas, NV (craps! more craps!). Certainly, a particular locale can be enticing for one reason or another.

If you want to immerse yourself in your category, seek out a specialized conference. The national events for the SCBWI are absolutely huge, and are constructed all around the genre(s), so you won't be short on relevant sessions or agents who will consider your story. Christian writing and screenwriting conferences can be a good option, as well.

If your whole goal is "The bigger the better," we can throw out some of the biggest events in the country. Again, we stress that while big conferences grow large for a reason (they are often awesome), that does not mean they're the absolute best option for you. Money, location, and goals must all be factored in. Plenty of small events are great and have seen attendees have success. That said, off the top of our heads, we would say some of the largest general conferences in the country (not genre specific) include the following: Pacific Northwest Writers Conference (Seattle), Willamette Writers Conference (Portland), San Francisco Writers Conference, our own Writer's Digest Conferences in New York and Los Angeles, the Rocky Mountain Fiction Writers Conference (Denver), Agents and Editors Conference (Austin), South Carolina Writers Workshop (Myrtle Beach), Muse & the Marketplace (Boston), and the Backspace Writers Conference (New York).

CHOOSE WISELY

Lots of events are competing for your attendance, which means you're in the driver's seat. So take your time, do some research, and see what a conference has to offer. If possible, use Google to find testimonials from writers who have been there and done that—and pay attention to what they liked and disliked about an event.

No matter what conference you choose, we simply urge you to go to conferences. Get out there! We at WD are huge proponents of events, as they are an incredible opportunity to learn, get critiques, meet professionals, and make writing friends for life. They are, without a doubt, worth the effort to attend.

We hope to see you at a conference this year!

By the way, if you're looking for a conference, perhaps one of these below is in your neck of the woods. WD editors will be presenting at the following events in 2013:

Feb. 2013: Pet Writing Conference (New York, NY), petwritingconference.com
Feb. 2013: San Francisco Writers Conference (San Francisco, CA), sfwriters.org
Spring 2013: Writer's Digest Conference (New York, NY), writersdigestconference.com
May 2013: PennWriters Conference (Pittsburgh, PA), pennwriters.org
Summer 2013: Pacific Northwest Writers Conference (Seattle/Bellevue, WA), pnwa.org

CONTESTS, AWARDS & GRANTS

Publication is not the only way to get your work recognized. Contests and awards can also be great ways to gain recognition in the industry. Grants, offered by organizations like SCBWI, offer monetary recognition to writers, giving them more financial freedom as they work on projects.

When considering contests or applying for grants, be sure to study guidelines and requirements. Regard entry deadlines as gospel and follow the rules to the letter.

Note that some contests require nominations. For published authors and illustrators, competitions provide an excellent way to promote your work. Your publisher may not be aware of local competitions such as state-sponsored awards—if your book is eligible, have the appropriate person at your publishing company nominate or enter your work for consideration.

To select potential contests and grants, read through the listings that interest you, then send for more information about the types of written or illustrated material considered and other important details. A number of contests offer information through websites given in their listings.

ALCUIN CITATION AWARD

P.O. Box 3216, Vancouver BC V6B 3X8 Canada. (604)732-5403. **Fax:** (604)985-1091. **E-mail:** awards@ alcuinsociety.com. **Website:** www.alcuinsociety.com. Previously published submissions from the year prior to the Award's Call for Entries (i.e. 2011 awards went to books published in 2010). Submissions made by the publisher, author or designer. Winning books are exhibited nationally and internationally at the Tokyo, Frankfurt, and Leipzig Book Fairs, and are Canada's entries in the international competition in Leipzig, "Book Design from all over the World" in the following spring. Winners are selected from books designed and published in Canada. Awards are presented annually at appropriate ceremonies held in each year. Alcuin Citations are awarded annually for excellence in Canadian book design. Deadline for entries: mid-March. Prize: Prizes: 1st, 2nd, and 3rd in each category (at the discretion of the judges). Judging by professionals and those experienced in the field of book design.

AMERICA & ME ESSAY CONTEST

P.O. Box 30400, 7373 W. Saginaw, Lansing MI 48909-7900. **E-mail:** lfedewa@fbinsmi.com. **Website:** www. farmbureauinsurance-mi.com/pages/events/essay.htm. Annual contest. Open to students only. The America & Me Essay Contest was founded by Farm Bureau Insurance to encourage Michigan youth to explore their roles in America's future. Since that time, nearly a half-million Michigan eighth graders have participated in the contest. Unpublished submissions only. Deadline for entries: mid-November. SASE for contest rules and entry forms. "We have a school mailing list. Any school located in Michigan is eligible to participate." Entries not returned. No entry fee. Cash awards, savings bonds, and plaques for state top ten ($1,000), certificates and plaques for top 3 winners from each school. Each school may submit up to 10 essays for judging. Judging by home office employee volunteers. Requirements for entrants: participants must work through their schools or our agents' sponsoring schools. No individual submissions will be accepted. Top 10 essays and excerpts from other essays are published in booklet form following the contest. State capitol/schools receive copies."

AMERICAN ASSOCIATION OF UNIVERSITY WOMEN AWARD IN JUVENILE LITERATURE

4610 Mail Service Center, Raleigh NC 27699-4610. (919)733-9375. **E-mail:** michael.hill@ncdcr.gov.

Contact: Michael Hill, awards coordinator. Annual award. Book must be published during the year ending June 30. Submissions made by author, author's agent or publisher. Deadline for entries: July 15. SASE for contest rules. Awards a cup to the winner and winner's name inscribed on a plaque displayed within the North Carolina Office of Archives and History. Requirements for entrants: Author must have maintained either legal residence or actual physical residence, or a combination of both, in the state of North Carolina for 3 years immediately preceding the close of the contest period. Only published work (books) eligible. Purpose of award: to recognize the year's best work of juvenile literature by a North Carolina resident. Judged by three-judge panel.

○ Competition receives 10-15 submissions per category.

AMERICAS AWARD

Website: http://www4.uwm.edu/clacs/aa/index.cfm. **Contact:** Julie Kline. Annual award. Purpose of contest: Up to 2 awards are given each spring in recognition of U.S. published works (from the previous year) of fiction, poetry, folklore or selected nonfiction (from picture books to works for young adults) in English or Spanish which authentically and engagingly relate to Latin America, the Caribbean, or to Latinos in the United States. By combining both and linking the "Americas," the intent is to reach beyond geographic borders, as well as multicultural-international boundaries, focusing instead upon cultural heritages within the hemisphere. Previously published submissions only. Submissions open to anyone with an interest in the theme of the award. Deadline for entries: January 15. Visit website or send SASE for contest rules and any committee changes. Awards $500 cash prize, plaque and a formal presentation at the Library of Congress, Washington DC. Judging by a review committee consisting of individuals in teaching, library work, outreach and children's literature specialists.

HANS CHRISTIAN ANDERSEN AWARD

Nonnenweg 12, Postfach Ba CH-4003 Switzerland. **E-mail:** liz.page@ibby.org. **Website:** www.ibby.org. **Contact:** Liz Page, director. Award offered every two years. Purpose of award: A Hans Christian Andersen Medal shall be awarded every two years by the International Board on Books for Young People (IBBY) to an author and to an illustrator, living at the time of the nomination, who by the outstanding value of their work are judged to have made a lasting contribution to literature for children and young people. The complete works of the author and of the illustrator will be taken into consideration in awarding the medal, which will be accompanied by a diploma. Candidates are nominated by National Sections of IBBY in good standing. The Hans Christian Andersen Award, is the highest international recognition given to an author and an illustrator of children's books. The Author's Award has been given since 1956, the Illustrator's Award since 1966. Her Majesty Queen Margrethe II of Denmark is the Patron of the Hans Christian Andersen Awards. The Hans Christian Andersen Jury judges the books submitted for medals according to literary and artistic criteria. The awards are presented at the biennial congresses of IBBY.

ATLANTIC WRITING COMPETITION FOR UNPUBLISHED MANUSCRIPTS

1113 Marginal Rd., Halifax NS B3H 4P7. (902)423-8116. **Fax:** (902)422-0881. **E-mail:** director@writers.ns.ca; talk@writers.ns.ca. **Website:** www.writers.ns.ca. **Contact:** Nate Crawford, program coordinator. "Annual contest for beginners to try their hand in a number of categories: novel, short story, poetry, writing for younger children, writing for juvenile/young adult. Only 1 entry/category is allowed. Established writers are also eligible, but must work in an area that's new to them. Because our aim is to help Atlantic Canadian writers grow, judges return written comments when the competition is concluded. Anyone residing in the Atlantic Provinces for at least 6 months prior to the contest deadline is eligible to enter." Deadline: First Friday in December. Prize: **Novel**—1st Place: $200; 2nd Place: $150; 3rd Place: $75. **Writing for Younger Children and Juvenile/Young Adult**—1st Place: $150; 2nd Place: $75; 3rd Place: $50. **Poetry and Short Story**—1st Place: $150; 2nd Place: $75; 3rd Place: $50. a team of 2-3 professional writers, editors, booksellers, librarians, or teachers.

MARILYN BAILLIE PICTURE BOOK AWARD

40 Orchard View Blvd., Suite 101, Toronto ON M4R 1B9 Canada. (416)975-0010. **Fax:** (416)975-8970. **E-mail:** meghan@bookcentre.ca. **Website:** www.bookcentre.ca. "To be eligible, the book must be an original work in English, aimed at children ages 3-8, written and illustrated by Canadians and first published in

Canada. Eligible genres include fiction, non-fiction and poetry. Books must be published between Jan. 1 and Dec. 31 of the previous calendar year. Honors excellence in the illustrated picture book format." Prize: $20,000.

BAKER'S PLAYS HIGH SCHOOL PLAYWRITING CONTEST

45 W. 25th St., New York NY 10010. **E-mail:** publications@bakersplays.com. **Website:** www.bakersplays.com. **Contact:** Roxanne Heinze-Bradshaw. **Open to any high school students.** Annual contest. Purpose of the contest: to encourage playwrights at the high school level and to ensure the future of American theater. Unpublished submissions only. Postmark deadline: January 30. Notification: May. SASE for contest rules and entry forms. No entry fee. Awards $500 to the first place playwright with publication by Baker's Plays; $250 to the second place playwright with an honorable mention; and $100 to the third place playwright with an honorable mention in the series. Judged anonymously. Plays must be accompanied by the signature of a sponsoring high school drama or English teacher, and it is recommended that the play receive a production or a public reading prior to the submission. To ensure return of manuscripts, please include SASE. Teachers must not submit student's work. The winning work will be listed in the *Baker's Plays Catalogue*, which is distributed to 50,000 prospective producing organizations.

JOHN AND PATRICIA BEATTY AWARD

950 Glenn Drive, Suite 150, Folsom CA 95630. (916)233-3298. **Fax:** (916)932-2209. **E-mail:** hollym@cla-net.org. **Website:** www.cla-net.org. **Contact:** Holly Macriss, executive director. Purpose of award: "The purpose of the John and Patricia Beatty Award is to encourage the writing of quality children's books highlighting California, its culture, heritage and/or future." Previously published submissions only. Submissions made by the author, author's agent or review copies sent by publisher. The award is given to the author of a children's book published the preceding year. Deadline for entries: Submissions may be made January-December. Contact CLA Executive Director who will liaison with Beatty Award Committee. Awards cash prize of $500 and an engraved plaque. Judging by a 5-member selection committee appointed by the president of the California Library Association. Requirements for entrants: "Any children's

or young adult book set in California and published in the U.S. during the calendar year preceding the presentation of the award is eligible for consideration. This includes works of fiction as well as nonfiction for children and young people of all ages. Reprints and compilations are not eligible. The California setting must be depicted authentically and must serve as an integral focus for the book." Winning selection is announced through press release during National Library Week in April. Author is presented with award at annual California Library Association Conference in November.

☼ THE GEOFFREY BILSON AWARD FOR HISTORICAL FICTION FOR YOUNG PEOPLE

40 Orchard View Blvd., Suite 217, Toronto ON M4R 1B9 Canada. (416)975-0010. **Fax:** (416)975-8970. **Website:** www.bookcentre.ca. **Contact:** Meghan Howe. Created in Geoffrey Bilson's memory in 1988. Awarded annually to reward excellence in the writing of an outstanding work of historical fiction for young readers, by a Canadian author, published in the previous calendar year. Open to Canadian citizens and residents of Canada for at least 2 years. Deadline: Mid-December. Prize: $5,000. Please visit website for submissions guidelines and eligibility criteria, as well as specific submission deadline.

THE IRMA S. AND JAMES H. BLACK BOOK AWARD

Bank Street College of Education, 610 W. 112th St., New York NY 10025-1898. (212)875-4458. **Fax:** (212)875-4558. **E-mail:** kfreda@bankstreet.edu;apryce@bankstreet.edu. **Website:** http://www.bankstreet.edu/childrenslibrary/irmasimontonblackhome.html. **Contact:** Kristin Freda. Purpose of award: "The award is given each spring for a book for young children, published in the previous year, for excellence of both text and illustrations." Entries must have been published during the previous calendar year (between January '11 and December '11 for 2012 award). Deadline for entries: mid-December. "Publishers submit books to us by sending them here to me at the Bank Street Library. Authors may ask their publishers to submit their books. Out of these, three to five books are chosen by a committee of older children and children's literature professionals. These books are then presented to children in selected first-, second-, and third-grade classes here and at a number

of other cooperating schools. These children are the final judges who pick the actual award winner. A scroll (one each for the author and illustrator, if they're different) with the recipient's name and a gold seal designed by Maurice Sendak are awarded in May."

WALDO M. AND GRACE C. BONDERMAN BIENNIAL NATIONAL YOUTH THEATRE PLAYWRITING COMPETITION AND DEVELOPMENT WORKSHOP AND SYMPOSIUM

Indiana Repertory Theatre, 140 W. Washington St., Indianapolis IN 46204. **E-mail:** dwebb@iupui.edu; bonderma@iupui.edu. **Website:** www.Irtlive.com. **Contact:** Janet Allen, artistic director. Open to professional and non-professional American playwrights. See website for deadline. Entries not returned. No entry fee. Judging by professional theatre directors, teachers, and artists. Requirements for entrants: Contest opens only to American playwrights with plays not previously produced professionally and not currently in development with a theatre.

BOSTON GLOBE-HORN BOOK AWARDS

56 Roland St., Suite 200, Boston MA 02129. (617)628-0225. **Fax:** (617)628-0882. **E-mail:** info@hbook.com; khedeen@hbook.com. **Website:** hbook.com/bghb/. **Contact:** Katrina Hedeen. Offered annually for excellence in literature for children and young adults (published June 1-May 31). Categories: picture book, fiction and poetry, nonfiction. Judges may also name several honor books in each category. Books must be published in the US, but may be written or illustrated by citizens of any country. The Horn Book Magazine publishes speeches given at awards ceremonies. Guidelines for SASE or online. Deadline for entries: May 15. Prize: Winners receive $500 and an engraved silver bowl; honor book recipients receive an engraved silver plate. Judged by a panel of 3 judges selected each year.

☼ ANN CONNOR BRIMER AWARD

Website: www.nsla.ns.ca/index.php/about/awards/ann-connor-brimer-award/ann-connor-brimer/. **Contact:** Heather MacKenzie, award director. Purpose of the contest: to recognize excellence in writing. Given to an author of a children's book who resides in Atlantic Canada. Previously published submissions only. Submissions made by the author's agent or nominated by a person or group of people. Must be published in previous year. Deadline for entries:

October 15. SASE for contest rules and entry forms. Please go to website for contest rules and entry forms: http://www.nsla.ns.ca/index.php/about/awards/ann-connor-brimer-award/ann-connor-brimer/. No entry fee but four copies of the title must accompany the submission. Awards $2,000 and framed certificate. Judging by a selection committee. Requirements for entrants: Book must be intended for use up to age 15; in print and readily available; fiction or nonfiction except textbooks

BUCKEYE CHILDREN'S BOOK AWARD

Website: www.bcbookaward.info. **Contact:** Christine Watters, president. Correspondence should be sent to Christine Watters via the website. **Open to Ohio students.** Award offered every year. Estab. 1981. Purpose of the award: The Buckeye Children's Book Award Program was designed to encourage children to read literature critically, to promote teacher and librarian involvement in children's literature programs, and to commend authors of such literature, as well as to promote the use of libraries. Nominees are submitted by students between January 1 and March 15. Votes are cast between September 1 and November 10. Winning titles are posted on the website on December 1.

RANDOLPH CALDECOTT MEDAL

50 E. Huron, Chicago IL 60611. (312)280-2163. **E-mail:** alsc@ala.org; lschulte@ala.org. **Website:** www.ala.org/alsc/caldecott.cfm. Purpose of the award: to honor the artist of the most outstanding picture book for children published in the U.S. (Illustrator must be U.S. citizen or resident.) Must be published year preceding award. Deadline for entries: December 31. SASE for award rules. Entries not returned. No entry fee. "Medal given at ALA Annual Conference during the Newbery/Caldecott Banquet."

CALIFORNIA YOUNG PLAYWRIGHTS CONTEST

2590 Truxton Rd., Ste. 202, San Diego CA 92106-6145. (619)239-8222. **Fax:** (619)239-8225. **E-mail:** write@playwrightsproject.org. **Website:** www.playwrightsproject.org. **Contact:** Cecelia Kouma, executive director. **Open to Californians under age 19.** Annual contest. Estab. 1985. "Our organization and the contest is designed to nurture promising young writers. We hope to develop playwrights and audiences for live theater. We also teach playwriting." Submissions required to be unpublished and not produced professionally. Submissions made by the author. Deadline

for entries: June 1. SASE for contest rules and entry form. No entry fee. Judging by professionals in the theater community, a committee of 5-7; changes somewhat each year. Works performed in San Diego at a professional theatre. Writers submitting scripts of 10 or more pages receive a detailed script evaluation letter upon request. "Offered annually for previously unpublished plays by young writers to stimulate young people to create dramatic works, and to nurture promising writers. Scripts must be a minimum of 10 standard typewritten pages; send 2 copies. Scripts will *not* be returned. If requested, entrants receive detailed evaluation letter. Guidelines available online."

CALLIOPE FICTION CONTEST

5975 W. Western Way, PMD 116Y, Tucson AZ 85713. **E-mail:** sreditor@clearwire.net. **Website:** www.calliopewriters.org. **Contact:** Sandy Raschke, fiction editor. **Open to students.** Annual contest. Purpose of contest: "To promote good writing and opportunities for getting published. To give our member/subscribers and others an entertaining and fun exercise in writing." Unpublished submissions only (all genres, no violence, profanity or extreme horror). Submissions made by author. Deadline for entries: Changes annually. Entry fee is $5 for nonsubscribers; subscribers get first entry fee. Awards small amount of cash (up to $75 for 1st place, to $10 for 3rd), certificates, full or mini-subscriptions to *Calliope* and various premiums and books, depending on donations. All winners are published in subsequent issues of *Calliope*. Judging by fiction editor, with concurrence of other editors, if needed. Requirements for entrants: winners must retain sufficient rights to have their stories published in the January/February issue, or their entries will be disqualified; one-time rights. Open to all writers. No special considerations—other than following the guidelines. Contest theme, due dates and sometimes entry fees change annually. Always send SASE for complete rules; available after March 15 each year. Sample copies with prior winners are available for $3.

☉ CANADA COUNCIL GOVERNOR GENERAL'S LITERARY AWARDS

350 Albert St., P.O. Box 1047, Ottawa ON K1P 5V8 Canada. (613)566-4410, ext. 5573. **Fax:** (613)566-4410. **Website:** www.canadacouncil.ca/prizes/ggla. Annual award. Purpose of award: given to the best English-language and the best French-language work in each of the 7 categories of Fiction, Literary Nonfiction, Po-

etry, Drama, Children's Literature (text), Children's Literature (illustration) and Translation. Books must be first-edition trade books that have been written, translated or illustrated by Canadian citizens or permanent residents of Canada. In the case of translation, the original work written in English or French, must also be a Canadian-authored title. Books must be submitted by publishers. Deadline depends on the book's publication date. For books published in English: March 15, June 1 and August 7. For books published in French: March 15 and July 15. The awards ceremony is scheduled mid-November. Amount of award: $25,000 to winning authors; $1,000 to non-winning finalists.

☯ CANADIAN SHORT STORY COMPETITION

Unit #6, 477 Martin St., Penticton BC V2A 5L2 Canada. (778)476-5750. **Fax:** (778)476-5750. **E-mail:** dave@redtuquebooks.ca. **Website:** www.redtuquebooks.ca. **Contact:** David Korinetz, contest director. Offered annually for unpublished works. Purpose of award is "to promote Canada and Canadian publishing. Stories require a Canadian element. There are three ways to qualify. They can be written by a Canadian, or written about Canadians, or take place somewhere in Canada." Deadline: December 31. Prize: 1st Place: $500; 2nd Place: $150; 3rd Place: $100; and 10 prizes of $25 will be given to honourable mentions. All 13 winners will be published in an anthology. They will each receive a complimentary copy. Judged by Canadian authors in the fantasy/sci-fi/horror field. Acquires first print rights. Contest open to anyone.

⊕ CHILDREN'S AFRICANA BOOK AWARD

c/o Rutgers University, 132 George St., New Brunswick NJ 08901. (732)932-8173; (301)585-9136. **Fax:** (732)932-3394. **E-mail:** africaaccess@aol.com. **Website:** www.africanstudies.org; www.africaaccessreview.org. **Contact:** Brenda Randolph, chairperson; Harriet McGuire. Purpose of contest: "The Children's Africana Book Awards are presented annually to the authors and illustrators of the best books on Africa for children and young people published or republished in the U.S. The awards were created by the Outreach Council of the African Studies Association (ASA) to dispel stereotypes and encourage the publication and use of accurate, balanced children's materials about Africa. The awards are presented in 2 categories:

Young Children and Older Readers. Since 1991, 63 books have been recognized." Entries must have been published in the calendar year previous to the award. No entry fee. Awards plaque, ceremony in Washington D.C., announcement each spring, reviews published at Africa Access Review website and in *Sankofa: Journal of African Children's & Young Adult Literature*. Judging by Outreach Council of ASA and children's literature scholars. "Work submitted for awards must be suitable for children ages 4-18; a significant portion of books' content must be about Africa; must by copyrighted in the calendar year prior to award year; must be published or republished in the US. New in 2010, the jury has added designation of 'Noteworthy Books,' flagged for special attention by teachers and librarians. Award winners, Honor Books and Noteworthy books will all be featured in our publicity materials."

CHILDREN'S BOOK GUILD AWARD FOR NONFICTION

E-mail: theguild@childrensbookguild.org. **Website:** www.childrensbookguild.org. Annual award. Purpose of award: "to honor an author or illustrator whose total work has contributed significantly to the quality of nonfiction for children." Award includes a cash prize and an engraved crystal paperweight. Judging by a jury of Children's Book Guild specialists, authors, and illustrators. "One doesn't enter. One is selected. Our jury annually selects one author for the award."

CHILDREN'S WRITER WRITING CONTESTS

93 Long Ridge Rd., West Redding CT 06896-1124. (203)792-8600. **Fax:** (203)792-8406. **Website:** www.childrenswriter.com. Contest offered twice a year by *Children's Writer*, the monthly newsletter of writing and publishing trends. Purpose of the award: To promote higher quality children's literature. "Each contest has its own theme. Any original unpublished piece, not accepted by any publisher at the time of submission, is eligible." Submissions made by the author. Deadline for entries: Last weekday in February and October. "We charge a $10 entry fee for nonsubscribers only, which is applicable against a subscription to *Children's Writer*. Awards: 1st place—$250 or $500, a certificate and publication in *Children's Writer*; 2nd place—$100 or $250, and certificate; 3rd-5th places—$50 or $100 and certificates. To obtain the rules and theme for the current contest go to the

website and click on "Writing Contests," or send a SASE to *Children's Writer* at the above address. Put "Contest Request" in the lower left of your envelope. Judging by a panel of 4 selected from the staff of the Institute of Children's Literature. "We acquire First North American Serial Rights (to print the winner in *Children's Writer*), after which all rights revert to author." Open to any writer. Entries are judged on age targeting, originality, quality of writing and, for nonfiction, how well the information is conveyed and accuracy. "Submit clear photocopies only, not originals; submission will not be returned. Mss should be typed double-spaced. No pieces containing violence or derogatory, racist or sexist language or situations will be accepted, at the sole discretion of the judges."

CHRISTIAN BOOK AWARDS

9633 S. 48th St., Suite 140, Phoenix AZ 85044. (480)966-3998. **Fax:** (480)966-1944. **E-mail:** info@ecpa.org; mkuyper@ecpa.org. **Website:** www.ecpa.org. **Contact:** Mark W. Kuyper, president. Categories include children, fiction, nonfiction, Bibles, Bible reference, inspiration, and new author. "All entries must be evangelical in nature and submitted through an ECPA member publisher." Submission period: September 1-30. See website for all details

COLORADO BOOK AWARDS

(303)894-7951, ext. 21. **Fax:** (303)864-9361. **E-mail:** long@coloradohumanities.org. **Website:** www.colo radocenterforthebook.org. **Contact:** Margaret Coval, executive director; Jennifer Long, program adjudicator. Offered annually for work published by December of previous year. "The purpose is to champion all Colorado authors, editors, illustrators, and photographers, and in particular, to honor the award winners raising the profiles of both their work and Colorado as a state whose people promote and support reading, writing, and literacy through books. The categories are generally: children's literature, young adult and juvenile literature, fiction, genre fiction (romance, mystery/thriller, science fiction/fantasy, historical), biography, history, anthology, poetry, pictorial, graphic novel/comic, creative nonfiction, and general nonfiction, as well as other categories as determined each year. Open to authors who reside or have resided in Colorado."

CRICKET LEAGUE

P.O. Box 300, Peru IL 61354. **E-mail:** cricket@ca ruspub.com. **E-mail:** mail@cricketmagkids.com.

Website: www.cricketmagkids.com. "The purpose of Cricket League contests is to encourage creativity and give young people an opportunity to express themselves in writing, drawing, painting or photography. There is a contest in each issue. Possible categories include story, poetry, art, or photography. Each contest relates to a specific theme described on each *Cricket* issue's Cricket League page and on the website. Signature verifying originality, age and address of entrant and permission to publish required. Entries which do not relate to the current month's theme cannot be considered." Unpublished submissions only. Deadline for entries: the 25th of the month. Cricket League rules, contest theme, and submission deadline information can be found in the current issue of *Cricket* and via website. "We prefer that children who enter the contests subscribe to the magazine or that they read *Cricket* in their school or library." No entry fee. Awards certificate suitable for framing and children's books or art/writing supplies. Judging by *Cricket* editors. Obtains right to print prizewinning entries in magazine and/or on the website.

CWW ANNUAL WISCONSIN WRITERS AWARDS COMPETITION

Website: www.wisconsinwriters.org. **Contact:** Geoff Gilpin; Karla Huston, awards co-chairs; and Carolyn Washburne, Christopher Latham Sholes Award and Major Achievement Award co-chair. Offered annually for work published by Wisconsin writers the previous calendar year. Nine awards: Major/life achievement alternate years; short fiction; short nonfiction; nonfiction book; poetry book; fiction book; children's literature; Lorine Niedecker Poetry Award; Sholes Award for Outstanding Service to Wisconsin Writers Alternate Years; Essay Award for Young Writers. Open to Wisconsin residents. Guidelines, rules, and entry form on website. Deadline: January 31 (postmark). Prize: Prizes: $500 and a week-long residency at Shake Rag Alley in Mineral Point. Essay Contest: $150.

MARGARET A. EDWARDS AWARD

50 East Huron St., Chicago IL 60611-2795. (312)280-4390 or (800)545-2433. **Fax:** (312)280-5276. **E-mail:** yalsa@ala.org. **Website:** www.ala.org/yalsa/edwards. Annual award administered by the Young Adult Library Services Association (YALSA) of the American Library Association (ALA) and sponsored by *School Library Journal* magazine. Purpose of award: ALA's Young Adult Library Services Association (YALSA),

recognizes an author and a specific work or works for significant and lasting contribution to young adult literature. Submissions must be previously published no less than five years prior to the first meeting of the current Margaret A. Edwards Award Committee at Midwinter Meeting. Nomination form is available on the YALSA website. No entry fee. Judging by members of the Young Adult Library Services Association. Deadline for entry: December 1. "The award will be given annually to an author whose book or books, over a period of time, have been accepted by young adults as an authentic voice that continues to illuminate their experiences and emotions, giving insight into their lives. The book or books should enable them to understand themselves, the world in which they live, and their relationship with others and with society. The book or books must be in print at the time of the nomination."

SHUBERT FENDRICH MEMORIAL PLAYWRITING CONTEST

P.O. Box 4267, Englewood CO 80155. (303)779-4035. **Fax:** (303)779-4315. **E-mail:** editors@pioneerdrama. com. **E-mail:** submissions@pioneerdrama.com. **Website:** www.pioneerdrama.com. **Contact:** Lori Conary, submissions editor. Purpose of the contest: "To encourage the development of quality theatrical material for educational and family theater." Previously unpublished submissions only. Open to all writers not currently published by Pioneer Drama Service. Deadline for entries: December 31. SASE for contest rules and guidelines or view online. No entry fee. Cover letter, SASE for return of ms, and proof of production or staged reading must accompany all submissions. Awards $1,000 royalty advance and publication. Upon receipt of signed contracts, plays will be published and made available in our next catalog. Judging by editors. All rights acquired with acceptance of contract for publication. Restrictions for entrants: Any writers currently published by Pioneer Drama Service are not eligible.

FIRST BOOK AWARD

100-2400 College Ave., Regina SK S4P 0K1 Canada. (306)569-1585. **Fax:** (306)569-4187. **E-mail:** director@bookawards.sk.ca. **Website:** www.bookawards. sk.ca. **Contact:** Executive director, book submissions. Offered annually. "This award is presented to a Saskatchewan author for the best first book, judged on the quality of writing." Books from the following

categories will be considered: Children's; drama; fiction (short fiction by a single author, novellas, novels); nonfiction (all categories of nonfiction writing except cookbooks, directories, how-to books, or bibliographies of minimal critical content); and poetry. Deadline: November 1. Prize: Prize: $2,000 (CAD).

DOROTHY CANFIELD FISHER CHILDREN'S BOOK AWARD

578 Paine Tpke. N., Berlin VT 05602. (802)828-6954. **E-mail:** grace.greene@state.vt.us. **Website:** www. dcfaward.org. **Contact:** Mary Linney, chair. Annual award. Purpose of the award: to encourage Vermont children to become enthusiastic and discriminating readers by providing them with books of good quality by living American or Canadian authors published in the current year. Deadline for entries: December of year book was published. E-mail for entry rules. No entry fee. Awards a scroll presented to the winning author at an award ceremony. Judging is by the children grades 4-8. They vote for their favorite book. Requirements for entrants: "Titles must be original work, published in the U.S., and be appropriate to children in grades 4-8. The book must be copyrighted in the current year. It must be written by an American author living in the U.S. or Canada, or a Canadian author living in Canada or the U.S."

THE NORMA FLECK AWARD FOR CANADIAN CHILDREN'S NONFICTION

40 Orchard View Blvd., Suite 217, Toronto ON M4R 1B9 Canada. (416)975-0010. **Fax:** (416)975-8970. **E-mail:** info@bookcentre.ca. **Website:** www.bookcentre.ca. **Contact:** Meghan Howe, library coordinator. The Norma Fleck Award was established by the Fleck Family Foundation in May 1999 to honour the life of Norma Marie Fleck, and to recognize exceptional Canadian nonfiction books for young people. Publishers are welcome to nominate books using the online form. Offered annually for books published between January 1 and December 31 of the previous calendar year. Open to Canadian citizens or landed immigrants. The jury will always include at least 3 of the following: a teacher, a librarian, a bookseller, and a reviewer. A juror will have a deep understanding of, and some involvement with, Canadian children's books. The Canadian Children's Book Centre will select the jury members. **Deadline: Mid-December (annually).** Prize: $10,000 goes to the author (unless 40% or more of the text area is composed of original

illustrations, in which case the award will be divided equally between the author and the artist).

FLICKER TALE CHILDREN'S BOOK AWARD

Morton Mandan Public Library, 609 W. Main St., Mandan ND 58554. **E-mail:** laustin@cdln.info. **Website:** www.ndla.info/ftaward.htm. **Contact:** Linda Austin. Purpose of award: to give children across the state of North Dakota a chance to vote for their book of choice from a nominated list of 20: 4 in the picture book category; 4 in the intermediate category; 4 in the juvenile category (for more advanced readers); 4 in the upper grade level nonfiction category. Also, to promote awareness of quality literature for children. Previously published submissions only. Submissions nominated by librarians and teachers across the state of North Dakota. Awards a plaque from North Dakota Library Association and banquet dinner. Judging by children in North Dakota. Entry deadline in April.

DON FREEMAN MEMORIAL GRANT-IN-AID

8271 Beverly Blvd., Los Angeles CA 90048. (323)782-1010. **Fax:** (323)782-1892. **E-mail:** scbwi@scbwi.org. **Website:** www.scbwi.org. Purpose of award: to "enable picture book artists to further their understanding, training and work in the picture book genre." Applications and prepared materials are available in October and must be postmarked between February 1 and March 1. Grant awarded and announced in August. SASE for award rules and entry forms. SASE for return of entries. No entry fee. Annually awards one grant of $1,500 and one runner-up grant of $500. "The grant-in-aid is available to both full and associate members of the SCBWI who, as artists, seriously intend to make picture books their chief contribution to the field of children's literature."

○ THEODOR SEUSS GEISEL AWARD

50 E. Huron, Chicago IL 60611. (800)545-2433. **E-mail:** ala@ala.org. **Website:** www.ala.org. The Theodor Seuss Geisel Award, established in 2004, is given annually beginning in 2006 to the author(s) and illustrator(s) of the most distinguished American book for beginning readers published in English in the United States during the preceding year. The award is to recognize the author(s) and illustrator(s) who demonstrate great creativity and imagination in his/her/their literary and artistic achievements to engage children in reading. Deadline for entries: December 31. Entries not returned. Not entry fee.

Medal given at awards ceremony during ALA Annual Conference.

○ AMELIA FRANCES HOWARD GIBBON AWARD FOR ILLUSTRATION

1150 Morrison Drie, Suite 400, Ottawa ON K 2H859 Canada. (613)232-9625. **Fax:** (613) 563-9895. **E-mail:** carol.mcdougall@iwk.nshealth.ca. **Website:** www.cla.ca. Purpose of the award: "to honor excellence in the illustration of children's book(s) in Canada. To merit consideration the book must have been published in Canada and its illustrator must be a Canadian citizen or a permanent resident of Canada." Previously published submissions only; must be published between January 1 and December 31 of the previous year. Deadline for entries: December 31. See website for award rules. Entries not returned. No entry fee. Judging by selection committee of members of Canadian Association of Children's Librarians. Requirements for entrants: illustrator must be Canadian or Canadian resident.

GOLDEN KITE AWARDS

8271 Beverly Blvd., Los Angeles CA 90048-4515. (323)782-1010. **E-mail:** awards@scbwi.org. **Website:** www.scbwi.org. Society of Children's Book Writers and Illustrators, 8271 Beverly Blvd.Los Angeles CA 90048. (323)782-1010. **E-mail:** scbwi@scbwi.org. **Website:** www.scbwi.org. **Contact:** SCBWI Golden Kite Coordinator. Annual award. Estab. 1973. "The works chosen will be those that the judges feel exhibit excellence in writing, and in the case of the picture-illustrated books—in illustration, and genuinely appeal to the interests and concerns of children. For the fiction and nonfiction awards, original works and single-author collections of stories or poems of which at least half are new and never before published in book form are eligible—anthologies and translations are not. For the picture-illustration awards, the art or photographs must be original works (the texts—which may be fiction or nonfiction—may be original, public domain or previously published). Deadline for entries: December 15. SASE for award rules. No entry fee. Awards, in addition to statuettes and plaques, the four winners receive $2,500 cash award plus trip to LA SCBWI Conference. The panel of judges will consist of professional authors, illustrators, editors or agents." Requirements for entrants: "must be a member of SCBWI and books must be published in that year."

Winning books will be displayed at national conference in August. Books to be entered, as well as further inquiries, should be submitted to: The Society of Children's Book Writers and Illustrators, above address. "The works chosen will be those that the judges feel exhibit excellence in writing and, in the case of the picture-illustrated books, in illustration, and genuinely appeal to the interests and concerns of children. For the fiction and nonfiction awards, original works and single-author collections of stories or poems of which at least half are new and never before published in book form are eligible—anthologies and translations are not. For the picture-illustration awards, the art or photographs must be original works (the texts—which may be fiction or nonfiction—may be original, public domain or previously published). Deadline for entries: December 15. SASE for award rules. No entry fee. Awards: In addition to statuettes and plaques, the 4 winners receive $2,500 cash award plus trip to LA SCBWI Conference. The panel of judges will consist of professional authors, illustrators, editors or agents." Requirements for entrants: "must be a member of SCBWI and books must be published in that year." Winning books will be displayed at national conference in August. Books to be entered, as well as further inquiries, should be submitted to: The Society of Children's Book Writers and Illustrators, above address.

☺ GOVERNOR GENERAL'S LITERARY AWARD FOR CHILDREN'S LITERATURE

(613)566-4414, ext. 5573. **Fax:** (613)566-4410. **Website:** www.canadacouncil.ca/prizes/ggla. Offered for the best English-language and the best French-language works of children's literature by a Canadian in 2 categories: text and illustration. Publishers submit titles for consideration. Deadline depends on the book's publication date. Books in English: March 15, June 1, or August 7. Books in French: March 15 or July 15. Prize: Each laureate receives $25,000; non-winning finalists receive $1,000.

☺☺ GOVERNOR GENERAL'S LITERARY AWARDS

350 Albert St., P.O. Box 1047, Ottawa ON K1P 5V8 Canada. (613)566-4414, ext. 4075. **Website:** www.canadacouncil.ca/prizes/ggla. (Specialized: Canadian citizens/permanent residents; English- and French-language works) Established by Parliament, the Canada Council for the Arts "provides a wide range of grants and services to professional Canadian artists and art organizations in dance, media arts, music, theater, writing, publishing, and the visual arts." The Governor General's Literary Awards, valued at $25,000 CAD each, are given annually for the best English-language and best French-language work in each of 7 categories, including poetry. Non-winning finalists each receive $1,000 CAD. Books must be first edition trade books written, translated, or illustrated by Canadian citizens or permanent residents of Canada and published in Canada or abroad during the previous year (September 1 through the following September 30). Collections of poetry must be at least 48 pages long, and at least half the book must contain work not published previously in book form. In the case of translation, the original work must also be a Canadian-authored title. Books must be submitted by publishers with a Publisher's Submission Form, which is available on request from the Writing and Publishing Section of the Canada Council for the Arts. Guidelines and current deadlines on the website and available by mail, telephone, fax, or e-mail.

HACKNEY LITERARY AWARDS

(205)226-4921. **E-mail:** info@hackneyliteraryawards.org. **Website:** www.hackneyliteraryawards.org. **Contact:** Myra Crawford, PhD, executive director. Offered annually for unpublished novels, short stories (maximum 5,000 words) and poetry (50 line limit). Guidelines on website. Deadline: September 30 (novels), November 30 (short stories and poetry). Prize: Prize: $5,000 in annual prizes for poetry and short fiction ($2,500 national and $2,500 state level). 1st Place: $600; 2nd Place: $400; 3rd Place: $250); plus $5,000 for an unpublished novel. Competition winners will be announced on the website each March.

☺ THE MARILYN HALL AWARDS FOR YOUTH THEATRE

P.O. Box 148, Beverly Hills CA 90213. **Website:** www.beverlyhillstheatreguild.com. **Contact:** Candace Coster, competition coordinator. Purpose of contest: "To encourage the creation and development of new plays for youth theatre." Unpublished submissions only. Authors must be U.S. citizens or legal residents and must sign entry form personally. Deadline for entries: between January 15 and last day of February each year (postmark accepted). Playwrights may submit up to two scripts. One nonprofessional production acceptable for eligibility. SASE for contest rules and entry forms. No entry fee. Awards: $700, 1st prize; $300, 2nd prize. Judging by theatre professionals cognizant of youth theatre and writing/producing.

HIGHLIGHTS FOR CHILDREN FICTION CONTEST

803 Church St., Honesdale PA 18431-1824. (570)253-1080. **Fax:** (570)251-7847. **E-mail:** eds@highlightscorp.com. **Website:** www.Highlights.com. **Contact:** Christine French Cully, fiction contest editor. Purpose of the contest: to stimulate interest in writing for children and reward and recognize excellence. Unpublished submissions only. Deadline for entries: January 31; entries accepted after January 1 only. SASE for contest rules and return of entries. No entry fee. Awards 3 prizes of $1,000 each in cash and a pewter bowl (or, at the winner's election, attendance at the Highlights Foundation Writers Workshop at Chautauqua) and a pewter bowl. Judging by a panel of Highlights editors and outside judges. Winning pieces are purchased for the cash prize of $1,000 and published in Highlights; other entries are considered for purchase at regular rates. Requirements for entrants: open to any writer 16 years of age or older. Winners announced in May. Length up to 800 words. Stories for beginning readers should not exceed 500 words. Stories should be consistent with Highlights editorial requirements. No violence, crime or derogatory humor. Send SASE or visit website for guidelines and current theme.

MARILYN HOLINSHEAD VISITING SCHOLARS FELLOWSHIP

113 Anderson Library, 222 21st Ave. South, Minneapolis MN 55455. **Website:** http://special.lib.umn.edu/clrc/kerlan/awards.php. Marilyn Hollinshead Visiting Scholars Fund for Travel to the Kerlan Collection will be available for research study in 2013. Applicants may request up to **$1,500**. Send a letter with the proposed purpose, plan to use specific research materials (manuscripts and art), dates, and budget (including airfare and per diem) to Marilyn Hollinshead Visiting Scholars Fellowship, 113 Andersen Library, 222 21st Ave. S. Mpls, MN 55455. The application deadline is **January 30.**

THE JULIA WARD HOWE/BOSTON AUTHORS AWARD

(617)783-1357. **E-mail:** bostonauthors@aol.com; lawson@bc.edu. **Website:** www.bostonauthorsclub.org. **Contact:** Alan Lawson. This annual award honors Ju-

lia Ward Howe and her literary friends who founded the Boston Authors Club in 1900. It also honors the membership over 110 years, consisting of novelists, biographers, historians, governors, senators, philosophers, poets, playwrights, and other luminaries. There are 2 categories: trade books and books for young readers (beginning with chapter books through young adult books). Works of fiction, nonfiction, memoir, poetry, and biography published in 2012 are eligible. Authors must live or have lived (college counts) within a 100-mile radius of Boston within the last 5 years. Subsidized books, cook books and picture books are not eligible. Fee is $25 per title.

HRC SHOWCASE THEATRE PLAYWRITING CONTEST

P.O. Box 940, Hudson NY 12534. (518)851-7244. **Website:** www.hrc-showcasetheatre.com. HRC Showcase Theatre is a not-for-profit professional theater company dedicated to the advancement of performing in the Hudson River Valley area through reading of plays and providing opportunities for new and established playwrights. Unpublished submissions only. Submissions made by author and by the author's agent. Deadlines for entries: May 1. SASE for contest rules and entry forms. Entry fee is $5. Awards $500 cash plus concert reading by professional actors for winning play and $100 for each of the four other plays that will be given a staged reading. Judging by panel selected by Board of Directors. Requirements for entrants: Entrants must live in the northeastern U.S.

⊕ CAROL OTIS HURST CHILDREN'S BOOK PRIZE

Westfield Athenaeum, 6 Elm St., Westfield MA 01085. (413)568-7833. **Website:** www.westath.org. **Contact:** Ralph Melnick, assistant director, Westfield Athenaeum. The Carol Otis Hurst Children's Book Prize honors outstanding works of fiction and nonfiction written for children and young adults through the age of 18. For a work to be considered, the writer must either be a native or a current resident of New England. While the prize (together with a monetary award of $500) is presented annually to an author whose work best exemplifies the highest standards of writing for this age group regardless of genre or topic or geographical setting, the prize committee is especially interested in those books that treat life in the region. Further, entries will be judged on how well they succeed in portraying one or more of the following elements: childhood, adolescence, family life, schooling, social and political developments, fine and performing artistic expression, domestic arts, environmental issues, transportation and communication, changing technology, military experience at home and abroad, business and manufacturing, workers and the labor movement, agriculture and its transformation, racial and ethnic diversity, religious life and institutions, immigration and adjustment, sports at all levels, and the evolution of popular entertainment. To date, award recipients have been Milton Meltzer for his young adultbook, *Tough Times* (Clarion), Kay Winters for her children's book, *Colonial Voices: Hear Them Speak* (Dutton), and Jane Yolan for her children's book treatment of Emily Dickinson in *My Uncle Emily* (Philomel). Established to celebrate the life and work of noted children's author Carol Otis Hurst. The book's cover, brief excerpts from the text, and its illustrations may be used to publicize the prize and its recipient.

INSIGHT WRITING CONTEST

Fax: (301)393-4055. **E-mail:** insight@rhpa.org. **Website:** www.insightmagazine.org. **Contact:** Dwain Esmond, editor. Annual contest for writers in the categories of student short story, general short story, and student poetry. Unpublished submissions only. General category is open to all writers; student categories must be age 22 and younger. Deadline: May 31. Prize: **Student Short Story** and **General Short Story:** 1st Prize: $250; 2nd Prize: $200; 3rd Prize: $150. **Student Poetry:** 1st Prize: $100; 2nd Prize: $75; 3rd Prize: $50. Entries must include cover sheet. Form available with SASE or on website. See website for rules and more information.

INTERNATIONAL READING ASSOCIATION CHILDREN'S BOOK AWARDS

P.O. Box 8139, 800 Barksdale Rd., Newark DE 19714-8139. (302)731-1600, ext. 221. **E-mail:** exec@reading.org. "This award is for newly published authors of children's books who show unusual promise in the children's book field." Offered annually for an author's first or second published book in fiction and nonfiction in 3 categories: primary (preschool-age 8), intermediate (ages 9-13), and young adult (ages 14-17). Guidelines and deadlines for SASE. Prize: 6 awards of $1,000 each, and a medal for each category. Categories: fiction and nonfiction. No entry fee. The book will be considered one time during the year of first copyright in English. **Deadline: November 1**. For

guidelines with specific information write to Executive Office, International Reading Association.

IRA CHILDREN'S AND YOUNG ADULT'S BOOK AWARD

(302)731-1600. **Fax:** (302)731-1057. **E-mail:** kbaughman@reading.org; exec@reading.org. **Website:** www.reading.org. **Contact:** Kathy Baughman. Awards are given for an author's first or second published book for fiction and nonfiction in 3 categories: primary (ages preschool-8), intermediate (ages 9-13), and young adult (ages 14-17). This award is intended for newly published authors who show unusual promise in the children's book field. Deadline for entries: See website. Awards $1,000. For guidelines, write or e-mail.

EZRA JACK KEATS/KERLAN MEMORIAL FELLOWSHIP

113 Elmer L. Andersen Library, 222 21st Ave. S., University of Minnesota, Minneapolis MN 55455. **Website:** http://special.lib.umn.edu/clrc/. This fellowship from the Ezra Jack Keats Foundation will provide $1,500 to a "talented writer and/or illustrator of children's books who wishes to use the Kerlan Collection for the furtherance of his or her artistic development." Special consideration will be given to someone who would find it difficult to finance a visit to the Kerlan Collection. The Ezra Jack Keats Fellowship recipient will receive transportation costs and a per diem allotment. See website for application deadline and for digital application materials. For paper copies of the application send a large (6×9 or 9×12) SASE with 97¢ postage.

THE EZRA JACK KEATS NEW WRITER AND NEW ILLUSTRATOR AWARDS

450 14th St., Brooklyn NY 11215. **E-mail:** jchang@nypl.org. **Website:** www.ezra-jack-keats.org. **Contact:** Julia Chang, program coordinator. Annual awards. Purpose of the awards: "The awards will be given to a promising new writer of picture books for children and a promising new illustrator of picture books for children. Selection criteria include books for children (ages 9 and under) that reflect the tradition of Ezra Jack Keats. These books portray: the universal qualities of childhood, strong and supportive family and adult relationships, the multicultural nature of our world." Submissions made by the publisher. Must be published in the preceding year. Deadline for entries: mid-December. SASE for contest rules and entry forms or e-mail Julia Chang at jchang@nypl.org.

No entry fee. Awards $1,000 coupled with Ezra Jack Keats Bronze Medal. Judging by a panel of experts. "The author or illustrator should have published no more than 3 children's books. Entries are judged on the outstanding features of the text, complemented by illustrations. Candidates need not be both author and illustrator. Entries should carry a 2011 copyright (for the 2012 award)." Winning books and authors to be presented at reception at The New York Public Library.

KENTUCKY BLUEGRASS AWARD

Lincoln County High School Media Center, 60 Education Way, Stanford KY 40484. (606)365-9111. **Fax:** (606)365-1750. **E-mail:** kay.hensley@lincoln.kyschools.us. **Website:** www.kyreading.org. Submit entries to: Kay Renee Hensley. Annual award. Estab. 1983. Purpose of award: to promote readership among young children and young adolescents. Also to recognize exceptional creative efforts of authors and illustrators. Previously published submissions only. Submissions made by author, made by author's agent, nominated by teachers or librarians. Must be published no more than 3 years prior to the award year. Deadline for entries: March 15. Contest rules and entry forms are available from the website. No entry fee. Awards a framed certificate and invitation to be recognized at the annual luncheon of the Kentucky Bluegrass Award. Judging by children who participate through their schools or libraries. "Books are reviewed by a panel of teachers and librarians before they are placed on a Master List for the year. These books must have been published within a three year period prior to the review. Winners are chosen from this list of preselected books. Books are divided into four divisions, K-2, 3-5, 6-8, 9-12 grades. Winners are chosen by children who either read the books or have the books read to them. Children from the entire state of Kentucky are involved in the selection of the annual winners for each of the divisions."

CORETTA SCOTT KING BOOK AWARDS

50 E. Huron St., Chicago IL 60611. (800)545-2433. **Website:** www.ala.org/csk. The Coretta Scott King Book Awards is an annual award celebrating African American experience. A new talent award may also be selected. An awards jury of Children's Librarians judge the books form the previous year, and select the winners in January at the ALA Midwinter meeting. A copy of an entry must be sent to each juror by December 1 of the juried year. A copy of the jury list

and directions for submitting titles can be found on website. Call or e-mail ALA Office for Literacy and Outreach Services for jury list. Awards breakfast held on Tuesday morning during ALA. Annual Conference in June. See schedule at website.

LEAGUE OF UTAH WRITERS CONTEST

420 W. 750 N., Logan UT 84321. (435)755-7609. **E-mail:** luwriters@gmail.com. **Website:** www.luwriters.org. **Contact:** Dianne Hardy, membership chair. Open to any writer, the LUW Contest provides authors an opportunity to get their work read and critiqued. Contest submission period opens March 1 and closes June 1. Multiple categories are offered; see webpage for details. Entries must be the original and unpublished work of the author. Winners are announced at the Annual Writers Round-Up in September. Those not present will be notified by e-mail. Cash prizes are awarded. Deadline: June 1. Entries are judged by professional authors and editors from outside the League.

MCLAREN MEMORIAL COMEDY PLAY WRITING COMPETITION

2000 W. Wadley, Midland TX 79705. (432)682-2544. **Fax:** (432)682-6136. **Website:** www.mctmidland.org. Open to students. Annual contest. Purpose of conference: "The McLaren Memorial Comedy Play Writing Competition was established in 1989 to honor longtime MCT volunteer Mike McLaren who loved a good comedy, whether he was on stage or in the front row." Unpublished submissions only. Submissions made by author. Deadline for entries: February 28th (scripts are accepted January 1 through the end of February each year). SASE for contest rules and entry forms. Entry fee is $10 per script. Awards $400 for full-length winner and $200 for one-act winner as well as staged readings for 3 finalists in each category. Judging by the audience present at the McLaren festival when the staged readings are performed. Rights to winning material acquired or purchased. 1st right of production or refusal is acquired by MCT. Requirements for entrants: "Yes, the contest is open to any playwright, but the play submitted must be unpublished and never produced in a for-profit setting. One previous production in a nonprofit theatre is acceptable. 'Readings' do not count as productions."

THE VICKY METCALF AWARD FOR CHILDREN'S LITERATURE

90 Richmond St. E., Suite 200, Toronto ON M5C 1P1 Canada. (416)504-8222. **Fax:** (416)504-9090. **E-mail:**

info@writerstrust.com. **Website:** www.writerstrust.com. **Contact:** Amanda Hopkins, program coordinator. "The Metcalf Award is presented to a Canadian writer for a body of work in children's literature at The Writers' Trust Awards event held in Toronto each Fall. Open to Canadian citizens and permanent residents only."

MIDLAND AUTHORS AWARD

P.O. Box 10419, Chicago IL 60610-0419. **E-mail:** writercc@aol.com. **Website:** www.midlandauthors.com. **Contact:** Carol Jean Carlson. "Established in 1915, the Society of Midland Authors Award (SMA) is presented to one title in each of six categories 'to stimulate creative effort,' one of SMA's goals, to be honored at the group's annual awards banquet in May." Annual. Competition/award for novels, story collections (by single author). Prize: cash prize of at least $300 and a plaque that is awarded at the SMA banquet. Categories: children's nonfiction and fiction, adult nonfiction and fiction, adult biography, and poetry. Judging is done by a panel of three judges for each category that includes a mix of experienced authors, reviewers, book sellers, university faculty and librarians. No entry fee. Guidelines available in September-November with SASE, on website, in publication. Accepts inquiries by e-mail, phone. **Deadline: Feb. 1.** Entries must be published in the prior calendar year, e.g. 2012 for 2013 award. "The contest is open to any title with a recognized publisher that has been published within the year prior to the contest year." Open to authors or poets who reside in, were born in, or have strong ties to a Midland state, which includes Illinois, Indiana, Iowa, Kansas, Michigan, Minnesota, Missouri, Nebraska, North Dakota, South Dakota, Ohio and Wisconsin. SMA only accepts published work accompanied by a completed award form. Writers may submit own work. Entries can also be submitted by the publisher's rep. "Write a great story and be sure to follow contest rules by sending a copy of the book to each of the three judges for the given category who are listed on SMA's website." Results announced at the SMA Awards Banquet each May. Other announcements follow in the media. Winners notified by mail, by phone. Results made available to entrants on website, in our monthly membership newsletter. Results will also go to local media in the form of press releases.

MILKWEED NATIONAL FICTION PRIZE

1011 Washington Ave. S., Suite 300, Minneapolis MN 55415. (612)332-3192. **Fax:** (612)215-2550. **E-mail:** editor@milkweed.org. **Website:** www.milkweed.org. **Contact:** Daniel Slager, award director. Purpose of the award: to recognize an outstanding literary novel for readers ages 8-13 and encourage writers to turn their attention to readers in this age group. Unpublished submissions only "in book form." Please send SASE or visit website for award guidelines. The prize is awarded to the best work for children ages 8-13 that Milkweed agrees to publish in a calendar year. The prize consists of a $5,000 advance against royalties agreed to at the time of acceptance. Submissions must follow our usual children's guidelines.

MINNESOTA BOOK AWARDS

325 Cedar Street, Suite 555, St. Paul MN 55101. **E-mail:** ann@thefriends.org; mnbookawards@thefriends.org; friends@thefriends.org. **Website:** www.thefriends.org. Annual award. Purpose of contest: To recognize and honor achievement by members of Minnesota's book community.

○ MUNICIPAL CHAPTER OF TORONTO IODE JEAN THROOP BOOK AWARD

40 St. Clair Ave. E.Suite 205, Toronto ON M4T 1M9 Canada. (416)925-5078. **Fax:** (416)925-5127. **E-mail:** iodtoronto@bellnet.ca. **Website:** www.bookcentre.ca/awards/iode_book_award_municipal_chapter_toronto. **Contact:** Jennifer Werry, contest director. Submit entries to: Theo Heras, Lillian Smith Library, 239 College St., Toronto. Annual contest. Estab. 1974. Previously published submissions only. Submissions made by author. Deadline for entries: November 1. No entry fee. Awards: $1,000. If the illustrator is different from the author, the prize money is divided. Judging by Book Award Committee comprised of members of Toronto Municipal Chapter IODE. Requirements for entrants: Authors and illustrators must be Canadian and live within the GTA.

NATIONAL BOOK AWARDS

The National Book Foundation, 90 Broad St., Suite 609, New York NY 10004. (212)685-0261. **E-mail:** nationalbook@nationalbook.org. **Website:** www.nationalbook.org. Presents $10,000 in each of 4 categories (fiction, nonfiction, poetry, and young people's literature), plus 16 short-list prizes of $1,000 each to finalists. Submissions must be previously published and **must be entered by the publisher.** General guidelines available on website; interested publishers should phone or e-mail the Foundation. Deadline: See website for current year's deadline.

NATIONAL CHILDREN'S THEATRE FESTIVAL

(305)444-9293, ext. 615. **Fax:** (305)444-4181. **E-mail:** maulding@actorsplayhouse.org. **Website:** www.actorsplayhouse.org. **Contact:** Earl Maulding. Purpose of contest: to bring together the excitement of the theater arts and the magic of young audiences through the creation of new musical works and to create a venue for playwrights/composers to showcase their artistic products. Submissions must be unpublished. Submissions are made by author or author's agent. Deadline for entries: April 1 annually. Visit website or send SASE for contest rules and entry forms. Entry fee is $10. Awards: first prize of $500, full production, and transportation to Festival weekend based on availability. Past judges include Joseph Robinette, Moses Goldberg and Luis Santeiro.

NATIONAL FOUNDATION FOR ADVANCEMENT IN THE ARTS

777 Brickell Ave., Suite 370, Miami FL 33131. (305)377-1140 ext 243. **Fax:** (305)377-1149. **E-mail:** info@nfaa.org. **Website:** www.youngARTS.org. **Contact:** Carla Hill. Created to recognize and reward outstanding accomplishment in cinematic arts, dance, jazz, music, photography, theater, voice, visual arts and/or writing. youngARTS is an innovative national program of the National Foundation for Advancement in the Arts (NFAA). Established in 1981, youngARTS touches the lives of gifted young people across the country, providing financial support, scholarships and goal-oriented artistic, educational and career opportunities. Each year, from a pool of more than 8,000 applicants, an average of 800 youngARTS winners are chosen for NFAA support by panels of distinguished artists and educators. Deadline for registration: June 1 (early) and October 1. Deadline for submission of work: Nov. 3. Entry fee is $35 (online)/$40(paper). Fee waivers available based on need. Awards $100-10,000—unrestricted cash grants. Judging by a panel of artists and educators recognized in the field. Rights to submitted/winning material: NFAA/youngARTS retains the right to duplicate work in an anthology or in Foundation literature unless otherwise specified by the artist. Requirements for entrants: Artists must be high school seniors or, if not enrolled in high school, must be 17 or 18 years old. Applicants must be U.S. citizens or residents, unless applying in jazz. Literary and visual works will be published in an anthology distributed during youngARTS Week in Miami when the final adjudication takes place. NFAA invites up to 150 finalists to participate in youngARTS Week in January in Miami-Dade County, Florida. youngARTS Week is a once-in-a-lifetime experience consisting of performances, master classes, workshops, readings, exhibits, and enrichment activities with renowned artists and arts educators. All expenses are paid by NFAA, including airfare, hotel, meals and ground transportation.

NATIONAL OUTDOOR BOOK AWARDS

(208)282-3912. **E-mail:** wattron@isu.edu. **Website:** www.noba-web.org. **Contact:** Ron Watters. "Nine categories: History/biography, outdoor literature, instructional texts, outdoor adventure guides, nature guides, children's books, design/artistic merit, natural history literature, and nature and the environment. Additionally, a special award, the Outdoor Classic Award, is given annually to books which, over a period of time, have proven to be exceptionally valuable works in the outdoor field. Application forms and eligibilty requirements are available online." Deadline: September 1. Prize: Winning books are promoted nationally and are entitled to display the National Outdoor Book Award (NOBA) medallion.

NATIONAL PEACE ESSAY CONTEST

1200 17th St. NW, Washington DC 20036. (202)457-1700. **Fax:** (202)429.6063. **E-mail:** essaycontest@usip.org. **Website:** www.usip.org/NPEC. "The contest gives students the opportunity to do valuable research, writing and thinking on a topic of importance to international peace and conflict resolution. Teaching guides are available for teachers who allow the contest to be used as a classroom assignment." Deadline for entries is February 1, 2012. "Interested students, teachers and others may visit the website to download or request contest materials. Please do not include SASE." Guidelines and rules on website. No entry fee. State-level awards are $1,000 college scholarships. National winners are selected from among the 1st place state winners. National winners receive scholarships in the following amounts: first place $10,000; second $5,000; third $2,500. National amount includes state award. First-place state winners invited to an expenses-paid awards program in Washington, DC in June.

Judging is conducted by education professionals from across the country and by the board of directors of the United States Institute of Peace. "All submissions become property of the U.S. Institute of Peace to use at its discretion and without royalty or any limitation. Students grades 9-12 in the U.S., its territories and overseas schools may submit essays for review by completing the application process. U.S. citizenship required for students attending overseas schools. National winning essays will be published by the U.S. Institute of Peace."

NATIONAL WRITERS ASSOCIATION NONFICTION CONTEST

10940 S. Parker Rd., #508, Parker CO 80134. (303)841-0246. **Fax:** (303)841-2607. **E-mail:** natlwritersassn@hotmail.com. **Website:** www.nationalwriters.com. **Contact:** Sandy Whelchel, director. Purpose of contest: "to encourage and recognize those who excel in nonfiction writing." Submissions made by author. Deadline for entries: December 31. SASE for contest rules and entry forms. Entry fee is $18. Awards 3 cash prizes; choice of books; Honorable Mention Certificate. "Two people read each entry; third party picks three top winners from top five." Judging sheets sent if entry accompanied by SASE. Condensed version of 1st place may be published in *Authorship*.

JOHN NEWBERY MEDAL

50 E. Huron, Chicago IL 60611. (800)545-2433, ext. 2153. **Fax:** (312)280-5271. **E-mail:** library@ala.org. **Website:** www.ala.org. Purpose of award: to recognize the most distinguished contribution to American children's literature published in the U.S. Previously published submissions only; must be published prior to year award is given. Deadline for entries: December 31. SASE for award rules. Entries not returned. No entry fee. Medal awarded at Caldecott/Newbery banquet during ALA annual conference. Judging by Newbery Award Selection Committee.

NEW ENGLAND BOOK AWARDS

297 Broadway, #212, Arlington MA 02474. (781)316-8894. **Fax:** (781)316-2605. **E-mail:** nan@neba.org. **Website:** www.newenglandbooks.org/Default.aspx?pageId=234046. **Contact:** Nan Sorenson, assistant executive director. Annual award. Previously published submissions only. Submissions made by New England booksellers; publishers. "Award is given to a specific title, fiction, non-fiction, children's. The titles must be either about New England, set in New England or by an author residing in the New England. The titles must be hardcover, paperback orginal or re-issue that was published between September 1 and August 31. Entries must be still in print and available. No entry fee. Judging by NEIBA membership. Requirements for entrants: Author/illustrator must live in New England. Submit written nominations only; actual books should not be sent. Member bookstores receive materials to display winners' books. Submission deadline: July 2.

NEW VOICES AWARD

Website: www.leeandlow.com. **Open to students.** Annual award. Purpose of contest: To encourage writers of color to enter the world of children's books. Lee & Low Books is one of the few minority-owned publishing companies in the country. We have published more than 90 first-time writers and illustrators. Winning titles include *The Blue Roses*, winner of a Patterson Prize for Books for Young People; *Janna and the Kings*, an IRA Children's Book Award Notable; and *Sixteen Years in Sixteen Seconds*, selected for the Texas Bluebonnet Award Masterlist. Submissions made by author. Deadline for entries: September 30. SASE for contest rules or visit website. No entry fee. Awards New Voices Award—$1,000 prize and standard publication contract (regardless of whether or not writer has an agent) along with an advance against royalties; New Voices Honor Award—$500 prize. Judging by Lee & Low editors. Restrictions of media for illustrators: The author must be a writer of color who is a resident of the U.S. and who has not previously published a children's picture book. For additional information, send SASE or visit Lee & Low's website.

NORTH AMERICAN INTERNATIONAL AUTO SHOW HIGH SCHOOL POSTER CONTEST

1900 W. Big Beaver Rd., Troy MI 48084-3531. (248)643-0250. **Fax:** (248)283-5148. **E-mail:** sherp@dada.org. **Website:** www.naias.com. **Open to students.** Annual contest. Submissions made by the author and illustrator. **Contact:** Detroit Auto Dealers Association (DADA) for contest rules and entry forms or retrieve rules from website. No entry fee. Awards in the High School Poster Contest are as follows: Chairman's Award—$1,000; State Farm Insurance Award—$1,000; Designer's Best of Show (Digital and Traditional)—$500; Best Theme—$250; Best Use of Color—$250; Most Creative—$250. A win-

CONTESTS, AWARDS & GRANTS

373

ner will be chosen in each category from grades 10, 11 and 12. Prizes: 1st place in 10, 11, 12—$500; 2nd place—$250; 3rd place—$100. The winners of the Designer's Best of Show Digital and Traditional will each receive $500. The winner of the Chairman's Award will receive $1,000. Entries will be judged by an independent panel of recognized representatives of the art community. Entrants must be Michigan high school students enrolled in grades 10-12. Winning posters may be displayed at the NAIAS 2012 and reproduced in the official NAIAS program, which is available to the public, international media, corporate executives and automotive suppliers. Winning posters may also be displayed on the official NAIAS website at the sole discretion of the NAIAS.

NORTHERN CALIFORNIA BOOK AWARDS

c/o Poetry Flash, 1450 Fourth St. #4, Berkeley CA 94710. (510)525-5476. **E-mail:** editor@poetryflash.org. **Website:** www.poetryflash.org. **Contact:** Joyce Jenkins, executive director. Annual Northern California Book Award for outstanding book in literature, open to books published in the current calendar year by Northern California authors. Annual award. NCBR presents annual awards to Bay Area (northern California) authors annually in fiction, nonfiction, poetry and children's literature. Purpose is to encourage writers and stimulate interest in books and reading." Previously published books only. Must be published the calendar year prior to spring awards ceremony. Submissions nominated by publishers; author or agent could also nominate published work. Deadline for entries: December. No entry forms. Send 3 copies of the book to attention: NCBR. No entry fee. Awards $100 honorarium and award certificate. Judging by voting members of the Northern California Book Reviewers. Books that reach the "finals" (usually 3-5 per category) displayed at annual award ceremonies (spring). Nominated books are displayed and sold at the Northern California Book Awards in the spring of each year; the winner is asked to read at the San Francisco Public Library's Main Branch.

OHIOANA BOOK AWARDS

274 E. First Ave., Suite 300, Columbus OH 43201-3673. (614)466-3831. **Fax:** (614)728-6974. **E-mail:** ohioana@ohioana.org. **Website:** www.ohioana.org. **Contact:** Linda Hengst, executive director. Offered annually to bring national attention to Ohio authors and their books, published in the last 2 years. (Books can only be considered once.) Categories: Fiction, nonfiction, juvenile, poetry, and books about Ohio or an Ohioan. Writers must have been born in Ohio or lived in Ohio for at least 5 years, but books about Ohio or an Ohioan need not be written by an Ohioan. Prize: certificate and glass sculpture. Judged by a jury selected by librarians, book reviewers, writers and other knowledgeable people. Each winter the jury considers all books received since the previous jury. No entry fee. **Deadline: December 31.** A copy of the book must be received by the Ohioana Library by December 31 prior to the year the award is given; literary quality of the book must be outstanding. No entry forms are needed, but they are available July 1 of each year. Specific questions should be sent to Ohioana. Results announced in August or September. Winners notified by mail in May.

OKLAHOMA BOOK AWARDS

200 NE 18th St., Oklahoma City OK 73105. (405)521-2502. **Fax:** (405)525-7804. **E-mail:** carmstrong@oltn.odl.state.ok.us. **Website:** www.odl.state.ok.us/ocb. **Contact:** Connie Armstrong, executive director. Purpose of award: "to honor Oklahoma writers and books about our state." Previously published submissions only. Submissions made by the author, author's agent, or entered by a person or group of people, including the publisher. Must be published during the calendar year preceding the award. Awards are presented to best books in fiction, nonfiction, children's, design and illustration, and poetry books about Oklahoma or books written by an author who was born, is living or has lived in Oklahoma. Deadline for entries: early January. SASE for award rules and entry forms. Entry fee $25. Awards a medal—no cash prize. Judging by a panel of 5 people for each category—a librarian, a working writer in the genre, booksellers, editors, etc. Requirements for entrants: author must be an Oklahoma native, resident, former resident or have written a book with Oklahoma theme. Winner will be announced at banquet in Oklahoma City. The Arrell Gibson Lifetime Achievement Award is also presented each year for a body of work.

ONCE UPON A WORLD CHILDREN'S BOOK AWARD

1399 S. Roxbury Dr., Los Angeles CA 90035-4709. (310)772-7605. **Fax:** (310)772-7628. **E-mail:** bookaward@wiesenthal.net. **Website:** www.wiesenthal.com/library. **Contact:** Adaire J. Klein, award director. Submissions made by publishers, author or author's agent. Suggestions from educators, libraries, and others accepted. Must be published January-December of previous year. Deadline for entries: March 31. SASE for contest rules and entry forms. Awards $1,000 each to two authors honoring a book for children age 6-10 and one for age 11 and up. Recognition of Honor Books if deemed appropriate. Judging is by 6 independent judges familiar with children's literature. Award open to any writer with work in English language on subjects of tolerance, diversity, human understanding, and social justice. Book Seals available from the library.

ORBIS PICTUS AWARD FOR OUTSTANDING NONFICTION FOR CHILDREN

1111 W. Kenyon Rd., Urbana IL 61801-1096. (217)328-3870. **Fax:** (217)328-0977. **E-mail:** dzagorski@ncte.org. **Website:** www.ncte.org/awards/orbispictus. Purpose of award: To promote and recognize excellence in the writing of nonfiction for children. Previously published submissions only. Submissions made by author, author's agent, by a person or group of people. Must be published January 1-December 31 of contest year. Deadline for entries: December 31. Call for award information. No entry fee. Awards a plaque given at the NCTE Elementary Section Luncheon at the NCTE Annual Convention in November. Judging by a committee. "The name Orbis Pictus commemorates the work of Johannes Amos Comenius, *Orbis Pictus— The World in Pictures* (1657), considered to be the first book actually planned for children."

OREGON BOOK AWARDS

224 NW 13th Ave., Suite 306, #219, Portland OR 97209. (503)227-2583. **E-mail:** susan@literary-arts.org. **Website:** www.literary-arts.org. **Contact:** Susan Denning. The annual Oregon Book Awards celebrate Oregon authors in the areas of poetry, fiction, nonfiction, drama and young readers' literature published between August 1, 2010 and July 31, 2011. Prize: Finalists are invited on a statewide reading tour and are promoted in bookstores and libraries across the state. Judged by writers who are selected from outside Oregon for their expertise in a genre. Past judges include Mark Doty, Colson Whitehead and Kim Barnes. Entry fee determined by initial print run; see website for details. Deadline: last Friday in August. Entries must be previously published. Oregon residents

only. Accepts inquiries by phone and e-mail. Finalists announced in January. Winners announced at an awards ceremony in November. List of winners available in April.

THE ORIGINAL ART

128 E. 63rd St., New York NY 10065. (212)838-2560. **Fax:** (212)838-2561. **E-mail:** kim@societyillustrators.org;info@societyillustrators.org. **Website:** www.societyillustrators.org. **Contact:** Kate Feirtag, exhibition director. Purpose of contest: to celebrate the fine art of children's book illustration. Previously published submissions only. Deadline for entries: July 18. Request "call for entries" to receive contest rules and entry forms. Entry fee is $30/book. Judging by seven professional artists and editors. Works will be displayed at the Society of Illustrators Museum of American Illustration in New York City October-November annually. Medals awarded; catalog published.

HELEN KEATING OTT AWARD FOR OUTSTANDING CONTRIBUTION TO CHILDREN'S LITERATURE

2920 SW Dolph Ct., Ste. 3A, Portland OR 97219. (503)244-6919. **Fax:** (503)977-3734. **E-mail:** csla@worldaccessnet.com. **Website:** www.cslainfo.org. **Contact:** Jeri Baker, chair of committee; Judy Janzen, administrator of CSLA. Annual award. "This award is given to a person or organization that has made a significant contribution to promoting high moral and ethical values through children's literature." Recipient is honored in July during the conference. Awards certificate of recognition, the awards banquet, and one-night's stay in the hotel. "A nomination for an award may be made by anyone. An application form is available by contacting Judy Janzen. Elements of creativity and innovation will be given high priority by the judges."

PATERSON PRIZE FOR BOOKS FOR YOUNG PEOPLE

One College Blvd., Paterson NJ 07505-1179. (973)523-6085. **Fax:** (973)523-6085. **E-mail:** mgillan@pccc.edu. **Website:** www.pccc.edu/poetry. **Contact:** Maria Mazziotti Gillan, executive director. Part of the Poetry Center's mission is "to recognize excellence in books for young people." Published submissions only. Submissions made by author, author's agent or publisher. Must be published between January 1-December 31 of year previous to award year. Deadline for entries: March 15. SASE for contest rules and entry forms or visit website. Awards $500 for the author in either of 3 categories: PreK-Grade 3; Grades 4-6, Grades 7-12. Judging by a professional writer selected by the Poetry Center. Contest is open to any writer/illustrator.

⊕ THE KATHERINE PATERSON PRIZE FOR YOUNG ADULT AND CHILDREN'S WRITING

Vermont College, 36 College St., Montpelier VT 05602. (802)828-8517. **E-mail:** hungermtn@vcfa.edu. **Website:** www.hungermtn.org. **Contact:** Miciah Bay Gault, editor. The annual Katherine Paterson Prize for Young Adult and Children's Writing offers $1,000 and publication in *Hunger Mountain* (see separate listing in Magazines/Journals); 3 runners-up receive $100 and are also published. Submit young adult or middle grade mss, and writing for younger children, short stories, picture books, or novel excerpts, under 10,000 words. Guidelines available on website. Deadline: June 30.

PENNSYLVANIA YOUNG READERS' CHOICE AWARDS PROGRAM

148 S. Bethelehem Pike, Ambler PA 19002-5822. (215)643-5048. **E-mail:** bellavance@verizon.net. **Website:** http://www.psla.org. **Contact:** Jean B. Bellavance, coordinator. Submissions nominated by a person or group. Must be published within 5 years of the award—for example, books published in 2007 to present are eligible for the 2011-2012 award. Deadline for entries: September 1. SASE for contest rules and entry forms. No entry fee. Framed certificate to winning authors. Judging by children of Pennsylvania (they vote). Requirements for entrants: currently living in North America. Reader's Choice Award is to promote reading of quality books by young people in the Commonwealth of Pennsylvania, to promote teacher and librarian involvement in children's literature, and to honor authors whose work has been recognized by the children of Pennsylvania. Four awards are given, one for each of the following grade level divisions: K-3, 3-6, 6-8, YA. View information at the Pennsylvania School Librarians website.

PEN/PHYLLIS NAYLOR WORKING WRITER FELLOWSHIP

588 Broadway, New York NY 10012. **E-mail:** awards@pen.org. **Website:** www.pen.org. **Contact:** Nick Burd, awards program director. Offered annually to a writer of children's or young-adult fiction in financial need, who has published 2 books for children and young adults which may have been well reviewed and warmly received by literary critics, but which have not generated sufficient income to support the author. Previous works must be released through a US publisher. Writers must be nominated by an editor or fellow writer. The nominator should write a letter of support, describing in some detail how the candidate meets the criteria for the Fellowship. The nominator should also provide: 1) A list of the candidate's published work, accompanied by copies of reviews, where possible. 2) Three copies of the outline of the current novel in progress, together with 50-75 pages of the text. Picture books are not eligible. 3) On a separate piece of paper, a brief description of the candidate's recent earnings and a statement about why monetary support will make a particular difference in the applicant's writing life at this time. If the candidate is married or living with a domestic partner, please include a brief description of total family income and expenses. Awards $5,000.

PLEASE TOUCH MUSEUM BOOK AWARD

Memorial Hall in Fairmount Park, 4231 Avenue of the Republic, Philadelphia PA 19131. (215) 578-5153. **Fax:** (215) 578.5171. **E-mail:** info@pleasetouchmuseum. org; hboyd@pleasetouchmuseum.org. **Website:** www. pleasetouchmuseum.org. **Contact:** Heather Boyd. Purpose of the award is "to recognize and encourage the publication of high-quality books for young children. The award is given to books that are imaginative, exceptionally illustrated, and help to foster a child's life-long love of reading while reflecting Please Touch Museum's philosophy of learning through play. Each year, the museum selects 1 winner in 2 age categories— ages 3 and under and ages 4 to 7. These age categories reflect the age of the children Please Touch Museum serves. The award now includes a Kid's Choice category where winning selections are chosen by area school children in our target age range. No entry fee. Publishing date deadlines apply." Please Touch Museum's Kid's Store purchases books for selling at Annual Book Award Ceremony and throughout the year. Winning author autographing sessions may be held at Please Touch Museum and at the Delaware Valley Association for the Education of Young Children' Annual Conference in Philadelphia. Contact Heather Boyd at hboyd@pleasetouchmuseum.org for official rules. "To be eligible for consideration, a book must:

(1) Be distinguished in text, illustration, and ability to explore and clarify an idea for young children (ages 7 and under); (2) be published within the last year by an American publisher; and (3) be by an American author and/or illustrator." SASE for award rules and entry forms. Judging by jury of select museum staff, children's literature experts, librarians, and early childhood educators.

PNWA LITERARY CONTEST

PMB 2717-1420 NW Gilman Blvd, Suite 2, Issaquah WA 98027. (425)673-2665. **Fax:** (206)824-4559. **E-mail:** staff@pnwa.org. **Website:** www.pnwa.org. **Contact:** Kelli Liddane. **Open to students.** Annual contest. Purpose of contest: "Valuable tool for writers as contest submissions are critiqued (2 critiques)." Unpublished submissions only. Submissions made by author. Deadline for entries: February 18, 2011. Entry fee is $35/entry for members, $50/entry for nonmembers. Awards $700-1st; $300-2nd. Awards in all 12 categories.

POCKETS FICTION-WRITING CONTEST

P.O. Box 340004, Nashville TN 37203-0004. (615)340-7333. **Fax:** (615)340-7267. **E-mail:** pockets@upper room.org; theupperroommagazine@upperroom.org. **Website:** www.pockets.upperroom.org. **Contact:** Lynn W. Gilliam, senior editor. *Pockets* is a devotional magazine for children between the ages of 6 and 11. Contest offered annually for unpublished work to discover new children's writers. Prize: $1,000 and publication in *Pockets*. Categories: short stories. Judged by *Pockets* staff and staff of other Upper Room Publications. No entry fee. Guidelines available on website or send #10 SASE. Deadline: Must be postmarked between March 1-August 15. Entries must be unpublished. Because the purpose of the contest is to discover new writers, previous winners are not eligible. No violence, science fiction, romance, fantasy or talking animal stories. Word length 1,000-1,600 words. Open to any writer. Winner announced November 1 and notified by U.S. mail. Contest submissions accompanied by SASE will be returned Nov. 1. "Send SASE with 4 first-class stamps to request guidelines and a past issue, or go to: http://pockets.upperroom.org."

"We do not accept mss sent by fax or e-mail."

EDGAR ALLAN POE AWARD

1140 Broadway, Suite 1507, New York NY 10001. (212)888-8171. **Fax:** (212)888-8107. **E-mail:** mwa@ mysterywriters.org. **Website:** www.mysterywriters. org. Mystery Writers of America is the leading association for professional crime writers in the United States. Members of MWA include most major writers of crime fiction and nonfiction, as well as screenwriters, dramatists, editors, publishers, and other professionals in the field. We welcome everyone who is interested in mysteries and crime writing to join MWA. Purpose of the award: to honor authors of distinguished works in the mystery field. Previously published submissions only. Submissions made by the author, author's agent; "normally by the publisher." Work must be published/produced the year of the contest. Deadline for entries: Must be received by November 30. Submission information can be found at: www.mysterywriters.org. No entry fee. Awards ceramic bust of "Edgar" for winner; scrolls for all nominees. Judging by professional members of Mystery Writers of America (writers). Nominee press release sent in mid January. Winner announced at the Edgar® Awards Banquet, held in late April/early May.

MICHAEL L. PRINTZ AWARD

50 E. Huron, Chicago IL 60611. **Fax:** (312)280-5276. **E-mail:** yalsa@ala.org. **Website:** www.ala.org/yalsa/ printz. Annual award. The Michael L. Printz Award is an award for a book that exemplifies literary excellence in young adult literature. It is named for a Topeka, Kansas school librarian who was a longtime active member of the Young Adult Library Services Association. It will be selected annually by an award committee that can also name as many as 4 honor books. The award-winning book can be fiction, nofiction, poetry or an anthology, and can be a work of joint authorship or editorship. The books must be published between January 1 and December 31 of the preceding year and be designated by its publisher as being either a young adult book or one published for the age range that YALSA defines as young adult, e.g. ages 12 through 18. The deadline for both committee and field nominations will be December 1.

PURPLE DRAGONFLY BOOK AWARDS

4696 W. Tyson St., Chandler AZ 85226-2903. (480)940-8182. **Fax:** (480)940-8787. **E-mail:** info@ fivestarpublications.com. **Website:** www.purple dragonflybookawards.com; www.fivestarpublica tions.com; www.fivestarbookawards.com. **Contact:** Lisa Goldman, Lynda Exley, contest coordinators. "Five Star Publications is proud to present the Purple

Dragonfly Book Awards, which were conceived and designed with children in mind. Not only do we want to recognize and honor accomplished authors in the field of children's literature, but we also want to highlight and reward up-and-coming, newly published authors and younger published writers. In our efforts to include everyone, the Purple Dragonfly Book Awards are divided into 35 distinct subject categories, ranging from books on the environment and cooking to sports and family issues. (Please click on the 'Categories' tab for a complete list.) The Purple Dragonfly Book Awards are geared toward stories that appeal to children of all ages. We are looking for stories that inspire, inform, teach or entertain. A Purple Dragonfly seal on your book's cover tells parents, grandparents, educators and caregivers they are giving children the very best in reading excellence. Our judges are industry experts with specific knowledge about the categories over which they preside. Being honored with a Purple Dragonfly Award confers credibility upon the winner, as well as provides positive publicity to further their success. The goal of these awards is to give published authors the recognition they deserve and provide a helping hand to further their careers." The awards are open to books published in any calendar year and in any country that are available for purchase. Books entered must be printed in English. Traditionally published, partnership published and self-published books are permitted, as long as they fit the above criteria. E-books are not permitted; although, Five Star does have plans for an e-book contest in the future, so please check www.FiveStarBookAwards.com periodically for notification of contest launch. Final deadline for submissions is May 1, 2013; to be eligible, submissions must be postmarked May 1, 2013 or earlier. The deadline is the same each year. Submissions postmarked March 1, 2013 or earlier that meet all submission requirements are eligible for the Early Bird reward: A free copy of "The Economical Guide to Self-Publishing" or "Promote Like a Pro: Small Budget, Big Show.". Prize: The grand prize winner will receive a $300 cash prize, 100 foil award seals (more can be ordered for an extra charge), 1 hour of marketing consultation from Five Star Publications, and $100 worth of Five Star Publications' titles, as well as publicity on Five Star Publications' websites and inclusion in a winners' news release sent to a comprehensive list of media outlets. The grand prize winner will also be placed in the Five Star Dragonfly Book Awards virtual

bookstore with a thumbnail of the book's cover, price, 1-sentence description and link to Amazon.com for purchasing purposes, if applicable. 1st Place: All first-place winners of categories will be put into a drawing for a $100 prize. In addition, each first-place winner in each category receives a certificate commemorating their accomplishment, 25 foil award seals (more can be ordered for an extra charge) and mention on Five Star Publications' websites. "Our judges are industry experts with specific knowledge about the categories over which they preside. Being honored with a Purple Dragonfly Award confers credibility upon the winner, as well as provides positive publicity to further their success. The goal of these awards is to give published authors the recognition they deserve and provide a helping hand to further their careers."

QUILL AND SCROLL INTERNATIONAL WRITING/PHOTO CONTEST

School of Journalism, Univ. of Iowa, 100 Adler Journalism Bldg., Iowa City IA 52242-2004. (319)335-3457. **Fax:** (319)335-3989. **E-mail:** quill-scroll@uiowa.edu; vanessa-shelton@uiowa.edu. **Website:** www.uiowa.edu/~quill-sc. **Contact:** Vanessa Shelton, contest director. **Open to students.** Annual contest. Previously published submissions only. Submissions made by the author or school newspaper adviser. Must be published within the last year. Deadline for entries: February 5. Visit website for more information and entry forms. Entry fee is $2/entry. Engraved plaque awarded to sweepstakes winners. Judging by various judges. *Quill and Scroll* acquires the right to publish submitted material in its magazine or website if it is chosen as a winning entry. Requirements for entrants: must be students in grades 9-12 for high school division. Entry form available on website. Winners will receive *Quill and Scroll*'s National Award Gold Key and, if seniors, are eligible to apply for one of the scholarships offered by *Quill and Scroll*. All winning entries are automatically eligible for the International Writing and Photo Sweepstakes Awards. Engraved plaque awarded to sweepstakes winners.

RED HOUSE CHILDREN'S BOOK AWARD

2 Bridge Wood View, Norsforth, Leeds VI LS18 5PEUnited Kingdom . **E-mail:** marianneadey@aol.com. **Website:** www.redhousechildrensbookaward.co.uk. Purpose of the award: "The R.H.C.B.A. is an annual prize for the best children's book of the year judged

by the children themselves." Categories: (I) books for younger children, (II) books for younger readers, (III) books for older readers. Estab. 1980. Works must be published in the United Kingdom. Deadline for entries: December 31. SASE or e-mail for rules. Entries not returned. Awards "a magnificent silver and oak trophy worth over €6,000." Silver dishes to each category winner. Portfolios of children's work to all Top Ten authors and illustrators. Judging by children. Requirements for entrants: Work must be fiction and published in the UK during the current year (poetry is ineligible). Top 50 Books of the year will be published in current "Pick of the Year" publication.

THE RED HOUSE CHILDREN'S BOOK AWARD

2 Bridge Wood View, Horsforth, Leeds, West Yorkshire LS18 5PEUnited Kingdom . **E-mail:** info@rhcba.co.uk. **Website:** www.redhousechildrensbookaward.co.uk. **Contact:** Sinead Kromer, national co-ordinator. (formerly The Children's Book Award), Owned and co-ordinated by the Federation of Children's Book Groups (Reg. Charity No. 268289). Purpose of the award is to enable children choose the best works of fiction published in the UK. Prize: trophy and silver bookmarks, portfolio of children's letters and pictures. Categories: Books for Younger Children, Books for Younger Readers, Books for Older Readers. No entry fee. **Closing Date is December 31.** Either author or publisher may nominate title. Guidelines available on website. Accepts enquiries by email and phone. Shortlist announced in February and winners announced in May. Winners notified at award ceremony and dinner at the Birmingham Botanical Gardens and via the publisher. For contest results, visit the website.

REGINA BOOK AWARD

100-2400 College Ave., Regina SK S4P 0K1 Canada. (306)569-1585. **Fax:** (306)569-4187. **E-mail:** director@bookawards.sk.ca. **Website:** www.bookawards.sk.ca. **Contact:** Executive director, book submissions. Offered annually. "In recognition of the vitality of the literary community in Regina, this award is presented to a Regina author for the best book, judged on the quality of writing." Books from the following categories will be considered: Children's; drama; fiction (short fiction by a single author, novellas, novels); nonfiction (all categories of nonfiction writing except cookbooks, directories, how-to books, or bibliographies of mini-

mal critical content); poetry. Deadline: November 1. Prize: Prize: $2,000 (CAD).

TOMÁS RIVERA MEXICAN AMERICAN CHILDREN'S BOOK AWARD

601 University Dr., San Marcos TX 78666-4613. (512)245-2357. **Website:** http://www.education.tx state.edu/about/Map-Directions.html. **Contact:** Dr. Jesse Gainer, award director. Competition open to adults. Annual contest. Competition open to adults. Annual contest. Estab. 1995. Purpose of award: "To encourage authors, illustrators and publishers to produce books that authentically reflect the lives of Mexican Americans appropriate for children and young adults in the United States." Unpublished mss not accepted. Submissions made by "any interested individual or publishing company." Must be published during the two years prior to the year of consideration for the appropriate category "Works for Younger Children" or " Works for Older Children." Deadline for entries: November 1 of publication year. Contact Dr. Jesse Gainer for information and send copy of book. No entry fee. Awards $2,000 per book. Judging of nominations by a regional committee, national committee judges finalists. Annual ceremony honoring the book and author/illustrator is held during the fall at Texas State University-San Marcos in collaboration with the Texas Book Festival.

ROCKY MOUNTAIN BOOK AWARD: ALBERTA CHILDREN'S CHOICE BOOK AWARD

Box 42, Lethbridge AB T1J 3Y3 Canada. (403)381-0855. **Website:** http://rmba.lethsd.ab.ca/. **Contact:** Michelle Dimnik, contest director. Submit entries to: Richard Chase, board member. **Open to students**. Annual contest. Purpose of contest: "Reading motivation for students, promotion of Canadian authors, illustrators and publishers." Previously unpublished submissions only. Submissions made by author's agent or nominated by a person or group. Must be published between 2010-2012. Register before January 15th to take part in the 2013 Rocky Mountain Book Award. SASE for contest rules and entry forms. No entry fee. Awards: Gold medal and author tour of selected Alberta schools. Judging by students. Requirements for entrants: Canadian authors and illustrators only.

ROYAL DRAGONFLY BOOK AWARDS

4696 W. Tyson St., Chandler AZ 85226. (480)940-8182. **Fax:** (480)940-8787. **E-mail:** info@fivestarpublica tions.com. **Website:** www.fivestarpublications.com; www.fivestarbookawards.com; www.royaldragonflybookawards.com. **Contact:** Lynda Exley. Offered annually for any previously published work to honor authors for writing excellence of all types of literature - fiction and nonfiction - in 50 categories, appealing to a wide range of ages and comprehensive list of genres. Open to any author published in English. Guidelines and entry forms available by request with SASE. Entry forms are also downloadable at www.royaldragonflybookawards.com. Entry fee is $50 for one title in one category, $45 per title when multiple books are entered or $45 per category when one book is entered in multiple categories. All entry fees are per title, per category. The Grand Prize winner receives $300, while another entrant will be the lucky winner of a $100 drawing. All first-place winners receive foil award seals and are included in a publicity campaign announcing winners. All first- and second-place winners and honorable mentions receive certificates.

☺ SASKATCHEWAN CHILDREN'S LITERATURE AWARD

100-2400 College Ave., Regina SK S4P 0K1 Canada. (306)569-1585. **Fax:** (306)569-4187. **E-mail:** director@bookawards.sk.ca. **Website:** www.bookawards. sk.ca. **Contact:** Executive director, book submissions. Offered annually award. "This award is presented to a Saskatchewan author or pair of authors, or to Saskatchewan author and a Saskatchewan illustrator, for the best book of children's literature, for ages 0-11, judged on the quality of the writing and illustration." Deadline: November 1. Prize: Prize: $2,000 (CAD).

☺ SASKATOON BOOK AWARD

100-2400 College Ave., Regina SK S4P 0K1 Canada. (306)569-1585. **Fax:** (306)569-4187. **E-mail:** director@bookawards.sk.ca. **Website:** www.bookawards. sk.ca. **Contact:** Executive director, book submissions. Offered annually. "This award is presented to a Saskatoon author (or pair of authors) for the best book, judged on the quality of writing." Books from the following categories will be considered: Children's; drama; fiction (short fiction by a single author, novellas, novels); nonfiction (all categories of nonfiction writing except cookbooks, directories, how-to books, or bibliographies of minimal critical content); poetry. Deadline: November 1. Prize: $2,000 (CAD).

SCBWI MAGAZINE MERIT AWARDS

Website: www.scbwi.org. **Contact:** Stephanie Gordon, award coordinator. Purpose of the award: "to recognize outstanding original magazine work for young people published during that year and having been written or illustrated by members of SCBWI." Previously published submissions only. Entries must be submitted between January 1 and December 15 of the year of publication. For rules and procedures see website. No entry fee. Must be a SCBWI member. Awards plaques and honor certificates for each of 4 categories (fiction, nonfiction, illustration, poetry). Judging by a magazine editor and two "full" SCBWI members. "All magazine work for young people by an SCBWI member—writer, artist or photographer—is eligible during the year of original publication. In the case of co-authored work, both authors must be SCBWI members. Members must submit their own work." Requirements for entrants: 4 copies each of the published work and proof of publication (may be contents page) showing the name of the magazine and the date of issue. The SCBWI is a professional organization of writers and illustrators and others interested in children's literature. Membership is open to the general public at large

SCBWI WORK-IN-PROGRESS GRANTS

Website: www.scbwi.org. "The SCBWI Work-in-Progress Grants have been established to assist children's book writers in the completion of a specific project." Four categories: (1) General Work-in-Progress Grant. (2) Grant for a Contemporary Novel for Young People. (3) Nonfiction Research Grant. (4) Grant for a Work Whose Author Has Never Had a Book Published. Requests for applications may be made beginning October 1. Completed applications accepted February 1-April 1 of each year. SASE for applications for grants. In any year, an applicant may apply for any of the grants except the one awarded for a work whose author has never had a book published. (The recipient of this grant will be chosen from entries in all categories.) Five grants of $1,500 will be awarded annually. Runner-up grants of $500 (one in each category) will also be awarded. "The grants are available to both full and associate members of the SCBWI. They are not available for projects on which there are already contracts." Previous recipients not eligible to apply.

SHABO AWARD FOR CHILDREN'S PICTURE BOOK WRITERS

The Loft Literary Center, 1011 Washington Ave. S., Suite 200, Open Book Minneapolis MN55415 . (612)215-2575. **Fax:** (612)215-2576. **E-mail:** loft@loft.org. **Website:** www.loft.org. "The Shabo Award is offered to children's picture book writers to develop 'nearly there' manuscripts into publishable pieces. Up to 8 advanced writers will be chosen annually. Participants should have few, or no, publications to date. Guidelines available online in April with an early June deadline." **Contact:** Jerod Santek. "The Shabo Award is offered to children's picture book writers to develop 'nearly there' manuscripts into publishable pieces. Up to 8 advanced writers will be chosen annually. Participants should have few, or no, publications to date. Guidelines available online in April with an early June deadline."

SKIPPING STONES BOOK AWARDS

Website: www.skippingstones.org. Open to published books, publications/magazines, educational videos, and DVDs. Annual awards. Purpose of contest: To recognize exceptional, literary and artistic contributions to juvenile/children's literature, as well as teaching resources and educational audio/video resources in the areas of multicultural awareness, nature and ecology, social issues, peace and nonviolence. Submissions made by the author or publishers and/or producers. Deadline for entries: February 1. Send request for contest rules and entry forms or visit website. Entry fee is $50; 50% discount for small nonprofit publishers. Each year, an honor roll of about 20 to 25 books and A/V with teaching resources are selected by a multicultural selection committee of editors, students, parents, teachers and librarians. Winners receive gold honor award seals, attractive honor certificates and publicity via multiple outlets. Many educational publications announce the winners of our book awards. "The reviews of winning books and educational videos/DVDs are published in the May-August issue of *Skipping Stones* and/or on our website."

SKIPPING STONES YOUTH HONOR AWARDS

P.O. Box 3939, Eugene OR 97403-0939. (541)342-4956. **E-mail:** editor@SkippingStones.org. **Website:** www.SkippingStones.org. **Open to students.** Annual awards. Purpose of contest: "to recognize youth, 7 to 17, for their contributions to multicultural awareness, nature and ecology, social issues, peace and nonviolence. Also to promote creativity, self-esteem and writing skills and to recognize important work being done by youth organizations." Submissions made by the author. Deadline for entries: June 25. SASE for contest rules or download from www.skippingstones.org/youthhonor-02.htm. Entries must include certificate of originality by a parent and/or teacher and a cover letter that included cultural background information on the author. Submissions can either be mailed or e-mailed. Entry fee is $3 fee is waived for low-income students. Everyone who enters the contest receives the September-October issue featuring Youth Awards. Judging by *Skipping Stones* staff. "Up to ten awards are given in three categories: (1) Compositions (essays, poems, short stories, songs, travelogues, etc.)—Entries should be typed (double-spaced) or neatly handwritten. Fiction or nonfiction should be limited to 1,000 words; poems to 30 lines. Non-English writings are also welcome. (2) Artwork (drawings, cartoons, paintings or photo essays with captions)—Entries should have the artist's name, age and address on the back of each page. Send the originals with SASE. Black & white photos are especially welcome. Limit: 8 pieces. (3) Youth Organizations—Tell us how your club or group works to: (a) preserve the nature and ecology in your area, (b) enhance the quality of life for low-income, minority or disabled or (c) improve racial or cultural harmony in your school or community. Use the same format as for compositions." The winners are published in the September-October issue of *Skipping Stones*. Now in its 25th year, *Skipping Stones* is a winner of N.A.M.E.EDPRESS, Newsstand Resources and Parent's Choice Awards.

KAY SNOW WRITERS' CONTEST

9045 SW Barbur Blvd. #5A, Portland OR 97219-4027. (503)452-1592. **Fax:** (503)452-0372. **E-mail:** wilwrite@teleport.com. **Website:** www.willamettewriters.com. **Contact:** Lizzy Shannon, contest director. Annual contest. **Open to students.** Purpose of contest: "to encourage beginning and established writers to continue the craft." Unpublished, original submissions only. Submissions made by the author. Deadline for entries: April 23rd. SASE for contest rules and entry forms. Entry fee is $10, Williamette Writers' members; $15, nonmembers; free for student writers grades 1-12. Awards cash prize of $300 per category (fiction, nonfiction, juvenile, poetry, script writing), $50 for students in three divisions: 1-5, 6-8, 9-12. Judges are anonymous.

SOUTHWEST WRITERS

3721 Morris NE, Suite A, Albuquerque NM 87111. (505)265-9485. **Fax:** (505)265-9483. **E-mail:** swwriters@juno.com. **Website:** www.southwestwriters.com. The SouthWest Writers Writing Contest encourages and honors excellence in writing. In addition to competing for cash prizes and the coveted Storyteller Award, contest entrants may receive an optional written critique of their entry from a qualified contest critiquer. Non-profit organization dedicated to helping members of all levels in their writing. Members enjoy perks such as networking with professional and aspiring writers; substantial discounts on mini-conferences, workshops, writing classes, and annual and quarterly SWW writing contest; monthly newsletter; two writing programs per month; critique groups, critique service (also for nonmembers); discounts at bookstores and other businesses; and website linking. Cost of membership: Individual, $60/year, $100/2 years; Two People, $50 each/year; Student, $40/year; Student under 18, $25/year; Outside U.S.$65/year; Lifetime, $750. See website for information. Submit first 20 pages and 1 page synopsis (using industry-standard formatting, Courier font, brad-bound). Deadline: May 1-May 16. Prize: Up to $1,000 grand prize. All mss will be screened by a panel and the top 10 in each category will be sent to appropriate editors or literary agents to determine the final top 3 places. The top 3 winners will also receive a critique from the judging editor or literary agent. Contacting any judge about an entry is an automatic disqualification. 12. Entrants retain all rights to their entries. By entering this contest, you agree to abide by the rules, agree that decisions by the judges are final, and agree that no refunds will be awarded.

SOUTHWEST WRITERS ANNUAL CONTEST

3721 Morris NE, Albuquerque NM 87111. (505)265-9485. **Website:** www.southwestwriters.com. **Open to adults and students.** Annual contest. Estab. Purpose of contest: to encourage writers of all genres. Also offers mini-conferences, critique service—for $60/year, offers 2 monthly programs, monthly newsletter, annual writing and bi-monthly writing contests, other workshops, various discount perks, website linking, e-mail addresses, classes and critique service (open to nonmembers). See website for more information or call or write.

⊕ SYDNEY TAYLOR BOOK AWARD

P.O. Box 1118, Teaneck NJ 07666. (212)725-5359. **E-mail:** chair@sydneytaylorbookaward.org; heidi@cbiboca.org. **Website:** www.sydneytaylorbookaward.org. **Contact:** Barbara Bietz, chair. Offered annually for work published during the current year. "Given to distinguished contributions to Jewish literature for children. One award for younder readers, one for older readers, and one for teens." Publishers submit books. Deadline: December 31, but we cannot guarantee that books received after December 1 will be considered. Guidelines on website. Awards certificate, cash award, and gold or silver seals for cover of winning book.

SYDNEY TAYLOR MANUSCRIPT COMPETITION

Sydney Taylor Manuscript Award Competition, 204 Park St., Montclair NJ 07042. **E-mail:** stmacajl@aol.com. **Contact:** Aileen Grossberg. **Open to students** and to any unpublished writer of fiction. Annual contest. Estab. 1985. Purpose of the contest: "This competition is for unpublished writers of fiction. Material should be for readers ages 8-11, with universal appeal that will serve to deepen the understanding of Judaism for all children, revealing positive aspects of Jewish life." Unpublished submissions only. Deadline for entries: December 15. Download rules and forms from website. No entry fee. Awards $1,000. Award winner will be notified in April, and the award will be presented at the convention in June. Judging by qualified judges from within the Association of Jewish Libraries. Requirements for entrants: must be an unpublished fiction writer; also, books must range from 64-200 pages in length. "AJL assumes no responsibility for publication, but hopes this cash incentive will serve to encourage new writers of children's stories with Jewish themes for all children."

↻ TD CANADIAN CHILDREN'S LITERATURE AWARD

40 Orchard View Blvd., Suite 217, Toronto ON M4R 1B9 Canada. (416)975-0010. **Fax:** (416)975-8970. **Website:** www.bookcentre.ca. "All books, in any genre, written and illustrated by Canadians and for children ages 1-12 are eligible. Only books first published in Canada are eligible for submission. Books must be published between January 1 and December 31 of the previous calendar year. Open to Cana-

dian citizens and/or permanent residents of Canada." "To honour the most distinguished book of the year for young people in both English and French." Submission deadline: Mid-December. Prize: Two prizes of $25,000, 1 for English, 1 for French. $10,000 will be divided among the Honour Book English titles and Honour Book French titles, to a maximum of 4; $2,500 shall go to each of the publishers of the English and French grand-prize winning books for promotion and publicity.

○ TORONTO BOOK AWARDS

100 Queen St. W., City Clerk's Office, 2nd floor, West Tower, Toronto ON M5H 2N2 Canada. (416)392-7805. **Fax:** (416)392-1247. **E-mail:** bkurmey@toronto.ca. **Website:** www.toronto.ca/book_awards. **Contact:** Bev Kurmey, protocol officer. The Toronto Book Awards honor authors of books of literary or artistic merit that are evocative of Toronto. Annual award for short stories, novels, poetry or short story collections. Prize: $15,000. Each short-listed author (usually 4-6) receives $1,000 and the winner receives the remainder. Categories: No separate categories—novels, short story collections, books of poetry, biographies, history, books about sports, children's books—all are judged together. Judged by jury of five who have demonstrated interest and/or experience in literature, literacy, books and book publishing. No entry fee. Cover letter should include name, address, phone, e-mail and title of entry. Six copies of the entry book are also required. **Deadline:** last week of March. Entries must be previously published. Guidelines available in September on website. Accepts inquires by fax, e-mail, phone. Finalists announced in June; winners notified in September at a gala reception. Guidelines and results available on website.

VEGETARIAN ESSAY CONTEST

P.O. Box 1463, Baltimore MD 21203. (410)366-VEGE. **Fax:** (410)366-8804. **E-mail:** vrg@vrg.org. **Website:** www.vrg.org. Annual contest. **Open to students.** Purpose of contest: to promote vegetarianism in young people. Unpublished submissions only. Deadline for entries: May 1 of each year. SASE for contest rules and entry forms. No entry fee. Awards $50 savings bond. Judging by awards committee. Acquires right for The Vegetarian Resource Group to reprint essays. Requirements for entrants: age 18 and under. Winning works may be published in *Vegetarian Journal*, instructional materials for students. Submit 2-3 page essay on any aspect of vegetarianism, which is the abstinence of meat, fish and fowl. Entrants can base paper on interviewing, research or personal opinion. Need not be vegetarian to enter.

VFW VOICE OF DEMOCRACY

406 W. 34th St., Kansas City MO 64111. (816)968-1117. **E-mail:** kharmer@vfw.org. **Website:** www.vfw.org. **Open to high school students.** Annual contest. Purpose of contest: to give high school students the opportunity to voice their opinions about their responsibility to our country and to convey those opinions via the broadcast media to all of America. Deadline for entries: November 1. No entry fee. Winners receive awards ranging from $1,000-30,000. Requirements for entrants: "Ninth-twelfth grade students in public, parochial, private and home schools are eligible to compete. Former first place state winners are not eligible to compete again. Contact your participating high school teacher, counselor, our website www.vfw.org or your local VFW Post to enter."

VIRGINIA LIBRARY ASSOCIATION/ JEFFERSON CUP

P.O. Box 56312, Virginia Beach VA 23456. (757)507-1097. **Fax:** (757)447-3478. **Website:** www.vla.org. Award director changes year to year. Purpose of award "The Jefferson Cup honors a distinguished biography, historical fiction or American history book for young people. Presented since 1983, the Jefferson Cup Committee's goal is to promote reading about America's past; to encourage the quality writing of United States history, biography and historical fiction for young people and to recognize authors in these disciplines." Entries must be published in the year prior to selection. Deadline for entries, January 31st. Additional information on the Jefferson Cup and criteria on making submissions is available on the VLA website. Judging by committee. The book must be about U.S. history or an American person, 1492 to present, or fiction that highlights the U.S. past; author must reside in the U.S. The book must be published especially for young people.

WESTERN HERITAGE AWARDS

1700 NE 63rd St., Oklahoma City OK 73111-7997. (405)478-2250. **Fax:** (405)478-4714. **E-mail:** ssimpson@nationalcowboymuseum.org. **Website:** www.nationalcowboymuseum.org. **Contact:** Shayla Simpson, PR director. Purpose of award: The WHA are presented annually to encourage the accurate and artistic telling of great stories of the West through 16 categories of western literature, television, film and music; including fiction, nonfiction, children's books and poetry. Previously published submissions only; must be published the calendar year before the awards are presented. Deadline for literary entries: November 30. Deadline for film, music and television entries: December 31. Entries not returned. Entry fee is $50/entry. Awards a Wrangler bronze sculpture designed by famed western artist, John Free. Judging by a panel of judges selected each year with distinction in various fields of western art and heritage. Requirements for entrants: The material must pertain to the development or preservation of the West, either from a historical or contemporary viewpoint. Literary entries must have been published between December 1 and November 30 of calendar year. Film, music or television entries must have been released or aired between January 1 and December 31 of calendar year of entry. Works recognized during special awards ceremonies held annually at the museum. There is an autograph party preceding the awards. Awards ceremonies are sometimes broadcast.

WESTERN WRITERS OF AMERICA

(307)329-8942. **Fax:** (307)327-5465 (call first). **E-mail:** wwa.moulton@gmail.com. **Website:** www.western writers.org. **Contact:** Candy Moulton, executive director. "17 Spur Award categories in various aspects of the American West." Send entry form with your published work. "The nonprofit Western Writers of America has promoted and honored the best in Western literature with the annual Spur Awards, selected by panels of judges. Awards, for material published last year, are given for works whose inspirations, image and literary excellence best represent the reality and spirit of the American West."

JACKIE WHITE MEMORIAL NATIONAL CHILDREN'S PLAY WRITING CONTEST

1800 Nelwood, Columbia MO 65202-1447. (573)874-5628. **E-mail:** bybetsy@yahoo.com. **Website:** www.cectheatre.org. Send scripts to 309 Parkade Blvd., Columbia MO 65202. Annual contest. Estab. 1988. Purpose of contest: "To encourage writing of family-friendly scripts." Previously unpublished submissions only. Submissions made by author. **Deadline:** June 1, 2013. SASE for contest rules and entry forms. **Entry fee:** $25. Awards $500 with production possible. "We reserve the right to award 1st place and prize monies

without a production." Judging by current and past board members of CEC and by non-board members who direct plays at CEC. Play may be performed during the following season. All submissions will be read by at least 3 readers. Author will receive a written evaluation of the script. **Contact:** Betsy Phillips, contest director. Send scripts to 309 Parkade Blvd., Columbia MO 65202. Annual contest. Purpose of contest: "To encourage writing of family-friendly scripts." SASE for contest rules and entry forms. Previously unpublished submissions only. Submissions made by author. Play may be performed during the following season. All submissions will be read by at least 3 readers. Author will receive a written evaluation of the script. Deadline: June 1, 2013. Prize: Awards $500 with production possible. "We reserve the right to award 1st place and prize monies without a production.". Judging by current and past board members of CEC and by non-board members who direct plays at CEC.

WILLA LITERARY AWARD

E-mail: slyon.www@gmail.com. **Website:** www.womenwritingthewest.org. **Contact:** Alice D. Trego, contest director; Suzanne Lyon, WILLA chair. The WILLA Literary Award honors the best in literature featuring women's or girls' stories set in the West published each year. Women Writing the West (WWW), a nonprofit association of writers and other professionals writing and promoting the Women's West, underwrites and presents the nationally recognized award annually (for work published between January 1 and December 31). The award is named in honor of Pulitzer Prize winner Willa Cather, one of the country's foremost novelists. The award is given in 7 categories: Historical fiction, contemporary fiction, original softcover fiction, creative nonfiction, scholarly nonfiction, poetry, and children's/young adult fiction/nonfiction. Deadline: February 1. Prize: Winner receives $100 and a trophy. Finalist receives a plaque. Award announcement is in early August, and awards are presented to the winners and finalists at the annual WWW Fall Conference. Judged by professional librarians not affiliated with WWW.

RITA WILLIAMS YOUNG ADULT PROSE PRIZE

E-mail: pennobhill@aol.com. **Website:** www.soul makingcontest.us. **Contact:** Eileen Malone. **Open to students.** Up to 3,000 words in story, essay, journal entry, creative nonfiction, or memoir by writers in grades 9-12. See judges online at website. Annual prize. Deadline: November 30. Guidelines for SASE or at www.soulmakingcontest.us. Charges $5/entry (make checks payable to NLAPW, Nob Hill Branch) International entrants please send Travelers Check drawn on a USA bank. Prize: 1st Place: $100; 2nd Place: $50; 3rd Place: $25. Open to any writer in grade 9-12 or equivalent. No e-mail entries or those mailed special delivery, certified or registered will be accepted. Do enclose SASE in your entry package if you wish to receive contest results.

PAUL A. WITTY OUTSTANDING LITERATURE AWARD

P.O. Box 10034, Lamar University, Beaumont TX 77710. (409)286-5941. **Fax:** (409)880-8384. **E-mail:** dorothy.sisk@lamar.edu. **Website:** www.reading.org. **Contact:** Dorothy Sisk, director. **Open to students.** Annual award. Categories of entries: poetry/prose at elementary, junior high and senior high levels. Unpublished submissions only. Deadline for entries: February 1. SASE for award rules and entry forms. SASE for return of entries. No entry fee. Awards $25 and plaque, also certificates of merit. Judging by 2 committees for screening and awarding. "The elementary students' entries must be legible and may not exceed 1,000 words. Secondary students' prose entries should be typed and may exceed 1,000 words if necessary. At both elementary and secondary levels, if poetry is entered, a set of five poems must be submitted. All entries and requests for applications must include a self-addressed, stamped envelope."

PAUL A. WITTY SHORT STORY AWARD

P.O. Box 8139, Newark DE 19714-8139. (302)731-1600, ext. 229. **Fax:** (302)731-1057. **E-mail:** committees@reading.org. **Website:** www.reading.org. "Offered to reward author of an original short story published in a children's periodical during 2010 which serves as a literary standard that encourages young readers to read periodicals. Write for guidelines or download from website." Deadline: December 1. Prize: $1,000.

ALICE WOOD MEMORIAL OHIOANA AWARD FOR CHILDREN'S LITERATURE

274 E. First Ave., Suite 300, Columbus OH 43201. (614)466-3831. **Fax:** (614)728-6974. **E-mail:** ohioana@ohioana.org. **Website:** www.ohioana.org. **Contact:** Linda R. Hengst. Offered to an author whose body of work has made, and continues to make, a significant contribution to literature for children or young adults, and through their work as a writer, teacher, administrator, and community member, interest in children's literature has been encouraged and children have become involved with reading. Nomination forms for SASE. Recipient must have been born in Ohio or lived in Ohio at least 5 years. Guidelines for SASE. Accepts inquiries by phone and e-mail. Results announced in August or September. Winners notified by letter in May. For contest results, call or e-mail Ohioana Library: Linda Hengst, executive director. Deadline: December 31. Prize: Prize is $1,000.

● WRITE A STORY FOR CHILDREN COMPETITION

Phone/Fax: (44)(148)783-2752. **E-mail:** enquiries@childrens-writers.co.uk. **Website:** www.childrens-writers.co.uk. **Contact:** Contest director. Annual contest for the best unpublished short story writer for children. Guidelines and entry forms online or send SAE/IRC. Open to any unpublished writer over the age of 18. Deadline: March 31. Prize: 1st Place: £2,000; 2nd Place: £300; 3rd Place: £200. Judged by a panel appointed by the Academy of Children's Writers.

WRITE IT NOW!

10823 Worthing Ave., San Diego CA 92126-2220. (858)689-2665. **E-mail:** editor@SmartWriters.com. **Website:** www.SmartWriters.com. **Contact:** Roxyanne Young, editorial director. Annual contest. "Our purpose is to encourage new writers and help get their manuscripts into the hands of people who can help further their careers." Unpublished submissions only. Submissions made by author. Deadline for entries: May 1. SASE for contest rules and entry forms; also see website. Entry fee is $15 for initial entry, $10 for additional entries. Awards a cash prize, books about writing, and an editorial review of the winning mss. Judging by published writers and editors. Requirement for entrants: "This contest is open to all writers age 18 and older. There are 5 categories: Young Adult, Mid-grade, Picture Book, Nonfiction, and Illustration." See website for more details, FAQ, and rules updates.

WRITER'S DIGEST INTERNATIONAL SELF-PUBLISHED BOOK AWARDS

(715)445-4612, ext. 13430. **E-mail:** writing-competition@fwmedia.com. **Website:** www.writersdigest.com. **Contact:** Nicole Florence. Contest open to all English-language self-published books for which the authors have paid the full cost of publication, or the cost of printing has been paid for by a grant or as part of a prize. Categories include: Mainstream/Literary Fiction, Nonfiction, Inspirational (spiritual/new age), Life Stories (biographies/autobiographies/family histories/memoirs), Children's Books, Reference Books (directories/encyclopedias/guide books), Poetry, Middle-Grade/Young Adult Books. Deadline: April 20. Prize: Grand Prize: $3,000, promotion in *Writer's Digest* and *Publishers Weekly*, and 10 copies of the book will be sent to major review houses with a guaranteed review in *Midwest Book Review*; 1st Place (9 winners): $1,000, promotion in *Writer's Digest*; Honorable Mentions: promotion in *Writer's Digest*, $50 of Writer's Digest Books, and a certificate.

WRITERS-EDITORS NETWORK ANNUAL INTERNATIONAL WRITING COMPETITION

E-mail: contest@writers-editors.com. **Website:** www.writers-editors.com. **Contact:** Dana K. Cassell, executive director. "Annual award to recognize publishable talent. Categories: Nonfiction (previously published article/essay/column/nonfiction book chapter; unpublished or self-published article/essay/column/nonfiction book chapter); fiction (unpublished or self-published short story or novel chapter); children's literature (unpublished or self-published short story/nonfiction article/book chapter/poem); poetry (unpublished or self-published free verse/traditional)." Guidelines available online. Open to any writer. Accepts inquiries by e-mail, phone and mail. Entry form online. Results announced May 31. Winners notified by mail and posted on website. Results available for SASE or visit website. Deadline: March 15. Prize: 1st Place: $100; 2nd Place: $75; 3rd Place: $50. All winners and Honorable Mentions will receive certificates as warranted. Judged by editors, librarians, and writers.

☺ WRITERS GUILD OF ALBERTA AWARDS

Percy Page Centre, 11759 Groat Rd., Edmonton AB T5M 3K6 Canada. (780)422-8174. **Fax:** (780)422-2663. **E-mail:** mail@writersguild.ab.ca. **Website:** www.writersguild.ab.ca. **Contact:** Executive Director. Offers the following awards: Wilfrid Eggleston Award for Nonfiction; Georges Bugnet Award for Fiction; Howard O'Hagan Award for Short Story; Stephan G. Stephansson Award for Poetry; R. Ross Annett Award for Children's Literature; Gwen Pharis Ring-

wood Award for Drama; Jon Whyte Memorial Essay Prize; James H. Gray Award for Short Nonfiction; Amber Bowerman Memorial Travel Writing Award. Eligible entries will have been published anywhere in the world between January 1 and December 31 of the current year; the authors must have been residents of Alberta for at least 12 of the 18 months prior to December 31. Unpublished mss, except in the drama, essay, and short nonfiction categories, are not eligible. Anthologies are not eligible. Works may be submitted by authors, publishers, or any interested parties. Deadline: December 31. Prize: Winning authors receive $1,500; essay prize winners receive $700. Other awards: Isabel Miller Young Writers Award; authors must be 12-18 years of age and a resident of Alberta.

WRITING CONFERENCE WRITING CONTESTS

P.O. Box 664, Ottawa KS 66067. (785)242-1995. **Fax:** (785)242-1995. **E-mail:** jbushman@writingconference.com. **Website:** www.writingconference.com. **Contact:** John H. Bushman, contest director. Purpose of contest: to further writing by students with awards for narration, exposition and poetry at the elementary, middle school and high school levels. Unpublished submissions only. Submissions made by the author or teacher. Deadline for entries: January 8. Consult website for guidelines and entry form. No entry fee. Awards plaque and publication of winning entry in The Writers' Slate online, April issue. Judging by a panel of teachers. Requirements for entrants: must be enrolled in school—K-12th grade—or home schooled.

YEARBOOK EXCELLENCE CONTEST

100 Adler Journalism Bldg, Room E346, U of Iowa, University of Iowa, Iowa City IA 52242-2004. (319)335-3457. **Fax:** (319)335-3989. **E-mail:** quill-scroll@uiowa.edu. **Website:** www.uiowa.edu/~quill-sc. **Contact:** Vanessa Shelton, executive director. **Open to students whose schools have Quill and Scroll charters.** Purpose of contest: to recognize and reward student journalists for their work in yearbooks and to provide student winners an opportunity to apply for a scholarship to be used freshman year in college for students planning to major in journalism. Previously published submissions only. Submissions made by the author or school yearbook adviser. Must be published between in the 12-month span prior to contest deadline. Deadline for entries: November 1. Visit our web site for list of current and previous winners.

☼ YOUNG ADULT CANADIAN BOOK AWARD

1150 Morrison Dr., Suite 400, Ottawa ON K2H 8S9 Canada. (613)232-9625. **Fax:** (613)563-9895. **Website:** www.cla.ca. This award recognizes an author of an outstanding English language Canadian book which appeals to young adults between the ages of 13 and 18. To be eligible for consideration, the following must apply; it must be a work of fiction (novel, collection of short stories, or graphic novel), the title must be a Canadian publication in either hardcover or paperback, and the author must be a Canadian citizen or landed immigrant. The award is given annually, when merited, at the Canadian Library Association's annual conference. Established in 1980 by the Young Adult Caucus of the Saskatchewan Library Association. Nominations should be sent by December 31, annually.

THE YOUTH HONOR AWARD PROGRAM

P.O. Box 3939, Eugene OR 97403. (514)342-4956. **E-mail:** editor@skippingstones.org. **Website:** www.skippingstones.org. **Contact:** Arun N. Toke, director of publicity/editor. Purpose of contest: "To recognize creative and artistic works by young people that promote multicultural awareness and nature appreciation." Unpublished submissions only. Submissions made by author. Deadline for entries: June 25. SASE for contest rules and entry forms also available on our website. Entry fee is $3; low-income entrants, free. "Ten winners and some noteworthy entries will be published in our fall issue. Winners will also receive an Honor Award Certificate, a subscription to *Skipping Stones* and five nature and/or multicultural books." Requirements for entrants: Original writing (essays, interviews, poems, plays, short stories, etc.) and art (photos, paintings, cartoons, etc.) are accepted from youth ages 7 to 17. Non-English and bilingual writings are welcome. Also, you must include a certificate of originality signed by a parent or teacher. "Include a cover letter telling about yourself and your submissions, your age, and contact information. Every student who enters will receive a copy of *Skipping Stones* fall issue featuring the 10 winning entries."

ANNA ZORNIO MEMORIAL CHILDREN'S THEATRE PLAYWRITING COMPETITION

Department of Theatre and Dance, PCAC, 30 Academic Way, Durham NH 03824. (603)862-3044. **Fax:** (603)862-0298. **E-mail:** mike.wood@unh.edu. **Website:** www.unh.edu/theatre-dance/zornio. **Contact:** Michael Wood. "Offered every 4 years for unpublished well-written plays or musicals appropriate for young audiences with a maximum length of 60 minutes. May submit more than 1 play, but not more than 3. All plays will be performed by adult actors. Guidelines and entry forms available as downloads on the website. Open to all playwrights in US and Canada. All ages are invited to participate." Purpose of the award: "to honor the late Anna Zornio, an alumna of The University of New Hampshire, for dedication to and inspiration of playwriting for young people, K-12th grade. Open to playwrights who are residents of the U.S. and Canada. Plays or musicals should run about 45 minutes." Unpublished submissions only. Submissions made by the author. Deadline for entries: March 2, 2012. No entry fee. Awards $500 plus guaranteed production. Judging by faculty committee. Acquires rights to campus production. For entry form and more information visit www.unh.edu/theatre-dance/zornio.

SUBJECT INDEX

CAREERS

HISTORY (NONFICTION)

HUMOR

HUMOR (NONFICTION)

INTERVIEW/PROFILE

SCIENCE FICTION

SPORTS (NONFICTION)

SUSPENSE/MYSTERY

EDITOR AND AGENT NAMES INDEX

AGE-LEVEL INDEX

PHOTOGRAPHY INDEX

POETRY INDEX

GENERAL INDEX

WD WRITER'S DIGEST

Is Your Manuscript Ready?

Trust 2nd Draft Critique Service to prepare your writing to catch the eye of agents and editors. You can expect:

- Expert evaluation from a hand-selected, professional critiquer
- Know-how on reaching your target audience
- Red flags for consistency, mechanics, and grammar
- Tips on revising your work to increase your odds of publication

Visit WritersDigestShop.com/2nd-draft for more information.

THE PERFECT COMPANION TO *WRITER'S MARKET*

The Writer's Market Guide to Getting Published

Learn exactly what it takes to get your work into the marketplace, get it published, and get paid for it!

Available from WritersDigestShop.com and your favorite book retailers.

To receive our weekly newsletter, plus a FREE download that will help improve your odds of getting published, go to: WritersDigest.com/enews

 Find more great tips, networking and advice by following @writersdigest

 And become a fan of our Facebook pa facebook.com/writersdigest